CHEMISTRY
FOR THE
CARIBBEAN

Also in this series

Physics for the Caribbean (Tom Duncan and Deniz Önaç)

CHEMISTRY
FOR THE
CARIBBEAN
A CXC Course

M. A. Atherton
and
J. K. Lawrence

Consultant editor: John Steward

JOHN MURRAY

© M. A. Atherton and J. K. Lawrence 1986

First published 1986
by John Murray (Publishers) Ltd
50 Albemarle Street, London W1X 4BD

Reprinted 1989

Typeset, printed and bound in Great Britain
by The Alden Press Ltd, Oxford

British Library Cataloguing in Publication Data

Atherton, M. A.
  Chemistry for the Caribbean: a CXC course.
  1. Chemistry
  I. Title   II. Lawrence, J.K.
  540   QD33

ISBN 0-7195-4234-0

Acknowledgements

We are much indebted to John Steward for his sound advice on all aspects of the book, but in particular for those relating to the Caribbean. He helped with the initial planning of the book, read and commented on the whole of the manuscript in detail, and provided a considerable amount of useful literature on chemistry in the Caribbean.

M.A.A.
J.K.L.

Photo credits

To the teacher

Chemistry for the Caribbean has been written to fulfil the requirements of the chemistry syllabus for the Secondary Education Certificate (S.E.C.) of the Caribbean Examination Council (C.X.C.).

The book has been devised as a course, based on a structured sequence of experiments and follow-up discussions, rather than as a reference book. There is a strong investigational flavour to the approach and the experiments contain questions (signalled by ►) which aim to encourage students to think carefully about their work. The important concepts and principles are developed and then used systematically throughout the book, so that students have many opportunities to reinforce their knowledge and understanding. On the other hand, we have not intended to prescribe a particular sequence of topics which the teacher must follow. The use of other sequences will be helped by the shortness of many of the chapters.

The inclusion of **Key words** and **Basic facts** at the end of most chapters should help students to ensure that they have understood the main points covered in these chapters. Questions are also included at the end of most chapters.

The text is divided into eight sections. The first of these, **First investigations** (Chapters 1 to 9), is a revision of elementary material. When the book is used just for the two years leading up to the C.X.C. examination, the text can then be picked up in the relevant places in the second section, **Metals, acids and salts** (Chapters 10 to 18), and the third section, **Particles, formulas and equations** (Chapters 19 to 26). If the book is used prior to this period, some expansion of the material in **First investigations** will be necessary, as this section does not contain the practical details of experiments.

One very important feature of the new C.X.C. syllabus is the emphasis on the applied and social aspects of chemistry. It is not possible, nor is it desirable, to separate the applications from the principles, so a lot of the former appear in the appropriate sections throughout the book. The bulk of the inorganic chemistry is in the fourth section, **Chemicals from nature I** (Chapters 27 to 34), and is approached via the available raw materials rather than the most 'convenient' laboratory chemicals: this obviously gives an applied slant to the work. The last section, **Chemistry in society** (Chapters 58 to 62), is almost totally devoted to applications with a Caribbean flavour.

We hope that the numerous references to applications throughout the text, together with the final section, will give students ideas for their special study of a local industry. Educational booklets and audio-visual aids from local and international companies should be available to assist students, and teachers may also be able to make a collection of relevant newspaper and magazine articles.

One of the most difficult decisions for a teacher is how and when to introduce the particulate theory, the mole concept, formulas and equations, ionic theory, atomic structure and bonding, chemical calculations and other aspects of chemical theory. This book collects these topics into two main parts, in the third and fifth sections (Chapters 19 to 26 and Chapters 35 to 45), but most teachers would prefer to interweave this work with more 'descriptive' chemistry rather than to tackle all the 'theory' in one go.

The organic chemistry is in the section **Chemicals from nature II** (Chapters 46 to 55), but it is not intended that this section should be covered without a break.

Pupils should be encouraged to use the data sheets and the periodic table at the end of the text. The answers to numerical problems and the identities of the substances used in the investigations in Chapter 56 are printed on one sheet which can be removed from the book if it is considered necessary.

Practical work

The new C.X.C. syllabus specifies a practical examination as well as continuous assessment by the teacher of students' practical skills and attitudes. We believe that the requirements of the former are fully covered in this book, especially in the section **Chemical analysis** (Chapters 56 and 57). The C.X.C. syllabus provides detailed guidelines for continuous assessment, but to some extent leaves open to the teacher the choice of which experiments the students should tackle. It is clear that as much as possible of the practical work should be student-based, and we hope that this book contains detailed instructions for a sufficient number of experiments which have due emphasis on careful observation, manipulation and organization, and which use an enquiry-based approach requiring students to interpret their results in a scientific way.

There is no separate teachers' guide, but the text contains material which will be of use to teachers and experimental instructions are thorough. The practical details for making up certain standard solutions for volumetric analysis are given in Chapter 57. Although some aspects of laboratory safety are dealt with in the text, the teacher must be primarily responsible for safety. In line with current international practice, we assume that eye protection will always be available whenever pupils are doing experiments and this is why we make no specific recommendations about eye protection for most experiments. Teachers should consult the various available publications on the use of chemicals and apparatus and potentially hazardous experiments.[1]

Unless otherwise stated, test-tube size is 125 mm × 16 mm and boiling-tube size is 150 mm × 25 mm.

Nomenclature

Nomenclature in a book of this sort has to be a compromise between the main need of unambiguously identifying a particular substance and the requirement to standardize names, at the same time bearing in mind the stage of development and the knowledge of the pupils.

The names sulphuric, sulphate, sulphurous, sulphite, nitric, nitrate, nitrous, nitrite and thiosulphate are used since these are preferred by I.U.P.A.C. and most national authorities and examination boards.[2]

Systematic names are introduced in Chapter 22 (Table 22.5) for both cations and anions. The use of numbers in naming cations is seen as referring to their ionic charges, but for anions the justification has to await the treatment of oxidation numbers in Chapter 40.

Prior to Table 22.5, oxidation numbers are not used. Ambiguity for substances such as the copper oxides is avoided by quoting colours, e.g. black or red copper oxide. The names 'dichromate' and 'permanganate' are used until their systematic names are introduced in Table 22.5. It is probable that 'dichromate' and 'permanganate' will continue to be used in some contexts and pupils who take up careers in chemistry-related fields need to know of the existence of more than one name for particular substances.

Systematic names are used for organic compounds but the trivial names are also given for important compounds.

M.A.A.
J.K.L.

1 (a) *Safeguards in School Laboratories* (A.S.E., 1981). Obtainable from Bookselling Department, Association for Science Education, College Lane, Hatfield, Hertfordshire AL10 9AA, U.K.

(b) *Topics in Safety* (A.S.E., 1982).

(c) *Hazards in the Chemical Laboratory*, editor L. Bretherick (Royal Society of Chemistry, 1981). Obtainable from R.S.C. Sales Distribution Centre, Blackhorse Road, Hatchworth, Hertfordshire SG6 1HN, U.K.

(d) *Hazardous Chemicals: a manual for schools and colleges*, Scottish Schools' Science Equipment Research Centre (Oliver and Boyd, 1979). Obtainable from Hugh Martin, Oliver and Boyd, Robert Stevenson Hse, 1 Baster Place, Edinburgh EH1 3BB, Scotland.

2 *Chemical Nomenclature, Symbols and Terminology for use in school science* (A.S.E., 1985).

Contents

To the student

The word **matter** can be used to describe all the different substances that are present in the world. Things as different as skin, water, air, rocks and so on are all made of different sorts of matter. **Chemistry** is mainly about how one sort of matter can be changed into another sort. The emphasis is, and always will be, on those materials of most use to mankind, in the home, in the factory, in medicine, in transportation, in agriculture and in many other areas. To appreciate these important applications more fully, it is necessary to acquire a basic knowledge of chemical facts and principles. This book deals with both the facts and principles and their applications in everyday life, in the Caribbean and elsewhere.

Chemistry is a laboratory-based subject and you will perform many experiments during your course. There are detailed instructions for experiments in most chapters which will enable you to carry them out for yourself. In doing so with care, you will learn how to make accurate observations, to use different types of equipment, to interpret your results and to develop your own explanations from them, and finally to present a report in a clear and logical form. The questions in the experimental instructions (signalled by ▶) are intended to help you to gain a better understanding of what you are doing. Make sure you can answer them well before you proceed to the next stage. The most important point is that experiments and 'theory' are very closely linked: experiments lead to new theories, and theories to more experiments.

Learning work for examinations is sometimes a difficult task. This is why we have included lists of **Key words** and **Basic facts** at the end of most chapters. When you look at the Key words, make sure that you can provide a definition of each one. If you cannot do this for some of them, look back through the chapter or at the list of Basic facts. The Basic facts are a brief summary of the main points in each chapter. Always read them carefully when you reach the end of a topic in your chemistry course. If there is anything in the statements you do not know or fully understand, look back through the chapter or ask your teacher.

This book should play an important part in your introduction to chemistry, both in the laboratory and outside it. We hope you will think that the content is interesting as well as instructive, and that the book will encourage you to take your study of the subject further at a later stage in your education.

M.A.A.
J.K.L.

x

First investigations

1 States of matter

Melting, boiling and sublimation

Water is the liquid that we know best. This liquid can be changed into a solid by cooling it to 0 °C and into a gas by heating it to 100 °C. These changes can be made to go in the opposite directions by cooling steam and by heating ice.

$$\text{solid} \underset{\text{cool}}{\overset{\text{heat}}{\rightleftharpoons}} \text{liquid} \underset{\text{cool}}{\overset{\text{heat}}{\rightleftharpoons}} \text{gas}$$
$$\text{(ice)} \qquad \text{(water)} \qquad \text{(water vapour)}$$

Many other substances behave in a similar way. Usually, when a solid is heated it melts to form a liquid, and when a liquid is heated it boils to form a gas. Cooling makes these changes happen the opposite way. (There are other changes which can happen to substances when they are heated, but these changes are usually not easy to reverse. These are called chemical changes.)

The temperature at which a solid melts to form a liquid is called its **melting point**. The temperature at which a liquid boils to form a gas is called its **boiling point**.

The melting point of ice is 0 °C and the boiling point of water (at sea level) is 100 °C. Other substances melt and boil at different temperatures.

Fig. 1.1 Two states of matter

Solid, liquid and gas are the three **states of matter** (or **phases** of matter). A change from one state to another is called a **change of state** or a **phase change**.

There is another change of state: when carbon dioxide gas is cooled to -78 °C, it changes straight into solid carbon dioxide. When solid carbon dioxide

below that temperature is heated to -78 °C, it changes straight into carbon dioxide gas. (The minus sign means that this temperature is 78° below 0 °C.) These changes are often called **sublimation**, and we say that during the change the solid **sublimes**.

$$\text{solid} \underset{\text{cool}}{\overset{\text{heat}}{\rightleftharpoons}} \text{gas}$$

Solutions

When salt is added to water, the solid salt disappears and the 'water' tastes salty. The salt has **dissolved** in the water to form a **solution** of salt in water. In this example, water is acting as a **solvent** when it dissolves the salt. The substance that dissolves (salt, in this case) is called the **solute**. There are many other substances that will dissolve in water, but there are also many that will not. The substances which do dissolve in water are said to be **soluble** in water. Those that do not dissolve in water are said to be **insoluble** in water.

Suspensions

Flour and finely powdered chalk are both insoluble in water. If they are mixed well with water, some of the solid stays floating in the water and the mixture looks cloudy. This mixture is called a **suspension**. Many insoluble solids will behave like this when they are finely powdered.

There are three important differences between solutions and suspensions:

1 Solutions, even if they are coloured, appear to be clear. Suspensions always look cloudy.
2 It is impossible to see the particles of solute in a solution. The particles in a suspension are large enough to be seen. (A lens or microscope may be needed if the particles are very small.)
3 The particles in a suspension can be removed by sieving the suspension through a fine sieve or a cloth. In the laboratory a filter funnel and the special porous paper called filter paper are used (see Fig. 2.1 on page 4). The process is called **filtration**. Particles of solute in solutions pass through even the best filter papers without being separated from the solvent.

Colloidal solutions

Two examples of **colloidal solutions** (or **colloids**) are egg-white dissolved in water and starch dissolved in water. The special properties of colloidal solutions are:

1 They appear to be clear when seen against a bright light, but they appear to be cloudy or smoky when seen at right angles to bright light (see Fig. 1.2).

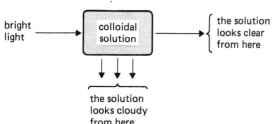

Fig. 1.2

2 Colloidal particles are too small to be seen even when a microscope is used.
3 Colloidal particles are too small to be caught by even the best filter paper.

We say a solution is colloidal when the particles in it are larger than particles in solutions but smaller than particles in suspensions.

Fig. 1.3

Colloidal solutions are very important in everyday life. They are found in many living things. Blood contains proteins (page 241) in colloidal solution. A styptic pencil used in shaving stops minor cuts from bleeding because the aluminium sulphate in the styptic pencil causes the proteins in the blood to come out of solution, clump together and form a solid. This is called the **coagulation** of a colloid.

A lot of industrial smokes contain solid particles which are colloidal. These particles are very difficult to remove from air and so it is difficult to prevent pollution. Smokes like this are colloidal solutions of very small solid particles in air (Fig. 1.3). Other colloidal solutions in air are produced by aerosol sprays. Scent sprays form colloidal solutions of very small liquid droplets in the air, while furniture polish sprays produce very small solid particles.

Table jelly is made from gelatin which has been coloured and flavoured. When a hot solution of gelatin is allowed to cool, it sets to form a jelly. The solution is sometimes called a **sol**, while the jelly-like solid is called a **gel**.

Emulsions are colloidal solutions of very small drops of one liquid in another. In salad creams, very small drops of oil are in colloidal solution in water. The oil does not form a separate layer (as in Fig. 2.7, page 6) because an **emulsifying agent** is added which helps to keep the oil drops in solution. The fat that is present in milk is in the form of an emulsion. But the emulsifying agent in milk is not completely successful, because cream slowly separates from milk. Soaps and detergents are useful in cleaning because they emulsify greasy dirt which otherwise would not dissolve in water.

QUESTIONS

1 What are the meanings of the terms: (*a*) sublimation, (*b*) melting point, (*c*) boiling point, and (*d*) the three states of matter?

2 Give some examples of changes of state between (*a*) solid and liquid, (*b*) liquid and gas, and (*c*) solid and gas.

3 Suggest two reasons why solid carbon dioxide is better than ice for keeping food cold.

4 Suggest answers for the following questions:
(*a*) Why is a solder used for joining parts of electrical circuits?
(*b*) Why are fuses put in electrical circuits?
(*c*) How does welding work?
(*d*) How is rain formed?

5 Solid iodine sublimes when it is heated gently, while sodium chloride melts at a high temperature. Suggest a method for separating a mixture of iodine and salt. Explain carefully how you would make sure that all the iodine is removed from the salt and how you would collect the iodine.

6 Explain how you would show that blood is a colloidal solution. (You may need to dilute the blood with water.)

7 When carbon dioxide is passed into limewater, a white solid is formed and the mixture looks very cloudy. How would you find out which of the following three statements is true?
(*a*) The mixture is a suspension.
(*b*) The mixture is a colloidal solution.
(*c*) The mixture is a colloidal solution with some solid suspended in it.

8 The table opposite gives the melting points and boiling points of some substances.
(*a*) Which substances are solids at room temperature?
(*b*) Which substance is a liquid at room temperature?
(*c*) Which substance is a gas at room temperature?

(*d*) Which one stays as a liquid over the widest range of temperature?
(*e*) Which one is solid at 0 °C and liquid at 100 °C?

Substance	Melting point in °C	Boiling point in °C
Iron	1535	3000
Magnesium	650	1110
Mercury	− 39	357
Oxygen	− 218	− 183
Sodium	98	890
Sulphur	115	445

Key words

change of state	solvent	insoluble	emulsions
melting point	solute	suspension	
boiling point	solution	filtration	
sublimation	soluble	colloidal solution	

Basic facts

- **Substances can exist as solids, liquids and gases.**
- **Changes between these states are called changes of state or phase changes.**
- **Solutions and suspensions most commonly involve solids dissolved or suspended in liquids.**
- **Colloidal solutions are very important in everyday life.**

2 Separating mixtures

Pure substances and mixtures

Some things you see around you are **mixtures** of more than one substance. Others consist of one substance only and are said to be **pure**.

How can you tell a pure substance from an **impure** one – a mixture? Sometimes the different substances in a mixture can be seen easily. If you look closely at some soil, you will see that it is a mixture of several substances. But many mixtures, such as beer or grass, *look* as if they contain only one substance. They can be shown to be mixtures by separating the substances in them.

How else can you find out if you are dealing with a pure substance? Another way is to look at the properties of the substance. Each pure substance has its own set of properties which are different from the

properties of any other pure substance. Mixtures may look like a pure substance, but their properties will be different from those of the pure substances in them. A solution of salt in water looks like pure water. But salt solution has a special taste and it does not boil at 100 °C or freeze at 0 °C. Many of its other properties are also different from those of pure water. You can tell pure water from other colourless liquids because it freezes at 0 °C and boils at 100 °C.

Purifying rock salt by recrystallization

In many parts of the world, salt can be found in a rock-like form. This is called **rock salt**. When it is dug out of the ground, it often contains sand which

Stage 1

Use a pestle and
mortar to grind
the rock salt.

Stage 2

Heat the ground
rock salt with enough
water to dissolve the salt.

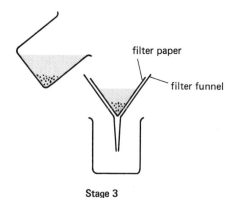

Stage 3

Filter the mixture of
salt solution and sand
to remove the sand.

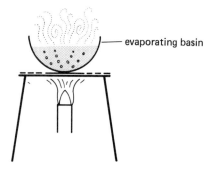

Stage 4

Evaporate the solution of
salt until crystals appear
and then let the mixture cool.

Fig. 2.1

makes it look dirty. The purification of rock salt to produce pure salt is shown in Fig. 2.1.

Stages 2, 3 and 4 work because the different substances in the mixture have different properties. In Stage 2, salt is soluble in water but the impurities are insoluble. In Stage 3, the insoluble impurities will not pass through the filter paper. The salt that is in solution passes through the filter paper. In Stage 4, water evaporates easily but the salt does not evaporate. Evaporating a solution to get crystals is called **crystallization**. When the experiment consists of dissolving crystals and then evaporating the solution to get purer crystals back, it is called **recrystallization**.

Separating substances by distillation

Substances which evaporate easily are said to be **volatile**. Substances which do not evaporate easily are said to be **non-volatile** or **involatile**. The separation of salt from salt solution in Stage 4 of Fig. 2.1 works because water is volatile while salt is involatile.

What would you have to do to collect the water that was evaporated? This would be an important question if you lived near the sea and had no supply of fresh water for drinking. Evaporation by itself is no good: the water vapour escapes into the air. You need to find a way to trap the water vapour and then turn it back into water. This is done on a large scale in some desalination plants like the one shown in Fig. 2.2.

Fig. 2.2 Desalination plant on Curaçao

4

A simple apparatus to trap the water is shown in Fig. 2.3. The method used in this experiment separates a solvent and a solute from a mixture of the two. But, unlike evaporation, this method allows you to get both substances and not just one of them. This is called separation by **distillation** and the liquid which is collected is called the **distillate**. Distillation is usually the easiest way to separate the substances in a solution of an involatile solute in a volatile solvent.

You probably realize that the apparatus used in Fig. 2.3 does not work very well. The plastic tubing becomes hot and some water vapour escapes into the air.

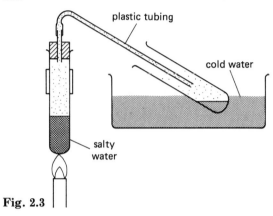

plastic tubing

cold water

salty water

Fig. 2.3

A more effective apparatus, called a **Liebig condenser**, is shown in Fig. 2.4. The tube that the steam passes along is kept cool by the cold water passing through the outer tube.

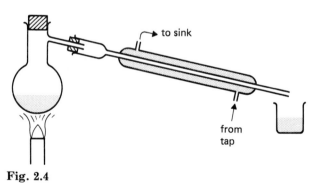

to sink

from tap

Fig. 2.4

Distillation is important for making some kinds of alcoholic drinks. When yeast is added to a solution that contains sugar, the mixture bubbles and the sugar is changed into ethanol (alcohol) by the yeast. This process is called **fermentation** (page 227), and it produces a solution containing only a small amount of ethanol in a lot of water. It is a **dilute** solution. Ethanol is more volatile than water so that, when the dilute solution is distilled, a more **concentrated** solution is obtained. This solution contains a higher proportion of ethanol than the first solution. Drinks such as rum, gin and whisky

are made by distillation after fermentation has produced a dilute solution of ethanol in water (see page 267).

If a solution of salt in water is distilled using the apparatus shown in Fig. 2.4, the salt and water can be completely separated. This is because salt is involatile at 100 °C. But when a solution of ethanol in water in distilled, complete separation is not possible because both liquids are volatile at the boiling point of the solution. In the manufacture of spirits such as rum, this incomplete separation is acceptable. Most spirits contain less than about 50% ethanol by volume.

If more complete separation is needed, the apparatus shown in Fig. 2.5 is used. The vapours given off from the boiling mixture are steadily cooled as they pass up the column. And they mix with liquid that has already condensed and is running back down the column. Because ethanol is more volatile than water, this mixing helps ethanol to evaporate and to

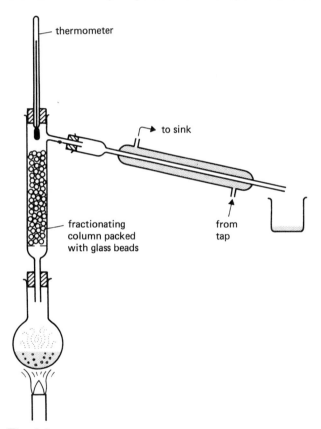

thermometer

to sink

fractionating column packed with glass beads

from tap

Fig. 2.5

pass up the column and water to be condensed and run back down. This procedure is called **fractional distillation**. It is used to separate the gases in the air (page 128) after the air has been liquefied, and to separate crude oil into **fractions** (groups of substances in this case) with different boiling point ranges (page 270). The fractional distillation of a dilute solution of ethanol in water can produce almost pure ethanol.

Separating substances by sublimation

Iodine is a solid that easily sublimes at a low temperature. This property means that it is easy to separate iodine from other substances which do not sublime. The apparatus in Fig. 2.6 shows how a mixture of iodine and salt could be separated. Here, the method of purifying iodine is to warm it gently so that it sublimes, while the impurities (in this case, salt) are left. The iodine collects as crystals under the dish of cold water. Other substances that sublime can be purified by this method.

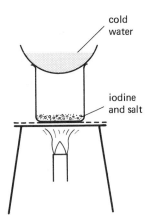

cold water

iodine and salt

Fig. 2.6

Separating liquids that do not mix

You already know that ethanol is soluble in water. Liquids that dissolve in one another are said to be **miscible**. Some liquids, such as oil and water, or paraffin and water, do not mix and are said to be **immiscible**. When two immiscible liquids are stirred together and then left to stand, they separate and form two layers, the denser liquid sinks to the bottom.

To separate two immiscible liquids, you could try pouring off the top liquid. Or you could try to remove the top liquid with a spoon. But neither of these methods is very effective.

If a **separating funnel** (Fig. 2.7) is used, the denser liquid can be drained away through a tap. The tap is closed just as the upper liquid reaches it.

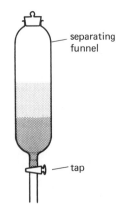

separating funnel

tap

Fig. 2.7

Separating substances by chromatography

Inks are usually solutions of dyes in water. The apparatus shown in Fig. 2.8 can be used to find out if the ink contains only one dye or several dyes. As the water spreads out through the filter paper, some of the dyes go with it. But as the ink spreads out, it is usually possible to see coloured bands. The number of coloured bands shows the number of dyes that are in the ink.

This method can be used to separate small amounts of substances in a mixture. It is called **paper chromatography**. After the experiment, the filter paper can be cut up so that each dye is separated from the others.

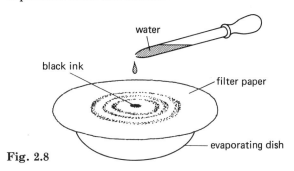

water

black ink

filter paper

evaporating dish

Fig. 2.8

Extracting coloured substances from plants

Chromatography can be used to investigate the coloured substances that are present in plants. For example, does grass contain a single green substance or does it contain several coloured substances?

Before you begin the chromatography, you need a solution of the coloured substances in grass. If you grind some grass with sand in a pestle and mortar and then add water, the green material does not dissolve. But if instead you add some ethanol, the green substance in the grass dissolves. This solution can then be used for a chromatography experiment.

Removing the green substances from ground grass using ethanol is an example of **solvent extraction**. The substances are extracted from a mixture by using a solvent which will dissolve only the substances that are needed. Water is used to dissolve sugar from crushed sugar cane. This is another example of solvent extraction.

QUESTIONS

1 Describe how you would make pure water from salty water, using objects in your home.

2 Tetrachloromethane is used to dissolve grease from clothes. Describe how pure tetrachloromethane could be obtained from a solution of grease in tetrachloromethane. (WARNING: do not try this experiment yourself as tetrachloromethane is poisonous.)

3 Sulphur is soluble in ethanol but not in water, while salt is soluble in water but not ethanol. Describe two ways of separating salt from a mixture of sulphur and salt.

4 Ammonium chloride is a solid that appears to sublime when it is heated. Suppose that you are given a mixture of ammonium chloride and sodium chloride (salt). Can you think of a way of getting both pure ammonium chloride and pure salt from it? Draw a diagram of the apparatus you could use.

5 Starting with a solution of salt in water which has some fine grains of sand in it, how would you separate (a) the sand, (b) the salt, and (c) the water?

6 Explain how you would find out if the ink in a ball-point pen contained only one dye or several dyes. Remember that the ink is not soluble in water.

7 You are given two bottles, one containing pure water and the other containing sugar solution. Describe a simple test, which does not rely on your sense of taste, to find out which is which.

Starting from the sugar solution, describe how you would obtain (a) some pure water, (b) some solid sugar.

Key words

pure	crystallization	volatile	distillation	concentrated	separating funnel
impure	recrystallization	involatile	distillate	miscible	chromatography
mixture	fractional distillation	condenser	dilute	immiscible	solvent extraction

Basic facts

- Each substance has its own set of properties, such as melting point and boiling point.
- A lot of things we meet in the world are mixtures. We can tell they are mixtures because they can be separated into different substances.
- The separation of a mixture depends on finding a difference between the properties of the substances in the mixture.
- The method used for separation depends on the differences in the properties of the substances being separated.

3 Acids, alkalis and indicators

Acids

Citrus fruits such as oranges, lemons and limes have a sharp taste. This is caused by an **acid** (citric acid) in the juices. If the juice of a citrus fruit is squeezed onto blue litmus paper, the paper turns red. This happens because litmus is a substance that changes colour when acids are added to it.

Many other substances are acidic and turn blue litmus paper red (Table 3.1), and there will be some in your own laboratory.

Table 3.1 Some common acids

Acid	Comments
Carbolic acid	Its chemical name is phenol; it is used as a disinfectant.
Carbonic acid	Soda water is a solution of this acid, made by dissolving carbon dioxide in water; rain water is a very dilute solution of this acid.
Citric acid	The acid in citrus fruits.
Ethanoic (acetic) acid	Vinegar is a very dilute solution of this acid; wines form ethanoic acid when they go sour.
Lactic acid	The acid in sour milk, and in human muscles after prolonged exercise.
Tartaric acid	A substance made from this acid (called 'cream of tartar') is used as the acid part of baking powder.
Hydrochloric acid Nitric acid Sulphuric acid	The three important laboratory acids.

Alkalis

Substances called **alkalis** can be recognized because they turn red litmus blue. Again, there will be alkaline substances in your own laboratory: some of them have a name ending in **hydroxide** (Table 3.2).

Table 3.2 Some common alkalis

Alkali	Comments
Ammonia solution	Used in some household cleaners
Calcium hydroxide	Its solution is known as limewater
Magnesium hydroxide	'Milk of magnesia'
Potassium hydroxide	Often called caustic potash
Sodium carbonate	Used as washing soda
Sodium hydrogencarbonate	Used as stomach powder
Sodium hydroxide	Often called caustic soda

Laboratory acids and alkalis must be used with a lot of care. Although a few, such as citric acid, are harmless, most are very dangerous and should never be tasted. If they come into contact with your skin, you should wash them off with plenty of water. Alkalis are particularly harmful if they splash into eyes. They damage the eye surface very rapidly. Care must be taken to pour alkalis without splashing, and eye protection should be worn whenever alkalis are used.

Indicators

Litmus is red when put into an acid and blue when put into an alkali. There are many other substances which show different colours when they are in acidic and alkaline solutions. These substances are called **indicators** and each one has its own acidic and alkaline colours. Many dyes that occur naturally in plants can be used as indicators.

Litmus comes from a lichen (a plant) that grows in West Africa. You can try to make your own indicator by extracting the coloured substances from plants. The coloured substances in the petals of blue and red flowers are often good indicators. A solution of the coloured substance can be made from the crushed petals by solvent extraction. Ethanol is a suitable solvent to use.

It is possible to classify substances as acidic, alkaline and **neutral** (neither acidic nor alkaline) using litmus paper. Some acids are so weakly acidic that they can be used in foods. Others are strongly acidic and are far too dangerous to use in food.

Universal indicators are mixtures of indicators. They show not only if a substance is acidic or alkaline but also how acidic or alkaline it is. The colours usually shown by universal indicators are given in Fig. 3.1.

It is easier to use a scale of numbers to describe how acidic or alkaline a substance is, rather than use colours. This scale is called the **pH scale** and the numbers are **pH values**. The pH values are shown in Fig. 3.1.

Solutions of strong acids have pH values of 0 or 1 while solutions of weak acids have pH values in the range 4 to 6. Solutions of strong alkalis have pH values of 13 or 14, while solutions of weak alkalis have pH values in the range 8 to 10. Neutral solutions, which are neither acidic nor alkaline, have pH value 7.

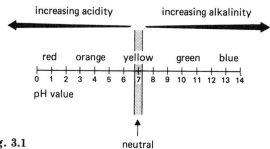

Fig. 3.1

Fig. 3.2 shows how to find the pH value of a solid. Everyday substances you could use include sugar, salt, soil, wood-ash or charcoal-ash, and soap. If you test a gas, remember first to make the paper damp with water, which should be neutral itself. Some of the results you might get are shown in Fig. 3.3.

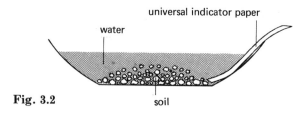

Fig. 3.2

Soils mostly have a pH value fairly close to 7: for many plants, the most suitable value is 6.5, though some plants prefer a more acidic soil than this and others like more alkaline soils.

The fairly high pH value of ash made by burning plant material, such as wood or seaweed, is due to the presence of a substance called 'potash'. In the past, the alkali potash was used in the manufacture of soap.

Soap was first made in Mediterranean countries by heating animal fat or vegetable oil with an alkali called 'soda' which is found naturally in the Nile Valley. But it is known from the writings of the day that the Romans made soap from goat's tallow (fat) and the ashes of beechwood. Modern soap-making uses vegetable oil and sodium hydroxide.

Some detergents have a very high pH value and are called heavy-duty detergents. They are able to clean very dirty clothes, but they unfortunately remove some dyes and are harmful to the skin. Other detergents have much lower pH values and are called light-duty detergents. These are not quite as good at getting dirt out of heavily soiled clothes but

neutral solution is evaporated, crystals of sodium chloride (common salt) are left. This is an example of a very common chemical reaction. The general way of showing this sort of reaction is

an acid + an alkali gives a salt + water

or   acid + alkali ⟶ salt + water

(This word-equation is a simple and short way of showing the change that is happening. Equations like this will usually be used in the first twenty chapters of this book.)

These neutralization reactions will be investigated more fully later in your chemistry course.

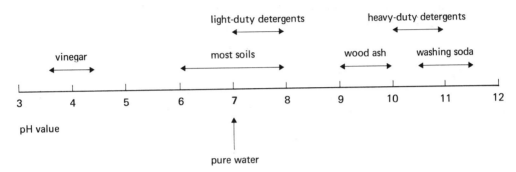

Fig. 3.3

they have the advantage of not removing the dyes from them and they do not cause irritation to the skin.

The pH value of fresh cow's milk is about 6.5. When milk goes sour, its pH value drops to about 5.5. This shows that an acid must be formed during the change.

Mixing acids and alkalis

Acids and alkalis have opposite effects on litmus and other indicators. By carefully mixing an acid with an alkali, it is possible to get a neutral solution. Acids and alkalis counteract one another but it is difficult to get an exactly neutral solution.

Mixing an acid and an alkali to get a neutral solution is called **neutralization**. If sodium hydroxide is neutralized with hydrochloric acid and the

QUESTIONS

1 If you spill some acid on your clothes, it should be neutralized before it can cause damage. What are the best substances for this job – water, sodium carbonate, sodium hydroxide or ammonia solution? What would you use to neutralize some sodium hydroxide which has been spilled?

2 Why does acid that has been accidentally spilled on a book often cause the colours of the book cover and the ink to change?

3 Wood ash contains a substance called potash which is an important fertilizer. Potash is very soluble in water and its solution is alkaline. If you had a bucket of wood ash, how would you get the potash from it? How would you know when no potash remained in the wood ash?

Can you suggest why wood ash should be kept dry when stored?

4 What substances are used to counteract acidity in soils? What is this process of counteracting acidity called?

Key words

acidic   alkaline   neutral   indicator   neutralization   pH scale   pH value

Basic facts

● **Acids and alkalis are recognized using indicators.**

● **The pH scale is used to measure how acidic or alkaline a substance is.**

● **Neutralizing an acid with an alkali produces a salt.**

4 Temporary and permanent changes: chemical changes

Temporary changes

A lot of changes have been mentioned in Chapters 1 and 2. Some examples are the changes of state of water, and either sugar or salt dissolving in water.

These changes are called **temporary** changes because they can be reversed easily. Ice melts on warming but is formed again when water is cooled. Salt disappears into solution when water is added to it but can be formed again when the solution is evaporated.

Making charcoal (coal) from wood

In many parts of the world, charcoal (or coal as it is called in the Caribbean area) is a useful fuel. It is made by heating wood without much air being present, so that the wood cannot burn (pages 107–8).

Charcoal can be formed in the laboratory by using the apparatus in Fig. 4.1. When charcoal is made, the wood always loses some mass: 100 kg of wood makes about 25 kg of charcoal. The other 75 kg just seems to 'disappear'. The experiment shown in Fig. 4.1 shows what happens to this extra mass. The wood gives off liquids and some gases that burn. A simple word-equation for this chemical reaction is

$$\text{wood} \xrightarrow{\text{heat}} \text{charcoal} + \text{liquids} + \text{gases}$$

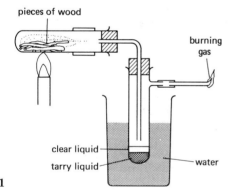

Fig. 4.1

Permanent changes and chemical changes

The results of the experiment shown in Fig. 4.1 show that wood can be broken down or **decomposed** into charcoal and some liquids and some gases.

Wood and charcoal have different appearances and different properties. Wood will bend, while charcoal is brittle. Charcoal but not wood can be used to write or draw on paper. Wood burns easily and forms a smoke when it burns, but charcoal is more difficult to burn and does not form a smoke.

The reason why wood and charcoal have different properties is because they are different substances. The change of wood to charcoal is not a temporary change because the change cannot be reversed. This sort of change can therefore be called a **permanent change**. But it is usually called a **chemical change** or ·a **chemical reaction** because different substances are made when the change happens.

Chemical reactions can be recognized because:

1 they always produce new substances;
2 most chemical reactions are permanent changes. But there are some chemical reactions that can be easily reversed.

The action of heat on some solids

When the green powder called copper carbonate is heated, a black powder is formed. It is easy to show that the black powder has a smaller mass than the green powder. This loss in mass suggests that something else, as well as the black powder, is formed when the change happens. Nothing else is seen to be formed, so the experiment can be repeated to catch any invisible gases that are formed. Three ways of trapping or collecting gases are shown in Fig. 4.2.

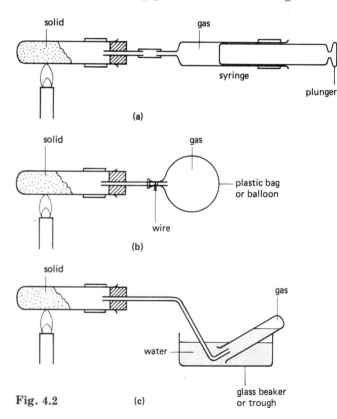

Fig. 4.2   (c)

If the gas given off is water vapour, it can be easily recognized. It condenses to give a colourless liquid with boiling point 100 °C and freezing point 0 °C. An apparatus for condensing the water vapour formed when a solid is heated is shown in Fig. 4.3.

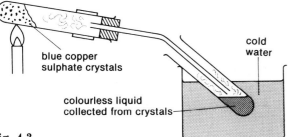

Fig. 4.3

Table 4.1

Carbon dioxide	Oxygen
1 Colourless	1 Colourless
2 Slightly acidic	2 Neutral
3 Extinguishes a glowing splint	3 Relights a glowing splint
4 Turns limewater cloudy	4 Has no effect on limewater

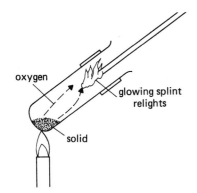

Fig. 4.4

The ways to recognize two other common gases are given in Table 4.1. The methods for doing the tests are shown in Figs. 4.4 and 4.5. In the method shown in Fig. 4.5*a*, the test-tube containing the lime-water and the gas has to be shaken to get the gas to react with the limewater.

The results of heating the solids copper carbonate, potassium permanganate, sodium hydrogencarbonate and blue copper sulphate are given in Table 4.2.

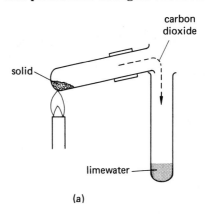

(a)

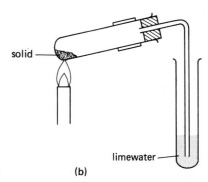

Fig. 4.5 (b)

All these changes are chemical reactions because new substances are formed. All but one of them are also permanent changes because there is no easy way to reverse them. They can all also be called **decomposition reactions** because, in each case, one substance is breaking down to give two or more simpler substances. Decomposition that is caused by *heating* a substance can be called **thermal decomposition**.

When blue copper sulphate is heated, the change is a chemical reaction because the blue crystals have different properties from the white powder and water. But if water is added to the white powder, blue copper sulphate is formed again.

The decomposition of blue copper sulphate to the white copper sulphate and water is an example of a chemical reaction which is not a permanent change. This chemical reaction is a **temporary change**.

The change from white to blue when water is added to white copper sulphate can be used as a test for water. Other liquids do not cause this colour change.

Table 4.2

Solid	Appearance before heating	Appearance after heating	Is there a loss in mass?	Gas given off
Copper carbonate	Green powder	Black powder	Yes	Carbon dioxide
Potassium permanganate	Purple crystals	Black powder	Yes	Oxygen
Sodium hydrogencarbonate	White powder	White powder	Yes	Carbon dioxide
Blue copper sulphate	Blue crystals	White powder	Yes	Water vapour

Water of crystallization

You now know that there are two kinds of copper sulphate – blue and white. The blue solid contains copper sulphate and water but the white solid is only copper sulphate. The water in this blue solid must be 'locked up' inside the crystals and it is lost only when the solid is heated: it is called **water of crystallization**.

Many other crystals also give off water when they are heated. Such crystals are said to be **hydrated**. The new solids formed after the water has been driven off do not have any water in them and these are said to be **anhydrous**.

The word-equation for the action of heat on blue copper sulphate can be written as either

$$\text{blue copper sulphate} \rightleftharpoons \text{white copper sulphate} + \text{water}$$

or

$$\text{hydrated copper sulphate} \rightleftharpoons \text{anhydrous copper sulphate} + \text{water}$$

In these equations the two half-arrows are used to show that the change is *reversible*.

Another substance that behaves like blue copper sulphate when it is heated is cobalt chloride. Hydrated cobalt chloride is pale pink, while anhydrous cobalt chloride is blue.

Exothermic changes

When a fuel such as charcoal or kerosine burns, a chemical reaction is happening. These reactions are very useful because they produce a lot of heat and they are used as sources of heat (page 207).

Many chemical reactions produce heat when they happen. If water is added to white copper sulphate, as in Fig. 4.6, a temperature rise is seen.

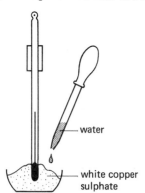

— water

— white copper
sulphate

Fig. 4.6

Changes that *produce* heat are called **exothermic changes**. The burning of a fuel and the reaction of water with white copper sulphate are both exothermic reactions.

Some changes *take in* heat as they happen. These are called **endothermic changes**. Although many chemical reactions are exothermic, there are some that are endothermic.

QUESTIONS

1 If you had a tin with a tightly fitting lid, a stone, a large nail, some small pieces of wood and a wood fire, describe how you would set about making a small amount of charcoal.

2 Do you think that the heating of grey crystals of iodine to form a purple vapour is an example of a chemical reaction? Explain your answer.

3 When a solid called barium carbonate is heated, there is no change of colour but the solid loses mass. How can this be explained?

4 When the white solid called zinc oxide is heated, it turns yellow. On cooling it becomes white again. How could you discover whether or not the white substance that remains, the white *residue*, is zinc oxide? If it is, can you say whether this is a temporary or a permanent change?

5 Cerium sulphate is a yellow solid. When it is heated, it turns orange, and a colourless liquid forms on the sides of the test-tube. No other gas is given off. Explain what has happened, using the words 'hydrated', 'anhydrous' and 'water of crystallization'. How could the orange solid be changed back to the yellow solid?

6 (*a*) Try to show by a simple experiment that washing soda crystals (hydrated sodium carbonate) contain water of crystallization.
(*b*) Now find the mass of a few lumps of these crystals on a watch glass. Leave the watch glass for at least a day and observe any changes that occur. Then find the new mass of the watch glass and the solid. What do you think has happened to at least some of the water of crystallization? Finally, find out by experiment whether or not the remaining solid is anhydrous.

7 Sodium hydrogencarbonate (bicarbonate of soda) can be added to cake mixes to make the cake rise when it is cooked. Try to explain how it works.

8 Explain why copper sulphate solution is useless as invisible ink but cobalt chloride solution is very effective. Someone gives you an invisible message written with cobalt chloride solution. How would you make it visible?

9 What happens to the gasoline (or diesel oil) that is used to run a car engine? What is the evidence that a chemical reaction occurs inside a car engine?

Key words

temporary change	decomposition	anhydrous	endothermic
permanent change	thermal decomposition	hydrated	
chemical change or chemical reaction	water of crystallization	exothermic	

Basic facts

- There are three things to look for when a chemical reaction occurs:
  1. New substances are formed.
  2. Chemical changes are often difficult to reverse.
  3. Chemical changes are often exothermic.

- The connection between permanent, temporary and chemical changes is summarized in a Venn diagram (Fig. 4.7). All permanent changes (such as the heating of copper carbonate) are chemical changes. Most temporary changes (such as changes of state and dissolving) are not chemical changes. A few temporary changes (such as heating blue copper sulphate) are chemical changes.

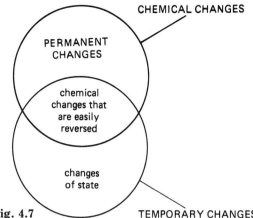

Fig. 4.7

- Tests for carbon dioxide are that it is a colourless gas that turns limewater milky, it is slightly acidic and it will extinguish a glowing splint.

- Tests for oxygen are that it is a neutral colourless gas that has no effect on limewater but that it relights a glowing splint.

- Tests for water are that it is a colourless neutral liquid with a boiling point of 100 °C and a freezing point of 0 °C. It will turn white copper sulphate blue and blue cobalt chloride pink.

5 Elements, compounds and mixtures

Elements

When blue copper sulphate is heated, it decomposes to form white copper sulphate and water. Can this process of decomposition be continued? It is possible to decompose white copper sulphate to three substances: copper, sulphur and oxygen. But, no matter what is done to the copper, the sulphur and the oxygen, they cannot be decomposed into other simpler substances.

The process of decomposition causes complicated substances to break down into two or more simpler substances. Sometimes these simpler substances can be broken down further, but a stage is always reached when no further decomposition is possible. The substances that are then left are known as **elements**.

Elements are the simplest substances that can be obtained by decomposition.

The elements formed by the decomposition of white copper sulphate are copper, sulphur and oxygen. These three elements are present, but combined together, in the white copper sulphate.

Substances that consist of two or more elements combined together are called compounds: compounds can always be broken down into simpler substances.

Another example of decomposition is the heating

of the red solid called mercury oxide. The results of this experiment are shown in Fig. 5.1. The silver-coloured liquid is called mercury and the gas is oxygen. Because neither of these substances can be broken down further, they are both elements. In this experiment the compound mercury oxide is broken down to give the elements mercury and oxygen.

The word-equation for this change is

$$mercury\ oxide \longrightarrow mercury + oxygen$$

So decomposition sometimes produces elements in one step but, more usually, several steps are necessary.

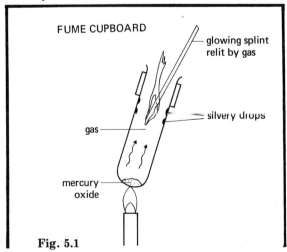

Fig. 5.1

Is it possible to make or **synthesize** a compound from its elements? If a compound consists of only two elements, it can often be made by heating the elements together. But many compounds, especially those like copper sulphate that consist of more than two elements, cannot be synthesized by heating the elements together.

There are 92 elements that occur in the world, and it has been possible to make another dozen or so using nuclear reactions (see page 275).

It is an interesting fact that the millions of compounds found in the world are all compounds of two or more of the known elements. Also, since only about forty of the elements are common, the vast majority of everyday materials are compounds of two or more of these forty elements. Substances as different as skin, hair, leather, wool, wood and muscle mainly contain compounds of the elements carbon, hydrogen, oxygen and nitrogen. Gasoline, kerosine and candle wax are all composed of compounds of carbon and hydrogen.

The two commonest elements are silicon and oxygen. Many man-made and natural materials contain compounds of these two elements together with other elements. Some examples are bricks, glass, sand, concrete, clay and granite.

Mixtures and compounds

Iron and sulphur are elements and each has its own set of properties. A mixture of iron and sulphur can be made by adding iron and sulphur to a beaker and stirring them. If a pestle and mortar are used to grind them together, they end up very well mixed indeed. But the separate grains of iron and sulphur can still be seen and each still keeps its own set of properties (see Table 5.1).

If a finely powdered mixture of 4 g of sulphur and 7 g of iron is made, then heated in a test-tube, a red hot glow is seen to spread through the mixture (Fig. 5.2). When the cool residue is removed from the tube, it is no longer possible to see individual grains of

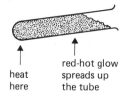

Fig. 5.2

heat here   red-hot glow spreads up the tube

Table 5.1

iron and sulphur. The solid has a uniform black appearance. And the solid has a new set of properties which are different from those of iron and sulphur and the mixture of iron and sulphur (Table 5.1). The black solid is a new substance and is a **compound** of iron and sulphur.

Some of the results of these experiments are shown in a diagram (Fig. 5.3).

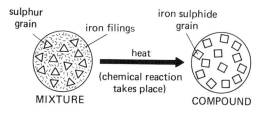

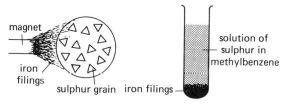

Separation of iron and sulphur from a mixture

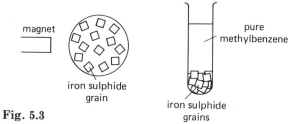

No separation of iron and sulphur from a compound

Fig. 5.3

There are three easy ways to separate the iron and sulphur from the *mixture*:
1. Use a hand lens and fine tweezers (very tedious).
2. Use a magnet.
3. Use methylbenzene.
None of these methods can separate the iron and sulphur from the *compound*.

The compound of iron and sulphur is called iron sulphide and the word-equation for its formation is

$$\text{iron} + \text{sulphur} \longrightarrow \text{iron sulphide}$$

The properties of this compound (iron sulphide) are very different from those of a mixture of iron and sulphur. It is easy to show the presence of iron and

Substance	Appearance	Effect of a magnet	Effect of methylbenzene
Iron filings	Small grey shiny specks	Attracted strongly	Does not dissolve
Sulphur	Dull yellow powder	Not attracted	Dissolves to form a pale yellow solution
Mixture of iron and sulphur	The separate specks of iron and sulphur can be seen	The iron is attracted; the sulphur is not attracted	The sulphur dissolves but the iron is unaffected
Compound of iron and sulphur	Uniform black powder	Not attracted	Does not dissolve

sulphur in the mixture but none of the properties of iron sulphide suggests that there is any separate iron or sulphur in it. This is evidence that a chemical reaction occurs when iron and sulphur are heated together.

More evidence comes from the observation that a red glow can be seen that spreads through the mixture when the bunsen burner is removed. This red glow means that heat energy is being produced in the tube. An *exothermic* change is happening.

You may be wondering why the mixture in the experiment has 7 g of iron and 4 g of sulphur. This is because these masses of the two elements react completely with one another (this is also true for 14 g and 8 g, 21 g and 12 g and so on). If 8 g of iron and 4 g of sulphur are heated together, the solid formed still contains 1 g of iron that has not reacted.

Two important facts about compounds are shown by the experiment.

Compounds have very different properties from their elements.

Compounds are made up of fixed proportions of their elements: they have a fixed composition.

The second fact means that a compound always has the same elements joined together in the same proportions. This is true however the compound is made. Scientists call this the **Law of Constant Composition.**

You should now be clear about the difference between a mixture and a compound. In a mixture the separate parts keep their properties, and they both show their own properties as if the other part were not present. So iron is attracted by a magnet and mixing it with sulphur does not change this property. Also, sulphur is soluble in methylbenzene and mixing it with iron does not change this property. But in a compound none of the properties of the original parts can be detected after the reaction. Iron sulphide is not magnetic and the sulphur which is combined in it cannot be dissolved in methylbenzene.

There is another difference between a mixture and a compound. If you add together 1 g of iron filings and 100 g of sulphur, a mixture of iron and sulphur is formed. Another mixture with a different composition is formed when 100 g of iron filings and 1 g of sulphur are mixed: so the composition of a mixture can vary whereas the composition of a compound is constant.

Atoms and molecules

The results of many experiments can best be explained by using the idea that all materials are made out of very small particles. Some of this evidence is given in Chapter 19.

It may be difficult for you to believe that your laboratory bench, the air around you, the water in

your tap, and all other materials (including yourself!) are made up of particles. After all, you cannot see them. If there are particles, they must be very small indeed.

Can the existence of elements and compounds be explained using the idea of particles? It is thought that different elements have different properties because they are made up of different kinds of particles. Also, an element cannot be broken down into simpler substances because it contains only one kind of particle. So we can say that a substance that is made up of only one kind of particle is an element.

Iron is an element and its particles are called **atoms**. An atom cannot be split into smaller particles; so elements are the simplest of all substances.

A lump of iron is made up of very many atoms. For the present, you can imagine that all these atoms are the same. Scientists have found that iron atoms have a diameter of about 0.000 000 1 mm and a mass of about 0.000 000 000 000 000 000 000 09 g. They are very small indeed!

A lump of sulphur is also made up of very small atoms, but these atoms are different from iron atoms and have different properties from iron atoms. So iron and sulphur have different properties and are different elements. Each element consists of its own special kind of atoms which are different from the atoms of all other elements.

When iron and sulphur react together to form iron sulphide, the compound has a new set of properties. These different properties must be due to the formation of a new sort of particle. This idea is shown in Fig. 5.4. The iron and sulphur atoms join together to form 'compound particles'.

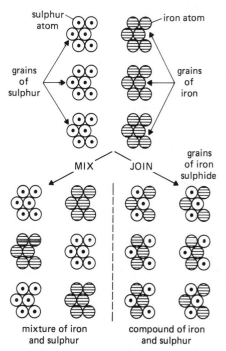

Fig. 5.4

(The grains are magnified to show a few of the atoms in them. Visible grains contain billions of atoms.)

5 Elements, compounds and mixtures

The 'compound particles' are usually called **molecules**. The properties of iron sulphide are different from those of iron and sulphur because iron sulphide is made of a new kind of particle.

If this idea of atoms is used to discuss chemical reactions, the atoms need to be represented in a quick and easy way. This is done by using a letter, or a pair of letters, to mean one atom of the element. So, when you want to write '1 atom of carbon', you write 'C'. This is called the **symbol** for one atom of carbon. The atomic symbols for some elements are given on page 279.

Think back to the reaction of iron and sulphur. The word-equation for the reaction is

$$iron + sulphur \longrightarrow iron\ sulphide$$

If you are to write this equation using symbols, you need to know how to write the **formula** of iron sulphide. In iron sulphide there are equal numbers of iron and sulphur atoms, and a 'compound particle' of iron sulphide contains one atom of iron and one atom of sulphur. So the formula of iron sulphide can be written as FeS. The equation for the formation of iron sulphide from iron and sulphur can now be written as

$$Fe + S \longrightarrow FeS$$

Over one hundred elements are known but there are only twenty-six letters in the alphabet, so pairs of letters have to be used for the symbols of some elements. Notice that, for these elements, only the first letter of the symbol is a capital letter.

The symbols for the elements calcium, carbon, copper and cobalt are Ca, C, Cu and Co, while the symbols for sulphur, sodium and silver are S, Na and Ag. The choices of Cu, Ag and Na appear strange, but these symbols come from the Latin words *cuprum* (copper), *argentium* (silver), and from the Arabic word for sodium carbonate, *natron*.

At this stage of your chemistry course, the symbol for an element is used to represent *one atom of the element*. This is a sort of chemical shorthand. Later in your course you will meet a different use of these symbols.

QUESTIONS

1 Make a list of elements that occur naturally on their own and not in a compound with other elements.

2 How could you show that copper sulphide consists of only the elements copper and sulphur? You can assume that copper sulphide, copper and sulphur are all available in the laboratory.

3 What are the everyday uses of the elements chlorine and argon?

4 Lead iodide is a compound made up of two elements. What are the names of these two elements? Describe one way in which you might try to break down lead iodide, and one way in which you might try to synthesize it from its elements.

5 One part by mass of zinc reacts completely with 4 parts by mass of iodine to form zinc iodide only. Suppose that you try to react 4 g of zinc with 18 g of iodine.
(a) Which of the two elements would not all react?
(b) What mass of this element would be left after the reaction?
(c) What mass of zinc iodide would be formed?

Key words

element	compound	atoms	molecules
mixture	synthesis	symbols for atoms	formulas for molecules

Basic facts

- **The components of a mixture show their own properties, while a compound has a set of properties of its own which are different from the properties of its component elements.**

- **Mixtures can usually be separated easily using differences in the properties of their components. There is usually no easy way to separate a compound into its component elements.**

- **Mixtures can have a very wide range of compositions, but the composition of a compound is fixed.**

- **The formation of a mixture does not usually produce much heat, but the formation of a compound is frequently very exothermic.**

6 Investigating air

The composition of air

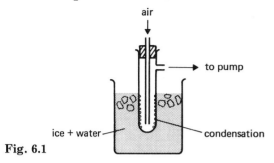

Fig. 6.1

When air is drawn through a cooled tube (Fig. 6.1), condensation is formed. The liquid can be shown to be water by testing its boiling point, freezing point and reaction with anhydrous copper sulphate. A similar apparatus can be used to show that there is some carbon dioxide in air by drawing air through limewater. A lot of air has to be used to get the limewater to turn milky. There must be only a small amount of carbon dioxide in air.

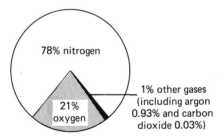

Fig. 6.2 The composition, by volume, of dry air

The composition of dry air is shown in Fig. 6.2. The percentage of water vapour in air varies between nearly zero and 4%, depending on the climate.

The 1% of dry air that is not oxygen or nitrogen is mainly made up of a group of gases called the **noble gases** (page 129). Like nitrogen, these are very inactive. The commonest of them is argon.

Liquefied air can be separated into nitrogen, oxygen and the noble gases by fractional distillation (page 128). This separation proves that air is a mixture of nitrogen, oxygen and other gases, and is not a compound.

The air also contains small amounts of gases produced in various ways by Man's activities. Two important examples are carbon monoxide (page 112) and sulphur dioxide (page 138).

Heating some elements in air

When hydrated copper sulphate is heated, it decomposes to give anhydrous copper sulphate and water. This thermal decomposition happens whether air is present or not. But when wood is heated, two quite different reactions can happen. If air is present, the wood burns and leaves a grey or white ash. But if no air is present when the wood is heated, charcoal is formed. Air is needed if wood is to burn. When wood *burns*, it is reacting with something that is present in the air. The effects of heating some elements in air are given in Table 6.1. The increases in mass are due to the magnesium and copper taking in something from the air to form new, solid compounds. Carbon and sulphur disappear because these elements react with something in the air to form compounds that are gases.

In the experiment in Fig. 6.3, the pump removes a lot of air from the tube before the copper is heated.

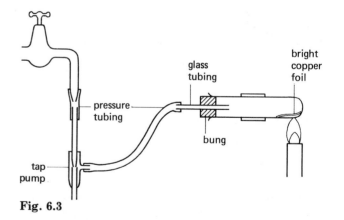

Fig. 6.3

Table 6.1

Element	Appearance before heating	Appearance after heating	Observations during heating
Magnesium	Shiny grey	White powder	The magnesium burns with a very bright flame. The residue has more mass than the magnesium.
Copper	Shiny red	Black coating	The copper slowly turns black. There is an increase in mass.
Carbon (graphite)	Shiny black solid	No residue	The graphite has to be heated strongly. It glows and disappears.
Sulphur	Yellow solid	No residue	The sulphur melts to give a brown liquid which burns with a blue flame. The gas given off makes people cough.

When the copper is heated, it does not turn black. But, if air is let into the tube while the copper is hot, the copper immediately goes black.

Experiments like this one show that the other elements also need air to be present if they are to react as described in Table 6.1.

Reactions like the burning of magnesium are often called **combustion reactions**. Although some metals, such as copper, do not burst into flames when they are heated in a crucible, they do react slowly. This kind of reaction is sometimes called **slow combustion**. The air is said to **support the combustion** of all these elements, because the combustions do not occur in the absence of air. In all combustion reactions, the element gives rise to a compound with entirely different properties from those of the element itself.

How much air is used in combustion reactions?

The apparatus shown in Fig. 6.4 can be used to heat copper in a known volume of air. The air is passed over the hot copper from syringe to syringe until the volume of air stays constant.

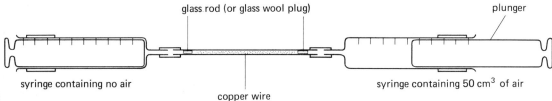

glass rod (or glass wool plug)   plunger

syringe containing no air

copper wire

syringe containing 50 cm^3 of air

Fig. 6.4

The results of the experiment show that about one-fifth, or 20%, of the air is used in the combustion of copper and that the four-fifths of the air left over does not react with hot copper. So only one-fifth of the air is active in forming the black compound of copper; the other four-fifths is inactive.

When this result is compared with the composition of air (Fig. 6.2), it becomes clear that it is the oxygen in the air that reacts with the copper. Similar results are obtained if the experiment is repeated with other elements.

If the experiment shown in Fig. 6.4 was repeated using oxygen, instead of air, in the syringe, it would be found that all the oxygen was used up.

Oxides

When copper is heated in air or oxygen, it combines with the oxygen to form a new compound which is called copper oxide. The word-equation for this reaction is

copper + oxygen ⟶ copper oxide

Similar reactions happen when most elements are heated in air or oxygen.

When the metal mercury is heated in air at its boiling point, it slowly reacts to form mercury oxide. If the mercury oxide is then heated more strongly, it decomposes (see Fig. 5.1). These reactions have enabled oxygen to be separated from the air and were very important in the discovery of oxygen and the understanding of combustion.

Changes in mass during combustion reactions

It is now possible to explain the changes in mass that are noted in Table 6.1.

Copper oxide has more mass than the copper from which it was made because it contains not only the copper but also the oxygen that has been taken from the air.

The word-equations for the combustions of carbon and sulphur are

carbon + oxygen ⟶ carbon dioxide

sulphur + oxygen ⟶ sulphur dioxide

Both of these oxides are gases and so escape into the air when the elements burn. Sulphur dioxide has a very irritating smell and makes people cough.

Would there still be a change in mass if the oxygen was weighed at the start of the reaction and if none of the oxide was allowed to escape? To answer this question your teacher may do the experiment shown in Fig. 6.5. White phosphorus is used because it catches fire very easily. But this property makes it a

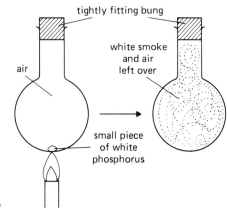

tightly fitting bung

air

white smoke and air left over

small piece of white phosphorus

Fig. 6.5

very dangerous element. It must be cut only if completely under water and it must not be touched: burns caused by phosphorus are very painful and take a long time to heal. In comparing the mass of the flask, bung and contents before and after the phosphorus is burnt, it is found that the mass does not change.

The same result would be found if substances other than phosphorus were used in the flask. In fact, the same result applies to all chemical reactions. The mass of the substances which react together equals the mass of the substances produced in the reaction. This is the **Law of Conservation of Mass** for a chemical reaction.

Burning substances in air

Many of the substances that burn in air, such as gasoline, kerosine, candle wax and ethanol, are used as fuels. Again, it is found that when they burn they use only one-fifth of the air. They react with oxygen from the air to form oxides. While an element burns to form only one oxide, a compound, which consists of two or more elements joined together, may burn to form several oxides. The oxides formed by the burning of a substance are often called the **products of combustion**.

The apparatus shown in Fig. 6.6 can be used to investigate the products of combustion of a fuel such as ethanol. The colourless liquid that is collected in the side-arm test-tube is slightly acidic, but otherwise has the properties of water. If the experiment is

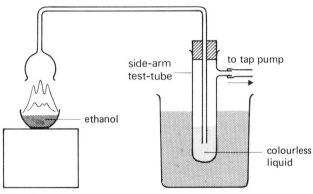

Fig. 6.6

repeated with limewater in the side-arm test-tube, the limewater quickly turns milky. It can be shown that ethanol burns to form water and carbon dioxide only, so the word-equation for the reaction is

ethanol + oxygen ⟶ carbon dioxide + water

The same method can be used to investigate the products of combustion of other fuels such as kerosine, candle wax and wood. In all these examples, carbon dioxide and water are produced (page 111).

Rusting of iron

The main disadvantage of using iron in, for example, bicycles, cars and bridges, is that it rusts very easily.

Fig. 6.7

You may have seen an old motor car or a piece of corrugated iron which has jagged holes where all the metal has corroded and completely broken up (Fig. 6.7). Because corrosion always begins on the surface, it seems likely that some reaction with the air is the cause.

The experiment shown in Fig. 6.8 shows that, when iron rusts, it uses one-fifth of the air. Again, it seems that oxygen is being used up.

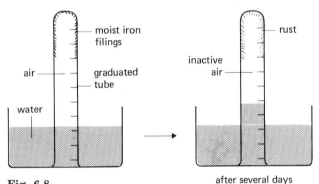

Fig. 6.8

But other experiments show that rusting is not as simple as combustion. The experiments shown in Fig. 6.9 prove that water is necessary for rusting to happen and that rusting happens faster when carbon dioxide is present. (Phosphorus pentoxide is a very good drying agent and sodium hydroxide reacts with carbon dioxide.)

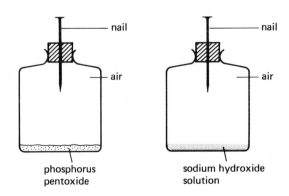

(a) air minus water vapour   (b) air minus carbon dioxide

Fig. 6.9

When a sample of rust is heated in a dry test-tube, condensation is formed on the cooler parts of the glass. This condensation can be shown to be water. A possible word-equation for the rusting of iron is therefore

$$\text{iron} + \text{oxygen} + \text{water} \longrightarrow \text{hydrated iron oxide}$$

But this does not explain why carbon dioxide speeds up rusting.

QUESTIONS

1 Leave a few lumps of anhydrous calcium chloride on a watch glass for at least a day and observe any change that occurs. Can you detect any new substance that has appeared on the watch glass? Where do you think it has come from? You could repeat this experiment using pellets of sodium hydroxide. (CARE: do not touch these pellets with your fingers as they are very corrosive.)
(*a*) Explain why chemists often use anhydrous calcium chloride for drying gases that contain water vapour or for removing traces of water from a liquid.
(*b*) Can you give one difference and one similarity between what happens to anhydrous calcium chloride and anhydrous (white) copper sulphate when they are exposed to the air?

2 Can you work out any other simple experiments to show that metals do not form their oxides when heated in the absence of air?

3 Explain the differences between the results of heating a metal in a vacuum and heating a metal in air.

4 Your friend does not know that air is a mixture of gases. He thinks it is a single substance. How would you convince him he is wrong?

5 White phosphorus burns slowly in air without first being heated. It is always kept under water because of this property. Describe an experiment in which you could use a small piece of white phosphorus to show that one-fifth of the air is used in burning. Draw a diagram of the apparatus you choose.

6 What mass of iron sulphide would be formed from the complete reaction of 7 g of iron filings and 4 g of sulphur? (All the iron and all the sulphur are used up in this reaction.) Which principle of science have you used in answering this question?

7 How could you try to discover what is formed when paper is burnt? Draw a diagram of the apparatus you would use.

8 Design a piece of apparatus that could be used to show that bottled gas such as Shellane burns to form carbon dioxide and water.

9 A liquid burns to form two products of combustion: carbon dioxide and sulphur dioxide.
(*a*) Which two elements must this liquid contain?
(*b*) Which other element could this liquid contain?
Explain your answers carefully.

10 Find as many ways as you can in which iron can be protected from rusting. Why do the following articles made of iron or steel not rust easily (if at all): cutlery, an iron bucket, the fenders of a motor car, a food can, and a metal bridge?

11 Do you expect rust to have more or less mass than the unrusted iron, or do you expect no change in mass to occur during rusting? Work out a suitable experiment that you could use to check your answer.

12 The air we breathe out has about 17% oxygen and 4% carbon dioxide. How are these percentages different from those for the air we breathe in? Can you explain these differences and so explain why it is essential for us to breathe in order to live?

Key words

combustion   **oxide**   **products of combustion**   **rusting**

Basic facts

- **Air is a mixture of several gases. The most important ones in dry air are nitrogen (78%), oxygen (21%), argon (0.9%), carbon dioxide (0.03%). The proportion of water in air varies.**

- **The percentage of oxygen in the air can be found by passing a known volume of air over a hot metal such as copper.**

- **Substances that burn in air react with the oxygen in air. Elements burn to form one oxide only, while the products of combustion of compounds usually contain more than one oxide.**

- **The Law of Conservation of Mass applies to all chemical reactions.**

- **Rust is formed by iron reacting with oxygen and water.**

7 Investigating water

Water as a product of combustion

When compounds such as ethanol and kerosine burn, one of their products of combustion is water. Combustion in air usually produces oxides, so it is reasonable to suggest that water might be an oxide. The other element(s) in water would be obtained if the oxygen could be taken away from water.

Do metals react with water?

When small pieces of calcium are added to water, a gas is given off and can be collected in an upside-down test-tube which has been filled with water (Fig. 7.1).

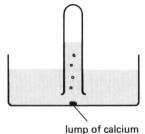

Fig. 7.1   lump of calcium

Tests on this gas show that it is neutral and that it burns with a blue flame. If some air is mixed with the gas before it is ignited, the mixture explodes in the test-tube with a pop or a squeak.

Magnesium also reacts with water, but the reaction is very slow. The apparatus shown in Fig. 7.2 has to be left for several hours before there is enough gas to test. The flammable gas is again formed.

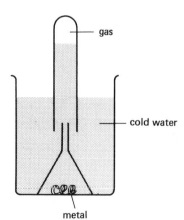

Fig. 7.2   metal

A high temperature can be used to speed up the reaction of magnesium and water. Using the apparatus shown in Fig. 7.3, the water is boiled to fill the tube with steam, then the magnesium is heated until it starts to react. If the water is then boiled again,

the magnesium burns very brightly and the flammable gas burns at the jet. A white powder is left in the tube. This reaction is difficult to start but then goes very quickly. If you do the experiment, hold the burner at arm's length.

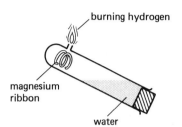

Fig. 7.3

Iron, zinc and copper do not appear to react with cold water. The apparatus shown in Fig. 7.4 can be used to try to react them with steam. Iron and zinc both react and the flammable gas is formed again, but copper will not react.

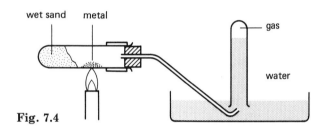

Fig. 7.4

The gas that is formed in all these reactions is called **hydrogen**. So water could be a compound of hydrogen and oxygen and it could be called hydrogen oxide. The reaction that happens when magnesium reacts with water could therefore be written

magnesium + hydrogen oxide
$\longrightarrow$ magnesium oxide + hydrogen

Is water hydrogen oxide?

The reaction of water with metals such as magnesium can be explained if we suppose that water is hydrogen oxide.

Another way of splitting up water is by *electrolysis* (page 25). Two gases are formed when electricity is passed through water. (Some sulphuric acid is usually added to the water to make the electrolysis go faster.) These gases are hydrogen and oxygen. This electrolysis therefore provides more evidence that water is a compound of hydrogen and oxygen.

But final proof that water is hydrogen oxide comes from the *synthesis* of water from hydrogen and oxygen. Only then is it possible to be sure that no other elements are present in water.

The apparatus shown in Fig. 7.5 can be used to show that water is formed when hydrogen burns in air. Strictly, the hydrogen should be burnt in pure oxygen but this experiment is too dangerous to attempt without special apparatus.

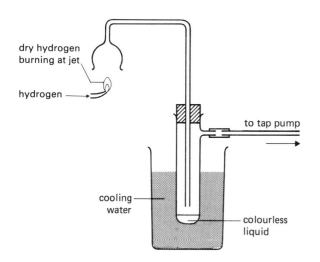

Fig. 7.5

The word-equation for this reaction is

hydrogen + oxygen ⟶ water

The word 'hydrogen' is derived from two Greek words which together mean 'water producer'.

The reaction of calcium oxide and water

When water is added, a drop at a time, to a lump of calcium oxide, the solid crumbles to a dry powder. This reaction is so exothermic that some of the water is boiled off as steam. The dry powder must be a compound of calcium oxide and water.

When the dry powder is shaken with water, an alkaline solution is formed. This is calcium hydroxide solution, or limewater, the solution that is used to test for carbon dioxide (page 11). The word-equation for the reaction of calcium oxide and water is

calcium oxide + water ⟶ calcium hydroxide

The formula of water

In each molecule of water there are two atoms of hydrogen and one of oxygen. This is shown by writing the formula of water as H_2O.

Hydrogen gas is made of molecules, each molecule containing two hydrogen atoms joined together. Oxygen molecules also contain two atoms joined together.

Fig. 7.6 shows how two hydrogen molecules can react with one molecule of oxygen to form two

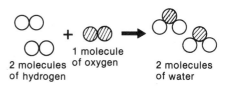

2 molecules of hydrogen   1 molecule of oxygen   2 molecules of water

Fig. 7.6

molecules of water. The equation for the reaction shown in Fig. 7.6 can be written

$$2H_2 + O_2 \longrightarrow 2H_2O$$

The reactions of metals with water

Some metals react with water. The metal takes the oxygen from the water and the metal oxide is formed. The hydrogen that is left appears as a gas. A general word-equation can be written for these reactions.

metal + water (hydrogen oxide)
⟶ metal oxide + hydrogen

This word-equation can be used for the reactions of magnesium, zinc and iron with water but not for the reaction of calcium with water. This is because calcium reacts to produce calcium hydroxide. (If any calcium oxide were formed, it would immediately react to form calcium hydroxide). So the word-equation is

calcium + water
⟶ calcium hydroxide + hydrogen

There are some other metals, such as sodium, which react in a similar way.

The equations for the reactions of magnesium and zinc with water are

$$Mg(s) + H_2O(g) \longrightarrow MgO(s) + H_2(g)$$
$$Zn(s) + H_2O(g) \longrightarrow ZnO(s) + H_2(g)$$

The letters which follow the formulas in the equations are called **symbols of state**. They tell us whether the substance is solid (s), liquid (l), gas (g) or is dissolved in water (aq). (See p. 61.)

The equation for the reaction of iron with water is complicated because the formula of the iron oxide formed is Fe_3O_4.

$$3Fe(s) + 4H_2O(g) \longrightarrow Fe_3O_4(s) + 4H_2(g)$$

The Law of Conservation of Mass (page 19) means that atoms are not destroyed or created during chemical reactions: they are just changed around, with their total numbers remaining constant. So it is important to note that there have to be equal numbers of each sort of atom on both sides of the equation.

Another method of preparing hydrogen

Acids are compounds of hydrogen and at least one other element. In some reactions, the hydrogen in the acids is 'pushed out' by another element. For example, hydrogen is formed when either dilute hydrochloric acid or dilute sulphuric acid reacts with the metals magnesium, zinc or iron. Two word-equations are

magnesium + hydrochloric acid
$$\longrightarrow \text{magnesium chloride} + \text{hydrogen}$$

zinc + sulphuric acid
$$\longrightarrow \text{zinc sulphate} + \text{hydrogen}$$

The other common laboratory acid, nitric acid, usually does not form hydrogen when it reacts with metals. The metals copper and lead do not react with either hydrochloric or sulphuric acids.

The laboratory preparation of hydrogen

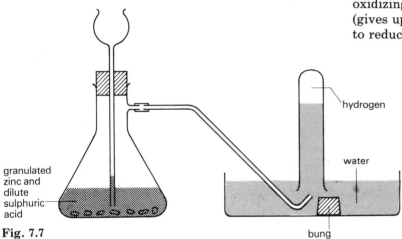

Fig. 7.7

The apparatus shown in Fig. 7.7 can be used to prepare hydrogen in the laboratory. When several test-tubes of gas have been collected, the apparatus should be taken to bits and washed out before any experiments are done with the hydrogen.

The pouring experiments shown in Fig. 7.8 can be used to show that hydrogen 'pours' upwards and is therefore less dense than air. To show which test-tube the hydrogen has poured into, its mouth should be held near to a flame

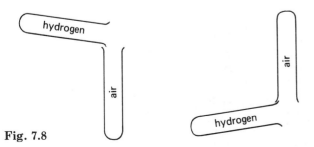

Fig. 7.8

Oxidation and reduction

When an element reacts to form its oxide, it is said to be **oxidized**. So magnesium is oxidized to magnesium oxide when it burns in oxygen or in air. The removal of oxygen from a compound is called **reduction**. When magnesium reacts with steam to produce hydrogen, the water is reduced to hydrogen. In this reaction also, the magnesium is oxidized to magnesium oxide.

Both oxidation and reduction take place at the same time in the same chemical reaction. The magnesium is called the **reducing agent** in this chemical reaction, while the steam is called the **oxidizing agent**.

Oxidation in a chemical reaction takes place when oxygen is added to a substance.
Reduction in a chemical reaction takes place when oxygen is removed from a substance.

The word-equation below shows that oxidation and reduction always go hand in hand.

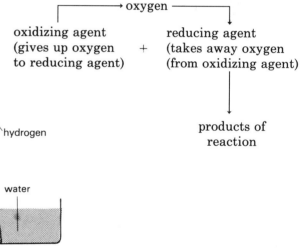

The apparatus shown in Fig. 7.9 can be used to pass hydrogen over heated copper oxide. To make sure that the apparatus is full of hydrogen (and so avoid an explosion when the jet is ignited), fill a test-tube with the gas issuing from the jet and ignite it at a burner one metre away. Then return the tube to the jet. If the gas was pure hydrogen, it will continue burning in the tube and ignite the gas at the jet. A safety screen should also be used.

The black copper oxide turns red and drops of

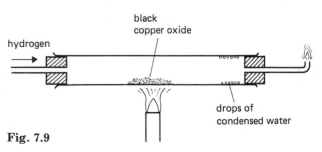

Fig. 7.9

water are formed on the cool parts of the tube. The word-equation is

hydrogen + copper oxide

$\longrightarrow$ hydrogen oxide (water) + copper

The copper oxide is the oxidizing agent because it oxidizes hydrogen to water. The hydrogen is the reducing agent because it reduces copper oxide to copper.

Reactions like these in which reduction and oxidation happen are called **redox** reactions.

The uses of hydrogen

Air is about fifteen times denser than hydrogen, and hydrogen is the least dense of all the gases. This explains why hydrogen has been used in airships. But hydrogen is also very flammable, so the gas helium is now used. Helium is twice as dense as hydrogen but is not flammable.

The reaction between hydrogen and oxygen is very exothermic and it has been used to produce high-temperature flames.

The major use of hydrogen is the manufacture of ammonia (page 133) which is used to make fertilizers, and it is also used to manufacture margarine from vegetable oils (page 238).

QUESTIONS

1 Water is formed when many fuels are burnt in air. What does this tell you about one of the elements of which fuels are made?

2 Kerosine contains compounds made up of only carbon and hydrogen, but propanone (acetone) is made up of carbon, hydrogen and oxygen. Could you tell these two liquids apart simply by burning them in air and identifying their products of combustion? Explain your answer carefully.

3 What kinds of materials can be used to make steam boiler tubes? Why would metals such as zinc or iron be unsuitable?

4 When a test-tube full of hydrogen is lit, there is a small explosion and a blue flame can be seen travelling down the tube; but when a test-tube full of a mixture of hydrogen and air is lit, there is a louder explosion and no blue flame is seen in the tube. Can you explain the difference?

5 Write a short description of the reaction between hot zinc and steam, using the words oxidized, reduced, oxidizing agent and reducing agent.

6 Heated zinc reacts with steam to form hydrogen.
(a) Draw a diagram of the apparatus you would use to make and collect some hydrogen from this chemical reaction.
(b) How would you prove that the gas collected is hydrogen?
(c) Write a word-equation and a symbol-equation for this reaction. (Write zinc oxide as ZnO.)
(d) Name the oxidizing agent and the reducing agent and so explain what happens to the oxygen in this reaction.

7 When hydrogen is passed over yellow lead oxide (PbO), lead and water are formed.
(a) Write down the word-equation and the symbol-equation for this reaction.
(b) Which substance, hydrogen or yellow lead oxide, acts as an oxidizing agent in this reaction, and which substance acts as a reducing agent? Explain your answers.
(c) What would you see happening to the solid (yellow lead oxide) during the experiment?

8 The densities of hydrogen, helium and air are approximately in the ratio $1:2:15$. Helium is inert: it does not react with other substances.
(a) Give one advantage and one disadvantage of using helium rather than hydrogen in an airship.
(b) If you were asked to design an airship, would you use hydrogen or helium in it? Explain your answer.
(c) Would you use hydrogen or helium in a balloon that was going to carry scientific instruments as high as possible into the atmosphere? Explain your answer.

9 Both hydrogen and methane (a gas which is a compound of carbon and hydrogen) burn with blue flames and form dangerously explosive mixtures with air. Also, they both produce water when they burn.

Suggest how to distinguish between the two gases.

Key words

formula   symbols of state   oxidation   reduction   redox   oxidizing agent   reducing agent

Basic facts

● **Water is hydrogen oxide.**

● **Several metals (such as magnesium, zinc, iron, calcium) will react with water or steam to produce hydrogen, but some metals (such as copper) do not react with either water or steam.**

● **Hydrogen is produced by reacting metals such as magnesium, zinc, iron with either dilute hydrochloric acid or dilute sulphuric acid, but some metals, such as copper, do not react.**

● **Hydrogen is usually produced in the laboratory by reacting zinc with dilute sulphuric or hydrochloric acid.**

● **Hydrogen is less dense than air and is flammable, forming dangerously explosive mixtures with air and oxygen.**

● **Hydrogen is used industrially in the manufacture of some fertilizers and margarine.**

8 The effects of electricity on substances

Which elements conduct electricity?

The apparatus in Fig. 8.1 can be used to find out if solid elements conduct electricity. The elements that do conduct electricity (conductors) are the metals, and carbon in the form of graphite. The elements that do not conduct electricity (insulators) are those elements which are not metals – the non-metals.

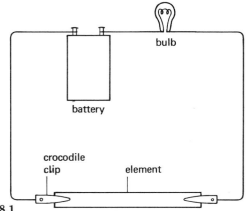

Fig. 8.1

The metal mercury is liquid at room temperature and conducts electricity.

When electricity passes through a metal, the only change that usually occurs is that the metal gets warm. There are no chemical changes. This sort of conduction is called **metallic conduction**.

Which compounds conduct electricity?

The apparatus shown in Fig. 8.2 can be used to find out which compounds conduct electricity. If it is possible to melt the compound, it can be tested when solid and also when molten.

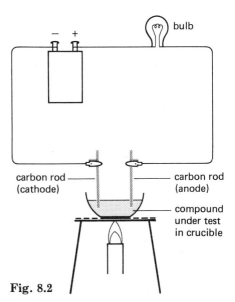

Fig. 8.2

In Fig. 8.2, the carbon rods used to make electrical contact with the substance being tested are called **electrodes**. The electrode that is attached to the negative battery connection is called the **cathode**, while the electrode attached to the positive battery connection is called the **anode**.

When lots of compounds are tested in this way, it is found that:

1 No **compounds** conduct when they are **solid**.
2 Some **compounds** conduct when they are **molten**. These are found to be **compounds of metals**.

When electricity passes through a molten metal compound, chemical changes occur at the electrodes and new substances are produced. This process of causing chemical reactions by passing electricity through a compound is called **electrolysis**. But not all compounds conduct electricity when they are molten. Those compounds that do conduct, and which are broken down by the electricity, are called **electrolytes**, and this sort of conduction is called **electrolytic conduction**. Those compounds that do not conduct are called **non-electrolytes**.

The results for the electrolysis of some molten compounds are given in Table 8.1. The flashes of light that are seen around the cathode are due to small particles of sodium (or potassium) catching fire and burning. In the electrolysis of molten electrolytes, two new substances are formed, one at the anode and one at the cathode. The substance formed at the cathode is the metal from the electrolyte. The substance formed at the anode is the non-metal from the electrolyte.

Do solutions conduct electricity?

Solutions can be tested to find out if they conduct electricity using the apparatus shown in Fig. 8.2. These four generalizations summarize the results:

1 Solutions of metal compounds conduct electricity. The substances found to conduct when molten also conduct when dissolved in water.

Table 8.1

Substance electrolysed	Observations at cathode	Observations at anode
Molten lead bromide	Beads of a grey metal are formed	Bubbles around anode. Red-brown gas given off.
Molten sodium chloride	Yellow flashes	Bubbles around anode. Gas smells like chlorine.
Molten potassium iodide	Occasional flashes	Bubbles around anode. Purple gas formed.

2 Solutions of acids conduct electricity.

3 Compounds that do not contain metals (with the exception of acids) do not conduct electricity when in solution. These are the compounds that were found to be non-conductors when molten.

4 When solutions conduct electricity, chemical changes happen at the electrodes. Passing electricity through solutions is another example of electrolysis and electrolytic conduction.

Gases are formed at the electrodes when some solutions are electrolysed. The apparatus shown in Fig. 8.3 can be used to collect the gases.

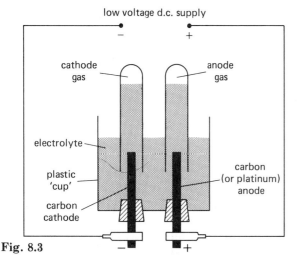

Fig. 8.3

The results for the electrolysis of some solutions are given in Table 8.2. The generalizations that arise from these results are:

1 At the cathode, either the metal from the solute or hydrogen is formed.

2 At the anode either the non-metal from the solute or oxygen is formed.

Electroplating – a use of electrolysis

Electrolysis is important in some industries. One use is in **electroplating**.

Many metal surfaces are covered with a thin layer of another metal. The handlebars of bicycles are covered with chromium so that the steel underneath is protected from the air. Shelf racks used in ovens may be plated with chromium (Fig. 8.4).

The plating is carried out by electrolysis. You know that a metal can be deposited around one of the electrodes during the electrolysis of some solutions. Suppose that you want to plate a shelf rack with chromium. The cathode must be the rack and the electrolyte must be a solution with a chromium compound

Fig. 8.4

Table 8.2

Solute	Observations at cathode	Product at cathode	Observations at anode	Product at anode
Sodium chloride			Pale yellow-green gas which bleaches litmus	Chlorine
Sodium bromide	A gas is produced which explodes when the tube mouth is held near to a flame	Hydrogen	Brownish red solution forms around anode	Bromine
Potassium iodide			Dark red-brown solution formed around anode	Iodine
Magnesium sulphate				
Sulphuric acid			A gas is produced which relights a glowing splint	Oxygen
Copper sulphate	The cathode becomes covered with a red solid	Copper		
Lead nitrate	Crystals, shiny and grey, form on the cathode	Lead		

dissolved in it. The anode could be of chromium, but this is not essential. When electricity is passed through the electrolyte, chromium metal is deposited in a thin layer on the rack (the cathode).

Electroplating can be done in the school laboratory, but it is not easy to get the metal properly 'stuck on' to the cathode. You can get better results by depositing the metal very slowly, but even then you will not be able to reach the quality of industrial electroplating.

Two ways of summarizing the work covered in this chapter are as follows.

Summary 1

(a) Elements
Metals conduct electricity but show no chemical changes when they conduct (metallic conduction). Non-metals do not conduct electricity. The main exception to these very simple generalizations is provided by carbon in the form of graphite.

(b) Compounds
Most compounds of metals conduct electricity when molten and when dissolved in water, but not when solid. Chemical changes occur during the conduction and the substances are called electrolytes. The process of breaking down a substance using electricity is called electrolysis. Compounds of non-metals usually do not conduct electricity in any state, the main exceptions being the acids in solution.

Summary 2

(a) Solids
The solid elements that conduct are the metals and graphite.

(b) Liquids
Mercury is the only metal that is a liquid at room temperature and the only liquid element to conduct electricity. (Other metals will conduct electricity when molten.)

Only compounds of metals will conduct electricity when molten and these usually have high melting points.

(c) Gases
Gases do not conduct electricity under normal conditions.

(d) Solutions
Solutions of metal compounds and solutions of acids in water conduct electricity and are electrolytes.

QUESTIONS

1 Try to construct your own electrolysis kit for solutions, similar to the one shown in Fig. 8.2 or 8.3, using these items:

the bottom half of a soft plastic bottle, two pencils, a dry battery and two pieces of wire.

Your main problem will be to find ways of attaching the wires to the battery and to the pencil leads, and to make the container reasonably watertight if you make the apparatus in Fig. 8.3.

Use your home-made apparatus to find out whether it is possible to electrolyse solutions in water of everyday materials, such as vinegar, 'bicarbonate of soda', detergent and tea.

2 Mercury is a conductor but not an electrolyte. Molten salt is a conductor and an electrolyte. Explain these two statements.

3 What are the likely products at the anode and at the cathode when these solutions are electrolysed: (a) copper bromide solution, and (b) potassium chloride solution?

4 When solid lead bromide is strongly heated, it melts. It is known that the liquid formed gives off small amounts of a red-brown gas (bromine) if heating is continued. When electricity is passed through molten lead bromide, bromine is again formed. Describe how you would try to show that the breakdown taking place in the second experiment is mainly because of the passing of the electricity and not because of the effect of heat.

5 The electrolysis of hydrochloric acid usually gives two substances: hydrogen and chlorine.
(a) How would you test for each of these gases?
(b) At which electrode is each gas likely to form?
(c) Does this result definitely show that hydrochloric acid is made up of only the elements hydrogen and chlorine? Give a reason for your answer.

Key words

conductor	electrode	electrolyte	electrolytic conduction
insulator	cathode	non-electrolyte	electroplating
metallic conduction	anode	electrolysis	

Basic facts
See Summary 1 and Summary 2.

9 Metals and non-metals

There are over one hundred elements known, so learning about the properties of each of them could be a formidable task. But, if the elements can be classified, this task is made much easier. There are many ways of classifying elements and one of the simplest methods is used in this chapter. Other ways, which involve more detail, are introduced later.

Classifying elements

One of the oldest methods of classifying elements is to pick out those that are metals and to have just two classes: **metals** and **non-metals**.

Most people can recognize metals quite easily by using a few simple tests: appearance, 'feel', and whether or not they are dense. The generalizations that can be made about metals are given in Table 9.1 and the boiling points of some elements are shown in Fig. 9.2. Carbon is included in the table where it has properties in common with metals. But generally, the properties of non-metals are the opposite of those of metals.

Some information about elements is given in Data Sheet 2 on page 280. You should use this information to decide how good the generalizations are that are given in Table 9.1.

Investigating oxides

The oxides of some elements can be prepared using the apparatus shown in Fig. 9.1. The element is heated in a bunsen flame until it starts to burn or glow. It is then put into a tube of oxygen.

When the element has stopped burning and the apparatus has cooled, some water is added to see if the oxide dissolves. The solution formed can be tested to find out if it is acidic or alkaline. The results of these experiments are given in Table 9.2.

The generalizations that can be made from these results are as follows.

1 Oxides of metals are solids while the oxides of non-metals are often gases.
2 Oxides of metals either do not react with water or react to give alkaline solutions. The oxides of non-metals react with water to form acidic solutions.

When the oxides of metals such as calcium are added to water, a reaction occurs to form the metal hydroxide (page 22). A general word-equation is

$$\text{metal oxide} + \text{water} \longrightarrow \text{metal hydroxide}$$

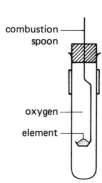

Fig. 9.1

combustion spoon

oxygen

element

Table 9.1

Property	Metals	Notes
Appearance	Usually shiny (metallic lustre); often 'ring' when tapped	It is often necessary to clean a corroded metal to reveal the clean shiny surface.
Melting point and boiling point	Usually high (Fig. 9.2)	All metals except mercury are solids at room temperature. Many cannot be melted in a bunsen flame. A few, e.g. sodium, potassium, have low melting points. (A few non-metals, e.g. carbon have very high melting points.)
Conduction of heat	Good	Metals often feel hot or cold because they are good conductors of heat. Some uses of metals depend on this property.
Conduction of electricity	Good	The ability of a metal to conduct electricity decreases as its temperature rises. Wires and cables that conduct electricity are made of metals. (Carbon in the form of graphite is a good conductor of electricity.)
Density	Usually high	A few metals, e.g. sodium and aluminium, have low densities.
Does it bend or is it brittle?	Metals can be hammered into thin sheets (they are malleable), and drawn into wires (they are ductile)	Engine blocks are 'cast' using molten metal but some metal objects are 'rolled' (sheet steel and girders) or 'pressed' into shape (car body panels) or 'drawn' (wires).

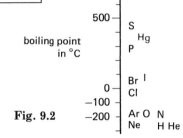

Table 9.2

Element	Reaction with oxygen	Effect of water on the oxide
Potassium Sodium Calcium	Burn brightly to form oxides that are white solids.	React with water to form alkaline solutions
Magnesium		Very slightly soluble in water to give an alkaline suspension
Copper	Slowly forms a black oxide.	Insoluble in water
Lead	Slowly forms a yellow oxide.	
Iron	Iron wool burns brightly to form a black oxide.	
Zinc	Burns brightly to form an oxide that is white when cold but yellow when hot.	
Phosphorus	Burns brightly to form an oxide that is a white solid.	React with water to form acidic solutions
Carbon	Burns brightly to form a colourless gas which turns limewater milky.	
Sulphur	Burns with a blue flame to form a colourless gas that has a choking smell.	

When metal hydroxides dissolve in water, they form alkaline solutions. These metal hydroxides are called alkalis.

When the oxides of non-metals are added to water, reactions occur to form acids:

carbon dioxide + water $\longrightarrow$ carbonic acid

sulphur dioxide + water $\longrightarrow$ sulphurous acid

phosphorus oxide + water $\longrightarrow$ phosphoric acid

Fig. 9.2

QUESTIONS

1 Suppose someone suggests that sodium cannot be a metal because it is soft, and that iodine must be a metal because it is grey and shiny. What would be your reply?

2 Here are some melting points of a selection of solid elements.

aluminium	660 °C	potassium	64 °C
carbon	3730 °C	sodium	98 °C
copper	1083 °C	sulphur	113 °C
iron	1535 °C	zinc	420 °C
phosphorus	44 °C		

Is there any link between the melting point of the element and whether it is a metal or a non-metal? Which melting points surprise you most?

3 What is the evidence in favour of carbon in the form of graphite being classed (a) as a metal, (b) as a non-metal?

4 What is the connection between the properties of metals and their uses in the following ways?

(a) iron for railway tracks

(b) aluminium for cooking pans

(c) copper for electricity cables

(d) chromium for plating iron in the making of door knobs and car fenders

(e) copper for making car radiators

(f) aluminium alloys for making aeroplanes

Key words

metal   non-metal

Basic facts

● Elements can be classified as metals and non-metals. These two classes of elements have characteristic physical properties.

● Metal oxides are solids and either do not react with water or react and form alkalis. Non-metal oxides react with water to form acids.

Metals, acids and salts

10 Investigating malachite

Some reactions of malachite

An ore is a rock from which a metal can be obtained. Your teacher may show you some lumps of an ore called malachite. You will do experiments on powdered malachite to try to find out what substance it is and which metal it contains.

The usual way to investigate a substance is to try to break it down into simpler substances in the hope that these simpler substances can be recognized.

Experiment 10.1 What happens when malachite is heated?

Heat some malachite powder in a small test-tube, gently at first and then more strongly.

▶ What happens when malachite is heated?
▶ Give reasons why the change must be a chemical reaction.
▶ How could you find out if malachite is reacting with something in the air?
▶ How could you find out if a gas is given off when malachite is heated?
▶ If a gas *is* given off, how would you try to identify it?
▶ How could you find out if malachite is simply losing water of crystallization when heated?

Try to plan an investigation so that you can find out more about what happens when malachite is heated. Talk about your ideas with your teacher. Do not do any experiments until you have your teacher's permission.

Experiment 10.2 Does malachite react with dilute sulphuric acid?

Put a spatula measure of malachite powder into a test-tube and add a few drops of bench dilute sulphuric acid. If there is a reaction, carefully add more acid until the reaction stops.

▶ Is a gas given off?

If a gas *is* given off, try to find out what it is.

▶ Is the change a chemical reaction? Give reasons for your answer.

Now find out if the black residue formed when malachite is heated also reacts with acids. Make some of the black powder by putting a spatula measure of malachite powder in a crucible lid and heating it until it turns black. Then transfer the black powder to a test-tube and add a small amount of bench dilute sulphuric acid.

▶ Does a reaction occur?

If you think that there is no reaction, gently warm the mixture for a few minutes.

▶ Is a gas given off?

At this stage of your investigation, you should draw a diagram in your book to show your results (Fig. 10.1). You should include in this the names of the gases.

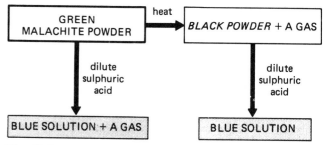

Fig. 10.1

It is very likely that the metal in malachite was first extracted by accident, by someone lighting a wood fire on some rock that contained malachite. If this did happen, the malachite would have been heated strongly next to some charcoal.

Experiment 10.3 Reacting the black powder with charcoal

Heat a spatula measure of malachite powder on a crucible lid until it has turned black. Let it cool and then mix in a spatula measure of powdered wood charcoal. Heat this mixture again.

▶ Is there any sign that a reaction occurs?

Look at the residue very closely and try to find some grains of metal. You will probably be disappointed with the amount of metal produced.

It is possible to separate the small amount of metal formed in the following way.

1. Grind up the residue, using a pestle and mortar. Then tip the finely powdered residue into a beaker.
2. Add some water and stir the mixture.
3. Gently pour away the liquid, which will be black because it has unreacted carbon suspended in it.
4. Repeat 2 and 3 until most of the black powder has been washed away and you are left with a residue that is not black.

▶ Why does this method of separation work?
▶ What colour is the residue?
▶ If it is a metal, can you suggest which metal it might be?
▶ Try to explan what happens to the carbon in this reaction.

Experiment 10.4 Is a gas given off when the black powder is heated with charcoal?

Heat a spatula measure of malachite powder on a crucible lid until it turns black, as in Experiment 10.3. Then decide what sort of apparatus you need to use to find out if a gas is given off when the black powder is heated with charcoal. Remember that if a gas is given off, you need to find out what it is.

Talk about your ideas with your teacher and either your teacher will show you the experiment or you will be allowed to do it for yourself.

One way of writing the equation for the reaction in Experiment 10.4 is

black powder + carbon $\longrightarrow$ metal + gas

You should now know the names of the metal and the gas. So the elements that must be present in the black powder are copper and oxygen.

When malachite is heated, the equation for the reaction can be written as

malachite $\xrightarrow{\text{heat}}$ black powder + carbon dioxide

When they are heated, many metal carbonates decompose to form the metal oxide and carbon dioxide. Metal carbonates also react with acids to form carbon dioxide and a soluble metal compound.

You should now be able to write the full word-equations for the action of heat on malachite and on the mixture of carbon and the black powder. The word-equation for the reaction of malachite with sulphuric acid is

copper carbonate + sulphuric acid
$\longrightarrow$ carbon dioxide + water
+ copper sulphate

The word-equation for the reaction of the black powder with sulphuric acid is

copper oxide + sulphuric acid
$\longrightarrow$ copper sulphate + water

You should now be able to put chemical names into Fig. 10.1 for all the solids and solutions.

Experiment 10.5 What happens when zinc or iron is added to copper sulphate solution?

Pour some of the blue solution from Experiment 10.2 into a test-tube and add either a clean iron nail or a clean piece of zinc foil.

▶ What happens on the surface of the added metal?
▶ What happens to the colour of the solution? (You may have to leave the experiment for half an hour or so to be able to answer this question.)
▶ Try to explain what is happening to the solution and also to the zinc or iron.

Experiment 10.6 Is the blue solution an electrolyte?

Design a suitable apparatus to find out if the blue solution is an electrolyte. Use carbon electrodes. When you do the experiment, note carefully what happens at each electrode.

▶ Try to explain what is happening at the cathode.

Summary

Malachite is copper carbonate. When it is heated, it decomposes.

copper carbonate
$\longrightarrow$ copper oxide + carbon dioxide

With dilute sulphuric acid, the word-equation for the reaction is

copper carbonate + sulphuric acid
$\longrightarrow$ copper sulphate + water
+ carbon dioxide

When copper oxide is added to dilute sulphuric acid, there is a slow reaction which can be speeded up by warming.

copper oxide + sulphuric acid
$\longrightarrow$ copper sulphate + water

When copper oxide is heated with carbon (charcoal), the word-equation for the reaction is

copper oxide + carbon $\longrightarrow$ copper + carbon dioxide

Copper can be extracted from copper sulphate solution by electrolysis or by adding a metal such as iron.

copper sulphate + iron
$\longrightarrow$ iron sulphate + copper

11 The reactivities of metals

The reactions of metals with oxygen

The reactions of some elements with oxygen have been described in Chapter 6 and the results are given in Table 6.1 on page 17. In each case the element reacts with oxygen to form an oxide.

The preparation of some more oxides, and an investigation of their properties, are described in Chapter 9. The results of the experiments are given in Table 9.2 on page 29. The generalizations that can be made about oxides from these results are given on page 28.

Some metals burn very brightly in air: sodium, potassium, calcium and magnesium. These metals burn even more brightly in oxygen. Zinc and iron burn slowly in air but much more rapidly and brightly in oxygen. Copper and lead do not burn in either air or oxygen, but form their oxides slowly without giving out any light.

For a metal to burn brightly, its reaction with oxygen must be very exothermic. The heat given out in the reaction raises the temperature of the metal until it is so hot that it glows.

Is it possible to measure how readily these metals react with oxygen? Two ways are to judge the amount of heat produced when the metal reacts, and how quickly the metal reacts. Metals like magnesium are said to be very **reactive** towards oxygen because the reaction goes very rapidly and a lot of heat is given out. Metals such as copper are not very reactive towards oxygen because they react slowly without producing a lot of heat.

From these experiments, metals can be arranged in their **order of reactivity** towards oxygen. The hardest part of this task is to decide how to classify the reactions that you have seen. One possible classification is as follows:

1 Metals that react fairly rapidly with oxygen at room temperature. These metals have to be stored under an oil to prevent oxidation occurring, e.g. sodium.
2 Metals which do not have to be stored in oil, but which burn brightly in air, e.g. magnesium.
3 Metals which burn slowly in air but which burn brightly in oxygen, e.g. iron.
4 Metals which do not burn in either air or oxygen but which form their oxides slowly, e.g. copper.

The most reactive metals are in the first group, while the least reactive metals are in the fourth group. You may be able to suggest some metals that would fit into a fifth group: those that do not form oxides when heated in air. These metals are often called the noble metals, an example being gold.

The reactions of metals with water

The reactions of some metals with water are discussed in Chapter 7 and the results are summarized on page 22.

We have seen that metals can be arranged in an order of reactivity by classifying their reactions with oxygen. Is it possible to arrange metals in an order of reactivity by using their reactions with water? Look back at the results given in Chapter 7 and put the metals calcium, copper, iron, magnesium and zinc in their order of reactivity with water.

Sodium is so reactive towards oxygen that it has to be stored underneath an oil such as paraffin. Is it also very reactive with water?

Your teacher may show you the spectacular reaction when a small piece of sodium is added to water. The apparatus shown in Fig. 11.1 is used. Sodium is less dense than water and also has a melting point just below 100 °C. The sodium floats on the water.

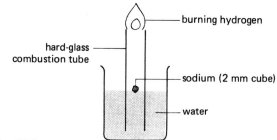

hard-glass combustion tube — burning hydrogen — sodium (2 mm cube) — water

Fig. 11.1

The reaction is sufficiently exothermic to melt the metal. The gas produced can be ignited and sometimes explodes safely or burns with a blue flame. If some red litmus is added to the solution left when the reaction has stopped, it turns blue.

You should be able to write a word-equation for the reaction of sodium and water. (If you are in doubt, refer back to the reaction of calcium with water on page 22.) You should also be able to decide how reactive sodium is in comparison with the other metals you have studied.

The metal potassium is similar to sodium. It also is stored under an oil. Its reaction with water is similar to that of sodium, but is even more exothermic and so is more dangerous.

How reactive is lead towards water? You may know that lead has been used for making water pipes, gutters and for roofing buildings. Your teacher may do the experiment shown in Fig. 7.4 using lead to show you that hot lead does not react with steam.

You should now try to arrange the metals in their order of reactivity towards water. A suitable classification could be as follows:

1 Metals which react rapidly with cold water, e.g. sodium.
2 Metals which react very slowly with cold water, but which burn when heated in steam, e.g. magnesium.
3 Metals which do not appear to react with cold water but which react when heated in steam, without burning, e.g. zinc.
4 Metals which will not react even when heated in steam, e.g. lead.

This order of reactivity is very similar to their order of reactivity towards oxygen.

The reactions of metals with acids

One way of preparing hydrogen is to react metals, such as magnesium, zinc or iron, with either dilute hydrochloric acid or dilute sulphuric acid (page 23).

Do other metals react with these acids to produce hydrogen? What is the order of reactivity of metals towards acids?

Experiment 11.1 *What is the order of reactivity of metals in their reactions with acids?*

For this experiment you will use foil of the metals: copper, iron, lead, magnesium and zinc.

Pour either dilute hydrochloric or sulphuric acid into a test-tube until it is one-quarter full. Add a 10 mm square of a metal foil and look to see if a reaction happens. If there is no reaction, gently warm the acid, shaking the tube and pointing it away from you. Do not heat the acid so that it boils. Is there a reaction now?

▶ Which metals react with the acids and which do not react?
▶ Which metals react most quickly?
▶ Try to arrange the metals in their order of reactivity with acids.

In the experiment, you may have noticed that some of the test-tubes get warm even when the acid is not heated. Many of these reactions are exothermic. The *amount of heat* given out in these reactions can be used as a measure of the reactivity of the metal towards the acid. Imagine an experiment in which 5 cm^3 of bench dilute hydrochloric acid is added to two spatula measures of several metal powders in separate test-tubes. Each tube is surrounded by cotton wool to cut down heat losses. The rises in temperature found in this experiment are given in this table.

Metal	*Rise in temp-erature in °C*
Magnesium	65
Zinc	10
Iron	5
Lead	1
Copper	0

The order of reactivity given here agrees well with those already obtained from the reactions of metals with oxygen and with water.

QUESTIONS

1 Gold, silver and platinum are used in jewellery.
(a) What chemical properties of these metals make them suitable for this use?
(b) Suggest one other reason (non-chemical) which helps to explain their use.
(c) How reactive are these metals towards oxygen and water? Where would you place them in the order of reactivity of metals?

2 Explain why magnesium is never found in rocks as an element, but occasionally copper is.

3 Which of the metals zinc, iron, copper would be suitable for making pipes to carry steam? Explain your answer.

4 Try to find out which are the so-called 'noble metals'. What is special about their properties?

5 Make a list of the metals that have uses in everyday life. Try to relate the uses of these metals to their properties.

6 What are the 'coinage metals'? Which properties of these metals make them suitable for this use?

Key words

reactivity

order of reactivity

Basic facts

● **It is possible to arrange metals in the order of their reactivities towards oxygen, water and acids:**
  1 by comparing the speeds of reaction,
  2 by comparing the amounts of heat given out by the reaction.

● **The orders of reactivity towards oxygen, water and acids are very similar.**

● **The order of reactivity for the metals, putting the most reactive one first, is potassium, sodium, calcium, magnesium, zinc, iron, lead, copper.**

12 Competition between metals

Metals competing for oxygen

Magnesium reacts with steam to form magnesium oxide and hydrogen.

magnesium + hydrogen oxide (steam)
$\longrightarrow$ magnesium oxide + hydrogen

In this reaction, magnesium takes the oxygen from steam, leaving the hydrogen on its own.

Fig. 12.1

You can imagine this reaction as a kind of 'tug-of-war' or competition between magnesium and hydrogen for the oxygen (Fig. 12.1): the magnesium tries to take the oxygen from the water while the hydrogen tried to hold on to it. Since magnesium forms magnesium oxide, magnesium must win the 'tug-of-war'. The magnesium must have a stronger attraction for the oxygen than the hydrogen has: magnesium is more *reactive* towards oxygen than hydrogen is.

But copper does not react with steam. In this 'tug-of-war', hydrogen manages to hold on to its oxygen in the face of a weaker pull from the metal. Copper is less reactive towards oxygen than hydrogen is, so when copper and hydrogen compete for oxygen, the hydrogen wins.

These results mean that magnesium is more reactive towards oxygen than copper is. So if magnesium and copper are made to compete for oxygen, the magnesium should win. Your teacher may show you the very spectacular reaction when magnesium is heated with copper oxide. This is a dangerous reaction and you must not try it for yourself. The word-equation for this reaction is

magnesium + copper oxide
$\longrightarrow$ magnesium oxide + copper

You should now understand why there is no reaction when copper is heated with magnesium oxide.

Experiment 12.1 Competition for oxygen between iron, copper and lead

Your teacher will provide you with copper powder, lead powder, iron filings, black copper oxide, yellow lead oxide and red iron oxide.
WARNING: On no account should you use any other metals because some of the reactions between metals and metal oxides can be extremely dangerous.

Try all the reactions that you think should occur, and at least one that you expect not to occur. Use a mixture of roughly equal volumes of metal and the metal oxide, and heat the mixture strongly on a crucible lid supported by a pipeclay triangle. Stand back while the mixture is being heated. Watch carefully for any signs of a reaction and look at the residue after it has cooled for any traces of the metal from the metal oxide.

▶ Write a word-equation for each reaction that occurs.
▶ Arrange the metals in the order of their reactivities to oxygen.

Competition for oxygen between metals and carbon

Experiment 10.3 shows that copper can be obtained from copper oxide by heating it with carbon.

copper oxide + carbon
$\longrightarrow$ copper + carbon dioxide

In this reaction the copper oxide is reduced (page 23) to copper and the carbon is oxidized to carbon dioxide. This reaction occurs because carbon is more reactive than copper towards oxygen. Which other metal oxides can be reduced in a similar reaction?

Experiment 12.2 Which metal oxides can be reduced by charcoal?

You are given some calcium oxide, yellow lead oxide and red iron oxide. Use the apparatus shown in Fig. 12.2 to find out which of these oxides can be

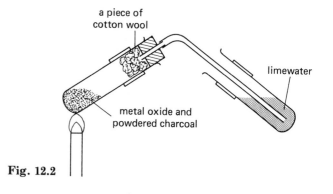

a piece of cotton wool

limewater

metal oxide and powdered charcoal

Fig. 12.2

reduced by heating them with wood charcoal. If reduction takes place, you may be able to see a change in the colour of the oxide as the metal is formed.

▶ What happens to the limewater if reduction takes place?
▶ Which gas causes this change and how is it formed during the reduction?
▶ Which metals are less reactive than carbon towards oxygen?
▶ Write word-equations for the reactions that occur.

Extracting iron from iron oxide

It is very difficult to produce any iron by heating iron oxide with carbon in the laboratory. But in industry, iron can be extracted using carbon, so long as the temperature of the mixture is kept as high as 1200 °C.

Fig. 12.3

Iron has been used by Man for a very long time. The first furnaces were much smaller than those shown in Fig. 12.3 and they were packed with charcoal instead of coke. Older people in some parts

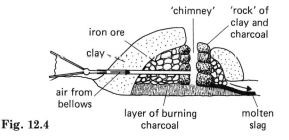

Fig. 12.4

of Africa still know how to extract iron in their villages. Fig. 12.4 shows what the inside of a furnace looks like.

The charcoal is the fuel that heats the furnace. But it also reacts with oxygen in the air pumped in by the bellows, to form carbon monoxide. Carbon monoxide is the reducing agent for the iron ore. At the end of the chemical reaction, the furnace can be opened to get out the hot, solid iron. When this has been cooled, it is ready to be beaten into the shape of a tool. Each furnace can make a few kilograms of iron at a time.

Competition for oxygen between metals and hydrogen

The reactions of metals with water are discussed in Chapters 7 (page 22) and 11 (page 32). The metals lead and copper do not react with either water or steam to produce hydrogen. The hydrogen holds on to its oxygen against the pull of the metals. It seems that hydrogen is more reactive towards oxygen than either copper or lead is.

This can be checked by finding out if hydrogen will take oxygen from lead oxide and copper oxide. Your teacher may show you these reactions using an

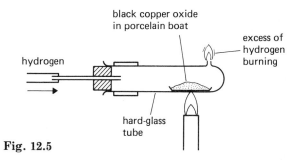

Fig. 12.5

apparatus like that in Fig. 12.5. In both cases, the metal oxide is reduced to the metal.

copper oxide + hydrogen ⟶ copper + water

Getting metals from solutions

When you put an iron nail into a solution of copper sulphate, the nail gets coated with a red solid (Experiment 10.5). This solid is copper and it has been 'pushed out' (displaced) from copper sulphate by the iron.

iron + copper sulphate
⟶ copper + iron sulphate

Reactions like these are called **displacement reactions**. By knowing the reactivity order for metals, we can predict if a metal is likely to displace another metal from a solution of one of its compounds. Iron is more reactive than copper and it also displaces copper from a solution of copper sulphate.

You should copy Table 12.1 into your notebook and fill it in with your forecast for each pair of metal and solution. If you think displacement will occur, put a tick in the box; if you think it will not, put a cross. (As an example, there is already a tick in the iron–coppper sulphate box, and a cross in the copper–iron sulphate box.)

You can see if your forecasts are correct by doing the next experiment.

Table 12.1

Metal \ Solution	Copper sulphate	Iron sulphate	Lead nitrate	Magnesium sulphate	Zinc sulphate
Copper		X			
Iron	√				
Lead					
Magnesium					
Zinc					

Experiment 12.3 Investigating some displacement reactions

Use the metals and solutions given in Table 12.1. In each case, add a small piece of cleaned metal (foil or nail) to a small volume of the solution in a test-tube.

▶ Can you see any new deposit on the surface of the metals?

If no change occurs straight away, leave the test-tube standing in a rack for a few minutes and then look at the metal again.

▶ What is the order of reactivity for the metals in these displacement reactions?
▶ Does this order agree with the order found in your earlier experiments?
▶ Write word-equations for the reactions that occur.

Which way round do copper and lead come in the order of reactivity? This question is difficult to answer. But Experiment 12.3 shows that when lead is put into copper sulphate solution, a reddish layer is formed on the surface of the lead. In this experiment copper is clearly less reactive than lead.

The position of aluminium in the order of reactivity

What are the everyday uses of aluminium? Do these provide any clues about how reactive aluminium is?

Aluminium is used to make cooking pans. This use relies on aluminium not reacting with either water or oxygen in the air, even when it is heated.

When aluminium is put into either dilute hydrochloric or sulphuric acids, there is no apparent reaction. But if aluminium is put into some fairly concentrated hydrochloric acid there is no reaction for a short time, and then a rapid exothermic reaction takes place.

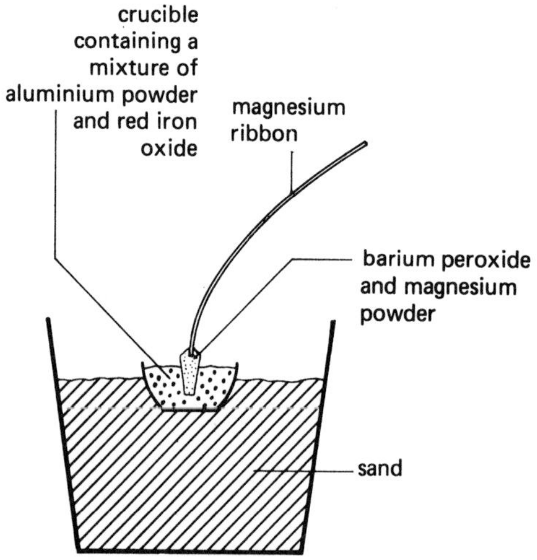

Fig. 12.6 The thermit reaction between aluminium and red iron oxide

Your teacher may show you the reaction between aluminium and red iron oxide. It is a reaction that is difficult to start and the special arrangement shown in Fig. 12.6 has to be used. The barium peroxide provides plenty of oxygen in which the magnesium ribbon can burn as a fuse. The burning fuse gives a high enough temperature for the reaction to begin. Once started, the reaction is spectacular and a great deal of heat is given out, so you must view it from a safe distance. Molten iron is formed, so the reaction must be very exothermic, because the melting point of iron is over 1500 °C. After the crucible has cooled, the contents can be tipped out to reveal the lump of iron.

This reaction shows that aluminium is more reactive than iron. The word-equation for the reaction is

aluminium + iron oxide

$\longrightarrow$ aluminium oxide + iron

The reaction of aluminium with a metal oxide is called the **thermit** reaction. It is not used to extract iron from iron oxide because aluminium is too expensive, but it is used for extracting chromium from chromium oxide. It is also used for welding together railway rails. The thermit mixture is packed into the joint between the rails in a special fire-resistant mould. The heat produced by the reaction is sufficient to melt and weld together the ends of the rails.

Experiment 12.4 A displacement reaction of aluminium

Leave a piece of aluminium foil in a few cm³ of copper sulphate solution in a test-tube for several minutes.

▶ Can you see a deposit of copper on the foil?

Carry out the experiment in Fig. 12.7. Take the foil from the acid just after the bubbles of gas start to form rapidly over the surface, and quickly rinse it in water and add it to the copper sulphate solution.

▶ What can you see now?

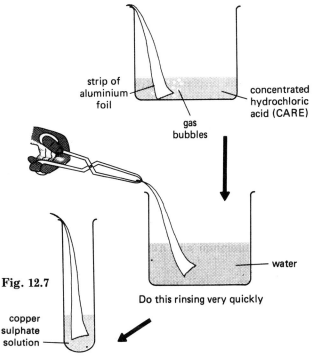

strip of aluminium foil

concentrated hydrochloric acid (CARE)

gas bubbles

water

Fig. 12.7

Do this rinsing very quickly

copper sulphate solution

Aluminium is a fairly reactive metal – not as reactive as magnesium but more reactive than iron. But it is usually reluctant to react because it gets quickly covered with a thin layer of aluminium oxide as soon as it meets the oxygen in the air. This thin layer of aluminium oxide acts as a protective layer. It prevents the metal underneath from reacting.

It is now possible to explain the peculiar reactions of aluminium. It does not react with an acid until the layer of aluminium oxide has been removed by reacting with the acid. Concentrated hydrochloric acid does this fairly quickly but dilute hydrochloric acid takes a long time. The thermit reaction is very difficult to start because of the protective oxide layer. Also there is no reaction beween copper sulphate solution and aluminium until the protective layer of aluminium oxide has been removed (as in Experiment 12.4).

The reason why aluminium can be used to make cooking pots is that the layer of aluminium oxide prevents the aluminium from reacting with water and oxygen under most conditions.

The reactivity series

The experiments in Chapter 11 demonstrate that metals show a similar order of reactivity towards oxygen, water and acids. The experiments in this chapter show that the idea of an order of reactivity can be extended to other reactions and that a similar order of reactivity is found in all cases. So it is possible to refer to a 'reactive metal' without saying what the metal is being reacted with. And a **reactivity order** or **reactivity table** or **reactivity series** can be made for the metals which applies to most of their reactions. A reactivity table is shown in Table 12.2.

Table 12.2

Metal	Air or oxygen	Water or steam	Dilute hydrochloric or sulphuric acids	Competition for oxygen between metals	Displacement reactions	Reduction of the metal oxide with:	
						carbon	hydrogen
Potassium Sodium Calcium	Burn to form oxides	React with cold water to form alkaline solutions and hydrogen	React giving off hydrogen	Each metal will reduce the oxides of metals lower in the series	Each metal will displace metals lower in the series	Not reduced	Not reduced (but the metal will reduce water)
Magnesium Aluminium Zinc Iron		React with steam to form metal oxide and hydrogen				Reduced only at very high temperature	Reduced
Lead Copper	Slow oxidation	No reaction	No reaction			Reduced	

There is another table, called the **electrochemical series** which compares the reactivities of metals in a different way. The order of the metals is nearly the same in both tables.

Some of the reactions suggested in Table 12.2 are too dangerous to carry out. For example, the metals potassium, sodium and calcium react rapidly with water and their reactions with acids would be dangerously explosive. Similarly, displacement reactions using sodium are not tried because the metal reacts too rapidly with water.

QUESTIONS

1 Suppose you were given a sample of tin metal. Describe how you would decide its position in the reactivity series. Your answer should include details of several different experiments, some of which you may like to try out after your teacher has given you permission.

2 Here are some facts about lead.

(*a*) When heated strongly, lead reacts slowly with air to form an oxide.

(*b*) It reacts with moderately concentrated hydrochloric acid when it is boiled, but it does not react with the dilute acid.

Say whether you think that lead is more or less reactive than (i) magnesium, (ii) copper, and (iii) iron. Give your reasons for your answers.

If you were given samples of lead powder, yellow lead oxide, copper powder, black copper oxide, iron filings and red iron oxide, how would you set about checking your answers to this question?

3 Write down the evidence you know for aluminium being placed between magnesium and iron in the reactivity series.

4 Explain why magnesium is not found in rocks as an element but silver is.

5 Iron is a cheap metal. Can you think of some reasons for this?

6 What are the 'coinage' metals? Which properties of these metals make them suitable for coin manufacture?

7 How would the possible uses of iron and aluminium be changed if iron formed a layer of iron oxide which protected it from further rusting, and aluminium was not protected by a layer of aluminium oxide?

Key words

displacement reaction   **thermit reaction**   **reactivity table (series), or electrochemical series**

Basic facts

- **Reactive metals can be used to reduce the oxides of less reactive metals.**

- **Carbon can reduce the oxides of the metals zinc and below in the reactivity table, but the temperatures needed for the carbon reduction of zinc oxide and iron oxide are too high to be reached in school laboratories.**

- **Hydrogen will reduce the oxides of the metals iron and below in the reactivity table.**

- **Reactive metals will displace less reactive metals from solutions of their compounds.**

- **In everyday life, aluminium appears to be a fairly unreactive metal. In fact it is fairly reactive but is protected by a thin layer of aluminium oxide.**

- **Metals can be arranged in an order of reactivity which applies to all their reactions.**

13 The action of heat on some metal compounds

The action of heat on metal carbonates

The investigation of malachite (Chapter 10) involves the heating of copper carbonate. The word-equation for this reaction is

copper carbonate

$\longrightarrow$ copper oxide + carbon dioxide

Do other metal carbonates decompose like this when they are heated?

Experiment 13.1 Do metal carbonates decompose when they are heated?

Put a spatula measure of a metal carbonate into a small test-tube and heat it, gently at first, but then more strongly if no reaction occurs.

Note any changes that happen. Test for the formation of carbon dioxide by holding the mouth of the small tube over a test-tube one-quarter filled with limewater. Remember to shake the tube of limewater occasionally.

Use some of the following carbonates:
either sodium carbonate or potassium carbonate, calcium carbonate, lead carbonate, magnesium carbonate, zinc carbonate (and copper carbonate if you need to revise that reaction).

Make a table such as that shown in Table 13.1, showing the results of your experiments. One line has been completed already.

The action of heat on metal nitrates

Experiment 13.2 Do metal nitrates decompose on heating?

Put a few crystals of a metal nitrate in a small tube (only enough to fill the rounded part at the bottom of the tube). Heat them, gently at first, but then more strongly if no reaction has occurred. Note any changes that happen.

CARE. Many crystals shatter when heated, and small pieces may fly out of the tube. Don't point the tube at anyone while the crystals are being heated.

Table 13.1 The effect of heat on carbonates

	Appearance before heating	Effect of heat	Is carbon dioxide given off?
Copper carbonate	Green powder	The powder quickly turns black	Yes. Only gentle heating is necessary

▶ Which carbonates decompose easily when they are heated gently? Which ones decompose only when heated strongly? Are there any which do not decompose?

▶ Try to arrange the carbonates in the order which shows how easily they decompose. Is there any link between this order and the position of the metal in the reactivity table?

When hydrated sodium carbonate is heated gently, the solid appears to melt, steam is given off and another white solid is formed. It is best to explain this 'melting' as the solid dissolving in its own water of crystallization.

Provided the samples of sodium and potassium carbonates are pure, they do not produce carbon dioxide when they are heated. The temperature of the bunsen burner flame is not high enough to cause them to decompose. All the other carbonates should give off carbon dioxide when they are heated, but calcium carbonate needs to be heated very strongly for it to decompose. The general word-equation for the reaction is

metal carbonate $\longrightarrow$ metal oxide + carbon dioxide

The carbonates of metals high in the reactivity series are the most difficult to decompose (sodium and potassium carbonates are not decomposed at the temperature of a bunsen burner flame and calcium carbonate decomposes only slowly). But the carbonates of metals lower in the reactivity table decompose more easily. There seems to be a connection between the position of the metal in the reactivity series and how easily its carbonate decomposes.

Test for the formation of oxygen by inserting a glowing splint into the tube, but **do not allow the splint to touch the hot metal nitrate.**

A brown gas may be given off. This gas, nitrogen dioxide, is very poisonous, **so you must stop heating the solid as soon as some of the brown gas has been formed.**

Use some of the following nitrates:
either sodium or potassium nitrate, calcium nitrate, copper nitrate, lead nitrate, magnesium nitrate and zinc nitrate.

Make a table of the results of your experiments similar to Table 13.1.

▶ Which nitrates decompose easily when they are heated gently? Which ones decompose only when heated strongly? Are there any which do not decompose?

▶ Try to arrange the nitrates in the order which shows how easily they decompose. Is there any link between this order and the position of the metal in the reactivity table?

You should have found that all the nitrates decompose when heated. Sodium and potassium nitrates first melt and then, on further heating, bubbles of a colourless gas are formed. The glowing splint test shows that this gas is oxygen. No nitrogen dioxide is formed and the word-equation for the decomposition of sodium nitrate is

sodium nitrate $\longrightarrow$ sodium nitrite + oxygen

The equation for the decomposition of potassium nitrate is similar.

All the other nitrates decompose more easily and produce both nitrogen dioxide and oxygen. The word-equation for the decomposition of lead nitrate is

lead nitrate $\longrightarrow$ lead oxide + oxygen + nitrogen dioxide

The word-equations for the decompositions of the other nitrates are similar to this. Some of the metal nitrates you used will have been hydrated and so may have behaved at first like sodium carbonate in Experiment 13.1.

The hydroxides of sodium and potassium do not decompose at bunsen burner temperatures, but the other metal hydroxides do decompose. The metal hydroxides that are easiest to decompose are generally those of the metals low in the reactivity table.

Summary

The ease with which metal carbonates, nitrates and hydroxides decompose depends on the position of the metal in the reactivity table. The results are summarized in Table 13.2.

Table 13.2

Metal	Action of heat on the metal carbonate	Action of heat on the metal nitrate	Action of heat on the metal hydroxide
Potassium Sodium	Will not decompose at bunsen burner temperatures.	Decompose when heated strongly, to form the metal nitrite and oxygen.	Will not decompose at bunsen burner temperatures.
Calcium Magnesium Zinc Lead Copper	Decompose to give the metal oxide and carbon dioxide. Carbonates of metals low in the series decompose most easily.	Decompose to give the metal oxide, oxygen and nitrogen dioxide. Nitrates of metals low in the series decompose most easily.	Decompose to give the metal oxide and water (steam). Hydroxides of metals low in the series decompose most easily.

There seems to be a connection between the position of the metal in the reactivity series and how easily the metal nitrate decomposes. The nitrates of sodium and potassium decompose only when heated very strongly. Even then, they do not produce any nitrogen dioxide but just oxygen. The nitrates of metals lower in the series decompose more easily and give off both oxygen and nitrogen dioxide. The nitrates of metals low in the series decompose most easily.

The action of heat on metal hydroxides

Your teacher may provide you with some metal hydroxides. You should plan your own investigation to find out if they decompose on heating. If you are doubtful about the reaction that may occur, look back to Chapter 7 (page 22). The reactions you will be trying to make happen are the *reverse* of the reactions studied there.

When you have done the experiments, answer the same sort of questions for the metal hydroxides that were asked at the ends of Experiments 13.1 and 13.2, page 39.

Some metal hydroxides decompose on heating, producing the metal oxide and water.

metal hydroxide $\longrightarrow$ metal oxide + water

QUESTIONS

1 Many metal oxides do not decompose when heated in a bunsen flame. Mercury oxide and silver oxide do decompose on heating to give the metal and oxygen. What do these results suggest about the positions of mercury and silver in the reactivity series?

2 The carbonate and nitrate of metal X were heated. The carbonate gave off carbon dioxide but only when it was heated strongly. The nitrate of X was seen to produce a brown gas when it was heated.
(a) Write word-equations for these two reactions, using X for the metal.
(b) Where would you expect X to be placed in the reactivity series? Explain your reasoning.

3 Strontium is a metal that is very similar to calcium in both reactivity and properties. What would you expect to happen in the following experiments? Write word-equations for any reactions.
(a) Strontium is added to water.
(b) Strontium nitrate is heated strongly.
(c) Strontium carbonate is heated strongly.

4 (a) Write a word-equation for the action of heat on lead nitrate.
(b) Suggest an apparatus and method that could be used to collect the nitrogen dioxide and oxygen separately. Some properties of the two gases are: oxygen is only sparingly soluble in water but nitrogen dioxide reacts to form an acidic solution; oxygen has a boiling point $-183\,°C$, while the boiling point of nitrogen dioxide is $20\,°C$.
(c) Describe one test you could use to find out if the oxygen you collected contains some nitrogen dioxide (too little to see).

14 Neutralizing acids with alkalis

Acidity and the pH scale

The pH scale (page 8) measures the acidity or alkalinity of solutions. The pH values of some substances are shown in Fig. 14.1 together with the ranges of colours of one sort of universal indicator.

out because the burette is marked to show volumes – it is **calibrated**. The advantages of this method are that the volumes of solutions are measured accurately and the experiment can be repeated until consistent results are obtained.

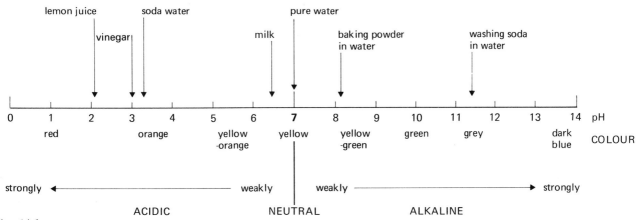

Fig. 14.1

The strong acids, hydrochloric, nitric and sulphuric acids, have pH values of 0, while the strong alkalis, sodium hydroxide and calcium hydroxide (limewater), have pH values of 14. The acids that can be used in foods or which are present in fruits are weak acids.

You know from Chapter 3 (page 9) that acids can be neutralized by substances such as sodium hydrogencarbonate (bicarbonate of soda) and sodium hydroxide. Are these neutralizations chemical reactions, or do the neutral solutions contain just the right amounts of acid and alkali to 'balance' one another? If the neutralization is a chemical reaction, a new substance will be formed during the process. Is it possible to produce a neutral solution and then find out what it contains?

Neutralizing hydrochloric acid with sodium hydroxide

It is quite difficult to produce a neutral solution by mixing hydrochloric acid and sodium hydroxide solutions. When the mixture of the solutions is nearly neutral, the addition of only a small volume of either the acid or the alkali causes the pH value to change a lot. So a special procedure called a **titration** is normally used. A **pipette** (Fig. 14.2) is used to measure out accurately a known volume of the alkali. A **burette** (Fig. 14.2) is then used for adding the acid. The volume of acid added can be worked

Experiment 14.1 Neutralizing sodium hydroxide with hydrochloric acid

Pour acid into the burette and then run a little acid through the tap to make sure that it is full of acid. Use a pipette filler to fill the pipette with sodium

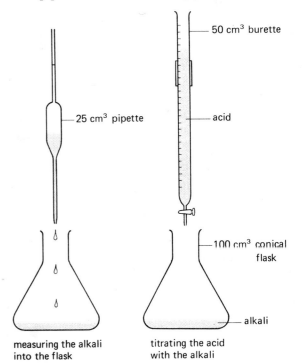

measuring the alkali into the flask

titrating the acid with the alkali

Fig. 14.2

hydroxide solution to the mark, and allow this alkali to empty into the flask.

Add a few drops of indicator (litmus or phenolphthalein or universal indicator) to the alkali. Read the level of the acid in the burette and then add acid to the alkali until it starts to change colour. The acid should then be added drop by drop, swirling the solution in the flask to mix it after each addition until the neutral colour or the first permanent acidic colour appears. This is called the **end-point** of the titration. Read the acid level in the burette and work out the volume of acid you have added.

You should then repeat the experiment to make sure that your first result was correct.

At this stage you have found out how to prepare a neutral solution, but the neutral solution is impure: it contains the indicator. Since it is difficult to remove the indicator from the solution, you should repeat the experiment with the same volumes of acid and alkali but without adding any indicator.

To find out what is left in the solution without indicator, the neutral solution should be evaporated until the crystals start to appear. The mixture should then be allowed to cool.

The crystals that are formed can be identified using the tests given in Chapter 56 on pages 251–3. The crystals are found to give an intense yellow colour when the flame test is used. When the crystals are dissolved in water and nitric acid and then silver nitrate solution is added, a white precipitate is formed.

These tests show that neutralizing hydrochloric acid with sodium hydroxide produces sodium chloride. This neutralization must be a *chemical* reaction because a *new substance* has been formed.

Hydrochloric acid is made by dissolving the substance hydrogen chloride in water. One way of writing the word-equation for the reaction is

hydrogen chloride + sodium hydroxide
$\longrightarrow$ sodium chloride + hydrogen hydroxide

Hydrogen hydroxide is another name for water, so the word-equation is usually written

hydrochloric acid + sodium hydroxide
$\longrightarrow$ sodium chloride + water

Other neutralization reactions

Your teacher may allow you to do other experiments similar to Experiment 14.1, but using other acids and other alkalis. The substances formed by the neutralization reactions can be identified using the tests given in Chapter 56.

When sulphuric acid is neutralized with alkalis, the substances produced are always *sulphates*. With nitric acid, *nitrates* are formed. If potassium hydroxide is used as an alkali, a *potassium* compound is formed, while the use of calcium hydroxide produces a *calcium* compound.

The word-equations for some of these reactions are

sodium hydroxide + sulphuric acid
$\longrightarrow$ sodium sulphate + water

potassium hydroxide + nitric acid
$\longrightarrow$ potassium nitrate + water

calcium hydroxide + hydrochloric acid
$\longrightarrow$ calcium chloride + water

The substances formed by these neutralization reactions are called **salts** (page 9). A general word-equation for this sort of neutralization reaction is

acid + alkali $\longrightarrow$ salt + water

The metal in the salt comes from the alkali, while the other part of the salt comes from the acid.

QUESTIONS

1 Two of your friends are having an argument about the neutralization of an alkali with an acid. One says that neutralization is not a chemical reaction and the neutral solution is a mixture of the acid and alkali in just the right proportions to give a neutral solution. The other says that neutralization is a chemical reaction.

How would you join in to settle the argument? Try to give as much evidence as possible to support your opinion.

2 Which acids and which alkalis would you use to prepare the following salts by titration?
(*a*) sodium nitrate
(*b*) potassium sulphate
(*c*) calcium nitrate.
Write a word-equation for each reaction.

Key words

titration   **pipette**   **burette**   **end-point**   **salts**

Basic fact

● **When an acid is neutralized with an alkali, a salt and water are produced.**

15 Other ways of neutralizing acids

Reacting metal oxides with acids

The alkalis that can be used to neutralize acids can be made by reacting metal oxides with water, for example:

sodium oxide + water $\longrightarrow$ sodium hydroxide
calcium oxide + water $\longrightarrow$ calcium hydroxide

But many metal oxides do not react with water, and so do not form alkaline solutions. So they cannot be used in titration experiments as in Chapter 14. Do these metal oxides react with acids even though they do not form alkaline solutions?

Experiment 15.1 Does copper oxide neutralize sulphuric acid?

Pour about $30\,cm^3$ of dilute sulphuric acid into a $100\,cm^3$ beaker and add a small amount of black copper oxide. If no reaction occurs, gently warm and stir the mixture.

▶ What is the evidence that a reaction occurs?

(You should be able to quote two observations in answer to this question.)

Carry on adding the copper oxide, a small amount at a time, stirring and warming the mixture, until some copper oxide is left that will not react. All the sulphuric acid has now been used up and the solution should be nearly neutral.

Filter the mixture and gently boil the filtrate in an evaporating basin until the first crystals appear. Then allow the solution to cool.

▶ What do you think the crystals will be?
▶ What would have happened if the filtrate had been evaporated until all the water had been boiled off?

Look at Chapter 56 to find suitable tests for identifying the crystals. You must consult your teacher before you try any of these tests.

The experiment can be repeated using other acids and other metal oxides. Some suitable experiments are:

zinc oxide and dilute sulphuric acid,
magnesium oxide and dilute sulphuric acid
yellow lead oxide and dilute nitric acid.

(But remember that lead compounds are very poisonous.)

▶ Write word-equations for the reactions that you try.

Reacting metal carbonates with acids

The investigation of malachite (Chapter 10) shows that copper carbonate reacts with dilute sulphuric acid. Do other metal carbonates react with dilute acids?

Experiment 15.2 Do metal carbonates react with acids?

Your teacher will provide you with a selection of metal carbonates, such as sodium carbonate, sodium hydrogencarbonate, potassium carbonate, calcium carbonate, magnesium carbonate, zinc carbonate, lead carbonate and copper carbonate. Put half a spatula measure of one of these compounds into a test-tube and add a few drops of one of the dilute acids, sulphuric, hydrochloric or nitric.
CARE: the mixture may bubble out of the tube. If this happens, hold the tube over a sink and rinse your hands with plenty of water.

To test the gas given off, pour it into a test-tube which is a quarter full of limewater, and then shake the tube to mix the gas and the limewater.

▶ Do all the carbonates react with all the acids?
▶ Is carbon dioxide formed in each reaction?
▶ Try to make a generalization about the reactions of acids and metal carbonates.

What is left in solution at the end of these reactions? To find out, it is necessary to neutralize completely an acid with a carbonate. The neutral solution can then be evaporated and the solid can be identified.

Some of the carbonates used in Experiment 15.2 are *soluble* in water (sodium carbonate, sodium hydrogencarbonate and potassium carbonate), and for these a titration can be used to form a neutral solution. The procedure is just the same as in Experiment 14.1, except that a different indicator, methyl orange, has to be used. Your teacher may arrange for you to do some experiments like this.

But most of the carbonates used in Experiment 14.1 are *insoluble* in water, so a titration cannot be used.

Experiment 15.3 What is formed when zinc carbonate reacts with dilute sulphuric acid?

Pour about $30\,cm^3$ of dilute sulphuric acid into a $100\,cm^3$ beaker and add a small amount of zinc carbonate.

Carry on adding the zinc carbonate in small amounts and stir the mixture after each bit of solid has been added.

▶ How will you know when all the acid has been neutralized?

Filter the mixture and evaporate the filtrate until the first crystals appear and then allow the solution to cool. Test the crystals to find out what they are after you have looked at Chapter 56, and consulted your teacher.

▶ Try to write a word-equation for the reaction.

(The equation for the reaction of copper carbonate with dilute sulphuric acid is given on page 31, and this may help you.)

Your teacher may allow you to try the reactions of other metal carbonates with acids. Write word-equations for any reactions that you do.

Reacting metals with acids

One method of preparing hydrogen is to react certain metals with either dilute sulphuric or hydrochloric acid (page 23). Plan your own investigations of these reactions using a method similar to that used in Experiments 15.1 and 15.3. Consult your teacher before you start any experiments. Try to identify the substances that have been formed and then write word-equations for the reactions.

QUESTIONS

1 Sodium sulphate can be prepared by titrating sodium hydroxide solution with dilute sulphuric acid, but zinc sulphate cannot be prepared in a similar way. Explain the reason for this difference.
   What methods can be used for preparing zinc sulphate?
2 Make a list of the methods you know for preparing salts. Suggest safe and suitable methods for preparing the following salts: potassium sulphate, zinc nitrate, copper chloride.
3 Starting from copper, how would you prepare some copper sulphate crystals?
4 You are given some copper powder which contains copper oxide as an impurity. How would you prepare pure copper from this mixture?
5 The mineral cerussite is thought to be lead carbonate. Explain how you would show that:
(a) it is a carbonate,
(b) it is a lead compound.

Basic facts

● **Acids can be neutralized by reacting them with metal oxides and metal carbonates or hydrogen-carbonates, as well as with alkalis. The general word-equations are as follows.**

$$\text{metal oxide} + \begin{array}{l}\text{sulphuric acid}\\\text{hydrochloric acid}\\\text{nitric acid}\end{array} \longrightarrow \begin{array}{l}\text{metal sulphate}\\\text{metal chloride}\\\text{metal nitrate}\end{array} + \text{water}$$

$$\begin{array}{l}\text{metal carbonate}\\\textit{or}\\\text{hydrogencarbonate}\end{array} + \begin{array}{l}\text{sulphuric acid}\\\text{hydrochloric acid}\\\text{nitric acid}\end{array} \longrightarrow \begin{array}{l}\text{metal sulphate}\\\text{metal chloride}\\\text{metal nitrate}\end{array} + \text{water} + \text{carbon dioxide}$$

● **Dilute sulphuric and hydrochloric acids react with metals not too low in the reactivity table according to the equation:**

$$\text{metal} + \begin{array}{l}\text{sulphuric acid}\\\text{hydrochloric acid}\end{array} \longrightarrow \begin{array}{l}\text{metal sulphate}\\\text{metal chloride}\end{array} + \text{hydrogen}$$

(Dilute nitric acid reacts with metals in a different way.)

● **The metal compounds formed in all these reactions are called salts (page 42). The metal in the salt comes from the metal oxide, carbonate (or hydrogencarbonate) or the metal itself, while the rest of the salt comes from the acid.**

16 Classifying oxides

Acidic and alkaline oxides

The ways in which the oxides of elements react with water are summarized on page 29. Using these reactions, it is possible to classify some oxides as **acidic oxides** or **alkaline oxides**. But a lot of oxides do not fit into this classification.

Acidic oxides react with water to form acids. Alkaline oxides react with water to form alkalis.

Acidic oxides:
carbon dioxide, phosphorus pentoxide, sulphur dioxide.
The word-equation for the reaction of carbon dioxide and water is

carbon dioxide + water ⟶ carbonic acid

Alkaline oxides:
calcium oxide, magnesium oxide, potassium oxide, sodium oxide.
The word-equation for the reaction of sodium oxide and water is

sodium oxide + water ⟶ sodium hydroxide

Oxides that are neither acidic nor alkaline:
copper oxide, hydrogen oxide, iron oxide, lead oxide, zinc oxide.

The oxides that are neither acidic nor alkaline do not react with water.

Oxides such as carbon dioxide, phosphorus pentoxide and sulphur dioxide are sometimes called **acid anhydrides**. Because these oxides react with water to form acids, they can be regarded as 'acids minus water'. The word anhydride means 'without water'.

Basic oxides

Most metal oxides do not react with water and so do not fit into the simple alkaline oxide and acidic oxide classification. But these metal oxides do react with acids to form salts and water (page 43).

Substances which *react with acids to form a salt and water only* are called **bases**. Metal oxides and metal hydroxides are bases.

acid + base ⟶ salt + water

So metal oxides which react like this can be called bases or **basic oxides**. Black copper oxide and iron oxide are basic oxides. Alkaline oxides are also basic oxides because they too will react with acids to form

salts and water only. But the usual way of neutralizing an acid with an alkaline oxide is to react the oxide with water first to form an alkali in solution. This alkali is then used to neutralize the acid (often using a titration method). So **alkaline oxides** are basic oxides which have the special property of *reacting with water to form alkalis*.

A classification of oxides

The classification of oxides as acidic and basic (with alkaline oxides being a sub-set of basic oxides) is shown as a Venn diagram in Fig. 16.1.

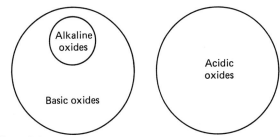

Fig. 16.1

This classification will need to be modified as more reactions of some of these oxides are met.

Some oxides do not appear to fit into this classification. One example is water, which is neither acidic nor basic. Another example is hydrogen peroxide, which has a special set of reactions of its own.

QUESTIONS

1 Lithium is a metal that is very similar to sodium. It burns in air or oxygen to form lithium oxide.
(*a*) Do you expect lithium oxide to be a solid, a liquid or a gas?
(*b*) How would you expect lithium oxide to react with water? Write a word-equation for the reaction.
(*c*) Would you expect lithium oxide to be:
 (i) an acidic oxide,
 (ii) a basic oxide but not an alkaline oxide,
 (iii) an alkaline oxide but not a basic oxide,
 (iv) an alkaline oxide and a basic oxide?
2 'All alkaline oxides are basic oxides, but not all basic oxides are alkaline oxides.'
Is this statement true? Explain your answer and give examples to justify your decision.
3 Would you expect silver oxide to be acidic, basic, or basic and alkaline? Explain your answer.
4 If you were given a sample of the metal cobalt, describe what experiments you would do to classify its oxide.

Key words

acidic oxide   **alkaline oxide**   **acid anhydride**   **base**   **basic oxide**

Basic facts

- The oxides of non-metals react with water to form acids and are called acidic oxides. Carbon dioxide forms carbonic acid, sulphur dioxide forms sulphurous acid and phosphorus pentoxide forms phosphoric acid.

- The oxides of very reactive metals react with water to form alkalis and are called alkaline oxides (e.g. sodium oxide, potassium oxide, calcium oxide).

- Most metal oxides are not alkaline oxides but are basic oxides (the oxides of magnesium, aluminium, zinc, iron, lead and copper).

- A base reacts with an acid to form a salt and water only.

- The classification of oxides into basic, alkaline and acidic is summarized in Fig. 16.1, but this classification is not complete.

17 Precipitation reactions

The solubilities of salts

When sodium chloride is added to water, it dissolves and a solution is formed. If more and more salt is added, a stage is reached when no more of it will dissolve and some solid stays undissolved. This solution is said to be **saturated**: it contains the maximum possible amount of dissolved salt.

The proportion of salt in the solution is known as its **solubility**, and this depends on the temperature. For example, at 20 °C, 36 g of sodium chloride dissolves in 100 g of water, and the solubility of sodium chloride is 36 g per 100 g of water.

If the experiment is done again at a different temperature, a different solubility is found. The ways in which the solubilities of some salts, including sodium chloride, change with temperature are shown in Fig. 17.1.

For most salts, the solubility *increases* as the temperature *rises*. This agrees with your observations in Experiments 14.1, 15.1 and 15.3. When a hot concentrated solution of a salt is cooled, crystals are formed because less salt dissolves in cold water than in hot water. But for a few salts the solubility decreases as the temperature rises.

The salts given in the graph are all soluble in water. Some salts are said to be insoluble in water because they *seem* not to dissolve when shaken with water. But accurate measurements show that small amounts of these salts do dissolve and so it is better to call them **sparingly soluble** salts.

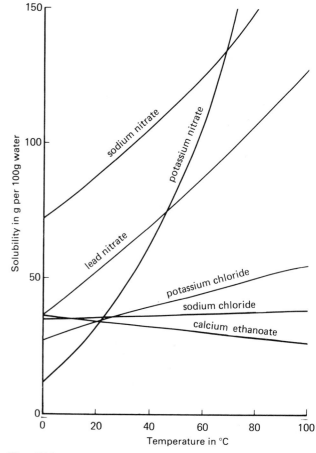

Fig. 17.1

Mixing solutions of some salts

When solutions of sodium carbonate and potassium chloride are mixed, a clear solution is formed: no reaction is seen. But if solutions of sodium carbonate and calcium chloride are mixed, a white solid is formed: in this case a reaction has occurred. When a solid is formed by a reaction in solution, it is called a **precipitate**.

Why is there a reaction in one case but not in the other? A precipitate in the reaction mixture shows that a new substance is formed which is sparingly soluble ('insoluble'). Sodium carbonate and calcium chloride react to give a sparingly soluble substance but sodium carbonate and potassium chloride do not.

What is this sparingly soluble substance which appears as a white precipitate? You should be able to answer this question for yourself after you have done the next experiment.

Experiment 17.1 Precipitating a salt from solution

Mix together roughly equal volumes of solutions of calcium chloride and sodium carbonate in a centrifuge tube. Stir the mixture using a glass rod, and then centrifuge it so as to get all the white precipitate at the bottom of the tube. Pour off the clear liquid from the white precipitate, add some pure water, and stir the mixture with the glass rod. Again centrifuge the mixture and pour off the clear liquid. Repeat the washing with distilled water and the centrifuging once more.

Pour off the clear liquid again and divide the white solid into three parts for the following tests.

(If centrifuges are not available, the mixture should be filtered and the solid washed with pure water while it is on the filter paper.)

1. Heat some of the solid very strongly in an ignition tube. Test for carbon dioxide in the usual way.
2. Add a few drops of dilute hydrochloric acid to the solid and again test for carbon dioxide.
3. Do the flame test on the solid using the method given in Chapter 56 (page 252).

▶ What do you think the white precipitate is?
▶ Write a word-equation for the reaction.

When solutions of calcium chloride and sodium carbonate are mixed, the calcium carbonate is formed as a white *precipitate* because it is sparingly soluble in water. When solutions of sodium carbonate and potassium chloride are mixed, no precipitate is formed because all the substances that might be formed (potassium carbonate and sodium chloride) are soluble in water.

Experiment 17.2 Some more reactions that produce precipitates

CARE: barium chloride, lead nitrate and copper sulphate are all poisonous.

Your teacher will provide you with some salt solutions and you can find out if a precipitate is formed when some of these solutions are mixed. The experiments to do are shown in Table 17.1.

Table 17.1

	Sodium carbonate	Potassium chloride	Sodium sulphate	Sodium nitrate
Copper sulphate				
Lead nitrate				
Barium chloride				

Each space needs to be filled with a result. For example, in the top right-hand space you should say if a precipitate is formed when solutions of copper sulphate and sodium nitrate are mixed. The other spaces are filled in in the same way.

If a precipitate is formed, the next problem is to find out what it is. If you think that the precipitate might be a metal carbonate (for the experiments in the sodium carbonate column), you can use the same method as in Experiment 17.1.

For the results in the other columns, try to work out what the precipitate is, using Fig. 17.1. For example, if you get a precipitate when you mix solutions of potassium chloride and lead nitrate, you can expect the precipitate to be either lead chloride or potassium nitrate. By looking at Fig. 17.1 you can see that potassium nitrate is soluble in water and so you would suggest that the precipitate is lead chloride.

▶ Write word-equations for the reactions that occur.

Precipitation reactions

Reactions that occur in solutions to produce precipitates are frequently called **precipitation reactions**.

The precipitates formed in these reactions are often *salts*, even though they have not been prepared by neutralizing an acid. These reactions can therefore be used as a method of preparing salts. But generally they are used only for the preparation of sparingly soluble salts.

Precipitation reactions are used a lot in analysing compounds. For example, it is possible to test for a *sulphate* by adding barium chloride and hydrochloric acid (page 251). A word-equation for the reaction is

barium chloride + metal sulphate

$\longrightarrow$ barium sulphate + metal chloride
(the precipitate)

This test is reliable only when hydrochloric acid is added. In Experiment 17.2, barium chloride forms a precipitate when mixed with sodium carbonate solution. This precipitate dissolves when hydrochloric acid is added. You should now understand why it is necessary to add hydrochloric acid when testing for a sulphate.

Another precipitation reaction used in analysis is the test for *chloride* (page 251). Silver nitrate is used and silver chloride is the white precipitate that is formed. Again an acid has to be added to stop other substances forming precipitates with the silver nitrate, but this time the acid used is dilute nitric acid.

Some generalizations about the solubilities of metal compounds

The following generalizations can be made about the solubilities of metal compounds.

1 All sodium, potassium and ammonium (page 130) compounds are soluble in water.

2 All nitrates are soluble in water.

3 Most chlorides are soluble in water. (The main exceptions are silver chloride and lead chloride.)

4 Most sulphates are soluble in water. (The main exceptions are barium sulphate and lead sulphate, but calcium sulphate is only slightly soluble.)

5 Most carbonates are sparingly soluble in water. (The main exceptions are covered in 1.)

6 Most hydroxides are sparingly soluble in water. (The main exceptions are covered in 1.)

7 Most lead compounds are sparingly soluble in water. (The main exception is lead nitrate.)

QUESTIONS

1 Explain the meanings of the following terms:
(*a*) saturated solution,
(*b*) solubility,
(*c*) sparingly soluble,
(*d*) precipitation reaction (give at least one example).

2 In which of the following experiments would you expect a precipitate to be formed? (Use Fig. 17.1 and the generalizations about solubilities if you are in doubt.)

For those experiments which produce a precipitate, say what the precipitate is and write a word-equation for the reaction.

(*a*) sodium chloride solution added to lead nitrate solution
(*b*) sodium carbonate solution added to zinc sulphate solution
(*c*) sodium sulphate solution added to aluminium chloride solution
(*d*) zinc sulphate solution added to copper chloride solution
(*e*) barium chloride solution added to silver nitrate solution.

3 A student was given some sodium carbonate crystals and asked to identify them. He dissolved some in water and added barium chloride solution. When he saw the white precipitate, he concluded that the crystals were a sulphate.
(*a*) What is the white precipitate that he saw?
(*b*) What mistake had the student made in his analysis?
(*c*) Say what the student should have done and explain how this would affect the result he got.

4 Use the information in Fig. 17.1 to arrange the following salts in the order of their solubilities (putting the most soluble one first), (*a*) at 50 °C, (*b*) at 10 °C:
 calcium ethanoate,
 potassium chloride,
 potassium nitrate,
 sodium chloride.

5 (*a*) From the information in Fig. 17.1, find a salt whose solubility decreases as the temperature rises.
(*b*) Explain how you would get crystals of this salt from solution.

Key words

saturated   solubility   sparingly soluble   precipitate   precipitation reaction

Basic facts

● **The solubility of a substance is the mass of the substance that will dissolve in 100 g of solvent to produce a saturated solution.**

● **Solubility varies with temperature. For most salts solubility increases as temperature increases.**

● **Sparingly soluble salts can be prepared by using precipitation reactions.**

● **Precipitation reactions are important in analysis, but care has to be taken to prevent incorrect results.**

18 Methods of preparing salts: a summary

Salt preparations starting with acids

The various reactions which neutralize acids (Chapters 14 and 15) all produce salts. These reactions can therefore be used to prepare salts. They are very useful methods because in each case the final solution contains only the salt. This means that no separation or purification is required apart from evaporating the solution until the crystals start to appear. The reactions that are possible are as follows.

1 Neutralization of an acid with an alkali

metal hydroxide + acid $\longrightarrow$ metal salt + water

To prepare the salt potassium nitrate, it would be necessary to start with **potassium** hydroxide solution and nitric acid (hydrogen **nitrate** solution). The metal part of the salt comes from the base while the other part of the salt comes from the acid.

2 Neutralization of an acid with a basic oxide

metal oxide + acid $\longrightarrow$ metal salt + water

To prepare the salt zinc sulphate, the reactants need to be **zinc** oxide and sulphuric acid (hydrogen **sulphate** solution).

3 Neutralization of an acid with a metal

metal + acid $\longrightarrow$ metal salt + hydrogen

Metals low in the reactivity table do not react with either dilute hydrochloric or sulphuric acids. Metals very high in the reactivity table that react rapidly with water react *explosively* with acids. So this method is restricted to the reactions of metals such as magnesium, aluminium, zinc and iron with hydrochloric and sulphuric acids.

4 Neutralization of an acid with a metal carbonate

metal carbonate + acid
$\longrightarrow$ metal salt + carbon dioxide + water

Hydrogencarbonates can be used as well as carbonates but the only common hydrogencarbonates that exist are those of sodium and potassium. If the carbonate is soluble in water, a titration method can be used for the neutralization. If it is sparingly soluble, the method in Experiment 15.3 has to be used.

Salt preparations using precipitation reactions

These reactions are discussed in Chapter 17. The reactions can be represented in the following way.

5 Precipitation of a sparingly soluble salt

soluble salt A + soluble salt B
$\longrightarrow$ sparingly soluble salt C
+ soluble salt D

For the preparation of the sparingly soluble salt lead sulphate, it is first necessary to choose a soluble lead salt and a soluble sulphate. Suitable choices for this reaction would be lead nitrate and either sodium or potassium sulphate, though other soluble sulphates could be used.

Salt preparations using synthesis reactions

Salts which are compounds of two elements only, can usually be prepared by reacting together a metal and a non-metal. The general equation can be written as follows.

6 Synthesis of salts

metal + non-metal $\longrightarrow$ salt

Both sodium and magnesium burn in chlorine and these reactions produce the salts sodium chloride and magnesium chloride respectively.

Other salts which can be prepared by synthesis reactions are bromides and iodides. These are salts of the acids hydrobromic acid (an aqueous solution of hydrogen bromide) and hydriodic acid (an aqueous solution of hydrogen iodide).

QUESTION

1 (a) Make lists of all the suitable methods of preparing the following compounds:
(i) sodium chloride
(ii) copper chloride.
(b) Explain why some of the general methods listed in this chapter are not suitable for the preparation of these salts.

Particles, formulas and equations

19 Is matter made up of particles?

Matter

Matter is the stuff of which everything in the world is made: the rocks and minerals, the vegetation, the air and the sea. *You* are also made of matter, and so are all the chemicals you have used in the laboratory. In Man's search for knowledge and in his desire to explain things, one of the central questions he has asked is: What is matter made of?

Following on from this is the question: What is it about one kind of matter that makes it different from every other kind?

Chapter 5 mentions the idea of particles, atoms and molecules, in connection with elements and compounds. But no evidence is given there for the existence of particles. In this chapter you will meet some of the evidence.

The evidence from experiments

Experiment 19.1 Dividing matter

Your teacher will provide you with a solution that contains 0.1 g of fluorescein dissolved in 1000 cm³ of solvent. Use a measuring cylinder to measure out 10 cm³ of this solution and pour it into a clean 1000 cm³ standard flask. Dilute this solution with water to the 1000 cm³ mark on the flask and shake the flask to mix the solution thoroughly.

Now use a pipette to remove 1 cm³ of this diluted solution and add it to a small test-tube. View the solution down the tube.

▶ Can you detect any colour?
▶ What is the mass of fluorescein in 10 cm³ of the first solution?
▶ What is the mass of fluorescein in 1000 cm³ of the diluted solution?
▶ What is the mass of fluorescein in 1 cm³ of the diluted solution?

Fluorescein can be 'spread out' a great deal. To explain this, scientists suggest that the particles (molecules) of the solid are separated and spread out in the water. The smallest amount of fluorescein that you can see in the above experiment has a mass of about 10^{-6} g (1/1 000 000 or one-millionth of a gram). This must be the *maximum* mass of any particles that exist. In fact, the molecules of fluorescein are known to be very much smaller than this.

Experiment 19.2 Watching crystals grow

Your teacher will provide you with warm concentrated solutions in water of substances such as copper sulphate, potassium chloride and potassium dichromate. Add a few drops of one solution to a microscope slide. Focus the microscope on the solution and observe the crystals as they form. Repeat the procedure with other solutions. If microscopes are not available, use magnifying glasses.

How can the regular way in which crystals grow be explained (Fig. 19.1)? If matter is made of particles, an explanation for this is possible. It looks as if the

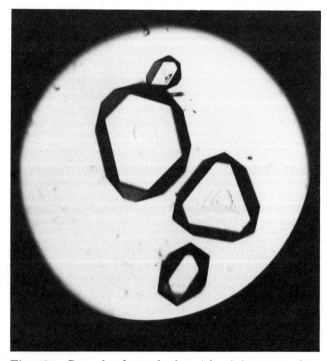

Fig. 19.1 Crystals of potash alum (aluminium potassium sulphate) growing on a microscope slide

particles in a crystal are packed together in an ordered way. And, for any one crystal, this packing is always in the same pattern. New particles are added to the crystal so that they fit with the pattern that is already there.

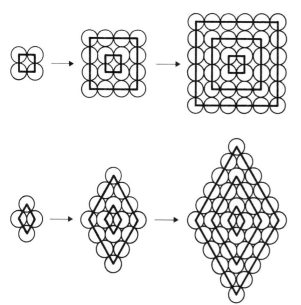

Fig. 19.2

You can imagine this process by thinking of sticking plastic spheres together in the ways shown in Fig. 19.2. These diagrams are in two dimensions but it is easy to see that three-dimensional shapes could also grow in the same way.

bromine gas. Figure 19.3 shows what happens when another gas jar is placed over the first one and the apparatus is left for about half an hour. This result is quite surprising when you realize that bromine gas is over five times as dense as air!

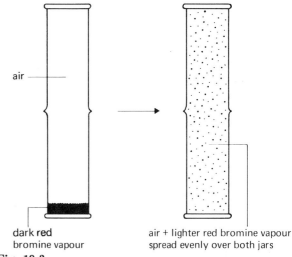

Fig. 19.3

When an open bottle of concentrated ammonia solution is held near to an open bottle of concentrated hydrochloric acid, a white smoke is formed by the reaction between ammonia gas and the acid gas (page 131). Using the apparatus shown in Fig. 19.4 it can be shown that these gases can diffuse much further than just past the top of the bottle. And since the white smoke is formed about two-thirds of the

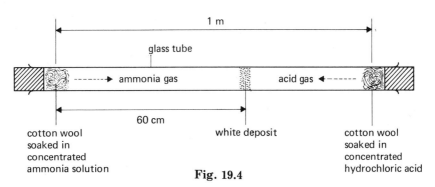

Fig. 19.4

Diffusion

If a few drops of a liquid called ethoxyethane are poured onto a watch glass, it is not long before they have all evaporated. But even if you were several metres away, you would notice the smell of the vapour. This spreading of a gas is called **diffusion**. Gases diffuse readily; 'smells' from a chemistry laboratory can spread a very long way throughout a school.

If a few drops of liquid bromine are placed at the bottom of a gas jar, they evaporate to form red-brown

way along the tube from the ammonia end, it is clear that ammonia diffuses about twice as fast as hydrogen chloride.

In these experiments on diffusion, the gases or vapours have not just been spreading into a larger volume; they have also been *mixing* with the other gases in the air. How can this very thorough mixing occur? The idea of particles can explain it easily if you assume that there is enough space between the particles of a gas into which the particles of other gases can move.

Gases can also diffuse through pores in unglazed porcelain. This can be shown using the apparatus in Fig. 19.5a. At first, the level of the water in tube A stays constant. But if a stream of hydrogen is directed into the large beaker around the container, gas is seen to bubble out of tube A.

The experiment can be repeated using other gases, after first removing the hydrogen from the container. If carbon dioxide is now passed into the space between the large beaker and the container, the apparatus must be rearranged (Fig. 19.5b) because this gas is denser than air. When the supply of carbon dioxide is turned on, water is seen to rise up tube A.

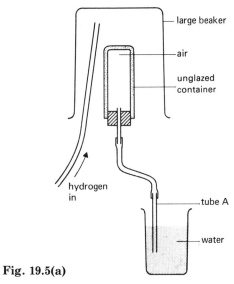

Fig. 19.5(a)

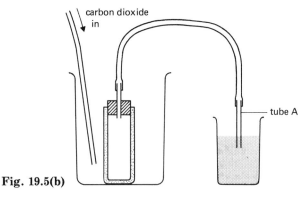

Fig. 19.5(b)

When the container is surrounded by hydrogen it seems that hydrogen must flow into the container. But when the container is surrounded by carbon dioxide, air flows out of the container. This can be explained by supposing that gases are *always* diffusing both in and out of the container. When there is air on both sides of the container, the rate of diffusion in and out is the same. But when there is a gas other than air outside the container, the rate of diffusion of this gas into the container is different from the rate of diffusion of the air out of the container.

You should now be able to work out that hydrogen diffuses faster than air but that air diffuses faster than carbon dioxide.

Diffusion, whether it be the mixing of several gases or the diffusion of gases through a porous solid, is strong evidence that matter is made of particles, *and that these particles must be moving.* The faster a gas diffuses, the faster its particles must be moving. Also, since a gas can diffuse in any direction, the particles must be moving in all directions.

Experiment 19.3 Looking at a diffusing liquid

Drop a large crystal of copper sulphate or ammonium dichromate into a beaker of cold water. Look for the movement of the blue or orange solution that forms around the crystal for at least a week, and longer if possible. (Do not move the beaker during this experiment.)

▶ Is the diffusion in liquids faster or slower than in gases?

▶ Can you explain your answer to the last question?

Brownian motion

This was first noticed in 1827 by Robert Brown, a botanist, when he was looking at extremely small and light pollen grains suspended (floating) in water. Under a microscope, he saw the grains moving short distances in an irregular zig-zag fashion. You can observe a similar effect if you look at grains of carbon in diluted Indian ink under a microscope.

The same effect is seen when very small grains of solid are suspended in a gas as well as in a liquid. Any kind of smoke is such a suspension. If some smoke is observed using a microscope, the grains are seen to be moving to and fro showing no signs of ever coming to rest. The smaller the grain, and also the higher the temperature, the more violent is this irregular motion.

How can Brownian motion be explained? You can imagine the very light smoke grains or pollen grains being jostled by the fast-moving particles of either the air or the water (Fig. 19.6). As with diffusion, you are led to the idea of matter being made of *moving particles.*

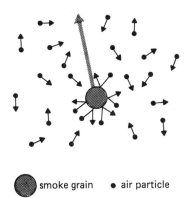

Fig. 19.6 ⬤ smoke grain   • air particle

Two mixing experiments

Ethanol (alcohol) is soluble in water. Is there a change of volume when these two liquids are mixed?

Your teacher may show you an experiment in which a burette is half-filled with water and then an approximately equal volume of ethanol is poured into the burette. At this stage, the two liquids do not mix very much because of the shape of the burette. The reading on the burette scale is noted and then the burette is inverted several times to mix the liquids. The volume is seen to decrease.

A similar result is obtained when salt dissolves in water. Fig. 19.7 shows an experiment in which about 100 g of salt is put into a 250 cm³ standard flask.

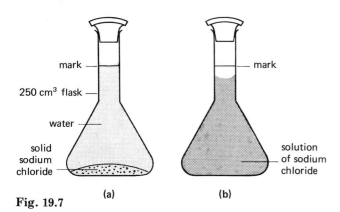

Fig. 19.7

Water is then gently added until the total volume is 250 cm³. When the flask is shaken to dissolve the salt, the volume of the solution is found to be less than 250 cm³.

The results of these experiments would be quite difficult to explain without using the idea of particles. But if you use this idea, you can suggest that in water (and in other liquids), the particles have small spaces between them and the salt and ethanol particles at least partly fill these spaces. In other words, there is some room between water particles that other particles can fit into.

Using particles to explain other observations

Some of the general properties of solids, liquids and gases are given in Table 19.1. Is it possible to explain the differences in properties that are shown in this table? The idea that matter is made of particles can be used to answer some questions about these differences such as:

Why do solids have a constant shape and volume whereas liquids have a constant volume but can change their shape?
Why do gases completely fill any container they are put into?
Why is it difficult to compress both solids and liquids, while gases can be compressed with ease? (The large increase in volume when a liquid boils and becomes a gas gives a useful clue here.)
Why do gases diffuse rapidly, liquids slowly and solids very slowly indeed?

Before you can answer these questions well, you need some more ideas about how the particles are arranged and how they can move. Figure 19.8 shows these extra ideas.

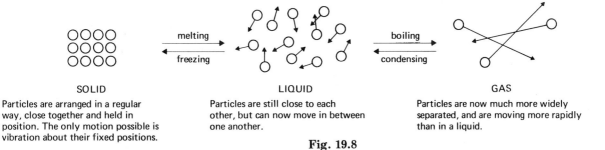

SOLID
Particles are arranged in a regular way, close together and held in position. The only motion possible is vibration about their fixed positions.

LIQUID
Particles are still close to each other, but can now move in between one another.

GAS
Particles are now much more widely separated, and are moving more rapidly than in a liquid.

Fig. 19.8

Table 19.1

	Shape	Volume	Compressibility	Diffusion	Effect of heat
Solids	Constant	Constant at constant temperature	Pressure hardly affects their volume	Very slow	Expand slightly as the temperature rises and melt usually with a slight increase in volume
Liquids	Variable	Constant at constant temperature		Slow	Expand slightly as the temperature rises and boil usually with a large increase in volume
Gases	Variable	Variable – will spread throughout any container	Easily compressible	Rapid	Expand much more than solids and liquids provided that the pressure stays constant

You can imagine solid particles to be arranged rather like the spectators at a cricket ground who have to sit in their seats. The particles in a liquid are then like the spectators standing in a half-full ground who can move a little way before they collide with someone else. The gas particles are like the players on the field who have plenty of room for movement.

You should now be able to explain why a gas exerts a pressure on the walls of its container, and also why the pressure of a gas in a container increases as the temperature increases. (Remember that the gas particles move faster at higher temperatures.)

Conclusions

You now know that the idea of particles can explain the regular shapes of crystals, the diffusion of gases and liquids, and Brownian motion. The general properties of solids, liquids and gases can also be explained so long as some extra ideas are added about how the particles are arranged and how they can move. On the other hand, it is difficult to account for all these observations and properties without using the idea of particles.

The evidence in this chapter points to matter being 'particulate'. But it does not *prove* that this is definitely so.

You should realize that it may be necessary to alter these simple ideas as new evidence is discovered. It is even possible that new evidence will change them completely.

No one has yet proved beyond all possible doubt that matter is particulate. But there is such a lot of evidence in its favour that all scientists use the idea of particles when they think about the way matter behaves.

QUESTIONS

1 Using the idea of particles, explain why it is more comfortable to ride a bicycle which is fitted with pneumatic tyres (tyres filled with compressed air) than one fitted with solid tyres.

2 A gas jar of hydrogen is placed on top of a gas jar of carbon dioxide (the arrangement is as in Fig. 19.3). After a few minutes a lighted splint produces a small explosion when applied to the mouth of the *bottom* jar, and some limewater turns cloudy when added to the *top* jar.

(*a*) Which gas is tested by means of limewater?

(*b*) After the experiment, which gas must be present in the bottom jar?

(*c*) The experiment is now repeated, but this time limewater is added to the *bottom* jar and a lighted splint applied to the mouth of the *top* jar. What do you think would happen in each case?

(*d*) Explain your answer to (*c*) using the idea of diffusion.

(*e*) Carbon dioxide is a denser gas than hydrogen. If the gas jar of hydrogen is placed *underneath* the gas jar of carbon dioxide, would diffusion occur more or less quickly than in the first case?

Key words

matter   diffusion   Brownian motion

Basic facts

- **Diffusion is the automatic spreading out of one substance into another. It is quite rapid for gases, much slower for liquids, and for solids it is so slow that it is difficult to observe.**

- **Different gases diffuse at different speeds but all can diffuse through porous solids.**

- **Many observations and the results of many experiments can be explained using the idea that matter is made of particles. This provides evidence in favour of the existence of particles but does not prove that matter consists of particles.**

20 Atoms and formulas

Elements and atoms

The ideas of elements and atoms have been used already. If you cannot answer the questions 'What is an element?' and 'What is an atom?' you should look back to Chapter 5 before you read any further.

How do atoms of different elements differ? Study Table 20.1, which gives the mass and diameter of an atom of several different elements. Different elements have different properties and so the atoms of different elements must also have different properties.

In Fig. 20.1, each circle represents one atom of an element, but each circle is 5×10^7 (50 million) times as large as the actual atom.

It is very difficult to imagine anything as small as these atoms. You can get some idea of size when you think that along the diameter of any of the circles in Fig. 20.1 you could fit fifty million atoms of the element side by side. Again, if a pair of calipers could be stretched across the diameter of an atom and then moved so as to stretch across the diameter of a marble, this would be equivalent to moving them from a marble to stretch across a sphere 1600 kilometres in diameter!

The atoms with the smallest mass are those of hydrogen, and the masses of all other atoms can be given in terms of the mass of an atom of hydrogen. These *atomic masses* (atomic weights) are *relative*. They are called **relative atomic masses**.

If you look at Data Sheet 1 on page 279, you will find a list of the relative atomic masses of some elements.

If the relative atomic mass of hydrogen is taken to be 1, then it follows that one atom of sodium has 23 times the mass of one atom of hydrogen. In other words, one atom of sodium has the same mass as 23 atoms of hydrogen.

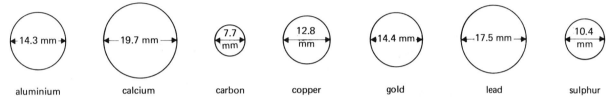

aluminium   calcium   carbon   copper   gold   lead   sulphur

Fig. 20.1

Lengths such as 2.86×10^{-7} mm are so small that scientists have found it handy to use a very small unit of length called the nanometre (nm). One nanometre is equal to

10^{-9} m (1/1 000 000 000 of a metre), or
10^{-6} mm (1/1 000 000 of a millimetre).

So a diameter of 2.86×10^{-7} mm can be written as 0.286×10^{-6} mm or 0.286 nm.

The masses of single atoms are also extremely small. The figures in Table 20.1 show that atoms have masses of about 10^{-22} g. The smallest object that even the best balance in your laboratory can detect probably has a mass of about 10^{-3} g (0.001 g). This very small object must contain about $10^{-3}/10^{-22}$ or 10^{19} (10 million million million) atoms.

Can the masses of atoms be found?

The mass spectrometer (page 155) deflects streams of moving, charged atoms of different masses into differently curved paths. These can then be collected separately and their relative masses found.

Table 20.1

Elements	Mass in g	Diameter in mm
Aluminium	4.5×10^{-23}	2.86×10^{-7}
Calcium	6.7×10^{-23}	3.94×10^{-7}
Carbon	2.0×10^{-23}	1.54×10^{-7}
Copper	11×10^{-23}	2.56×10^{-7}
Gold	33×10^{-23}	2.88×10^{-7}
Lead	34×10^{-23}	3.50×10^{-7}
Sulphur	5.3×10^{-23}	2.08×10^{-7}

(Note: 10^{-23} is $1/10^{23}$ or 1/100 000 million million million; 10^{-7} is $1/10^7$ or 1/10 million.)

Some years ago, a new standard was chosen and all masses of atoms are now compared to the mass of one atom of carbon.

The formulas of black and red copper oxides

In this section, you will see how the relative atomic masses of elements can be used, together with other information, to work out the formulas of some compounds. Two important principles are used in these chemical calculations: the Law of Conservation of Mass (page 19) and the Law of Constant Composition (page 15).

Black copper oxide is a compound of copper and oxygen. To write its formula, you need to know how many copper atoms combine with one oxygen atom. You can start by finding the *masses* of copper and oxygen which combine with one another.

Your teacher may show you an experiment in which a known mass of black copper oxide is heated in hydrogen. The apparatus may be similar to that shown in Fig. 20.2. Bottled gas can be used for the reaction if a cylinder of hydrogen is not available. The word-equation for the reaction is

copper oxide + hydrogen $\longrightarrow$ copper + water

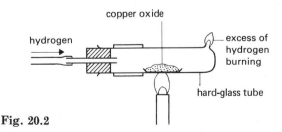

Fig. 20.2

During the reaction, the black copper oxide changes to red copper and the reaction is obviously exothermic.

When the reduction is complete, the mass of copper is found. The results of an experiment like this one are

mass of black copper oxide	3.08 g
mass of copper	2.46 g

So that the results of different experiments (which start with different amounts of the oxide) can be easily compared, it is usual to find the percentage of copper in the copper oxide. Taking the results above, the percentage of copper in the oxide is

$$\frac{2.46}{3.08} \times 100 = 79.9\%$$

Therefore, in black copper oxide, 80% of the mass is copper, leaving 20% as oxygen.

Now that you know the percentage of copper in black copper oxide, how can the formula of black copper oxide be found?

Imagine that you go to a store to buy some sugar and coffee and that the sugar is sold in 1 kg packets while the coffee is sold in $\frac{1}{4}$ kg packets. You come home with 2 kg of sugar and 1 kg of coffee. Work out how many bags of sugar and coffee you bought.

This calculation, which you probably did in your head, can be set out like this:

	Sugar	Coffee
Mass bought in kg	2	1
Mass in one packet in kg	1	$\frac{1}{4}$
Number of packets	$\frac{2}{1} = 2$	$\frac{1}{\frac{1}{4}} = 4$

Now imagine that you come home with 2 kg of sugar and 1 kg of coffee, but that you have forgotten the mass of each packet of sugar and coffee, and you do not look to see the number of packets of each. You can only remember that one packet of sugar has four times the mass of one packet of coffee. The above calculation now becomes

	Sugar	Coffee
Mass bought in kg	2	1
Ratio of the masses of the packets	4 to	1
Ratio of the number of packets bought	$\frac{2}{4}$ to	$\frac{1}{1}$

The ratio $\frac{2}{4}$ to 1 can be written as $\frac{1}{2}$ to 1 or as 1 to 2.

This calculation tells you that, for each packet of sugar bought, two packets of coffee were bought. It does not tell you the actual numbers of packets of each which were bought. The result agrees with the first calculation: 2 to 4 is the same as 1 to 2. But from the second calculation you can find only the ratio of the number of packets bought, not the actual numbers.

Can this kind of calculation be repeated, using the results of the copper oxide experiment? There are 80 g of copper to every 20 g of oxygen in black copper oxide. To find out how many copper atoms are present for each oxygen atom, you have to allow for the masses of copper atoms and oxygen atoms being different. This is like allowing for the masses of packets of sugar and coffee being different.

The calculation is set out below. If you have difficulty with any of the steps, look back to the corresponding step in the sugar and coffee calculation.

	Copper		Oxygen
Mass in g present in 100 g of black copper oxide	80		20
Ratio of masses of copper and oxygen atoms	63.5	to	16
Ratio of number of atoms present	$\frac{80}{63.5}$	to	$\frac{20}{16}$

When you work out these fractions, you will find that they are equal (or very nearly so).

This calculation shows that there are equal numbers of copper and oxygen atoms in black copper oxide. Or, for every copper atom there is one oxygen atom. This is the answer you need if you are going to write the formula of black copper oxide: CuO. But because the ratio we get is the *simplest* one (1 to 1 is simpler than 2 to 2 and so on), the formula you write is sometimes called the **empirical formula**.

What is the formula of red copper oxide?

There are two oxides of copper; one is black and the other is red.

To find the formula of red copper oxide, you can follow the same method as for black copper oxide. In an experiment like the one shown in Fig. 20.2, it is found that when 4.21 g red copper oxide is reduced, 3.74 g copper is left.

If you follow through the steps of the calculation for black copper oxide but use these figures, you will find that there are two atoms of copper for every atom of oxygen in red copper oxide. So the formula for red copper oxide is Cu_2O.

You should now understand how these two elements can combine together to form two different compounds.

QUESTIONS

Relative atomic mass values can be found in Data Sheet 1 on page 279.
1 Use relative atomic mass values to calculate:
(a) the number of hydrogen atoms which have the same mass as one atom of aluminium (take the relative atomic mass of hydrogen to be 1.0);

(b) the number of carbon atoms that have the same mass as one silver atom;

(c) the number of nitrogen atoms that have the same mass as one cadmium atom;

(d) the number of helium atoms that have the same mass as ten oxygen atoms;

(e) the number of nitrogen atoms that have the same mass

as five iron atoms (take the relative atomic mass of iron to be 56.0).

2 Sodium chloride contains 39.3% sodium by mass. Calculate its empirical formula.

3 When 1.00 g of magnesium is heated in chlorine, 3.92 g of magnesium chloride is formed. Calculate the empirical formula of magnesium chloride.

Key words
relative atomic mass   empirical formula

Basic facts

- Each element is made up of its own sort of atoms. Atoms of different elements have different sizes and masses as well as different properties.

- Atoms are so small that special units are used for their sizes (nanometers), and their masses are compared using the relative atomic mass scale.

- The relative atomic mass scale once compared masses of atoms to the mass of a hydrogen atom, but the modern scale uses the mass of a carbon atom as the basis.

- The empirical formula of a compound shows the simplest ratio in which the atoms of the elements in the compound are combined.

- The empirical formula of a compound can be calculated from its composition by mass by taking into account the different masses of the atoms present in the compound.

21 The chemical mole and writing equations

Packets of atoms

It is very handy to buy sugar and coffee in packets of different mass. Chemists often use 'packets of elements' of different mass. In this section, you will see why this is done.

When copper and oxygen combine to form black copper oxide,

1 atom of copper combines with 1 atom of oxygen.

This could be written as

33 atoms of copper combine with 33 atoms of oxygen,

or again, using n to stand for a whole number,

n atoms of copper combine with n atoms of oxygen.

In this reaction, what would be a handy size for 'a packet of oxygen atoms' and 'a packet of copper atoms'? The answer is that they can be any size

provided they both contain the same number of atoms. Then 1 'packet of copper atoms' would react with 1 'packet of oxygen atoms''.

What size should be chosen for these packets? For the packets of copper and oxygen atoms to hold the same number of atoms, the masses of the packets must be in the ratio of 63.5 to 16. (The masses of single copper and oxygen atoms are in the ratio of 63.5 to 16. The same mass ratio will apply whenever you compare masses of equal numbers of copper and oxygen atoms.)

Since the mass ratio has to be 63.5 to 16, the size of the packets is chosen so that *1 packet of copper atoms has a mass of 63.5 g* and then *1 packet of oxygen atoms will have a mass of 16 g.*

'1 packet of copper atoms' with mass 63.5 g is usually called *1 mole of copper atoms* and '1 packet of oxygen atoms' with mass 16 g is called *1 mole of oxygen atoms.*

So, when copper and oxygen react to form black copper oxide,

1 copper atom reacts with 1 oxygen atom

or 1 mole of copper atoms reacts with 1 mole of oxygen atoms

or 63.5 g of copper reacts with 16 g of oxygen.

Now think about copper and oxygen combining to form red copper oxide. In this compound, 2 copper atoms react with 1 oxygen atom, or 2 moles of copper atoms react with 1 mole of oxygen atoms. These ideas can be used with other elements:

1 mole of sodium atoms has a mass of 23 g.
1 mole of magnesium atoms has a mass of 24.3 g.
2 moles of nitrogen atoms have a mass of
$2 \times 14.0 = 28.0$ g.
$\frac{1}{2}$ mole of aluminium atoms has a mass of
$\frac{1}{2} \times 27.0 = 13.5$ g.

The important fact is that 1 mole of atoms of any element always contains the same number of atoms. To find the mass (in g) of one mole of atoms of an element, all you have to do is to look up its relative atomic mass.

A more exact definition of the mole

The relative atomic mass of an element used to be worked out by comparing the mass of one atom of the element with the mass of one atom of hydrogen.

In the modern definition of relative atomic mass, the masses of atoms are compared with the mass of 1 atom of carbon.* The relative atomic mass of carbon is defined as being 12 exactly. So the relative atomic mass of an element is defined as

$$\frac{\text{the mass of 1 atom of element}}{\text{the mass of 1 atom of carbon}} \times 12$$

The 12 has to be included because the relative atomic mass of carbon is 12.

Now look at the relative atomic masses of the elements carbon, sodium and oxygen. The masses of one atom of carbon, sodium and oxygen are in the ratio 12 to 23 to 16. Also, if you compare the masses of n atoms (where n is any whole number) of each element, the ratio is still 12 to 23 to 16.

In order to define the mole, the value of n is chosen so that n carbon atoms have a mass of exactly 12 g. It follows that the same number of sodium atoms will have a mass of 23 g and the same number of oxygen atoms will have a mass of 16 g.

This number of atoms is obviously a very special one. It is called the **Avogadro constant** and it is usually written as L. (You should realize that you are now back to the special 'packets' of atoms that are mentioned on page 57.)

1 mole of atoms of an element is defined as that amount of the element which contains L atoms. Its mass in grams is numerically the same as the relative atomic mass of the element. The value of L is defined as the number of carbon atoms in exactly 12 g of carbon.†

What is the value of the Avogadro constant? If you look back at Table 20.1, you will see that the actual masses of atoms are very small indeed, so that L has to be enormously large. Its value is 6.02×10^{23}, or about six hundred thousand million million million.

It is very difficult to get any idea of how big such a number is. The following calculation may help to give you an idea of its size.

Suppose that one year there is a huge rice crop and that 6×10^{23} rice grains (1 mole of rice grains) are harvested. How long would this rice last if it were used to feed the world's population three meals a day?

A fairly generous helping of rice contains about 5000 grains, so that, for one day, one person would need 15 000 or 1.5×10^4 grains of rice for three meals. The world population, about five thousand million or 5×10^9, would eat $5 \times 10^9 \times 1.5 \times 10^4$ or 7.5×10^{13} grains for its three meals in one day. In one year, the consumption would be $7.5 \times 10^{13} \times 365$, which is about 2700×10^{13} or 2.7×10^{16} grains. This can be called 3×10^{16}.

This number of rice grains is nowhere near 6×10^{23}. In fact, 1 mole of rice grains would last $6 \times 10^{23}/3 \times 10^{16}$ or 2×10^7 years – 20 million years!

Using the idea of moles with compounds

The idea of the mole has been used so far only with elements and atoms. It can also be used with compounds:

1 mole of a compound can be defined as that amount of compound which contains L molecules.

A general definition of the mole now becomes:

1 mole of a substance is that amount of substance which contains L chemical units.

'Chemical units' means atoms for those substances like sodium which consist of atoms, and molecules for those substances like carbon dioxide which consist of molecules. In later chapters you will see that it can also apply to other kinds of particles.

---

* Strictly, this is one atom of carbon-12, the commonest isotope (page 158) of carbon.

† Again strictly, this should be carbon-12.

What is the mass of 1 mole of carbon dioxide molecules? From its formula, CO_2, you see that 1 mole of CO_2 contains 1 mole of C atoms combined with 2 moles of O atoms. So its mass is therefore $12 + (2 \times 16) = 44\,g$. The mass of 1 mole of molecules of a compound is called its **molar mass**.

If you write the molar mass of a compound without the units (grams), then this is the **relative molecular mass**. So the relative molecular mass of carbon dioxide is 44.

One way of describing the formation of carbon dioxide from its elements is to say that 1 mole of C atoms combines with 2 moles of O atoms to form 1 mole of CO_2 molecules. But oxygen gas consists of O_2 molecules (page 22), so it is better to say 1 mole of C *atoms* combines with 1 mole of O_2 *molecules*.

A statement such as '1 mole of oxygen' is not a good one to make because it could mean one of two things; either 1 mole of O atoms (mass 16 g) or 1 mole of O_2 molecules (32 g). In order to avoid misunderstandings, you should always state whether you mean atoms or molecules. This is simply done by writing 1 mole of O or 1 mole of O_2, rather than 1 mole of oxygen. Abbreviated, mole is written mol.

So, for the synthesis of carbon dioxide, you should write

$$1\,mol\ C + 1\,mol\ O_2 \longrightarrow 1\,mol\ CO_2$$

For the synthesis of black copper oxide, the statement is

$$1\,mol\ Cu + \tfrac{1}{2}\,mol\ O_2 \longrightarrow 1\,mol\ CuO$$

or $\quad 2\,mol\ Cu + 1\,mol\ O_2 \longrightarrow 2\,mol\ CuO$

Equations

The statements above about the formation of carbon dioxide and black copper oxide are usually shortened by leaving out the words mole or mol:

$$C + O_2 \longrightarrow CO_2$$

and $\quad 2Cu + O_2 \longrightarrow 2CuO$

And this way of representing a reaction using formulas is called the **symbol equation** (or just the **equation**) for the reaction. The symbol equation for a reaction not only shows which substances are involved in the reaction, it also shows the amounts (in moles) of each substance involved.

The Law of Conservation of Mass (page 19) says that, in chemical reactions, the total mass of the reactants always equals the total mass of the products: no new matter is produced and no old matter is destroyed. Since matter is made of atoms, this is like saying that atoms cannot be created or destroyed during a reaction.

To *balance* a symbol equation means making sure that the quantities of each kind of atom are the same on either side of the equation. The equations given above for the synthesis of carbon dioxide and black

copper oxide are balanced because there is the same number of moles of each sort of atom on each side of the equations. Now consider the equation for the combustion of methane (which has the formula CH_4). The word-equation is

$$\text{methane} + \text{oxygen} \longrightarrow \text{carbon dioxide} + \text{water}$$

Putting in formulas gives

$$CH_4 + O_2 \longrightarrow CO_2 + H_2O$$

There is the same number of moles of carbon atoms on both sides but there are different numbers of moles of hydrogen and oxygen atoms. Because each mole of methane contains four moles of hydrogen atoms, it must produce two moles of water when it burns:

$$CH_4 + O_2 \longrightarrow CO_2 + 2H_2O$$

And since four moles of oxygen atoms are present on the right-hand side, there must be the same number on the left:

$$CH_4 + 2O_2 \longrightarrow CO_2 + 2H_2O$$

This equation is now balanced.

Calculations using moles

Example 1 Converting masses to moles

How many moles of atoms are there in 4 g of oxygen? (O = 16.0)
1 mole of O atoms has a mass of 16 g, so that 1 g of oxygen is $\frac{1}{16}$ mole of O atoms.
Therefore 4 g of oxygen is $\frac{4}{16}$ or $\frac{1}{4}$ mole of O atoms.

Example 2 Converting moles to masses

What is the mass of 0.3 mole of Na atoms? (Na = 23.0).
1 mole of Na atoms has a mass of 23.0 g so that 0.3 mole has a mass of $0.3 \times 23 = 6.9\,g$.

Example 3 Finding a formula

Black copper oxide contains 80% copper by mass. What is its formula? (Cu = 63.5, O = 16.0)
100 g of black copper oxide contains 80 g of copper and 20 g of oxygen.
80 g of copper is $\frac{80}{63.5} = 1.26$ mole of Cu atoms
20 g of oxygen is $\frac{20}{16} = 1.25$ mole of O atoms
More accurate analysis figures would give equal numbers of moles of atoms of each element, so 1 mole of Cu atoms reacts with 1 mole of O atoms. The formula must be CuO.

You should compare this calculation with the one on page 56. The two calculations are similar, but the reasoning is different.

You should now realize that the formula of any substance can be worked out, provided the composition by mass of the substance can be found by analysis.

Working out some formulas and equations

(a) What is the formula of magnesium oxide?

The method used to find the formulas of the copper oxides (Fig. 20.2) does not work for magnesium oxide because it is not reduced by hydrogen. But magnesium readily combines with oxygen when it is hot.

Experiment 21.2 What is the formula of magnesium oxide?

Accurately find the mass of a crucible and lid and then find its mass again when it contains between 0.2 and 0.3 g of cleaned magnesium ribbon.

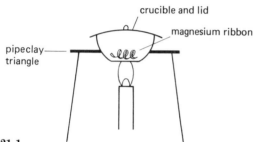

Fig. 21.1

Heat the crucible strongly as shown in Fig. 21.1 until the metal begins to burn. Then heat it gently, raising and lowering the lid with tongs so that the metal burns slowly and as little as possible of the white oxide is lost to the air. When most of the burning is finished, heat the crucible strongly with the lid off. Finally, let the crucible cool and then find its new mass (with the lid).

▶ Work out the number of mol Mg used.
▶ Work out the number of mol O that the magnesium reacted with.
▶ How many mol Mg combine with 1 mol O?
▶ Write the formula for magnesium oxide.

You may be dissatisfied with the result of this experiment.

▶ What do you think is the largest source of error?

It is difficult to get accurate results with Experiment 21.2. The formula of magnesium oxide is MgO.

What is the equation for its formation? The word-equation is

magnesium + oxygen $\longrightarrow$ magnesium oxide

Putting in formulas gives

$$Mg + O_2 \longrightarrow MgO$$

The balanced equation is

$$2Mg + O_2 \longrightarrow 2MgO$$

(b) What is the formula of copper carbonate?

The formula of copper carbonate could be found by analysing it to find the percentages of copper, carbon and oxygen. But when copper carbonate is heated, it decomposes to produce black copper oxide and carbon dioxide. From the numbers of moles of CuO and CO_2 produced, it is possible to work out the formula of copper carbonate.

Experiment 21.2 Finding the formula of copper carbonate

Find the mass of a crucible and then find its mass again when it contains two or three spatula measures of copper carbonate. Heat the crucible strongly until reaction is complete.

▶ How do you know when the reaction has finished?

Let the crucible cool and then find its mass.

▶ Set out your results and calculations:
Mass of crucible
Mass of crucible and copper carbonate
Mass of crucible and copper oxide
Mass of copper oxide left
Number of mol of CuO left
Mass of carbon dioxide given off
Number of mol of CO_2 given off
Ratio of number of mol of CuO : number of mol of CO_2

You should find that 1 mol CuO is formed at the same time as 1 mol CO_2. Both of these substances are produced by the decomposition of the copper carbonate:

copper carbonate $\longrightarrow$ CuO + CO_2

So the formula of copper carbonate must be $CuCO_3$.

(c) What is the formula of hydrated magnesium sulphate?

The formula of anhydrous magnesium sulphate is $MgSO_4$, but crystals of magnesium sulphate contain water of crystallization. When hydrated magnesium sulphate is heated it decomposes to anhydrous magnesium sulphate and water. The formula of the hydrated crystals can be written $MgSO_4 \cdot xH_2O$. Your job in the next experiment is to find the value of x.

Experiment 21.3 What is the formula of hydrated magnesium sulphate?

Accurately find the mass of a crucible and then find its mass again when it contains about 3 g of magnesium sulphate crystals. Heat the crucible strongly as shown in Fig. 21.1 (but without the crucible lid) for about ten minutes.

▶ Do you think that the reaction has finished?
▶ If you are not sure that the reaction has finished, can you think of a way of making sure?

Let the crucible cool and find its new mass. Record the masses in a table.

▶ Work out from your results:
1. the mass of water of crystallization originally present in the crystals;
2. the number of mol H_2O originally present in the crystals;
3. the mass of anhydrous magnesium sulphate originally present in the crystals;
4. the number of mol $MgSO_4$ originally present in the crystals;
5. the number of mol H_2O which combine with 1 mol $MgSO_4$. (The answer is a whole number, so round off your answer to the nearest whole number.)

You should now be able to write the formula for hydrated magnesium sulphate crystals and also the equation for its thermal decomposition.

Symbols of state

Symbols of state are used to show the physical states of substances when equations are written. They are (s) for solid, (l) for liquid, (g) for gas and (aq) for substances in aqueous solution (i.e. dissolved in water). Some examples of their use are

$$C(s) + O_2(g) \longrightarrow CO_2(g)$$
$$CuCO_3(s) \longrightarrow CuO(s) + CO_2(g)$$
$$MgSO_4 \cdot 7H_2O(s) \longrightarrow MgSO_4(s) + 7H_2O(g)$$

Note that in the last equation, water is given the symbol of state (g) because it is produced as a gas. You should include symbols of state in all the equations that you write.

QUESTIONS

Look at Data Sheet 1 (page 279) where necessary.

1 Work out the mass, in grams, of the following:
(a) 1 mol S
(b) 0.2 mol Cl
(c) 0.1 mol N
(d) 6 mol Na
(e) 0.5 mol P
(f) 0.25 mol C
(g) 0.6 mol Mg
(h) 0.75 mol Cu
(i) 4.2 mol Zn
(j) 0.01 mol Fe

2 How many moles of atoms are there in the following amounts of elements?
(a) 4 g of carbon
(b) 11.5 g of sodium
(c) 4 g of magnesium
(d) 96.3 g of sulphur
(e) 54 g of aluminium
(f) 62 g of phosphorus
(g) 48 g of oxygen
(h) 7 g of nitrogen
(i) 1.08 g of silver
(j) 603 g of mercury

3 Work out the relative molecular masses of the following compounds:
(a) NO_2 (b) Al_2O_3 (c) $Mg(NO_3)_2$ (d) H_2O (e) $CuSO_4$

4 Write out the following statements, putting in the missing words and numbers:
(a) A mole of Cu atoms with a mass of ... g and a mole of S atoms with a mass of ... g combine to form a ... of CuS with a mass of ... g.
(b) ... g of lead combines with ... g of oxygen to form 1 mole of Pb_3O_4 which has a mass of ... g.
(c) In 308 g of CCl_4 there are ... moles of C atoms with a mass of ... g and ... moles of Cl atoms with a mass of ... g.

5 Two samples of white mercury chloride are changed to mercury by heating with a suitable reducing agent. These are the results obtained:

	Sample 1	Sample 2
Mass of mercury chloride in g	4.47	4.40
Mass of mercury formed in g	3.80	3.24

(a) What mass of chlorine combines with 3.80 g of mercury in sample 1?
(b) How many moles of Cl atoms is this?
(c) How many moles of Hg atoms is 3.80 g of mercury? (The relative atomic mass of mercury may be taken as 200.)
(d) From your answers to (b) and (c), work out the formula of mercury chloride in sample 1.
(e) Carry out a similar calculation to that in (a) to (d) in order to find the formula of mercury chloride in sample 2.
(f) What conclusion can you reach from your answers to (d) and (e)?

6 Hydrogen is passed over heated black copper oxide which has been dried very throughly. Water is produced and collected in a suitable piece of apparatus. The copper oxide is changed to copper. These results are obtained:

mass of black copper oxide =	2.650 g
mass of copper formed =	2.117 g
mass of water formed =	0.600 g

(a) What is the name of the process in which oxygen is removed from a substance?
(b) The oxygen in the black copper oxide is removed by hydrogen. What happens to the oxygen?
(c) Work out the mass of hydrogen and the mass of oxygen in 0.600 g of water using the above results.
(d) Write these masses in (c) as numbers of moles of H and O atoms.
(e) What is the formula of water shown by the answers to (d)?
(f) Describe a suitable piece of apparatus in which the water could be collected and its mass found.

7 The compositions by mass of some compounds are given below. Work out the formula of each compound by finding the simplest ratio of moles of atoms.
(a) Sodium chloride: 11.7 g of this compound contains 4.6 g of sodium and 7.1 g of chlorine.
(b) Carbon dioxide: 1.32 g of this compound contains 0.36 g of carbon and 0.96 g of oxygen.
(c) Yellow lead oxide: 2.23 g of this compound contains 2.07 g of lead and 0.16 g of oxygen.
(d) Red iron oxide: 6.40 g of red iron oxide contains 4.48 g of iron and 1.92 g of oxygen.
(e) Lead carbonate: 5.34 g of lead carbonate contains 4.14 g of lead, 0.24 g of carbon and 0.96 g of oxygen.

21 The chemical mole and writing equations

The composition by mass in the three examples below are given in percentages. These tell you the number of grams of each element in 100 g of the compound.

(*f*) Sodium carbonate: this compound contains 43.4% of sodium, 11.3% of carbon, 45.3% of oxygen.

(*g*) Sodium hydroxide: this compound contains 57.5% of sodium, 40% of oxygen, and 2.5% of hydrogen.

(*h*) Nitric acid: this compound contains 1.6% of hydrogen, 22.4% of nitrogen and 76% of oxygen.

8 An oxide of iron was reduced by heating it in hydrogen. 1.50 g of the iron oxide left a residue of 1.05 g of iron.

(*a*) Write the word-equation for the reaction.

(*b*) Calculate the empirical formula of the iron oxide.

(*c*) Write the balanced equation (including symbols of state) for the reaction.

9 1.40 g of aluminium was heated in chlorine and produced 6.92 g of aluminium chloride.

(*a*) Calculate the empirical formula of aluminium chloride.

(*b*) Write a balanced equation (including symbols of state) for the reaction.

10 The formula of sodium thiosulphate crystals is

$$Na_2S_2O_3 \cdot 5H_2O.$$

(*a*) How many moles each are there of Na, S, and O atoms in 1 mole of $Na_2S_2O_3$ (anhydrous sodium thiosulphate)?

(*b*) What is the relative molecular mass of $Na_2S_2O_3$?

(*c*) How many moles of H_2O are there in 1 mole of $Na_2S_2O_3 \cdot 5H_2O$?

(*d*) What is the mass in grams of this water?

(*e*) Work out the relative molecular mass of $Na_2S_2O_3 \cdot 5H_2O$.

11 7.50 g of hydrated copper sulphate crystals are gently heated until the loss of water of crystallization appears to be complete. After cooling, they have a mass of 5.35 g. They are then reheated and cooled and their mass is then found to be 4.80 g. Further heating does not change this mass.

(*a*) In this experiment, how would you judge if the reaction is complete?

(*b*) Do you think the reaction is finished after the first heating? Explain your answer.

(*c*) Do you think the reaction is finished after the second heating? Explain your answer.

(*d*) Work out the number of mol H_2O and the number of mol $CuSO_4$ originally present in the crystals.

(*e*) Work out the number of mol H_2O which combine with 1 mol $CuSO_4$ in the crystals.

(*f*) Write the formula for hydrated copper sulphate and the equation for its thermal decomposition to anhydrous copper sulphate.

12 The formula of anhydrous sodium carbonate is Na_2CO_3. Two hydrated forms of sodium carbonate contain 14.5% and 62.9% of water of crystallization. Calculate the formulas of the two hydrated forms of sodium carbonate.

Key words

mole	**relative atomic mass**	**molar mass** **balanced**
Avogadro constant	**relative molecular mass**	**equation**

Basic facts

- **One mole of a substance is that amount of the substance that contains L chemical units.**

- **For the present, the Avogadro constant, L, is defined as the number of atoms in exactly 12 g of carbon.**

- **The relative atomic mass of an element is the mass of one of its atoms compared to one-twelfth of the mass of a carbon atom. Relative molecular mass is defined in a similar way.**

- **Molar mass is the mass of one mole of a substance. (The chemical units which make up the substance should be noted.)**

- **The relative atomic mass of an element and the mass of one mole of atoms of that element have the same numerical value. But the molar mass has the units of mass (grams), while relative atomic mass has no units. There is a similar relationship between the relative molecular mass of a compound and its molar mass.**

- **Equations show not only which substances are involved in a reaction, they also show the relative quantities of the different substances.**

- **Equations have to be balanced so that they do not contradict the Law of Conservation of Mass.**

- **Symbols of state are used to show the physical states of substances involved in reactions.**

22 The idea of ions

More about electrolysis

The electrolysis of some molten compounds and some aqueous solutions has been dealt with in Chapter 8. The results for the electrolysis of molten compounds are straightforward but for aqueous solutions, the presence of water sometimes affects what is formed at the electrodes.

It seems that metals that are high in the reactivity series are *not* produced at the cathode (the electrode attached to the negative battery connection) when aqueous solutions of their salts are electrolysed. Instead, hydrogen is given off. But metals which are low in the reactivity series *are* produced at the cathode when aqueous solutions of their salts are electrolysed.

For the products at the anode (the electrode attached to the positive battery connection), it seems that the electrolysis of solutions of sulphates and nitrates gives oxygen at the anode. But solutions of chlorides, bromides and iodides give chlorine, bromine and iodine, respectively.

There are some exceptions to these statements so they should be used only as rough guides. You will meet two of the exceptions in Experiments 22.1 and 22.2.

Experiment 22.1 What happens when copper sulphate solution is electrolysed using copper electrodes?

Set up the apparatus as shown in Fig. 22.1. Find the mass of each electrode and then clamp each one firmly between the two halves of a split cork so that they are held upright in the same place for the whole of the electrolysis. Adjust the rheostat so that the current is about 0.1 A. It does not matter if this current changes during the experiment.

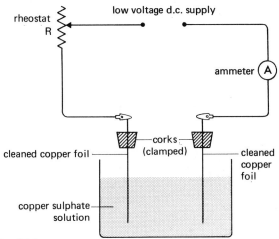

Fig. 22.1

Electrolyse the solution for about 45 minutes and then remove the electrodes from the solution. The anode should be dipped into water and into propanone (acetone), allowed to dry, and its new mass found. The cathode should be treated in the same way, but do this carefully so that the deposit of copper stays on the foil and is not washed off.

Allowing for experimental error, it is always found in the above experiment that the anode loses the same mass of metal as the cathode gains. The copper is dissolved from the anode and an equal mass is deposited on the cathode.

Compare this result with the result of the electrolysis of copper sulphate solution between platinum electrodes (Table 8.2). The results are summarized in Table 22.1.

Table 22.1

Electrodes	Change at anode	Change at cathode	Change in electrolyte
Platinum	Oxygen evolved	Copper deposited	Blue colour fades
Copper	Copper dissolved	Copper deposited	No change in blue colour

Experiment 22.2 Does changing the concentration of hydrochloric acid affect what is produced at the electrodes?

Your teacher will provide you with two solutions of hydrochloric acid. One solution is fairly concentrated and the other is very dilute. Use the apparatus shown in Fig. 8.3 (page 26) to electrolyse the solutions and to collect samples of the gases formed at the electrodes. A platinum anode should be used for the electrolysis of the dilute solution.

▶ Try to decide what the gases produced could be.
▶ Then use the appropriate tests (Chapter 56, page 250) to identify the gases.

Similar results to these would be obtained if solutions of other chlorides were used. The results are summarized in Table 22.2.

Table 22.2

	Product at cathode	Product at anode
Fairly concentrated hydrochloric acid	Hydrogen	Chlorine
Very dilute hydrochloric acid	Hydrogen	Oxygen

Charged particles

So far, you know a lot of *facts* about electrolysis. But how can electrolysis be explained? It may seem strange that passing electricity through a substance can cause chemical reactions to happen. A *theory* is required which can successfully answer the following questions:

1. How is the electric current carried through the electrolyte?
2. Why do some elements form at the cathode while others form at the anode?
3. What happens at the electrodes to cause elements to be released?

Question 1 deals only with the conduction of electricity and not with any chemical reactions. Questions 2 and 3 deal with the chemical reactions caused by electricity. It is obviously important to note that such reactions always occur *at the electrodes* and not in the body of the electrolyte.

Your teacher may show you the electrolysis of a green solution of copper chromate in dilute ammonia solution (Fig. 22.2). The gelatin makes the solution set like a jelly and stops any mixing by diffusion. After electrolysis has gone on for a few minutes, the solution above the green jelly on the cathode side goes blue and the solution on the anode side goes yellow. After one or two hours, definite bands can be seen, blue near the cathode and yellow near the anode.

The green solution of copper chromate has separated into a blue part which moves towards the cathode and a yellow part which moves towards the anode. If small equal amounts of the blue and yellow solutions are mixed, green copper chromate is produced again. Why does this separation occur when a current is passed through the electrolyte?

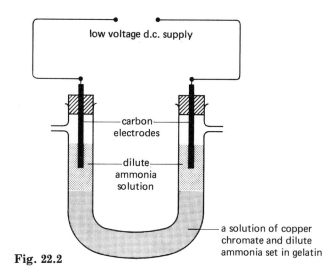

Fig. 22.2

A likely explanation is that some particles in the solution are blue. If these blue particles are positively charged, they will be attracted towards the negative cathode. Other particles are yellow and negatively charged, and are attracted towards the positive anode.

Since a green solution of copper chromate is electrically neutral, the charges on the blue and yellow parts must exactly balance each other when the two parts are mixed in certain proportions.

So copper chromate consists of two kinds of charged particle, a positive kind and a negative kind. These charged particles are called **ions**. An electric current is carried across a solution, or flows through a solution, by the movement of the ions.

Positively charged ions are called **cations**; negatively charged ions are called **anions**. Cations move to the cathode and anions move to the anode. Question 1 (above) has now been answered. Fig. 22.3 shows what has been concluded so far.

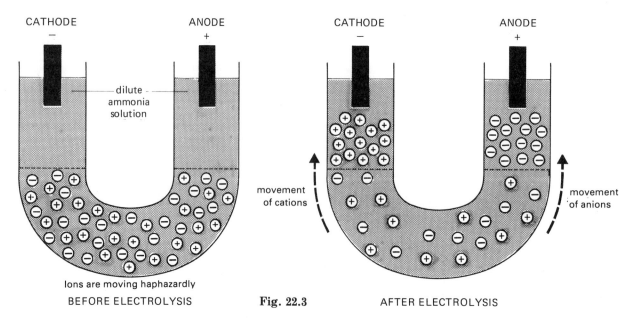

Fig. 22.3

BEFORE ELECTROLYSIS   AFTER ELECTROLYSIS

Which part of the copper chromate is blue and positively charged, and which part is yellow and negatively charged? A glance round the laboratory shelves might suggest the answer. Solutions of copper sulphate and copper nitrate are blue but solutions of sodium chromate and potassium chromate are yellow. It seems likely that copper cations are blue in colour and chromate anions yellow.

Another way of investigating the movement of coloured ions during electrolysis is shown in Fig. 22.4. If the strip of filter paper is moistened with water and a crystal of potassium permanganate is placed in the middle of it, a patch of purple slowly moves towards the *anode* when the current is passed between the crocodile clips acting as electrodes.

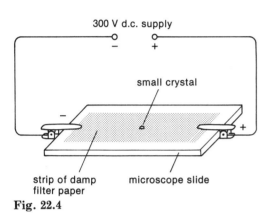

Fig. 22.4

Potassium permanganate is purple. Because nothing is seen to move to the cathode, at first sight it looks as if the whole substance moves towards the anode. Sodium permanganate is also purple and does the same thing. Since solutions of many sodium and potassium salts are known to be colourless, it seems more likely that it is only the permanganate part of the substance that moves towards the anode. So the permanganate ion must be an anion. This means that the sodium and potassium ions are the cations and must be colourless, and this is why their movement cannot be seen during this experiment.

You now have a theory that explains why electrolytes conduct electricity. It appears that all electrolytes consist of cations and anions which exactly balance each other in charge and which move to the cathode and anode respectively during electrolysis.

Table 22.3

| Cations | Anions | |
	Containing only one element	Containing more than one element
All metal ions Hydrogen ions	Chloride ions Bromide ions Iodide ions	Sulphate ions Nitrate ions Hydroxide ions Chromate ions Permanganate ions

You can decide the kind of charge on a coloured ion by looking at its movement in experiments like those described above: it is also possible to decide this by noting at which electrode elements tend to be formed (Table 22.3).

Think again about the questions asked at the beginning of this section. Answers have been found for the first two questions. You still have to attempt to answer the third question: what happens at the electrodes to cause elements to be released? This could be re-phrased to: How can charged ions be changed to neutral particles of elements (atoms) at the electrodes?

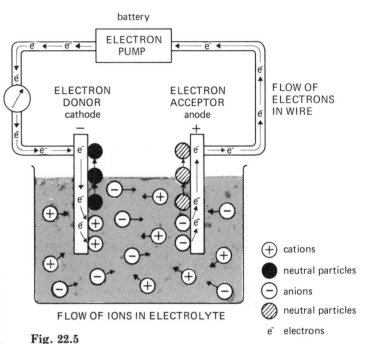

Fig. 22.5

⊕ cations

● neutral particles

⊖ anions

▨ neutral particles

e⁻ electrons

What happens at the electrodes during electrolysis?

What is happening inside a wire when electricity flows through it? It is thought that the flow of electricity is caused by the movement of very small particles called *electrons* (page 150). These electrons carry a *negative electric charge* and they move from the negative terminal of the battery, round the circuit and back to the positive terminal of the battery.

Look at Fig. 22.5 which tries to show what happens in the various parts of the circuit during an electrolysis experiment.

In the wires there is a flow of electrons. The flow is from the battery to the cathode and from the anode back to the battery.

In the electrolyte, there is a flow of ions. Cations (positively charged) move towards the cathode and anions (negatively charged) move towards the anode.

What happens at the surface of the electrodes? Remember that you have to explain how elements are formed. In other words, how are ions changed into atoms?

Positively charged ions arrive at the cathode from the electrolyte and negatively charged electrons come to the cathode from the battery. The cations can combine with electrons to form neutral particles. The cations lose their charge and are said to be discharged.

So, at the cathode,

cations	+	electrons	⟶	atoms
(positively charged ions)		(taken from the cathode)		(formed at the cathode)

(The cathode *donates* electrons to the cations and so is called the electron donor).

If the electrolyte is molten lead bromide, lead ions combine with electrons to form lead atoms and you see a deposit of lead on the cathode. If the electrolyte is dilute sulphuric acid or sodium chloride solution, hydrogen ions combine with electrons to form hydrogen atoms. These atoms combine to form hydrogen molecules and you see hydrogen gas given off.

At the anode, negatively charged ions arrive from the electrolyte and electrons flow from the anode to the battery. When anions reach the anode, they lose electrons which the anode accepts and the ions become neutral atoms. So, at the anode anions are discharged by losing electrons:

anions	⟶	atoms	+	electrons
(negatively charged ions)		(formed at the anode)		(given to the anode)

If the electrolyte is molten lead bromide, bromide ions arrive at the anode, lose electrons to the anode and form bromine atoms. The atoms then form molecules and you see bromine gas given off.

Question 3 (page 64) has nearly been answered now. The part that remains to be answered is: How many electrons have to be gained or lost for an ion to be changed into an atom? This is what the next section is about.

The size of ionic charges

In the electroplating experiment (22.1) you found the loss in mass of the anode and the gain in mass of the cathode. But you made no measurements to find the *amount* of electricity needed to produce these particular changes in mass.

Experiment 22.3 What amounts of electricity are needed to deposit 1 mol Cu and 1 mol Ag?

Some groups in the class should repeat Experiment 22.1 with the following differences.

1. Keep the current steady at about 0.5 A for the whole experiment by adjusting the rheostat. Write down your value for this steady current.

2. Time the period of the electrolysis to the nearest minute; this should be about 30 minutes.

3. Find the mass of the anode before and after the electrolysis and write down its loss of mass. This loss is equal to the gain in mass of the cathode.

The other groups should do the experiment using silver electrodes and silver nitrate solution. The method is the same as that described for the copper plating. Again, you need only find the loss in mass of the anode.

The following examples show you how to work out the amount of electricity required to form either 1 mole of metal atoms or 1 mole of atoms of a gas.

Examples

1. *Suppose a current of 0.20 A is passed for exactly 30 minutes and forms a deposit of 0.40 g of silver. What amount of electricity deposits 1 mole of Ag atoms?*

Now $Q = I \times t$, where Q is the amount of electricity in coulombs (C), I the current in amperes (A) and t the time in seconds (s).

In this experiment, $Q = 0.20 \times 30 \times 60 = 360$ C. So, 0.40 g of silver is deposited by 360 C. 1 mole of silver atoms has a mass of 108 g, so that to produce 1 mole of Ag atoms, the number of coulombs needed is $360 \times 108/0.40$.

And so 1 mole of Ag atoms is deposited by *9.7 × 10^4 C.*

You should repeat this calculation using your results from Experiment 22.3 for the electrolysis of copper sulphate.

Accurate experiments show that the value for this amount is 9.65×10^4 C mol^{-1} for silver and 1.93×10^5 C mol^{-1} for copper. If your own results do not agree too well with these, try to decide where errors could have arisen during the experiment. Notice that the result for copper is twice that for silver.

2. *What amount of electricity is needed to deposit 1 mole of Pb atoms?*

This amount could be found by a similar electroplating experiment. (Which electrodes and electrolyte would you choose?) But the electrolysis of a molten lead compound such as lead bromide gives very good results. The apparatus is shown in Fig. 22.6. Molten lead collects below the cathode. The molten lead bromide can be poured from the container leaving lead at the bottom (Fig. 22.6).

When cold, the bead of lead can be prised from the container and its mass found.

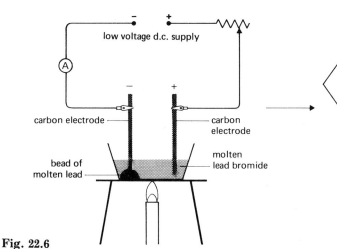

Fig. 22.6

Using a current of 1.5 A for 20 minutes gives a mass of 1.94 g of lead. The amount of electricity needed to deposit 1 mole of Pb atoms can be worked out as for copper and silver and comes to about *1.9 × 10⁵ C*.

3. What amount of electricity is needed to release 1 mole of H atoms?

The apparatus shown in Fig. 22.7 is suitable for this investigation. In one experiment, 68 cm³ of hydrogen is collected after a current of 0.60 A is passed for 15 minutes. The density of hydrogen under normal laboratory conditions is about 8.3×10^{-5} g cm⁻³.

The mass of hydrogen released is $8.3 \times 10^{-5} \times 68 = 5.6 \times 10^{-3}$ g. The number of coulombs passed through the solution is $0.60 \times 15 \times 60 = 540$ C.

Since 5.6×10^{-3} g hydrogen is released using 540 C, 1 g hydrogen would be released by $540 \times 1/(5.6 \times 10^{-3}) = 9.6 \times 10^{4}$ C.

The amount of electricity necessary to produce 1 mole of atoms of several elements is given in Table 22.4. These amounts can all be found by the kinds of

Table 22.4

Element	Relative atomic mass	Q in C mol⁻¹
Aluminium	27.0	2.89×10^5 or $3F$
Iron	55.8	2.89×10^5 or $3F$
Lead	207	1.93×10^5 or $2F$
Zinc	65.4	1.93×10^5 or $2F$
Tin	119	1.93×10^5 or $2F$
Copper	63.5	1.93×10^5 or $2F$
Silver	108	9.65×10^4 or $1F$
Hydrogen	1.01	9.65×10^4 or $1F$
Chlorine	35.5	9.65×10^4 or $1F$

method given above. Because of these results, a constant can be introduced called the **Faraday constant**. This is given the symbol F and is taken to equal 9.65×10^4 C mol⁻¹.

You can see from this table that electricity is used in 'packets' when 1 mole of any element's atoms is

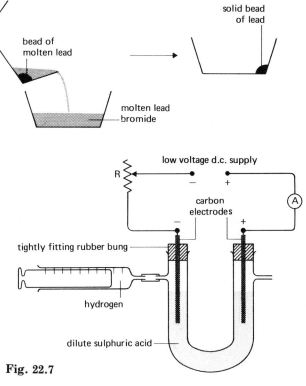

Fig. 22.7

formed at the electrodes during electrolysis. The smallest 'packet' is 9.65×10^4 C mol⁻¹, $(= 1 F)$, but some elements require two or three 'packets' ($2F$ or $3F$) before 1 mole is formed at the electrode.

It is like the situation in a store where some people only take one box of half a dozen eggs whereas others may want two or three boxes; it is not usual for someone to remove one egg from a box and buy just that.

In the same way, 1 mole of any element's atoms is never formed by any amount of electricity less than 9.65×10^4 C. Another interesting point about the table is that iron sometimes needs $2F$ to deposit 1 mole of atoms and sometimes $3F$. This is like the same person taking two boxes of eggs on one day and three boxes on another.

You know that the *amount* of electricity that passes through a circuit is measured in coulombs. If you think of this amount of electricity as an electric charge, then you can work out the amount of charge held by a mole of ions. If the ions are cations, it is positive charge, while for anions it is negative charge.

So, from Table 22.4 you can see that a mole of either silver or hydrogen ions has a total positive charge of $1F$, while a mole of chloride ions has a negative charge of $1F$. A mole of either zinc or lead ions has a positive charge of $2F$ while a mole of aluminium ions has a positive charge of $3F$, and so on.

To form 1 mole of Ag atoms at the *cathode*, 1 mole of silver ions has to gain 9.65×10^4 C of negative charge from the cathode. The cathode supplies this negative charge as electrons. How many electrons does each silver ion have to gain for it to become a silver atom?

The charge on the electron is about 1.6×10^{-19} C. How much negative charge does a mole (6×10^{23}, the Avogadro constant) of electrons carry? The amount can be found by multiplying 1.6×10^{-19} by 6×10^{23}, and comes to 9.6×10^4 C mol^{-1}. You should see that this amount of charge is about equal to the Faraday constant. If accurate values are taken for the charge on the electron and the Avogadro constant, this answer equals the accurate value of the Faraday constant found by experiments on electrolysis.

So, in order to form 1 mole of Ag atoms from 1 mole of silver ions, about 6×10^{23} electrons with a total charge of 9.65×10^4 C need to be added.

The discharge of a mole of silver ions can be written as:

$$\begin{array}{ccc} \text{1 mole of} & + \; 1F \text{ of negative} & \longrightarrow \; \text{1 mole of} \\ \text{silver ions} & \text{charge} & \text{Ag atoms} \end{array}$$

$$\text{or} \quad \begin{array}{ccc} 6 \times 10^{23} & + \; 9.65 \times 10^4 \text{ C} & \longrightarrow \; 6 \times 10^{23} \\ \text{silver ions} & \text{provided by} & \text{Ag atoms} \\ & 6 \times 10^{23} & \\ & \text{electrons} & \end{array}$$

$$\text{or} \quad \text{1 silver ion} + \text{1 electron} \longrightarrow \text{1 Ag atom}$$

In view of this result, you can see that 1 mole of silver ions is 1 mole of Ag atoms which has lost 1 mole of electrons, or that a silver ion is a silver atom which has lost one electron. If a mole of silver ions is written as Ag$^+$ and a mole of electrons as e$^-$, the equation for the reaction at the cathode is

$$\begin{array}{cccc} \text{Ag}^+(\text{aq}) & + & \text{e}^- & \longrightarrow & \text{Ag(s)} \\ \text{1 mole } (6 \times 10^{23}) & & \text{1 mole} & & \text{1 mole } (6 \times 10^{23}) \\ \text{of Ag}^+ \text{ ions} & & (6 \times 10^{23}) & & \text{of Ag atoms} \\ & & \text{of electrons} & & \end{array}$$

But, in order to produce a mole of lead atoms at the cathode, $2F$ of negative charge must be provided.

$$\begin{array}{ccc} \text{1 mole of} + 2F \text{ of negative} & \longrightarrow \text{1 mole of} \\ \text{lead ions} \quad \text{charge} & \text{Pb atoms} \end{array}$$

$$\text{or} \quad \begin{array}{ccc} 6 \times 10^{23} & + \; 2 \times 9.65 \times 10^4 \text{ C} & \longrightarrow \; 6 \times 10^{23} \\ \text{lead ions} & \text{provided by} & \text{Pb atoms} \\ & 2 \times 6 \times 10^{25} & \\ & \text{electrons} & \end{array}$$

So 1 mole of lead ions is 1 mole of Pb atoms which has lost 2 moles of electrons, or a lead ion is a lead

atom which has lost two electrons. The charge carried by a mole of lead ions is double that carried by a mole of silver ions. A mole of lead ions is written as Pb^{2+} and the equation for the reaction at the cathode during the discharge of lead ions in the electrolysis of, say, molten lead bromide is

$$\begin{array}{cccc} \text{Pb}^{2+}(\text{l}) & + & 2\text{e}^- & \longrightarrow & \text{Pb(s)} \\ \text{1 mole } (6 \times 10^{23}) & & \text{2 mole} & & \text{1 mole } (6 \times 10^{23}) \\ \text{of Pb}^{2+} \text{ ions} & & (2 \times 6 \times 10^{23}) & & \text{of Pb atoms} \\ & & \text{of electrons} & & \end{array}$$

For the reaction at the cathode during the electrolysis of lead nitrate solution, the equation is the same except that (l) is replaced by (aq).

A similar sort of argument shows that aluminium ions are aluminium atoms that have lost three electrons, so their symbol is Al^{3+}. And iron atoms can form two sorts of ions, either Fe^{2+} or Fe^{3+}.

What happens at the *anode* during electrolysis? When negatively charged ions are discharged, they need to lose electrons. Taking the formation of chlorine as an example,

$$\begin{array}{ccc} \text{1 mole of} - & 1F \text{ of} & \longrightarrow \text{1 mole of} \\ \text{chloride} & \text{negative} & \text{Cl atoms} \\ \text{ions} & \text{charge} & \end{array}$$

$$\text{or} \quad \begin{array}{ccc} 6 \times 10^{23} - & 9.65 \times 10^4 \text{ C} & \longrightarrow 6 \times 10^{23} \\ \text{chloride} & \text{removed as} & \text{Cl atoms} \\ \text{ions} & 6 \times 10^{23} & \\ & \text{electrons} & \end{array}$$

$$\text{or} \quad \text{1 chloride ion} - \text{1 electron} \longrightarrow \text{1 Cl atom}$$

Using symbols, the equation can be written as

$$\begin{array}{cccc} \text{Cl}^-(\text{aq}) & - & \text{e}^- & \longrightarrow & \text{Cl(g)} \\ \text{1 mole } (6 \times 10^{23}) & \text{1 mole } (6 \times 10^{23}) & & \text{1 mole } (6 \times 10^{23}) \\ \text{of Cl}^- \text{ ions} & \text{of electrons} & & \text{of Cl atoms} \end{array}$$

This is followed by

$$\text{Cl(g)} + \text{Cl(g)} \longrightarrow \text{Cl}_2(\text{g})$$

At the anode, electrons are always *given up* by the anions. In one example of electrolysis, no atoms are formed at the anode. Instead the anode dissolves as, for example, in Experiment 22.1. Can this be explained using electrons? The copper atoms in the anode must dissolve to form Cu^{2+} (aq) ions, and this process can be represented by

$$\begin{array}{cccc} \text{Cu(s)} & - & 2\text{e}^- & \longrightarrow & \text{Cu}^{2+}(\text{aq}) \\ \text{1 mole} & & \text{2 moles} & & \text{1 mole} \\ (6 \times 10^{23}) & & (2 \times 6 \times 10^{23}) & & (6 \times 10^{23}) \\ \text{of Cu atoms} & & \text{of electrons} & & \text{of Cu}^{2+} \text{ ions} \end{array}$$

Again, the reaction at the anode involves electrons being given to the anode and then being returned to the battery. In this case, they are produced by atoms in the anode forming cations with the release of electrons.

Ionic charges and the formulas of electrolytes

A list of ions together with their charges is given in Table 22.5. Some ions are 'compound ions', that is, they contain more than one atom. The atoms in these compound ions are joined together very strongly and they often stay joined together during chemical reactions.

Some elements appear under two separate columns showing that they can form two kinds of ion with different charges. In these cases, the ions are written or spoken about by putting a number after the name of the element. For example, Cu^+ is called a copper(I) iron and Fe^{3+} an iron(III) ion. You could refer to Ca^{2+} as a calcium(II) ion, but there is no need to do this because there is only one kind of calcium ion. From now on, in naming compounds that contain elements which can form cations of different charges, you must include this number so that it is clear which cation is present in the compound. For example, red copper oxide is called copper(I) oxide and black copper oxide is called copper(II) oxide.

Numbers are also included in the names of some of the anions in Table 22.5. The reasons for including these numbers are explained in Chapter 40.

How can formulas be worked out using Table 22.5? An electrolyte has no *overall* charge. In other words, the total positive charges on the cations must balance the total negative charges on the anions.

Table 22.5

Cations

Charge + 1	Charge + 2	Charge + 3
Hydrogen H^+	Calcium Ca^{2+}	Iron(III) Fe^{3+}
Sodium Na^+	Magnesium Mg^{2+}	Aluminium Al^{3+}
Potassium K^+	Lead Pb^{2+}	
Lithium Li^+	Zinc Zn^{2+}	
Silver Ag^+	Barium Ba^{2+}	
Copper(I) Cu^+	Strontium Sr^{2+}	
Ammonium $NH_4{}^+$	Iron(II) Fe^{2+}	
	Copper(II) Cu^{2+}	

Anions

Charge − 1	Charge − 2
Fluoride F^-	Oxide O^{2-}
Chloride Cl^-	Sulphide S^{2-}
Bromide Br^-	Sulphite $SO_3{}^{2-}$
Iodide I^-	Sulphate $SO_4{}^{2-}$
Hydroxide OH^-	Carbonate $CO_3{}^{2-}$
Nitrate $NO_3{}^-$	Chromate(VI) $CrO_4{}^{2-}$
Hydrogen-sulphate $HSO_4{}^-$	Dichromate(VI) $Cr_2O_7{}^{2-}$
Hydrogen-carbonate $HCO_3{}^-$	
Manganate(VII) $MnO_4{}^-$	

Fig. 22.8 shows how this balance can be reached for three different electrolytes.

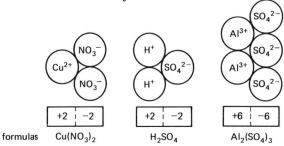

Fig. 22.8 These diagrams do not show particles of $Cu(NO_3)_2$, H_2SO_4, or $Al_2(SO_4)_3$: they just show the proportions in which the cations and anions are linked in each compound; nor do they show the relative sizes of the ions

If the formula of aluminium sulphate were $AlSO_4$, there would be an overall charge of $+3 − 2$ or $+1$, which does not agree with the solid being electrically neutral. To balance the positive and negative charges, two charges of size $+3$ and three charges of size $−2$ are needed, so that the formula is $Al_2(SO_4)_3$. Notice that the number of ions is shown by a number *following* the symbol as a subscript. Also, if the number follows a 'compound ion' as in $Cu(NO_3)_2$ or $Al_2(SO_4)_3$, then brackets have to be used.

Explaining the electrolysis of aqueous solutions

Pure water is a very poor conductor of electricity. This suggests that there are very few ions present to carry the current. The ions that are present in pure water are hydrogen and hydroxide ions. One way of writing the equation for their formation is

$$H_2O(l) \rightleftharpoons H^+(aq) + OH^-(aq)$$

(The sign $\rightleftharpoons$ is explained on page 196.)

The electrolysis of aqueous solution often causes the decomposition of water rather than the decomposition of the electrolyte dissolved in the water. This happens, for example, when very dilute sodium chloride solution is electrolysed. The cathode product is hydrogen and the anode product is oxygen.

During the electrolysis, sodium and hydrogen ions move towards the cathode while chloride and hydroxide ions move towards the anode. Why are hydrogen ions and hydroxide ions discharged even though there are far more sodium ions and chloride ions present?

The answer to this question cannot be given very definitely as there are several rival theories. One idea is that the few ions that are present from the water are discharged more easily than the other ions. So, $H^+(aq)$ ions are discharged more easily than the $Na^+(aq)$ ions at the cathode, and the $OH^-(aq)$ ions are discharged more easily than the $Cl^-(aq)$ ions at the anode.

At the *cathode*, $H^+(aq) + e^- \longrightarrow H(g)$
followed by $\quad H(g) + H(g) \longrightarrow H_2(g)$

So the overall equation is

$$2H^+(aq) + 2e^- \longrightarrow H_2(g)$$

At the *anode*, $OH^-(aq) - e^- \longrightarrow OH(aq)$
followed by $\quad OH(aq) + OH(aq) \longrightarrow O(g) + H_2O(l)$
and $\quad O(g) + O(g) \longrightarrow O_2(g)$

The overall equation is

$$4OH^-(aq) - 4e^- \longrightarrow 2H_2O(l) + O_2(g)$$

The water then produces a few more $H^+(aq)$ and $OH^-(aq)$ ions which are discharged, and so on.

The uses of electrolysis

Electrolysis is very important in industry and it is used for a variety of purposes.

In electroplating (page 26) a thin layer of a metal is deposited on the surface of another metal to improve resistance to corrosion.

Very pure copper can be produced from impure copper by electrolysis (page 100).

Some metals, such as aluminium (page 99), have to be extracted by electrolysis, and the electrolysis of brine (page 122) produces the important chemicals sodium hydroxide, chlorine and hydrogen.

Although aluminium is fairly high in the reactivity table, it is unreactive under most conditions because of a thin layer of aluminium oxide which protects it from attack (page 37). This resistance to corrosion can be improved by a process called anodizing. The metal is used as the anode for the electrolysis of a solution which produces oxygen at the anode. This oxygen reacts with the aluminium and produces a thicker and very protective layer of aluminium oxide. The aluminium can be coloured at the same time by including a dye in the electrolyte.

QUESTIONS

1 What are the main differences between conduction in metals and conduction in electrolytes? Would you class graphite as a metallic conductor or an electrolyte?

2 What products would you expect at the cathode and at the anode when the following are electrolysed using platinum electrodes?

(a) molten magnesium bromide
(b) aqueous magnesium bromide
(c) copper(II) nitrate solution
(d) a solution containing copper(II) sulphate and potassium sulphate.

What might be the effect of using copper electrodes in (d)?

3 When a deep purple solution of copper(II) manganate(VII) is electrolysed in a U-tube, a blue colour appears around the cathode and a lighter purple colour around the anode.

(a) What kind of charge must the particles that cause the blue colour have?
(b) What kind of charge must the particles that cause the light purple colour have?
(c) Name the ions that cause the blue colour.
(d) Name the ions that cause the light purple colour.
(e) Given that the formula of copper(II) manganate(VII) is $Cu(MnO_4)_2$, which can you say about the *relative* sizes of the charges on the two kinds of ion?
(f) Predict what colour the liquid in the *middle* of the U-tube well away from the electrodes would be.

4 During the electrolysis of an iron salt, 0.10 g of iron is deposited on the cathode when 0.50 A is passed through the electrolyte for 17 minutes. Work out:
(a) the number of coulombs passed through the electrolyte;
(b) the number of coulombs that would be necessary to produce 1 mole of Fe atoms (Fe = 56);
(c) the charge on the iron ions ($F = 9.65 \times 10^4 \, C \, mol^{-1}$).

Write the equation for the reaction at the cathode.

5 In the electrolysis of molten sodium hydride (NaH), $100 \, cm^3$ of hydrogen is collected at the *anode*. During the experiment a steady current of 1.0 A is passed for exactly 13.5 minutes.
(a) What is formed at the cathode?
(b) Work out the mass of hydrogen released, assuming the density of the gas under the conditions of the experiment to be $8.33 \times 10^{-5} \, g \, cm^{-3}$.
(c) How many coulombs of electricity are passed through the electrolyte during the experiment?
(d) Using your answers to (b) and (c), work out the number of coulombs required to release 1 mole of H atoms.
(e) What is the likely charge on the hydride ion? Write the symbol for 1 mole of hydride ions in molten sodium hydride. (The Faraday constant is $9.65 \times 10^4 \, C \, mol^{-1}$.)
(f) What is the likely charge on the sodium ion in view of your answer to (e)?

6 Using Table 22.5, write down the formulas for 1 mole of:
(a) sodium iodide, (b) calcium hydroxide, (c) copper(I) chloride, (d) iron(II) sulphate, (e) aluminium sulphide, (f) lithium hydroxide, (g) lead(II) iodide, (h) sodium hydrogencarbonate, (i) potassium carbonate, (j) ammonium sulphate.

Key words

electrolytic conduction   **ions**   **cations**   **anions**   **ionic charges**   **Faraday constant**   **anodizing**

Basic facts

- **The ionic theory proposes that electrolytes consist of electrically charged particles which are called ions. During electrolysis the cations (positively charged) move towards the cathode and the anions (negatively charged) move towards the anode.**

- During the electrolysis of a molten salt, the ions from the salt are discharged (lose their charges) when they reach the electrode and they become neutral atoms. So the salt is decomposed to its elements.

- At the cathode, the cations gain electrons while at the anode, the anions lose electrons.

- Water is a very poor conductor of electricity but contains a small proportion of hydrogen and hydroxide ions.

- During the electrolysis of aqueous solutions, either the ions from the salt or the ions from water are discharged at the electrodes.

- Metallic conduction is the movement of electrons through a metal. Electrolytic conduction is the movement of ions through an electrolyte and the discharge of ions at the electrodes.

- During the electrolysis of aqueous solutions, factors which affect the products at the electrodes include the position of the metal in the reactivity table, the type of electrode (inert or reactive) and the concentration of the electrolyte.

- The Faraday constant is the amount of electric charge carried by one mole of electrons.

- By using ionic charges it is possible to work out the formulas for electrolytes and also to write equations for the reactions that occur at the electrodes during electrolysis.

23 Ions and the reactions of acids, bases and salts

What are acids?

The various ways of neutralizing acids are discussed in Chapters 14 and 15 and these reactions (together with some others) are summarized in Chapter 18.

Using these reactions, it is possible to write a list of characteristic acidic properties and this list also describes in practical terms what is meant by the term 'acid'.

A definition of an acid

An acid is a substance that has the following properties when it is dissolved in water:

1 It has a sharp taste (but it is far too dangerous to apply this test to most acids).
2 It has a pH value less than 7 and causes indicators to show their acidic colours.
3 It reacts with many metals to form salts and hydrogen.
4 It reacts with an alkali to form a salt and water.
5 It reacts with a basic oxide to form a salt and water.
6 It reacts with a carbonate or a hydrogencarbonate to form a salt, carbon dioxide and water.
7 It is an electrolyte.

This list summarizes what you already know about acids and it can also be used to decide if a substance should be classified as an acid. However, it describes only what acids will do and says nothing about *why* acids behave like this.

What are alkalis?

The alkalis that you have used in your chemistry course so far are metal hydroxides which are soluble in water. There are not many of these and the common ones are sodium hydroxide, potassium hydroxide and calcium hydroxide. One other alkali that is used frequently is ammonia solution. This is made by dissolving the gas ammonia (page 131) in water. Although ammonia solution does not contain a metal hydroxide, it is an alkali and has the same general properties of other alkalis.

A definition of an alkali

An alkali is a substance (often a metal hydroxide) which has the following properties when dissolved in water.

1 It feels slippery when rubbed between your fingers and has a bitter taste. See Warning below.
2 It has a pH value greater than 7 and causes indicators to show their alkaline colours.
3 It reacts with acids, neutralizing the acid and producing a salt and water.
4 It is an electrolyte.

This list summarizes what you already know about alkalis and also enables you to decide if a substance is an alkali. Again it does not explain why alkalis have these particular properties.

WARNING: It is far too dangerous to taste most alkalis. Also alkalis dissolve the grease in skin, so that any alkali accidentally spilt on the skin must be washed off immediately with plenty of water. Alkalis are particularly damaging to the surfaces of eyes: safety goggles must be worn when alkalis are being used.

A theory about acidity and alkalinity

Many metals decompose acids. The usual gaseous product of the decomposition is hydrogen. Because of this, Sir Humphry Davy in 1816 defined acids as *hydrogen producers* and obviously thought that all acids must be compounds of hydrogen.

All acids are electrolytes and so their solutions must contain ions. What are these ions?

Table 23.1

Acid	Formula	Product at cathode	Product at anode
Hydrochloric	HCl	Hydrogen	Chlorine
Hydrobromic	HBr	Hydrogen	Bromine
Hydriodic	HI	Hydrogen	Iodine
Nitric	HNO_3	Hydrogen	Oxygen
Sulphuric	H_2SO_4	Hydrogen	Oxygen
Ethanoic	CH_3CO_2H	Hydrogen	Oxygen

Some acids are listed in Table 23.1 together with their formulas and the substances produced when they are electrolysed using platinum electrodes. It follows from this that

1 hydrogen is always produced at the cathode during the electrolysis of an acid;
2 at the anode, the product is either oxygen, or the non-metal that is combined with hydrogen in the acid.

From the formulas of acids and their behaviour when they are electrolysed, it seems that they all form hydrogen ions in aqueous solution.

The formation of hydrogen at the cathode is due to the discharge of hydrogen ions:

$$H^+(aq) + e^- \longrightarrow H(g)$$
$$2H(g) \longrightarrow H_2(g)$$

The product at the anode depends on the anion. Some alkalis are listed in Table 23.2 together with

Table 23.2

Alkali	Formula	Product at cathode	Product at anode
Sodium hydroxide	NaOH	Hydrogen	Oxygen
Potassium hydroxide	KOH	Hydrogen	Oxygen
Calcium hydroxide	$Ca(OH)_2$	Hydrogen	Oxygen

their formulas and the products of the electrolysis of their solutions using platinum electrodes. During electrolysis, alkalis are similar to acids in that hydrogen is produced at the cathode. But in the case of alkalis, the hydrogen formed at the cathode must come from the water.

The behaviour of alkalis can be explained by suggesting that the ions they form in solution are metal ions and hydroxide ions.

The hydroxide ions are discharged at the anode during electrolysis (page 70):

$$4OH^-(aq) \longrightarrow 2H_2O(l) + O_2(g) + 4e^-$$

New definitions of acids and alkalis

You know that all acids have certain properties in common and it can be suggested that all acids in aqueous solution form $H^+(aq)$ ions. Could it be that the common properties of all acids are due to the presence of $H^+(aq)$ ions in their aqueous solutions? Also, could it be that the common properties of all alkalis are due to the presence of $OH^+(aq)$ ions in their aqueous solutions? If these ideas are correct, new definitions of what is meant by acids and alkalis can now be given.

An acid is a substance that gives rise to H^+ (aq) ions in aqueous solution.
An alkali is a substance that gives rise to OH^- (aq) ions in aqueous solution.

These definitions suggest that $H^+(aq)$ ions cause blue litmus to turn red, and $OH^-(aq)$ ions cause red litmus to turn blue. They also suggest that when an alkali neutralizes an acid, or vice versa, the acidity or alkalinity disappears because the $H^+(aq)$ or $OH^-(aq)$ ions are no longer present.

You should be careful to distinguish between these definitions which offer an *explanation* for acidity and alkalinity, and the definitions given earlier in this chapter which *describe* how acidity or alkalinity can be recognized in practice.

Think about these two definitions of the conductor of a steel band.

1. A conductor is a person who stands on a small platform in front of a steel band and waves his baton around in time to the music.
2. A conductor is a person who has a deep appreciation and understanding of music and can help a steel band to interpret it satisfactorily.

The first definition gives clear-cut instructions on how to decide whether or not a given person is the conductor of a steel band. All you have to do to recognize him is to look for the small platform and watch who is holding the baton. This is like the first definitions of acidity and alkalinity which are just statements about what acids and alkalis do.

The second definition of a conductor offers an explanation of *why* he is chosen for this job. It goes further than the first one because it contains more information about the skills involved and it is not obvious that a conductor is really like that. In the same way, the second definitions of acidity and alkalinity go further because they include the knowledge of why an acid or an alkali has its particular properties.

You must never think of these new definitions of acids and alkalis as statements of fact in the same way as the first definitions are. They certainly seem to explain the observations very well, but in science it is always possible to probe more deeply into a subject and to find new and more helpful explanations. The discussion of acids and alkalis and why they are acidic and alkaline is continued in Chapter 24.

The concentration of solutions

The concentration of a solution is often written as the number of grams of the solid dissolved in $1000 \, cm^3$ (1 litre or $1 \, dm^3$) of solution. But to a chemist, it is much more useful to say how many *moles* of the solid are dissolved in a given volume rather than how many grams. In chemistry, the concentration of a solution is usually written as:

the number of moles of dissolved substance in 1 litre of solution

and the units are $mol \, l^{-1}$. These units are sometimes shortened to M.

Here are some concentrations written in these units.

1 mol l⁻¹ (or 1 M):

a solution containing 1 mole of dissolved substance in 1 litre of solution.

0.1 mol l⁻¹ (or 0.1 M):

a solution containing 0.1 mole of dissolved substance in 1 litre of solution.

If concentrations are given in $mol \, l^{-1}$ (or M), then it follows that:

equal volumes of solutions of the same concentration contain the same number of moles of their different solutes

This fact is very useful when you try to discover how many moles of reacting substances there are in a chemical reaction.

Examples of the use of concentration in $mol \, l^{-1}$

1 How many moles of $Pb(NO_3)_2$ (lead (II) nitrate) are there in $50 \, cm^3$ of a $0.1 \, mol \, l^{-1}$ (0.1 M) solution of this salt in water?

1 litre of a $0.1 \, mol \, l^{-1}$ solution contains 0.1 mole of $Pb(NO_3)_2$; $1 \, cm^3$ of the same solution contains $0.1/1000$ mole of $Pb(NO_3)_2$; and $50 \, cm^3$ of the same solution contains $0.1 \times 50/1000$ mole of $Pb(NO_3)_2$.

So $50 \, cm^3$ of a $0.1 \, mol \, l^{-1}$ solution contains *0.005 mole of $Pb(NO_3)_2$.*

2 What is the concentration in $mol \, l^{-1}$ of a solution that contains 20 g of sodium hydroxide in $500 \, cm^{-3}$? (NaOH: relative molecular mass = 40)

$500 \, cm^3$ of solution contains 20 g of sodium hydroxide, and 1 litre of solution contains 40 g of sodium hydroxide (i.e. 1 mole of NaOH).

So the concentration of the solution is *1 mol l⁻¹ (or 1 M).*

3 How many grams of potassium iodide are there in $100 \, cm^3$ of a $0.2 \, mol \, l^{-1}$ (0.2 M) solution? (KI: relative molecular mass = 166)

1 litre of a $0.2 \, mol \, l^{-1}$ solution contains 0.2 mole of KI; $100 \, cm^3$ of solution contains 0.02 mole of KI; but 1 mole of KI has a mass of 166 g, therefore $100 \, cm^3$ of solution contains 0.02×166 g of KI.

So there are *3.32 g of KI in $100 \, cm^3$ of a 0.2 M solution.*

The equations for the neutralizations of acids with alkalis

The titration of an alkali with an acid is described in Chapter 14. The experiments in Chapter 14 are done to find out what is produced, and word-equations are written to describe the reactions. In order to write equations using formulas, it is necessary to find out the molar ratios in which the acid and alkali react and in which the salt is formed.

Experiment 23.1 Titrating sodium hydroxide and hydrochloric acid

The procedure is similar to that described for Experiment 14.1 (page 41) with the following modifications.

The concentrations of the acid and alkali should be known and preferably should be 1 M.

When consistent titration results have been obtained, prepare a neutral solution that does not contain any indicator. Pour this solution into a previously dried evaporating basin whose mass has been found. Evaporate the solution taking care to avoid loss of solid when the crystals start to form. When all the water has been evaporated, allow the basin and crystals to cool and then find their mass. The mass of the sodium chloride crystals can now be calculated.

Suppose that $25.0\,cm^3$ of $1.0\,M$ sodium hydroxide solution is neutralized by $24.5\,cm^3$ of $1.0\,M$ hydrochloric acid and that the mass of sodium chloride left after the evaporation is $1.46\,g$.

$1000\,cm^3$ of $1.0\,M$ sodium hydroxide solution contains $1.0\,mol$ NaOH. So $25.0\,cm^3$ of this solution contains

$$\frac{25}{1000} \times 1.0$$
$$= 0.025\,mol\ NaOH.$$

Similarly, $24.5\,cm^3$ of $1.0\,M$ hydrochloric acid contains

$$\frac{24.5}{1000} \times 1.0$$
$$= 0.0245\,mol\ HCl.$$

The molar mass of sodium chloride is $58.5\,g$, so that $1.46\,g$ of sodium chloride is $\frac{1.46}{58.5} = 0.025\,mol$ NaCl. So the molar ratio is

	NaOH	HCl	NaCl
	0.025	0.0245	0.025
or	1	1	1

This result means that 1 mol NaOH reacts with 1 mol HCl to form 1 mol NaCl, and part of the equation for the reaction can now be written

$$1NaOH(aq) + 1HCl(aq) \longrightarrow 1NaCl(aq)$$

Because of the large amount of water present as the solvent for this reaction, it is not easy to find by experiment how many moles of water molecules are formed. But for the equation to be balanced, one mol of H_2O must be included and the final balanced equation is

$$NaOH(aq) + HCl(aq) \longrightarrow NaCl(aq) + H_2O(l)$$

(The figure 1 need not be placed in front of the formulas.)

Reactions between other acids and alkalis

Experiments like the one for hydrochloric acid and sodium hydroxide can be done using other acids and other alkalis. Some results are given in Table 23.3.

Equations can be written for the three reactions in this table. The first two reactions have equations like that for hydrochloric acid and sodium hydroxide, but in the third reaction only 0.5 mole of H_2SO_4 is used and 0.5 mole of Na_2SO_4 is formed. So the equation is

$$\tfrac{1}{2}H_2SO_4(aq) + NaOH(aq) \longrightarrow \tfrac{1}{2}Na_2SO_4(aq) + H_2O(l)$$

Multiplying through the equation by two gets rid of the fractions:

$$H_2SO_4(aq) + 2NaOH(aq) \longrightarrow Na_2SO_4(aq) + 2H_2O(l)$$

The substance formed by the neutralization of hydrochloric acid and sodium hydroxide is common salt. The substances made in other neutralization reactions are also salts (page 44).

Salts are electrolytes: they contain a cation (usually a metal cation) and an anion. The anion comes from the 'parent' acid: sulphuric acid produces sulphates, $SO_4^{2-}(aq)$; hydrochloric acid produces chlorides, $Cl^-(aq)$; and nitric acid produces nitrates, $NO_3^-(aq)$. When the salt is prepared by neutralization, the cation comes from the 'parent' alkali.

Explaining neutralization using the idea of ions

Think about the reaction between sodium hydroxide and hydrochloric acid. Here are the ions that are in the reactants and in the products:

$Na^+(aq) + OH^-(aq)$ from sodium hydroxide

$H^+(aq) + Cl^-(aq)$ from hydrochloric acid

$\longrightarrow$ $Na^+(aq) + Cl^-(aq)$ from sodium chloride + $H_2O(l)$

Reactants   *Products*

Water is a very weak electrolyte and contains very few ions, and so it must still be written as $H_2O(l)$. Fig. 23.1 shows this reaction in the form of a diagram.

The reaction in Fig. 23.1 seems very different from the one in the 'non-ionic' equation. It looks as if the $Na^+(aq)$ and $Cl^-(aq)$ ions do not 'do' anything during the reaction. Like the spectators at a football match, they 'watch' the action but take no part in it: they could be called the *spectator ions*. The 'action' appears to be the joining of $H^+(aq)$ and $OH^-(aq)$ ions in a molar ratio of $1:1$ to form water. Using this

Table 23.3

Acid	Alkali	Number of moles of acid that react with 1 mole of alkali	Number of moles of product formed by 1 mole of alkali
HCl	KOH	1	1 (of KCl)
HNO_3	NaOH	1	1 (of $NaNO_3$)
H_2SO_4	NaOH	0.5	0.5 (of Na_2SO_4)

new idea an *ionic* equation can be written for the neutralization:

$$H^+(aq) + OH^-(aq) \longrightarrow H_2O(l)$$

This equation is still balanced for moles of oxygen atoms and hydrogen atoms but it is also balanced for *charges*: on the left-hand side there are a -1 and a $+1$ charge, making an overall charge of zero, and on the right-hand side there is also zero charge.

Ionic equations must be balanced for charges as well as for moles of atoms

All acids supply $H^+(aq)$ ions and all alkalis supply $OH^-(aq)$ ions. So this new equation suggests that whichever acid or alkali is used, the *neutralization* reaction simply involves each mole of $H^+(aq)$ ions joining with 1 mole of $OH^-(aq)$ ions.

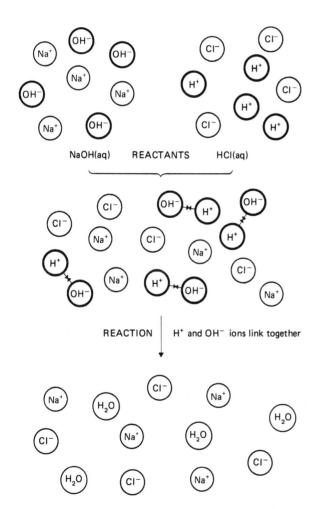

Fig. 23.1 Note that only those particles of water produced in the reaction are shown

The reaction between sodium carbonate and hydrochloric acid

Sodium carbonate solution, $Na_2CO_3(aq)$, is quite strongly alkaline and it can be used to neutralize

acids. How many moles of HCl react with 1 mole of Na_2CO_3, and what is formed by the reaction?

It is easy to show that the reaction produces carbon dioxide; also, when the remaining solution is evaporated to dryness, sodium chloride is left. A titration method can be used to find out more about this reaction.

Experiment 23.2 Titrating sodium carbonate solution with dilute hydrochloric acid

Follow the method given for the titration of sodium hydroxide with dilute hydrochloric acid (Experiment 23.1). Run 25 cm³ of 0.05 M sodium carbonate solution into a flask and use 0.1 M hydrochloric acid in the burette. The best indicator for this titration is *methyl orange*, which is yellow in alkaline solution and red in acidic solution. The end-point is shown by an orange colour in the mixture.

Do not evaporate a neutral solution to dryness in this experiment. Too little sodium chloride is formed for you to determine its mass accurately.

Suppose that 24.9 cm³ of the acid is needed to react with 25 cm³ of 0.05 M sodium carbonate.

1 litre of 0.1 M acid contains 0.1 mole of HCl; so 24.9 cm³ of the same solution contains $0.1 \times 24.9/1000$ or 0.00249 mole of HCl.

1 litre of 0.05 M sodium carbonate contains 0.05 mole of Na_2CO_3; so 25 cm³ of the same solution contains $0.05 \times 25/1000$ or 0.00125 mole of Na_2CO_3.

The molar ratio $HCl : Na_2CO_3$ is $0.00249 : 0.00125$ or very nearly $2:1$, so that *2 moles of HCl react with 1 mole of Na_2CO_3.*

So the left-hand side of the equation for this reaction is

$$2HCl(aq) + Na_2CO_3(aq) \longrightarrow \ldots$$

More of the equation could be written if the number of moles of CO_2 which are formed from 1 mole of Na_2CO_3 could be found. One way of doing this is to find the mass of carbon dioxide produced by a known mass of sodium carbonate.

One piece of apparatus that can be used is shown in Fig. 23.2. The test-tube holds a known mass of sodium carbonate and there is an excess of hydrochloric acid in the flask.

The mass of the whole apparatus is found and the flask is then tipped so that the acid reacts with the

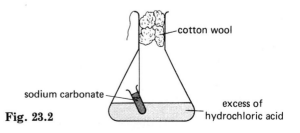

Fig. 23.2

sodium carbonate. When the reaction is finished, the mass of the apparatus is found again. The loss in mass of the apparatus is equal to the mass of carbon dioxide that has been given off.

Suppose that in an experiment like this one, the mass of anhydrous sodium carbonate is 0.50 g and the loss in mass of the flask and contents is 0.20 g.

0.50 g of sodium carbonate (relative molecular mass = 106) produces 0.20 g of carbon dioxide (relative molecular mass = 44), so that 0.50/106 mole of Na_2CO_3 produces 0.20/44 mole of CO_2. And the molar ratio of Na_2CO_3 to CO_2 is 0.0047 : 0.0045, or very nearly 1 : 1.

So *1 mole of Na_2CO_3 produces 1 mole of CO_2.*

$$2HCl(aq) + Na_2CO_3(aq) \longrightarrow CO_2(g) + \ldots$$

The rest of the equation can now be worked out since you know that the only other product is an aqueous solution of sodium chloride:

$$2HCl(aq) + Na_2CO_3(aq)$$
$$\longrightarrow 2NaCl(aq) + CO_2(g) + H_2O(l)$$

The acid, the carbonate and the salt are all electrolytes. If this equation is written out using ions, it can be seen that the sodium ions and chloride ions again behave as spectator ions:

$$\left. \begin{array}{l} 2H^+(aq) + 2Cl^-(aq) \\ \text{(from the acid)} \\ 2Na^+(aq) + CO_3^{2-}(aq) \\ \text{(from the carbonate)} \end{array} \right\} \rightarrow \begin{array}{l} 2Na^+(aq) + 2Cl^-(aq) \\ + CO_2(g) \\ + H_2O(l) \end{array}$$

So the equation can be simplified to give the ionic equation:

$$2H^+(aq) + CO_3^{2-}(aq) \longrightarrow CO_2(g) + H_2O(l)$$

This equation can be used to represent the reaction of any carbonate with any acid.

Other methods of neutralizing acids

The experiments in Chapter 15 show that metals, metal oxides and metal carbonates can all be used to neutralize acids.

1. When magnesium reacts with hydrochloric acid, the equation for the reaction can be written as

$$Mg(s) + 2HCl(aq) \longrightarrow MgCl_2(aq) + H_2(g)$$

If the electrolytes (hydrochloric acid and magnesium chloride) are written as ions, the equation becomes

$$Mg(s) + 2H^+(aq) + 2Cl^-(aq)$$
$$\longrightarrow Mg^{2+}(aq) + 2Cl^-(aq) + H_2(g)$$

The chloride ions are spectator ions and can be left out of the equation, so the ionic equation is

$$Mg(s) + 2H^+(aq) \longrightarrow Mg^{2+}(aq) + H_2(g)$$

This equation can be used for the reactions of most acids (but not nitric acid) with magnesium. Similar

equations can be written for the reactions of other metals with acids.

2. Basic oxides neutralize acids. Taking the reaction of copper(II) oxide and sulphuric acid as an example, the equation can be written

$$CuO(s) + H_2SO_4(aq) \longrightarrow CuSO_4(aq) + H_2O(l)$$

The sulphate ions do not change and so are spectator ions.

$$CuO(s) + 2H^+(aq) \longrightarrow Cu^{2+}(aq) + H_2O(l)$$

3. The neutralization of a metal carbonate, such as zinc carbonate, with an acid can be written either as

$$ZnCO_3(s) + 2HNO_3(aq)$$
$$\longrightarrow Zn(NO_3)_2(aq) + CO_2(g) + H_2O(l)$$

or as

$$ZnCO_3(s) + 2H^+(aq)$$
$$\longrightarrow Zn^{2+}(aq) + CO_2(g) + H_2O(l)$$

All these ways of neutralizing acids (with alkalis, metals, basic oxides and carbonates) are very useful ways of preparing salts because in each reaction, the only substances left in solution are the ions of the salt. Evaporation of this solution produces crystals of the salt.

Precipitation reactions and the idea of ions

You may need to revise the work on precipitation reactions in Chapter 17 before you work through this section.

When solutions of lead(II) nitrate and potassium iodide are mixed, a yellow precipitate is formed. Use the generalizations about the solubilities of salts given on page 48 to work out what the yellow precipitate should be.

The experiment in Fig. 23.3 shows that the reaction between lead(II) nitrate and potassium iodide involves ions. The microscope slides are covered with strips of filter paper moistened with water. The crocodile clips are connected to a fairly high voltage d.c. supply and act as either anodes or cathodes. The areas around each electrode are spotted with the solutions. When the current is switched on, the ions begin to move: cations to the cathode and anions to the anode. A yellow precipitate is seen to form in the middle of only *one* of the two strips of filter paper.

From Fig. 23.3 it is clear that the ions which meet and form the yellow precipitate are lead ions and iodide ions because these are the ions that move across the paper in part (b). In part (a), potassium ions and nitrate ions move across the paper but no precipitate is formed. This result should agree with the answer obtained by looking at the generalizations about solubilities of salts.

Another experiment which shows the movement of ions and the formation of precipitates is shown in

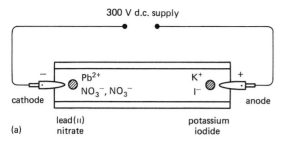

Fig. 23.3 No precipitate forms in (a), but a yellow precipitate forms in (b)

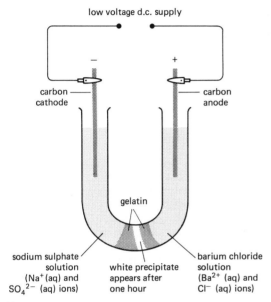

Fig. 23.4

Fig. 23.4. This method works well, even when the precipitate is white.

The gelatin prevents the ions diffusing together quickly, but when the electrodes are connected to a battery, the ions move through the gelatin quite quickly. The result, shown in Fig. 23.4, where a white precipitate is formed when barium ions and sulphate ions meet in the gelatin, should agree with the result you would expect from the generalizations about solubilities (page 48). If the electrodes were connected to the battery the other way round, no precipitate would be formed because sodium ions would meet chloride ions in the gelatin, and sodium chloride is a soluble salt.

The equation for a precipitation reaction can be worked out by using different volumes of the solutions of the two reactants, mixing them and comparing the amounts of precipitate formed.

One way of measuring the amount of precipitate would be to filter off the solids and wash and dry them before finding their masses. This would take a very long time but this can be shortened by using another method. If the reaction mixtures are all centrifuged, or left to stand for several hours, the precipitates collect at the base of each test-tube: and

if the tubes all have the same shape and size, the heights of the precipitates can be taken as a rough measure of their masses. This method has the advantage of being easy and quick, although the results may not always be reliable because the grains of the precipitates may not pack together equally.

The results of an experiment using 1 M solutions of lead(II) nitrate and potassium iodide are given in Table 23.4, and the results are plotted in Fig. 23.5. It

Table 23.4

Volume of 1.0 M $Pb(NO_3)_2$ solution in cm^3	Volume of 1.0 M KI solution in cm^3	Height of precipitate, in mm
1.0	11.0	8.0
2.0	10.0	11.0
3.0	9.0	15.0
5.0	7.0	16.5
6.0	6.0	15.0
8.0	4.0	13.0
9.0	3.0	11.5
10.0	2.0	10.0

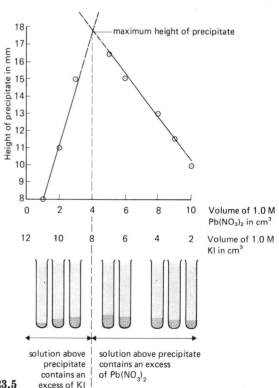

Fig. 23.5

77

is necessary to plot a graph because the volumes needed to give the maximum amount of precipitate may not have been used in any of the tubes in the experiment.

Because solutions of the same molar concentrations are used, equal volumes of them contain equal numbers of moles of solute.

From the graph you should see that the maximum amount of reaction occurs when 2 moles of KI react with 1 mole of $Pb(NO_3)_2$. In an equation this can be written as

$$Pb(NO_3)_2(aq) + 2KI(aq) \longrightarrow \ldots$$

The experiment in Fig. 23.3 shows that $Pb^{2+}(aq)$ and $I^-(aq)$ are the ions that react. The results in Fig. 23.5 show that 1 mole of $Pb(NO_3)_2$ reacts with 2 moles of KI. So in this reaction $Pb^{2+}(aq)$ and $I^-(aq)$ ions combine in the molar ratio of 1:2 to form a precipitate of lead(II) iodide. The ionic equation is

$$Pb^{2+}(aq) + 2I^-(aq) \longrightarrow PbI_2(s)$$

Whenever the equation for a precipitation reaction is needed, an experiment like the one in Fig. 23.5 could be done. But this would take a long time and there is a quicker way of writing the equation so long as the formula of the precipitate is known. Think about the formation of 1 mole of $PbCl_2$. This amount of lead chloride contains 1 mole of Pb^{2+} ions and 2 moles of Cl^- ions, so that the ionic equation for its precipitation is

$$Pb^{2+}(aq) + 2Cl^-(aq) \longrightarrow PbCl_2(s)$$

The equation for the formation of barium sulphate (Fig. 23.4) is

$$Ba^{2+}(aq) + SO_4^{2-}(aq) \longrightarrow BaSO_4(s)$$

QUESTIONS

1 Work out the concentration in $mol\,l^{-1}$ of the following solutions:
(a) sodium hydroxide solution containing $20\,g\,l^{-1}$,
(b) sodium chloride solution containing $5.85\,g$ in $500\,cm^3$,
(c) sulphuric acid containing $4.9\,g$ in $200\,cm^3$.

2 Work out the mass of the solute in each of the following solutions:
(a) $1000\,cm^3$ of $2.0\,M$ potassium nitrate,
(b) $500\,cm^3$ of $0.50\,M$ sodium sulphate,
(c) $200\,cm^3$ of $4.0\,M$ nitric acid.

3 Balance these equations for moles of atoms of each kind. (*Note*: there are no other products apart from those given.)
(a) $Ca(OH)_2(aq) + HCl(aq) \longrightarrow CaCl_2(aq) + H_2O(l)$
(b) $CuO(s) + HNO_3(aq) \longrightarrow Cu(NO_3)_2(aq) + H_2O(l)$
(c) $Fe(s) + HCl(aq) \longrightarrow FeCl_2(aq) + H_2(g)$
(d) $PbCO_3(s) + HNO_3(aq)$
$$\longrightarrow Pb(NO_3)_2(aq) + CO_2(g) + H_2O(l)$$

4 Balance these equations for moles of atoms of each kind and for charges. (*Note*: there are no other products apart from those given.)
(a) $Mg(s) + H^+(aq) \longrightarrow Mg^{2+}(aq) + H_2(g)$
(b) $PbO(s) + H^+(aq) \longrightarrow Pb^{2+}(aq) + H_2O(l)$
(c) $CO_3^{2-}(aq) + H^+(aq) \longrightarrow CO_2(g) + H_2O(l)$
(d) $Na(s) + H_2O(l) \longrightarrow Na^+(aq) + H_2(g) + OH^-(aq)$
Equations (a) to (c) are for reactions in which a salt is formed. To which method of salt preparation does each reaction belong?

5 $10\,g$ of calcium carbonate ($CaCO_3$) just dissolves in $100\,cm^3$ of $2\,M$ hydrochloric acid, leaving no excess of acid, and $4.4\,g$ of carbon dioxide (CO_2) is evolved.
(a) How many moles of calcium carbonate is $10\,g$? (Relative atomic masses: $C = 12$, $Ca = 40$, and $O = 16$.)
(b) How many moles of hydrochloric acid are there in $100\,cm^3$ of $2\,M$ acid?
(c) How many moles of carbon dioxide is $4.4\,g$?
(d) Using your answers to parts (a), (b) and (c), write down part of the equation for this reaction.
(e) What other information would you need in order to complete the equation?

6 Two people are having a discussion about how to prepare some potassium chloride crystals. The first suggests mixing solutions of potassium carbonate and sodium chloride and then evaporating the solution. The second suggests mixing solutions of potassium carbonate and hydrochloric acid and then evaporating the solution. You are asked to decide between the two suggestions.
(a) Will both of these two methods work? Explain your answer.
(b) Describe how you would prepare potassium chloride crystals using one of these methods.

7 You are given some powdered copper and some dilute sulphuric acid and told to prepare some copper(II) sulphate crystals. You can use any apparatus you need but no other laboratory chemicals. Describe how you would do it and write equations for the reactions.

8 Balance these equations for moles of atoms of each kind. (*Note*: there are no other products apart from those given.) Then write ionic equations for the reactions.
(a) $Pb(NO_3)_2(aq) + K_2SO_4(aq) \longrightarrow PbSO_4(s) + KNO_3(aq)$
(b) $Ba(NO_3)_2(aq) + Na_2CrO_4(aq)$
$$\longrightarrow BaCrO_4(s) + NaNO_3(aq)$$
(c) $Na_2CO_3(aq) + Ca(OH)_2(aq)$
$$\longrightarrow CaCO_3(s) + NaOH(aq)$$
(d) $CuSO_4(aq) + NaOH(aq)$
$$\longrightarrow Cu(OH)_2(s) + Na_2SO_4(aq)$$
(e) $AlCl_3(aq) + NaOH(aq) \longrightarrow Al(OH)_3(s) + NaCl(aq)$

9 Using the patterns in solubility given on page 48, predict whether or not a precipitate of a sparingly soluble salt is likely to form when the following pairs of solutions are mixed:
(a) calcium nitrate and potassium sulphate solutions,
(b) iron(III) sulphate and sodium nitrate solutions,
(c) barium chloride and potassium carbonate solutions,
(d) lead(II) nitrate and calcium chloride solutions,
(e) zinc sulphate and magnesium chloride solutions.
   If you think that a precipitate will form, then name it, and write the ionic equation for the reaction.

10 Certain volumes of 0.5 M $Hg(NO_3)_2$ solution are mixed with 50 cm³ portions of 0.5 M KI solution. A precipitate is formed in each case which is washed and dried before its mass is found. The results are shown in Fig. 23.6.

(a) What is the maximum amount of precipitate that forms?

(b) What are the volumes of the reactants that first give this maximum amount?

(c) Explain why the mass of precipitate rises as the volume of $Hg(NO_3)_2$ solution rises, but eventually reaches a maximum and stays there.

(d) Work out the numbers of moles of $Hg(NO_3)_2$ and of KI required to give the maximum amount of precipitate.

(e) Using your answer to (d) write down the left-hand side of the equation for the reaction.

(f) Someone suggests to you that the precipitate is mercury(II) iodide, HgI_2. Does this idea agree with your answer to (e)? Explain your answer.

(g) Complete the ionic equation for this reaction and name the spectator ions.

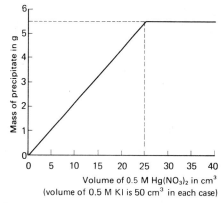

Fig. 23.6

11 How would you set about convincing someone with a little knowledge of chemistry that vinegar is a solution of an acid?

Key words

M, concentration in mol l⁻¹   **spectator ion**   **ionic equation**

Basic facts

- Acids can be recognized by their reactions with many metals, alkalis, basic oxides and carbonates. They also have pH values of less than 7 and are electrolytes.

- Acids can be defined as substances that produce hydrogen ions in aqueous solution. Their characteristic reactions are the reactions of aqueous hydrogen ions.

- Alkalis can be recognized because they have pH values above 7, they neutralize acids to give a salt and water only and are electrolytes.

- Alkalis can be defined as substances that produce hydroxide ions in aqueous solution. Their characteristic reactions are the reactions of aqueous hydroxide ions.

- Mol l⁻¹ is a concentration unit that is very useful to chemists. Equal volumes of different solutions with the same concentration (in mol l⁻¹) contain equal numbers of moles of their respective solutes.

- Salts are electrolytes. Their cations are usually metal ions while their anions are produced from acids.

- Neutralization of an acid with an alkali is the reaction of aqueous hydrogen ions with aqueous hydroxide ions to produce water.

- A precipitation reaction occurs when the ions of a sparingly soluble salt come together.

24 Some more ideas about acids and alkalis

Is water important in acidity and alkalinity?

All the discussion so far has concerned *aqueous* solutions. Do acids show acidity and alkalis show alkalinity in solvents other than water?

Experiment 24.1 The acidity of tartaric acid and ethanoic (acetic) acid

For this experiment, anhydrous tartaric acid and dry ethanoic acid are required. You also need dry blue litmus paper and some dry propanone (acetone).

1. Touch the crystals of tartaric acid with dry blue litmus paper. Then add dry blue litmus paper to a few cm³ of dry ethanoic acid in a *dry* test-tube. (WARNING: the smell of this liquid is very unpleasant; do not breathe its vapour.)
2. Shake a few crystals of tartaric acid with a few cm³ of dry propanone in a *dry* test-tube. Shake the tube gently to complete the dissolving. (CARE: propanone is highly flammable.) Add a piece of dry blue litmus paper to this solution.
3. Shake a few crystals of tartaric acid with a few cm³ of distilled water in a test-tube, and warm to dissolve. Again, test the solution with litmus paper.
4. Repeat tests 2 and 3, shaking the dry propanone and the distilled water with a few drops of ethanoic acid from a dropper, and test each solution with blue litmus paper.

▶ Do the solutions that turn blue litmus red also show the other properties of acids?

5. Check this by adding a small strip of cleaned magnesium ribbon to one portion of each solution and either a small amount of dry sodium hydrogencarbonate or a small marble chip to another portion of each.

▶ Do the solutions that do not turn blue litmus red show any of the other properties of acids?

6. Repeat test 5 using the solutions that have no effect on litmus paper.

From the results of these experiments it seems that neither of the acids shows acidic properties when dissolved in propanone, and that water is necessary for the acidic properties to show.

Hydrogen chloride gas dissolves in water to give an acidic solution (page 124), while ammonia gas dissolves in water to form an alkaline solution (page

131). Do these gases show the same acidic and alkaline properties if they are dissolved in solvents other than water?

A solution of dry hydrogen chloride in either dry methylbenzene (toluene) or dry propanone can be prepared using the apparatus in Fig. 24.1. An aqueous solution of hydrogen chloride is always readily available in laboratories as dilute hydrochloric acid.

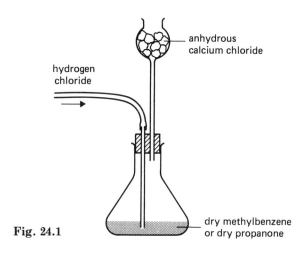

Fig. 24.1

Tests on the aqueous solution and the methylbenzene or propanone solution produce the results and explanations given in Table 24.1.

It looks as if hydrogen ions are produced only when an acid dissolves in water. This suggests that

Table 24.1

Observation	Explanation
1. Hydrogen chloride in methylbenzene or propanone does not conduct electricity	There are no ions in this solution
2. Hydrogen chloride in water is a good conductor of electricity	There are many ions in this solution
3. Hydrogen chloride in methylbenzene or propanone has no effect on dry blue litmus paper and does not react with magnesium ribbon or dry sodium hydrogencarbonate	No acidic properties are shown by this solution because there are no hydrogen ions present in it
4. Hydrogen chloride in water turns blue litmus red and shows all the other properties of acids	Acidic properties are shown because hydrogen ions are present in the solution

the dissolving process is really a *reaction* which produces new materials:

hydrogen chloride + water

$\longrightarrow$ hydrogen ions + chloride ions

But when hydrogen chloride dissolves in either methylbenzene or propanone, no similar reaction occurs: the hydrogen chloride in the solution is present as molecules.

Other acids behave in a similar way to hydrogen chloride. When they are pure and dry they consist of molecules and do not show acidic properties. But when they are added to water, they react to form ions. These reactions can be represented by the following equations.

$$HCl(g) + water \longrightarrow H^+(aq) + Cl^-(aq)$$

$$H_2SO_4(l) + water \longrightarrow 2H^+(aq) + SO_4^{2-}(aq)$$

$$HNO_3(l) + water \longrightarrow H^+(aq) + NO_3^-(aq)$$

Note that, like pure ethanoic acid, hydrogen sulphate and hydrogen nitrate are liquids at room temperature. The addition of hydrogen sulphate and hydrogen nitrate to water produces sulphuric acid and nitric acid respectively.

Does alkalinity also require the presence of water? Your teacher may prepare a solution of dry ammonia in dry trichloromethane (chloroform) using the apparatus in Fig. 24.2.

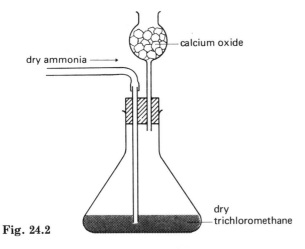

Fig. 24.2

The ammonia gas can be prepared either by heating an ammonium salt with an alkali (page 131) or by warming a very concentrated solution of ammonia in water. In both cases, the ammonia then needs to be thoroughly dried. This can be done by passing the gas through a tube containing lumps of quicklime (calcium oxide). Most other common drying agents react with ammonia.

The solution of ammonia in trichloromethane can be compared with the aqueous solution of ammonia available on the shelves of your laboratory. The results of the tests applied to these solutions are as follows.

1. A solution of dry ammonia in dry trichloromethane does not conduct electricity.
2. A solution of ammonia in water does conduct electricity, although not very well.
3. A solution of dry ammonia in dry trichloromethane does not turn dry red litmus paper blue.
4. A solution of ammonia in water does turn litmus paper blue.

Again, it looks as if ammonia *reacts* with water, in this case to produce hydroxide ions.

ammonia + water

$\longrightarrow$ hydroxide ions + ammonium ions

The solution of ammonia in dry trichloromethane does not shown any alkaline properties because the ammonia exists as molecules in this solvent.

Most alkalis are metal hydroxides. These are ionic in the solid state and so dissolving them in water allows the ions to become separated. The reaction of ammonia with water is discussed on page 131.

The strengths of acids and alkalis

You know that the pH value is a measure of the strength of an acid or an alkali. A rough measure of pH can be made using wide-range universal indicator paper, but this method is not sensitive enough to find accurately the relative strengths of many laboratory acids or alkalis. To do this, it is much better to use narrow-range paper.

Experiment 24.2 Measuring the pH values of some laboratory acids and alkalis

Your teacher will provide you with solutions of hydrochloric acid, ethanoic acid, ammonia and sodium hydroxide, containing 0.01 mole of the substance per 1000 cm^3 of solution.

First, use wide-range universal indicator paper to find the approximate pH value of each solution. Then choose a suitable narrow-range paper and measure each pH value more accurately.

An even more accurate way of finding the pH value of a solution is by using an electrical instrument called a pH meter. Your teacher may show you how a pH meter is used.

Some pH values are given below for solutions containing 0.01 mole of certain acids and alkalis in 1000 cm^3 of solution.

hydrochloric acid $\big\}$ nitric acid	2.0
ethanoic acid	3.5
sodium hydroxide $\big\}$ potassium hydroxide	12.0
ammonia solution	10.5

Another way of comparing the strengths of *acids* is to observe the rates at which hydrogen is evolved when acids of the same concentration are added to similar pieces of magnesium ribbon or the rates at which carbon dioxide is formed when the acids are added to lumps of marble.

Experiment 24.3 Comparing the reactions of hydrochloric acid and ethanoic acid with marble chips and magnesium ribbon

Your teacher will provide you with solutions of hydrochloric acid and ethanoic acid which have the same concentration: they both contain the same number of moles of acid in 1000 cm³ of solution.

Half-fill a test-tube with the hydrochloric acid and put a similar amount of ethanoic acid in another tube.

Choose two small marble chips of about the same size and shape and put one of these into each test-tube of acid. Compare the rates at which the gas is produced in the two tubes.

Repeat the experiment using similar pieces of magnesium ribbon instead of the marble chips. Again compare the rates at which the gas is produced in each tube.

What makes one acid react more quickly than another? A clue to the answer is provided by the experiments shown in Fig. 24.3. Hydrochloric acid is

These results are obtained because a solution of a weak acid contains very few ions. So ethanoic acid is weak because most of the ethanoic acid molecules in solution remain as molecules. Very few of the molecules split up to form ions. The equation which represents this is

$$CH_3CO_2H(l) \; + \; water$$
$$\rightleftharpoons CH_3CO_2^-(aq) \; + \; H^+(aq)$$

The half-arrows mean that the reaction is reversible: it can go in both directions (page 196).

But a **strong acid** has a low pH value, it reacts rapidly with carbonates and metals and it is a good conductor of electricity. These properties can be explained by saying that in aqueous solution, most of the molecules of the acid react with water to form ions:

$$HCl(aq) \; + \; water \longrightarrow H^+(aq) \; + \; Cl^-(aq)$$

In the same sort of way, sodium hydroxide is a strong alkali because in solution it consists entirely as ions. But ammonia is a weak alkali because in solution most of the ammonia stays as molecules and only a very small proportion of the molecules react with water molecules to form ions.

Most acids are far too acidic to taste safely. Because ethanoic acid is a weak acid, it can be used to flavour food, provided that only a dilute solution is used.

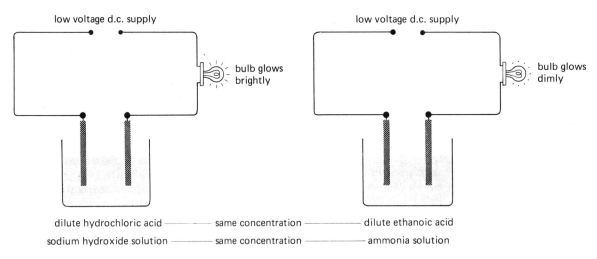

low voltage d.c. supply — bulb glows brightly
low voltage d.c. supply — bulb glows dimly

dilute hydrochloric acid ———— same concentration ———— dilute ethanoic acid
sodium hydroxide solution ———— same concentration ———— ammonia solution

Fig. 24.3

a good conductor of electricity but ethanoic acid conducts very poorly.

A **weak acid** has the following properties.

1 Its pH value is not very low.
2 It reacts slowly with carbonates.
3 It reacts slowly with metals.
4 It is a poor conductor of electricity.

You should be careful to distinguish between the terms *concentrated* and *dilute*, and *strong* and *weak*. The first two just refer to the relative amounts of acid or alkali present in 1000 cm³ of solution and say nothing about the relative numbers of ions present; the last two refer to the relative numbers of H⁺(aq) ions or OH⁻(aq) ions present in acidic or alkaline

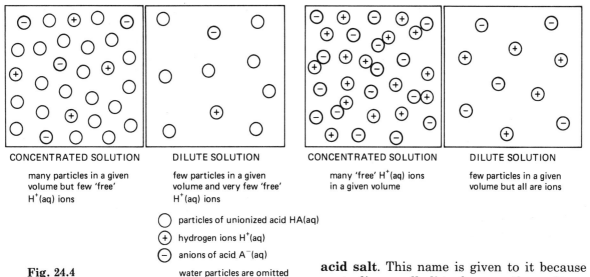

WEAK ACID

CONCENTRATED SOLUTION

many particles in a given volume but few 'free' $H^+(aq)$ ions

DILUTE SOLUTION

few particles in a given volume and very few 'free' $H^+(aq)$ ions

STRONG ACID

CONCENTRATED SOLUTION

many 'free' $H^+(aq)$ ions in a given volume

DILUTE SOLUTION

few particles in a given volume but all are ions

◯ particles of unionized acid HA(aq)

⊕ hydrogen ions $H^+(aq)$

⊖ anions of acid $A^-(aq)$

water particles are omitted

Fig. 24.4

solutions (Fig. 24.4). For example, whereas a concentrated solution of ethanoic acid is only weakly acidic, even dilute solutions of hydrochloric acid are strongly acidic.

The basicity of acids

When a **monobasic** acid reacts with water, each mole of the acid can give a maximum of one mole of hydrogen ions. Examples of monobasic acids are hydrochloric, nitric and ethanoic acids.

$$\left.\begin{array}{l} HCl \\ HNO_3 \\ CH_3CO_2H \\ 1\,mole \end{array}\right\} \xrightarrow{\text{water}} \begin{array}{l} H^+(aq) + Cl^-(aq) \\ H^+(aq) + NO_3^-(aq) \\ H^+(aq) + CH_3CO_2^-(aq) \\ \text{a maximum} \\ \text{of 1 mole} \end{array}$$

An example of a **dibasic** acid is sulphuric acid. One mole of sulphuric acid can give a maximum of two moles of hydrogen ions when it reacts with water:

$$H_2SO_4(aq) + water \longrightarrow 2H^+(aq) + SO_4^{2-}(aq)$$

The neutralization of a monobasic acid with sodium hydroxide can produce one salt only. But a dibasic acid can react with sodium hydroxide to form two salts:

$$H_2SO_4(aq) + 2NaOH(aq)$$
$$\longrightarrow Na_2SO_4(aq) + 2H_2O(l)$$

$$H_2SO_4(aq) + NaOH(aq)$$
$$\longrightarrow NaHSO_4(aq) + H_2O(l)$$

The salt shown in the second equation is called sodium hydrogensulphate and is an example of an

acid salt. This name is given to it because it can neutralize an alkali to form another salt:

$$NaHSO_4(aq) + NaOH(aq)$$
$$\longrightarrow Na_2SO_4(aq) + H_2O(l)$$

The salt formed in the first equation, $Na_2SO_4(aq)$ (sodium sulphate), is called a **normal salt**.

There are also **basic salts**, so called because they can neutralize acids. One example is the mineral malachite which has the formula $CuCO_3 \cdot Cu(OH)_2$.

Sodium sulphate and sodium hydrogensulphate can be prepared by titration. Sulphuric acid is titrated into a known volume of sodium hydroxide solution using an indicator such as phenolphthalein. The endpoint shows the volumes of acid and alkali needed to produce the normal salt, and evaporation of the neutral solution produces crystals of sodium sulphate. But if the volume of acid is doubled (or the volume of alkali is halved) the solution contains the acid salt. (Look back at the equations for the formation of the two salts if you are unsure of the reason for changing the volumes like this.)

Solutions of sodium sulphate and sodium hydrogensulphate have some similar properties because they both contain sulphate ions. (They both give a precipitate with barium chloride solution.) But while sodium sulphate solution is neutral, sodium hydrogensulphate solution is strongly acidic because it contains hydrogen ions:

$$NaHSO_4(s) + water$$
$$\longrightarrow Na^+(aq) + H^+(aq) + SO_4^{2-}(aq)$$

So sodium hydrogensulphate solution shows all the properties of acids.

A well-known acid salt is sodium hydrogencarbonate (sodium bicarbonate). Its formula is $NaHCO_3$. The corresponding normal salt is sodium carbonate. Although it is called an acid salt, the pH value of its aqueous solution is about 8 and it reacts with acids (because it is similar to a carbonate) as well as with alkalis.

24 Some more ideas about acids and alkalis

Experiment 24.4 Some properties of sodium hydrogencarbonate

1. Put a small amount of sodium hydrogencarbonate into a test-tube and then add a few drops of dilute hydrochloric acid. Identify the gas given off.

▶ Write the ionic equation for the reaction.

2. Put a small amount of sodium hydrogencarbonate in a small tube (an ignition tube) and gently heat it. Identify the gases given off. Retain the residue in the tube.

▶ Why is it difficult to write an equation for this reaction?

3. Continue heating the residue from part 1 of the experiment until no further reaction occurs.

▶ How can you tell when the reaction is complete?

Allow the small tube and the residue to cool and then drop the residue into a test-tube containing dilute hydrochloric acid. Shake the tube so that the acid comes into contact with the residue. Identify the gas given off.

▶ What do you now think is formed when sodium hydrogencarbonate is heated?
▶ Write an equation for the action of heat on sodium hydrogencarbonate.

There are several everyday uses of sodium hydrogencarbonate. It is used in indigestion tablets because it cures indigestion that is caused by an excess of acidity in the stomach. It is safe to eat small quantities of sodium hydrogencarbonate because it is only very slightly alkaline. But it still neutralizes acid effectively:

$$HCO_3^-(aq) + H^+(aq) \longrightarrow H_2O(l) + CO_2(g)$$

It can also be used in making cakes. When the cake is being cooked, the sodium hydrogencarbonate in the cake mix decomposes and produces bubbles of gas which make the cake rise:

$$2NaHCO_3(s) \longrightarrow Na_2CO_3(s) + H_2O(l) + CO_2(g)$$

(This is the same reaction that occurs in part 2 of Experiment 24.4.) But sodium carbonate has a soapy taste, and it affects the flavour of the cake. This problem can be avoided by mixing solid sodium hydrogencarbonate with a solid weak acid such as tartaric acid. (This mixture is called baking powder.) When water is added to the cake mix, the acid reacts with the sodium hydrogencarbonate and produces carbon dioxide. (This is similar to the reaction that occurs in part 1 of Experiment 24.4.)

The formation of the acid salt calcium hydrogencarbonate from the normal salt calcium carbonate (and the reverse reaction) is very important in nature (pages 118–119).

Monobasic acids cannot form acid salts. When a dibasic acid reacts with an acid, two salts are possible (one acid and the other normal) because there are two hydrogen atoms in each molecule of the acid which may be replaced during the neutralization reaction. If the dibasic acid is represented as H_2X, the formation of the two salts can be shown as follows.

(a)
$$H_2X(aq) + 2NaOH(aq) \longrightarrow 2H_2O(l) + Na_2X(aq)$$

or

$$H_2X(aq) + 2OH^-(aq) \longrightarrow 2H_2O(l) + X^{2-}(aq)$$
$$\text{normal salt}$$

(b)
$$H_2X(aq) + NaOH(aq) \longrightarrow H_2O(l) + NaHX(aq)$$

or

$$H_2X(aq) + OH^-(aq) \longrightarrow H_2O(l) + HX^-(aq)$$
$$\text{acid salt}$$

In reaction (a), one mole of the acid reacts with two moles of the sodium hydroxide. But in reaction (b), one mole of acid reacts with only one mole of alkali.

The basicity of an acid can be found by titrating the acid with an alkali and calculating the number of moles of hydroxide ions that are required to neutralize the acid and produce the normal salt. A monobasic acid requires one mole of hydroxide ions for each mole of acid but a dibasic acid requires two moles of hydroxide ions for each mole of acid.

Experiment 24.5 What is the basicity of ethanedioic acid?

CARE: ethanedioic acid is very poisonous. Wash your hands very well when you have completed the experiment.

Your teacher will provide you with solutions of ethanedioic acid and sodium hydroxide of known concentrations (in $mol \, l^{-1}$). Use a pipette and pipette filler to measure out a known volume of the alkali. Titrate this with the acid solution using phenolphthalein as indicator. (The phenolphthalein shows the end-point for the formation of the normal salt.) Repeat the titration until you obtain consistent results.

Calculate the number of moles of alkali used in each titration, and the number of moles of acid needed to neutralize the alkali.

▶ How many moles of alkali are needed to neutralize one mole of acid?
▶ What is the basicity of ethanedioic acid?
▶ The formula of ethanedioic acid is $H_2C_2O_4$. Write equations for the reactions that can occur when it reacts with sodium hydroxide.

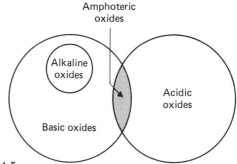

Amphoteric oxides and hydroxides

You should revise the section on the classification of oxides (Chapter 16, page 45) before you work through this section.

Suppose you were asked to find out if a substance is acidic or basic. You could answer this question by investigating the reactions of the substance with an acid and an alkali. If the substance is acidic, it reacts with an alkali to give a salt and water, but if the substance is basic, it reacts with an acid to give a salt and water.

Experiment 24.6 An investigation of the acid–base properties of some metal hydroxides

Start with a test-tube containing about a 1 cm depth of zinc sulphate solution. To this solution add dilute sodium hydroxide solution, a small amount at a time until a precipitate is formed.

▶ What is this precipitate?

Shake the mixture and pour about half of it into another test-tube. To one half add a dilute acid.

▶ Does the precipitate react? Is the precipitate showing basic properties?

To the other half add dilute sodium hydroxide solution.

▶ Does the precipitate react? Is the precipitate showing acidic properties?

Repeat this whole procedure using solutions of iron(II) sulphate, iron(III) chloride, copper(II) sulphate, aluminium sulphate and lead(II) nitrate. Note that in the experiments with lead(II) nitrate, the acid added to the precipitate must be dilute nitric acid. (Both lead(II) sulphate and lead(II) chloride are sparingly soluble in water.)

▶ Make a list of metal hydroxides that show only basic properties and a list of those that show both basic and acidic properties.

The addition of sodium hydroxide solution to zinc sulphate solution produces a precipitate of zinc hydroxide:

$$Zn^{2+}(aq) + 2OH^-(aq) \longrightarrow Zn(OH)_2(s)$$

Zinc hydroxide shows basic properties when it reacts with an acid:

$$Zn(OH)_2(s) + 2H^+(aq) \longrightarrow Zn^{2+}(aq) + 2H_2O(l)$$

But it also reacts with sodium hydroxide solution:

$$Zn(OH)_2(s) + 2OH^-(aq) \longrightarrow ZnO_2{}^{2-}(aq) + 2H_2O(l)$$
the zincate ion

The final solution contains the ions of the salt sodium zincate. In this reaction, the zinc hydroxide is behaving as an acid because it reacts with an alkali to give a salt and water. Note that the zinc ends up as part of an anion, just like the non-metal atoms in the anions sulphate and nitrate.

A substance which shows both acidic and basic properties is said to be **amphoteric**. From your results for Experiment 24.6 it should be clear that aluminium and lead(II) hydroxides are also amphoteric. You should be able to write equations for their reactions with acids. For their reactions with alkalis, the equations are

$$Al(OH)_3(s) + OH^-(aq) \longrightarrow AlO_2{}^-(aq) + 2H_2O(l)$$
the aluminate ion
$$Pb(OH)_2(s) + 2OH^-(aq) \longrightarrow PbO_2{}^{2-}(aq) + 2H_2O(l)$$
the plumbate ion

The *oxides* of these metals are also amphoteric. Using zinc oxide as an example,

$$\underset{\text{base}}{ZnO(s)} + \underset{\text{from the acid}}{2H^+(aq)} \longrightarrow \underset{\substack{\text{cations of}\\\text{a salt}}}{Zn^{2+}(aq)} + \underset{\text{water}}{H_2O(l)}$$

$$\underset{\text{acid}}{ZnO(s)} + \underset{\substack{\text{from the}\\\text{alkali}}}{2OH^-(aq)} \longrightarrow \underset{\substack{\text{anion of}\\\text{a salt}}}{ZnO_2{}^{2-}(aq)} + \underset{\text{water}}{H_2O(l)}$$

The classification of oxides shown in Fig. 16.1 (page 45) now needs to be modified to allow for amphoteric oxides. The new Venn diagram is shown in Fig. 24.5.

Fig. 24.5

Your teacher may show you the reaction between aluminium and sodium hydroxide solution. When aluminium powder is added to the alkali there is no obvious reaction for a few minutes because of the protective layer of aluminium oxide (page 37). But when the reaction starts, it frequently occurs rapidly because it is exothermic and the reaction mixture quickly gets hot. The flammable gas that is given off is hydrogen and the equation for the reaction is

$$2Al(s) + 2OH^-(aq) + 2H_2O(l)$$
$$\longrightarrow 2AlO_2{}^-(aq) + 3H_2(g)$$

This reaction involves the formation of aluminate ions and so depends on the amphoteric nature of aluminium and its compounds.

24 Some more ideas about acids and alkalis

QUESTIONS

1 Criticize each of these statements about acids.
(*a*) All acids contain oxygen.
(*b*) Acids show acidic properties only when they are dissolved in a liquid.
(*c*) Acids turn universal indicator solution red.
(*d*) Every solution which, during electrolysis, produces hydrogen at the cathode, must contain an acid.
(*e*) Acids are decomposed by metals to give hydrogen.

2 Dry hydrogen iodide gas, HI(g), does not turn blue litmus red. It dissolves in both water and a solvent called xylene (1,2-dimethylbenzene). Some properties of these two solutions are listed below.

Hydrogen iodide in xylene	Hydrogen iodide in water
1. Does not conduct electricity	1. Conducts electricity well
2. Neutral to litmus paper	2. Turns blue litmus paper red
3. Does not react with magnesium ribbon	3. Gives off hydrogen with magnesium ribbon
4. Does not react with anhydrous sodium carbonate	4. Gives off carbon dioxide with anhydrous sodium carbonate

(*a*) Which of these solutions is acidic?
(*b*) How can you explain that one solution conducts electricity and the other is a non-conductor?
(*c*) Hydrogen iodide in water is an electrolyte. What are the likely products at the cathode and anode when this solution is electrolysed?
(*d*) Some water (pH = 7) is added to a few cm^3 of the solution of hydrogen iodide in xylene in a test-tube, and the mixture shaken. After a few seconds, two colourless layers can be seen in the tube. Universal indicator paper is added to the bottom (water) layer. Is this layer likely to be acidic, alkaline or neutral? Explain your answer.
(*e*) Would you expect a temperature change when dry hydrogen iodide is bubbled into water?

3 Ethanedioic acid (oxalic acid) crystals have the formula $H_2C_2O_4 \cdot 2H_2O$. Solutions of ethanedioic acid in water have a low pH value. A solution of the crystals in dry propanone is also slightly acidic.
(*a*) How many moles of water does 1 mole of $H_2C_2O_4 \cdot 2H_2O$ contain?
(*b*) What happens to the water in the crystals when they are dissolved in water?
(*c*) What is the most likely reason why a solution of the crystals in dry propanone is slightly acidic?
(*d*) Would it be possible to prepare a *neutral* solution of ethanedioic acid in propanone? If you think so, say how this could be done. If you think that it is impossible, say why.

4 When a solution of sodium sulphate is electrolysed, hydrogen is collected at the cathode and oxygen at the anode. A few drops of litmus solution added to the solution around the cathode turn blue during the electrolysis, whereas around the anode the litmus turns red. Experiments show that none of the sodium sulphate is used up during the electrolysis.
(*a*) What are the names of the cation and the anion in sodium sulphate?
(*b*) Is it likely that either of these ions is discharged during electrolysis?
(*c*) What is the ion that causes the blue colour around the cathode?
(*d*) What is the ion that causes the red colour around the anode?
(*e*) Which particles could be discharged at the cathode to produce both hydrogen and the blue colour, and at the anode to produce both oxygen and the red colour?
(*f*) Write equations for the reaction at each electrode.

5 (*a*) Explain what is meant by the terms 'strong acid' and 'weak acid'.
(*b*) A 1 M solution of hydrochloric and reacts rapidly with both magnesium ribbon and lumps of calcium carbonate but a 1 M solution of ethanoic acid reacts only slowly with the substances. Explain these observations.
(*c*) Outline one other experiment you could do to support your explanation given in answer to part (*b*).

6 A solution of ethanoic acid (molecular formula $H_4C_2O_2$) in water has the concentration $6.0\,g\,l^{-1}$.
  $25\,cm^3$ of this solution is titrated with 0.20 M sodium hydroxide solution and is found to need $12.5\,cm^3$ for neutralization using phenolphthalein indicator.
(*a*) From the concentration of the acid in $g\,l^{-1}$, calculate the concentration of the acid in $mol\,l^{-1}$.
(*b*) How many mols of $H_4C_2O_2$ are used in the titration?
(*c*) How many mol of OH^- are needed in the titration?
(*d*) How many mol of OH^- react with 1 mol of $H_2C_2O_2$?
(*e*) What is the basicity of the acid?
  Write the equation for the neutralization reaction.

7 A white powder shows the following reactions:
(*a*) It gives a lilac colour when used in the flame test.
(*b*) It gives off carbon dioxide when added to an acid.
(*c*) It gives off carbon dioxide when heated.
(*d*) The residue from test (*c*) gives off carbon dioxide when added to an acid.
  Identify the white powder and explain the results of the above tests, writing equations for the reactions.

8 Explain what is meant by an 'amphoteric oxide'. Name one such oxide and describe the reactions you would do to demonstrate its amphoteric properties.

Key words

strong acid	**basicity**	**dibasic**	**normal salt**	**amphoteric**
weak acid	**monobasic**	**acid salt**	**basic salt**	**spectator ions**

Basic facts

● **Acids show their characteristic properties only when they 'dissolve' in water. The 'dissolving' is in fact a reaction between water molecules and the molecules of the acid in which ions are produced.**

- Ammonia is alkaline only in aqueous solution. When it is dry, it consists of molecules. When it is added to water, ammonia molecules react to produce ammonium ions and hydroxide ions.

- In aqueous solutions of strong acids, the vast majority of the molecules of the acid have reacted to form ions. In aqueous solutions of weak acids, only a very small proportion of the molecules of the acid have reacted to form ions.

- The differences between the reactions of strong acids and weak acids (of equal concentrations in $mol\,l^{-1}$) are due to the differences in the concentrations of the hydrogen ions.

- The basicity of an acid is the maximum number of moles of hydrogen ions that can be formed from one mole of acid molecules.

- Dibasic acids can form two sorts of salts: normal salts and acid salts.

- Amphoteric oxides and hydroxides can show both acidic and basic properties.

25 Reactions of gases

Gas volumes

When a chemical reaction is studied for the first time, a very important question is, What is the equation for the reaction? To answer this question, experiments are done which measure the amounts of reactants that react and the amounts of the products that are formed. You have already done some experiments of this kind in your work from Chapters 21, 22, 23 and 24.

Usually, the *masses* of the substances in the reaction are measured, and from these, the number of moles of substances can be worked out.

What happens for a reaction between gases? Although the masses of gases can be measured, it is far easier to measure their *volumes*. In school laboratories, this is often done using syringes.

This chapter deals with measuring the volumes of gases which take part in reactions and then tries to explain the results.

But there is a complication when the volumes of gases are measured. If you have pumped up a bicycle tyre you will know that it is fairly easy to compress a gas. The answer to the question

'What is the volume of 1 g of hydrogen?'

should be

'It depends on the pressure and temperature of the hydrogen'.

1 g of hydrogen can occupy either a large volume (at a low pressure) or a small volume (at a high pressure, Fig. 25.1).

The volume of 1 g of hydrogen *at a given pressure* depends on the temperature (Fig. 25.2). Gases expand when they are heated and contract when they are cooled.

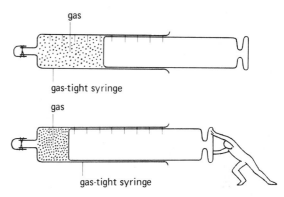

Fig. 25.1 The volume of a fixed mass of gas decreases as the pressure increases

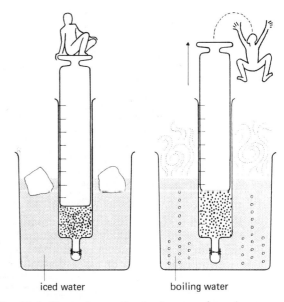

Fig. 25.2 The volume of a fixed mass of gas increases as the temperature increases

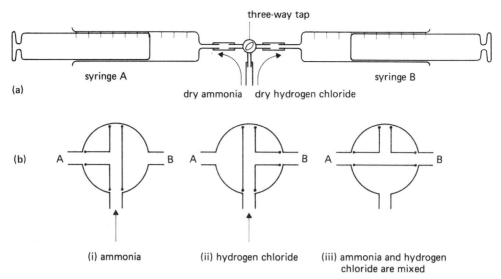

Fig. 25.3 (b) shows details of the three-way tap in (a)

Measuring gas volumes in reactions

The reaction between ammonia and hydrogen chloride (page 51) is an easy one to investigate. The apparatus for the experiment is shown in Fig. 25.3.

Syringe A is filled with a known volume of dry ammonia, and then the three-way tap is turned so that syringe B can be filled with a known volume of dry hydrogen chloride. The three-way tap is finally turned so that the two gases can be mixed by alternately pushing in each plunger.

Here is a result for this experiment.

Initial volume	Final volume
60 cm³ hydrogen chloride	19 cm³ hydrogen chloride
40 cm³ ammonia	0 cm³ ammonia (plus a white solid of negligible volume)

The remaining gas turns wetted blue litmus paper red, and so it is hydrogen chloride.

These results show that 41 cm³ (60–19) of hydrogen chloride reacts with 40 cm³ of ammonia to give a white solid, or, roughly equal volumes of hydrogen chloride and ammonia react.

You will find the results of another gas-volume experiment on page 90. All such experiments show that the volumes of gases that react are in a simple whole-number ratio to one another. So 30 cm³ of one gas may be found to react with 15 cm³, 30 cm³ or 60 cm³ of another gas. But 30 cm³ of one gas is never found to react with 23 cm³ or 37 cm³ of another gas. Also, when the products of the reaction are gases, their volumes are also in a simple whole-number ratio with the volumes of the reactants. These results are obtained only when all gas volumes are measured at the same temperature and pressure.

Results like these were summarized in 1808 by the French scientist Gay Lussac when he proposed a **Law of Volumes** which applies to reactions which involve gases.

> The volumes of the gases that react together and the volumes of any gases that are formed in a reaction are in a simple whole-number ratio. The only condition is that all the gas volumes have to be measured at the same temperature and pressure.

Working out equations from gas volumes

The molar gas volume

The density of a gas can be found by measuring the volume of a known mass of the gas and then dividing the mass by the volume. But because the volume of the gas depends on the temperature and pressure, the density of the gas also depends on the temperature and pressure.

So that results for different gases can be compared easily, scientists have chosen a standard temperature and pressure. These are 0 °C (273 K) and 1 atmosphere pressure ($1.01 \times 10^5 \, \mathrm{N\,m^{-2}}$). *Standard temperature and pressure* is usually shortened to S.T.P. Information about gases, such as density, is often given for these standard conditions.

The densities of four gases, at S.T.P., are given in Table 25.1. From these figures it is possible to work

Table 25.1	Relative atomic mass	Formula of molecules	Density at S.T.P., in g l⁻¹
Argon	39.9	Ar	1.78
Hydrogen	1.01	H₂	0.0902
Nitrogen	14.0	N₂	1.25
Oxygen	16.0	O₂	1.43

out the volume which 1 mole of molecules of each gas would occupy at S.T.P. For hydrogen, the calculation is

0.0902 g of hydrogen at S.T.P. occupies 1 litre,

so 2.02 g of hydrogen at S.T.P. occupies

$$\frac{2.02}{0.0902} = 22.4 \text{ litres}$$

You should work out the volumes occupied by 1 mole of molecules of the other gases in Table 25.1. (Remember that argon exists as atoms.) Similar calculations can be carried out for all other gases and the rather surprising result is that the answers are always very close to one another. (The results are not always exactly the same, but at this stage in your chemistry course the differences are not important.)

The volume occupied by 1 mole of molecules of any gas is called the **molar gas volume**. Its value at S.T.P. is 22.4 litres.

If the volumes are worked out for another temperature and pressure, again a constant value is found. At 25 °C and 1 atmosphere pressure, the molar gas volume is about 24 litres.

The molar gas volumes of hydrogen, nitrogen and oxygen were worked out using the idea that the molecules of these gases are **diatomic**, that is, each molecule consists of two atoms. Most of the evidence for this idea is too complicated to include in this book but it should be clear that it is a very useful idea. Not only can it be used to explain some of the properties of gases, it can also be used to explain the results obtained when gases react. For example, the idea is used later in this section when the reaction between hydrogen and oxygen is discussed. It would be very difficult indeed to explain the experimental results for this reaction if the idea were not used.

Most of the elements that are gases at room temperature are diatomic but the noble gases (such as argon, mentioned above) are **monatomic**: they exist as atoms.

Avogadro's Principle

You know from Chapter 21 that 1 mole of any substance always contains the same number of particles. It has now been shown that 1 mole of molecules of any gas at S.T.P. always occupies 22.4 litres. This means that 22.4 litres of any gas at S.T.P. contains the same number (6.02×10^{23}) of molecules. It also means that, for example, 100 cm³ of *any* gas at S.T.P. contains the same number of molecules.

The same kind of result also holds for other temperatures and pressures. For example, 24 litres of any gas at 25 °C and 1 atmosphere pressure contain 1 mole of molecules.

These ideas were first put forward by an Italian scientist called Avogadro and are summarized in the following statement which is called **Avogadro's Principle**.

Equal volumes of all gases measured at the same temperature and pressure contain the same number of molecules.

This is accepted by modern chemists because it makes sense of a lot of results of experiments on gases. Also, it fits in with the idea that gases consist of molecules that are very widely separated from each other. Fig. 25.4 shows that equal numbers of molecules of two gases, one made up of small molecules and one of larger molecules *can* occupy the same volume so long as the molecules are a long way apart. But if the same molecules were packed tightly together, equal numbers of molecules would occupy different volumes. So no generalizations exist about the volumes occupied by 1 mole of molecules in the liquid or solid states.

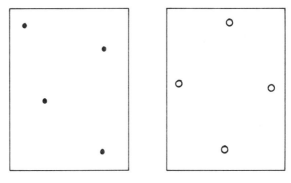

molecules widely separated
equal volumes–equal number of molecules

molecules packed tightly together
unequal volumes–equal number of molecules

Fig. 25.4

By using Avogadro's Principle for experiments that involve reactions of gases, results obtained as gas volumes can be changed into the relative numbers of molecules of reactants and products.

Think again about the reaction between ammonia and hydrogen chloride (page 88). It was found that equal volumes of ammonia and hydrogen chloride react together. So equal numbers of molecules of the two gases must react with one another.

ammonia + hydrogen chloride
40 cm³   40 cm³
X molecules   X molecules

⟶ white solid
negligible volume

By using Avogadro's Principle, X molecules of ammonia react with X molecules of hydrogen chloride, and so one molecule of ammonia reacts with one molecule of hydrogen chloride. Avogadro's Principle cannot be applied to the white solid because it is not a gas. But the left-hand side of the equation for this reaction can be written if you know the formulas of ammonia (page 130) and hydrogen chloride (page 124).

$$NH_3(g) \quad + \quad HCl(g) \quad \longrightarrow \text{white solid}$$

1 molecule   +   1 molecule
or 1 mole of NH_3 +   1 mole of HCl

The white solid ammonium chloride has the formula NH_4Cl.

The equation for the synthesis of steam can be worked out in the same way. In this reaction the product is also a gas, provided the temperature is kept over 100 °C. The results of a gas-volume experiment (at a temperature above 100 °C) are:

$$\text{hydrogen} + \text{oxygen} \longrightarrow \text{steam}$$
$$2x\,cm^3 \quad + \quad x\,cm^3 \longrightarrow 2x\,cm^3$$

Using Avogadro's Principle and then dividing by X:

$2X$ molecules $+$ X molecules $\longrightarrow 2X$ molecules

2 molecules   +   1 molecule $\longrightarrow$ 2 molecules

So one molecule of steam is made up of one molecule of hydrogen and half a molecule of oxygen. Both hydrogen and oxygen are diatomic, (their molecules are made of *two* atoms). So a molecule of steam has two atoms of hydrogen and one atom of oxygen: the formula of steam is H_2O. The equation for the reaction is (Fig. 25.5)

$$2H_2(g) \quad + \quad O_2(g) \quad \longrightarrow \quad 2H_2O(g)$$

2 molecules   +   1 molecule $\longrightarrow$ 2 molecules
or 2 moles of H_2 + 1 mole of O_2 $\longrightarrow$ 2 moles of H_2O

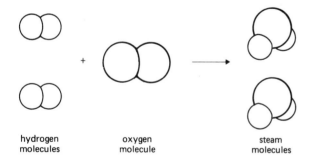

hydrogen   oxygen   steam
molecules   molecule   molecules

Fig. 25.5

The results of other experiments on reacting gases can be used in the same way as the results for the synthesis of steam.

But the problem is more difficult if you want to find the formula of a gaseous compound using a reaction involving solids as well as gases. For example, carbon dioxide is made by burning carbon in oxygen.

Only the volumes of carbon dioxide and oxygen can be used because Avogadro's Principle cannot be applied to solids. So the number of atoms of carbon in a molecule of carbon dioxide cannot be worked out directly from the results of the gas-volume experiment. Extra information is needed before you can get the complete formula for carbon dioxide.

If 50 cm^3 of oxygen is passed over hot carbon until the reaction stops, it is found that 50 cm^3 of carbon dioxide is formed.

$$\text{carbon} + \text{oxygen} \longrightarrow \text{carbon dioxide}$$
$$50\,cm^3 \qquad\qquad 50\,cm^3$$

Using Avogadro's Principle,

$$X \text{ molecules} \longrightarrow X \text{ molecules}$$
$$1 \text{ molecule} \longrightarrow 1 \text{ molecule}$$

So a molecule of carbon dioxide contains 2 atoms of oxygen. The formula of carbon dioxide can be written as C_nO_2. n is a small whole number which cannot be found using a gas-volume experiment.

The extra information comes from finding the density of carbon dioxide and then using the molar gas volume. At room temperature and pressure, this density is $1.8\,g\,l^{-1}$ and the molar gas volume is 24 litres. Since 1 litre of carbon dioxide has a mass of 1.8 g, then 24 litres have a mass of 1.8×24 or 43 g. This is the mass of 1 mole of carbon dioxide.

Now 1 mole of C_nO_2 contains n moles of C atoms and 2 moles of O atoms. 1 mole of C atoms has a mass of 12 g and 1 mole of O atoms has a mass of 16 g.

So 1 mole of C_nO_2 has a mass of $[12n + (16 \times 2)]$ g, and

$$43 = 12n + 32$$

Because n is a whole number, it must equal 1. The formula of carbon dioxide is CO_2, and the equation for its synthesis is

$$C(s) + O_2(g) \longrightarrow CO_2(g)$$

Empirical and molecular formulas

The formula of a gas may be found in two completely different ways:

1. by the use of the results of combining *volume* experiments as shown above for steam and carbon dioxide;
2. by the use of results from combining *mass* experiments; this kind of calculation is done on page 59 for a solid compound, but it can be used for gases as well.

Usually the formula found by each method is the same for a gaseous compound. For example, method 1 gives the formula of steam (water) as H_2O. Method 2 gives the result that 2g of hydrogen combines with 16g of oxygen when hydrogen gas reduces copper(II) oxide to copper. This means that hydrogen atoms and oxygen atoms are combined in the ratio 2 to 1, so the formula of water is again H_2O.

But in a few cases, the two methods give different formulas for a compound. An example is the formula of a gas called ethane. This gas contains only carbon and hydrogen and can be burnt in oxygen to give carbon dioxide and steam. It is possible to obtain the formula by measuring either volumes or masses.

Volume measurements

When it is burnt, one volume of ethane produces two volumes of carbon dioxide and three volumes of steam; so one molecule of ethane produces two molecules of CO_2 and three molecules of H_2O.

It is known that two molecules of CO_2 contain two atoms of C, and that three molecules of H_2O contain six atoms of H. Because these atoms must have come from one molecule of ethane, the formula of ethane must be C_2H_6. This result agrees with the observed relative molecular mass of ethane which is about 30 g.

Mass measurements

It is found that 0.60 g of ethane contains 0.48 g of carbon and 0.12 g of hydrogen. But

0.48 g carbon = 0.48/12.0 or 0.04 mole of C atoms,
and
0.12 g hydrogen = 0.12/1.0 or 0.12 mole of H atoms.

So, 0.04 mole of C atoms combines with
0.12 mole of H atoms.

This gives a whole-number molar ratio C : H of 1 : 3, and so the formula is CH_3.

Two formulas have been found for ethane, C_2H_6 and CH_3. Why are they different? Which is the 'right' one? C_2H_6 is an example of a **molecular formula**: it shows the actual number of carbon and hydrogen atoms in one molecule of ethane. CH_3 is an example of an **empirical formula**: the calculated result is a ratio and shows only the *proportions* in which the two kinds of atom are combined. It does not give the number of atoms of each element in the molecule.

Another example of a gas whose empirical and molecular formulas are different is dinitrogen tetraoxide. Its empirical formula is NO_2 but its relative molecular mass is 92. If NO_2 were also the molecular formula, then the relative molecular mass would be (14 + 32) or 46. The fact that the relative molecular mass is exactly twice this value suggests that the molecular formula is $(NO_2)_2$ or N_2O_4. In other words, 1 mole of dinitrogen tetraoxide contains 2 moles of N atoms and 4 moles of O atoms, and one molecule of it contains two atoms of nitrogen and four atoms of oxygen.

Finding equations for reactions in which gases are formed

Think about the reaction between sodium hydrogencarbonate and dilute sulphuric acid. A titration method can be used to find the left-hand side of the equation and shows that 1 mole of $NaHCO_3$ reacts with $\frac{1}{2}$ mole of H_2SO_4. But a gas, carbon dioxide, is one of the products, and a method such as the one described in Experiment 25.1 can be used to find how many moles of CO_2 are produced by 1 mole of $NaHCO_3$.

Experiment 25.1 Finding the volume of a gas produced in a reaction

First saturate about 50 cm³ of 1 M sulphuric acid with carbon dioxide by adding to it three spatula measures of sodium hydrogencarbonate. (Any carbon dioxide given off in the main experiment cannot now dissolve in the acid.) Add this acid to a 250 cm³ flask fitted with a bung and a delivery tube (Fig. 25.6). Accurately find the mass of about 0.20 g of

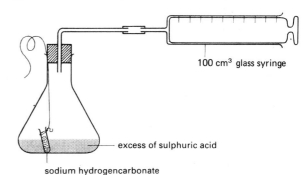

100 cm³ glass syringe

excess of sulphuric acid

sodium hydrogencarbonate

Fig. 25.6

sodium hydrogencarbonate in a small test-tube which should then be hung by a thread in the conical flask.

After making sure that the plunger of the syringe is at zero on the scale, shake the flask and contents so that the solid and the acid come into contact: all the solid reacts and some excess of acid remains. Find the volume of carbon dioxide given off when the reaction is complete.

▸ Work through these steps using the results of your experiment.
1. Knowing that 1 mole of $NaHCO_3$ has a mass of 84 g, work out the fraction of a mole of the solid that you used for the experiment.
2. Your teacher will tell you the molar gas volume for your laboratory conditions. Work out the fraction of a mole of carbon dioxide that you collected in the syringe.
3. Use the results of 1 and 2 to find how many moles of CO_2 are produced by 1 mole of $NaHCO_3$.
▸ Write down the complete balanced equation for the reaction of sodium hydrogencarbonate and sulphuric acid.

QUESTIONS

1 The density of air under the usual laboratory conditions is about $1.2 \, \mathrm{g\,l^{-1}}$. Will this density increase, decrease or stay the same
(i) if the pressure of the air is increased (while the temperature stays the same), and
(ii) if the temperature is increased (while the pressure stays the same)?

2 Calculate:
(a) the number of molecules of chlorine in 1.2 litres of the gas at 25 °C and 1 atmosphere pressure;
(b) the number of molecules in $100 \, \mathrm{cm^3}$ of a gas at S.T.P.;
(c) the volume occupied by 1.6 g of the gas methane (CH_4) at S.T.P.;
(d) the volume occupied by 1.6 g of the gas methane at 25 °C and 1 atmosphere pressure;
(e) the number of moles of CO_2 in 6 litres of the gas at 25 °C and 1 atmosphere pressure.

3 Arrange these gases in order of decreasing volume at room temperature and pressure. (The relative molecular masses of the gases are given in brackets.)
(u) 2 g of carbon monoxide (28)
(b) 2 g of carbon dioxide (44)
(c) 2 g of chlorine (71)
(d) 2 g of oxygen (32)
(e) 2 g of nitrogen dioxide (46)

Explain the reasoning behind your answer.

4 A gas called arsine consists only of the elements arsenic (As) and hydrogen (H). At room temperature and pressure, $40 \, \mathrm{cm^3}$ of arsine decomposes to give $60 \, \mathrm{cm^3}$ of hydrogen. The relative molecular mass of arsine is between 75 and 80.
(a) Work out the number of atoms of hydrogen in one molecule of arsine assuming that hydrogen is diatomic.
(b) Explain why it is not possible to write down the complete formula for arsine using your answer to (a).
(c) Work out the formula for arsine given that the relative atomic mass of arsenic is 74.9.
(d) Is (c) a molecular or an empirical formula?
(e) Name a common gas whose formula is like that of arsine.

5 When ammonia (NH_3) reacts with oxygen (O_2) it can do so in two ways. The incomplete equations for these reactions are:

$$4NH_3(g) + 5O_2(g) \longrightarrow \ldots + 6H_2O(g) \qquad (1)$$
$$4NH_3(g) + 3O_2(g) \longrightarrow \ldots + 6H_2O(g) \qquad (2)$$

(a) What is the difference between the volumes of ammonia and oxygen that react with another in 1 and 2?
(b) Here is a list of substances containing nitrogen:

$N_2(g)$
$NO(g)$
$NO_2(g)$
$N_2O(g)$
$N_2O_4(g)$
$N_2O_5(g)$

Which one of these is the only possible second product in reaction 1, and how many molecules of it are formed by four molecules of ammonia?

(c) Which one of the gases listed in (b) is the only possible second product in reaction 2, and how many molecules of it are formed by four molecules of ammonia?

6 Two volumes of hydrogen fluoride gas, HF(g), combined with 1 volume of a gas X to form 2 volumes of a gas Y and no other product. Gas X has an empirical formula NF(g) and its relative molecular mass is 66.
(a) What is the molecular formula of gas X? (Relative atomic masses: N = 14.0 and F = 19.0.)
(b) What is the name of gas X likely to be?
(c) Which of these equations is likely to be the correct one for the reaction between HF(g) and gas X?

(i) $HF(g) + N_2F_2(g) \longrightarrow N_2HF_3(g)$
(ii) $HF(g) + N_3F_3(g) \longrightarrow N_3HF_4(g)$
(iii) $2HF(g) + N_2F_2(g) \longrightarrow 2NHF_2(g)$
(iv) $2HF(g) + NF(g) \longrightarrow NH_2F_3(g)$
(v) $2HF(g) + 2N_2F_2(g) \longrightarrow 2N_2HF_3(g)$

Explain how you arrive at your answer.

7 $30 \, \mathrm{cm^3}$ of a gaseous oxide of nitrogen is completely reacted with hot iron wire. It is found that $30 \, \mathrm{cm^3}$ of nitrogen is formed at the same temperature and pressure. In another experiment, the same oxide of nitrogen is found to have a density of $1.83 \, \mathrm{g\,l^{-1}}$ at room temperature and pressure. (Relative atomic masses: N = 14.0, O = 16.0.)

(a) How many atoms of nitrogen must one molecule of the oxide contain?
(b) What must happen to the oxygen when the oxide reacts with iron wire?
(c) Work out the relative molecular mass of the oxide assuming that the molar gas volume is 24 litres at room temperature and pressure.
(d) Using your answers to (a) and (c), work out the molecular formula for the oxide.

8 (i) Nitrogen monoxide, NO(g), reacts with oxygen, $O_2(g)$, at room temperature to form a *single* gaseous product which is known to be either nitrogen dioxide, $NO_2(g)$, or dinitrogen tetraoxide, $N_2O_4(g)$.
(ii) An experiment with gas syringes shows that $60 \, \mathrm{cm^3}$ of NO(g) combines with $30 \, \mathrm{cm^3}$ of oxygen to give about $30 \, \mathrm{cm^3}$ of the product.

(a) Describe how you would attempt to obtain the results in (ii) by experiment.
(b) Write down the two possible balanced equations for the reaction using only the information given in (i).
(c) Using the results in (ii), say which of the two equations in answer (b) is the correct one.

9 The gas ethene is a compound of hydrogen and carbon. $20 \, \mathrm{cm^3}$ of ethene is burnt in an apparatus that is kept at a temperature of 120 °C and $40 \, \mathrm{cm^3}$ of carbon dioxide and $40 \, \mathrm{cm^3}$ of steam are formed.

(a) Work out the molecular formula of ethene and write the equation for its combustion.
(b) What is the empirical formula of ethene?
(c) Explain why the temperature of the apparatus is
(i) kept constant and
(ii) above 100° C.

Key words

Gay Lussac's Law of Volumes	monatomic molecules
S.T.P.	Avogadro's Principle
molar gas volume	empirical formula
diatomic molecules	molecular formula

Basic facts

- The volume of a given mass of gas depends on its pressure and temperature. If the pressure on a gas is increased (while the temperature is kept constant), the volume of the gas decreases. If the temperature of a gas is increased (while the pressure is kept constant) the volume of the gas increases.

- Gases react in simple whole-number ratios by volume. The volumes of any gases produced are also in a simple whole-number ratio to the volumes of the reactants, provided all volume measurements are made at the same temperature and pressure (Gay Lussac's Law of Volumes).

- The volume occupied by one mole of molecules of any gas (its molar gas volume) is constant at a given temperature and pressure. At S.T.P. the molar gas volume is $22.4 \, l \, mol^{-1}$.

- Most elements that are gases at room temperature and pressure consist of diatomic molecules (each molecule contains two atoms). But the noble gases have monatomic molecules.

- Equal volumes of all gases at the same temperature and pressure contain equal numbers of molecules (Avogadro's Principle).

- The formulas of gaseous compounds can be worked out from the volume ratios for reactions involving their synthesis or decomposition, provided the other substances involved in the reaction are gases of known formulas.

- The molar mass of a gas can be worked out from its density at a particular temperature and pressure, and the molar gas volume at that temperature and pressure.

26 Chemical calculations

The part of this book called *Particles, formulas and equations* contains several kinds of calculations. To conclude this part, this chapter summarizes these calculations and gives more examples with a wider range. All the examples are based on ideas which you have already met.

Equations and reacting masses

An equation is a shorthand way of representing a change that has been found to occur. So before an equation can be written, the change that occurs must be known.

Think of the reduction of iron(III) oxide by aluminium, for which the equation has been found to be:

$$2Al(s) + Fe_2O_3(s) \longrightarrow Al_2O_3(s) + 2Fe(s)$$

This equation gives the following information.

1. Iron(III) oxide reacts with aluminium to form aluminium oxide and iron. All the reactants and products are solids.
2. 2 moles of Al react with 1 mole of Fe_2O_3 to produce 1 mole of Al_2O_3 and 2 moles of Fe:

$$2Al(s) + Fe_2O_3(s) \longrightarrow Al_2O_3(s) + 2Fe(s)$$

2 moles	1 mole	1 mole	2 moles
$2 \times 27.0 \, g$	$159.6 \, g$	$102.0 \, g$	$2 \times 55.8 \, g$

The equation shows how many moles of each substance react or are formed. From the number of moles of each substance, the mass of each substance can be worked out as shown. This is the kind of information about a reaction that allows a chemist to work out the proportions in which the reactants should be mixed and the amount of product (the **yield**) he can expect.

93

Example 1

What is the maximum mass of iron that can be obtained by reacting 100 kg of aluminium with iron(III) oxide?

From the equation, 2 moles of Al (relative atomic mass = 27.0) produce 2 moles of Fe (relative atomic mass = 55.8).

So 54.0 g of aluminium produces 111.6 g of iron, 54.0 kg of aluminium produces 111.6 kg of iron and 100 kg of aluminium produces 111.6 × 100/54 kg of iron.

The maximum mass of iron obtained by the reaction of 100 kg of aluminium is *207 kg.*

In working this out, you have to assume two things:

1. that *all* the aluminium reacts to form iron (the reaction goes to completion), and
2. that the reaction shown by the equation is the only one that happens, that is, there are no side-reactions such as the aluminium reacting with oxygen from the air.

For the reactions dealt with in this chapter, both these things are true. But some reactions are reversible and do not always go to completion (page 200). In these cases, the amount of product is always *lower* than that predicted by the equation.

Mass–mass and mass–gas volume calculations

All calculations of this kind need three main steps.

In the first step, the equation is used to find the numbers of moles of the substances involved in the reaction. In the second step, these are changed into the units of mass or volume that you want. Finally, the particular masses or volumes given in the question are used together with those from the second step to find the answer.

A summary of these processes is given in Fig. 26.1. Try to find each of these steps in Example 1.

Example 2

500 kg of sodium hydrogencarbonate is completely decomposed by heat. Work out the yield of sodium carbonate in kg and the yield (at S.T.P.) of carbon dioxide in litres.

1. $2NaHCO_3(s) \longrightarrow Na_2CO_3(s) + CO_2(g) + H_2O(l)$
   2 moles   1 mole   1 mole

2. | 1 mole has mass 84.0 g | 1 mole has mass 106 g | 1 mole of CO_2 occupies 22.4 litres at S.T.P. |
   2 moles have mass 168 g | | |
   168 kg | 106 kg | 22 400 litres

3. (a) 168 kg of sodium hydrogencarbonate produces 106 kg of sodium carbonate. So 500 kg produces 106 × 500/168 = *315 kg of sodium carbonate.*

   (b) 168 kg of sodium hydrogencarbonate produces 22 400 litres of carbon dioxide at S.T.P. So 500 kg produces 22 400 × 500/168 = *66 700 litres of carbon dioxide.*

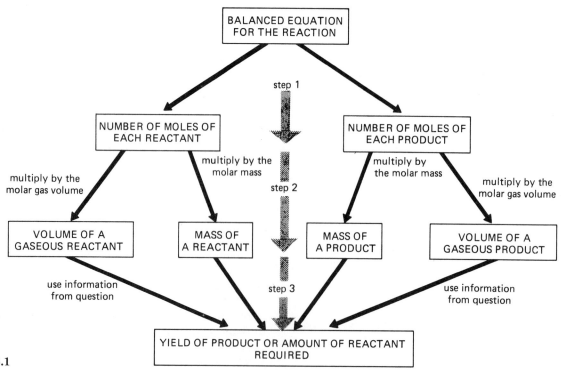

Fig. 26.1

Gas volume–gas volume calculations

These problems can be solved by using Avogadro's Principle. There is no need to change moles of gas to volumes using the molar gas volume as in Example 2.

Example 3

Ammonia can react with oxygen in two ways:

$$4NH_3(g) + 3O_2(g) \longrightarrow 2N_2(g) + 6H_2O(g) \quad (1)$$
$$4NH_3(g) + 5O_2(g) \longrightarrow 4NO(g) + 6H_2O(g) \quad (2)$$

In each of two experiments, $80\,cm^3$ of ammonia is reacted with $150\,cm^3$ (an excess) of oxygen. All volumes are measured at the same temperature and pressure.

Work out (a) the volume of nitrogen produced in reaction 1, (b) the volume of nitrogen monoxide (NO) produced in reaction 2, and (c) the volumes of oxygen remaining, after each reaction has finished.

(a) In reaction 1, 4 moles of ammonia produce 2 moles of nitrogen. Using Avogadro's Principle, it can be said that 4 *volumes* of ammonia produce 2 *volumes* of nitrogen. In other words, ammonia forms half of its own volume of nitrogen. So $80\,cm^3$ of ammonia forms *$40\,cm^3$ of nitrogen.*

(b) Using the same reasoning, ammonia produces its own volume of nitrogen monoxide in reaction 2, that is, *$80\,cm^3$ of nitrogen monoxide.*

(c) In reaction 1, 4 volumes of ammonia react with 3 volumes of oxygen. So *$80\,cm^3$ of ammonia reacts with* $80 \times \frac{3}{4}$ or $60\,cm^3$ of oxygen.

The volume of oxygen left over is the initial volume minus the volume reacted $= 150 - 60 = 90\,cm^3$.

In the same way, it can be worked out that $80 \times \frac{5}{4}$ or $100\,cm^3$ of oxygen is used in reaction 2, and the volume of oxygen left over is $150 - 100$ or *$50\,cm^3$.*

Calculations involving solutions

Chemists usually give the concentration of a substance in a solution in $mol\,l^{-1}$ (M). If the volume and concentration of a solution are known, the number of moles of solute in that solution can be worked out. In this way, measuring out a certain volume of a solution whose concentrations is known is one way of measuring out moles of solute.

Example 4

How many moles of copper(II) sulphate are there in $250\,cm^3$ of a $0.50\,M$ solution?

In $1000\,cm^3$ of $1.0\,M$ solution there is $1\,mol\ CuSO_4$.

So in $1000\,cm^3$ of $0.50\,M$ solution there is $0.50\,mol$ $CuSO_4$.

And in $250\,cm^3$ of $0.50\,M$ solution there is $0.50 \times 250/1000 = 0.125\,mol\ CuSO_4$.

Example 5

How many cm^3 of $0.50\,M$ sodium carbonate solution are required to react with $100\,cm^3$ of $0.10\,M$ hydrochloric acid?

The equation for the reaction is

$$Na_2CO_3(aq) + 2HCl(aq)$$
$$\longrightarrow 2NaCl(aq) + CO_2(g) + H_2O(l)$$

$100\,cm^3$ of $0.10\,M$ hydrochloric acid contains $0.10 \times 100/1000$ or $0.010\,mol$. From the equation, $2\,mol$ HCl reacts with $1\,mol\ Na_2CO_3$, so that $0.010\,mol$ HCl reacts with $0.0050\,mol\ Na_2CO_3$. There is 0.50 $mol\ Na_2CO_5$ in $1\,litre$ of $0.50\,M$ sodium carbonate solution.

So there is $0.0050\,mol\ Na_2CO_3$ in *$10\,cm^3$* of the same solution.

Calculations using the Avogadro constant

From the definition of the mole (page 58) it follows that $1\,mole$ of any substance contains 6.02×10^{23} particles. The particles can be atoms (for elements like sodium or argon), molecules (for compounds like water or carbon dioxide) or groups of ions (for compounds like sodium chloride).

Example 6

Work out the number of
(a) atoms in $0.27\,g$ of silver,
(b) molecules in $1.12\,litres$ of hydrogen at S.T.P.,
(c) ions in $50\,cm^3$ of $1.0\,M$ sodium sulphate solution.

(a) $1\,mol\ Ag$ contains 6.02×10^{23} atoms. So $108\,g$ of silver contains 6.02×10^{23} atoms, and $0.27\,g$ of silver contains $6.02 \times 10^{23} \times 0.27/108 = 1.505 \times 10^{21}$ *atoms.*

(b) $1\,mol\ H_2$ contains 6.02×10^{23} molecules. So $22.4\,litres$ of hydrogen at S.T.P. contain 6.02×10^{23} molecules, and $1.12\,litres$ of hydrogen at S.T.P. contain $6.02 \times 10^{23} \times 1.12/22.4 = 3.01 \times 10^{22}$ *molecules.*

(c) $1\,mol\ Na_2SO_4$ contains $2 \times 6.02 \times 10^{23}\ Na^+$ and $6.02 \times 10^{23}\ SO_4{}^{2-} = 18.06 \times 10^{23}$ ions. So $1\,litre$ of $1.0\,M$ sodium sulphate solution contains 18.06×10^{23} ions, and $50\,cm^3$ of $1.0\,M$ sodium sulphate solution contains $18.06 \times 10^{23} \times 50/1000 = 9.03 \times 10^{22}$ *ions.*

Calculations using the Faraday constant

The link between the amount of electricity and the chemical changes in electrolysis is dealt with in Chapter 22. The total amount of electric charge carried by one mole of electrons is 9.65×10^4 C.

Example 7

Electricity is passed in series through solutions of silver nitrate and dilute sulphuric acid. If a current of 1.93 A is used for 1 min 40 s, work out:
(a) *the mass of silver produced, and*
(b) *the volume of hydrogen produced (at S.T.P.).*

The amount of electricity passed through the solutions is $1.93 \times 100 = 1.93 \times 10^2$ C.

(a) The equation for the discharge of silver ions is

$$Ag^+(aq) + e^- \longrightarrow Ag(s)$$

so that
1 mol electrons produces 1 mol Ag, or
96 500 C produces 108 g of silver, so
1.93×10^2 C will produce $108 \times 1.93 \times 10^2/$
$9.65 \times 10^4 = 0.216$ g of silver.

(b) The equation for the discharge of hydrogen ions is

$$2H^+(aq) + 2e^- \longrightarrow H_2(g)$$

so that
2 mol electrons produces 1 mol H_2, or
$2 \times 96 500$ C produces 2 g of hydrogen, or
22.4 litres at S.T.P. So,
193 C produces $22.4 \times 193/2 \times 96 500$
$= 0.0224$ litres of hydrogen at S.T.P.
(that is, 22.4 cm^3).

QUESTIONS

Look at Data Sheet 1, page 279, where necessary.
1 Work out the mass in kg of iron(III) oxide that is reduced to iron by 100 kg of aluminium.

2 Titanium(IV) chloride may be reduced by magnesium to titanium metal. The equation for the reaction is:

$$TiCl_4(l) + 2Mg(s) \longrightarrow 2MgCl_2(s) + Ti(s)$$

Work out the mass in kg of titanium(IV) chloride that would be required to produce 500 kg of titanium metal.

3 Limestone can be decomposed to quicklime and carbon dioxide by heat:

$$CaCO_3(s) \longrightarrow CaO(s) + CO_2(g)$$

Work out:
(a) the mass of quicklime in kg, and
(b) the approximate volume of carbon dioxide at room temperature and pressure that would be produced by 1000 kg of limestone. (Assume the molar gas volume to be 24 litres at room temperature and pressure, and the relative atomic mass of calcium to be 40.)

4 The overall equation for the electrolysis of molten sodium chloride is:

$$2NaCl(l) \longrightarrow 2Na(l) + Cl_2(g)$$

Work out:
(a) the mass of sodium metal, and
(b) the approximate volume of chlorine at room temperature and pressure that would be produced by the decomposition of 70 g of sodium chloride (assume the molar gas volume to be 24 litres at room temperature and pressure).

5 720 cm^3 carbon dioxide (measured at 25 °C and 1 atmosphere pressure) is slowly passed through an excess of limewater. Work out the mass of calcium hydroxide that reacts with the carbon dioxide and the maximum mass of calcium carbonate that can be precipitated. (At 25 °C and 1 atmosphere pressure, the molar gas volume is 24 litres.)

6 The gas propane, C_3H_8, burns in an excess of air or oxygen to form carbon dioxide and water vapour. Starting with 100 cm^3 of propane, what volume of oxygen is needed for its complete combustion and what volume of carbon dioxide is formed? All gas volumes are measured at the same temperature and pressure.

7 Natural gas (mostly CH_4) burns in air or oxygen to form carbon dioxide and steam:

$$CH_4(g) + 2O_2(g) \longrightarrow CO_2(g) + 2H_2O(g)$$

10 cm^3 of natural gas is burnt in 100 cm^3 of *oxygen* in one experiment, and in another experiment 10 cm^3 of natural gas is burnt in 100 cm^3 of *air*. Assume all volumes are measured at the same temperature and pressure.
(a) Work out the volume of oxygen which is *not* used up in the first experiment.
(b) What volume of carbon dioxide is formed in the first experiment?
(c) About what volume of oxygen is there in 100 cm^3 of air?
(d) Is there any excess of oxygen left over after the second experiment is complete?
(e) What volume of carbon dioxide is formed in the second experiment?

8 Hydrazine, N_2H_4, is used as a rocket fuel. When it is burnt in oxygen it produces nitrogen and water.
(a) Write down the balanced equation for the combustion of hydrazine.
(b) Work out the volume of oxygen (measured at S.T.P.) that would be required to complete the combustion of 1 kg of hydrazine. (Assume the molar gas volume to be 22.4 litres at S.T.P.)

9 Petrol consists partly of octane (C_8H_{18}). When octane gas is burnt in an excess of air, carbon dioxide and water vapour are the only products.
(a) Write down the balanced equation for this reaction.
(b) Work out the volume of octane gas that reacts with the oxygen in 500 cm^3 of *air*. Assume that air contains 20% of oxygen by volume. Both volume measurements are made at the same temperature and pressure.

10 (a) Work out the number of moles of sodium chloride in 100 cm^3 of 0.01 M solution.
(b) Work out the volume of 0.50 M sulphuric acid which is required to neutralize 25 cm^3 of 0.10 M sodium hydroxide solution.

11 The equation for one reaction of sodium hydroxide with sulphuric acid is:

$$2NaOH(aq) + H_2SO_4(aq) \longrightarrow Na_2SO_4(aq) + 2H_2O(l)$$

How many cm^3 of 0.05 M sodium hydroxide solution react with:
(*a*) 25 cm^3 of 0.1 M sulphuric acid, and
(*b*) 50 cm^3 of 0.05 M sulphuric acid?

12 Using the fact that the formulas of hydrogen sulphide and hydrogen chloride are $H_2S(g)$ and $HCl(g)$ respectively, try to decide which of these two gases has the higher density.

13 When sodium sulphate solution is added to barium chloride solution, a precipitate of the sparingly soluble salt barium sulphate is formed. In one experiment, 100 cm^3 of 1 M sodium sulphate solution is added to 150 cm^3 of 1 M barium chloride solution.
(*a*) Write the non-ionic equation for the reaction.
(*b*) Work out the number of mol Na_2SO_4 and the number of mol $BaCl_2$ which are used in the experiment.
(*c*) Which reactant is present in excess?
(*d*) Work out the maximum mass of barium sulphate which could be made in the experiment.

(*e*) Describe briefly how you would get the barium sulphate in a pure and dry state.

14 Work out the number of:
(*a*) molecules of 0.11 g of carbon dioxide,
(*b*) molecules in 1 g of hydrogen,
(*c*) ions in 1.17 g of sodium chloride,
(*d*) potassium ions in 500 cm^3 of 0.50 M potassium sulphate solution.

15 Work out the masses of copper and chlorine that can be obtained by passing 1 A for 386 s through molten copper(II) chloride. The Faraday constant is $9.65 \times 10^4 C\,mol^{-1}$.

16 Work out the number of:
(*a*) molecules in 560 cm^3 of oxygen at S.T.P.,
(*b*) atoms in 1.04 g of chromium,
(*c*) magnesium ions in 500 cm^3 of 0.5 M magnesium sulphate solution.

17 Work out the number of coulombs required to produce:
(*a*) 5.4 g of aluminium by the electrolysis of a molten aluminium salt,
(*b*) 280 cm^3 of chlorine measured at S.T.P. by the electrolysis of a molten metal chloride.
($F = 9.65 \times 10^4 C\,mol^{-1}$, and the molar gas volume at S.T.P. is 22.4 litres)

Basic facts

- **The steps in working out problems involving calculations are usually as follows:**
  1 Write the balanced equation for the reaction.
  2 From the equation, write down in moles the relationship you will need to use.
  3 Change the relationship in moles to the units you need.
  4 Then use the information you are given in the question.
  Compare these steps with the directions contained in Fig. 26.1, page 94.

Chemicals from nature I

27 Metals from rocks

Metals and ores

A **mineral** is a single substance found in rocks. Rocks can be made of one mineral only or, more usually, several different minerals. **Ores** are minerals from which a metal can be extracted (Fig. 27.1). Most ores are compounds of metals, though a few are elements: gold and silver are often found in rocks as the elements. But metals higher than gold and silver in the reactivity series are almost always found in compounds.

Whenever a metal is *extracted* from one of its compounds, the chemical reaction is called *reduction*, even if the compound is not an oxide. This is a new use of the word reduction compared with the way it is used on page 23.

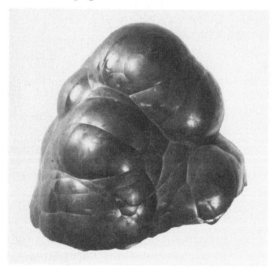

Fig. 27.1 *left* Kidney iron ore (haematite)   *upper right* Galena   *lower right* Copper pyrites

Fig. 27.2 shows the most common metals that are found, either alone or joined with other elements in the earth's rocks. Most of the well-known metals, such as copper, lead and zinc, are really quite rare. Some scientists think that at the rate we are using these rarer metals, we shall have used up all the known deposits of their ores in another few decades.

Metal extractions and the reactivity series

Table 27.1 describes how four well-known metals are extracted from their common ores. The order of these metals is their order in the reactivity series.

Fig. 27.2

the rest (Cu, Pb, Zn, etc)

Ti (titanium)

Al

Mg

K

Na

Ca

Fe

Very reactive metals form compounds which are difficult to reduce, while less reactive metals form compounds which are easier to reduce. Reduction by electrolysis is the usual extraction process for reactive metals, though it is possible (but expensive) to extract them by heating the ore with an even more reactive metal. It is certainly not possible to reduce the ores of reactive metals using carbon in the form of coke. (Coke is made by strongly heating coal in the absence of air.)

Coke is a common reducing agent in the extraction of metals which are found in the middle or the lower half of the reactivity series. For the sulphide ores of metals low in the reactivity series, the extraction is sometimes carried out just by heating the ore in a carefully controlled supply of air.

The reduction process is one of three main stages in the production of a pure metal from the rocks containing its ore.

1 Preliminary concentration (the separation of the metal compound from other substances present in the ore).
2 Reduction of the ore to the metal.
3 Refining (purification) the metal.

The production of a particular metal may involve one, two or all three of these stages.

Stage 1 may include a process called **flotation**. The crushed mixture of ore and soil or rock is shaken with a liquid (water or oil) containing a 'frothing' agent. The ore floats in the froth while the waste material is 'wetted' and sinks.

A different and simpler separation process (called **panning**) is being used in Fig. 27.3. Two old-timers are prospecting for gold in the United States of America. The gold has a density of $19.3\,\mathrm{g\,cm^{-3}}$ and sinks to the bottom of the 'pan' of water, while the less dense rock is washed away.

Other processes are used to concentrate ores besides flotation, and some may involve chemical reactions. An example of this kind of purification process is found in the production of aluminium (page 101).

Stage 3 (refining the metal) is used if a metal is required in a very pure form and if the process employed in stage 2 does not produce metal with this high level of purity. **Electrorefining** (purification by electrolysis) is used for making very pure copper (see below).

You should be able to identify some or all of the three stages in each of the metal extractions that follow. The first metal dealt with is not very reactive (it comes near the bottom of the reactivity series) and the last ones are reactive (they come towards the top of the reactivity series).

Fig. 27.3

Extracting copper

The main ore of copper is copper pyrites (a sulphide, see Table 27.1) but some copper is also extracted from malachite (a carbonate: copper(II) carbonate dihydroxide).

Table 27.1

Metal	Ore	Method of extraction
Sodium	Rock salt (sodium chloride)	Electrolysis of molten ore
Aluminium	Bauxite (aluminium oxide)	
Iron	Haematite (iron(III) oxide)	Reduction of ore using coke (carbon)
Copper	Copper pyrites (copper(II) iron(II) disulphide)	Heating ore alone in air

The first stage is to separate the copper pyrites from the unwanted earthy material dug up along with it. This is done by flotation. Copper pyrites also contains iron which is removed by roasting the ore with sand, when the iron reacts to form a molten slag of iron silicate. The residue from this process is then heated with a controlled amount of air. This oxidizes the sulphur to sulphur dioxide but the copper, being unreactive, is left as the metal.

$$Cu_2S(s) + O_2(g) \longrightarrow 2Cu(l) + SO_2(g)$$

The copper produced in this way is 99.8% pure, but this is still not pure enough to use the metal in electrical wiring because even small traces of impurities lower its conducting properties.

Fig. 27.5 Removing the cathodes during the electrorefining of copper

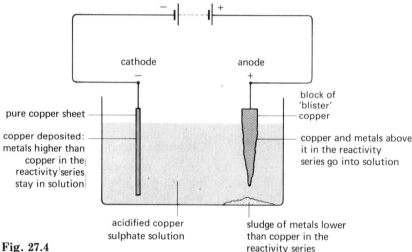

Fig. 27.4

Figs. 27.4 and 27.5 show the way the electrorefining of 'blister' copper is carried out. The copper is the anode dissolved and pure copper is deposited on the cathode. Some of the impurities in the 'blister' copper, such as iron, also dissolve from the anode, but they are not deposited on the cathode. A few of the impurities, such as gold and silver, do not dissolve and they fall to the bottom of the cells as sludge. This sludge is a valuable by-product of the process.

Extracting iron

In the laboratory it is more difficult to extract iron from an iron ore than to extract copper from malachite. This is because iron is higher than copper in the reactivity series and so is more strongly bound to other elements in its ores.

Even so, iron can be extracted in industry using coke if the temperature of the mixture is kept around 1200 °C. Hot air is blown into the blast furnace (Fig. 27.6) through nozzles called tuyeres (pronounced twee-yairs). This air reacts with the hot coke to form carbon monoxide.

$$2C(s) + O_2(g) \longrightarrow 2CO(g)$$

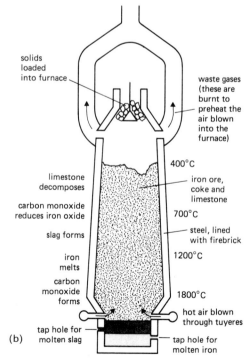

Fig. 27.6(a) Blast furnace in eastern England

Fig. 27.6(b) Diagram of blast furnace

Carbon monoxide is a very good reducing agent (page 23) and it is this, not the carbon, that is mainly responsible for reducing the iron ore to iron. If the iron ore is haematite (iron(III) oxide), the equation for this extraction is

$$Fe_2O_3(s) + 3CO(g) \longrightarrow 2Fe(l) + 3CO_2(g)$$

However, just in the hottest part of the furnace next to the tuyeres where the temperature is about 180 °C, coke is the reducing agent.

$$Fe_2O(s) + 3C(s) \longrightarrow 2Fe(l) + 3CO(g)$$

Both these equations show that the temperature is high enough for the iron to be produced in the molten (liquid) state.

The iron ore contains sandy and dirty impurities which have to be removed. The limestone in the furnace is used to do this job. First it decomposes to form calcium oxide which then reacts with the impurities to form molten slag. This trickles down the furnace to collect on top of the molten iron. Both the slag and the iron can be run off from separate tap holes.

The iron produced by the blast furnace contains between 2.5 and 4.5 % carbon. This causes the iron to be strong but brittle. Steel is made by reducing this percentage of carbon in the iron (page 105).

Extracting reactive metals

Both sodium and magnesium are reactive metals that are produced by the electrolysis of their molten chlorides. Sodium chloride comes from rock salt deposits underground, while magnesium chloride is often extracted from sea water. Electrolytic extractions always produce very pure metals and so there is no need for further purification.

Large electrical currents are needed for these electrolyses to provide enough energy to break down the compounds and also to keep the electrolytes in the molten state. A cheap supply of electricity, often from hydroelectric power (HEP), is a big advantage.

Aluminium is extracted by the electrolysis of molten aluminium oxide. The main ore of aluminium is bauxite, which is an impure form of this oxide, so in the first stage of the extraction, the bauxite is purified. It is heated with hot sodium hydroxide solution under pressure. Because aluminium oxide is amphoteric (page 85), it reacts with the alkali.

$$Al_2O_3(s) + 2NaOH(aq) \longrightarrow 2NaAlO_2(aq) + H_2O(l)$$
$$\text{sodium aluminate}$$

The solution is then filtered to remove all the insoluble impurities. When the reverse of the reaction represented by the above equation occurs, hydrated aluminium oxide is precipitated from the solution. This is then heated to drive off the water to form pure aluminium oxide.

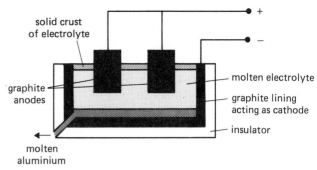

Fig. 27.7

The second stage of the extraction process is the electrolysis. The electrolysis of pure molten aluminium oxide is not possible because its melting point is very high (over 2000 °C) and the liquid is a poor conductor. But the pure aluminium oxide dissolves in molten cryolite (Na_3AlF_6) at 900 °C to give a mixture that conducts well. This mixture is electrolysed using graphite (carbon) anodes and the carbon lining of the cell as the cathode (Fig. 27.7). Aluminium is produced at the cathode and this collects at the bottom of the cell as a liquid.

$$Al^{3+}(l) + 3e^- \longrightarrow Al(l)$$

Oxygen is formed at the anodes.

$$2O^{2-}(l) - 4e^- \longrightarrow O_2(g)$$

Because of the high temperature needed for this electrolysis, the oxygen reacts with the carbon anodes. This means that the anodes are gradually burnt away and have to be replaced periodically.

QUESTIONS

1 (a) Name *two* gases and *one* solid that can be used as reducing agents in the extraction of metals from their ores.
(b) Which one of these three would you use to reduce malachite to copper in the laboratory? Give reasons for your answer.
(c) What are the hazards (if any) associated with the use of each of the reducing agents you named in (a)?

2 Here is some information about the extraction of four metals.

Metal	Method of extraction
Chromium	Reduction of oxide by aluminium
Lead	Reduction of oxide by coke
Magnesium	Electrolysis of molten chloride
Titanium	Reduction of chloride by magnesium

(a) Which two of these metals are extracted using a more reactive metal as a reducing agent?
(b) What other extraction method could possibly have been used for these two metals?
(c) What is the third extraction method given in the table?
(d) Using the information in the table and your knowledge of the reactivity series, write down an order of reactivity for the four metals, putting the most reactive one first.

3 Fig. 27.8 shows some dates in the history of the extraction of metals. What is the pattern in this that links with the reactivity series for metals?

Key words

ore

extraction (of metals)

reduction (of ores)

concentration (of ores)

flotation

electrorefining

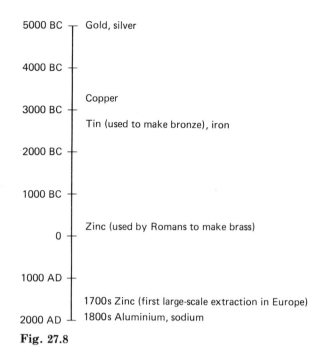

5000 BC	Gold, silver
4000 BC	
3000 BC	Copper
	Tin (used to make bronze), iron
2000 BC	
1000 BC	
0	Zinc (used by Romans to make brass)
1000 AD	
	1700s Zinc (first large-scale extraction in Europe)
2000 AD	1800s Aluminium, sodium

Fig. 27.8

Basic facts

- The ease with which a metal can be extracted from its ore is related to the position of the metal in the reactivity series.

- The oxides of moderately reactive or less reactive metals can be reduced by heating them with carbon (charcoal or coke). Carbon monoxide is also a suitable reducing agent for these oxides.

- Reactive metals are usually extracted by the electrolysis of their molten oxides or chlorides.

28 Using metals

Metals and alloys

The important properties of metals are discussed in Chapter 9. You should be able to link these properties with the three uses of metals shown in Figs. 28.1 to 28.3. There are no other materials which have this set of most useful properties.

For some uses, metals need to be very pure. This is why electrorefining of the 'impure' metal produced by the extraction process is sometimes carried out, for example with copper (page 100).

For many purposes, mixtures of two or more metals are used. These mixtures (called **alloys**) are made by melting the purified metals together and letting them cool and solidify. Alloys have different properties from the separate metals, and nowadays metallurgists can often make alloys with the properties they want for a particular job.

Generally, alloys are harder and stronger than the separate metals and have lower melting points. They may also be more resistant to **corrosion** (page 104).

Tables 28.1 and 28.2 on page 103 show the properties and uses of some common alloys.

Fig. 28.1

Table 28.1 Some common non-steel alloys

Alloy	Percentage composition	Important properties	Uses
Brass	Cu 60 Zn 40	Harder and stronger than copper but just as corrosion-resistant	Ornaments
Bronze	Cu 85 Sn 15	As for brass	Statues, plaques, ships' propellers
Cupro-nickel	Cu 75 Ni 25	As for brass, looks silvery	'Silver' coins
Duralumin	Al 95 Cu 4 Traces of Mn and Mg	Density just as low as aluminium or magnesium but much stronger and more corrosion-resistant	Aircraft construction, kitchen utensils
Magnalium	Al 70 Mg 30		
Solder	Pb 67 Sn 33	Harder than lead and has an even lower melting point	Joining wires and pipes
Pewter	Sn 80 Pb 20		Ornaments
Type metal	Pb 80 Sb 15 Sn 5	Harder than lead and has an even lower melting point	Printing
9 carat gold	Cu 67 Au 33	Harder (and cheaper) than pure gold	Jewellery, decorative work

Table 28.2 Some common steel alloys

Alloy	Percentage composition	Important properties	Uses
Mild steel	Fe > 99 C < 1 Traces of other elements	Much stronger than iron	Motor car bodies
Invar steel	Fe 63 Ni 36 Trace of C	Much lower coefficient of expansion than iron	In thermostats and clock pendulums
Stainless steel	Fe 85 Cr 14 Ni 1	Harder than ordinary steel and much more corrosion-resistant	Cutlery, ornaments

Fig. 28.2

Fig. 28.3

The choice of the best metal or alloy for a particular use depends on which properties are most important.

1 Where lightness (low density) is not so important (as in cars, ships, bridges and so on), steel is the usual choice because it is *strong* but also relatively *cheap*.
2 Where *lightness* is important (as in aircraft and spacecraft), the less dense and more expensive aluminium alloys are often chosen.
3 Where *corrosion-resistance* is important (as in turbine blades, ships' propellers, ships' hulls and coinage), either a special alloy must be used or the metal/alloy chosen must be treated to minimize corrosion (see below). A ship's propeller made of bronze is shown in Fig. 28.4. Car exhaust pipes are usually made of mild steel but this rusts quite quickly. Much more expensive stainless steel exhaust pipes are sometimes used and these have the advantage of lasting far longer.

Fig. 28.4

4 Where *appearance* is important (as in ornaments and jewellery), metals or alloys with an attractive colour or lustre are chosen. Gold (Fig. 28.5) is an obvious example but it is usually alloyed with copper and silver to make it harder (and cheaper). Brass and bronze are also attractive alloys and they have the extra advantages of being stronger and easier to cast than pure copper.

There is one pure metal that has many of the useful properties possessed by alloys. This is the

Fig. 28.5 Gilding iron and leather decorated with gold leaf

metal called titanium. Its density is only $4.5\,\mathrm{g\,cm^{-3}}$, it is very strong, resists quite high temperatures and it has excellent resistance to corrosion. Added to the fact that it occurs quite widely in rocks (Fig. 27.2), you might expect to find titanium in common use. However, it is a reactive metal and difficult to extract from its ores. It is necessary to employ an expensive process involving the reduction of titanium(IV) chloride ($TiCl_4$) by magnesium in an inert atmosphere of argon. Titanium is used in the form of the pure metal where no other metal is suitable and when the cost of the titanium can be justified (Fig. 28.6).

Fig. 28.6 A titanium tank which holds the liquid fuel used to power the lunar module of one of the American space missions

The best-known alloys are the various steels. Mild steel contains iron and very small amounts of a non-metal (carbon) rather than another metal. Other steels, like stainless steel and invar steel, contain iron and other metals as well as traces of carbon.

The iron produced by a blast furnace contains

Fig. 28.7

many impurities and it is very brittle because of the relatively high proportion of carbon (up to about 4.5%). To produce a steel from this impure iron, the unwanted impurities must first be removed. This is done by blowing oxygen onto the surface of molten iron in a furnace (Fig. 28.7). The impurities are oxidized and either they are given off as gaseous oxides or else they combine with calcium oxide (from added limestone) to form a slag which floats on the surface of the iron. When the purity of the iron has reached the right level, the furnace is tapped. If an 'alloy steel' is being produced (stainless steel, invar steel, and so on), then the required metals are added at this stage.

If a source of cheap electricity is available, steel can also be made from iron in an electric arc furnace. There are two such furnaces at the Point Lisas industrial estate in Trinidad.

The corrosion of metals

Everyone knows that iron forms a layer of brown crumbly rust on its surface when it is exposed to the 'weather'. Rusting is caused by the reaction of iron with oxygen and water in the air (page 20).

Many other metals corrode in air. You can tell this because they lose their shine and sometimes change colour as well. The surfaces of copper water-tanks and bronze statues start off copper-coloured but slowly go brownish, grey and then green as they corrode.

The layer formed on most metals by corrosion is an oxide or a carbonate of the metal. Unlike rust itself, this layer does not usually flake off quickly. Instead it stays there and helps to stop the air from attacking the metal underneath. So these metals have their own 'do-it-yourself' protection. This is why some metals like aluminium resist corrosion better than

iron even though they are higher in the reactivity series than iron (Data Sheet 3, page 282).

It is very difficult to stop iron and ordinary steel from rusting, though regular painting or greasing does help. One of the best ways is to make an alloy of iron and another metal: stainless steel (Table 28.2) is a good example.

But steel alloys can be much more expensive than mild steel. No-one would think of making very long underground pipelines or large ships out of stainless steel; and yet the mild steel in these items could rust very quickly because acids in the soil and salt in the sea speed up the process a lot.

Another obvious way to rustproof iron or steel is to cover it with another metal that is more resistant to corrosion. This is being done with the shelf racks shown in Fig. 8.4 (page 26). The shelf racks act as cathodes, pure chromium is used as the anode and the electrolyte is a solution of chromic acid. The chromium is dissolved from the anode and deposited on the cathode. Car fenders which are made of steel are chromium plated in this way.

Two other metals used to protect iron are zinc and tin:

1. In a process called **galvanizing**, the iron or steel is dipped into molten zinc. A coating of zinc is left on the iron as it is removed and is allowed to cool slowly.
2. The layer of tin on 'tin' cans used as food containers is usually electroplated on to the steel.

Galvanized iron is used in the form of corrugated iron for constructing some buildings (Fig. 28.8). It cannot be used for food containers because it is possible that a layer of zinc could dissolve in the contents of the can to form zinc compounds, which are poisonous.

Fig. 28.8

Galvanized iron has a big advantage over tin-plated iron. If the layer of zinc is scratched, it is the zinc that is corroded in preference to the iron. In contrast, if a tin can is scratched, the steel begins to corrode even more rapidly than if the tin were not present. You should be able to explain both these observations after you have performed Experiment 28.1.

Experiment 28.1 Investigating the rusting of iron nails

Use three shiny iron nails in this experiment. Wrap a small piece of zinc foil tightly round a 1 cm length of one nail, and do the same to another nail with a small piece of copper or tin foil. (CARE: the edges of the foils may be sharp.) Leave the third nail as it is.

Put each nail into a separate Petri dish and cover it with sodium chloride solution (Fig. 28.9). Rusting can take place in the solution because it contains dissolved air as well as sodium chloride.

Leave the nails for at least a day. After this, look for signs of brown rust on each nail.

☛ Which nail has rusted the most, and which one has rusted the least?

The order of reactivity towards oxygen of the three metals is (most reactive first): zinc, iron, tin/copper. When a metal such as zinc is wrapped round the iron nail, the zinc corrodes rather than the iron. This is because zinc is more reactive than iron. But if the metal wrapped round the nail is less reactive than iron, the iron rusts quickly while the unreactive metal (in this case, copper or tin) does not change at all.

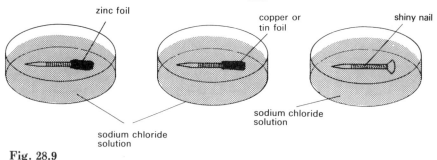

Fig. 28.9

QUESTIONS

1 (a) What is an *alloy*?
(b) Why are alloys often better than the pure metals for a whole variety of uses in the home and in industry? Give at least one example.
(c) State *one* reason why some alloys are not widely used despite having very useful properties.

2 Type-metal is an alloy with the percentage composition lead (Pb) 80, antimony (Sb) 15, tin (Sn) 5. It is used in printing because it is hard, melts at a low temperature (240 °C) and expands on solidifying.
(a) What are the differences in composition between type-metal and solder?
(b) Give one property which type-metal and solder have in common.
(c) Would you expect the melting point of pure lead to be higher or lower than 240 °C? Give a reason for your answer.

3 (a) Find as many ways as you can in which iron or steel can be protected from rusting, and make a list of these.
(b) Why do the following articles made of iron or steel not rust easily (if at all): cutlery, the fenders of cars, a can for storing food, a metal bridge?

4 The processes of burning and rusting have some features in common. Make a list of their differences and a list of their similarities.

5 Fig. 28.10 shows some zinc blocks on the steel hull of a ship. Explain how these help to protect the hull from the corrosive effects of sea water.

6 Name a metal that is used for:
(a) the cases of 'dry' cells for flashlights,
(b) a paint primer for coating iron or steel,
(c) electrical wiring,
(d) making car batteries (accumulators).

Fig. 28.10 Zinc alloy bars fitted to the rudder and stern of an oil tanker. At intervals of a few years, the hull needs to be refitted with new bars when the old ones have completely corroded

7 Explain why iron does not rust if its galvanized coating is scratched whereas the iron in a scratched or damaged 'tin' can rusts very quickly indeed.

Key words

alloys   corrosion   electroplating   galvanizing

Basic facts

- Alloys are usually mixtures of two or more metals, though the best-known alloy (mild steel) is a mixture of a metal (iron) and a non-metal (carbon).

- Alloys often have improved properties over pure metals and so have a wide variety of uses.

- All but the very least reactive metals tarnish in air but the corroded layer on the surface usually protects the metal from further attack.

- The rust that forms on iron and mild steel does *not* protect the metal underneath. However, there are several ways in which steel can be rust-proofed.

- A more reactive metal placed in contact with iron will corrode in preference to the iron and so protect it from rusting.

29 Where do fuels come from?

Wood and charcoal

Wood is sometimes used as a fuel but only on a small scale. It burns quite quickly and has a lower heating value than most other fuels (page 207). Charcoal (called 'coal' in Caribbean countries) is a better fuel because it burns more slowly and has twice the heating value of wood.

Charcoal is a useful fuel in parts of the world where there is a lot of wood and where other fuels are not easily available. The traditional method used to make charcoal from wood is shown in Fig. 29.1.

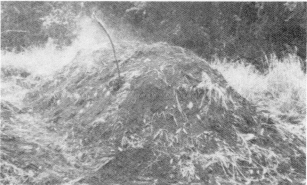

Fig. 29.1 *above* Pieces of wood are put into a neat pile and covered with grass and then soil
upper right A small hole is left in the grass and soil where the burning of the wood can be started
lower right Some of the wood burns and heats the rest of the wood. In a few days, most of the wood is changed to charcoal

The pieces of wood are piled up and heated under a covering of grass and soil. The heat comes from the burning of a small amount of the wood. The rest of the wood is then decomposed to charcoal by this heat. The process takes a few days.

When charcoal is produced for fuel on a small scale, the trees that have been used are replaced naturally as more trees grow. But if charcoal is made on a large scale, it is important to plan the cutting of trees carefully and to plant young trees to replace those that have been used. If this is not done, forests can be destroyed and the nature of the countryside can be completely changed. Such a change is almost always harmful and in some countries serious soil erosion occurs because the roots of trees no longer help to bind the soil grains together.

Fossil fuels

When living things die, their remains are usually broken down by bacteria to simple compounds such as carbon dioxide, water and ammonia. But sometimes in the past this total decay has been prevented because of the local geology, relief and climate, and other chemical changes have occurred to form **fossil fuels**. The word *fossil* shows that the fuels were formed from once-living material. The formation of fossil fuels – coal, crude oil (petroleum) and natural gas – is shown in the carbon cycle (Fig. 30.1, page 111). You should note that this diagram does not show the 'normal' decay of dead material to carbon dioxide, water and ammonia in the atmosphere.

Coal is formed by the chemical alteration of wood from ancient forests. It occurs in thin layers between other layers of *sedimentary* rocks (rocks formed by the hardening of layers of sediment). Some natural gas may also originate in this way. Oil and the rest of the natural gas come from the chemical alteration of ancient marine organisms rather than from ancient forests. Unlike coal, oil and gas do not stay where they were formed. Instead they move upwards through *permeable* rocks, that is rocks that either have joined-up spaces between their grains or have a network of fissures and cracks. Oil and gas cannot move through impermeable rocks unless they are cut by **faults** (large displacements of the rocks which occur during earthquakes).

If you were to drill a hole from the surface down through the layers of rocks, you would find that some layers are permeable and others are impermeable. These layers control what happens to the oil or gas as it rises towards the surface.

Suppose that a layer of permeable rock is 'sandwiched' between sloping layers of impermeable rock (Fig. 29.2). Oil or gas could keep on moving upwards through the permeable layer, even though it could not enter the impermeable layer above. But if the

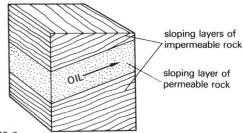

Fig. 29.2

'sandwich' is folded into a 'hill' of rock layers (Fig. 29.3), the oil or gas would then be trapped in a place where it could not move upwards or sideways. The

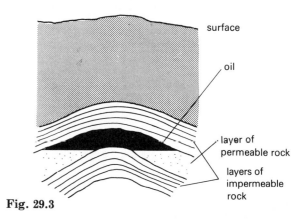

Fig. 29.3

oil or gas would also be trapped if the permeable rock was cut by an impermeable barrier (Fig. 29.4).

The 'hill' of rock under the ground is called an **anticline**, and the sudden break in the rocks (Fig. 29.4) is a fault. These are two of the most common kinds of oil and gas traps, but there are other kinds as well.

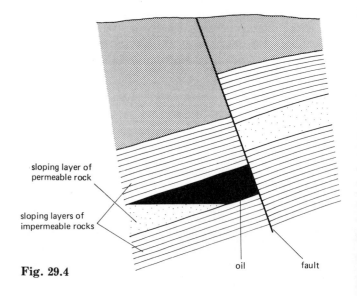

Fig. 29.4

It is possible for some oil or gas to continue rising through permeable rocks and along faults until it reaches the surface. The gas, of course, is then lost but the oil may accumulate. This is the origin of the famous pitch-lake of Trinidad (Fig. 29.5). The pitch (asphalt) was formed by the loss of the volatile fractions and the partial oxidation of surface oil by the oxygen in the air.

Fig. 29.5

Finding oil and gas

The search for fossil fuels is being carried out all over the world, both under land and under the sea. Oil and gas were first extracted from fields which were under land, but recent advances in technology have given rise to the development of many offshore fields such as those off the East Coast of Trinidad and in the Gulf of Paria.

The first task of the oil prospectors is to find certain arrangements of rock layers that might act as oil or gas traps (see Figs. 29.3 and 29.4). One way of searching is to make a **seismic survey**.

Small explosions are set off at the surface of the land or the sea and the shock waves from these move through the rocks. One kind of wave is like a sound wave travelling through the air: a 'pulse of vibration' moves through the rock. Detectors 'listen' for the waves that arrive back at the surface after they have been reflected by some of the rock layers. Fig. 29.6 shows the method that is used.

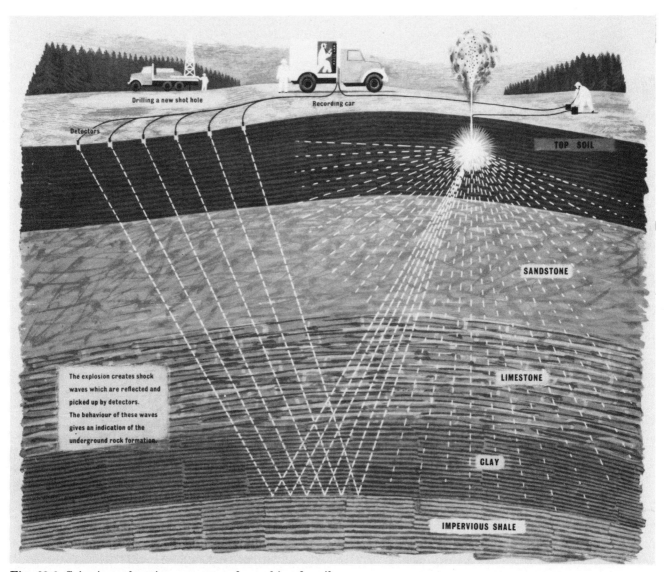

Drilling a new shot hole

Recording car

Detectors

TOP SOIL

SANDSTONE

LIMESTONE

CLAY

The explosion creates shock waves which are reflected and picked up by detectors. The behaviour of these waves gives an indication of the underground rock formation.

IMPERVIOUS SHALE

Fig. 29.6 Seismic exploration: one way of searching for oil

Once some promising arrangements of rock layers have been found, the next task is to drill some boreholes. A diamond core head or drill bit is used at the end of a 10 m length of pipe. When the 10 m of pipe have disappeared into the rock, another length is screwed onto the end (Fig. 29.7) and drilling begins again.

Fig. 29.7

The head or bit gets very hot, and specially prepared 'mud' has to be pumped down the drill pipe to cool it. If a drill bit is used for the drilling, this circulating mud carries rock chippings up to the surface where they are examined. If the core head is used, whole cores of rock are lifted up to the surface. Whichever method is used, geologists aim to discover the order of the rocks in the borehole and whether any of them contain fossil fuels or other useful materials.

Boreholes for oil and gas may go down to a depth of several thousand metres. In offshore drilling, the main problem is to keep the drilling rig completely steady, despite the movement of the wind and the waves.

Most boreholes produce no gas or oil at all. But if a strike of oil or gas is made, the next step is to drill several more boreholes around it to see how large the field is. It is also important to find out how easy it will be to get the oil or gas out. Finally, a decision is made about whether or not to go into full production.

Looking for fossil fuels of all kinds is now very big business. Immense sums of money are required to carry out seismic surveys and to drill boreholes. But the rewards for success are much larger still.

QUESTIONS

1 Making charcoal from wood is often referred to as 'charcoal burning'. Explain why the word 'burning' is not a very appropriate word to use for this process.

2 Explain why the burning of wood causes much more air pollution than using charcoal as a fuel.

3 'Fuels such as oil, natural gas and our food have stored-up energy from the sun which is released when we burn the fuels in air or oxidize the food in our bodies.'

Write a short essay explaining this statement.

4 (a) If your country has reserves of crude oil or natural gas, use reference books to complete a table with these headings.

Kind of fossil fuel	Places where fossil fuel comes from	Places where prospecting for fossil fuel is going on

(b) If your country imports fossil fuels, find out which countries are the main suppliers.

Key words

fossil fuels   oil and gas traps   seismic survey

Basic facts

- **Charcoal is made when wood is decomposed by heat in the absence of oxygen.**

- **Charcoal is a better fuel than wood, but neither is often used on a very large scale. However, charcoal is increasingly used in the Caribbean because of the rising costs of imported fossil fuels.**

- **Coal is a fossil fuel which is found in seams in sedimentary rocks.**

- **Crude oil and natural gas are fossil fuels which are usually found trapped underground in permeable rocks.**

- **Seismic surveys and trial drillings are two important methods of prospecting for oil and gas, both on land and under the sea.**

30 The chemistry of fuels

What are fuels made of?

Carbon dioxide is the only product of the combustion of charcoal. This result suggests that charcoal contains carbon and perhaps some oxygen. In fact, charcoal consists mainly of carbon (together with small amounts of metal compounds that were originally present in the wood).

Many fuels burn to produce carbon dioxide and water and a lot of these fuels are hydrocarbons (natural gas, kerosine, gasoline and so on). These fuels, apart from natural gas, are products of the fractional distillation of crude oil (page 270). The fuel ethanol is a compound of carbon, hydrogen and oxygen and so this also burns to form carbon dioxide and water.

The carbon cycle

The part of the carbon cycle that involves fuels is shown in Fig. 30.1. In various compounds, carbon (like nitrogen, page 134) is circulated between the air, the earth's surface and the rocks beneath the surface. On the surface, many of these compounds are in living things. Coal, crude oil and natural gas are formed by the death, burial and partial decay of some of these living things.

'burnt' as fuel in the oxygen from the air, and carbon dioxide and water vapour are produced. Respiration occurs in both animals and plants, though plants use up more carbon dioxide in photosynthesis than they produce in respiration.

Normally, all these processes might be expected to keep a constant amount of carbon dioxide in the air. But it seems that Man has interfered with this balance by burning more and more fuel. Scientists estimate that over the last century, the percentage of carbon dioxide in the air has risen from 0.030 to 0.033, an increase of about 10%.

This increase is only about half of what it should be according to a calculation based on all the fuel burnt during that time. This might be explained by saying that the rest of the carbon dioxide has been dissolved by water on the earth's surface (Fig. 30.1). You can find out more about this other part of the carbon cycle on page 118.

Fuels and air pollution

In a good supply of oxygen, a hydrocarbon fuel burns to form carbon dioxide and water vapour (gases already present in the air). For example, the equation for the burning of methane, the main component of

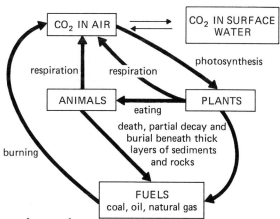

Fig. 30.1 Part of the carbon cycle

Green plants use carbon dioxide from the air, along with water and energy from the sun's rays, to synthesize carbohydrates (page 226). The green pigment in plants (chlorophyll) is essential for this process called **photosynthesis**. The simplest equation for photosynthesis is

$$6CO_2(g) + 6H_2O(l) \longrightarrow C_6H_{12}O_6(s) + 6O_2(g)$$

The reverse of this reaction happens in **respiration** (breathing). The carbohydrates (food) are

natural gas, is

$$CH_4(g) + 2O_2(g) \longrightarrow CO_2(g) + 2H_2O(g)$$

But if the supply of oxygen is limited, other products can be formed. For example, soot (carbon) can be seen on the inside of an upturned beaker placed over a burning candle when there is not enough air entering from outside. Other fuels can also burn to form carbon (soot).

$$CH_4(g) + O_2(g) \longrightarrow C(s) + 2H_2O(g)$$

Fig. 30.2

Soot in the air is a **pollutant**, that is a substance not present in 'pure' air but which is added to it, usually by man-made processes (Fig. 30.2).

Between the extremes of complete burning of a hydrocarbon fuel (which forms carbon dioxide) and very incomplete burning (which forms carbon), there is a half-way stage at which there is enough oxygen to oxidize the carbon, but not all the way to carbon dioxide. The products of this burning are carbon monoxide and water vapour.

$$2CH_4(g) + 3O_2(g) \longrightarrow 2CO(g) + 4H_2O(g)$$

Carbon monoxide is a very poisonous gas. People can be killed within half an hour if they breathe air containing as little as 0.1% by volume of carbon monoxide. It is particularly dangerous because it has no smell, taste or colour to indicate its presence in the air.

When we breathe, oxygen is absorbed in our blood and is then carried around our bodies. The oxygen does not dissolve in blood, but forms a compound with haemoglobin in a reversible reaction:

haemoglobin(aq) + oxygen(g) $\rightleftharpoons$
               oxyhaemoglobin(aq)

If we breathe a mixture of air and carbon monoxide, another reaction is possible:

haemoglobin(aq) + carbon monoxide(g) $\rightleftharpoons$
               carboxyhaemoglobin(aq)

Haemoglobin reacts more readily with carbon monoxide than oxygen. So if we breathe mixtures of air and carbon monoxide, carboxyhaemoglobin is formed in our blood, so lowering the blood's ability to carry oxygen around our bodies. This oxygen shortage can result in unconsciousness and then death.

When gasoline (mostly octane, C_8H_{18}) burns in a car engine, some carbon monoxide is formed and is passed into the air through the exhaust pipe. This kind of air pollution can be a serious problem in busy city centres. In the worst areas, police directing traffic can work for short periods only before they are affected by it (Fig. 30.3).

Fig. 30.3

There is another dangerous pollutant that comes from gasoline. To improve the efficiency with which the car engine burns its fuel, a compound of lead called lead tetraethyl, $Pb(C_2H_5)_4$ is often added to the gasoline. Another compound, dibromoethane, is also added so that the lead is swept out with the exhaust fumes rather than deposited on the walls of the engine cylinders. So in areas with a lot of traffic, there are lead compounds in the air we breathe.

Even though the concentrations of these are small, the lead accumulates in our blood and body tissues and is not easily released. Lead is a poison and can cause abnormal behaviour, brain damage and even death.

Scientists differ over how much harm can be done by the lead pollution from car exhausts. However, it is known that lead compounds from this source can cause the death of plants on roadside verges. Many countries are introducing laws to reduce or even eliminate the amount of lead that is put into gasoline.

Two other pollutants in the air are sulphur dioxide and the oxides of nitrogen. Sulphur dioxide comes mainly from the burning of sulphur-containing coal and oil in power stations (page 144).

Nitrogen oxides are formed by the sparking of air in car engines. Los Angeles in the USA is a city with a smog problem caused partly by these oxides (Fig. 30.4). A million cars and some large oil refineries add thousands of tonnes of pollutants to the air each day. Because of the bowl-shaped local relief and light winds, the pollutants cannot easily disperse. The ultraviolet radiation from the sun starts off reactions involving hydrocarbons and nitrogen oxides which produce a yellowy brown haze.

Fig. 30.4

QUESTIONS

1 When a beaker containing cold water is held over a bunsen flame, moisture quickly forms on the outside. After a short time, this disappears and the outside of the beaker gets dry again. Explain these changes.

2 Describe an experiment you can carry out to show that bottled gas or natural gas contains carbon. Explain how the results of your experiment would prove this.

3 Depending on the conditions, hydrocarbon fuels can burn to form carbon, carbon monoxide or carbon dioxide.
(a) Explain why this is so.
(b) Which two of these products are undesirable? What effects can each of them have on our environment?
(c) The third of these products is already present in the air and is not a pollutant. Which one is this?

4 Could a charcoal stove (coal pot) produce carbon monoxide rather than carbon dioxide? Explain your answer carefully.

5 Find an example given in this book of an important use of carbon monoxide.

6 A small percentage of wood charcoal is not made up of carbon and cannot be burnt in air. It is left as ash after all the carbon has formed carbon dioxide.

Describe an experiment you could perform to find the percentage of ash in a piece of charcoal.

Key words

hydrocarbon fuels   **photosynthesis**   **air pollution**   **pollutant**

Basic facts

- **Many fuels are hydrocarbons (compounds made from hydrogen and carbon only) or mixtures of hydrocarbons.**

- **Hydrocarbon fuels burn to form carbon dioxide and water vapour when there is a plentiful supply of air. If the air supply is restricted, then some carbon monoxide or carbon (soot) may be formed. These are pollutants.**

- **The element carbon is circulated between the air, the earth's surface and some rocks in a series of chemical reactions that make up the carbon cycle.**

31 Chemicals from limestone

The flow-chart (Fig. 31.1) summarizes the chemical reactions that are mentioned in this chapter. Study it carefully as you work through the chapter.

What is limestone?

Limestone is a sedimentary rock (Fig. 31.2). Some limestones were formed from layers of shells on the sea floor and some others from the coral reefs along ancient tropical coastlines. In both cases the layers of material were pressed down by huge thicknesses of newer materials and, usually, crystals of calcium carbonate were formed which bound the grains and shells together.

Chalk is a special kind of limestone made from microscopic shells of marine organisms. It is very soft and usually contains no crystals of calcium carbonate to bind the shells together. **Marble** is limestone which has been altered by being heated to a high temperature, for example, by a volcanic eruption.

Fig. 31.2

▶ What colour of flame can be seen?
▶ What does this observation tell you about the nature of limestone?

Use the apparatus shown in Fig. 31.3 to heat a small lump of limestone (a marble chip) very strongly.

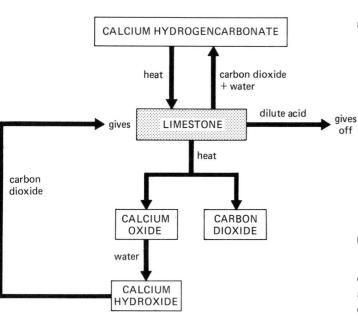

Fig. 31.1

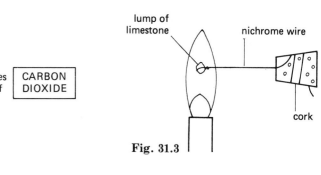

Fig. 31.3

▶ What can you see during heating?

After about 15 minutes, let the solid cool. This is quicklime. Put the quicklime on a watchglass and add one drop of water to it. (CARE: do not let the quicklime come into contact with your skin or your eyes because it can cause burns.)

▶ What happens?

Add more water to the solid, drop by drop, until the chemical reaction stops. The dry solid is now slaked lime.

Put a *little* of the slaked lime in a test-tube and shake it with water. Let the mixture settle and then find the pH value of the solution. Also pass carbon dioxide through some of the *clear* solution.

▶ What happens?
▶ What is the chemical name of slaked lime?

Experiment 31.1 Some tests on limestone

Add a few drops of bench dilute (2 M) hydrochloric acid to a small lump of limestone in a test-tube. Test the gas given off with limewater.

▶ What is this gas?
▶ What does this observation tell you about the nature of limestone?

Carry out the flame test (page 252) on a small amount of powdered limestone.

Table 31.1 shows a chemical analysis of a limestone.

Table 31.1

Test	Result	Conclusion
Dilute hydrochloric acid is added to limestone	The limestone 'fizzes': a gas is given off. This gas (carbon dioxide) makes lime water go cloudy	There is a CARBONATE in limestone
Some crushed limestone is held on a nichrome wire in a Bunsen flame	The flame goes brick red for a time	There is a CALCIUM compound in limestone

Dilute hydrochloric acid reacts with the calcium carbonate, releasing carbon dioxide.

$$CaCO_3(s) + 2HCl(aq)$$
$$\longrightarrow CaCl_2(aq) + CO_2(g) + H_2O(l)$$

When limestone is heated strongly, it forms calcium oxide (quicklime).

$$CaCO_3(s) \longrightarrow CaO(s) + CO_2(g)$$

When a small amount of water is added to calcium oxide, an exothermic reaction called **slaking** takes place and solid calcium hydroxide (slaked lime) is formed.

$$CaO(s) + H_2O(l) \longrightarrow Ca(OH)_2(s)$$

Calcium hydroxide is not very soluble in water. Its solution is alkaline and is often called 'limewater'.

Limestones often contain impurities. This extra material could perhaps be something that reacts with dilute acid without giving off carbon dioxide, or it could be something that is left over as a solid at the end of the reaction.

Experiment 31.2 *Finding the purity of a limestone*

(a) Use the apparatus shown in Fig. 25.6 (page 91). Add exactly 0.30 g of pure calcium carbonate from a bottle to the small test-tube in the flask. When the reaction stops and no more gas collects in the syringe, read its volume on the scale.

(b) Do the experiment again, this time using 0.30 g of finely crushed limestone.

▶ What volume of carbon dioxide do you now collect?
▶ Try to explain any difference between the two volumes collected in parts (a) and (b).

Filter the mixture after all the gas has been given off.

▶ Is there any solid residue on the filter paper?
▶ From the results in (a) and (b), do you think your limestone seems to be pure calcium carbonate?

Using limestone

Limestone has many uses. The rock may be cut into blocks and used as a building stone, or it may be broken up into small chippings and used in a tarmac road surface. It is also an important raw material in a number of industries (Fig. 31.4). Chalk is used in

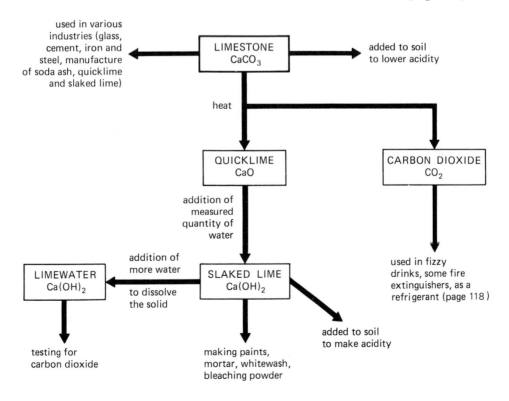

used in various industries (glass, cement, iron and steel, manufacture of soda ash, quicklime and slaked lime) ← **LIMESTONE CaCO₃** → added to soil to lower acidity

heat

QUICKLIME CaO

CARBON DIOXIDE CO₂

addition of measured quantity of water

addition of more water

SLAKED LIME Ca(OH)₂

to dissolve the solid

LIMEWATER Ca(OH)₂

used in fizzy drinks, some fire extinguishers, as a refrigerant (page 118)

added to soil to make acidity

testing for carbon dioxide

making paints, mortar, whitewash, bleaching powder

Fig. 31.4

the cement industry in particular, and marble is a very attractive ornamental stone, especially when polished.

To make glass, a mixture of ground limestone ($CaCO_3$), sand (silica, SiO_2) and sodium carbonate (soda ash, Na_2CO_3) is melted together by heating it to a high temperature. The reaction produces the familiar soda glass, which is made of sodium silicate and unchanged silica.

Fig. 31.5

In a cement works, ground limestone is mixed with clay and water and heated to about 1500 °C in a long rotary kiln (Fig. 31.5). The reaction between the calcium carbonate and the clay (which can be thought of as containing aluminium oxide and silicon dioxide, silica) produces calcium aluminate and calcium silicate. The dry powder made from these two chemicals is what we call cement.

Limestone is also used in the extraction of iron (page 100) and in the manufacture of sodium carbonate (page 126).

Two other important chemicals that can be made from limestone are quicklime and slaked lime (see Experiment 31.1 and Fig. 31.4). The decomposition of limestone by heat is carried out on a large scale in lime-kilns (Fig. 31.6) where the temperature is over 900° C.

Calcium hydroxide is a much cheaper alkali than sodium hydroxide (the cost of the electricity used in the manufacture of sodium hydroxide makes this

alkali expensive). So slaked lime is used in industry as a cheap alternative to sodium hydroxide.

Whitewash is a suspension of calcium hydroxide in water. Mortar is made by mixing sand, slaked lime and water. The setting of mortar is partly the reaction of calcium hydroxide with carbon dioxide in the air as the crystals of calcium carbonate formed make the grains of sand stick together. The weathering of mortar is due to the reaction of the calcium carbonate with water and more carbon dioxide (page 118).

Calcium hydroxide can be used to neutralize the excess of acidity in acidic soils. Powdered limestone can also be used for this purpose. The agricultural fertilizer 'Nitrochalk' is a mixture of ammonium nitrate and calcium carbonate.

Fig. 31.6

More about carbon dioxide

Carbon dioxide is a product in the following reactions.

1 The action of heat on most carbonates (page 38)

e.g. $$CuCO_3(s) \longrightarrow CuO(s) + CO_2(g)$$

2 The reactions between dilute acids and carbonates (page 43) or hydrogencarbonates,

e.g. $Na_2CO_3(s) + 2HCl(aq)$
$$\longrightarrow 2NaCl(aq) + CO_2(g) + H_2O(l)$$

3 The burning of carbon or hydrocarbon fuels in air (page 111)

e.g. $$C(s) + O_2(g) \longrightarrow CO_2(g)$$

The most convenient method for preparing carbon dioxide in the laboratory is the second one because it does not involve the use of heat and the reaction can be controlled by the amount of acid added.

Experiment 31.3 Making and testing carbon dioxide

The apparatus for this experiment is the same as for making hydrogen (Fig. 7.7, page 23), but the chemicals used are calcium carbonate, as limestone (marble) chips, and dilute hydrochloric acid. Because carbon dioxide is only slightly soluble in water, the gas can be collected in the same way as hydrogen.

Make at least four test-tubes full of the gas. Close each tube with a bung. Test the gas with:

(a) damp universal indicator paper or damp blue litmus paper,
(b) a few cm^3 of limewater,
(c) a burning splint plunged into the tube.

Try also to find a way of showing that carbon dioxide has a higher density than air.

Carbon dioxide does not support the combustion of most substances (including a glowing wood splint). However, an exception is magnesium. If a piece of burning magnesium ribbon is quickly lowered into a gas jar of carbon dioxide, it continues to form a residue of white magnesium oxide and black carbon.

$$2Mg(s) + CO_2(g) \longrightarrow 2MgO(s) + C(s)$$

The pouring experiment in Fig. 31.7 shows that carbon dioxide does not support the combustion of candle wax. It also shows that the gas is denser than air.

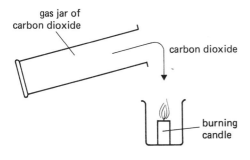

The carbon dioxide extinguishes the burning candle.

Fig. 31.7

If carbon dioxide is bubbled into water, the pH value of the water falls from 7 to 4. If this water is then boiled to drive off the carbon dioxide, the pH value slowly reverts to 7. At room temperature, a given volume of water dissolves about its own volume of carbon dioxide to give a slightly acidic solution, sometimes called carbonic acid. The acidity arises from the reaction of the gas with water to form H$^+$(aq) ions. Since the gas contains no hydrogen, all

these ions must come from the water. One equation for this reaction is

$$CO_2(aq) + H_2O(l) \rightleftharpoons 2H^+(aq) + CO_3^{2-}(aq) \quad (1)$$
carbonate ions

Because the solution does not have a very low pH value and because it is a rather poor conductor of electricity, carbonic acid is a weak acid (page 82). One way of looking at this is to say that the reaction can go in either direction but that it goes much less readily from left to right than from right to left. This explains why relatively few hydrogen ions and carbonate ions are produced by every mole of carbon dioxide and water, and also why hydrogen ions react with carbonate ions to produce carbon dioxide (page 115).

Another possible way in which carbon dioxide could react with water is by this equation:

$$CO_2(aq) + H_2O(l) \rightleftharpoons H^+(aq) + HCO_3^-(aq) \quad (2)$$
hydrogen-
carbonate ions

You should now see that carbonic acid can form two kinds of salt: carbonates and hydrogencarbonates.

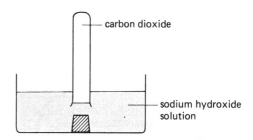

Fig. 31.8

The apparatus for the reaction of carbon dioxide with an alkali is shown in Fig. 31.8. The level of sodium hydroxide solution rises some way up the test-tube as the gas reacts with it. Two reactions are possible depending on the proportions in which the carbon dioxide and alkali are used.

$$2NaOH(aq) + CO_2(g) \longrightarrow Na_2CO_3(aq) + H_2O(l)$$
sodium carbonate
$$NaOH(aq) + CO_2(g) \longrightarrow NaHCO_3(aq)$$
sodium
hydrogencarbonate

Sodium carbonate and sodium hydrogencarbonate are both salts. Acids which can form two kinds of salts when neutralized with an alkali are called **dibasic** acids (page 83).

Carbon dioxide forms a white solid when it is passed into limewater. (This is the limewater test for carbon dioxide.) If this solid is filtered off and tested with a dilute acid, carbon dioxide is reformed. This shows that the white solid is probably a carbonate. Because it is formed from calcium hydroxide (limewater), it must be calcium carbonate.

$$Ca(OH)_2(aq) + CO_2(g) \longrightarrow CaCO_3(s) + H_2O(l)$$

When carbon dioxide is passed into limewater for several minutes, the white precipitate of calcium carbonate slowly disappears. The reaction that occurs is

$$CaCO_3(s) + H_2O(l) + CO_2(g)$$
$$\rightleftharpoons Ca^{2+}(aq) + 2HCO_3^-(aq)$$

Calcium hydrogencarbonate is soluble in water and exists as calcium ions and hydrogencarbonate ions. So the precipitate of calcium carbonate disappears as this reaction occurs. But calcium hydrogencarbonate decomposes easily on heating. When its solution is heated, bubbles of carbon dioxide are given off and the white precipitate of calcium carbonate is formed again.

Uses of carbon dioxide

Because it forms a *weak* acid, carbon dioxide is used for putting the acid taste in drinks. All 'fizzy' drinks are solutions of carbon dioxide in water which have been coloured, sweetened and flavoured. Carbon dioxide is much more soluble in water when it is at a high pressure than at atmospheric pressure. 'Fizzy' drinks and soda water are made by dissolving carbon dioxide in water under pressure. You should now know why they fizz when the pressure is released.

Because carbon dioxide does not support the combustion of most substances, is non-flammable and is denser than air, the gas is often used in fire extinguishers. The carbon dioxide is stored in a cylinder under pressure and is released by squeezing a lever (Fig. 31.9).

Fig. 31.9

Carbon dioxide freezes at $-78\,°C$ to form a white solid called 'dry ice'. This is used as a refrigerant for foods (Fig. 31.10). It is especially convenient because it sublimes directly to the gas and does not leave any residue.

Fig. 31.10

Recycling limestone

The part of the carbon cycle involving limestone (Fig. 31.11) can be 'plugged into' the part given in

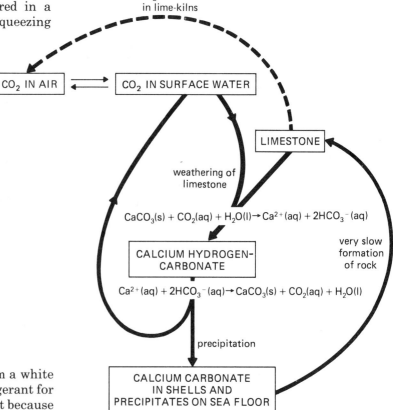

heating of limestone in lime-kilns

CO₂ IN AIR ⇌ CO₂ IN SURFACE WATER

LIMESTONE

weathering of limestone

$$CaCO_3(s) + CO_2(aq) + H_2O(l) \rightarrow Ca^{2+}(aq) + 2HCO_3^-(aq)$$

very slow formation of rock

CALCIUM HYDROGEN-CARBONATE

$$Ca^{2+}(aq) + 2HCO_3^-(aq) \rightarrow CaCO_3(s) + CO_2(aq) + H_2O(l)$$

precipitation

CALCIUM CARBONATE IN SHELLS AND PRECIPITATES ON SEA FLOOR

Fig. 31.11 Another part of the carbon cycle

Fig. 30.1 (page 111). It shows that limestone rock is formed from sea-shells and any precipitate of calcium carbonate on the sea floor. It also shows that calcium carbonate and calcium hydrogencarbonate are changed into one another in nature.

Rainwater and the water in rivers, lakes and the sea always contains dissolved carbon dioxide. This carbon dioxide has been dissolved from the air and also from the soil where it is produced by living organisms. Limestone is **weathered** by reaction with this dissolved carbon dioxide.

$$CaCO_3(s) + H_2O(l) + CO_2(g)$$
$$\rightleftharpoons Ca^{2+}(aq) + 2HCO_3^-(aq)$$

The reaction produces calcium hydrogencarbonate in solution and this is carried by rivers to the sea. Animals which live in the sea can use the dissolved calcium hydrogencarbonate to make shells and bones that contain calcium carbonate, and carbon dioxide is released at the same time. Also, if the sea is warm enough, some water will evaporate and calcium carbonate will be precipitated, again with the formation of carbon dioxide.

Fig. 31.12

The stalactites and stalagmites in the limestone cave shown in Fig. 31.12 are also an example of the recycling of limestone. The water draining through the limestone contains calcium hydrogencarbonate from the weathering of the rock. When drops of this solution evaporate, they lose carbon dioxide to the air and the weathering reaction is reversed. This leaves a thin layer of calcium carbonate on the roof of the cave. The same reaction can leave a layer of calcium carbonate on the floor of the cave where the drops fall. The stalactites grow downwards from the cave roof and the stalagmites grow upwards. Sometimes a stalactite and a stalagmite join together to form a continuous growth from roof to floor.

When limestone dissolves in surface water, there is an important effect on the water supply of the area. For the next experiment, you need a solution of calcium hydrogencarbonate. This can be obtained by bubbling carbon dioxide into limewater for several

minutes until it goes clear again. But you can also get it directly from limestone by putting a lump of it in a bottle of soda water.

Soda water has a much higher concentration of carbon dioxide than surface water and so the limestone dissolves much more quickly in it. The lump should be left in the soda water for about a week to give time for the calcium hydrogencarbonate to be formed.

Experiment 31.4 Investigating hard water

1. Shake a few cm³ of the solution of calcium hydrogencarbonate with a soap flake or one or two drops of soap solution in a test-tube. Next, shake a few cm³ of distilled water with the same amount of soap.

▶ In which sample of water is it harder to make a lather?

2. Now boil another few cm³ of the solution of calcium hydrogencarbonate for a few minutes. Then let it cool and test it with a soap flake as in 1.

▶ Is it now easier to get a lather with this water?

Water containing calcium ions is always **hard**, that is, it does not lather very easily with soap. The hardness caused by calcium hydrogencarbonate can be removed by boiling because the calcium ions form a precipitate of calcium carbonate. The equation is the reverse of the one given above for the formation of calcium hydrogencarbonate by the weathering of limestone. Other soluble calcium salts can cause water to be hard but it is only with calcium hydrogencarbonate that the hardness can be removed by boiling.

All kinds of hard water can be softened using sodium carbonate. This provides carbonate ions which can react with the calcium ions in the water, again to form a precipitate of calcium carbonate:

$$Ca^{2+}(aq) + CO_3^{2-}(aq) \longrightarrow CaCO_3(s)$$
in hard water   from sodium
carbonate

Water containing calcium hydrogencarbonate can be a problem in industry. Fig. 31.13 shows the 'scale' of calcium carbonate which can form in boiler pipes after they have been carrying hot water for some time.

Fig. 31.13

Temporary hard water, usually caused by dissolved calcium hydrogencarbonate, can be softened by boiling. Water which contains other calcium salts such as calcium sulphate is not affected by boiling and is called **permanent** hard water. Magnesium salts behave in a similar way and can also produce permanent and temporary hardness.

QUESTIONS

1 (a) Name *two* uses of limestone that do not involve changing it to another chemical.
(b) Write the symbol equation for the chemical reaction of limestone with dilute nitric acid.
(c) Suppose that 100 g of limestone gives off 20 litres of carbon dioxide at a certain temperature and pressure when it is added to an excess of dilute nitric acid. Is this limestone pure or impure calcium carbonate? Explain your answer. (Relative atomic masses: Ca = 40, C = 12, H = 1; the volume occupied by 1 mole of any gas at the given temperature and pressure is 24 litres.)

2 Slaked lime is used to make lime mortar, a material that is sometimes used in brick and stone buildings. When lime mortar is fresh, it gives no chemical reaction with dilute hydrochloric acid, but older lime mortar gives off carbon dioxide.
(a) What compound is there likely to be in older lime mortar?
(b) Explain, using an equation, how the slaked lime in fresh lime mortar could be changed to this compound by one of the gases in the air.

3 Calcite is $CaCO_3$, magnesite is $MgCO_3$ and dolomite is $CaCO_3 \cdot MgCO_3$. The equation for the reactions of these minerals with dilute hydrochloric acid may be written as:

$$XCO_3(s) + 2HCl(aq) \longrightarrow XCl_2(aq) + H_2O(l) + CO_2(g)$$

where X is Ca or Mg.
(a) Write the equation for the reaction of dolomite with dilute hydrochloric acid.
(b) If 0.1 mol $CaCO_3$ produces 2.4 litres of carbon dioxide under certain conditions, how much gas would be produced by (i) 0.1 mol $CaCO_3 \cdot MgCO_3$, and (ii) 0.1 mol $MgCO_3$, under the same conditions?
(c) What are the percentages by mass of calcium in calcite and dolomite? (Relative atomic masses: Ca = 40, Mg = 24, O = 16, C = 12.)
(d) Here are some suggestions for extracting calcium or magnesium from their carbonates. In each case the carbonate is first heated to produce the oxide:
  (i) reduce the oxide with carbon,
  (ii) decompose the oxide at a very high temperature,
  (iii) reduce the oxide using either hydrogen or carbon monoxide,
  (iv) electrolyse the molten oxide (melting points: CaO 2700 °C, MgO 2640 °C),
  (v) convert the oxide to the chloride and electrolyse the molten anhydrous chloride (melting points: $CaCl_2$ 772 °C, $MgCl_2$ 712 °C).
Which method would you choose? Consider each method in turn and explain why you think it is a good method, a poor method or a method which might not work at all.

4 The concentration of calcium ions (Ca^{2+}) in sea water is much lower than their concentration in river water. Use the carbon cycle (Fig. 31.11) to explain this large discrepancy.

5 What is boiler scale? Explain why it is formed only when *hot* water containing calcium hydrogencarbonate is passed through the pipes.

6 What tests would you use to show that some sea shells contain calcium carbonate? (Say what you would expect to happen in each test and give equations for the reactions that should occur.)
  How would you find out if a piece of sea shell is *pure* calcium carbonate?

7 If you were given a sample of limestone, explain how you would convert it into calcium hydroxide. Write equations for any reactions you suggest.
  How would you show that you had succeeded in producing calcium hydroxide?

8 Describe how you would prepare a few gas jars of carbon dioxide in the laboratory. Choose three everyday uses of carbon dioxide and explain why the properties of carbon dioxide make it suitable for these uses.

Key words

slaking	**weathering of limestone**	**temporary hardness**
dibasic acid	**stalactites and stalagmites**	**permanent hardness**

Basic facts

- Limestones are sedimentary rocks which consist mainly of calcium carbonate. Chalk and marble are also composed mainly of calcium carbonate.

- Like other carbonates, limestone reacts with dilute acids to produce carbon dioxide. It is difficult to decompose by heating but produces calcium oxide (quicklime) and carbon dioxide.

- The reaction of calcium oxide with water (slaking of quicklime) is very exothermic and produces calcium hydroxide which is the cheapest alkali available on an industrial scale. In the laboratory, calcium hydroxide solution (limewater) is used to test for carbon dioxide.

- Calcium carbonate, calcium oxide (quicklime) and calcium hydroxide (slaked lime) have many important uses. Lime-kilns are used to produce quicklime from limestone.

- Carbon dioxide is usually produced in the laboratory by reacting an acid with a carbonate. The most important properties of carbon dioxide are: that it is denser than air, forms a weakly acidic
- solution in water, is non-flammable and does not support combustion; and that solid carbon dioxide sublimes at a fairly low temperature. These properties account for the uses of carbon dioxide in fizzy drinks, as a fire extinguisher and as a refrigerant.
- Carbonic acid is a dibasic acid and so can form two salts (carbonates and hydrogencarbonates) when reacted with an alkali. Whereas calcium carbonate does not dissolve in carbon dioxide-free water, calcium hydrogencarbonate is soluble. The reversible reaction between calcium carbonate, water and carbon dioxide to give calcium hydrogencarbonate is very important in nature.

32 Chemicals from salt

The flow-chart (Fig. 32.1) summarizes the experiments that are mentioned in this chapter. Study it carefully as you work through the chapter.

Salt from seas and lakes

When sea water is evaporated, solid salts are always left. A cubic metre of sea water contains about 27 kg of sodium chloride, about 5 kg of magnesium salts, about 1 kg of calcium sulphate and smaller amounts of other substances. Over two-thirds of the earth's surface is covered by seas which means that a huge amount of dissolved substances is present in them.

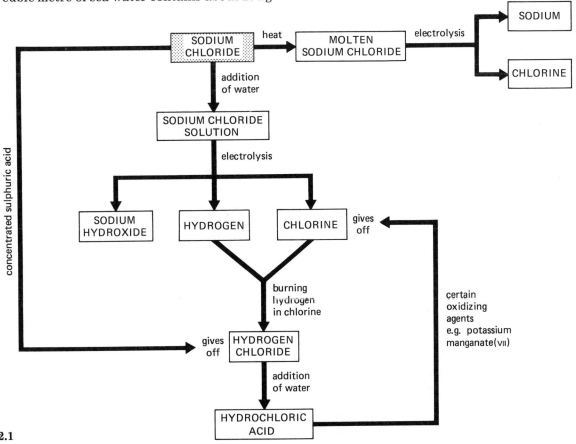

Fig. 32.1

32 Chemicals from salt

In some tropical countries, salt for cooking comes from the sea. The sea water is trapped in shallow 'ponds' (Fig. 32.2) and is slowly evaporated.

Fig. 32.2

However, a lot of salt, called rock salt, comes from underground deposits. These were formed many millions of years ago by the evaporation of large salty lakes or almost completely enclosed seas. Over many years, thick layers of salt crystals formed on the floors of these lakes and seas. Since then, the crystals have been covered by sediments and pressed down and hardened to make rock salt.

Electrolysing sodium chloride solution

If the electrolysis of sodium chloride solution is carried out in a U-tube, the pH value of the solution in the cathode arm rises from its original value of 7 (Fig. 32.4). This is because there is an increase in the concentration of hydroxide ions (the ions present in all solutions of alkalis in water) around the cathode as the hydrogen ions from the water combine with electrons to form hydrogen atoms (and then molecules). Chloride ions move to the anode where they lose electrons to form chlorine atoms (and then molecules).

In industry, this electrolysis is carried out with a concentrated solution of sodium chloride called brine. One kind of cell used is called the mercury-cathode cell (Fig. 32.5). The anodes are made of titanium and the cathode is a stream of mercury flowing across the bottom of the cell. Although this cell does not work in the same way as the one shown in Fig. 32.4, the three products are still the same.

Sodium, not hydrogen, is discharged at the mercury cathode and it then dissolves in the mercury to form a liquid alloy called sodium amalgam.

$$Na^+(aq) + e^- \longrightarrow Na \text{ (amalgam)}$$

This amalgam then flows out of the cell to be reacted with water. The products are sodium hydroxide and

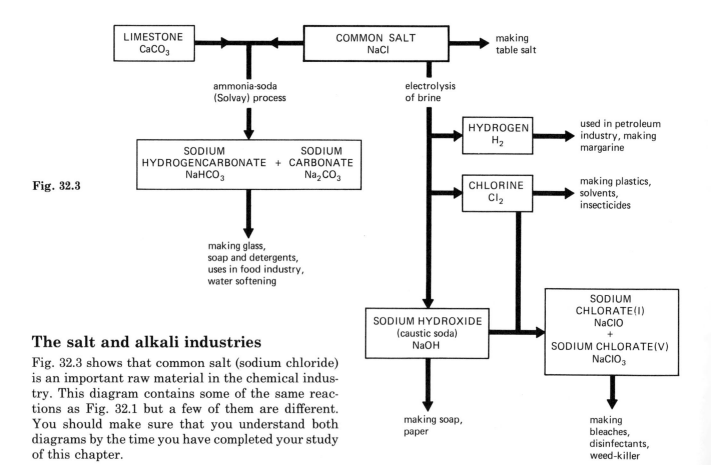

Fig. 32.3

The salt and alkali industries

Fig. 32.3 shows that common salt (sodium chloride) is an important raw material in the chemical industry. This diagram contains some of the same reactions as Fig. 32.1 but a few of them are different. You should make sure that you understand both diagrams by the time you have completed your study of this chapter.

hydrogen, along with pure mercury which can be re-used in the cell.

$$2Na + 2H_2O(l)$$
(amalgam)

$$\longrightarrow \underbrace{2Na^+(aq) + 2OH^-(aq)} + H_2(g)$$
sodium hydroxide
solution

It is necessary to use a flowing mercury cathode in this process so that the chlorine and the sodium hydroxide are kept separate. If they were not, they would react to form sodium chlorate(I) (hypochlorite) or possibly even sodium chlorate(V) (page 126).

The use of mercury in this cell has its problems. Mercury is a very expensive material and so there is a high capital cost in setting up the cells. Also,

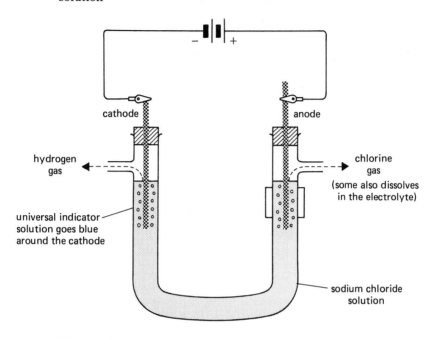

Fig. 32.4

At the cathode:

$2H^+(aq) + 2e^- \rightarrow H_2(g)$,

where the H^+ (aq) ions are produced by the ionization of water.
$2H_2O(l) \rightleftharpoons 2H^+(aq) + 2OH^-(aq)$

The overall reaction is obtained by combining the above two equations:
$2H_2O(l) + 2e^- \rightarrow H_2(g) + 2OH^-(aq)$

At the anode:

$2Cl^-(aq) - 2e^- \rightarrow Cl_2(g)$

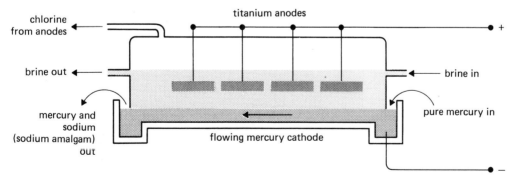

Fig. 32.5

Currents up to 400 kA can be used in a modern cell. A complete cell installation (with perhaps over 100 individual cells) can consume about 100 MW of electricity. Since this is about the output of a large modern power station, it is not surprising that such an installation requires a specially built power station on the same site.

although the process is operated very efficiently, there is a small loss of mercury (as the metal or as mercury(II) chloride). The mercury is discharged along with the waste materials and is one of the main sources of mercury pollution in the industrial environment.

Mercury effluent can be absorbed, as organic compounds, in the tissues of marine animals and plants and so get into the food chain. In the 1950s at Minamata, in Japan, some serious cases of mercury poisoning were reported. This was an area where people ate marine fish close to a works which was discharging mercury into the sea.

Fig. 32.3 shows the uses of the chlorine and sodium hydroxide produced by the electrolysis of brine, and one of these is featured in Fig. 32.6.

Fig. 32.6 A drum of solid sodium hydroxide at a soap factory

Hydrogen chloride

Fig. 32.7 shows how hydrogen chloride can be made

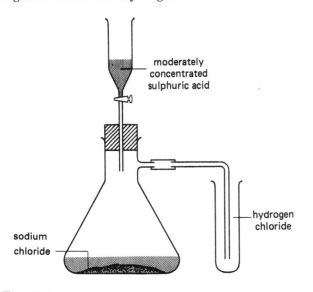

Fig. 32.7

from sodium chloride and moderately concentrated sulphuric acid.

$$NaCl(s) + H_2SO_4(l) \longrightarrow NaHSO_4(aq) + HCl(g)$$

Tests on the gas show that it is denser than air, it does not support the combustion of a wood splint, and it is very soluble in water (Fig. 32.8).

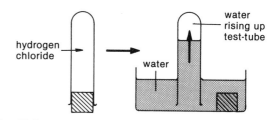

Fig. 32.8

Hydrogen chloride is an acidic gas: it dissolves in water to form hydrochloric acid. It also fumes in air because it reacts with any water vapour that is present.

$$HCl(g) + water \longrightarrow H^+(aq) + Cl^-(aq)$$

or

$$HCl(g) + H_2O(l) \longrightarrow H_3O^+(aq) + Cl^-(aq)$$

Water must be essential for hydrogen chloride to behave as an acid because a solution of *dry* hydrogen chloride in methylbenzene has no acidic properties at all (page 80).

To make hydrochloric acid from hydrogen chloride, the gas is passed into water as shown in Fig. 32.9. The typical acidic properties of dilute hydrochloric acid are listed on page 71.

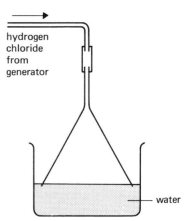

Fig. 32.9 Note the position of the funnel just below the surface of the water

Being an acidic gas, hydrogen chloride reacts with ammonia, an alkaline gas, to form a white 'smoke' of ammonium chloride, a salt.

$$NH_3(g) + HCl(g) \longrightarrow NH_4Cl(s)$$

Hydrogen chloride can be synthesized from its elements (Fig. 32.10).

$$H_2(g) + Cl_2(g) \longrightarrow 2HCl(g)$$

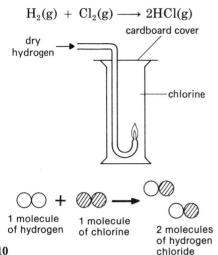

Fig. 32.10

Oxidizing hydrochloric acid

Concentrated hydrochloric acid can react with some oxidizing agents (substances that can release some or all of their oxygen to another substance). So the acid can act as a reducing agent by taking up this oxygen. The hydrogen part of the acid joins with the oxygen to form water, so leaving chlorine behind. You can always tell whether concentrated hydrochloric acid has been oxidized by finding out if any chlorine gas is given off from the mixture. Sodium chlorate(I) (hypochlorite, NaClO) or potassium manganate(VII) ($KMnO_4$) are suitable oxidizing agents for concentrated hydrochloric acid.

Chlorine

Fig. 32.7 shows apparatus suitable for making chlorine, but the sodium chloride must be replaced by sodium chlorate(I) solution and the concentrated sulphuric acid by moderately concentrated hydrochloric acid.

Tests on the gas show that it is denser than air,

it bleaches the dye in moist litmus paper and it supports the combustion of a wide range of elements and compounds.

For example, magnesium burns in chlorine to form magnesium chloride while iron wool burns to form iron(III) chloride.

$$Mg(s) + Cl_2(g) \longrightarrow MgCl_2(s)$$
$$2Fe(s) + 3Cl_2(g) \longrightarrow 2FeCl_3(s)$$

It should be noted that heated iron wool reacts with hydrogen chloride to form iron(II) chloride.

$$Fe(s) + 2HCl(g) \longrightarrow FeCl_2(s) + H_2(g)$$

The synthesis of hydrogen chloride (see page 124) also illustrates the reaction of an element, a non-metal in this case, with chlorine.

In fact, the reactions of chlorine with elements and compounds can be compared with the burning of the same substances in oxygen. Chlorine, like oxygen, is a good oxidizing agent.

Fuels can also burn in chlorine. The paraffin wax in a candle or a wax taper is a hydrocarbon (page 214). When this burns in chlorine, carbon (soot) and hydrogen chloride are formed.

Compound of C and H + chlorine
$$\longrightarrow \text{carbon} + \text{hydrogen chloride}$$

This is equivalent to the burning of a hydrocarbon in a limited supply of air (page 111).

Many chlorides (metal chlorides, hydrogen chloride, ammonium chloride) form Cl^- (aq) ions when mixed with water. The usual test for the presence of chloride ions is discussed on page 48. The properties of chloride salts are summarized in Fig. 32.11.

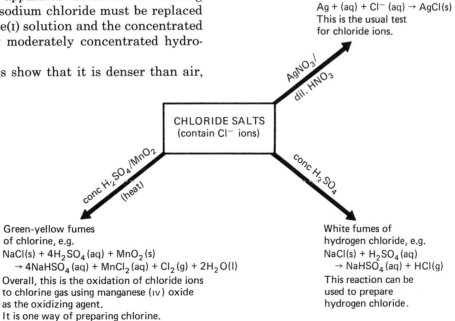

White precipitate of silver chloride.
$Ag^+(aq) + Cl^-(aq) \rightarrow AgCl(s)$
This is the usual test for chloride ions.

$AgNO_3$ / dil. HNO_3

CHLORIDE SALTS (contain Cl^- ions)

conc H_2SO_4/MnO_2 (heat)

conc H_2SO_4

Green-yellow fumes of chlorine, e.g.
$NaCl(s) + 4H_2SO_4(aq) + MnO_2(s)$
$\rightarrow 4NaHSO_4(aq) + MnCl_2(aq) + Cl_2(g) + 2H_2O(l)$
Overall, this is the oxidation of chloride ions to chlorine gas using manganese (IV) oxide as the oxidizing agent.
It is one way of preparing chlorine.

White fumes of hydrogen chloride, e.g.
$NaCl(s) + H_2SO_4(aq)$
$\rightarrow NaHSO_4(aq) + HCl(g)$
This reaction can be used to prepare hydrogen chloride.

Fig. 32.11

Uses of chlorine

Dry chlorine has no bleaching properties, but in the presence of even small amounts of water chlorine bleaches many dyes, including the red or blue dye in litmus paper.

Two acids are formed when chlorine reacts with water – hydrochloric acid and chloric(I) (hypochlorous) acid (HClO).

$$Cl_2(g) + H_2O(l) \rightleftharpoons HCl(aq) + HClO(aq)$$

The hydrochloric acid turns universal indicator paper or blue litmus paper red but the chloric(I) acid is a bleaching agent. So if the indicator paper is left in the gas for long enough, all the colour is removed by the bleaching action of chloric(I) acid. The equation below shows that this happens when the dye is oxidized.

$$HClO(aq) + \underset{\text{(coloured)}}{dye} \longrightarrow HCl(aq) + \underset{\text{(colourless)}}{oxidized\ dye}$$

When sodium hydroxide solution is shaken with chlorine gas, the colour and smell of chlorine disappear because the salts sodium chloride and sodium chlorate(I) (NaClO) are formed.

$$2NaOH(aq) + Cl_2(aq)$$
$$\longrightarrow NaCl(aq) + NaClO(aq) + H_2O(l)$$

If sodium chlorate(I) solution is made slightly acidic, it releases chloric(I) acid and so it becomes a bleaching agent. Sodium chlorate(I), commonly known as 'sodium hypochlorite', is the main component in many commercial bleaches and sterilizing agents.

'Bleaching powder' has similar properties to sodium chlorate(I) solution but it is a solid made by absorbing chlorine gas in solid calcium hydroxide (slaked lime).

If chlorine is passed into a hot, concentrated solution of sodium hydroxide, sodium chloride and sodium chlorate(v) (NaClO_3) are produced.

$$3Cl_2(g) + 6NaOH(aq)$$
$$\longrightarrow 5NaCl(aq) + NaClO_3(aq) + H_2O(l)$$

Sodium chlorate(v) is used as a non-selective weedkiller.

Both sodium chlorate(I) and sodium chlorate(v) are made in industry by mixing the chlorine and sodium hydroxide from the electrolysis of brine in a controlled way (Fig. 32.3).

The ammonia-soda (Solvay) process

This is the way in which sodium hydrogencarbonate (NaHCO_3) and sodium carbonate (soda ash, Na_2CO_3 or washing soda, Na_2CO_3 · 10H_2O) are made on a large scale. Fig. 32.3 shows some of the very many uses of these compounds.

The stages in the ammonia-soda process are shown

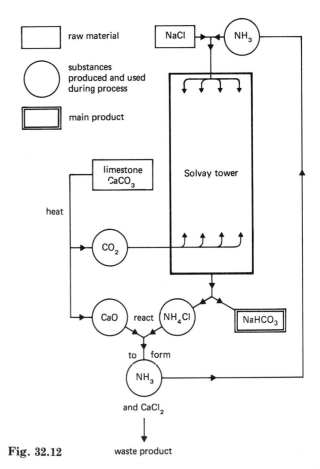

Fig. 32.12

in Fig. 32.12. For the main reaction, brine with dissolved ammonia is passed down a tower and carbon dioxide is forced up the tower. The equation for this reaction can be written as:

$$\underset{\text{from brine}}{Na^+(aq)} + NH_3(aq) + CO_2(g) + H_2O(l)$$
$$\longrightarrow NaHCO_3(s) + \underset{\substack{\text{present in solution as}\\\text{ammonium chloride}}}{NH_4^+(aq)}$$

The chloride ions are spectator ions and play no part in the reaction. The least soluble salt in the reaction mixture is sodium hydrogencarbonate and this is formed as a sludge when the concentration of hydrogencarbonate ions becomes high enough.

The carbon dioxide required for the process is made by heating limestone (page 115). The calcium oxide is reacted with water to form calcium hydroxide which is used to produce ammonia from the ammonium chloride left in solution at the end of the main reaction.

$$Ca(OH)_2(s) + 2NH_4Cl(s)$$
$$\longrightarrow 2NH_3(g) + 2H_2O(g) + CaCl_2(s)$$

The sodium hydrogencarbonate is filtered off and decomposed by heat to form anhydrous sodium carbonate. If sodium carbonate is crystallized from solution, washing soda (Na_2CO_3 · 10H_2O) is produced.

The ammonia-soda process is economical because the starting materials are cheap, the ammonia can be recirculated, and the only waste material is calcium chloride.

The liquid effluent (waste material) is a mixture of sodium chloride and calcium chloride in water, as well as some suspended solids originating from impurities in the limestone. Disposal of this can be a problem but nowadays most of it is returned to the boreholes from which the brine was obtained. The remaining liquid effluent can then be safely discharged into an adjacent river.

QUESTIONS

1 (a) Why does the sea contain much higher concentrations of dissolved salts than the rivers that flow into them?
(b) Why do a few lakes such as the Dead Sea in the Middle East (Fig. 32.13) contain higher concentrations of dissolved salts than the sea itself?

Fig. 32.13

2 Hydrogen chloride reacts with zinc to form a white solid and hydrogen.
(a) Write an equation for this chemical reaction.
(b) Draw a diagram of the apparatus you would use in order to carry out the chemical reaction and to collect the hydrogen free from any excess of hydrogen chloride.

3 When a mixture of hydrogen and chlorine is left for a few days, the green colour gradually fades and an acidic gas is produced. But if a similar mixture is passed over a hot platinum wire, the green colour fades very quickly indeed. (WARNING: this experiment could produce a dangerous explosion.)
(a) What is happening to the mixture as the green colour fades?
(b) What effect does the platinum wire have on the mixture?
(c) What word can be used to describe the effect of the wire?
(d) For which gas is the chemical reaction a synthesis?
(e) Describe another way in which this gas could be synthesized.

4 Starting with solid sodium chloride as your only compound containing chlorine, describe *two* ways in which you could make a few test-tubes of chlorine gas.

5 Explain, with equations where possible, the following observations:
(a) A piece of magnesium ribbon gives off hydrogen gas when added to a solution of chlorine in water.
(b) A piece of damp blue litmus paper held in chlorine gas first turns red and then goes white.

6 (a) What raw materials does a country need in order to establish an alkali industry?
(b) Make a list of the main products of this industry and explain (with equations where appropriate) one use of each product.

Key words
bleaching agent　　ammonia-soda process

Basic facts

● Salt comes from the sea or from underground deposits.

● Salt (together with limestone) is the essential raw material of the alkali industry.

● The electrolysis of sodium chloride solution produces hydrogen, chlorine and sodium hydroxide. A mercury-cathode cell is used in the large-scale process. This is a very important process because all three products have many industrial uses.

● Hydrogen chloride is made in the laboratory by reacting sodium chloride with moderately concentrated sulphuric acid. It dissolves in water to form hydrochloric acid.

● Concentrated hydrochloric acid can be oxidized to form chlorine.

● Chlorine reacts with water to form hydrochloric and chloric(I) acids. Chloric(I) acid (hypochlorous acid) acts as a bleaching agent and and as a disinfectant.

● Sodium chloride solution, ammonia and limestone are the raw materials used to make sodium carbonate in the ammonia-soda process.

● Chlorides can be detected by their reaction with silver nitrate. Other tests include the formation of hydrogen chloride (with concentrated sulphuric acid) and chlorine when reacted with a suitable oxidizing agent.

33 Chemicals from air

Fig. 33.1 shows that air is an important raw material in the chemical industry. It can be separated into its components (Fig. 33.2) and, along with water (steam) and petroleum or natural gas, it is used to produce ammonia and nitric acid.

The fractional distillation of liquid air

This process is summarized in Fig. 33.3. During the fractional distillation, nitrogen evaporates first because it has the lowest boiling point ($-196\,°C$) and oxygen evaporates last because it has the highest

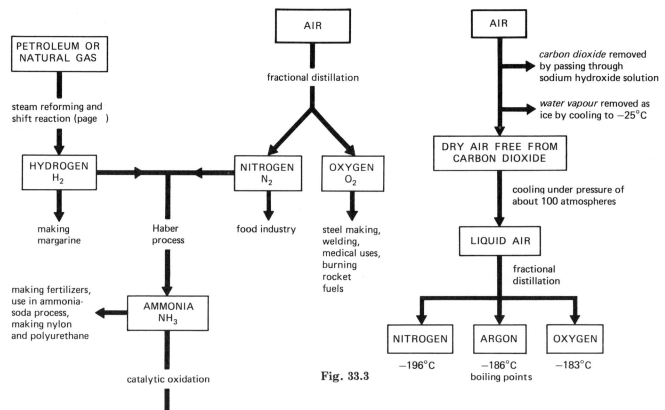

Fig. 33.1

Fig. 33.3

boiling point ($-183\,°C$). The separated gases are stored under pressure in large spherical containers (Fig. 33.4) or steel cylinders.

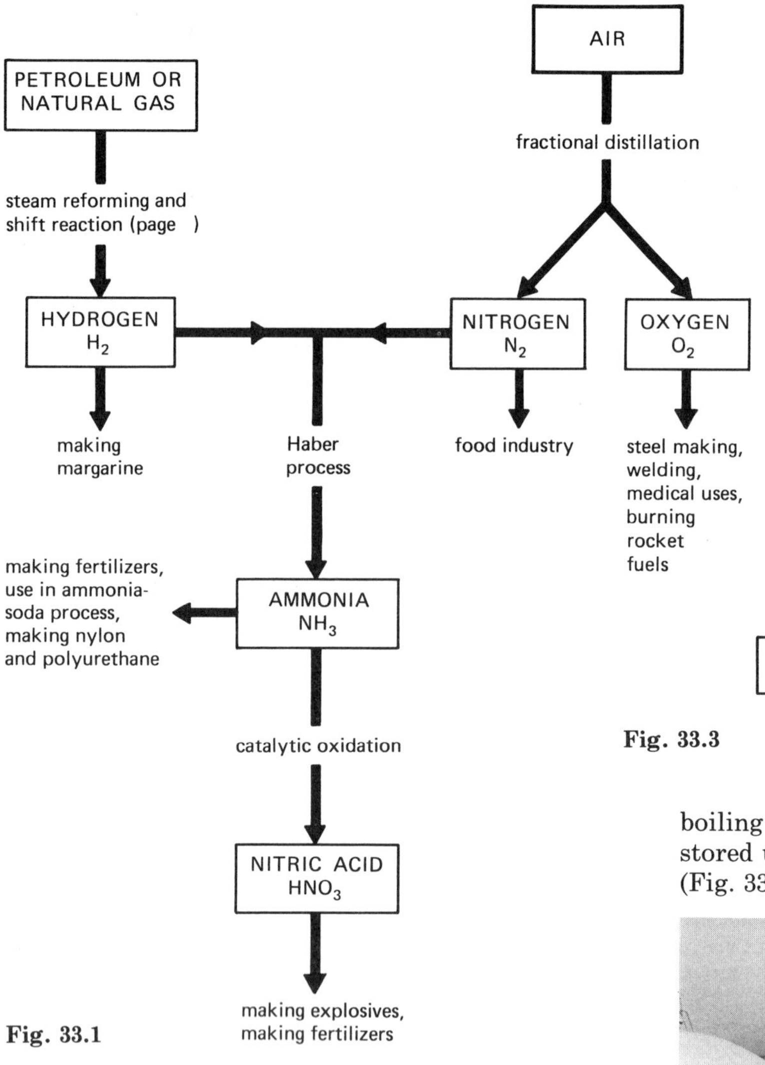

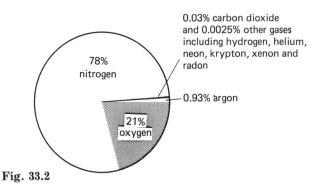

Fig. 33.2

Fig. 33.4 Storage tanks for liquid oxygen and nitrogen. The taller tower is where the fractional distillation is carried out

Liquid nitrogen is used in the food industry. When sprayed directly onto food, it causes very rapid freezing which helps to preserve the flavour and texture. But by far the most important use of nitrogen is in the manufacture of ammonia (page 133).

Pure oxygen has many uses, especially in steelmaking (page 105) and in welding and cutting metals where the burning fuel has to provide a high temperature. It is widely used to assist breathing.

Pure argon is used in welding in order to provide an inert atmosphere that stops the welded metal from forming its oxide (Fig. 33.5). Argon is often used at low pressure to fill electric light bulbs. This helps to prolong the life of the filament.

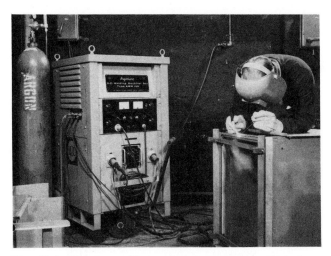

Fig. 33.5 Argon provides an inert atmosphere that stops the welded metal forming its oxide

Neon, like argon, is a noble gas that is made by the fractional distillation of liquid air. When electricity is passed through neon, the gas gives out a brilliant red-orange light. Because this light penetrates fog, neon lights are used for airport runways as well as for advertising signs.

Helium is even less common in air than neon but it is also sometimes found in natural gas. It has a very low density and is used for filling balloons. Mixtures of helium and oxygen are preferred to those of nitrogen and oxygen for deep-sea divers and spacemen.

The preparation and properties of oxygen

Oxygen is a reactive gas that supports the combustion of very many elements and compounds. Like nitrogen, it is essential to life, but unlike nitrogen, it is used in the elemental form and plays a vital part in the process of respiration (breathing). The digested foods in our bodies are oxidized by compli-cated reactions involving the inhaled oxygen carried in the blood stream, and we exhale (breath out) the products of the oxidation, namely carbon dioxide and water vapour. The oxidation reactions provide us with the energy our bodies need to keep warm and to do work.

Oxygen is often available in the laboratory from a cylinder. But if it needs to be prepared, the apparatus and chemicals shown in Fig. 33.6 can be used.

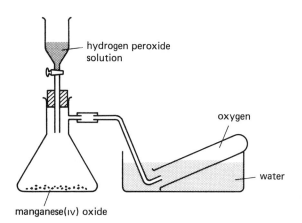

Fig. 33.6

The hydrogen peroxide solution decomposes to water and oxygen, and the decomposition is speeded up by the use of a catalyst of manganese(IV) oxide.

$$2H_2O_2(aq) \longrightarrow 2H_2O(l) + O_2(g)$$

The properties of nitrogen

Nitrogen is an unreactive gas. It is neutral to indicators and does not support the combustion of most elements and compounds. One of the few substances that just manages to burn in nitrogen is magnesium, which forms magnesium nitride (Mg_3N_2).

$$3Mg(s) + N_2(g) \longrightarrow Mg_3N_2(s)$$

In the form of nitrogen-containing compounds, nitrogen is essential to life. But atmospheric nitrogen exists in the form of the element. The conversion of elemental nitrogen to nitrogen compounds is called **fixation**. The fixation of nitrogen occurs in nature, by organisms and in thunderstorms, or it can be achieved by man-made processes.

One way of fixing nitrogen is to pass an electric spark through a mixture of nitrogen and oxygen.

$$N_2(g) + O_2(g) \longrightarrow 2NO(g)$$
$$\text{nitrogen monoxide}$$

But the most important way of fixing nitrogen is through its reaction with hydrogen in the Haber process (page 133).

Ammonia

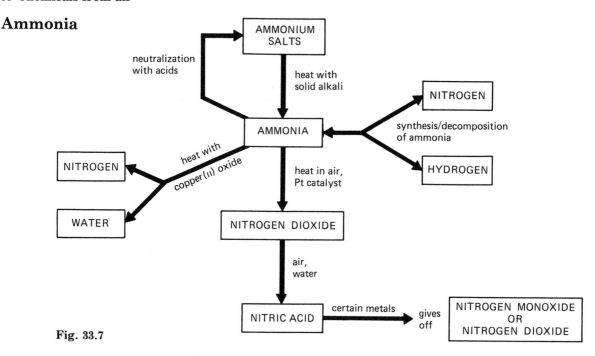

Fig. 33.7

Ammonia (NH_3) is a very important compound and much of this chapter deals with how it is made and with some of its reactions. The flow-chart (Fig. 33.7) summarizes the reactions that are mentioned below. Study it carefully as you work through the chapter. You should also make sure that you understand fully the flow-chart in Fig. 33.1 which contains some of the same reactions.

A solution of ammonia in water is alkaline and can be used to neutralize acids. The salts made in these reactions are called ammonium salts. Two examples are ammonium chloride (NH_4Cl) and ammonium sulphate ((NH_4)$_2SO_4$).

Experiment 33.1 Can ammonia be prepared from an ammonium salt?

Gently warm separate samples of solid ammonium sulphate and ammonium chloride in a test-tube.

▶ Can you smell any ammonia?

CARE: do not take a deep breath of this poisonous gas.

Moisten a mixture of one spatula measure of solid ammonium chloride with one spatula measure of solid calcium hydroxide or soda lime with a little water and gently warm the mixture in a test-tube.

▶ Can you smell any ammonia again?

Repeat the experiment using solid ammonium sulphate and calcium hydroxide or soda lime.

To collect some ammonia gas, set up the apparatus shown in Fig. 33.8. Collect four test-tubes of the gas, closing each tube with a bung. Assume that a tube is full when ammonia has been passed into it for 10 seconds. The density of ammonia at 25 °C and

1 atmosphere pressure is $0.706 \times 10^{-3}\,\mathrm{g\,cm^{-3}}$. The density of air under the same conditions is $1.18 \times 10^{-3}\,\mathrm{g\,cm^{-3}}$.

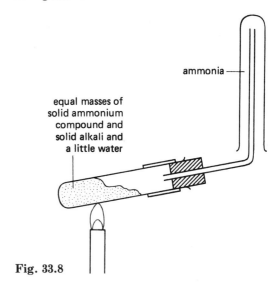

Fig. 33.8

▶ Explain why ammonia has to be collected by passing the gas upwards into the test-tube rather than downwards.

Carry out these tests on the gas you have collected:

1. Hold an open tube of ammonia near to a test-tube containing a few cm^3 of concentrated hydrochloric acid.

▶ What happens?

2. You should already know how ammonia solution affects universal indicator. If you are in doubt about this result, add a few cm^3 of universal indicator to a tube of ammonia and shake the mixture.

▶ Which ion must ammonia produce with water?

3. Hold a burning splint at the mouth of an open tube.

▶ Does ammonia burn in air?

4. Find a way of showing that ammonia is very soluble in water.

The equation for this preparation of ammonia is

$$(NH_4)_2SO_4(s) + Ca(OH)_2(s)$$
$$\longrightarrow 2NH_3(g) + 2H_2O(g) + CaSO_4(s)$$

Or, more generally, any ammonium salt reacts with any alkali to produce ammonia.

$$NH_4{}^+(s) + OH^-(s) \longrightarrow NH_3(g) + H_2O(l)$$

In test 1, the alkaline gas (ammonia) is reacting with the acidic gas (hydrogen chloride) given off by concentrated hydrochloric acid, to give a white smoke of a salt, ammonium chloride.

$$NH_3(g) + HCl(g) \longrightarrow NH_4Cl(s)$$

can be reacted with acids to form salts, in this case ammonium salts. (See Experiment 33.3, page 134.)

Water is essential for ammonia to behave as an alkali. If the gas is dissolved in another solvent such as propanone (acetone), the solution that is formed has no alkaline properties (page 81).

Ammonia solution is prepared from ammonia gas in the same way that hydrochloric acid is prepared from hydrogen chloride (Fig. 32.9, page 124). The dilute solution smells strongly of ammonia but is fairly safe to use. The concentrated solution is called 0.88 ammonia because its density is $0.88\,\text{g cm}^{-3}$. It is much more dangerous and you should never attempt to smell the ammonia in a bottle of this solution.

The oxidation of ammonia

The oxygen in the air can be used as an oxidizing agent (see Experiment 33.1), but ammonia burns more easily in pure oxygen. Fig. 33.10 shows a suitable piece of apparatus for the experiment. No

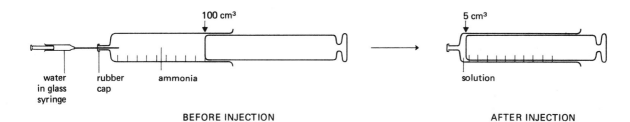

Fig. 33.9

The very high solubility of ammonia in water is well demonstrated by the experiment shown in Fig. 33.9. A syringe is filled with $100\,\text{cm}^3$ of *dry* ammonia and a little water is injected into it. The piston of the syringe then moves to about the $5\,\text{cm}^3$ mark.

The solution formed is alkaline because of the production of hydroxide ions.

$$NH_3(g) + H_2O(l) \rightleftharpoons NH_4{}^+(aq) + OH^-(aq)$$

The $\rightleftharpoons$ sign is used to show that the reverse reaction can also occur. (It is, of course, the equation for the preparation of ammonia from an ammonium salt and an alkali.) This sign also shows that not all of the NH_3 and H_2O are converted into ions. A balance point (position of equilibrium, page 197) is achieved, and both reactants and products are present in the reaction mixture in certain proportions. This incomplete ionization is why ammonia is a much weaker alkali than sodium hydroxide or potassium hydroxide. However, just like strong alkalis, ammonia solution (ammonium hydroxide)

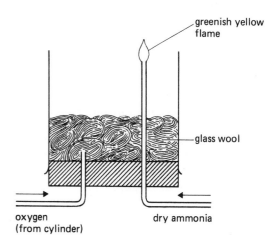

Fig. 33.10

products of the reaction can be seen, but if a beaker of cold water is held just above the flame a mist appears on the outside of it. This may remind you of the burning of many other substances in air or oxygen, such as candle wax and the gas you get from the taps in your laboratory. The equation for this reaction is

$$4NH_3(g) + O_2(g) \longrightarrow 2N_2(g) + 6H_2O(g)$$

Ammonia can also be oxidized in other ways than burning. Fig. 33.11 shows an experiment in which oxygen is bubbled through concentrated ammonia solution. A coil of hot platinum wire is held in the mixture of ammonia and oxygen above the solution.

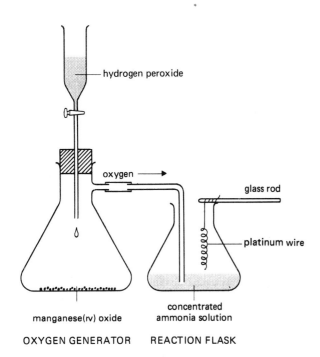

OXYGEN GENERATOR   REACTION FLASK

Fig. 33.11

Some explosions occur and the wire gets noticeably hotter as heat is produced by the reaction. A coil of copper wire could be used in place of the platinum, but this tends to break up and drop into the solution as it gets hotter.

The equation for this reaction is

$$4NH_3(g) + 5O_2(g) \longrightarrow 4NO(g) + 6H_2O(g)$$

The gas with the formula NO is called nitrogen monoxide. This reaction is rather violent because the platinum wire acts as a **catalyst**, a substance that speeds up the reaction without itself being consumed (page 190). The **catalytic oxidation** of ammonia is an important stage in the industrial production of nitric acid (page 136).

Experiment 33.2 Do any compounds oxidize ammonia?

Use each of the following solids in turn in the apparatus shown in Fig. 33.12.
1. Wire-form copper(II) oxide
2. Lead(II) oxide
3. Magnesium oxide

Each of these solids contain oxygen and could possibly act as an oxidizing agent.

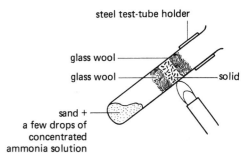

Fig. 33.12

Heat the solid strongly, and sometimes heat the sand soaked in ammonia solution very gently to keep a steady stream of ammonia gas passing over the solid. Do not overheat the ammonia solution because an excess of ammonia might blow the solid out of the tube.

▶ Do any of the solids change colour?
▶ Which of them seem to be reduced to the metal and so act as oxidizing agents?

In some of these cases, the ammonia is oxidized by the metal oxide and the metal oxide is reduced to the metal, e.g.

$$2NH_3(g) + 3CuO(s)$$
$$\longrightarrow N_2(g) + 3Cu(s) + 3H_2O(l)$$

So, like hydrogen, carbon and carbon monoxide, ammonia is a reducing agent.

Decomposing ammonia

Ammonia is not easy to decompose by heat except at high temperatures. But in the presence of a catalyst the decomposition by heat does happen much more readily (Fig. 33.13). All the air is flushed out of the

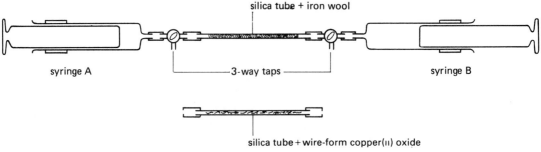

syringe A   ─3-way taps─   syringe B

silica tube + wire-form copper(II) oxide

Fig. 33.13

apparatus and 50 cm³ of dry ammonia is passed into syringe A via the three-way tap. The iron wool catalyst is heated strongly and the taps adjusted so that the ammonia can be pushed backwards and forwards over the catalyst. After all the ammonia has been decomposed and the apparatus has cooled, there is 100 cm³ of gas left.

To find out what this 100 cm³ contains, the three-way taps must be closed so that no gas escapes, and the silica tube containing the iron wool must be replaced by another silica tube containing wire-form copper(II) oxide. When the taps are opened and the gas is passed over the hot oxide, the volume drops to about 25 cm³ and the oxide is reduced to copper.

Since all the ammonia has been decomposed, this reduction must have been carried out by the hydrogen, one of the products of its decomposition. The remaining 25 cm³ of gas is nitrogen.

The results of this experiment can be written as follows (all volumes are measured at the same temperature and pressure).

$$\text{ammonia} \underset{\substack{\text{iron} \\ \text{catalyst}}}{\overset{\text{heat}}{\rightleftharpoons}} \text{nitrogen} + \text{hydrogen}$$
$$50\,\text{cm}^3 \qquad\qquad 25\,\text{cm}^3 \qquad 75\,\text{cm}^3$$

Avogadro's principle (page 89) can be used to find the formula of ammonia from these results.

$$2x\,\text{cm}^3 \text{ of ammonia}$$
$$\longrightarrow x\,\text{cm}^3 \text{ of } N_2(g) + 3x\,\text{cm}^3 \text{ of } H_2(g)$$

Using Avogadro's principle, it can be concluded that

2 molecules of ammonia
$$\longrightarrow 1 \text{ molecule of } N_2(g) + 3 \text{ molecules of } H_2(g)$$

This is shown in Fig. 33.14, and the molecules in the two boxes must each possess one nitrogen atom and three hydrogen atoms.

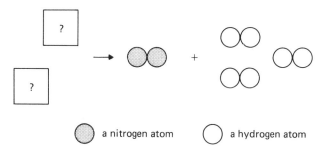

○ a nitrogen atom   ○ a hydrogen atom

Fig. 33.14

Synthesizing ammonia – the Haber process

Ammonia can be made from nitrogen and hydrogen only. But, because of the unreactivity of nitrogen, this is not easy to carry out in the school laboratory. The problem was solved on a large scale by a German chemist called Fritz Haber at the beginning of the century. A reasonable yield of ammonia at a fast enough rate can be obtained in the so-called **Haber process** using a high pressure (200 atmospheres), a moderate temperature (about 500 °C) and an iron catalyst. The reasons why these conditions are chosen are discussed on page 200.

$$N_2(g) + 3H_2(g) \rightleftharpoons 2NH_3(g)$$

The mixture of gases coming out of the reaction vessel contains about 15 per cent of ammonia. Because of the high pressure, the cooling of these gases causes the ammonia to liquefy and so separate out. The unchanged nitrogen and hydrogen can then be recycled.

The importance of ammonia

The world production of ammonia has increased dramatically in the latter half of the twentieth century. This is because about 80 per cent of ammonia is used for making artificial fertilizers (Figs. 33.15 and 33.16) which are increasingly needed to supplement the nitrogen that is naturally absorbed into the soil. The rapidly growing population of many countries means that fertilizers are needed to use the existing land more efficiently and to develop new, perhaps more marginal land for cultivation.

Fig. 33.15 Solid nitrogenous fertilizer

Fig. 33.16 Transferring liquid nitrogenous fertilizer from tank to sprayer

Experiment 33.3 *Making a fertilizer from ammonia*

Add about 20 cm³ of bench dilute (1 M) sulphuric acid to an evaporating basin. Stirring all the time, add to this some bench dilute (2 M) ammonia solution until the liquid in the basin smells slightly of ammonia.

Then begin to evaporate the solution. From time to time, remove a small sample of the solution on the end of a glass rod and let it cool. If crystals form, then stop the evaporation and leave the partially evaporated solution to crystallize.

The white crystals which form are of ammonium sulphate ('sulphate of ammonia').

The two most important fertilizers are ammonium sulphate and ammonium nitrate (called 'Nitram') and they are produced by reacting ammonia gas with solutions of either sulphuric acid or nitric acid, e.g.

$$2NH_3(g) + H_2SO_4(aq) \longrightarrow (NH_4)_2SO_4(aq)$$

There are three important elements that are added to the soil via fertilizers: nitrogen (N), phosphorus (P) and potassium (K). The so-called NPK fertilizers usually contain ammonium nitrate (NH_4NO_3), ammonium phosphate (($NH_4)_2HPO_4$) and potassium chloride (KCl) in varying proportions (Fig. 33.17).

Fig. 33.17

The first two salts are made by reacting ammonia gas with a mixture of nitric acid and phosphoric(v) acid solutions.

$$NH_3(g) + HNO_3(aq) \longrightarrow NH_4NO_3(aq)$$
$$NH_3(g) + H_3PO_4(aq) \longrightarrow (NH_4)_2HPO_4(aq)$$

The potassium chloride is obtained from mineral deposits.

The selection of the NPK fertilizer that adds the correct proportions of each element to the particular soil and crop is very important. It would be very wasteful and expensive to add more of an element than was necessary. Also, the water in rivers and lakes become polluted by any excessive amounts of fertilizers being washed into them.

The high concentration of nitrates and phosphates in water encourages the growth of large numbers of green algae and hence bacteria. As they grow, these bacteria use up all the oxygen dissolved in the water with the disastrous result that it can no longer support any animal life. The nitrates and phosphates in untreated sewage also have the same effect. This kind of **water pollution** can be dealt with only by restricting the use of nitrate fertilizers and by treating sewage before it is pumped into rivers and lakes.

The nitrogen cycle

The use of nitrogen-containing (nitrogenous) fertilizers is one process in the **nitrogen cycle** (Fig. 33.18). In this cycle nitrogen, in the form of various compounds or as the element itself, gets circulated between the air, soils and living things. Like the carbon cycle (page 111), it is very important to life.

Soils always have nitrates in solutions which move between the soil grains. Plants are able to absorb these solutions through their roots. For some plants like peas, beans and clover, nitrogen from the air is converted directly to nitrates by nitrifying bacteria living on their roots. But most plants cannot use the nitrogen in the air like this. Instead, they have to rely on other processes to provide them with nitrates.

The fixation of nitrogen (page 129) is carried out both naturally and by Man. Because of the low yield of ammonia in the Haber process (15 per cent), attempts have been made to imitate the much more efficient fixation carried out in nature by the nitrifying bacteria, so far without commercial success. (The opposite of fixation is carried out by denitrifying bacteria on compounds containing nitrogen.)

Plants use the nitrates they absorb from the soil together with some of the carbohydrates they have made by photosynthesis (page 111), and convert them to **proteins**. Proteins are compounds made from the elements carbon, hydrogen, oxygen and nitrogen, and a few also contain sulphur. Animals use proteins in the plants they eat to form, for example, flesh, muscle and blood.

Nitric acid

Nitric acid is an oxidizing agent, with the concentrated acid having a more powerful effect than the dilute acid. In this way dilute nitric acid is different from dilute sulphuric or hydrochloric acids.

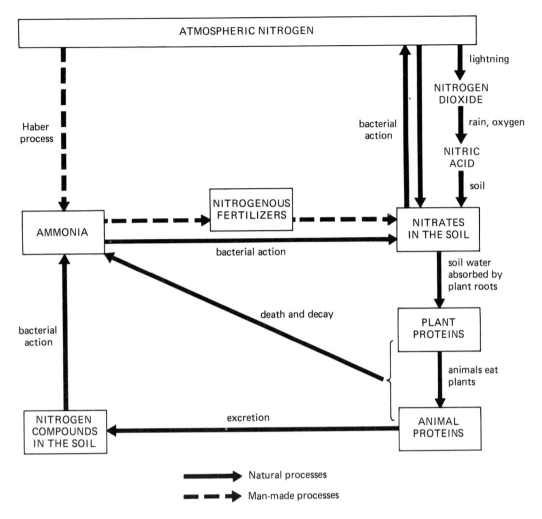

Natural processes
Man-made processes

Fig. 33.18

But dilute nitric acid is a typical acid in its reactions with alkalis, basic oxides and carbonates (page 71).

Your teacher may show you just how powerful an oxidizing agent nitric acid is by carefully adding a few drops of the concentrated acid to some warm sawdust. The sawdust bursts into flames straight away and a lot of brown fumes of nitrogen dioxide are given off. (In no circumstances should you try this for yourself.) The word-equation for this reaction can be written as

nitric acid   +   wood   ⟶   nitrogen dioxide
(concentrated)   (compound   + carbon dioxide
              of C, H & O)   + water

Concentrated nitric acid also oxidizes pure carbon and many other compounds containing carbon.

Experiment 33.4 Can nitric acid oxidize a metal?

1. Put two or three copper turnings in a small beaker kept in a fume cupboard. Carefully add to them a few drops of concentrated nitic acid from a dropper.

CARE: *do not inhale the gas. If you spill any acid onto your skin or clothes, wash it immediately with a large amount of water.*
Test the gas evolved with moist red and blue litmus paper.

▸   What is the gas?
▸   What colour is the solution formed in the reaction?
▸   To which substances has the acid been reduced?

2. Add a few cm³ of bench dilute (2 M) nitric acid to some copper turnings in a boiling tube. If no reaction occurs, or if the reaction is slow, warm the mixture *gently*. Test the gas with moist red and blue litmus paper.

▸   In what ways is this reaction like the reaction in 1?
▸   Is there any difference between them?

Both concentrated and dilute nitric acid react with most metals to form the metal nitrate in solution and one or more of the oxides of nitrogen. For example, copper and concentrated nitric acid give copper(II) nitrate solution and nitrogen dioxide.

Fig. 33.19 shows what happens in the reaction between copper and dilute nitric acid. If you look closely at the boiling tube, you may notice that the gas becomes coloured only some distance above the level of the acid. This is because the gas produced at

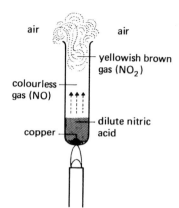

Fig. 33.19

the surface is colourless nitrogen monoxide (NO) which reacts with oxygen from the air in the upper part of the tube to produce some nitrogen dioxide (NO_2).

$$2NO(g) + O_2(g) \longrightarrow 2NO_2(g)$$

In its reaction with metals, dilute nitric acid does not behave like a typical dilute acid: it reacts with most metals, whereas dilute sulphuric acid and dilute hydrochloric acid react only with metals which are above hydrogen in the reactivity series. When dilute nitric acid reacts with a metal, nitrogen monoxide is usually formed, but when other acids react with metals, hydrogen is formed.

Nitrates

Nitrates are salts of nitric acid and can be prepared by the usual methods (Chapter 18). As mentioned above, dilute nitric acid is not a typical acid in its reaction with metals: the nitrate is formed even with metals low in the reactivity series, and a different gas is given off.

All nitrates are soluble in water and this makes them suitable as fertilizers (page 134).

All nitrates can be decomposed by heat. The extent of the decomposition (to a metal nitrite or an oxide) is linked to the position of the metal in the reactivity series.

Nitrate of metal high in reactivity series, e.g.

$$2NaNO_3(s) \longrightarrow 2NaNO_2(s) + O_2(g)$$
$$\text{sodium nitrite}$$

Nitrate of metal lower in reactivity series, e.g.

$$2Zn(NO_3)_2(s) \longrightarrow 2ZnO(s) + 4NO_2(g) + O_2(g)$$

Ammonium nitrate is decomposed to an oxide of nitrogen and water.

$$NH_4NO_3(s) \longrightarrow N_2O(g) + 2H_2O(g)$$

When nitrates are warmed with concentrated sulphuric acid, nitric acid is formed. If copper is present in the reaction mixture, the nitric acid reacts to give brown fumes of nitrogen dioxide. This reaction is often used as a test for nitrate ions (page 251).

The manufacture and uses of nitric acid

Nitric acid is manufactured by the oxidation of ammonia using a catalyst made of a platinum–rhodium alloy. The reaction is carried out at a pressure of about 4 atmospheres.

$$4NH_3(g) + 5O_2(g) \longrightarrow 4NO(g) + 6H_2O(g)$$

Air, water and the nitrogen monoxide are then passed into the absorption tower at a pressure of about 10 atmospheres where further oxidation occurs to form nitrogen dioxide (NO_2) and nitric acid.

$$2NO(g) + O_2(g) \longrightarrow 2NO_2(g)$$

$$4NO_2(g) + 2H_2O(l) + O_2(g) \longrightarrow 4HNO_3(aq)$$

Each reaction vessel for the oxidation of ammonia contains several expensive platinum–rhodium gauze sheets. Although the catalyst is not used up in the reaction itself (page 191), it does need to be replaced from time to time.

Fig. 33.20 Quarry blasting using a TNT/ammonium nitrate explosive

About 75 per cent of the nitric acid made in this process is used in fertilizer manufacture. But quite a lot is also used to make explosives such as TNT, nitroglycerine and ammonium nitrate (Fig. 33.20).

QUESTIONS

1 Explain why the Haber process is so important to modern food production.

2 (a) Use Fig. 33.18 to identify (i) *two* ways in nature that nitrogen in the air is fixed as nitrates, and (ii) *one* way in nature that the nitrogen in nitrates is returned to the soil after being taken up by plants.
(b) How does Man 'fix' nitrogen?

3 A grey metal *A* reacts with concentrated nitric acid giving off a brown gas *B* and forming a colourless solution. On evaporation and crystallization, the colourless solution forms white crystals *C*. When *C* is heated, it decomposes very readily to give the gas *B* and another gas *D* which relights a glowing splint. The solid residue *E*, left after the decomposition is complete, is a good conductor of electricity.
(a) What is the name of the gas *B*?
(b) What is the name of the gas *D*?
(c) Name two other elements which *C* must contain besides *A*.
(d) Is the solid residue *E* likely to be:
  (i) a metal,
  (ii) a metal oxide,
  (iii) a metal nitrate?
(e) In view of your answer to (d), do you think that *A* is a reactive or an unreactive metal? Give reasons for your answer.
(f) Suppose the metal *A* is silver. Write an equation for the decomposition of *C* to give *B*, *D* and *E*.

4 Dry ammonia is passed over a heated sample of dry copper(II) oxide of mass 2.40 g. After the reduction is finished, the resulting copper has a mass of 1.92 g. The water produced is collected by passing the gases through a drying agent. It is found that the water has a mass of 0.54 g. The remaining gases are passed through acid to remove the excess of ammonia and it is found that the volume of nitrogen collected is 240 cm³ under the conditions of the experiment. (Relative atomic masses: N = 14, H = 1.)
(a) What mass of oxygen is there in the copper(II) oxide?
(b) What mass of oxygen must there be in the water?
(c) What mass of hydrogen is there in the water and from which substance must it have come?
(d) What is the fraction of a mole of H atoms present in the sample of ammonia used?
(e) What is the mass of 240 cm³ of nitrogen given that the density of the gas under the conditions of the experiment is 1.17×10^{-3} g cm⁻³?
(f) What is the fraction of a mole of N atoms which your answer to (e) represents?
(g) From which substance must the nitrogen have come?
(h) How many moles of H atoms combine with 1 mole of N atoms to form 1 mole of ammonia?

5 (a) Work out the percentage by mass of nitrogen in each of the following fertilizers:

  ammonium sulphate, $(NH_4)_2SO_4$
  ammonium nitrate, NH_4NO_3
  calcium nitrate, $Ca(NO_3)_2$
  carbamide (urea), $CO(NH_2)_2$
  ammonia, NH_3

(b) Ammonium sulphate solution has a pH value of about 5. Why is this a disadvantage for a substance that is used as a fertilizer?
(c) Although calcium nitrate contains a fairly low percentage of nitrogen, there is a good reason why it is still a valuable fertilizer. What is this reason?
(d) All the above fertilizers are soluble in water. Why is this property essential for a fertilizer?
(Relative atomic masses: N = 14, H = 1, O = 16, S = 32, Ca = 40, C = 12.)

Key words

fractional distillation   **catalytic oxidation**   **nitrifying bacteria**

fixation of nitrogen   **Haber process**

Basic facts

- **Pure nitrogen and oxygen are made on a large scale by the fractional distillation of liquid air.**

- **Ammonia can be made in the laboratory by heating an ammonium salt with a solid alkali.**

- **Ammonia can be oxidized either to nitrogen or, in a catalysed reaction, to nitrogen monoxide.**

- **Ammonia is made from nitrogen and hydrogen on a large scale by the Haber process.**

- **Nitric acid is made by the catalytic oxidation of ammonia.**

- **Both ammonia and nitric acid are used to make nitrogenous fertilizers.**

- **Nitrogen is circulated between the air, soils and living things by way of the nitrogen cycle.**

- **Nitric acid is different from sulphuric and hydrochloric acids in that both in dilute and concentrated solutions it can act as an oxidizing agent towards metals.**

34 Chemicals from sulphur

The flow-chart (Fig. 34.1) summarizes most of the chemical reactions mentioned in this chapter starting from either rock sulphur or metal sulphides. Study it carefully as you work through the chapter.

produces almost pure sulphur because the other rocks do not melt. Since bulk liquids are more easy to handle than bulk solids, sulphur is frequently transported as a liquid.

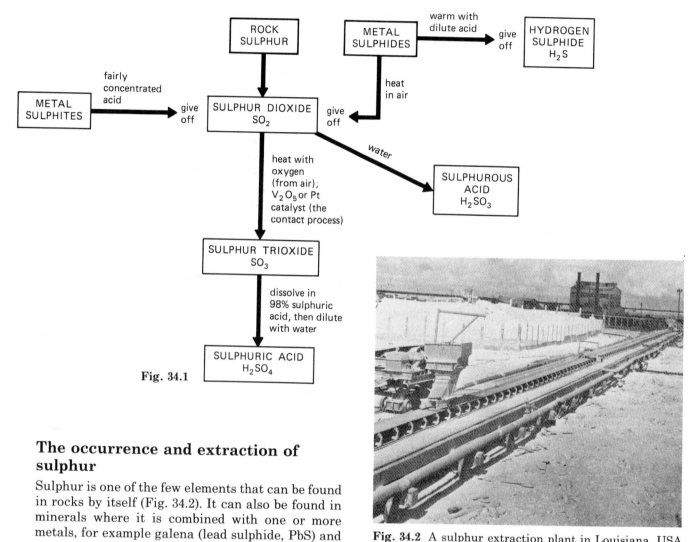

Fig. 34.1

The occurrence and extraction of sulphur

Sulphur is one of the few elements that can be found in rocks by itself (Fig. 34.2). It can also be found in minerals where it is combined with one or more metals, for example galena (lead sulphide, PbS) and copper pyrites (copper iron sulphide $CuFeS_2$). There are photographs of these two minerals on page 98. Sulphur also commonly occurs in fossil fuels. It can be removed from crude oil in one step of the refining process but it cannot easily be removed from coal, and the burning of sulphur-containing coal is the major source of sulphur dioxide as an atmospheric pollutant (page 144).

Sulphur is extracted from underground deposits of rock sulphur by the Frasch process. Three concentric pipes are lowered down a borehole to the deposit of sulphur. Superheated water and hot air are forced down two of the pipes; the sulphur, which has a fairly low melting point, becomes molten and is forced up the third pipe (Fig. 34.3). This method

Fig. 34.2 A sulphur extraction plant in Louisiana, USA

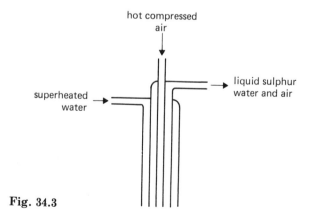

Fig. 34.3

The allotropes of sulphur

Experiment 34.1 Trying to make crystals of sulphur

1. Gently heat some powdered roll sulphur in an evaporating basin until it is just molten, and then allow it to cool. When a skin of crystals has covered the surface of the sulphur, punch a hole in the skin with a glass rod and rapidly but carefully pour out the sulphur which is still molten into another container (Fig. 34.4). (CARE: remember that the temperature of the molten sulphur will be over 100 °C.) Look at the residue in the evaporating basin.

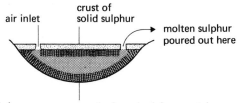

air inlet · crust of solid sulphur · molten sulphur poured out here

Fig. 34.4   needle-shaped sulphur crystals

▶ Describe the shape and colour of the crystals. If you have a microscope, look closely at one or two of the crystals under low power. Then put them aside for a few days and look at them again.
▶ Does their appearance change during this time?

2. Prepare a warm solution of sulphur in methylbenzene by heating a boiling tube half-full of methylbenzene in a beaker of warm water and adding small amounts of powdered roll sulphur until no more will dissolve. Keep the temperature of the water-bath at about 40 °C. (CARE: methylbenzene is extremely flammable: no bunsen burners should be alight when it is being used.)

Allow the solution to cool and look at the crystals produced using a low-power microscope.

▶ In what way are they different from the crystals prepared in 1?

These experiments give two different kinds of yellow crystal. There are two questions that can be asked about this:

1. What substance are the crystals made from?
2. Why are there two kinds of crystals and not just one?

The answer to the first question is easy to find. No chemical reaction has occurred in the experiments and the crystals must both be made from sulphur. This is confirmed by burning a sample of the crystals on a crucible lid: a colourless choking gas characteristic of sulphur is produced in each case and no residue remains. Also, equal masses of the two kinds of crystal burn to give the same volume of this gas, called sulphur dioxide (SO_2). This volume is what you would expect to be formed from samples of pure sulphur.

Sulphur exists as two **allotropes**, each with its own arrangement of sulphur particles. These allotropes have slightly different melting points and densities (Table 34.1). The needle-shaped allotrope is called **monoclinic sulphur** (β-sulphur) and the octahedral allotrope is called **rhombic sulphur** (α-sulphur).

Table 34.1

Property	Rhombic sulphur (α-sulphur)	Monoclinic sulphur (β-sulphur)
Density in g cm^{-3}	2.07	1.96
Melting point in °C	113	119
Temperature range of stability in °C	Up to 95.5	95.5 to 119
Volume of 1 mole of S atoms at 95.5 °C in cm^3	15.5	16.4
Chemical properties	← Identical →	

Crystals of monoclinic sulphur slowly change to rhombic sulphur when they are kept at room temperature. Also, if crystals of rhombic sulphur are kept at about 100 °C for a few days, they change into monoclinic crystals. The temperature above which monoclinic crystals are formed and below which rhombic crystals are formed is 95.5 °C. This is called the **transition temperature** and at this temperature both forms can exist together (Fig. 34.5).

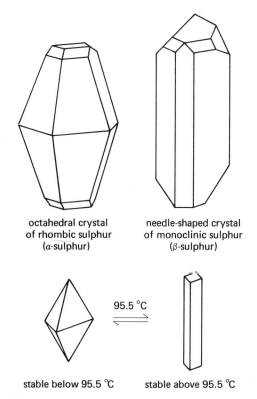

octahedral crystal of rhombic sulphur (α-sulphur)

needle-shaped crystal of monoclinic sulphur (β-sulphur)

95.5 °C

stable below 95.5 °C   stable above 95.5 °C

Fig. 34.5

You should now see why you get two kinds of crystal in Experiment 34.1. The freezing point of molten sulphur is 119 °C and so only monoclinic crystals can be obtained by cooling molten sulphur. But when a solvent is used, the kind of crystal obtained depends on the temperature at which crystallization occurs, and in part 2 of Experiment 34.1 the temperature is well below the transition temperature.

It has been shown that both allotropes of sulphur are made from molecules that contain eight atoms of sulphur in a bent ring (Fig. 34.6). These molecules can pack together in two ways depending on the temperature and so two kinds of crystal are possible. The rate of change from one allotrope to the other is slow because the S_8 molecules are held quite firmly in the crystalline arrangement and cannot easily alter their positions.

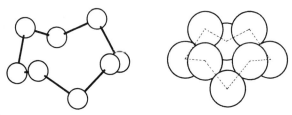

Fig. 34.6 Two ways of representing the S_8 ring

The chemical properties of these allotropes of sulphur are very similar.

The action of heat on sulphur

Experiment 34.2 Heating sulphur

Heat about three spatula measures of powdered roll sulphur in a small test-tube. At first, you should heat the sulphur very gently using a small luminous bunsen flame and so obtain a pale coloured liquid. If the liquid has a dark colour, you have heated it too strongly and you should let it resolidify and then start again.

After the sulphur has just melted, raise its temperature slowly, and carefully note any changes in colour. From time to time, tip the tube slightly so that you can see how easily the liquid flows. (Be careful not to let any liquid run out of the tube.) When each marked change has occurred, let the liquid cool and decide whether or not the changes are reversible.

Finally, heat the sulphur until it is boiling and then quickly pour the liquid into a small beaker of cold water. The solid that is formed is called **plastic sulphur**.

Fig. 34.7 shows the main changes which occur when sulphur is heated. These remarkable changes can be explained only by knowing what happens to

the S_8 molecules as the temperature rises. The molecules bump into each other and at a high enough temperature the collisions are energetic enough to cause some of the rings to break. The short chains of eight sulphur atoms so formed then link together to give much longer chains: this process of forming long molecules from many short ones is called polymerization (page 222). These long chains get tangled up and cannot easily move past one another. As the temperature rises further, there is enough energy for some of them to 'depolymerize', that is, break up into much shorter chains which can move past one another more easily than the longer chains.

The very viscous ('sticky') black liquid has many long molecules that cannot move past one another easily, whereas the very mobile ('runny') pale yellow liquid has mostly ring molecules that readily move past one another. The dark red-brown liquid is a little less viscous than the black liquid because the shorter chains get less tangled up than the longer chains and so more movement is possible.

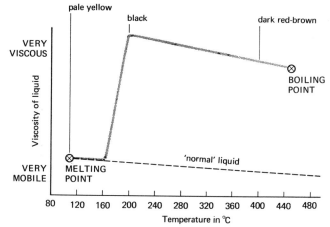

Fig. 34.7

When sulphur that is nearly boiling is cooled very quickly, none of the changes back to a crystalline solid have time to occur. The arrangement of the particles in the dark red-brown liquid gets trapped or 'frozen' into the solid. This explains why plastic sulphur has rubber-like properties at first. But in a few days the solid goes crystalline and brittle as the chains gradually break into S_8 chains which then form S_8 rings.

The chemical properties of sulphur

Sulphur is immediately below oxygen in the periodic table. Are oxygen and sulphur chemically similar?

Sulphur combines with many metals when a mixture of sulphur and the metal is heated. (Some of these reactions are very dangerous.) The compounds formed are called metal **sulphides** and many of them contain the sulphide ion, S^{2-}. In compounds with other non-metals, sulphur atoms often form two covalent bonds (page 169), as in hydrogen sulphide (H_2S).

The atomic numbers of oxygen and sulphur are 8 and 16 respectively. This means that each of their atoms has 6 electrons in the outer energy level (page 153). To achieve the stable number of 8 outer electrons, these atoms need to gain 2 more electrons. This explains why the anions of sulphur and oxygen have a charge of -2 and why the formulas of water and hydrogen sulphide are H_2O and H_2S. To understand this argument fully, you will need to read Chapter 39 on chemical bonding.

But this comparison of the chemistry of oxygen and sulphur cannot be taken very far. In a lot of sulphur compounds (such as sulphur dioxide) the sulphur atoms form more than two covalent bonds.

Sulphur is a non-metal and its oxides, sulphur dioxide and sulphur trioxide, are both acidic as expected (see below).

Sulphur dioxide

Sulphur burns with a blue flame in either oxygen or air to form sulphur dioxide which is acidic and has a choking smell.

$$S(s) + O_2(g) \longrightarrow SO_2(g)$$

Many metals sulphides, when heated in air, produce the metal oxide and sulphur dioxide. This kind of reaction is used in industry both for the manufacture of sulphur dioxide and for the production of metal oxides which are later reduced to the metal.

Another way of making sulphur dioxide is by warming fairly concentrated hydrochloric acid with a metal sulphite such as sodium sulphite (Na_2SO_3).

The acidic properties of sulphur dioxide

Sulphur dioxide is very soluble in water and it reacts with water to produce an acidic solution called sulphurous acid.

$$SO_2(g) + H_2O(l) \rightleftharpoons H^+(aq) + HSO_3^-(aq) \quad (1)$$
$$\text{hydrogensulphite ion}$$

$$HSO_3^-(aq) \rightleftharpoons H^+(aq) + SO_3^{2-}(aq) \quad (2)$$
$$\text{sulphite ion}$$

Both these reactions can go in either direction and sulphur dioxide is given off when sulphurous acid is heated. As in the reaction of carbon dioxide and water (page 117), the $H^+(aq)$ ions giving rise to acidity come from the water, not from the oxide

itself. Both acids are weak and are also readily decomposed.

$$CO_2(g) + \boxed{H}_2O(l) \qquad SO_2(g) + \boxed{H}_2O(l)$$

reversible $\updownarrow$ reaction reversible $\updownarrow$ reaction

$$\boxed{H}CO_3^-(aq) + \boxed{H^+(aq)} \qquad \boxed{H}SO_3^-(aq) + \boxed{H^+(aq)}$$

reversible $\updownarrow$ reaction reversible $\updownarrow$ reaction

$$CO_3^{2-}(aq) + \boxed{2H^+(aq)} \qquad SO_3^{2-}(aq) + \boxed{2H^+(aq)}$$

When sulphurous acid is neutralized with an alkali, a metal sulphite is produced. For example, with sodium hydroxide solution, the salt sodium sulphite is formed.

$$2NaOH(aq) + SO_2(g) \longrightarrow Na_2SO_3(aq) + H_2O(l)$$

The reaction of sodium sulphite with acids can be written as

$$SO_3^{2-}(s) + 2H^+(aq) \longrightarrow SO_2(g) + H_2O(l)$$

This is the reverse of the reaction that occurs when sulphur dioxide reacts with water.

The oxidizing properties of sulphur dioxide

Magnesium ribbon burns in sulphur dioxide to form a yellow residue of sulphur and a white residue of magnesium oxide.

$$Mg(s) + SO_2(g) \longrightarrow MgO(s) + S(s)$$

This is the oxidation of magnesium by the transfer of oxygen from sulphur dioxide. The gas is itself reduced by the removal of all its oxygen.

The reducing properties of sulphur dioxide

Sulphur dioxide has many more reactions in which it is a reducing agent rather than as an oxidizing agent. It can be oxidized to sulphur trioxide (SO_3) by reaction with oxygen (page 142). When the oxidizing agent is in aqueous solution, the sulphur dioxide is oxidized to sulphate ions (SO_4^{2-}). For example, sulphur dioxide reduces hydrogen peroxide solution.

$$H_2O_2(aq) + SO_2(g) \longrightarrow 2H^+(aq) + SO_4^{2-}(aq)$$

The usual test for sulphur dioxide is to hold a piece of filter paper soaked in acidified potassium dichromate(VI) solution in a stream of the gas. The colour of the solution changes from orange to very pale green. In a similar way a purple solution of potassium manganate(VII) goes colourless in a stream of sulphur dioxide. Most oxidizing agents convert sulphur dioxide to sulphate ions.

The uses of sulphur dioxide

The main use of sulphur dioxide is in the manufacture of sulphuric acid (see below). Sulphur dioxide is very poisonous to most forms of life and in low concentration is a permitted food preservative. In foods, its concentration has to be sufficiently low to be harmless to humans but high enough to kill moulds and bacteria.

The properties of sulphuric acid

When sulphur trioxide reacts with water, sulphuric acid is formed.

$$H_2O(l) + SO_3(g) \longrightarrow H_2SO_4(aq)$$

A dilute solution of sulphuric acid has all the properties of a typical acid (page 71). The usual test for sulphate ions is to add barium chloride solution to the solution under test that has already been acidified with dilute hydrochloric acid. The formation of a white precipitate of barium sulphate shows the presence of sulphate ions.

$$Ba^{2+}(aq) + SO_4{}^{2-}(aq) \longrightarrow BaSO_4(s)$$

Pure hydrogen sulphate is a rather viscous liquid with a high boiling point (330 °C) which rapidly absorbs moisture from the atmosphere. It reacts very exothermically with water and great care has to be taken when it is diluted to prevent explosive boiling. The hydrogen sulphate is added, a small amount at a time, to a large volume of water and the mixture has to be stirred and cooled.

Its powerful dehydrating properties are shown in the following reactions (*a*), (*b*) and (*c*):

(*a*) When concentrated sulphuric acid is added to hydrated copper sulphate, the blue crystals gradually turn white and the mixture gets hot.

$$CuSO_4 \cdot 5H_2O(s) \xrightarrow{-5H_2O} CuSO_4(s)$$

(*b*) Carbon monoxide is formed when concentrated sulphuric acid is added to methanoic acid.

$$HCO_2H(aq) \xrightarrow{-H_2O} CO(g)$$

(*c*) When concentrated sulphuric acid is added to sugar (sucrose), the sugar slowly darkens in colour until it is black and the mixture froths as it gets hot.

$$C_{12}H_{22}O_{11}(s) \xrightarrow{-11H_2O} 12C(s)$$

Concentrated sulphuric acid reacts with metal chlorides and nitrates to produce hydrogen chloride and hydrogen nitrate respectively. These reactions occur because hydrogen sulphate has a higher boiling point than either hydrogen chloride or hydrogen nitrate.

$$H_2SO_4(l) + Cl^-(s) \longrightarrow HCl(g) + HSO_4{}^-(s)$$

$$H_2SO_4(l) + NO_3{}^-(s) \xrightarrow{warm} HNO_3(g) + HSO_4{}^-(s)$$

The manufacture of sulphuric acid

The main stage in the manufacture of sulphuric acid, the so-called **contact process**, is the oxidation of sulphur dioxide by oxygen in the presence of a catalyst to produce sulphur trioxide, SO_3. A good yield of sulphur trioxide at a fast enough rate can be obtained using a fairly high temperature (450–500 °C), atmospheric pressure and a catalyst of vanadium(v) oxide, V_2O_5. The reasons why these conditions are chosen are discussed on page 200.

$$2SO_2(g) + O_2(g) \longrightarrow 2SO_3(g)$$

Fig. 34.8 shows how sulphur trioxide can be made from sulphur dioxide in the laboratory. It is essential that both the sulphur dioxide and the oxygen are completely dry because the sulphur trioxide produced reacts very vigorously with water.

Sulphur dioxide and oxygen (in the approximate ratio of 2:1 by volume) are passed over hot platinized mineral wool, which acts as the catalyst. The gases are then passed through a cooled tube at 0 °C to form silky white crystals of sulphur trioxide. A platinum catalyst is not used in the industrial process because it too easily absorbs impurities from the gases. This 'poisoning' of the catalyst makes it far less effective in speeding up the reaction.

The sulphur trioxide forms a mist in damp air as it reacts with the water vapour. To avoid this mist

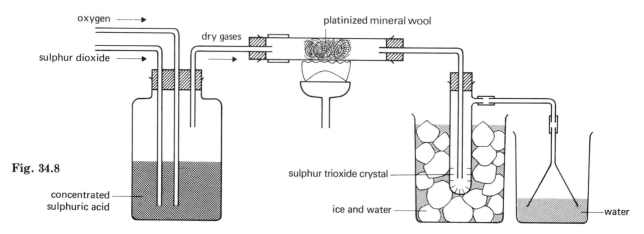

Fig. 34.8

oxygen ⟶

dry gases

sulphur dioxide ⟶

platinized mineral wool

concentrated sulphuric acid

sulphur trioxide crystal

ice and water

water

formation in the industrial process, the sulphur trioxide is first dissolved in concentrated sulphuric acid before being diluted with water to the required concentration. The overall chemical reaction can be represented by the equation

$$SO_3(g) + H_2O(l) \longrightarrow H_2SO_4 aq$$

This equation shows that the dense white fumes that form when sulphur trioxide meets damp air are small droplets of sulphuric acid. This is why you must never try to smell sulphur trioxide: the formation of sulphuric acid in your lungs would be very harmful.

The uses of sulphuric acid

In the nineteenth century, sulphuric acid was the most important substance in the chemical industry, and the amount used by a country was considered to be an excellent indication of its commercial prosperity. With the growth in this century of several new industries that do not use sulphuric acid, it is not such a vital material as it used to be. Even so, sulphuric acid is still a very important chemical because it is one of the reactants used for the manufacture of a whole range of useful substances, in particular fertilizers, paints, detergents, and natural and man-made fibres.

Sulphate of ammonia (ammonium sulphate, page 134) and superphosphate are fertilizers which are made using sulphuric acid. For superphosphate, rock phosphate (calcium phosphate) is reacted with sulphuric acid.

$$Ca_3(PO_4)_2(s) + 2H_2SO_4(aq)$$
$$\longrightarrow \underbrace{Ca(H_2PO_4)_2(s) + 2CaSO_4(s)}_{\text{superphosphate}}$$

The product is more soluble in water than rock phosphate and so is a more useful fertilizer.

Modern paints contain a very white compound called titanium(IV) oxide, TiO_2. One way this is made is by treating the titanium mineral called ilmenite with sulphuric acid. When the resulting titanium sulphate is converted back to titanium(IV) oxide, the impurities in the mineral are left in solution in the acid.

Sulphuric acid is also used in the manufacture of many detergents (page 239).

Hydrogen sulphide

Hydrogen sulphide (H_2S) is a very toxic gas with a characteristic 'bad eggs' smell. It is produced by the reaction of a metal sulphide with a dilute acid.

$$S^{2-}(s) + 2H^+(aq) \longrightarrow H_2S(g)$$

Like sulphur dioxide, it reduces oxidizing agents such as acidified potassium dichromate(VI) solution

and acidified potassium manganate(VII) solution. The colour changes are the same (page 141) except that a yellow precipitate of sulphur is formed with hydrogen sulphide but not with sulphur dioxide because hydrogen sulphide (and sulphides generally) are oxidized to sulphur.

$$S^{2-} \xrightarrow{-2e^-} S \quad \text{(see page 173)}$$

Sulphur dioxide does not react with moist lead ethanoate (lead acetate) paper but hydrogen sulphide gives a black precipitate of lead sulphide.

$$Pb^{2+}(aq) + S^{2-}(aq) \longrightarrow PbS(s)$$
$$\text{(from } H_2S \text{ in water)}$$

This reaction is used as a test for sulphide ions. Many other metal sulphides are also insoluble in water.

'White lead' (basic lead carbonate) was often used as a white pigment in oil paints. When this pigment is exposed to an industrial atmosphere containing hydrogen sulphide, it turns to black lead sulphide. Restoration of the white colour is achieved by using hydrogen peroxide solution which oxidizes lead sulphide to white lead sulphate.

$$\underset{\text{black}}{PbS(s)} + 4H_2O_2(aq) \longrightarrow \underset{\text{white}}{PbSO_4(s)} + 4H_2O(l)$$

Sulphides, sulphites and sulphates

Sulphides, sulphites and sulphates are all salts of acids. Sulphides contain the S^{2-} anion and are salts of the weak acid formed when hydrogen sulphide (H_2S) is dissolved in water. Sulphites contain the SO_3^{2-} anion and are salts of sulphurous acid, another weak acid (page 82). Sulphates contain the SO_4^{2-} anion and are salts of sulphuric acid, a strong acid.

Experiment 34.3 Do sulphides, sulphites and sulphates react with an acid and with an oxidizing agent?

Add a few drops of bench dilute (2 M) hydrochloric acid to a small quantity of each of the following solids: sodium sulphide (CARE: do not get any sodium sulphide on your skin), sodium sulphite and sodium sulphate. Warm the test-tube gently and test any gas given off in two ways:

1. with a strip of filter paper soaked in acidified potassium dichromate solution;
2. with moist lead ethanoate (lead acetate) paper.

Use the table on page 250 to identify the gases.

To the acidified solutions, add potassium manganate(VII) solution a few drops at a time.

▶ Is the potassium manganate(VII) solution decolorized?
▶ Is any other change apparent?

The salts formed from weak acids readily react with the dilute hydrochloric acid to produce the gas (either H_2S or SO_2) from which their 'parent' acid is made. The salt formed from the strong acid (that is, from sodium sulphate) does not give off any gas with dilute hydrochloric acid.

Sulphites and sulphides are both rapidly oxidized by potassium manganate(VII) solution. Sulphite ions are oxidized to sulphate ions (which can be detected by their reaction with barium chloride solution), while sulphides are oxidized to sulphur which appears as an off-white or yellow cloudiness in the solution.

Some reactions of sulphides, sulphites and sulphates are given in Table 34.2. These reactions can be used as tests for compounds that contain these ions.

Sulphur compounds in the air

Sulphur compounds, especially sulphur dioxide and hydrogen sulphide, are among the main causes of air pollution. Certain fuels contain sulphur and when they burn, sulphur dioxide is given off: coal and fuel oil contain up to 3% sulphur, and petrol about 0.05%. Hydrogen sulphide is released into the air by the decay of dead animal and plant material, and by the decomposition of human waste.

The amounts of these pollutants in the air are not very high. On average there is a little less than a millionth of a gram (10^{-6} g) each of sulphur dioxide and hydrogen sulphide in a cubic metre of air. Over cities there is usually much more sulphur dioxide: the concentration may reach a thousandth of a gram (10^{-3} g) per cubic metre close to large sources of pollution.

You may think that such small amounts of these gases would not have any serious effects. But this is not so. Quite low concentrations of sulphur dioxide can damage the leaves of plants and stunt their growth, and they can also make people's respiratory illnesses much worse. Also, sulphur dioxide and hydrogen sulphide are both oxidized in the atmosphere to sulphuric acid. As well as being harmful to plants and animals, this acid attacks the stonework of buildings, especially limestone (Fig. 34.9) and causes it to crumble.

Fig. 34.9

Table 34.2

	Add dilute hydrochloric acid	Add potassium manganate(VII) solution to an acidified solution	Other tests
Sulphates, SO_4^{2-}	No reaction	No decolorization	White precipitate of $BaSO_4$ is formed when $BaCl_2$ is added to a solution acidified with dilute HCl
Sulphites, SO_3^{2-}	Cough-inducing smell of SO_2 $SO_3^{2-}(s) + 2H^+(aq) \longrightarrow SO_2(g) + H_2O(l)$	Decolorization of $KMnO_4$ leaving a clear solution $SO_3^{2-}(aq) \xrightarrow{oxidation} SO_4^{2-}(aq)$	Oxidize SO_3^{2-} to SO_4^{2-} and then test for SO_4^{2-}
Sulphides, S^{2-}	'Bad eggs' smell of H_2S $S^{2-}(s) + 2H^+(aq) \longrightarrow H_2S(g)$	Decolorization of $KMnO_4$ leaving a cloudy suspension of sulphur $S^{2-}(aq) \xrightarrow{oxidation} S(s)$	Black precipitate of PbS is formed when a soluble lead salt is added

'**Acid rain**' is rain that contains dissolved sulphur dioxide. The main sources of this gas are coal- and oil-burning power stations. These power stations usually have tall chimneys so that the waste gases are dispersed into the air, and the area around the power station is often not badly polluted. But the pollution occurs downwind from the power station and can cause serious damage to both forests and animal life. The sulphur dioxide can be carried for hundreds of kilometres in the air. It is claimed that the sulphur dioxide produced by power stations in the USA is causing serious damage to forests in Canada, and by British power stations to forests in Scandinavia.

Experiment 34.4 *What effect does sulphur dioxide in the air have on metals?*

Set up on the apparatus shown in Fig. 34.10. Leave the metal foils in the plastic box for at least a week.

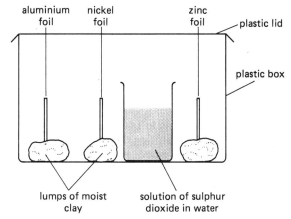

Fig. 34.10

▶ What signs of corrosion are there on the metals? (Compare the foils from the box with foils of the same metals from your laboratory shelves.)
▶ What further experiment is necessary to show that the corrosion is caused by the sulphur dioxide, and not by something else in the air of the box?

The corrosion of metals in an atmosphere containing sulphur dioxide is thought to be caused by sulphuric acid. This is formed on the surface of the metal and reacts with its protective layer. Once the fresh metal is exposed to the air, corrosion can take place much more quickly.

The protective layer on most metals is an oxide or a carbonate of the metal. Both these classes of compounds react with acids to form salts, and so the substances formed by this kind of corrosion are sulphates.

QUESTIONS

1 Both carbon dioxide and sulphur dioxide turn limewater cloudy. Describe one way (apart from smell) that you could use to distinguish between these two gases.

2 A country has reserves of crude oil and copper pyrites. Draw a flow-diagram to show how the fertilizer 'sulphate of ammonia' (ammonium sulphate) could be made on a large scale starting from these two materials, and air and water.

3 Describe how you would make crystals of copper(II) sulphate starting from copper metal and dilute sulphuric acid. Write equations for the chemical reactions.

4 List some of the ways in which man has caused pollution of the air.

5 Look at Table 34.1 which gives some of the properties of rhombic and monoclinic sulphur. Would you expect either a mass change or a volume change when monoclinic sulphur changes to rhombic sulphur at room temperature? Explain your answer.

6 When rhombic sulphur is heated very slowly it begins to melt at a temperature close to 119 °C. If it is heated very quickly it melts at about 113 °C. If a freshly prepared sample of monoclinic sulphur is heated, it melts at 119 °C, but if it has been prepared several days before, then it melts at a temperature nearer 113 °C. Write a short account explaining these observations using the idea of a transition temperature.

7 The extraction of sulphur from underground deposits of rock-like sulphur is carried out by passing very hot water under pressure into the deposits. The sulphur melts and is then pumped up to the surface where it solidifies and separates from the water.
(*a*) Explain what the temperature of the very hot water has to be in this extraction, and so why the water is under pressure.
(*b*) Why is the molten material pumped up to the surface along with the water made only of sulphur and not of sulphur mixed up with other molten rocks?
(*c*) Which allotrope of sulphur first forms at the surface as the molten sulphur solidifies? What eventually happens to this allotrope at ordinary temperatures?

8 A colourless gas X has the following reactions:
(i)   when it is burnt in oxygen, it forms water and sulphur dioxide;
(ii) when it is passed over heated tin, a flammable gas Y is produced and a solid residue remains;
(iii) when it is heated to a high temperature it forms two products, a yellow solid and gas Y.
Answer these questions about X and Y.
(*a*) What is Y likely to be?
(*b*) What is the name of the yellow solid in (iii)?
(*c*) From your answers to (*a*) and (*b*) say which two elements X must contain.
(*d*) Explain why water and sulphur dioxide are the products of the burning of X.
(*e*) Explain what is happening to X in reaction (ii).
(*f*) Name one other substance which would probably decompose X in the same way as tin does.

9 You are given four unlabelled bottles, each of which contains one of the following solutions: sodium sulphate, sodium sulphite, sodium sulphide, and sodium carbonate. Explain what tests you would carry out to identify each solution. You should say what each solution would do in each test that you use.

10 Starting with solid sulphur, outline how you would prepare samples of: (a) iron sulphide, (b) hydrogen sulphide, (c) sulphur dioxide, (d) sulphuric acid.

Write equations for the reactions involved.

11 Explain what is meant by the statement 'dilute sulphuric acid is a typical strong acid'.

12 Selenium is the element immediately below sulphur in the periodic table. By assuming that the chemistries of sulphur and selenium are similar, answer the following questions.

(a) Write the equation for the reaction that occurs when selenium (symbol Se) is heated in air.
(b) How would you expect the substance formed in (a) to react with water? Write an equation for the reaction.
(c) What would be formed if the substance formed in (a) was mixed with oxygen and passed over a hot catalyst? Write the equation for the reaction and for the reaction that occurs when the product of this reaction is added to water.
(d) How would the solution formed in (c) react with (i) magnesium, (ii) sodium carbonate solution and (iii) copper oxide?

Key words

allotrope   transition temperature   catalyst poisoning

allotropy   contact process   acid rain

Basic facts

- Sulphur exhibits allotropy. The transition temperature between rhombic and monoclinic sulphur is 95.5 °C.

- Sulphur is obtained from underground deposits by the Frasch process.

- The main chemical properties of sulphur are its reactions with metals to form metal sulphides and with oxygen to form sulphur dioxide.

- Sulphurous acid is formed when sulphur dioxide reacts with water. The salts of sulphurous acid are the sulphites.

- Sulphur dioxide is usually prepared in the laboratory by reacting a sulphite with hydrochloric acid. It is a powerful reducing agent and reduces most oxidizing agents, but occasionally it reacts as an oxidizing agent.

- Sulphur trioxide is made by the oxidation of sulphur dioxide and with water forms the strong acid sulphuric acid.

- Dilute sulphuric acid is a typical strong acid.

- Concentrated sulphuric acid behaves as a powerful dehydrating agent (with sugar, hydrated copper sulphate and methanoic acid) and as an involatile acid (with nitrates and chlorides).

- Sulphuric acid is a very important industrial chemical and has many uses.

- Hydrogen sulphide is prepared by reacting a metal sulphide with an acid. With water it forms a weakly acidic solution. Its salts are called sulphides.

- Hydrogen sulphide and sulphides are easily oxidized to sulphur by most oxidizing agents.

- Many metal sulphides are insoluble in water and the formation of a black precipitate of lead sulphide is used as a test for sulphide ions.

- Compounds of sulphur are responsible for some serious pollution of the atmosphere.

Ideas and explanations

35 The story of the periodic table

The importance of classification

Classifying things is a common activity of all scientists. It is one step in the process of making sense of the world around us and developing explanations for what we observe.

There are several examples of classifications in this book. An important one is the division of elements into metals and non-metals (page 28). Elements can be further divided by finding out more about their physical and chemical properties.

Throughout the nineteenth century, chemists had suspected that there was some link between the relative atomic masses of the elements and their properties. But their work was hampered by two problems: only about half the elements we know today had been discovered and isolated, and their relative atomic masses were often not determined accurately. It took many years for a form of the **periodic table** to be developed.

Early developments

J. W. Döbereiner, a German chemist, was the first person to see a connection between relative atomic masses and chemical properties. In 1817 he noticed that certain groups of three elements with closely similar properties have relative atomic masses which increase in a regular way. An example of such a '**triad**' is the series of elements calcium, strontium, and barium: the relative atomic mass of strontium is about midway between those of calcium and barium (the accurate relative atomic mass of strontium is 87.6).

$$\frac{40.1(Ca) + 137.3(Ba)}{2} = 88.7$$

This is not an isolated coincidence and the relative atomic masses of three other triads, chlorine/bromine/iodine, sulphur/selenium/tellurium, and lithium/sodium/potassium show a similar pattern. However, it is also possible to find triads (for example, copper/silver/gold) of similar elements whose relative atomic masses do not rise in a regular way. Döbereiner's discovery was a first step towards a classification of elements based on their relative atomic masses but it is a long way from the modern periodic table.

It was in the 1860s that the crucial steps were taken. In 1862 De Chancourtois arranged the known elements in order of their relative atomic masses in a spiral around a vertical cylinder. He divided the cylinder into sixteen vertical groups and discovered that similar elements occur in the same group. A flattened version of this type of periodic table is shown in Fig. 35.1 for the first twenty elements. Notice that, as in the modern periodic table, it is difficult to place hydrogen in any particular group.

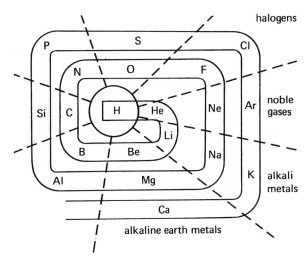

Fig. 35.1

A similar type of discovery was made in 1864 by J. A. R. Newlands, a British chemist. He said that when the elements were arranged in order of their relative atomic masses every *eighth* element was similar. (It was not every *ninth* element because at that time the noble gases were not known.) Newlands' idea became known as the Law of Octaves because of the similarity between the variation of chemical properties and the repetition of a musical note at the same position in each octave. Newlands' periodic table was criticized because it contained many exceptions to the Law of Octaves. For example, he was forced to place cobalt and nickel in the same family as the halogens, and iron in the same family as oxygen and sulphur.

Also in 1864, a German chemist called Lothar Meyer plotted the 'atomic volume' of a series of solid

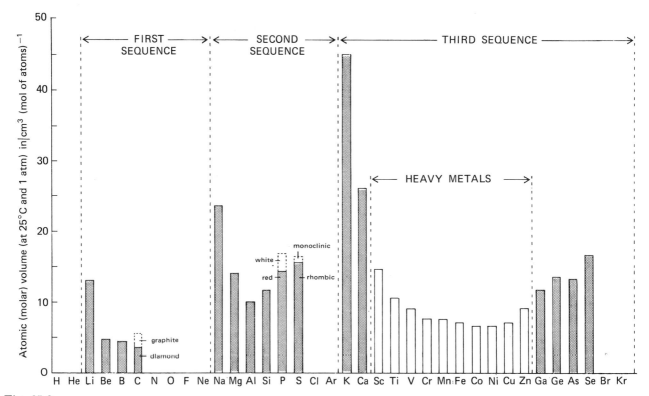

Fig. 35.2

elements against relative atomic mass. A histogram similar to his graph is shown in Fig. 35.2: the 'atomic volume' is the volume of a mole of atoms at 25 °C and normal atmospheric pressure. This 'graph' is different from Lothar Meyer's graph in that the order of the elements is the one used in the modern periodic table.

There is a pattern to these 'atomic volumes'. If you ignore the 'heavy metals', each sequence of eight elements (marked with a tint) shows a fall and then a rise in 'atomic volumes'. The 'heavy metals' do not interrupt the overall pattern but merely extend the sequence to eighteen elements.

Other properties of the elements also show a repeating pattern when their values are plotted against relative atomic mass. This repeating pattern of properties is called **periodicity**.

Fig. 35.3

Mendeleev's periodic table

It is the famous Russian chemist Dimitri Mendeleev (Fig. 35.3) who deserves the credit for proposing the first detailed periodic table in 1869. This table owed much to the work of the other chemists already mentioned, but Mendeleev succeeded in building up a far better scheme with fewer elements which did not fit the pattern (Fig. 35.4). This was because he was prepared to move some of the elements around the table until he found a suitable position for them. It sometimes meant that he had to switch a pair of elements and have the order of increasing relative atomic mass reversed.

Another adjustment to the table that Mendeleev sometimes made was to leave gaps between certain elements when it was clear that to place them next to each other would destroy the pattern. He assumed that these gaps would eventually be filled by elements yet to be discovered. He surprised his fellow chemists by boldly predicting in great detail the properties of these unknown elements, and his predictions encouraged the search for new elements. When some of these were discovered, chemists found that Mendeleev's predictions were surprisingly close to their observations. The periodic table had passed its most rigorous test.

In the periodic table, there are horizontal rows called **periods** and vertical columns called **groups**. It is in the groups that you are most likely to find elements with properties in common.

Mendeleev was very confident of his pattern even though the evidence for it was far from complete:

ОПЫТ СИСТЕМЫ ЭЛЕМЕНТОВ,

основанной на их атомном весе и химическом сходстве.

(Разослано Д. И. Менделеевым

в феврале 1869 года некоторым из химиков).

```
                      Ti=50    Zr=90    ?=180
                       V=51    Nb=94   Ta=182.
                       C:=52   Mo=96    W=186.
                       Mn=55   Rh=104,4 Pt=197,4
                       Fe=56   Ru=104,4 Ir=198.
                    Ni-Co=59   Pl=106,6 Os=199.
H=1                       Cu=63,4 Ag=108  Hg=200.
     Be=9,4  Mg=24     Zn=65,2  Cd=112
     B=11    Al=27,4   ?=68     Ur=116   Au=197?
     C=12    Si=28     ?=70     Sn=118
     N=14    P=31      As=75    Sb=122   Bi=210
     O=16    S=32      Se=79,4  Te=128?
     F=19    Cl=35,5   Br=80    I=127
Li=7 Na=23   K=39      Rb=85,4  Cs=133   Tl=204
             Ca=40     Sr=87,6  Ba=137   Pb=207.
             ?=45      Ce=92
             ?Er=56    La=94
             ?Yt=60    Di=95
             ?In=75,6  Th=118?
```

Fig. 35.4 Mendeleev's periodic table, first published in Russian

only sixty-three elements were known at the time and there were many gaps in his table. His ideas were an imaginative leap into the unknown. The following extract from his writings shows his great confidence in his own ideas:

'...although I have had my doubts about some obscure points, yet I have never once doubted the universality of this law, because it could not possibly be the result of chance.'

The 'obscure points' to which Mendeleev refers are the minor irregularities in his table. Apart from the changes in the order of increasing relative atomic mass, it was also necessary for him to group several elements such as iron, cobalt, and nickel in the same vertical group. What Mendeleev did not realize was that these 'obscure points' could be cleared up once scientists had found an *explanation* for the periodic variation of properties in terms of the arrangement of electrons in the atoms.

QUESTIONS

1 In Mendeleev's time, the relative atomic mass of beryllium (Be) was thought to be about 13.5. Beryllium is known to be a metallic element with some properties in common with magnesium.
(a) If the relative atomic mass of beryllium were 13.5, between which two elements would it be placed in Mendeleev's periodic table?
(b) Is this a likely position for this element in view of its observed properties? Give a reason for your answer.
(c) In which family of elements do you think that beryllium should be placed?
(d) Is the modern value for the relative atomic mass of beryllium consistent with its position in the periodic table? Explain your answer.

2 In Mendeleev's periodic table, there was a gap in the group of elements containing silicon (Si) and tin (Sn). Mendeleev called this element ekasilicon (Es), but it was renamed germanium after its discovery.

Molar volume in cm³ (mol of atoms)⁻¹	Density in g cm⁻³	Relative atomic mass	Elements	
11.6	2.42	28.1	Si	Increasing
?	?	?	Es	metallic
16.4	7.31	118.7	Sn ↓	character

(a) Use the table above to estimate the relative atomic mass, the density and the molar volume of ekasilicon.
(b) What is the formula of the oxide of ekasilicon likely to be?
(c) Is ekasilicon likely to be a metal, a non-metal or an element showing some metallic properties and some non-metallic properties?

Key words

periodic table   **triads**   **molar volume ('atomic volume')**   **periodicity**   **period**   **group**

Basic facts

- **When elements are arranged in order of increasing relative atomic mass, they show a periodicity in their properties, that is, there is a repeating pattern in the way the properties vary.**

- **This periodicity is not satisfactory unless the order of some elements is slightly changed. This means that in a few cases an element with a higher relative atomic mass is placed *before* an element with a lower relative atomic mass.**

- **Mendeleev's periodic table makes this pattern very clear and was used successfully to predict the properties of some undiscovered elements.**

36 Atomic structure and the periodic table

Mendeleev discovered a periodicity (a repeating pattern of properties) when the elements are arranged in order of increasing relative atomic mass. It is now known that to explain this periodicity, we need to know about the structure of the atoms that make up the elements.

The sub-atomic particles

In Mendeleev's time, atoms were pictured as very small, hard spheres which could not be broken down into smaller parts. Scientists now think of atoms as being made from collections of much smaller particles, the **sub-atomic particles**. You will have used the idea of **electrons** to explain the observations made during electrolysis experiments (page 66).

The first direct evidence for electrons was obtained in 1897 by the British physicist J. J. Thomson. A diagram of the apparatus he used is given in Fig. 36.1. The tube contained a gas at a very low pressure and the cathode was heated by passing an electric current through it. When a high voltage was applied between the cathode and the anode, an electric current flowed across the tube and a faint green glow appeared on a screen beyond the anode ring. On a closer look, this glow was found to be made up of thousands of tiny flashes of light.

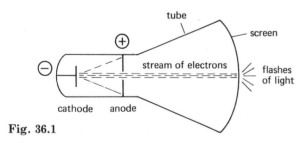

Fig. 36.1

Thomson decided that the flashes were due to particles with a negative charge given off from the hot cathode (the negative electrode) and accelerated across the tube towards the anode (the positive electrode). Some of the particles passed through the hole in the anode and travelled on to hit the screen.

The same kind of particles are produced no matter which metal is used for the cathode and which gas is in the tube. The particles are electrons. Their charge has been found to be 1.60×10^{-19} C and their mass 9.11×10^{-28} g. On the relative atomic mass scale, this mass becomes a relative mass of 5.43×10^{-4} (or 1/1840) which is obviously very much lower than even the value for hydrogen, the element with the lowest relative atomic mass.

The working of television tubes relies on the emission of electrons from a hot metal in a tube containing a gas at low pressure. The kind of tube used by Thomson is called a cathode ray tube. In a television set, electrons flowing through a cathode ray tube strike a screen and produce the picture.

Atoms are electrically neutral, that is, they have no net negative or positive charge. If atoms contain electrons, then they must also contain enough particles with a *positive* charge to balance the negative charge of the electrons. These positively charged particles are called **protons**.

A proton has nearly two thousand times the mass of an electron, that is, it has a mass very nearly equal to the mass of a hydrogen atom. So on the relative atomic mass scale, the relative mass of a proton is written as 1.

The positive charge carried by a proton has been found to be 1.60×10^{-19} C. This charge is equal, but of opposite sign, to that carried by one electron. So an electrically neutral atom must contain equal numbers of protons and electrons, but ions must contain different numbers of protons and electrons (Fig. 36.2).

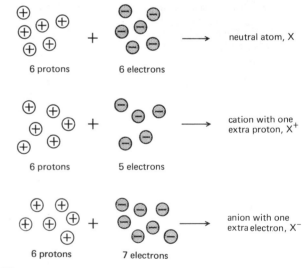

Fig. 36.2

How are the protons and electrons arranged in the atom? The famous experiments of Ernest Rutherford (Fig. 36.3) and his co-workers gave part of the answer to this question. Rutherford was able to 'fire' fast-moving streams of positively charged particles from a radioactive isotope (page 157) at very thin gold foil. These particles were moving very fast and had much more mass than either a proton or an

Fig. 36.3

about 10^{-7} mm whereas the radius of a nucleus is only about 10^{-12} mm: the nucleus takes up about as little space in an atom as a small ball-bearing placed in the middle of a large school laboratory.

The protons must be very tightly packed together in the nucleus. This is surprising when you remember that they all have a positive charge and so can be expected to repel each other. But the discovery of a second nuclear particle, the **neutron**, partly solves this problem. The neutron has zero charge but a mass equal to the mass of a proton (Table 36.1).

Fig. 36.5 shows that this newer picture of the atom is a long way from the idea of a hard, unbreakable sphere.

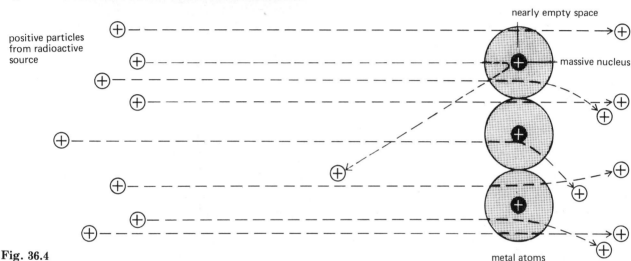

Fig. 36.4

electron. So he expected them all to pass through the foil almost undeflected. But, to his surprise, about one in every thousand particles bounced off the gold foil. In Rutherford's own words, 'it was almost as incredible as if you fired a 15-inch shell at a piece of tissue paper as it came back and hit you.'

If was clear that the positive part of the atom (the part that would repel the positively charged particles) must be concentrated into a very small, but dense, part of the atom. Fig. 36.4 pictures the results of the experiment and shows that a very large part of the atom is simply empty space.

Rutherford concluded that there are protons in the centre of the atom (the **nucleus**) and electrons in the space around the nucleus. The radius of an atom is

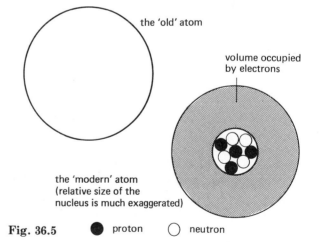

Fig. 36.5

Table 36.1

Name of particle	Relative mass on relative atomic mass scale	Mass in g	Relative charge	Charge in C
Electron	1/1840	9.11×10^{-28}	-1	-1.60×10^{-19}
Proton	1	1.67×10^{-24}	$+1$	$+1.60 \times 10^{-19}$
Neutron	1	1.67×10^{-24}	0	0

Henry Moseley, who was a research student working under Rutherford, discovered that the amount of positive charge (the number of protons) carried by the nucleus of an atom is a fixed amount for all atoms of the same element. For example, he found that atoms of hydrogen always contain one proton, atoms of carbon six protons, and atoms of oxygen eight protons. The atoms of no other element contain one, six or eight protons, and so this number must be a unique property of an element. It is called the **atomic number** of that element:

atomic number

= **number of protons in the atom**

= **number of electrons in the neutral atom**

The elements with atomic numbers 1 to 10 are given in Table 36.2. You will recognize these as the first ten elements of the periodic table in the order in which they occur. This link between the atomic number of an element and its position in the periodic table is found to apply for all elements. Each

Table 36.2

Element	H	He	Li	Be	B	C	N	O	F	Ne
Atomic number	1	2	3	4	5	6	7	8	9	10

succeeding element in the periodic table has one extra proton in its nucleus. In this way, the position of an element in the table is fixed by its atomic number: the element with atomic number 12 must be twelfth, and so on.

When the elements are arranged in the periodic table according to their relative atomic masses, it is found that in three cases pairs of elements have to be changed round. For example, iodine and tellurium have relative atomic masses of 126.9 and 127.6 respectively, but they should be switched over, with tellurium before iodine so that each element appears in the right family. As the atomic numbers are tellurium 52 and iodine 53, they are already in the order that allows tellurium to fall in group VI and iodine in the halogen family. Other 'misplaced' elements are also correctly placed by their atomic numbers.

The arrangement of electrons in atoms

How are the electrons in an atom arranged in the space around the nucleus? All the evidence suggests that the arrangement is not a haphazard one but that there is a pattern. Most of this evidence is too advanced to be given here but you can get some impression of it in the following way.

A magnesium atom has twelve protons in its nucleus and so there are twelve electrons in the space around the nucleus. To remove one electron from an atom requires energy to overcome the force of attraction between the positively charged nucleus and the negatively charged electron.

When one electron has been removed from a magnesium atom, the 'atom' left over still has twelve protons but only eleven electrons, and so has a charge of $+1$. The second electron is more difficult to remove than the first because it has to be removed from what is now a positively charged ion. Its removal produces a cation with twelve protons and ten electrons and so there is an increase in charge to $+2$. This means that the third electron is even more difficult to remove than the second. In the same way, the fourth is more difficult to remove than the third, and so on. So a steady increase in the amounts of energy required to remove electrons one by one from an atom would be expected.

Is there a steady increase such as this in practice? A method has been found for measuring the energies which are required to remove electrons from atoms. The energies required to remove electrons one by one from, say, a magnesium atom do not increase steadily (Fig. 36.6); each electron requires more energy to be removed than the one before, but the greatest difference is between the energies required to remove the second and third electrons. For an atom of sodium, a similar large 'jump' occurs between the energies required to remove the first and second electrons, and for an atom of aluminium between the energies required to remove the third and fourth electrons (Fig. 36.6).

How can these large differences in energy be explained? Suppose that you have to remove heavy books arranged in layers from a large box. Particularly if you are feeling very unfit, you are sure to find that the first book is the easiest to remove and that later books are more difficult to remove as you get more tired. This is like the process of removing electrons from an atom that is mentioned above.

But there is something else that affects how easy it is to lift the books. The books in the top layer can be removed fairly easily because you do not have to lift them very far to get them out of the box. But when the top layer has been removed, the ones in the second layer are more difficult to remove because they have to be lifted further. Each time a deeper layer is reached, removal gets more laborious. So the job gets gradually harder as you grow more tired, but occasionally there are much larger increases in the difficulty of the job as a new layer is reached.

These ideas can be used in thinking about the 'lifting' of electrons from an atom. The large increase in the energy required to remove some electrons from an atom can be explained if you think of the electrons as being arranged in 'layers' like the books in the box.

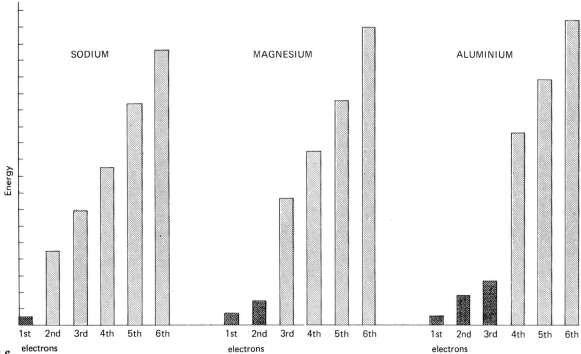

Fig. 36.6

So Fig. 36.6 shows that there are three electrons in the top 'layer' of an aluminium atom, two electrons in the top 'layer' of a magnesium atom, and one electron in the top 'layer' of a sodium atom.

The electrons in this outer 'layer' of an atom are called the **outer electrons** or the **valence electrons**. These are the electrons that can be removed most readily from an atom because they are furthest away from the positively charged nucleus.

The other electrons in an atom are also arranged in one or more 'layers' between the nucleus and the outer 'layer'. It is usual to call the 'layers' **energy levels** because electrons in different 'layers' have different energies while those in any one 'layer' have similar (but not always identical) energies. The electrons in the energy levels of a magnesium atom are shown in Fig. 36.7.

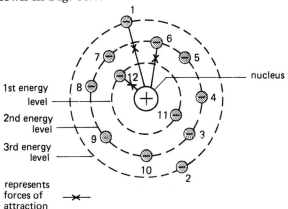

Fig. 36.7 The forces of attraction are strongest between the nucleus and the electrons in the first (innermost) energy level (11 and 12), and weakest between the nucleus and the electrons in the third (outer) energy level (1 and 2)

For each kind of atom, the total number of electrons and also the number of outer electrons are known. These numbers are given in Table 36.3 for the first twenty elements in the periodic table.

Table 36.3

Element	Atomic number	Number of outer electrons	Outer energy level	Number of inner electrons
Hydrogen	1	1	1st	0
Helium	2	2		0
Lithium	3	1		2
Beryllium	4	2		2
Boron	5	3		2
Carbon	6	4	2nd	2
Nitrogen	7	5		2
Oxygen	8	6		2
Fluorine	9	7		2
Neon	10	8		2
Sodium	11	1		10
Magnesium	12	2		10
Aluminium	13	3		10
Silicon	14	4	3rd	10
Phosphorus	15	5		10
Sulphur	16	6		10
Chlorine	17	7		10
Argon	18	8		10
Potassium	19	1	4th	18
Calcium	20	2		18

It is clear that when elements are arranged in the order of their atomic numbers, the numbers of outer electrons in their atoms vary in a regular way.

153

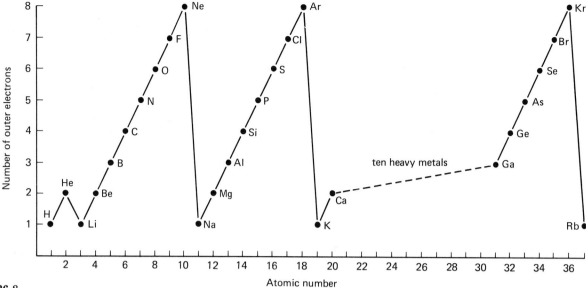

Fig. 36.8

Elements in the same vertical column (group) of the periodic table have the same number of outer electrons.

Fig. 36.8 shows the pattern, but it also shows that it is broken by a series of metals called the **heavy (or transition) metals**.

The properties of an element are controlled by the number of outer electrons in its atoms because these are the parts of an atom that are used to make *bonds* between elements (page 166). So lithium, sodium and potassium show similar properties because their atoms *all* have *one* outer electron. Fluorine and chlorine show very different properties from these metals because they have a different number of outer electrons. But fluorine and chlorine are very alike because their atoms all have the same number (seven) of outer electrons.

Of course, in other ways the atoms of elements in the same group are very different. For example, the atoms of lithium, sodium and potassium have different *total* numbers of protons (and of electrons); for these elements they number 3, 11 and 19 respectively. It is only the number of outer electrons that is the same.

The periodicity in the properties of elements when they are arranged in order of increasing atomic number is the result of the regular way in which the number of outer electrons varies with atomic number.

You should also see that for many elements,

the number of outer electrons in their atoms is equal to the number of the group in the periodic table in which the element is found.

But heavy metals must be excluded from this rule because they break the regular pattern in the number of outer electrons in the atoms of the elements. These elements seem to stand apart from the main trends in the table.

QUESTIONS

1 The atomic number of sulphur is 16.

(a) How many protons are there in the nucleus of a sulphur atom?

(b) How many electrons are there surrounding the nucleus?

(c) How many electrons are there is the 1st, 2nd and 3rd energy levels respectively?

(d) How many electrons are there in a sulphide anion, S^{2-}?

2 Explain how Rutherford established that the atom consists of a small, dense and positively charged nucleus surrounded by mainly empty space.

3 'There is a periodic variation in the properties of the elements when they are arranged in order of increasing atomic number.'

(a) Explain the terms *periodic variation* and *atomic number*.

(b) What is the reason for this periodic variation?

Key words

sub-atomic particles	**neutrons**	**outer (valence) electrons**
electrons	**nucleus**	**energy levels**
protons	**atomic number**	

Basic facts

- An atom is made of a very small and dense nucleus containing protons and neutrons, which is surrounded by a relatively large volume containing electrons.

- Protons and neutrons have equal masses, but protons carry a positive charge while neutrons have no charge. An electron has a much smaller mass than a proton but carries a negative charge equal in size to the positive charge on a proton.

- Each element has a unique number called its atomic number, which is equal to the number of protons in the atom (and to the number of electrons in the neutral atom and also to the positional number of the element in the periodic table).

- Electrons are arranged in various energy levels around the nucleus.

- The properties of an element are controlled by the number of outer electrons in its atoms. Elements in any one group (vertical column) of the periodic table show some chemical similarities because their atoms all contain the same number of *outer* electrons.

- The periodicity in the properties of elements arranged in order of increasing atomic number is explained by the regular way in which the number of outer electrons varies with atomic number.

37 Isotopes

Isotopes and relative atomic mass

Until the discovery of the sub-atomic particles it was thought that the atoms of any one element were the same in every way. It is now known that atoms of the same element can have different masses.

The atoms of neon can have relative atomic masses of 20, 21 or 22. But they all have ten protons in their nuclei and ten electrons outside the nuclei. Eight of these electrons are outer electrons in each kind of neon atom. This is why the properties of these atoms with different masses are very alike.

A sample of an element containing only one kind of atom is called an **isotope** of that element. Naturally occurring elements are usually a mixture of several isotopes, each with its own relative atomic mass. Because their properties are very alike, isotopes of an element are difficult to separate. But it can be done using an instrument called a **mass spectrometer**.

Imagine first that the problem is not to separate atoms of different masses but different sizes of steel ball-bearings. Suppose that the ball-bearings are rolled down a slope onto a wooden board (Fig. 37.1). They roll across the board and travel past a powerful horseshoe magnet. If the experiment is arranged so that all the ball-bearings travel past this magnet at

the same constant speed, then they are bent into differently curved paths depending on their masses.

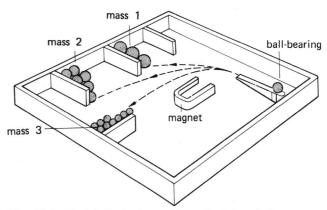

Fig. 37.1 Model that shows the principle of the mass spectrometer

The ball-bearings with the largest mass travel past with only a slight bending but those with the smallest mass are bent into a tight curve. In this way, the ball-bearings can be separated according to their masses.

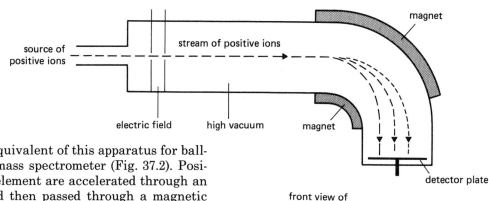

Fig. 37.2

The 'atomic' equivalent of this apparatus for ball-bearings is the mass spectrometer (Fig. 37.2). Positive ions of the element are accelerated through an electric field and then passed through a magnetic field. If the charge on all the ions is the same and if they are all moving at about the same speed, the magnetic field bends the paths of the ions by different amounts depending only on the masses of the ions. These ions then strike a detector. So ions of the same charge and mass are all bent towards the same place on the detector plate; but ions with different masses are found at different places. The paths of the lightest ions are bent the most and those of the heaviest are bent the least.

A pure element usually produces several lines on the detector plane. Each line is for a particular isotope of that element. The trace for neon is shown in Fig. 37.2. Notice that the line for neon-20 is much more intense than the others. Neon-20 is by far the commonest of the three isotopes of neon.

How can atoms of the same element have different masses? They must have the same number of protons and electrons because Moseley showed that this number (the atomic number) is a fixed and unique number for each element. The answer must be that they contain different numbers of neutrons.

The **mass number** of an isotope is the total number of neutrons and protons in the nucleus of the atom: so it is a whole number, and is very nearly the same as the relative atomic mass of the isotope. You should make sure that you understand the difference between the mass number and the atomic number of an isotope.

$$\textbf{mass number} = \textbf{number of protons} + \textbf{number of neutrons}$$
$$\textbf{atomic number} = \textbf{number of protons}$$

Table 37.1 gives the numbers of the three kinds of sub-atomic particles in the isotopes of some elements. The commonest isotope for each element is printed in bold type. It is usual to write an isotope as $_b^a\text{X}$, where a is the mass number, b its atomic number, and X is the symbol for the element. (Another way of writing about an isotope is used above for neon. This is to give the name of the element followed by the mass number of the isotope: $_{12}^{24}\text{Mg}$ is magnesium-24 or Mg-24.)

Table 37.1

Element	Isotopes	Mass number	Atomic number	Number of protons ($=$ number of electrons)	Number of neutrons
Neon	$_{10}^{20}\textbf{Ne}$	20	10	10	10
	$_{10}^{21}\text{Ne}$	21	10	10	11
	$_{10}^{22}\text{Ne}$	22	10	10	12
Carbon	$_{6}^{12}\textbf{C}$	12	6	6	6
	$_{6}^{13}\text{C}$	13	6	6	7
	$_{6}^{14}\text{C}$	14	6	6	8
Oxygen	$_{8}^{16}\textbf{O}$	16	8	8	8
	$_{8}^{17}\text{O}$	17	8	8	9
	$_{8}^{18}\text{O}$	18	8	8	10
Magnesium	$_{12}^{24}\textbf{Mg}$	24	12	12	12
	$_{12}^{25}\text{Mg}$	25	12	12	13
	$_{12}^{26}\text{Mg}$	26	12	12	14

The overall relative atomic mass of an element depends on

the relative atomic mass of each of its isotopes, and the proportions of each isotope that are present.

You should realize this as you work through the following example.

Examples

1 Natural neon consists of about 90.92% of neon-20, 0.26% of neon-21, and 8.82% of neon-22. What is the relative atomic mass of neon?

In every 10 000 atoms of neon there are 9092 atoms of neon-20, 26 atoms of neon-21 and 882 atoms of neon-22. So 10 000 atoms of neon have a relative mass of

$(9092 \times 20) + (26 \times 21) + (882 \times 22)$ or 201 790.

And one atom of neon (on average) has a relative mass of 201 790/10 000, or 20.2. The relative atomic mass of naturally occurring neon is *20.2.*

2 Natural potassium consists of about 93.10% of potassium-39, 0.01% of potassium-40, and 6.89% of potassium-41. What is the relative atomic mass of potassium?

In every 10 000 atoms of potassium there are 9310 atoms of potassium-39, 1 atom of potassium-40 and 689 atoms of potassium-41. So 10 000 atoms of potassium have a relative mass of

$(9310 \times 39) + (1 \times 40) + (689 \times 41)$ or 391 379.

And one atom of potassium (on average) has a relative mass of 391 379/10 000, or 39.1. The relative atomic mass of naturally occurring potassium is *39.1.*

Radioactive isotopes

In a chemical reaction, it is usually only the number of outer electrons in the atoms of the reacting substances that changes. The number of inner electrons and the nuclei of the atoms do not change at all.

But some elements are **radioactive** and their atoms break down spontaneously in a process called **radioactive decay**. In this process, atoms of one element change to atoms of another element with a different atomic number. So radioactive decay must involve changes in the *nuclei* of the atoms.

Most elements do not have any radioactive isotopes: in other words, the nuclei of their atoms are stable. Whatever it is that holds the particles together tightly in the nucleus must have a very powerful 'adhesive effect'. But the 'nuclear adhesive' cannot be strong enough to hold the particles together in the nuclei of the atoms of radioactive isotopes, and so the nuclei are unstable and occasionally they break into smaller parts.

For some elements, only one isotope is radioactive; for others, all the isotopes are radioactive. All isotopes of elements with atomic numbers greater than 83 are radioactive; only a few isotopes with atomic numbers less than 83 are radioactive.

The rate of radioactive decay (that is, the number of decays in a given time) varies a lot from one isotope to another, but it always depends only on the number of undecayed atoms present. Unlike the rate of a chemical reaction, it does not depend on temperature, pressure, or the presence of a catalyst. The **half-life** of a radioactive isotope is a measure of the rate at which it decays; it is the time taken for exactly half of the original number of radioactive atoms to decay. Some half-lives are given in Table 37.2 to show how different these can be.

Table 37.2

Isotope	Half-life
$^{238}_{92}$U	4.5×10^9 years
$^{14}_{6}$C	5.6×10^3 years
$^{226}_{88}$Ra	1.6×10^3 years
$^{234}_{90}$Th	24 days
$^{234}_{91}$Pa	70 seconds
$^{214}_{84}$Po	1.6×10^{-4} seconds

Suppose you have 8 g of thorium-234 to start with. After 24 days there will be only 4 g of undecayed thorium-234, and after a further 24 days the mass of thorium-234 will have halved again (Fig. 37.3).

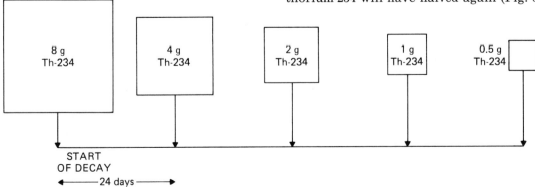

8 g
Th-234

4 g
Th-234

2 g
Th-234

1 g
Th-234

0.5 g
Th-234

START
OF DECAY

Fig. 37.3   ◄——— 24 days ———►

As the atoms of radioactive isotopes are decaying, they emit radiation consisting of very small particles and energy. The radiation can be of three kinds (Table 37.3).

Table 37.3

Kind of radiation	Nature of radiation	
α	Nuclei of helium atoms	Particles
β	Electrons	
γ	High-energy X-rays	

You can work out which new isotope is formed by the decay of a radioactive isotope if you know which kind of radiation is emitted. For example, the radioactive isotope carbon-14 emits β-radiation which consists of an electron coming from the nucleus. Because the electron has very little mass compared with the other sub-atomic particles (page 151), the mass number of the new isotope is the same as the mass number of carbon-14.

But the loss of one electron by each atom is equivalent to the *gain* of one *proton* in the nucleus: so the atomic number of the new isotope is one higher than the atomic number of carbon-14. The nuclear equation for this process is

$$\underset{\text{carbon-14}}{^{14}_{6}\text{C}} \longrightarrow \underset{\text{nitrogen-14}}{^{14}_{7}\text{N}} + \underset{\text{electron}}{^{0}_{-1}\text{e}}$$

The new isotope is nitrogen-14 which is not radioactive. Notice that the numbers on the 'top line' (the mass numbers) add up to 14 on each side of this equation, and the numbers on the 'bottom line' (the atomic numbers) add up to 6 on each side.

Another example is the radioactive decay of uranium-238. This emits α-radiation and each decaying atom loses a helium nucleus consisting of two protons and two neutrons. So the mass number of the atom drops by four (2 protons + 2 neutrons) and the atomic number by two (2 protons). The nuclear equation for this process is

$$\underset{\text{uranium-238}}{^{238}_{92}\text{U}} \longrightarrow \underset{\text{thorium-234}}{^{234}_{90}\text{Th}} + \underset{\text{helium nucleus}}{^{4}_{2}\text{He}}$$

But the process does not stop at thorium-234 because this is also a radioactive isotope. In fact, there is a whole series of steps which begins with uranium-238 and goes through several radioactive isotopes before ending with a non-radioactive isotope, lead-206.

Using radioactive isotopes

Radioactive isotopes have many important uses. You can read about nuclear fission in Chapter 62.

Uranium-238 can be used to find the age of certain rocks. When the rock containing uranium was first formed, none of this isotope would have decayed to $^{206}_{82}$Pb. After 4.5×10^9 years, exactly half the original radioactivity remains, and after 9.0×10^9 years, there is only one quarter of the original radioactivity left. If analyses using a mass spectrometer showed that

$$\frac{\text{number of atoms of } ^{238}_{92}\text{U}}{\text{number of atoms of } ^{206}_{82}\text{Pb}} = 1$$

then the rock would be assumed to be 4.5×10^9 years old.

The age of archaeological remains can also be found by radioactive dating. But for these a radioactive isotope is needed which has a half-life of a few thousand years rather than many millions of years. The charcoal from the fires made by primitive men, the skulls of 'ape-men', leather and so on, all contain carbon, and some of this is the radioactive isotope carbon-14, which has a half-life of 5600 years. Recently, 'carbon dating' has been used to show that the wrappings around the famous Dead Sea Scrolls are about 2000 years old.

Radioactive isotopes are also important as **tracer elements** in investigations in medicine, chemistry and biology. They are useful in this way because they behave chemically like non-radioactive isotopes of the same element. But they have the great advantage that the radiation they emit is harmless and can easily be detected, so providing information about any diseased organs or tissues.

Radioactive elements which emit higher energy radiation are also used in medicine, to destroy diseased tissue. In Fig. 37.4 the patient has a cancerous growth deep in his body, and the computer-controlled instrument is used to focus a beam of γ-rays from radioactive cobalt-60 onto the growth to destroy the diseased cells.

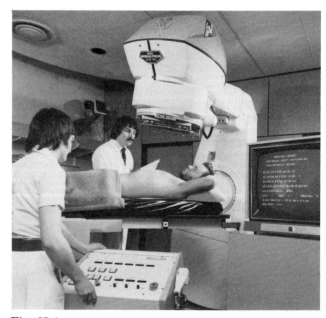

Fig. 37.4

A radioactive isotope of phosphorus (phosphorus-32, half-life 14.3 days) can be used to track the movement of phosphate ions in a living organism. For example, if a fish is kept for a few days in water in which is dissolved radioactive sodium phosphate (containing radioactive phosphorus-32), the fish takes in phosphate ions from the water. If the fish is killed after a few days and its skeleton laid on photographic paper which is still inside its protective covering, an auto-radiogram such as that in Fig. 37.5 is obtained.

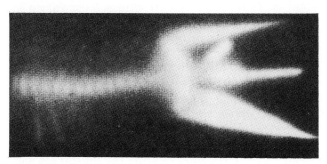

Fig. 37.5

Both iodine-131 and phosphorus-32 have relatively short half-lives. Safe isotopes with short half-lives are useful in tests on living things because they give good readings with small doses.

QUESTIONS

1 Complete each of the following statements.
(a) The mass number of $^{14}_{7}$N is ...
(b) The atomic number of $^{23}_{11}$Na is ...
(c) There are... protons and... neutrons in an atom of $^{23}_{11}$Na.
(d) $^{16}_{8}$O and $^{18}_{8}$O are... of oxygen.
(e) When the radioactive isotope $^{24}_{11}$Na decays, it emits ... -radiation to form $^{24}_{12}$Mg.

2 The relative atomic masses of argon and potassium are 39.9 and 39.1 respectively, and so potassium ought to be placed before argon in a periodic table in which the elements are arranged in order of increasing relative atomic mass. But Mendeleev altered the order so that argon came before potassium. The proportions of the isotopes present in a sample of these two elements are:

argon-36	0.34%	potassium-39	93.1%
argon-38	0.06%	potassium-40	0.01%
argon-40	99.6%	potassium-41	6.89%

(a) Can you suggest why Mendeleev insisted on reversing the order based on the relative atomic masses of these two elements?
(b) Can you explain why in the modern periodic table argon naturally comes before potassium?
(c) Explain why the relative atomic mass of potassium is lower than that of argon.

3 Natural chlorine consists of 75.5% of the isotope chlorine-35 and 24.5% of the isotope chlorine-37.
(a) Given that the atomic number of chlorine is 17, work out how many neutrons there are in an atom of each of these isotopes.
(b) In 1000 atoms of natural chlorine how many atoms are there of each of the isotopes?
(c) From your answer to (b), work out the relative atomic mass of chlorine.

4 Use Tables 37.2 and 37.3 to answer these questions.
(a) How long will it take for 8 g of thorium-234 to have decayed to only 1 g?
(b) If you start with 8 g of thorium-234, what mass of this radioactive isotope will be left after 96 days?
(c) Thorium-234 emits β-radiation when it decays. Work out the mass number and the atomic number of the new isotope that is formed.

5 Work out the numbers of protons, neutrons and electrons that each of the following particles contains. Also show how the electrons in these particles are arranged in energy levels.
(a) $^{27}_{13}$Al (b) $^{39}_{19}$K (c) $^{41}_{19}$K (d) $^{23}_{11}$Na^{+} (e) $^{37}_{17}$Cl^{-}
(f) $^{16}_{8}$O^{2-} (g) $^{24}_{12}$Mg^{2+}

Key words

isotope	**mass number**	**half-life**
mass spectrometer	**radioactive decay**	**tracer elements**

Basic facts

- **An isotope of an element has a unique mass number (the number of protons plus the number of neutrons) as well as a unique atomic number.**

- **A naturally occurring element may be composed of several isotopes. Each isotope has the same atomic number but a different mass number. This explains why many elements have relative atomic masses which are not whole numbers.**

- **In the process of radioactive decay, atoms of certain elements change spontaneously to atoms of a different element.**

- **The half-life of a radioactive isotope is the time taken for exactly half of the original number of radioactive atoms to decay.**

38 The structures of some solids

Strong and weak structures

Many solids form crystals with a definite shape. This is true of salts made by evaporating their solutions, of solids like sulphur which are formed by cooling their liquids, and of metals deposited at the cathode during electrolysis. The regular shape of crystals strongly suggests that there is a pattern underlying the way the particles making up the crystals are arranged (pages 50–1). These regular arrangements are called **structures**.

One way of investigating and then classifying solid structures, is to try to destroy the pattern by heating the solids. In other words, how easy is it to melt the solids and then boil their liquids? What are their melting points and boiling points?

The particles in a solid are held together in a regular arrangement by forces of attraction between them. They can only vibrate around their fixed positions. But if the solid is heated, the extra energy given to the particles causes stronger vibrations and this works against these forces of attraction. Eventually a temperature is reached (the melting point of the solid) when the forces of attraction can no longer hold the particles together in a regular arrangement against the vibration of the particles. At a higher temperature still (the boiling point of the liquid), the particles are moving with so much energy that the liquid becomes a gas and the particles get much more widely separated (page 53).

When a solid melts to form a liquid, there is usually a small expansion. The particles have been separated by only a small amount. But when a liquid boils, there is a very large expansion. The particles have been separated by a large amount. So the boiling point of a substance is a better measure than the melting point of the 'strength' of the forces of attraction between particles. For a few solids, the temperature at which they vaporize (sublime) directly to the gas has to be used.

There are very big differences among boiling points and vaporization (sublimation) points of substances. This shows that structures must vary a lot in 'strength'. For example, a crystal of iodine can be vaporized by gently warming it in a test-tube, whereas graphite has to be heated to a temperature of over 3700 °C before it vaporizes. The iodine structure must be rather 'weak' and the graphite structure very 'strong' indeed.

Fig. 38.1 shows the pattern of the boiling points of the first eighteen elements in the periodic table and some of their compounds. The temperature range is divided into 100 °C intervals and the substances with boiling points within each 100 °C interval are listed.

The boiling points seem to fall into two classes, and this is even more obvious if the element sodium is ignored.

The best way of explaining why substances can be classified like this is to suggest that there are two main kinds of solid structure. These are often called **molecular structures** and **giant structures**. Some conclusions about these two kinds of substances are given in Table 38.1.

Because solids with molecular structures have low boiling points, it appears that the forces of attraction between the particles in the solid are weak and can easily be overcome. But a glance at Fig. 38.1 should show you that there is considerable variation: these forces are stronger in substances such as ice and solid ethanol (C_2H_5OH) than they are in substances such as solid argon and solid hydrogen.

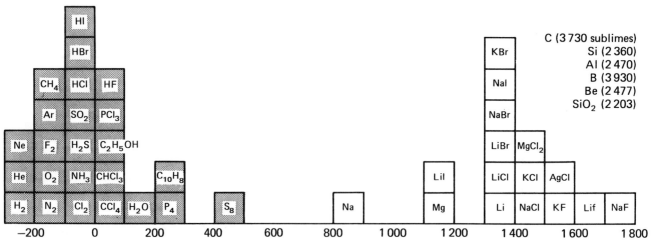

b.p. in °C

Fig. 38.1

Solids with giant structures have high boiling points showing that the forces of attraction between the particles in the solid are strong. Here again, though, there must be differences in the size of these forces of attraction. In sodium and magnesium they are quite weak for giant structures, whereas in boron and silicon they are very strong indeed.

In the rest of this chapter you can find the answers to these two questions about structures.

1. What kinds of particles are there in solids?
2. How are the particles arranged in solids?

In the next chapter you can find the answer to a third question:

3. What are the forces of attraction between the particles?

Some molecular structures

The particles that make up solids with molecular structures are molecules. In the case of carbon dioxide, the molecules have the formula CO_2. These molecules are not easy to decompose into smaller particles because it is difficult to separate the carbon

and oxygen atoms: the forces of attraction that hold the carbon atom and the two oxygen atoms together *within* each molecule of carbon dioxide must be strong.

When solid carbon dioxide vaporizes to form gaseous carbon dioxide, there is enough energy to separate the molecules because the forces of attraction *between* them are very weak, but there is not enough energy to break down the molecules themselves. So both gaseous and solid carbon dioxide consist of CO_2 molecules. In the same way, when most other solids with molecular structures melt or vaporize and when their liquids evaporate, the molecules stay the same.

You can imagine a solid with a molecular structure to be like a wall built of strong bricks and weak mortar. Because the mortar is weak, the wall is quite easy to knock down (Fig. 38.2), but because the bricks are strong, they stay undamaged in the rubble left over.

Fig. 38.2

The element iodine has a molecular structure. Fig. 38.3 shows how I_2 molecules are arranged in iodine crystals. As in all molecular structures, the molecules pack together as closely and as neatly as their shape allows. In this case they do not line up parallel to each other but half of them tilt one way and half the other way.

Table 38.1

Property	Substances with molecular structures	Substances with giant structures
Boiling point	Low: below about 400 °C	High: above about 800 °C
Nature of elements	Non-metals	Metals
Nature of compounds	Compounds of non-metals	Compounds of metals and non-metals, i.e. salts
Conduction of electricity (compounds)	Non-electrolytes	Mainly electrolytes but a few non-electrolytes

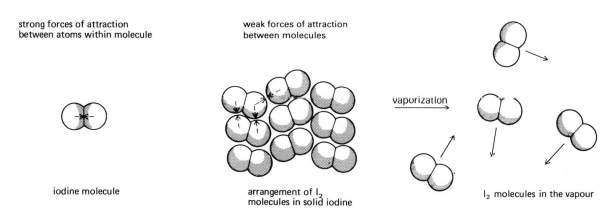

strong forces of attraction between atoms within molecule

weak forces of attraction between molecules

vaporization

iodine molecule

arrangement of I_2 molecules in solid iodine

I_2 molecules in the vapour

Fig. 38.3 The middle diagram is of a space-filling model. You should read the comments on pages 162 and 163 about the advantages of this kind of model

Molecular substances are non-electrolytes because the liquids formed by melting the solids, and the solutions formed by dissolving the solids in a suitable solvent, contain molecules and not ions.

Sulphur is also an example of a solid with a molecular structure. Each sulphur molecule consists of a puckered ring of eight sulphur atoms (page 139). What happens when sulphur is heated is rather unusual. In most solids with molecular structures, the forces of attraction between the molecules are usually overcome before the forces of attraction within the molecules. But the forces of attraction within the sulphur molecules are not strong enough to prevent the S_8 rings in liquid sulphur from opening out to form chains of atoms (page 140).

Some giant structures

In giant structures, each particle has a strong force of attraction for all the other particles close to it. These forces extend all through the crystal to form a very rigid structure. It requires a lot of energy to break down the forces of attraction between the particles.

Fig. 38.4

A solid with a giant structure is like a wall built of strong bricks and strong mortar. Such a wall is very difficult indeed to knock down (Fig. 38.4). Also, just as the wall may be built out of one kind of brick or two or more different kinds of brick, the particles in the giant structure may all be the same or there may be two or more different kinds.

Giant structures of ions

The particles in an electrolyte like sodium chloride are ions. The ions are packed together so that each cation is surrounded most closely by anions and each anion is surrounded most closely by cations.

Fig. 38.5 shows how this could be done in two dimensions.

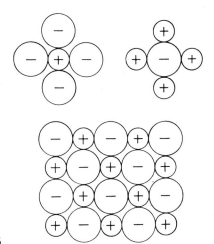

Fig. 38.5

A very common arrangement for the ions is the so-called rock salt structure (Fig. 38.6). This is the structure for substances such as potassium iodide, lithium bromide, sodium bromide and magnesium oxide as well as for sodium chloride (rock salt) itself. It is a cubic structure and its shape is the same as the commonest shape for rock salt crystals (Fig. 38.7). It is an extension to three dimensions of the arrangement shown in Fig. 38.5.

Either of the two diagrams in Fig. 38.6 may be used to show the structure of rock salt. The diagram of the ball-and-spoke model separates the spheres using a line. It has the advantage that the arrangement of the ions can be clearly seen, and the lines represent

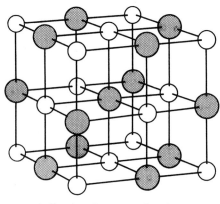

ball-and-spoke model of rock salt

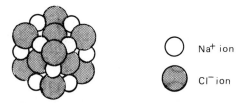

space-filling model of rock salt

○ Na⁺ ion

● Cl⁻ ion

Fig. 38.6 The two models are of different parts of a rock salt crystal

the strong forces of attraction between the cations and anions. But since it is thought that the ions are very close to each other, the space-filling model is more realistic.

Fig. 38.7 Cubic crystals of colourless rock salt

Fig. 38.6 shows that each sodium ion is in contact with six chloride ions, and each chloride ion is in contact with six sodium ions.

In the structure of sodium chloride, there are equal numbers of sodium ions, Na^+, and of chloride ions, Cl^-, and the structure as a whole has no charge. The formula of solid sodium chloride is written as $NaCl(s)$ or $Na^+Cl^-(s)$. You should realize that this formula *cannot* represent molecules of sodium chloride because there are no separate molecules in the structure: it only shows the proportions of sodium and chloride ions present.

Fig. 38.6 shows that the chloride ion is larger than the sodium ion. Anions are usually larger than cations.

What happens to this ionic structure when rock salt is heated? You can imagine that the ions vibrate with more energy (Fig. 38.8). Eventually, when the vibrations become vigorous enough, the structure breaks up: liquid sodium chloride consists of a mixture of sodium ions and chloride ions that are fairly free to move around one another. When the liquid is boiled, each cation seeks out an anion and they are removed together to form a gaseous pair of ions, $Na^+Cl^-(g)$.

These ideas explain why liquid sodium chloride is a good conductor of electricity: when a potential difference is applied across the liquid, the ions are free enough to move to the cathode or anode.

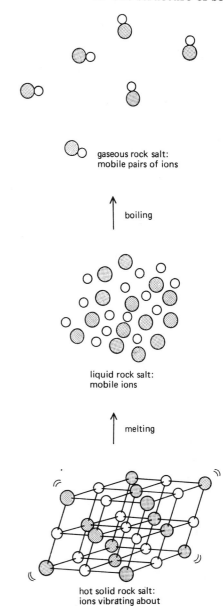

gaseous rock salt:
mobile pairs of ions

↑ boiling

liquid rock salt:
mobile ions

↑ melting

hot solid rock salt:
ions vibrating about
fixed positions

Fig. 38.8

Giant structures of atoms

In some giant structures, it is atoms and not ions that are held together by strong forces of attraction. Elements with giant structures contain only one kind of atom while compounds with giant structures contain more than one kind of atom.

You should remember that in molecular structures the forces of attraction between the atoms within the molecules are very strong but that there are only weak forces between the molecules. But the strong forces of attraction in a giant atomic structure extend through the whole structure. It is very difficult to break down giant atomic structures: it requires even more energy to melt and boil some substances with giant atomic structures than to melt and boil those with giant ionic structures.

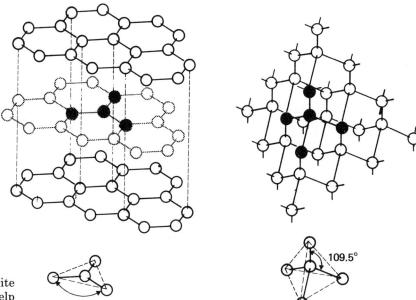

Fig. 38.9 Ball-and-spoke models of graphite and diamond. The spokes are included to help to emphasize the arrangement of the atoms. Note that alternate layers are aligned directly over each other in graphite

layered structure of
GRAPHITE

three-dimensional (tetrahedral) structure of
DIAMOND

Two examples of giant atomic structures are shown in Fig. 38.9. Both are composed only of carbon atoms. The different arrangements of carbon atoms in diamond and graphite explains why carbon exists in these allotropic forms, or allotropes (page 139).

Diamond and graphite have very similar chemical properties but very different physical properties (Table 38.2, and Figs. 38.10 and 38.11).

In diamond, each carbon atom is surrounded by four other carbon atoms in a regular three-dimensional arrangement. For diamond to be so hard, the atoms must be held together very strongly (page 170). In graphite, each carbon atom is surrounded by three others in a layered arrangement. Whereas the atoms within any one layer are held together firmly, the layers are only loosely bound together. The slipping of these layers over one another helps to explain the lubricating properties of graphite. The layered structure of graphite also explains why it is soft and easily cleaved (broken) into flat flakes. Graphite conducts electricity because electrons can move along the planes (page 171).

Table 38.2

Property	Diamond	Graphite
Appearance	Shiny, colourless and transparent	Fairly dull and dark grey
Hardness	Very hard	Quite soft
Conduction of electricity	Non-conductor	Good conductor
Density in g cm^{-3}	3.51	2.25
Ignition temperature in °C	800–900	about 700

Fig. 38.10 Raw uncut diamonds used as abrasives for cutting rock and concrete

Fig. 38.11 Graphite

QUESTIONS

1 Use Fig. 38.1 to find:
(a) *two* elements which are non-metals and yet seem to have a giant structure.
(b) *one* compound which is a non-electrolyte and yet seems to have a giant structure.

2 Explain these observations.

(*a*) Diamond is a very poor conductor of both heat and electricity.

(*b*) Pyrographite (a special form of graphite in which all the separate crystals are arranged in the same direction) may be used as a heat shield in the nose-cone of a space rocket. Such a substance is able to conduct heat along the nose-cone but allows almost no heat to pass through the nose-cone into the rocket.

(*c*) A solid non-conductor such as diamond, or a metal that conducts heat in all directions, would both be unsuitable for the job that graphite does in space rockets.

3 Explain these statements.

(*a*) Solid sodium conducts electricity but is not an electrolyte.

(*b*) Solid iodine does not conduct electricity.

(*c*) Solid sodium iodide has a giant ionic structure but does not conduct electricity whereas liquid sodium iodide and an aqueous solution of sodium iodide are both electrolytes.

4 Here are the boiling points and the melting points for a selection of compounds.

Compound	m.p. in °C	b.p. in °C
Benzene	5.5	80.1
Hydrogen chloride	− 114	− 85.1
Magnesium chloride	712	1420
Potassium iodide	681	1320
Sodium chloride	801	1470
Tetrachloromethane	− 23.0	76.8

(*a*) Which compounds are liquids at room temperature?

(*b*) Which compound is a gas at room temperature?

(*c*) List the compounds whose solids probably have molecular structures.

(*d*) List the compounds whose solids probably have giant structures.

(*e*) Which of the compounds would you expect to be electrolytes when molten? What does your answer suggest about the kind of particles which may be present in the crystals of these compounds?

5 Fig. 38.12 is a diagram of part of the ionic structure for a compound with the formula XY. The anion in this structure is Y_2^{2-}.

(*a*) How many atoms of Y are there in one Y_2^{2-} ion?

(*b*) What is the charge on the cation in this compound?

(*c*) Which of these statements about the ionic structure is true?

   (i) there are twice as many cations as anions in the structure;

   (ii) there are twice as many anions as cations in the structure;

   (iii) there are equal numbers of anions and cations in the structure.

(*d*) How many anions are in contact with each cation, and how many cations are in contact with each anion?

(*e*) Name another ionic compound which has a structure with the same shape as the one in Fig. 38.12.

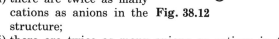

○ cation ⬤ anion Y_2^{2-}

Fig. 38.12

6 'The elements boron and helium are extreme examples of the two main kinds of structure in solids.'

Element	Boron, B	Helium, He
b.p. in °C	3930	− 269

(*a*) Carefully explain the meaning of this statement using the above data.

(*b*) Given that both solid and liquid boron are poor conductors of electricity, can you say whether the solid is likely to have:

(i) a giant structure of atoms, (ii) a giant structure of ions, or (iii) a giant structure of cations in a 'sea' of mobile electrons (page 170)?

(*c*) Use the periodic table and the data sheets at the end of the book to find an element close to boron in the periodic table that has similar physical properties to those of boron. Which form of this element is more like boron in its conductance of electricity?

Key words

molecular structures   **giant structures of ions**   **giant structures of atoms**   **allotropy/allotropes**

Basic facts

- **Crystals are composed of regular arrangements (structures) of atoms, molecules or ions.**

- **Molecular structures have weak forces of attraction between the molecules but (usually) strong forces of attraction between the atoms within the molecules. Solids with molecular structures are easily melted and boiled. Many elements that are non-metals exist in molecular structures. Most compounds which contain only non-metals are also molecular.**

- **Giant structures are composed of either atoms or ions with strong forces of attraction between them. Solids with giant structures are difficult to melt and boil. Metals and their compounds almost always have giant structures, but a few non-metals (carbon and silicon) and some of their compounds (silicon dioxide) also have giant structures.**

- **Substances with giant ionic structures conduct electricity only when the ions are able to move to the electrodes, that is, when the substances are in the liquid state or in aqueous solution.**

- **Graphite is unusual in having a giant atomic structure and yet being a good conductor of electricity. This is because it has mobile electrons that are able to move along the planes of carbon rings.**

39 Chemical bonding

What are bonds?

The forces that hold atoms and ions together are called **bonds**. To understand why there are forces of attraction between particles, you need to think again about the arrangement of electrons around the nuclei of atoms.

You can start by looking at the atoms of the noble gases. This family of elements is unusual in being very unreactive indeed. How can this be explained?

When atoms come into contact, it is their outermost parts that are affected and so it must be these parts that control how they react. The total number of electrons and the number of outer electrons in the atoms of the noble gases are given in Table 39.1. Since the noble gases are very unreactive, these arrangements of electrons must be particularly difficult to disrupt. In other words, these arrangements of electrons must very stable indeed.

In this chapter, you will see how the numbers in Table 39.1 can be used to think about some of the forces that hold atoms and ions together.

Table 39.1

Element	Atomic number	Total number of electrons in one atom	Number of outer electrons
He	2	2	2
Ne	10	10	8
Ar	18	18	8
Kr	36	36	8
Xe	54	54	8
Rn	86	86	8

Bonds between ions

When sodium and chlorine react to form sodium chloride ($Na^+ Cl^-$), sodium atoms must each lose one electron to form sodium ions and chlorine atoms must each gain one electron to form chloride ions. The numbers of electrons in these atoms and ions are given in Table 39.2. If you compare Tables 39.1 and

Table 39.2

Atom or ion	Atomic number	Total number of electrons in one atom or ion
Na	11	11
Na^+	11	10
Cl	17	17
Cl^-	17	18

39.2, you should see that a sodium ion has the same number of electrons as a neon atom and that a chloride ion has the same number of electrons as an argon atom.

Whereas sodium and chlorine are very reactive elements, their compound (sodium chloride) is very difficult to decompose into its elements. For example, the best way of extracting sodium from sodium chloride, that is, of changing sodium ions to sodium atoms, is by electrolysis (page 122): an extraction process using carbon as a reducing agent does not work and it is very difficult indeed to decompose sodium chloride by heating.

So it is not easy to change sodium ions to sodium atoms or chloride ions to chlorine atoms. It can be suggested that these ions are stable because they have the same (stable) number of electrons as neon and argon atoms.

You know that all the other alkali metals form compounds that are difficult to decompose and in which the metal is present as a cation with a $+1$ charge. Can the stability of these cations be explained in the same way as for Na^+?

Table 39.3

Element	Atomic number	Total number of electrons in an atom	Total number of electrons in a cation
Li	3	3	2
Na	11	11	10
K	19	19	18
Rb	37	37	36
Cs	55	55	54

The numbers of electrons in the atoms and ions of the alkali metals are given in Table 39.3. The atoms of each alkali metal have one electron more than the atoms of the noble gas just before it in the periodic table.

The ions of each alkali metal have the same number of electrons as the atoms of the noble gas just before it in the periodic table.

The halogens are very reactive non-metals and they form ions with a single negative charge. The numbers of electrons in their atoms and ions are given in Table 39.4. The atoms of each halogen have one electron less than the atoms of the noble gas just after it in the periodic table.

The ions of each halogen have the same number of electrons as the atoms of the noble gas just after it in the periodic table.

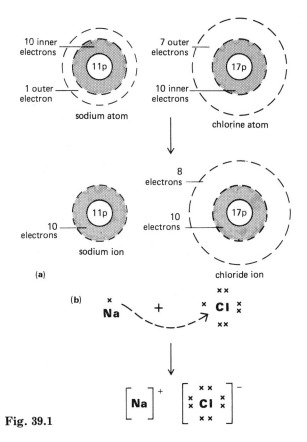

Fig. 39.1

Fig. 39.1 is a way of showing how Na^+ and Cl^- ions are formed from their atoms. Each sodium atom loses one electron to a chlorine atom. You should realize that the diagram shows a theory that successfully explains why there are sodium and chloride ions in solid sodium chloride. It also explains why the formula of sodium chloride is NaCl and not, say, $NaCl_2$ or Na_2Cl. But it does not necessarily suggest that the reaction between sodium and chlorine occurs in this way. The reaction occurs between sodium metal and *molecules* of chlorine gas, not between *separate atoms* of sodium and chlorine.

In solid sodium chloride, each sodium ion is surrounded by chloride ions and each chloride ion by sodium ions (Fig. 38.6, page 162). So adjacent ions attract each other because of their opposite charges. The strong electrostatic forces of attraction between oppositely charged ions are called **ionic bonds**. In a crystal of sodium chloride, these bonds extend in three dimensions all through the structure.

Can the ideas used to explain the formation of sodium ions and chloride ions be applied to other elements? The elements in group II of the periodic table (except beryllium) are all very reactive metals and their atoms form ions with a charge of $+2$. Aluminium can form ions with a charge of $+3$ and oxygen forms ions with a charge of -2.

Table 39.5 shows the total numbers of electrons in the ions Mg^{2+}, Ca^{2+}, Al^{3+} and O^{2-}. These numbers are the same as the total numbers of electrons in the atoms of the nearest noble gas in the periodic table, either neon (10 electrons) or argon (18 electrons).

The parts of the periodic table that contain the elements dealt with above are shown in Fig. 39.2.

Table 39.4

Element	Atomic number	Total number of electrons in an atom	Total number of electrons in an anion
F	9	9	10
Cl	17	17	18
Br	35	35	36
I	53	53	54

Table 39.5

Element	Atomic number	Total number of electrons in an atom	Total number of electrons in an ion
Mg	12	12	10
Ca	20	20	18
Al	13	13	10
O	8	8	10

Fig. 39.2

Group number	VIII	I	II		III	IV	V	VI	VII	VIII
	2 He	3 Li						8 O	9 F	10 Ne
	10 Ne	11 Na	12 Mg		13 Al				17 Cl	18 Ar
	18 Ar	19 K	20 Ca						35 Br	36 Kr
									53 I	54 Xe
Number of outer electrons	8	1	2		3	4	5	6	7	8
Charge on ion		+1	+2		+3			−2	−1	

When elements that come just after a noble gas in the periodic table form ions, their atoms lose all their outer electrons. This number is equal to the number of the group in which the element lies. So the charge on cations is equal to the group number of the element.

When elements that come just before a noble gas form ions, the number of outer electrons in their atoms is increased to the number in the atoms of the following noble gas. Since the atoms of all the noble gases from neon to radon have eight outer electrons, the charge on an anion of any element in periods 2 to 6 is equal to the difference between eight and the group number of the element.

The rule is a very useful one but it cannot explain the charges on all ions. For example, it does not work with the cations of heavy metals such as iron or copper. None of the cations Fe^{2+}, Fe^{3+} and Cu^{2+} has the same number of electrons as there are in the atoms of one of the noble gases.

There is also the problem of why some elements like carbon do not form ions. The numbers of electrons in the atoms of helium, carbon and neon are given in Table 39.6. If carbon atoms were to form

Table 39.6

Element	Total number of electrons in an atom
He	2
C	6
Ne	10

ions with the same number of electrons as the atoms of a noble gas, each carbon atom would either have to lose four electrons to form the C^{4+} ion or gain four electrons to form the C^{4-} ion. Most of the ions you know have charges of $+1$, $+2$ or -1 and less often $+3$ and -2. Ions that are monatomic, that is, consist of only one atom, rarely have charges greater than these because the energy needed to remove more than three outer electrons from an atom is very large. So it can be suggested that carbon atoms do not form ions because the formation of such ions, involving the transfer of four electrons, requires too much energy.

Bonds between atoms

Why are there strong forces of attraction between atoms within molecules and between atoms in giant atomic structures?

Covalent bonding in molecules

Hydrogen molecules (H_2) are the simplest of all molecules. A single hydrogen atom has one proton and one electron. What happens to the two electrons when the atoms join to form a hydrogen molecule?

When the two hydrogen atoms are a long way from one another, each electron is attracted only by the proton in its own atom. As the two atoms approach one another (Fig. 39.3a) each electron is now attracted by both protons, while the two electrons repel one another and the two protons repel one another. When the protons are close enough together (Fig. 39.3b), a strong bond is formed. The region in which the electrons are most likely to be found is where they are most strongly attracted by both protons at the same time. This region is shaded in Fig. 39.3b.

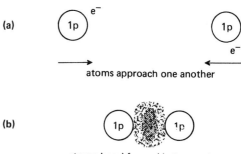

Fig. 39.3

atoms approach one another

strong bond formed between atoms

There is another way of thinking about the bond between two hydrogen atoms. Both atoms are trying to get the same number of electrons as a helium atom. They can do this by each gaining one extra electron. But it is impossible for both atoms to gain complete control of both electrons. Instead, they have to *share* the two electrons between them (Fig. 39.4). So, in effect, both atoms now have two outer electrons even though this pair of electrons is being shared between them.

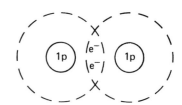

Fig. 39.4

The atoms are held together as a molecule because both nuclei are attracting and holding on to the same thing – the shared pair of electrons. The two approaches (Figs. 39.3 and 39.4) give a similar picture of the hydrogen molecule.

Hydrogen atoms readily react to form hydrogen molecules and it is very difficult to decompose these molecules by heating the gas. So the bond formed between two hydrogen atoms must be strong. It seems that this is so because the hydrogen atoms in a hydrogen molecule have the same number of electrons as a helium atom, and noble gas atoms have a very stable arrangement of electrons.

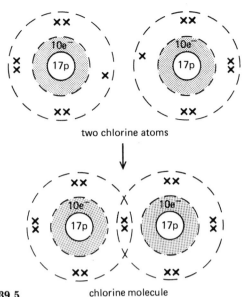

Fig. 39.5

two chlorine atoms

chlorine molecule

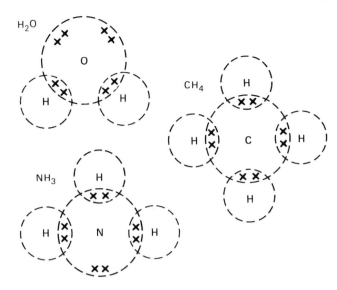

Fig. 39.6

These ideas can be applied to more complicated molecules such as those of chlorine (Fig. 39.5) and the other halogens. There are seventeen electrons in a chlorine atom and eighteen in an atom of the nearest noble gas, argon. A chlorine atom needs to gain a share of one more electron to achieve a very stable arrangement of electrons. Fig. 39.5 shows that both chlorine atoms in a molecule of chlorine have, in effect, eight outer electrons, which is the same number of outer electrons in an argon atom.

This kind of bond, in which two atoms attract the same pair of electrons and so are held together, is known as a **covalent bond**. The shared pair of electrons is sometimes called a **bonding pair**. Because the inner electrons do not take any part in forming a covalent bond, they need not be represented by crosses in diagrams such as those in Fig. 39.5.

A covalent bond is often shown as a line between the atomic symbols. So a hydrogen molecule can be written as H—H, and a chlorine molecule as Cl—Cl.

You should now be clear about the difference between an ionic bond and a covalent bond. An ionic bond is formed by the *transfer* of one or more electrons between atoms. A covalent bond is formed by the *sharing* of a pair of electrons.

The atoms in the molecules of compounds are also held together by covalent bonds. Fig. 39.6 shows the arrangement of outer electrons in molecules of water, ammonia and methane.

The number of covalent bonds an atom forms is closely linked to its position in the periodic table. Fig. 39.7 shows that this number of usually the same as the number of electrons needed to achieve the electronic arrangement of the nearest noble gas.

Fig. 39.7

Group number	I	II		III	IV	V	VI	VII	VIII
					6 C	7 N	8 O	9 F	10 Ne
								17 Cl	18 Ar
								35 Br	36 Kr
								53 I	54 Xe
Number of outer electrons					4	5	6	7	8
Number of electrons needed to reach the same number as the atoms of a noble gas					4	3	2	1	0
Number of covalent bonds formed with other atoms or with its own atoms					4	3	2	1	0

There are, however, some exceptions to this rule. For example, phosphorus is in group V of the periodic table and you might have expected that a phosphorus atom would form three covalent bonds. But there are two chlorides of phosphorus, PCl_3 and PCl_5, and the rule cannot be used to explain how phosphorus can form PCl_5.

Elements that form covalent bonds are found towards the middle and on the right-hand side of the periodic table. But elements in groups VI and VII can also form anions. They can form both ionic and molecular compounds because there are two ways their atoms can gain electrons and reach the number in an atom of one of the noble gases.

Covalent bonding in giant structures of atoms

In diamond, each carbon atom forms a covalent bond with each of four other carbon atoms. The arrangement of outer electrons around one carbon atom is shown in Fig. 39.8. The central carbon atom has eight outer electrons and each of the other four carbon atoms has eight outer electrons when the other atoms to which it is bonded are included. These strong covalent bonds extend all through the structure.

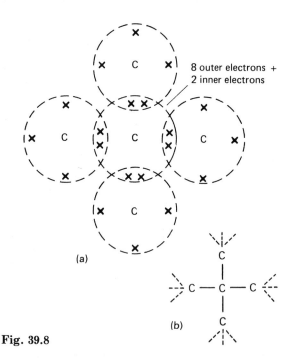

Fig. 39.8

Molecular structures and giant atomic structures both have covalent bonds between atoms. Yet molecular structures are weak and easily broken down by heat whereas giant atomic structures are strong and not easily broken down by heat. To understand why this is so, you have to look at where the covalent bonds are found. In molecular structures they bind together only the atoms *within*

the molecules: there are no covalent bonds *between* the molecules. The forces of attraction between the molecules are very much weaker than covalent bonds. There are no such weak links in a giant atomic structure: each atom is joined to others by strong covalent bonds and these bonds form a network all through the crystal.

The bonds in metals

A look at Fig. 38.1 and Table 38.1 (pages 160 and 161) will show you that metals have giant structures. Some of these are very strong structures but a few, like the sodium structure, are a bit weaker than the rest. What kind of bond holds the particles together so well?

It is difficult to imagine the bonds being ionic, like those in rock salt. Although the metal atoms could form cations, there are no non-metal atoms around to take up the electrons released and so form anions. You may think that the bonds might be covalent. But if they were, it would not be possible to explain why metals are so different in many of their properties from other substances with giant atomic structures. In particular, any idea of the bonds in metals must explain why they are such good conductors of electricity and heat.

The atoms of metals readily form cations. Can it be that the particles of metals are cations and not atoms? If they are, then a lump of metal consists of cations together with the outer electrons which have been lost from the atoms. The cations and electrons produce an electrically neutral material. This means that the outer electrons do not belong to any particular cation. Instead, you can imagine that they are able to move among the ions: they are said to be **delocalized** or **mobile**.

This picture of the structure of a metal is sometimes described as a regular array of metal cations in an 'atmosphere' or 'sea' of mobile electrons. Using the word 'atmosphere' or 'sea' shows that an electron is not **localized** (fixed) near to any one cation. You should contrast this with a covalent bond between two atoms. Here, two electrons are localized between two particular nuclei and they are not free to move away from this region.

How are the cations held together in the structure? They must repel one another because they all have a positive charge. The electrons also repel one another. But there must be forces of attraction between the cations and the electrons. So the forces holding the cations together must be the forces of attraction between the cations and the electrons distributed among them.

The idea of mobile electrons seems a good one because it can explain the conduction of electricity and heat by metals. When a potential difference is applied across a metal, the mobile electrons start to

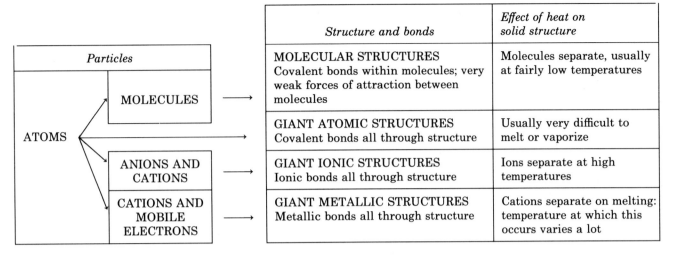

Particles	Structure and bonds	Effect of heat on solid structure
MOLECULES	**MOLECULAR STRUCTURES** Covalent bonds within molecules; very weak forces of attraction between molecules	Molecules separate, usually at fairly low temperatures
ATOMS	**GIANT ATOMIC STRUCTURES** Covalent bonds all through structure	Usually very difficult to melt or vaporize
ANIONS AND CATIONS	**GIANT IONIC STRUCTURES** Ionic bonds all through structure	Ions separate at high temperatures
CATIONS AND MOBILE ELECTRONS	**GIANT METALLIC STRUCTURES** Metallic bonds all through structure	Cations separate on melting: temperature at which this occurs varies a lot

Fig. 39.9

move in one direction. Electrons are supplied to one end of the metal from the battery and an equal number of electrons are removed from the other end of the metal. This process does not change the metal in any way because there is no overall change in the number of mobile electrons and the way that they are distributed through the structure.

When one end of a metal is heated, the mobile electrons at that end are given more kinetic energy. These electrons are able to move through the structure, colliding with other electrons and in this way passing on their own increased energy through the structure.

Substances with structures in which all the bonding electrons are *localized* between two atoms are poor conductors of electricity and heat. This is because the electrons are not free to move through the structure.

There is one non-metal that is a very good conductor of electricity and heat. The graphite structure (Fig. 38.9, page 164) does not contain cations but it does have delocalized electrons. Each carbon atom in graphite has only three covalent bonds and yet there is a total of four outer electrons. This means that one electron per carbon atom is not used in the covalent bonding within each layer of rings. Each of these electrons is free to move.

When a single graphite crystal is tested, it is found to conduct heat and electricity well in the direction along the layers, while it acts as an insulator in the direction which is at right angles to the layers. So it is clear that the delocalized electrons cannot move from one layer to another but they can move along the layers.

Structures and bonds

Fig. 39.9 is a summary of the main types of structures and bonds discussed in Chapters 38 and 39.

QUESTIONS

1 Potassium (atomic number 19) and fluorine (atomic number 9) react to form potassium fluoride.
(a) What is the arrangement of electrons in a potassium atom and in a fluorine atom?
(b) How would you expect potassium atoms and fluorine atoms to react? (Would they gain electrons, lose electrons or share electrons?)
(c) What sort of a compound would you expect potassium and fluorine to form? Explain your answer, give the formula of the compound and show the arrangement of electrons in the particles in the compound.
(d) How would you expect fluorine to react with hydrogen? Again say what sort of compound would be formed, give its formula and show how the electrons are arranged in the particles in the compound.

2 This question is about the following compounds: phosphine (a compound of phosphorus and hydrogen), caesium fluoride, hydrogen iodide and strontium oxide. Use the periodic table (page 283) and your knowledge of Chapters 38 and 39 to answer these questions.
(a) For each of these compounds, say whether it is likely to contain ionic bonds or covalent bonds. (Base your answer on the positions of the elements in the periodic table.)
(b) Write down the likely formula of each of the compounds. For those with giant ionic structures give the charges on the ions.

3 An element X forms a bromide that is a liquid at room temperature and that has the formula XBr_3. Neither the element nor its bromide conducts electricity.
(a) In which group of the periodic table is X likely to be found?
(b) Give two reasons why solid XBr_3 is likely to have a molecular structure.
(c) How many outer electrons are there in an atom of (i) X and (ii) bromine?
(d) Draw a diagram to show how the outer electrons are arranged in order that atoms of X and bromine in XBr_3 molecules all get the number of electrons in a noble gas atom. How many outer electrons are there in the atoms of X and of bromine in the molecules?

4 Here are two ways in which a hydrogen atom may form bonds with other atoms:

A it may gain one electron;
B it may share its electron with another atom in a covalent bond.

Hydrogen has an atomic number of 1 and helium has an atomic number of 2.
(*a*) Write down the formula of the ion formed by process A.
(*b*) Can you give one reason why a hydrogen atom is likely to gain an electron?
(*c*) In which of these compounds do you think that the bond formed by process *A* may be found: (i) $H_2Se(g)$, (ii) $HCl(g)$, (iii) $CH_4(g)$, (iv) $NaH(s)$? Give a reason for your choice.

(*d*) Molecules of hydrogen sulphide (H_2S) have two bonds formed by process *B*. Given that a sulphur atom has six outer electrons and ten inner electrons, draw a diagram showing the formation of these two bonds in a molecule.
(*e*) How many electrons does (i) a sulphur atom and (ii) a hydrogen atom have in a molecule of hydrogen sulphide?
5 Lithium fluoride (LiF) has a giant ionic structure and lithium has a metallic structure.
(*a*) Which kinds of strong bonds are present in these solids?
(*b*) Starting with one lithium atom and one fluorine atom, show what happens to the outer electrons of each atom to give the kind of bond present in lithium fluoride.
(*d*) Which of the solids would you expect to conduct electricity (i) when solid, and (ii) when liquid?

Key words

ionic bond	**bonding pair (of electrons)**	**delocalized (mobile) electrons**
covalent bond	**metallic bonding**	**localized electrons**

Basic facts

- The atoms of noble gases have particularly stable arrangements of electrons.

- To form an ionic bond, one or more electrons are transferred from one atom to another. The total number of electrons and the number of outer electrons in cations and anions are often the same as those in the atoms of noble gases.

- To form a covalent bond, a pair of electrons is shared between two atoms. The total number of electrons and the number of outer electrons in each atom are the same as those in the atoms of noble gases.

- Ionic bonds are the forces holding ions together in giant ionic structures. Covalent bonds are the forces holding atoms together in molecules and in giant atomic structures.

- The structures of metals are composed of metal cations in a 'sea' of mobile electrons. It is the mobile electrons which explain why metals are good conductors of electricity and heat.

40 Redox reactions

Transfer of oxygen and hydrogen

A substance is oxidized when it has oxygen added to it or hydrogen removed from it. A substance is reduced when it has oxygen removed from it or hydrogen added to it.

These are the simplest ways of considering reactions in which **red**uction and **ox**idation take place (**redox reactions**).

The burning of magnesium in steam or carbon dioxide are examples of the transfer of oxygen.

$$Mg(s) + H_2O(g) \longrightarrow MgO(s) + H_2(g)$$
$$2Mg(s) + CO_2(g) \longrightarrow 2MgO(s) + C(s)$$

In each case, the oxygen is removed from one compound by the magnesium to form magnesium oxide. So the **reducing agent** is magnesium and the **oxidizing agent** is steam or carbon dioxide (page 23). The magnesium is **oxidized** and the steam or carbon dioxide is **reduced**.

The burning of ammonia or methane in oxygen are examples of the transfer of hydrogen.

$$4NH_3(g) + 6O_2(g) \longrightarrow 2N_2(g) + 6H_2O(g)$$
$$CH_4(g) + 2O_2(g) \longrightarrow CO_2(g) + 2H_2O(g)$$

In each case, the hydrogen is removed from the compound by the oxygen to form water vapour.

Oxidation takes place when hydrogen is removed from a substance and reduction takes place when hydrogen is added to a substance. So the ammonia or methane is oxidized by oxygen and the oxygen is reduced by ammonia or methane.

But oxygen is not necessary for a redox reaction to occur. The reactions of hydrogen sulphide with bromine and ammonia with chlorine are redox but do not involve oxygen.

$$H_2S(aq) + Br_2(aq) \longrightarrow 2H^+(aq) + 2Br^-(aq) + S(s)$$

$$2NH_3(aq) + 3Cl_2(aq)$$
$$\longrightarrow N_2(g) + 6H^+(aq) + 3Cl^-(aq)$$

In the rest of this chapter, other more general definitions of redox reactions are discussed. These extend the idea of oxidation and reduction well beyond the simple idea of the transfer of oxygen or hydrogen.

Redox reactions and electron transfer

Think of the burning of magnesium in oxygen.

$$2Mg(s) + O_2(g) \longrightarrow 2MgO(s)$$

This reaction can be split into two parts. The magnesium atoms in the element magnesium form magnesium cations in magnesium oxide, and the oxygen atoms in the oxygen molecules form oxide anions in magnesium oxide.

$$Mg \longrightarrow Mg^{2+}$$
$$O \longrightarrow O^{2-}$$

These equations are not balanced. To form its cation, a magnesium atom must lose two electrons, and to form its anion, an oxygen atom must gain two electrons. The full **half-equations** for these two **half-reactions** are

$$2Mg(s) - 4e^- \longrightarrow 2Mg^{2+}(s)$$
$$O_2(s) + 4e^- \longrightarrow 2O^{2-}(s)$$

If you combine these two half-equations together, you get the full equation for the reaction. There has been a transfer of electrons from the magnesium atoms to the oxygen atoms. You know that the burning of magnesium in oxygen is a redox reaction in which the magnesium is being oxidized to magnesium oxide.

Chemists call all reactions that occur by electron transfer 'redox reactions', and the following definitions then apply.

A substance is oxidized when it loses electrons.
A substance is reduced when it gains electrons.

From these definitions it follows that:

an oxidizing agent is a substance that accepts electrons;
a reducing agent is a substance that gives up electrons.

The idea of electron transfer can be applied to many reactions involving solutions of electrolytes, that is, substances which exist as ions when dissolved in water. An example is the displacement of copper by zinc from a solution of copper(II) sulphate. The ionic equation is

$$Zn(s) + Cu^{2+}(aq) \longrightarrow Zn^{2+}(aq) + Cu(s)$$

The full half-equations for the two half-reactions are

$$Zn(s) - 2e^- \longrightarrow Zn^{2+}(aq)$$
$$Cu^{2+}(aq) + 2e^- \longrightarrow Cu(s)$$

There has been a transfer of electrons from the zinc atoms to the copper(II) cations. So zinc atoms have been oxidized (oxidizing agent, $Cu^{2+}(aq)$) and copper(II) cations have been reduced (reducing agent, $Zn(s)$).

You can read more about electron transfer in Chapters 41 and 42.

Oxidation numbers

Redox reactions can also be defined in terms of **oxidation numbers** (see p. 175). The advantage of using these rather than the idea of electron transfer is that they can be applied to *any* redox reaction whether or not it involves ionic substances.

Oxidation numbers are assigned to each individual element in a compound. Sometimes they appear in the name of a compound (e.g. copper(II) oxide, iron(III) chloride), and here they refer to the element after whose name they are written. The four rules for deciding which number to assign are as follows:

1 The oxidation number of the atoms in an element is zero, e.g.

In Mg, O_2, Cl_2 and S_8, the oxidation numbers of the atoms are all zero.

2 For elements which exist in compounds in the form of simple cations or anions, the oxidation number is equal to the charge on the ion, e.g.

The formula for sodium chloride is Na^+Cl^-, so the oxidation number of sodium in sodium chloride is $+1$ and of chlorine in sodium chloride is -1.
The formula for magnesium oxide is $Mg^{2+}O^{2-}$, so here the oxidation number of magnesium is $+2$ and of oxygen is -2.
The formula of zinc chloride is $Zn^{2+}(Cl^-)_2$, so here the oxidation number of zinc is $+2$ and of chlorine is -1.

The sum of the ionic charges in a compound must always be zero (page 163), and this rule means that the sum of the oxidation numbers in a compound must also be zero.

3 For compounds which are not ionic, it is necessary to invent rules for deciding oxidation numbers. These rules are as follows.

In their compounds:

(**a**) hydrogen has an oxidation number of $+1$;

(**b**) oxygen has an oxidation number of -2;

(**c**) chlorine has an oxidation number of -1 (except in compounds with oxygen).

(If you continue your study of chemistry you will learn that there are exceptions to some of these rules and also why these rules are made.)

	H$_2$	S	O$_4$
o.n.	$(+1) \times 2$	x	$(-2) \times 4$

so that $+2 + x - 8$ has to equal zero because H$_2$SO$_4$ is a neutral molecule. So $x = +6$.

Similarly it can be shown that in the sulphite ion (SO$_3^{2-}$) the oxidation number of sulphur is $+4$ and in the nitrate ion (NO$_3^-$) the oxidation number of nitrogen is $+5$. These oxidation numbers can be used to name compounds. This means that sodium sulphate is sometimes called sodium sulphate(VI) while sodium sulphite can be called sodium sulphate(IV).

Table 40.1

	Oxidation numbers of electrons in compounds
Group I (Li Na K)	Always $+1$, e.g. NaCl, KBr, Li$_2$O, Na$_2$SO$_4$, KNO$_3$
Group II (Mg Ca Ba)	Always $+2$, e.g. MgCl$_2$, CaO, Ba(NO$_3$)$_2$
Group III (Al)	Always $+3$, e.g. AlCl$_3$, Al$_2$O$_3$
Group IV (C Pb)	Carbon: common values are $+4$ in CO$_2$ and CCl$_4$ and -4 in CH$_4$; other possible values include $+2$ in CO Lead: often $+2$ as in PbO and Pb(NO$_3$)$_2$ but sometimes $+4$ as in PbO$_2$
Group V (N)	Nitrogen: -3 in NH$_3$ but other values possible
Group VI (O S)	Oxygen: always -2, e.g. O^{2-}, H$_2$O, CuO Sulphur: -2 in H$_2$S and S^{2-}, $+4$ in SO$_2$ and $+6$ in SO$_3$
Group VII (halogens)	Fluorine: always -1, e.g. F$^-$ Chlorine: always -1, e.g. Cl$^-$ except in compound with oxygen Bromine and iodine: -1 in halides but other values possible
Transition (heavy) metals	Variable positive values, e.g. $+2$ or $+3$ for iron in Fe^{2+} and Fe^{3+}, and other values possible

Using these rules, it is possible to work out the oxidation numbers of elements in many compounds and some examples are given in Table 40.1. In every case the sum of the oxidation numbers in the formula of the compound must be zero, e.g.

NH$_3$ (each H atom is 'worth' $+1$ making $+3$ altogether, so the N atom must be 'worth' -3 to give a total of zero).

CO$_2$ (each O atom is 'worth' -2, making -4 altogether, so the C atom must be 'worth' $+4$).

4 In the compound sodium sulphate, the oxidation number of sodium is $+1$ and the oxidation number of the sulphate ion as a whole is -2 (SO$_4^{2-}$). What is the oxidation number of sulphur here? The sum of the oxidation numbers of the one sulphur atom and four oxygen atoms in the sulphate ion has to be -2. Since each oxygen atom is given the oxidation number -2, the oxidation number of sulphur has to be $+6$.

Similarly in sulphuric acid, the oxidation number of sulphur is $+6$:

Transition metal atoms are sometimes found in anions. Their oxidation numbers can be worked out in a similar way. The correct name for potassium permanganate (KMnO$_4$) is potassium manganate(VII) since the rules give the oxidation numbers of potassium and oxygen as $+1$ and -2 respectively. So the oxidation number of the manganese atom has to be $+7$. Potassium dichromate (K$_2$Cr$_2$O$_7$) is known as potassium dichromate(VI) because the oxidation number of the chromium atom is $+6$. This is explained more fully:

	K	Mn	O$_4$
o.n.	$+1$	x	$(-2) \times 4$

so that $+1 + x - 8$ has to equal zero and x must be $+7$.

	K$_2$	Cr$_2$	O$_7$
o.n.	$(+1) \times 2$	$2x$	$(-2) \times 7$

so that $+2 + 2x - 14$ has to equal zero and x must be $+6$.

Oxidation numbers and redox reactions

We can now write definitions of oxidation and reduction using the idea of oxidation numbers:

A substance is oxidized when the oxidation number of one of its elements increases.
A substance is reduced when the oxidation number of one of its elements decreases.

Example 1

(a) Magnesium is oxidized by oxygen to magnesium oxide.

$$Mg \longrightarrow MgO$$
o.n. of magnesium $\quad Mg(0) \quad Mg(+2)$
$$O_2 \longrightarrow MgO$$
o.n. of oxygen $\quad O(0) \quad O(-2)$

Magnesium has its oxidation number increased (this is oxidation) while oxygen has its oxidation number decreased (this is reduction).

(b) Carbon reduces copper(II) oxide to copper (page 30, Experiment 10.3).

$$CuO \longrightarrow Cu$$
o.n. of copper $\quad Cu(+2) \quad Cu(0)$
$$C \longrightarrow CO_2$$
o.n. of carbon $\quad C(0) \quad C(+4)$

Copper has its oxidation number decreased (this is reduction) while carbon has its oxidation number increased (this is oxidation).

Example 2

Sulphides and sulphites convert acidified potassium manganate(VII) (potassium permanganate) to manganese(II) ions. They themselves become sulphates (page 144).

$$S^{2-} \longrightarrow SO_4^{2-}$$
o.n. of sulphur $\quad S(-2) \quad S(+6)$
$$SO_3^{2-} \longrightarrow SO_4^{2-}$$
o.n. of sulphur $\quad S(+4) \quad S(+6)$
$$MnO_4^- \longrightarrow Mn^{2+}$$
o.n. of manganese $\quad Mn(+7) \quad Mn(+2)$

In this reaction, sulphur has its oxidation number increased and manganese has its oxidation number decreased. So sulphides and sulphites are oxidized, and acidified potassium manganate(VII) (potassium permanganate) is reduced.

Example 3

Various substances convert iron(II) ions to iron(III) ions and others perform the reverse process. Oxidation occurs when the oxidation number of iron goes from +2 to +3 and reduction occurs when it goes from +3 to +2.

When carrying out the next experiment, try to decide in each redox reaction which other element, besides iron, is undergoing a change in oxidation number.

Experiment 40.1 Redox reactions of iron(II) and iron(III) ions

1. To separate volumes of iron(II) sulphate solution acidified with bench dilute (1 M) sulphuric acid, add the same volume of:

(a) bench dilute (2 M) nitric acid, and then warm the mixture;
(b) dilute bromine solution;
(c) potassium manganate(VII) (potassium permanganate) solution;
(d) potassium dichromate(VI) (potassium dichromate) solution;
(e) a solution of sodium sulphate(IV) (sodium sulphite) or sulphur dioxide, and then warm.

In each case, test the final solution in order to find the kind or kinds of iron ions present. Carry out the same tests on the original solution of iron(II) sulphate as a control. Remember that not all the iron(II) ions may have reacted. But what is important is to decide whether or not any change at all takes place. Look at Chapter 56 for details of the tests.

▶ Which of the substances (a) to (e) change iron(II) ions to iron(III) ions and so act as oxidizing agents?

2. Repeat 1, using a solution of iron(III) sulphate acidified by adding bench dilute (1 M) sulphuric acid. Again, try to discover whether or not a reaction occurs. As a control, carry out all your tests on the original solution of iron(III) ions as well as on the final solution.

▶ Which one of the substances (a) to (e) changes iron(III) ions to iron(II) ions and so acts as a reducing agent?

QUESTIONS

1 Iron(II) ions are formed when iron filings react with dilute hydrochloric or sulphuric acid, but iron(III) ions are formed with dilute nitric acid.
(a) Describe how you would carry out these two experiments and prove that iron(II) ions were formed in one case and iron(III) ions in the other.
(b) Which gas would you expect to be given off with (i) the dilute hydrochloric or sulphuric acid and (ii) the dilute nitric acid?
(c) Use the idea of (i) electron transfer and (ii) oxidation number to explain why the conversion of iron to iron(II) ions is oxidation.

2 The following reactions are all redox reactions. Decide in each case whether the reaction can be considered as involving electron transfer or as involving the addition or removal of oxygen or hydrogen atoms. Also identify both the oxidizing agent and the reducing agent in each reaction.

(a) $2H_2S(aq) + SO_2(aq) \longrightarrow 3S(s) + 2H_2O(l)$
(b) $H_2S(aq) + Cl_2(aq) \longrightarrow 2H^+(aq) + 2Cl^-(aq) + S(s)$
(c) $Mg(s) + 2H_2O(l) \longrightarrow Mg^{2+}(aq) + 2OH^-(aq) + H_2(g)$

Finally, explain each reaction in terms of changes in oxidation number of the appropriate elements.

3 Acidified potassium dichromate(VI) (potassium dichromate) solution ($K_2Cr_2O_7$) is involved in a lot of redox reactions. The partly completed half-equation is:

$$Cr_2O_7{}^{2-}(aq) + 14H^+(aq) \longrightarrow 2Cr^{3+}(aq) + 7H_2O(l)$$

(a) What is the oxidation number of chromium in $Cr_2O_7{}^{2-}$ and in Cr^{3+} ions?
(b) Complete the above half-equation by adding or subtracting the appropriate number of electrons to or from the left-hand side.
(c) Give *two* explanations for regarding $Cr_2O_7{}^{2-}$ ions as an oxidizing agent.

Key words

redox reactions	reducing agent
oxidation	electron transfer
oxidizing agent	oxidation number
reduction	

Basic facts

- Oxidation can be defined as:
  - the addition of oxygen to a substance
  - the removal of hydrogen from a substance
  - the loss of electrons from a substance
  - an increase in the oxidation number of one element in a substance.

- Reduction can be defined as the opposite of the above statements.

- The widest definition of redox reactions involves the use of oxidation numbers.

- There are rules governing the assignment of oxidation numbers to each element, on its own or in a compound.

41 Trends in the periodic table: I Groups

The periodicity of chemical properties shown by elements enabled Mendeleev to arrange similar elements in vertical **groups** in his periodic table (page 283). In this chapter, you can study the groups of elements with the most marked similarities within them. Not all groups in the table have elements with such closely similar properties.

The alkali metals (group I)

Sodium and potassium are quite like one another and very unlike most other metals. They are very soft and they quickly burst into flames when they are heated. They have to be stored in oil so that they cannot come into contact with oxygen or water vapour in the air. Their melting points are low, and the trend is towards lower melting points as you go down the group (Table 41.1).

Table 41.1

Alkali metals	m.p. in °C
Lithium	180
Sodium	97.8
Potassium	63.7
Rubidium	38.9
Caesium	28.7

The reaction of sodium with water is quite dramatic (page 32). Hydrogen is given off, and sodium hydroxide is formed. The equation for this reaction is:

$$2Na(s) + 2H_2O(l) \longrightarrow 2NaOH(aq) + H_2(g)$$

Potassium reacts with water even more dramatically than sodium. A very small piece splutters vigorously and quickly disappears. Hydrogen is given off and again the solution left over goes blue when some drops of universal indicator solution are added.

$$2K(s) + 2H_2O(l) \longrightarrow 2KOH(aq) + H_2(g)$$

Lithium is a metal that is similar in appearance to sodium and potassium. In the next experiment you can find out how similar it is in its chemical reactions.

Experiment 41.1 Two reactions of lithium

1. Your teacher may show you what happens when a very small piece of lithium (no bigger than a rice grain) is heated on a tin lid covered by a gauze (Fig. 41.1).

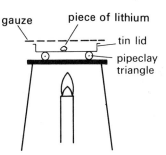

Fig. 41.1

2. Add a very small piece of lithium (no bigger than a rice grain) to some cold water in a beaker. (CARE: lithium is a reactive metal. Do not touch it with your fingers: use dry tongs.)

▶ What can you see?

Test the final solution with a few drops of universal indicator solution.

▶ Is the final solution acidic or alkaline?
▶ Is lithium more reactive or less reactive towards water than solution?

Lithium, sodium and potassium belong to a chemical 'family' called the **alkali metals** which make up group I of the periodic table. They can be put in the same family because they have a lot in common and the differences between them are not great. Not only are they all soft, very reactive metals, they all react to form compounds which are ionic and in which the metal ions have a charge of + 1.

However, there is a trend going down the group because potassium is more reactive than sodium, which in turn is more reactive than lithium. In fact, the most reactive alkali metal is caesium (Cs).

By 'most reactive' in this case we mean that the atom of the element is most ready to form a cation by losing an electron. In other words, the alkali metals show increasing strength as reducing agents (page 173) the lower they are situated in their group.

increasing strength as a reducing agent

$$Li(s) - e^- \longrightarrow Li^+(aq)$$
$$Na(s) - e^- \longrightarrow Na^+(aq)$$
$$K(s) - e^- \longrightarrow K^+(aq)$$
$$Rb(s) - e^- \longrightarrow Rb^+(aq)$$
$$Cs(s) - e^- \longrightarrow Cs^+(aq)$$

increasing reactivity or increasing tendency for atoms to react to form ions

The alkaline earth metals (group II)

The **alkaline earth metals** form group II of the periodic table. The two most familiar metals in this family are magnesium and calcium. How alike are they?

They do look very alike. Both are grey, rather soft, and shiny when fresh; but both get coated with a dull layer of white or grey oxide when exposed to the air. This last fact suggests that they are reactive metals. But they are not stored under oil so they are obviously not quite as reactive as the alkali metals. They all have much higher melting points than the alkali metals but again there is a trend towards lower melting points as you go down the group (Table 41.2).

Table 41.2

Alkaline earth metals	m.p. in °C
Beryllium	1280
Magnesium	650
Calcium	850
Strontium	768
Barium	714

Both magnesium and calcium burn in air to form alkaline oxides (page 45).

$$2Mg(s) + O_2(g) \longrightarrow 2MgO(s)$$
$$2Ca(s) + O_2(g) \longrightarrow 2CaO(s)$$

They also react with water or steam (page 21). In this case, it is clear that calcium is more reactive than magnesium because calcium reacts rapidly with cold water whereas magnesium reacts very slowly with water. For a rapid reaction to occur, steam has to be passed over heated magnesium.

Table 41.3

Halogen	Appearance	Melting point in °C	Boiling point in °C	Density in g cm^{-3}
Fluorine	Pale yellow gas	− 220	− 188	1.11 (at b.p.)
Chlorine	Yellow-green gas	− 101	− 34.7	1.56 (at b.p.)
Bromine	Dark red liquid which forms a dark red-brown gas	− 7.2	58.8	3.12
Iodine	Grey solid with a shiny appearance which forms a purple gas	114	184	4.93

$$Mg(s) + H_2O(g) \longrightarrow MgO(s) + H_2(g)$$
$$Ca(s) + 2H_2O(l) \longrightarrow Ca(OH)_2(aq) + H_2(g)$$

Calcium is also more reactive than magnesium towards dilute acids. Magnesium reacts very rapidly with dilute acids and the reaction is strongly exothermic. The reaction of calcium with dilute acids is too rapid and exothermic for it to be done safely.

The increasing reactivity going down group II is illustrated by the fact that the lowest metal (barium, Ba) has to be stored under oil just like the alkali metals. Again, the reactivity is linked with the ease with which the atoms of the element lose electrons to form cations. As for the group I metals, reactivity is highest for the metals that are lowest in the group.

increasing strength as a reducing agent →

$$Mg(s) - 2e^- \longrightarrow Mg^{2+}(aq)$$
$$Ca(s) - 2e^- \longrightarrow Ca^{2+}(aq)$$
$$Sr(s) - 2e^- \longrightarrow Sr^{2+}(aq)$$
$$Ba(s) - 2e^- \longrightarrow Ba^{2+}(aq)$$

increasing reactivity or increasing tendency for atoms to react to form ions →

The halogens (group VII)

Some of the chemistry of chlorine is dealt with in Chapter 32. At first sight, chlorine, bromine and iodine appear to be very different from one another. Whereas chlorine is a yellow-green gas at room temperature, bromine is a dense very dark red-brown liquid, and iodine is a nearly-black solid. But bromine and iodine can both be vaporized very easily. The boiling points, melting points and densities of the **halogens** are given in Table 41.3. If you examine the values in this table you will see that these properties show fairly steady trends. It is the existence of trends in properties like these that enabled Mendeleev to predict the properties of elements that had not been discovered when he developed the periodic table (page 148).

Chlorine, bromine and iodine have all been used as germicides: chlorine and bromine in swimming baths and iodine in 'tincture of iodine' which is a solution of iodine in methylated spirit used for preventing cuts from becoming infected.

The halogens show striking similarities in the sorts of compounds they form. With metals, they form ionic compounds in which the charge on their anions is − 1. In their compounds with non-metals the halogen atoms often form one covalent bond (e.g. HCl, HBr, HI). The **halide** ions are Cl$^-$, Br$^-$ and I$^-$ and salts containing these ions are often referred to as **halides**.

Three experiments using chlorine are shown in Fig. 41.2. When you have looked at these, study the experiments shown in Fig. 41.3 (page 180) for bromine. You should decide that chlorine and bromine show similar chemical reactions but that chlorine is the more reactive element.

Fig. 41.2

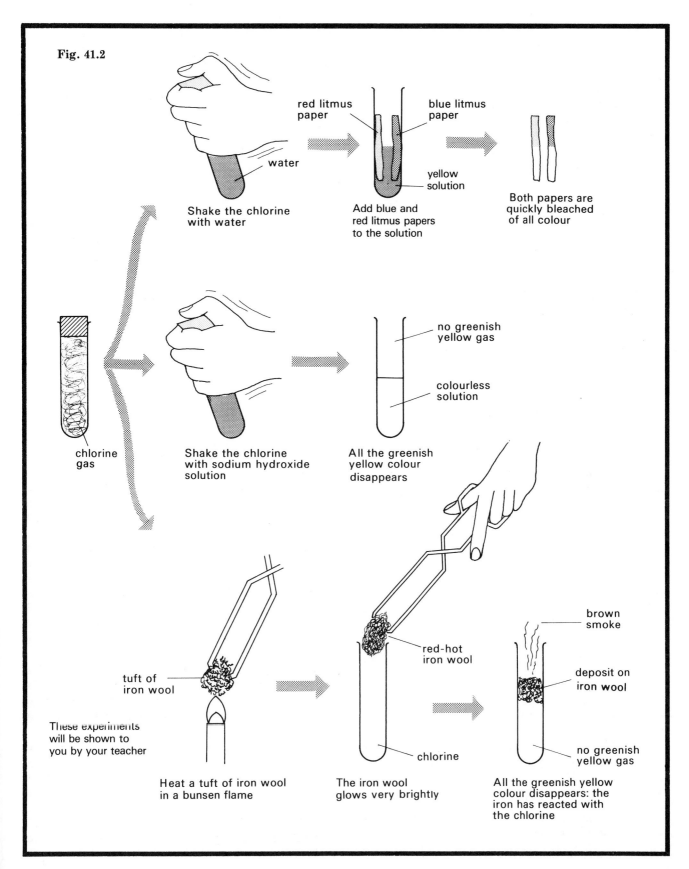

red litmus paper

blue litmus paper

water

yellow solution

Shake the chlorine with water

Add blue and red litmus papers to the solution

Both papers are quickly bleached of all colour

chlorine gas

no greenish yellow gas

colourless solution

Shake the chlorine with sodium hydroxide solution

All the greenish yellow colour disappears

brown smoke

tuft of iron wool

red-hot iron wool

deposit on iron wool

These experiments will be shown to you by your teacher

chlorine

no greenish yellow gas

Heat a tuft of iron wool in a bunsen flame

The iron wool glows very brightly

All the greenish yellow colour disappears: the iron has reacted with the chlorine

Fig. 41.3

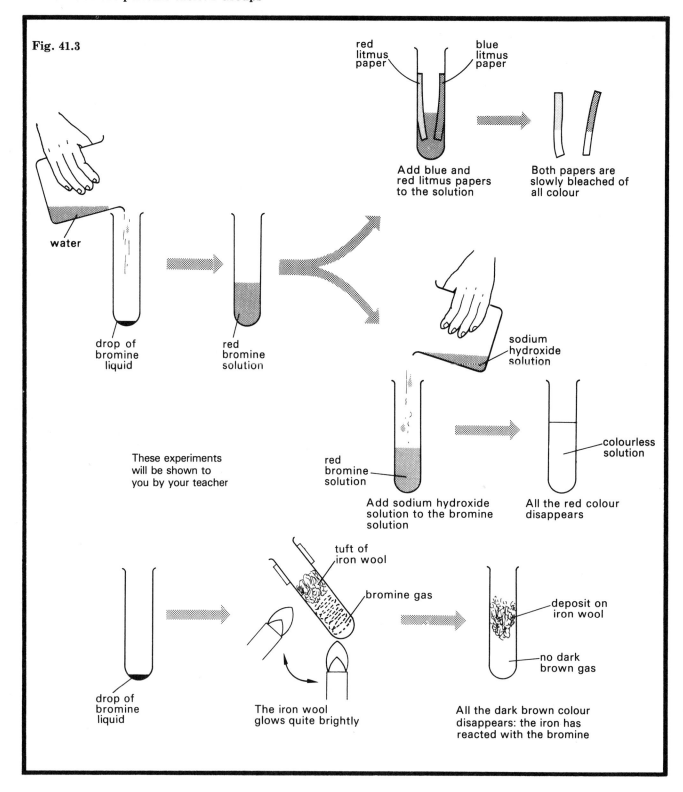

Experiment 41.2 Is iodine like chlorine and bromine?

1. Use some tongs to add a small crystal of iodine to a test-tube half full of water. Close the tube with a bung and shake it.

▶ Has the iodine dissolved?

Now warm the water.

▶ Has any more iodine dissolved?

Add a piece of blue litmus paper and a piece of red litmus paper to the water.

▶ Is there any sign of bleaching?

2. Use some tongs to add a small crystal of iodine to a test-tube half full of sodium hydroxide solution. Warm it gently with the mouth of the tube pointing well away from yourself or anyone else.

▶ What happens?

3. Use the apparatus in Fig. 41.4 in a fume cupboard and heat the iron wool very strongly. Then move the Bunsen flame under the iodine crystal so that some iodine vapour passes through the iron wool.

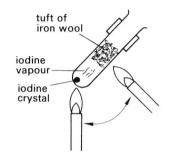

tuft of iron wool

iodine vapour

iodine crystal

Fig. 41.4

▶ What happens?
▶ What is left on the iron wool at the end of the experiment?

These experiments show that chlorine is more reactive than bromine which, in turn, is more reactive than iodine. This is the reverse of the trend for groups I and II because reactivity increases going *up*, not down the group. This can be explained by saying that, of the three, chlorine is the halogen whose molecules most readily gain electrons to form anions. In other words, chlorine is the strongest oxidizing agent (page 173).

| increasing strength as an oxidizing agent | $Cl_2(g) + 2e^- \longrightarrow 2Cl^-(aq)$
$Br_2(g) + 2e^- \longrightarrow 2Br^-(aq)$
$I_2(g) + 2e^- \longrightarrow 2I^-(aq)$ | increasing reactivity, or increasing tendency for atoms to form ions |

These ideas can be tested in the following experiments.

Experiment 41.3 What is the order of reactivity for the halogens?

1. Add a few drops of chlorine solution to about 3 cm^3 of potassium bromide solution in a test-tube.

▶ Is there any change in colour?
▶ Has bromine been displaced by chlorine from the bromide solution?

2. Do 1 again, using iodine solution instead of chlorine water.

▶▶ Is there any change in colour?

If you think that the change may only be due to the dilution of the iodine solution, carry out a control experiment. Add the same volume of iodine solution to 3 cm^3 of water in another test-tube. Compare the colour obtained with the colour of the iodine/potassium bromide mixture.

▶ Has bromine been displaced by iodine from the bromide solution?

3. Complete this series of experiments by finding if there is a reaction when the following are mixed:

(*a*) chlorine solution and potassium iodide solution,
(*b*) bromine solution and potassium chloride solution,
(*c*) bromine solution and potassium iodide solution,
(*d*) iodine solution and potassium chloride solution.

Carry out a control experiment whenever you are not sure about the colour change.

▶ Do these results agree with the idea that, of these three halogens, chlorine is the strongest oxidizing agent and iodine is the weakest one?

Ionic equations can be written for each reaction in which a halogen element displaces another halogen element from a solution containing its ions. For the displacement of iodine by chlorine from a solution of potassium iodide, the equation is

$$Cl_2(aq) + 2I^-(aq) \longrightarrow 2Cl^-(aq) + I_2(aq)$$

The half-equations (page 173) are

$Cl_2(aq) + 2e^- \longrightarrow 2Cl^-(aq)$ reduction of chlorine molecules to ions (with chlorine as the oxidizing agent)

$2I^-(aq) - 2e^- \longrightarrow I_2(aq)$ oxidiation of iodide ions to atoms and then molecules with iodide ions as the reducing agent)

The equations for the displacement of bromine by chlorine, and of iodine by bromine are similar.

QUESTIONS

1 This is a question about rubidium (Rb).
(*a*) To which family of elements does rubidium belong?
(*b*) What would you expect rubidium to look like?
(*c*) What is likely to happen when a piece of rubidium is added to cold water? What would you see when some drops of red litmus solution are added to the solution that is formed?
(*d*) Write a balanced equation for the reaction mentioned in (*c*).

2 Here are some statements about barium:
  (i) It is a silvery white metal which bursts into flame in air without having to be warmed first.
  (ii) With oxygen, it forms barium oxide which will react with water to form an alkaline solution.
  (iii) It reacts with water forming an alkaline solution and giving off a gas.
  (iv) The formula of its main oxide is BaO.
  (*a*) What is the name of the alkaline solution formed in (ii) and (iii)?
  (*b*) What is the name of the gas given off in (iii)?
  (*c*) From your knowledge of the reactions of magnesium, is barium more or less reactive than magnesium?
  (*d*) Which of the reactions mentioned are also shown by sodium and the other alkali metals.
  (*e*) Which of the evidence given above suggests that barium is an alkaline earth metal and not an alkali metal?
  (*f*) Write balanced equations for the reaction of barium with (i) oxygen and (ii) water.

3 (*a*) What is the order of reactivity for the elements chlorine, bromine and iodine?
  (*b*) Where does fluorine come in the periodic table in relation to these three other halogens?
  (*c*) Is fluorine likely to be a stronger or weaker oxidizing agent than chlorine?
  (*d*) In view of your answer to (*c*), predict what would happen when:
  (i) fluorine gas is bubbled into chlorine solution;
  (ii) burning magnesium ribbon is lowered into a gas jar of fluorine.
  (*e*) Write an ionic equation for the reaction in (i) and a non-ionic equation for the reaction in (ii).
  (*f*) From the position of astatine in the halogen group, predict:
  (i) whether it is likely to be a solid, a liquid or a gas at room temperature;
  (ii) whether or not it is likely to be very soluble in water.

Key words

group   **alkali metals**   **alkaline earth metals**   **halogens**   **halides**

Basic facts

- **The elements in a group on the extreme left-hand or right-hand side of the periodic table have similar chemical reactions. They are more similar than elements in a mid-table group.**

- **There is an increase in the strength of the metal as a reducing agent going down groups I and II.**

- **There is an increase in the strength of the halogen element as an oxidizing agent going up group VII.**

42 Trends in the periodic table: II Periods

In this chapter you can study the trends in properties across a row or **period** of the periodic table. The row discussed most is the **third short period** which includes the elements from sodium (Na) to argon (Ar). But there is a mention of a **long period** from potassium (K) to krypton (Kr). Fig. 42.1 shows these periods.

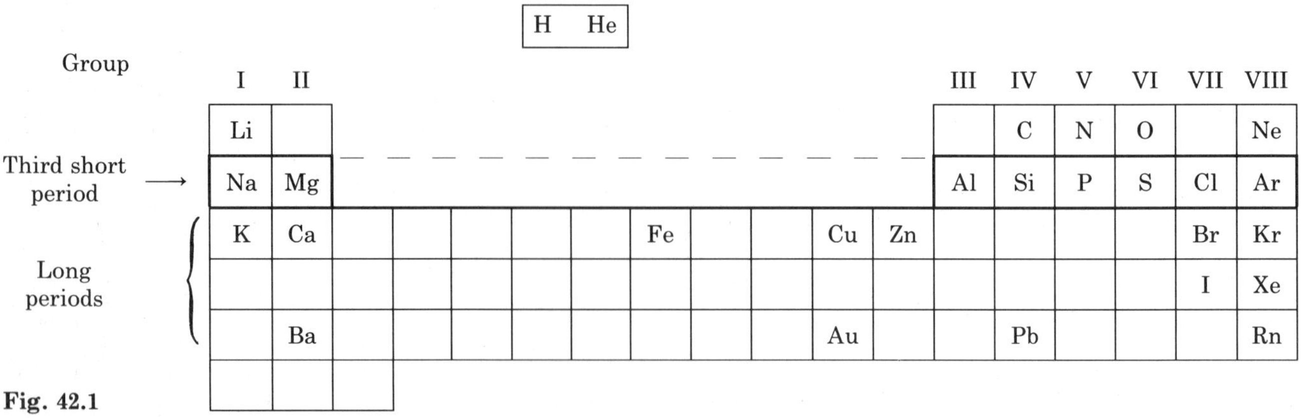

					H	He							

Group	I	II							III	IV	V	VI	VII	VIII
	Li									C	N	O		Ne
Third short period →	Na	Mg							Al	Si	P	S	Cl	Ar
Long periods	K	Ca				Fe		Cu	Zn					Br	Kr
														I	Xe
		Ba					Au			Pb				Rn

Fig. 42.1

182

Metals and non-metals

One important pattern in the properties of elements is that most can be classified as metals or non-metals. Chapter 9 deals with some of the physical properties of metals and non-metals. Two chemical properties are shown in Table 42.1.

Table 42.1

Property	Metals	Non-metals
Kind of ions formed	Often form simple cations; do not form simple anions	Some form simple anions; do not form simple cations
Action of acids	Sufficiently reactive metals react and form salts	Do not react

Group

Group	I	II		III	IV	V	VI	VII	VIII
	Li	Be		B	C	N	O	F	Ne
	Na	Mg		Al	Si	P	S	Cl	Ar
	K	Ca		Ga	Ge	As	Se	Br	Kr
	Rb	Sr		In	Sn	Sb	Te	I	Xe
	Cs	Ba		Tl	Pb	Bi	Po	At	Rn

↑
heavy metals
Fig. 42.2 omitted   METALS ┊ NON-METALS

A dividing line can be drawn between metals and non-metals in the periodic table (Fig. 42.2). In this figure, the heavy metals (transition metals) are omitted. Notice that the dashed line goes through the symbols Ge (germanium) and As (arsenic). These elements lie midway between the extremes of metallic and non-metallic behaviour and they have both metallic and non-metallic properties; they are called **semimetals** or **metalloids**.

Semimetals highlight the fact that a lot of elements can show *both* metallic and non-metallic behaviour. Even a 'typical' metal can be said to be more or less metallic than another metal, and a 'typical' non-metal more or less non-metallic than another non-metal. There is a gradual change in all groups and periods towards more metallic or more non-metallic elements. This does not mean, of course, that there must be both 'typical' metals and 'typical' non-metals in every group, though it is certainly true for periods.

Redox reactions across the third short period

Metals form cations and so must act as reducing agents whereas non-metals form anions and so must act as oxidizing agents. This means that there is a change from reducing properties to oxidizing properties for the elements across a short period.

You can now look again at the reaction of some elements, this time from the point of view of electron transfer. The first three elements in the third short period are sodium, magnesium and aluminium. You know from the position of these elements in the reactivity series for metals that they are in the order of decreasing reactivity going from left to right. Another way of putting this is to say that, of the three, sodium atoms lose electrons most readily and aluminium atoms lose electrons least readily.

$$Na - e^- \longrightarrow Na^+$$
$$Mg - 2e^- \longrightarrow Mg^{2+}$$
$$Al - 3e^- \longrightarrow Al^{3+}$$

decreasing strength of the metal as a reducing agent because of decreasing readiness of atoms to lose electrons

At the other end of the third short period, argon is chemically inert and need not be discussed any further. But the next element, chlorine, is a very reactive non-metal. Its atoms readily gain electrons to form chloride ions.

$$Cl + e^- \longrightarrow Cl^-$$

(The full half-equation is

$$Cl_2(g) + 2e^- \longrightarrow 2Cl^-(aq)$$

or $$Cl_2(g) + 2e^- \longrightarrow 2Cl^-(s))$$

So chlorine is a strong oxidizing agent, just like oxygen itself.

Sulphur is like chlorine in that it reacts with metals to form an ion. Magnesium burns in chlorine to form magnesium chloride, $Mg^{2+}(Cl^-)_2$, and, when heated to a high temperature, it reacts with powdered sulphur to form magnesium sulphide, $Mg^{2+}S^{2-}$. In the reaction of sulphur with magnesium, sulphur atoms gain electrons and so sulphur acts as an oxidizing agent.

$$S + 2e^- \longrightarrow S^{2-}$$

(The full half-equation is

$$S_8(s) + 16e^- \longrightarrow 8S^{2-}(s))$$

Like chlorine and unlike sodium and magnesium, sulphur does not form cations by its atoms losing electrons: in this sense, sulphur does not act as a reducing agent. But it is possible for sulphur to be oxidized in a different way, as these equations show:

$$S_8(s) + 8O_2(g) \longrightarrow 8SO_2(g)$$
$$2SO_2(g) + O_2(g) \longrightarrow 2SO_3(g)$$

In contrast, it is very difficult to oxidize chlorine. For example, chlorine does not react with oxygen gas to form an oxide. So chlorine usually acts as an oxidizing agent but sulphur can be either oxidized or reduced depending on the substance it is reacting with.

Are the reactions of silicon and phosphorus related to the redox reactions of the elements on each side of them in the third short period? Silicon powder burns in oxygen to form silicon dioxide, and white phosphorus burns in oxygen to form phosphorus(v) oxide, P_2O_5.

$$Si(s) + O_2(g) \longrightarrow SiO_2(s)$$
$$P_4(s) + 5O_2(g) \longrightarrow 2P_2O_5(s)$$

So phosphorus continues the trend across the third short period from right to left away from strong oxidizing properties and towards stronger reducing properties. Although phosphorus does oxidize strong reducing agents such as magnesium, its atoms are far less likely to gain electrons and form anions than the atoms of sulphur or chlorine. On the other hand, phosphorus readily acts as a reducing agent in its reaction with oxygen.

There is a pattern in the redox reactions of the elements in the third short period (Table 42.2). At the extreme left-hand side of the period, the elements are strong reducing agents, and at the extreme right-hand side (excluding argon), the elements are strong oxidizing agents. Reducing properties are not so important in elements towards the right-hand side of the period while oxidizing properties become more important. Elements such as phosphorus that are in the middle of the period tend to show both reducing and oxidizing properties but are generally less reactive than the elements at either end of the period.

Oxides in the third short period

The oxides of the elements from sodium to sulphur can be prepared by heating the elements in oxygen, and you will have already seen most of these combustion reactions. An oxide of chlorine cannot be prepared in this way because all the oxides of this element (there are several) are unstable when heated and decompose readily.

Table 42.3 contains the melting points and boiling points of the oxides. The oxides of sodium, magnesium, aluminium and silicon clearly have giant structures (page 162). When molten, the first three oxides are good conductors of electricity whereas silicon dioxide is not. This shows that the metal oxides probably have giant ionic structures while silicon dioxide has a giant atomic structure.

Table 42.3

Formula of oxide	m.p. in °C	b.p. in °C
Na_2O	Sublimes at 1275 °C	
MgO	2640	3600
Al_2O_3	2045	3000
SiO_2 (quartz)	1610	2230
P_4O_{10}	569	591
SO_2	−73	−10
Cl_2O	−20	2

Sulphur dioxide and chlorine monoxide (Cl_2O) obviously have molecular structures (page 161). But it is difficult to decide about phosphorus(v) oxide (P_2O_5). This melts and boils at temperatures that are neither particularly high nor particularly low. It has, however, been proved that the solid is a polymer made from macromolecules (page 222).

Sodium oxide (Na_2O) and magnesium oxide react with water to form OH^-(aq) ions: they are examples of alkaline oxides, a special kind of basic oxide. But aluminium oxide shows both basic and acidic properties, and so there is a trend from left to right across the period towards less basic and more acidic oxides.

On the right-hand side of the period, sulphur dioxide and sulphur trioxide both react with water to form acidic solutions: they also react with alkalis to form salts. Phosphorus(v) oxide has similar reactions though it does not form such a strongly acidic solution with water as does sulphur trioxide. Silicon dioxide continues this trend away from strongly acidic character. It does not react with water under normal conditions, and it reacts with alkalis only when they are molten.

Table 42.2

Element	Na	Mg	Al	Si	P	S	Cl
Redox reactions of element	←Strong reducing→ agents			Forms SiO_2 by oxidation	Forms P_4O_{10} by oxidation	Forms SO_2 by oxidation and S^{2-} by reduction	Forms Cl^- by reduction − strong oxidizing agent

Strength as reducing agent increasing ←———————————

Strength as oxidizing agent increasing ———————————→

Table 42.4

Element	Na	Mg	Al	Si	P	S	Cl
Oxide	Na_2O	MgO	Al_2O_3	SiO_2	P_4O_{10}	SO_3, SO_2	Cl_2O_7
Nature of oxide	Alkaline and basic		Amphoteric	←————————Acidic————————→			

Basic character increasing

←————————————————

Acidic character increasing

————————————————→

The trend in the acidic or basic character of these oxides is summarized in Table 42.4.

Chlorides in the third short period

The chlorides of all the elements from sodium to sulphur can be prepared by heating the element in chlorine. Table 42.5 shows their melting points and boiling points, as well as their conductivity when liquids.

Table 42.5

Formula of chloride	Electrical conductivity of liquid	m.p. in °C	b.p. in °C
NaCl	Good	801	1470
$MgCl_2$	Good	712	1420
$AlCl_3$	Very poor	sublimes at 180 °C	
$SiCl_4$	Very poor	− 68	57
PCl_3	Very poor	− 91	74
SCl_2	Very poor	− 80	59

Solid sodium chloride and magnesium chloride obviously have giant ionic structures. Their formulas can be explained by the transfer of either one or two electrons from each atom of the metal to one or two atoms of chlorine respectively.

The chlorides of silicon, phosphorus and sulphur obviously have molecular structures. Each atom shares electrons with the surrounding chlorine atoms. The number of shared pairs of electrons (4 for silicon, 3 for phosphorus and 2 for sulphur) is equal to the extra number of outer electrons each atom needs to achieve the electronic structure of argon, the nearest noble gas (page 166).

Aluminium chloride is a rather special case, and an account of its structure and bonding must be left for a more advanced course.

Trends across a long period

The first long period has ten elements more than a short period. These ten elements are the **heavy** or **transition metals**. If you take these away, then you are left with a series of elements that show the usual trends in properties across any short period.

The fourth period is the first long period. The ten elements that lie between calcium and gallium are all metals and there is no obvious trend from metallic to non-metallic properties.

The heavy or transition metals have a number of properties in common. The term 'heavy' refers to their densities (page 281). They are much denser than the metals in groups I and II, and only a few other metals, such as tin and lead, have similar densities.

The heavy metals are not only very alike in their densities. They are also quite hard; they have a lustre when clean; they are good conductors of electricity and heat; and most of them are strong and yet malleable (easily beaten into a thin sheet) and ductile (easily drawn through a small hole to form wire).

There is a lot of variation in their reactivities, ranging from fairly reactive metals, such as iron, to very unreactive metals, such as gold. Heavy metals are not found in one small section of the reactivity series, although they are generally in the lower half. From this point of view, the family likeness in chemical properties is not all that striking.

But most heavy metals do have a lot in common. The exceptions to this appear to be the elements at the two extremes of the rows, like scandium (Sc) and zinc.

Heavy metals:

1 **form compounds that are sometimes coloured in the solid state but which always give coloured irons in solution;**

2 **form at least two cations with different charges, i.e. show variable oxidation numbers (page 173);**

3 **are often used as catalysts.**

(Sometimes the catalyst is a compound of the heavy metal rather than the element itself. You can find several examples in this book.)

QUESTIONS

1 (*a*) Find a group in the periodic table that contains both metals and non-metals.

(*b*) Find a group that contains only metals. Which of these metals is likely to show the least metallic behaviour?

(*c*) Find a group that contains only non-metals. Which of these non-metals is likely to show the most metallic behaviour?

2 Use your periodic table to find the position of the element (Ga). In the light of this position, try to predict:

(*a*) the formula of its chloride.

(*b*) the formula of its oxide.

(*c*) the nature of its oxidic (acidic, basic or amphoteric),

(*d*) whether the element is likely to be a reducing agent or an oxidizing agent.

3 A sample of the very reactive non-metallic element *boron* can be obtained by heating its oxide, B_2O_3, with magnesium. The product can be purified by washing it separately with hydrochloric acid and with sodium hydroxide solution.

(*a*) Would B_2O_3 be regarded as an acidic or a basic oxide? Give a reason for your answer.

(*b*) Write an equation to represent the reaction between B_2O_3 and magnesium. This reaction can be said to involve both oxidation and reduction. Explain why this is so.

(*c*) Suggest possible reasons for washing with hydrochloric acid and sodium hydroxide solution in the purification process.

(*d*) Why should this way of extracting boron be expensive on a large scale? What alternative, and cheaper, method is available?

(Hint: consider the large-scale extraction of another group III element.)

4 Here are some data about two chlorides with the formula XCl and YCl_4.

Chloride	m.p. in °C	b.p. in °C
XCl	610	1360
YCl$_4$	− 23	77

When a spatula measure of XCl is dissolved in about $10\,cm^3$ of distilled water, a small temperature rise is observed and a neutral solution is produced. YCl_4 does not dissolve in water at all. Molten XCl conducts electricity well, whereas liquid YCl_4 is a non-conductor.

(*a*) In which group of the period table would you expect to find element X?

(*b*) Describe all the evidence given above that suggests that solid XCl has a giant ionic structure.

(*c*) Draw a diagram to show how the ionic bond between an X atom and a chlorine atom is formed (include only the outer electrons of the atoms).

(*d*) Describe all the evidence given above that suggests that solid and liquid YCl_4 consists of YCl_4 molecules.

(*e*) Name and give the formulas of two chlorides that you would expect to have closely similar properties to XCl.

Key words

short period   long period   semimetal (metalloid)   heavy (transition) metal

Basic facts

- **Ignoring the heavy (transition) metals, there is a gradual trend across a period from strongly metallic properties to strongly non-metallic properties.**

- **In the middle of the periodic table, there are elements called semimetals or metalloids that have both metallic and non-metallic properties.**

- **Across a short period, there is a trend from:**
  - **reducing properties to oxidizing properties for the elements**
  - **basic properties to acidic properties for the oxides**

- **Giant structures of atoms or ions are found in the compounds of elements on the left-hand side of the periodic table, while molecular structures (with covalent bonding within the molecules) are found in the compounds of elements on the right-hand side.**

- **Heavy (transition) metals form a family of elements in a horizontal row. They have coloured ions in solution, show variable oxidation numbers, and are quite often used as catalysts.**

43 Rates of reaction

Different reactions go at different speeds

Think back to some of the reactions you have seen and carried out in the laboratory. Many familiar reactions occur so quickly that they seem to happen in an instant: most reactions involving the formation of a precipitate are like this. But some reactions in which a gas is produced when a solid (such as a carbonate or a metal) is added to an acid take a few minutes to complete.

$$Ag^+(aq) + Cl^-(aq) \longrightarrow AgCl(s) \qquad (1)$$
$$CO_3{}^{2-}(s) + 2H^+(aq) \longrightarrow CO_2(g) + H_2O(l) \qquad (2)$$

Reaction 1 is 'instantaneous', while reaction 2 is over in a few minutes.

In contrast to most laboratory reactions, natural processes are often very slow indeed. The weathering of rocks such as granite and limestone due to the action of water and gases in the air and in the soil is an example of a very slow change. The weathering of the stonework in the building in Fig. 34.9 (page 144) happens at the rate of only a few millimetres every 100 years. The corrosion of metals such as iron and copper by the air is also slow, although it is on a time scale of years, not hundreds of years. One of the slowest natural processes is the radioactive decay of certain elements such as uranium (page 158): these may take many millions of years.

So reactions can occur at very widely different speeds. The fastest reactions seem to be instantaneous because they happen as soon as the reactants are mixed (Fig. 43.1). Many reactions in solution are very fast, particularly those between a cation and an anion.

The fastest reaction of all occurs so quickly that it is almost complete in 10^{-10} seconds! The slowest reactions, for example geological processes, are often those between two solids or a solid and a gas.

In this chapter, you can study the 'in-between' reactions, that is, reactions that are slow enough for you to follow their progress from start to finish (Fig. 43.2) but not so slow that your patience is too sorely tried. You can have a first look at some of these 'in-between' reactions by carrying out Experiment 43.1.

Experiment 43.1 A first look at some reaction rates

Carry out each of these reactions in a test-tube. After you have mixed the substances, stand the tube in a rack and watch the reaction mixture carefully until no further change occurs.

1. Measure $10\,cm^3$ of dilute sodium thiosulphate solution into a test-tube and add to it about $1\,cm^3$ of bench dilute (2 M) hydrochloric acid.

Fig. 43.1 The 'instantaneous' reaction between iodine solution and sodium thiosulphate solution. (The products of this reaction are colourless.)

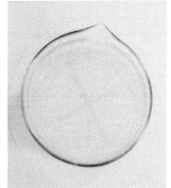

Fig. 43.2 The reaction between sodium thiosulphate solution and an acid (Experiment 43.1) takes about a minute. The cross below the beaker fades as more and more sulphur is formed

2. Dissolve one spatula measure of potassium iodide in about 5 cm³ of water and add to it two drops of bench dilute (1 M) sulphuric acid. Add about 5 cm³ of dilute hydrogen peroxide solution to this mixture and then quickly pour the reaction mixture into another test-tube.

3. Make a solution of potassium manganate(VII) by dissolving *one or two* crystals of the solid in a few cm³ of water in a test-tube. To another test-tube, add about 5 cm³ of ethanedioic acid (oxalic acid) solution and about 5 cm³ of bench dilute (1 M) sulphuric acid. Add 1 or 2 cm³ of the manganate(VII) solution to this mixture and then pour the pink reaction mixture into an empty test-tube. CARE: ethanedioic acid is poisonous.

In each experiment, you know that a reaction is taking place because the reaction mixture changes in some way.

▶ What property of the reaction mixture changes in each case as the reaction occurs?

How can the rate of a reaction be measured?

What is meant by the rate (speed) of a chemical reaction? To answer this question, you should first think about some everyday examples of rate. The speed of a car is usually given as the number of kilometres travelled per hour: in cricket, the run rate is the number of runs scored per hour; and the rate of flow of water through a tap might be measured in cubic centimetres or litres per minute. All rates are a quantity (like volume, mass or length) achieved in a given time so that the units of rate are quantities per unit time.

$$\text{Rate} = \frac{\text{measured change in a given property}}{\text{time taken for the change to occur}}$$

What quantities change during a chemical reaction, and can these changes be easily measured? *Concentration* changes with time, but this is not always easy to measure directly during a reaction. It is sometimes easier to measure some other property that changes as the concentrations change. Examples of some of these properties are

1. volume of a gaseous product,
2. colour intensity,
3. pH,
4. conductivity of an electrolyte,
5. amount of a precipitate,
6. pressure of a gaseous mixture,
7. temperature.

Average rate and rate at a given time

Think of a motorist who travels 40 km in one hour. His *average* speed for the journey is 40 km h⁻¹. But this is unlikely to have been his speed at every stage of the journey. At any one instant, he might have been travelling at 80 km h⁻¹ or may even have been stationary. An average rate cannot say much about the way in which the rate varies at different stages during the journey.

In a chemical reaction, the rate does not stay the same over the whole reaction, as you can see in some of the experiments that follow. When describing the rate of reaction, you must be careful to say whether the rate is the average rate over the whole reaction, or whether it is the average rate over a particular part of the reaction, or whether it is the rate at a particular instant during the reaction.

Investigating the rate of the reaction between magnesium and dilute hydrochloric acid

The equation for this reaction is

$$\text{Mg(s)} + 2\text{H}^+(\text{aq}) \longrightarrow \text{Mg}^{2+}(\text{aq}) + \text{H}_2(\text{g})$$

The rate at which the magnesium is used up would not be easy to measure throughout the reaction, but it is easy to find the *average* rate of this over the whole reaction by timing how long it takes for the strip of magnesium to 'disappear'. The longer the time taken, the lower is the average rate.

In the next experiment, you are going to study the average rate of the magnesium–acid reaction under different conditions. You may already have some ideas on how to speed up or slow down a reaction, and you can test these ideas here.

Experiment 43.2 Changing the rate of the reaction between magnesium and dilute hydrochloric acid

For each separate experiment in the table on page 189, add the magnesium to the acid and find the time taken for the metal to dissolve.

In part 1, you should thoroughly mix the acid and the water before adding the magnesium. In part 2, you can heat the acid to a temperature of 2 or 3 °C above the value you want so as to allow for some cooling during the reaction. Do not heat the acid after you have added the magnesium. In part 3, the different samples of magnesium all have about the same mass.

▶ What is being varied in each part of the experiment?
▶ What effect does each change have on the average rate over the whole reaction?

Part	Temperature	Amount of magnesium	Volume of dilute (2 M) hydrochloric acid in cm³	Volume of water in cm³
1	Room temperature	30 mm strips of clean ribbon	(a) 50 (b) 40 (c) 30 (d) 20	0 10 20 30
2	(a) 30 °C (b) 40 °C (c) 50 °C (d) 60 °C	30 mm strips of clean ribbon	30	20
3	Room temperature	(a) 0.03 g of powder (b) 0.03 g of turnings (c) 30 mm of clean ribbon (d) 9 mm of clean wire	50	0

Your results for this experiment tell you nothing about how the rate varies throughout the reaction. One way to get information about this is to collect the hydrogen evolved and measure its volume at different times.

Experiment 43.3 Measuring the rate at which hydrogen is evolved

Clean about 80 mm of magnesium ribbon with some emery paper and then coil it loosely. Measure about 50 cm³ of 0.5 M hydrochloric acid into the conical flask (Fig. 43.3). Before starting the reaction, put the

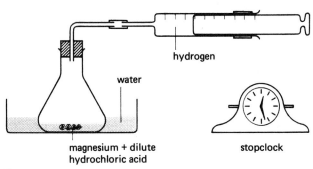

Fig. 43.3

bung tightly in the neck of the flask and note the volume of air displaced. Remove the bung, push the plunger to zero on the scale of the syringe, add the coil of magnesium to the acid, and then put the bung into the neck of the flask as quickly as you can. At the same time start the stopclock.

Read the volume of hydrogen in the syringe every half minute until all the magnesium has reacted. Before each reading, rotate the plunger of the syringe to make sure that it has not become jammed. The reaction flask stands in cold water because the

reaction is exothermic: it is important to keep a fairly steady temperature all through the reaction.

Take the volume of the air displaced by the bung away from all your volume measurements. Then plot a graph of volume of hydrogen in cm³ along the y-axis against time in minutes along the x-axis. Draw a smooth curve through as many of the points as possible.

Your curve should look like the one in Fig. 43.4; it is called a **rate curve**. Notice that it is steep at first but gets less steep as time goes on until at the end of the reaction it is horizontal. So V_f is final (maximum) volume of gas produced by the reaction under the particular conditions of temperature and pressure of the experiment.

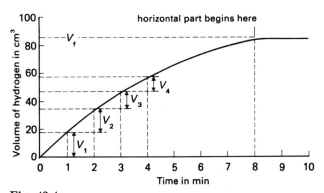

Fig. 43.4

V_1, V_2, V_3 and V_4 are the volumes of gas collected in each of the first four minutes of the reaction. These give the **average** rate of the reaction in cm³ of hydrogen per minute over each one-minute interval. Each succeeding average rate is less than the previous one, and this is shown by the gradual flattening out of the curve.

Fig. 43.5 shows some tangents drawn to a rate curve. Each tangent can be used to find the rate at a particular instant, rather than an average rate over an interval of time.

The slope of the tangent at a point on the rate curve equals the rate of the reaction at that particular instant in the reaction.

The steepest tangent is the one drawn to the point of the curve at time 0. This shows that the highest rate during the reaction is the rate at the start (the **initial rate**). As the reaction goes on, the curve begins to flatten and the slope of the tangent decreases. So the rate of reaction decreases steadily throughout the reaction until it becomes zero when the reaction has stopped.

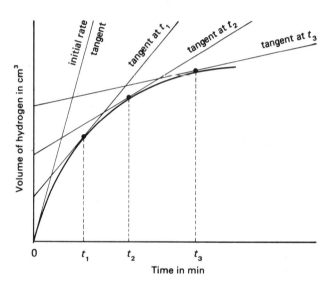

Fig. 43.5

Experiment 43.2 shows you one way of investigating how changes in the conditions affect the rate of the reaction between magnesium and dilute hydrochloric acid. Another way is to plot a rate curve for each set of conditions, though this would be a much bigger investigation. The effect of an increase in temperature could be studied more satisfactorily because you could then make sure that the temperature stayed the same throughout the reaction (in Experiment 43.2, the temperature varies by a few degrees Celsius).

Some results for such an investigation are shown in Figs. 43.6 and 43.7.

In each experiment, the same mass of magnesium is used and there is always an excess of acid, so that the same *mass* of hydrogen should always be produced when the reaction has finished. But the *volume* of hydrogen varies with the temperature at which the experiment is carried out.

Rates and catalysis

Adding certain substances (which are not reactants) to some reaction mixtures can increase the rate considerably. These substances are called **catalysts**. Catalysts are widely used in industry to speed up reactions which otherwise would be uneconomically slow.

A catalysed reaction can be used to prepare oxygen in the laboratory. The decomposition of hydrogen peroxide solution gives oxygen, but the reaction is slow at room temperature unless a catalyst is used.

$$2H_2O_2(aq) \longrightarrow 2H_2O(l) + O_2(g)$$

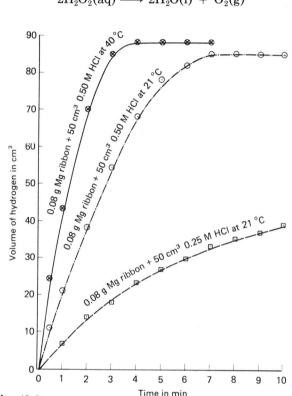

Fig. 43.6

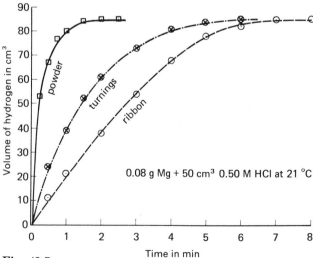

Fig. 43.7

Experiment 43.4 Which substances are catalysts for the decomposition of hydrogen peroxide solution?

1. Add small amounts of the following solids to separate test-tubes containing a few cm³ of '20 volume' hydrogen peroxide solution: lead(IV) oxide, manganese(IV) oxide, sand, copper(II) oxide, lead(II) oxide.
2. Add a few drops of concentrated ammonia solution (CARE) to a small volume of cobalt(II) nitrate solution until you get a brown solution. Add two drops of this solution to some '20 volume' hydrogen peroxide solution. Carry out a control experiment by adding some concentrated ammonia solution to some '20 volume' hydrogen peroxide solution.

Manganese(IV) oxide is a good catalyst for this reaction, and it is the one that is usually chosen when you want to prepare oxygen from hydrogen peroxide solution.

Some of the questions that could be asked about this catalysed reaction, and about any other reaction catalysed by a solid, are:

1. Does the mass of the catalyst change during the reaction?
2. Does the catalyst look any different at the end of the reaction?
3. What effect (if any) does an increase in the mass of catalyst used have on the rate of the reaction?
4. What effect (if any) does the physical form of the catalyst have on the rate of the reaction?

Questions 1 and 2 are about the catalyst itself and do not involve any measurements of rate. Questions 3 and 4 do require that you measure the rate of decomposition accurately.

The most convenient rate to measure is the initial rate, and this can be done by drawing a tangent to the rate curve at the origin (page 190).

Experiment 43.5 Investigating a reaction catalysed by a solid

Decide on a suitable piece of apparatus for the measurement of the initial rate of decomposition of hydrogen peroxide solution when catalysed by manganese(IV) oxide. Use 5.0 cm³ of '20 volume' hydrogen peroxide solution in 45 cm³ of water and 0.05 g of manganese(IV) oxide. But when you do not want to measure the rate, the reaction can be completed quickly by using about 1 g of catalyst and undiluted '20 volume' hydrogen peroxide solution.

Plan your own series of experiments to investigate one or more of the above four questions. Talk to your teacher about your plans before you start.

Now that you know something about catalysts and catalysed reactions, you may be wondering how catalysts work. It is known that catalysts are not used up during the reaction because they do not lose any mass. But it is difficult to imagine how catalysts can affect the rate of a reaction without, in some way, taking part in the reaction. The great Swedish chemist, J. J. Berzelius believed in a 'catalyst force' which somehow accelerated the reaction. We now realize that such a 'theory' is not an explanation at all because the nature of this mysterious force has still to be explained.

One hint that a catalyst may not just be a spectator in any reaction is that it sometimes looks different at the end of the reaction. For example, granular manganese(IV) oxide gets more powdery after it has catalysed the decomposition of hydrogen peroxide. And further evidence to support this idea comes from the next experiment.

Experiment 43.6 Does the catalyst take part in the reaction between sodium potassium tartrate and hydrogen peroxide?

Dissolve about 2 g of sodium potassium tartrate in about 50 cm³ of water in a beaker. Warm the water to about 80 °C and then add 10 cm³ of '20 volume' hydrogen peroxide solution. Add a few crystals of cobalt(II) chloride (the catalyst) and stir the mixture to dissolve them.

▶ Which substances causes the pink colour?
▶ What colour changes occur?
▶ At what stage in the colour changes is the gas evolved?

When no more changes in colour occur, add a further 10 cm³ of the hydrogen peroxide.

It looks as if this catalyst takes an active part in the reaction, but is re-formed at the end of the reaction and so, unlike the reactants, it is *not* used up (Fig. 43.8). It is thought that all catalysts are like this.

A POSSIBLE ROUTE FOR THE CATALYSED REACTION

THE UNCATALYSED REACTION

reactant particles   product particle

Fig. 43.8

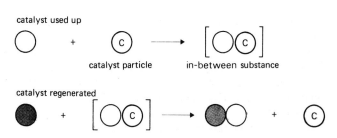

catalyst used up

catalyst particle   in-between substance

catalyst regenerated

They react with one or more of the reactants to form a new compound which then rapidly reacts to form the products and re-forms the catalyst at the same time.

The overall reaction is exactly the same as the uncatalysed reaction. But the reactions involved in the catalysed reaction must occur more quickly than the uncatalysed reaction.

The effect of light on the rate of some reactions

Experiment 43.7 What is the effect of light on a silver halide?

(Note: because of the cost of silver nitrate, this experiment may have to be a teacher demonstration.) Add about 15 cm³ of dilute silver nitrate solution to about 15 cm³ of dilute potassium chloride solution in a boiling tube. Filter off the precipitate and spread out on the bench the filter paper containing the precipitate.

Cover about half the surface of the white precipitate with a strip of metal (e.g. zinc) or a coin. Either put the filter paper in sunlight or light a 50 mm strip of cleaned magnesium ribbon held by tongs, and hold this half a metre above it. Finally, remove the strip of metal or the coin. CARE: do not look directly at the magnesium flame.

▶ What difference in colour is there between the covered and uncovered parts of the precipitate?

The effect of light on some reactions is rather like the effect of raising the temperature: light or heat provide the energy needed for the reaction to be speeded up.

Not many reactions are **photosensitive**, but one of them occurs in the vitally important process of photosynthesis (page 111).

A theory about rates

Chemical reactions occur when the atoms in the particles of the reactants regroup themselves into other arrangements and so form new particles of new substances. How do these changes come about?

It is obvious that the particles of the reactants must meet, that is, they must collide with each other. The particles in any substance must always be moving (page 52), and it is reasonable to assume that a lot of collisions occur in any reaction mixture.

Think about the reaction of hydrogen with iodine gas:

$$H_2(g) + I_2(g) \longrightarrow 2HI(g)$$

In the reaction mixture, there are collisions between pairs of hydrogen molecules, between pairs of iodine molecules and between hydrogen and iodine molecules (Fig. 43.9). Do all of these collisions cause a

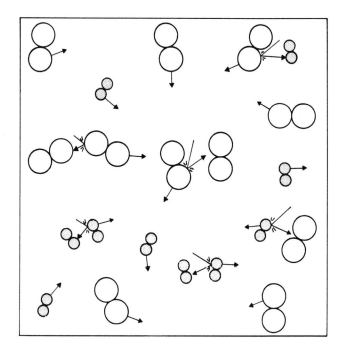

iodine molecule

hydrogen molecule

Fig. 43.9

reaction to occur? Clearly, a collision of two hydrogen molecules or of two iodine molecules cannot produce hydrogen iodide. For hydrogen iodide to be produced, hydrogen and iodine molecules must be involved in collisions. But do *all* collisions between hydrogen and iodine molecules produce hydrogen iodide?

Chemists have worked out the rate of this reaction, assuming that all collisions between hydrogen and iodine molecules produce hydrogen iodide. They found that this rate would be so high, even at room temperature, that the reaction would nearly be completed in as little as 10^{-9} s. And yet experiment has shown that this reaction goes very slowly at room temperature. Some reactions have been found to have rates as high as this, but most reactions are *much* slower than expected.

So chemists have been led to the following idea:

Only a fraction of all the collisions between reactant particles of the right kind cause a reaction to occur.

What kind of collision is likely to be successful?

Think of the head-on collision of two motor cars travelling at high speed (Fig. 43.10). The energy of the collision is very high indeed and much damage would be done to the vehicles. But a glancing blow would not cause as much damage, and a collision at lower speeds, even if head-on, would cause only minor damage (Fig. 43.11).

Fig. 43.10

Fig. 43.11

If particles of the reactants are moving at different speeds, then some collisions must be high-energy ones and some must be low-energy ones. It is likely that the highly energetic, head-on collisions cause the greatest 'molecular damage', that is, are successful in rearranging atoms and so producing a reaction.

You can now use these ideas to think about the changes in conditions that affect the rate of a reaction.

The effect of pressure and concentration

An increase in the pressure of a mixture of gases, or an increase in the concentration of a reactant in solution, both increase the number of reactant particles in a given volume. This results in a higher frequency of collisions between reactant particles and so a higher frequency of high-energy collisions (Fig. 43.12).

> **An increase in the concentration of the reactants (or pressure, for reactions between gases) increases the rate of a reaction.**

The effect of heat and light

When a reaction mixture is heated the reactant particles get more energy and they move more quickly. An increase in speed has two effects:

1. it increases the frequency of all collisions;
2. it increases the energy of the collisions.

Chemists have found that it is the increase in the frequency of *high-energy collisions* that mainly causes an increase in the rate of the reaction.

> **An increase in temperature increases the rate of a reaction**

The effect of temperature is often very marked. For many reactions, an increase in temperature from 15 °C to 25 °C roughly doubles the rate. But there are exceptions and a careful study of Fig. 43.6 (page 190)

Fig. 43.12 the reaction between  and

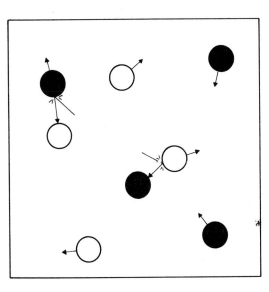

lower concentration – lower collision frequency

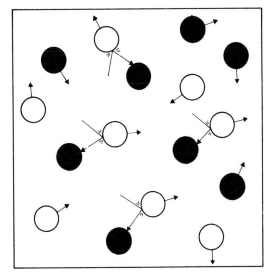

higher concentration – higher collision frequency

gives one good example: an increase of nearly 20 °C, not 10 °C, produces a doubling of the rate of the reaction between magnesium and hydrochloric acid.

If a reaction mixture can absorb light energy (and not all can), then this also causes a large increase in the rate of the reaction. The reaction between bromine and an alkane is a good example of this (page 217).

The effectiveness of catalysts can be improved if they are used in forms like powders, pellets and gauze, all of which have large surface areas. Different physical forms for catalysts seem to suit different reactions. The catalysts are pellets in the Haber process (page 133) and the contact process (page 142), whereas a gauze is used in the manufacture of nitric acid (page 136).

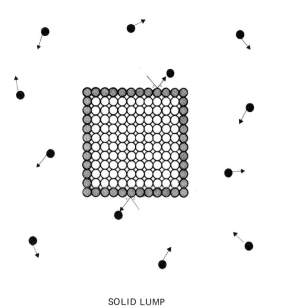

SOLID LUMP
44 particles of solid exposed to collisions with liquid or gas particles

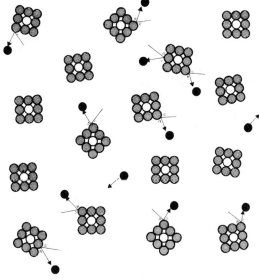

SOLID BROKEN INTO SMALLER LUMPS
128 particles of solid exposed to collisions with liquid or gas particles

Fig. 43.13

The effect of the state of subdivision of a solid reactant

Reactions involving solids must take place at the surface of the solid because it is only there that collisions with particles of other reactants can take place (Fig. 43.13). If the other reactant is a liquid or a gas, particles of it collide with the particles at the surface of the solid. So the larger the surface area of the solid, the greater are the chances of successful collisions occurring.

An increase in the state of subdivision of a solid increases the rate of a reaction.

Very fine-grained (finely-divided) solids have very large surface areas. The grains of a small amount of such a solid (just enough to cover the palm of your hand) have a surface area the same as the floor area of two average-sized school laboratories.

Fine powders of combustible materials can be dangerous when suspended in air. If a combustion reaction is started it occurs so quickly that there can be an explosion. A flour mill is one place where this kind of reaction could take place, and so great care needs to be taken to prevent flour getting into the air.

The effect of a catalyst

Catalysts must take part in the reaction they are catalysing (page 191). But why do they have the effect of increasing the rate of the reaction?

In the reaction mixture, there are collisions between the reactant particles themselves and between the reactant particles and the catalyst particles. *Successful* collisions between the reactant particles must be *very* energetic because the uncatalysed reaction is quite slow: but successful collisions between the reactant particles when they are associated with the catalyst particles need lower collisional energies and the catalysed reaction is quite fast. The presence of the catalyst provides a different and easier way in which the reactants can form the products.

Inhibitors

Inhibitors are substances which slow down the rate of a reaction. These act by preventing a reaction from proceeding along its normal 'route'. A well-known example is the use of lead additives in gasoline (page 112) which prevents the gasoline from being ignited on the compression strokes.

QUESTIONS

1 Use the rate curves in Figs. 43.6 and 43.7 to answer the following questions:

(a) Why is the final volume of hydrogen slightly higher for the 40 °C curve than for the others?
(b) Sketch the rough shapes and positions of the rate curves you would get if you added:

  (i) 0.08 g of magnesium ribbon to 50 cm³ of 1 M hydrochloric acid at 21 °C,
  (ii) 0.08 g of magnesium wire to 50 cm³ of 0.5 M hydrochloric acid at 21 °C,
  (iii) 0.08 g of magnesium ribbon to 50 cm³ of 0.5 M hydrochloric acid at 5 °C.

2 Explain these facts.

(a) Cork does not react with air at room temperature, but cork dust suspended in air has been known to explode.
(b) A mixture of hydrogen and oxygen may be left indefinitely without appearing to react, but if a spark is passed, or heat is applied, the mixture may explode.
(c) It takes a long time to hard-boil an egg at high altitudes.

3 A geologist is interested in investigating the reaction between water containing dissolved carbon dioxide and limestone (calcium carbonate). She knows that in nature the reaction is very slow.

(a) Describe three ways in which the geologist could speed up the reaction so that she could study it in the laboratory.
(b) Dolomite (calcium magnesium carbonate) also reacts slowly with water containing dissolved carbon dioxide. How would it be possible to compare the rate of this reaction with the rate of the limestone reaction?

4 In an experiment to investigate the rate of the reaction between marble chips and dilute hydrochloric acid, about 1 g of the solid is reacted with 25 cm³ of 2 M hydrochloric acid in a flask with a plug of cotton wool in its neck. The mass of the flask is found at two-minute intervals and the results obtained are plotted in Fig. 43.14.

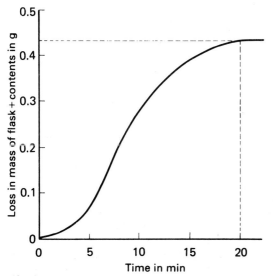

Fig. 43.14

(a) What is the plug of cotton wool in the neck of the flask used for?
(b) Explain why there is a loss in mass.
(c) At what time does the reaction finish?
(d) At roughly what time is the rate of reaction highest?
(e) The pupil carrying out this experiment does not saturate the hydrochloric acid with carbon dioxide before adding the marble chips. What unusual feature of the rate curve results from this mistake? Explain your answer carefully.
(f) Suggest another way in which the rate of this reaction could be measured.

5 In an industrial process, there is often a choice between using a high pressure or a high temperature (or both) to speed up the reaction, and using a catalyst.

(a) Why is a reasonably high rate of reaction important in industry?
(b) Why is a catalyst preferred to an increase in the pressure or temperature of the reaction mixture? (The full answer to this question can only be given if you look forward to page 200.)
(c) Catalysts are not used up in a reaction and yet industrial catalysts do need replacing from time to time. Why is this so?

6 (a) Describe an experiment you could carry out to decide how effective each of the following solids is in catalysing the decomposition of hydrogen peroxide solution: copper(II) oxide (CuO), lead(IV) oxide (PbO₂) and manganese(IV) oxide (MnO₂).
(b) The following results are obtained in a series of experiments using equal volumes of hydrogen peroxide solution of the same concentration.

Solid	Mass of solid added in grams	Volume of oxygen given off in the first minute of the reaction, in cm³
Powdered MnO₂	0.1	24
Powdered MnO₂	0.2	56
Granular MnO₂	0.1	3
Powdered PbO₂	0.1	90
Powdered CuO	0.1	0

  (i) Which of the solids in the above table does not act as a catalyst in the decomposition of hydrogen peroxide solution?
  (ii) Explain the differences between the results for the three kinds of manganese(IV) oxide.
  (iii) Which of the solids is the most effective catalyst for this reaction?

7 Find an example of:

(a) a solid catalyst used to speed up a chemical reaction between two gases,
(b) a solid catalyst used to speed up the preparation of a common gas from a solution,
(c) a very fast reaction between two solutions that is finished as soon as the solutions are mixed.

Key words

rate of reaction	initial rate	photosensitive reactions	state of subdivision
rate curve	catalyst	high-energy collisions (between molecules)	inhibitors

Basic facts

• Different reactions go at different rates.

• In most reactions, the initial rate is the highest, and the rate then decreases gradually as the reactants are used up.

• The rate of a reaction can be increased by (i) increasing the concentration (or pressure for gases) of the reactants, (ii) increasing the temperature of the reaction mixture, (iii) increasing the state of subdivision of any solid reactant, and (iv) using an appropriate catalyst.

• A catalyst takes an active part in a reaction but, unlike a normal reactant, is continually re-formed.

• Some reactions are photosensitive, that is, their rates are considerably increased by the reactants being exposed to light.

• Only high-energy collisions between reactant particles result in the products being formed.

• Inhibitors are substances which slow down the rate of a reaction.

44 Reversible reactions

Some processes that go both ways

In Chapter 4, changes are divided into two kinds, temporary and permanent changes. Changes of state are examples of temporary changes; the molecules of the substance stay the same but their spacing is changed.

Some temporary changes produce new substances and so must be chemical reactions. When hydrated copper(II) sulphate is heated, it breaks down to form two new substances which recombine on cooling. It is a reversible change and the sign $\rightleftharpoons$ means that the reaction can go both ways.

$$CuSO_4 \cdot 5H_2O(s) \rightleftharpoons CuSO_4(s) + 5H_2O(l)$$
hydrated copper(II) anhydrous copper(II)
sulphate (blue)   sulphate (white)

This kind of chemical reaction, in which a compound is decomposed by heat but re-forms from the products on cooling, is called **thermal dissociation**. If the products cannot re-form the original compound, the reaction is a thermal decomposition (page 11).

Experiment 44.1 What happens when ammonium chloride is heated?

1. Gently warm a small amount of ammonium chloride in a test-tube. Take care to heat only the bottom of the test-tube.

▶ What can you see happening?
▶ Do you think that the change is a temporary or a permanent change?
▶ Do you think that the change is a chemical reaction?

2. Set up the apparatus shown in Fig. 44.1. CARE: handle glass wool with tongs and not with your fingers.

Use about 0.1 g of solid and heat it gently over a low bunsen flame.

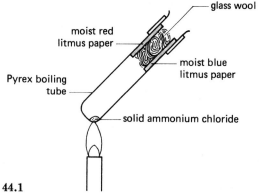

Fig. 44.1

▸ What happens to the two pieces of litmus paper?

▸ Which change occurs first?

Stop heating when there is no more solid at the bottom of the tube.

▸ To which two gases is ammonium chloride decomposed?

▸ Which one of these gases diffuses more quickly?

Ammonium chloride breaks down on heating into ammonia and hydrogen chloride, and these gases join up again in the cooler parts of the tube. This reaction is an example of thermal dissociation.

$$NH_4Cl(s) \rightleftharpoons NH_3(g) + HCl(g)$$

Another example is the thermal dissociation of mercury(II) oxide.

$$2HgO(s) \rightleftharpoons 2Hg(l) + O_2(g)$$

This was a key reaction in the first investigations into the composition of the air (Chapter 6). In 1774, Joseph Priestley decomposed the 'red calx of mercury' (mercury(II) oxide) into mercury and oxygen, using a very large glass lens and the sun's rays as his source of heat. Three years after this, Antoine Lavoisier made mercury(II) oxide by keeping mercury near its boiling point in the presence of air for a few days. In this way, Lavoisier was able to show that the active gas (oxygen) obtained from the 'red calx of mercury' (and other compounds) must be one of the gases in the air.

In a thermal dissociation, the conditions needed for the products to join up again and form the original substance vary from reaction to reaction. But the required temperature is usually lower than the temperature needed for the complete breakdown of that substance. For example, ammonium chloride breaks down on gently warming and the products recombine at room temperature; but mercury(II) oxide breaks down at about 500 °C and the products recombine at about 300 °C.

Balance points in reversible reactions

When litmus solution is added to an acidic solution it turns red, whereas in alkaline solutions it is blue. You know that, by mixing acidic and alkaline solutions in the right amounts, the litmus can show a purple colour.

The colour change of litmus is a reversible reaction. What does the purple colour represent? The colour purple is made by mixing red and blue colours. This means that purple litmus is at a **balance point** or in-between stage between the two extremes of litmus entirely in its red form and litmus entirely in its blue form. Are there balance points for other reversible reactions?

Experiment 44.2 Looking for balance points in some reversible reactions

1. What is the effect of alkali on bromine water?

Add bench dilute (2 M) sodium hydroxide solution, drop by drop, to a few cm³ of bromine water until you can see no further change in colour. Find out if this reaction is reversible by adding to the solution obtained above a substance which you might expect to produce the opposite effect to the alkali. If it is reversible, try to get a balance point for this reaction between the two extremes of colour. It may help you to compare any in-between colour you get with samples of the two extremes of colour in separate test-tubes.

2. What is the effect of alkali on potassium dichromate(VI) solution?

Repeat 1, using potassium dichromate(VI) solution instead of bromine water. Again try to find a balance point between the two extremes of colour.

The equation for the reaction between bromine water and alkali can be written as

$$Br_2(aq) + 2OH^-(aq)$$
red-brown
$$\rightleftharpoons Br^-(aq) + OBr^-(aq) + H_2O(l) \quad (1)$$
colourless

When enough alkali has been added to bromine water, the solution goes colourless, showing that the reaction has occurred and that the bromine has been changed to bromide ions and bromate(I) (hypobromite) (OBr⁻) ions. When an acid is added to the colourless solution, the red-brown colour of the bromine returns, showing that the reaction has occurred from right to left. Any in-between colour you get is at a stage of the reaction between the two extremes produced above. There are then bromine atoms in both reactant, $Br_2(aq)$, and products, $Br^-(aq)$ and $OBr^-(aq)$.

Think about a balance point in more detail. As long as the conditions stay the same, the colour intensity of the reaction mixture also stays the same. This means that the amounts of reactants and products in this mixture are constant: it seems that no reaction is occurring even though there are still some reactant particles left in the reaction mixture. (More is said about this in the next section.)

This is not like a reaction mixture where the reaction is still going on. In such a mixture, the amounts of reactants and products are changing as more and more of the products are being formed.

A balance point at which no reaction can be seen to be occurring is called a **position of equilibrium**. This can be achieved in a reversible reaction for *any* amounts of reactants and products.

What decides the stage of the reaction at which an equilibrium is established? In the reaction between bromine and alkali, the colour intensity changes each time a drop of alkali or acid is added to the mixture but then stays the same unless more drops are added. So each time the pH value of the solution is changed, the equilibrium moves to a new position with different amounts of reactants and products. In this reaction, it seems that the position of equilibrium depends on the pH value of the reaction mixture.

Another way of writing the equation for the reaction occurring in bromine water is

$$Br_2(aq) + H_2O(l)$$
$$\rightleftharpoons Br^-(aq) + OBr^-(aq) + 2H^+(aq) \quad (2)$$

Equations 1 and 2 look different but they represent the same reaction. The first equation is useful for thinking about the effect of hydroxide ions on the reaction from left to right, while the second equation is useful for thinking about the effect of hydrogen ions on the reaction from right to left.

The equation for the reaction between dichromate(VI) ions and hydroxide ions is

$$Cr_2O_7{}^{2-}(aq) + 2OH^-(aq)$$
dichromate(VI)
ions
(orange)

$$\rightleftharpoons 2CrO_4{}^{2-}(aq) + H_2O(l) \quad (3)$$
chromate(VI)
ions
(yellow)

In alkaline solution (high concentration of hydroxide ions), the position of equilibrium lies to the right, while in acid solution (low concentration of hydroxide ions), the position of equilibrium lies to the left.

Again, it is possible to write the equation in a different way.

$$Cr_2O_7{}^{2-}(aq) + H_2O(l)$$
$$\rightleftharpoons 2CrO_4{}^{2-}(aq) + 2H^+(aq) \quad (4)$$

Increasing the concentration of hydrogen ions causes dichromate(VI) ions to be formed, while lowering the concentration of hydrogen ions (by the addition of alkali) causes chromate(VI) ions to be formed.

The idea of dynamic equilibrium

At equilibrium, no changes in the reaction mixture seem to be occurring. There is very good evidence that this is not really so. The equilibrium is **dynamic**. Particles of the reactants are still forming products, and particles of the products are still forming reactants, *but these two opposing effects are equal and cancel one another out.*

An example of dynamic equilibrium is the unlikely event of someone running along a conveyor belt at the same speed at which it is travelling in the other direction (Fig. 44.2). The person stays in the same position, but both the belt and the person are moving all the time. The effects of the moving conveyor belt and the person running in the other direction exactly balance one another.

Fig. 44.2 Dynamic equilibrium

Now imagine the same person standing still on a conveyor belt that is not moving. Again her position does not change, but this is now an example of a **static** equilibrium like the one in Fig. 44.3. Equilibria in chemistry are always of the dynamic kind.

Fig. 44.3 Static equilibrium

One piece of evidence for this comes from the use of **radioactive tracers** (page 158). Particles can be put into a mixture at equilibrium, which are radioactive but which in other ways are exactly the same as some of those already in the mixture. These 'labelled' particles do not disturb the equilibrium so long as only a very small number are added. After a short time, it can be shown that *both* reactants *and* products in the mixture are radioactive, not just the reactants. Some of the radioactive particles have reacted to form product particles, *even though the position of equilibrium stays the same all through the experiment.*

The best way to explain this is to use the idea of dynamic equilibrium. It would be very difficult indeed to explain it by using the idea of static equilibrium.

A radioactive tracer can be used to investigate the equilibrium set up when a solid is in contact with its saturated solution. Think of the equilibrium between solid lead chloride and its saturated solution. When the equilibrium has been reached, a little of the solid lead(II) chloride is replaced by radioactive lead(II) chloride. After a short time, the *solution* is found to be radioactive. An exchange of particles between the solid and solution must have occurred, even though equilibrium has been kept all through the experiment. Fig. 44.4 is a way of showing what happens.

Equilibrium between the solid and its solution is reached when the rate at which the solid dissolves exactly equals the rate at which the lead chloride is being crystallized from the solution:

$$PbCl_2(s) \underset{crystallizing}{\overset{dissolving}{\rightleftharpoons}} Pb^{2+}(aq) + 2Cl^-(aq)$$

When the radioactive solid lead(II) chloride is put into the mixture, it takes part in this reversible reaction and radioactive lead ions go into the solution.

Many other equilibria are also dynamic. When ice is in contact with water at 0 °C in an insulated container, there is no change in the amounts of ice and water. When water is in contact with the air in a closed container at constant temperature, the concentration of water vapour in the air stays the same. But all the time, water molecules are being exchanged between the solid and the liquid, and between the liquid and the gas. Equilibrium is reached when the rates of the opposing processes are equal. Fig. 44.5 is a way of showing what happens in the case of water and water vapour.

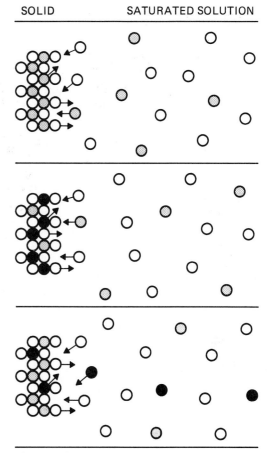

SOLID   SATURATED SOLUTION

DYNAMIC EQUILIBRIUM EXISTS IN ALL THREE STAGES

○ non-radioactive Pb particles
● radioactive Pb particles
○ non-radioactive Cl particles

Fig. 44.4

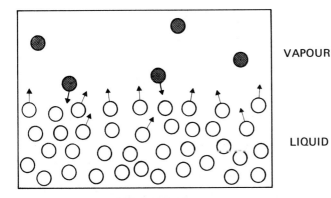

NO EQUILIBRIUM

The number of vapour particles entering the liquid per second is less than the number of liquid particles entering the vapour. Hence the number of vapour particles is increasing.

Fig. 44.5

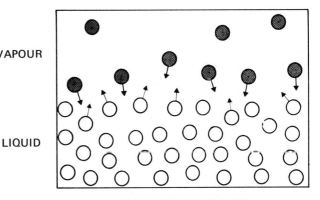

VAPOUR

LIQUID

DYNAMIC EQUILIBRIUM

The number of particles moving out of the liquid per second equals the number moving into the liquid per second. Hence there is no *net* change in the number of particles in either the liquid or the vapour.

Yield and rate in the chemical industry

Many important reactions in the chemical industry are reversible, and under the conditions used they reach equilibrium. This means that not all the reactants are changed to the required product. The percentage conversion of reactants to product is called the **yield** of the reaction.

When a chemical engineer is planning an industrial process, he must think of both the *yield* he wants and the *rate* at which the product is to be formed. So he has to adjust the operating conditions to produce as high a yield as possible at a reasonable rate. Unfortunately, conditions which produce a high yield can be expensive and sometimes also result in a low rate. It is often necessary to decide on some kind of compromise. These are the *optimum* (best) operating conditions for the reaction.

The optimum conditions for the Haber process

$$N_2(g) + 3H_2(g) \rightleftharpoons 2NH_3(g) \quad \text{(heat given out)}$$

Fig. 44.6 shows the yield of ammonia in the Haber process for different pressures and temperatures. At constant pressure, the yield decreases as the temperature increases. At constant temperature, the yield increases as the pressure increases.

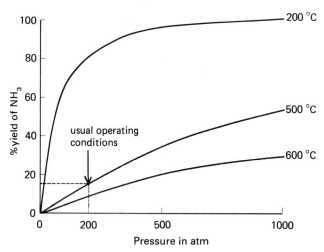

Fig. 44.6

Table 44.1 shows the effects on the rate, the yield and the cost of changing the pressure and temperature of the reaction mixture.

The table shows two problems which require a compromise to be found:

1. the expense of using a high pressure,
2. the very different effects on the rate and the yield of using a high temperature, which in any case would also be expensive.

The optimum operating conditions for the Haber process are shown in Fig. 44.6. At a temperature of 500 °C and a pressure of 200 atmospheres, the yield of ammonia is about 15%.

The fairly low rate achieved at 500 °C can be increased considerably by the use of an iron catalyst. This can be done at low cost because the catalyst does not need to be replaced very often. The catalyst does *not* affect the yield in any way at all.

The optimum conditions for the contact process

$$2SO_2(g) + O_2(g) \rightleftharpoons 2SO_3(g) \quad \text{(heat given out)}$$

Like the Haber process, a high yield of product is formed at low temperatures and high pressures. But, unlike the Haber process, the yield is as high as 98% at 450 °C and *normal* atmospheric pressure. So it is obviously not worth using a higher pressure. Again, the temperature chosen is a compromise between a high one for a high rate and a low one for a high yield. The use of a vanadium(v) oxide catalyst means that a high rate can be achieved at the moderate temperature of 450 °C, and the yield at this temperature is still very high.

A final word

The effects of pressure, temperature and catalysts on the rate of reactions involving gases are similar whatever the reaction. But this is not true for the effects of pressure and temperature on the yield. For example, a low temperature favours a high yield for a gaseous reaction that gives out heat (as in the Haber process and the contact process), but it favours a low yield for a reaction that absorbs heat.

Also, a high pressure does not necessarily favour a high yield. It does for the Haber process and the contact process but it does not for the manufacture of nitric acid from ammonia. In this case, it does not matter whether the reaction gives out or absorbs heat. What is important is the change in the number of molecules as the reactants form the products.

There is a general rule (called **Le Chatelier's principle**) underlying these conclusions for a reaction mixture that is in dynamic equilibrium. Whatever external change is made to the reaction mixture (temperature, pressure, concentration), the change produced has the opposite effect. A new equilibrium position is then established with different proportions of reactants and products.

Table 44.1

Conditions		Rate	Yield	Cost
Pressure	High	High	High	High
	Low	Low	Low	High
Temperature	High	High	Low	High
	Low	Low	High	Low

If the *temperature* is increased, the reaction that is favoured is the one that absorbs heat, that is, the reaction that lowers the temperature.

If the *pressure* is increased, the reaction that is favoured is the one that lowers the pressure, that is, the reaction that reduces the number of molecules present in the reaction mixture.

If the *concentration* of one of the reactants or products is increased, the reaction that is favoured is the one that decreases this concentration, that is, the reaction that removes some of the reactant or product from the reaction mixture.

QUESTIONS

1 The equation for the reversible reaction of bismuth(III) chloride with water is:

$$BiCl_3(aq) + H_2O(l) \rightleftharpoons BiOCl(s) + 2H^+(aq) + 2Cl^-(aq)$$
white (bismuth
oxide chloride)

(*a*) When the reaction goes from left to right, what would you expect to see?

(*b*) Explain why it is impossible to prepare a clear solution of bismuth(III) chloride in water by adding some solid to pure water.

(*c*) Use your knowledge of the reaction of bromine with water to decide what the effect would be of adding dilute hydrochloric acid to the mixture at equilibrium.

(*d*) What would be the effect of adding solid sodium hydroxide to the mixture at equilibrium and stirring so that it dissolves?

2 The reaction between zinc sulphate solution and hydrogen sulphide is reversible. The equation for the reaction is

$$Zn^2(aq) + H_2S(aq) \rightleftharpoons ZnS(s) + 2H^+(aq)$$
colourless   colourless   white

(*a*) How would you carry out the reaction from left to right and what would you expect to see?

(*b*) How would you carry out the reaction from right to left and what would you expect to see?

(*c*) Why would it be difficult to be sure about the position of equilibrium in a mixture containing both reactants and products?

(*d*) What substance (other than one of the reactants or products) could you add to the mixture at equilibrium to make more zinc sulphide?

3 The graphs in Fig. 44.7 are plots of concentration against time for two different reactions. Plots A and B are for the same reaction, and plot C traces the change in concentration of the reactant in another reaction.

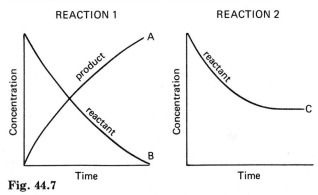

Fig. 44.7

(*a*) Why does curve A start at the origin, rise steeply at first and then gradually flatten out?

(*b*) Why does curve B drop steeply at first and then gradually flatten out before finally meeting the *x*-axis?

(*c*) Curve C flattens out well before curve B and never meets the *x*-axis. What does this tell you about the reactant concentration at the end of the reaction? What is an important difference between this reaction and the reaction represented by curves A and B?

(*d*) Sketch the kind of curve you would expect for the change in the product concentration in the second reaction.

Key words

reversible reaction	**balance point (or position of equilibrium)**	**yield (in a chemical reaction)**
thermal dissociation	**dynamic equilibrium**	**Le Chatelier's principle**

Basic facts

- **A reversible reaction is one that can go both ways.**

- **A position of equilibrium in a reversible reaction is a balance point between reactants and products.**

- **At equilibrium, no overall change in the proportion of reactants and products occurs unless certain conditions (e.g. temperature and pressure) are altered.**

- **A chemical equilibrium is dynamic, reactants are forming products at the same rate as products are forming reactants. This explains why there is no overall change.**

- **A knowledge of chemical equilibria is important in deciding on the optimum conditions for the manufacture of certain industrial chemicals. The yield of product in a gaseous reaction which gives out heat can be increased by increasing the pressure and decreasing the temperature.**

45 Energy in chemistry

What is energy?

Everyone talks about energy, and yet the term is difficult to define. It is easier, at first, to describe what energy can do and how it can be recognized.

Our bodies produce energy that keeps us warm and makes it possible for us to move and do work. The energy produced by the combustion of fuels is used to propel vehicles, ships, aeroplanes and rockets (Fig. 45.1) as well as for the production of electricity for heating, lighting and the many machines that are driven by electricity. The energy used in striking a tuning fork produces a disturbance in the air, which we experience as sound. Light makes the needle of a lightmeter move over a scale, and in solar batteries is used to produce electricity.

Fig. 45.1

Energy can be recognized because it can make things move. Because work is done when an object is made to move, it is possible to define energy as *the capacity for doing work*.

There are many kinds of energy. When a ball is rolled uphill, energy has to be expended. Yet if you look at the ball at the top of the hill, it is not at all obvious that it has more energy than it had at the bottom. But it must contain more energy; it can roll downhill without any help. The energy of a moving body is called **kinetic energy**. The energy stored in the ball at the top of the hill is called **potential energy**.

There is no difference in the appearance of a bottle when it is on a shelf from when it is on the floor, but energy has to be put in to lift the bottle, against gravity, onto the shelf. So the bottle has more energy when it is on the shelf than when it is on the floor. This extra energy is also potential energy. Other examples of objects that have potential energy are a stretched elastic band, and the string of a musical instrument when it is being plucked but before it has been released. When these objects begin to move, the stored potential energy changes into kinetic energy (Fig. 45.2).

Fig. 45.2

Heat is also a kind of energy. It used to be thought that it was a fluid called 'caloric' which flowed from a hot body to a cold body. But in the nineteenth century, a British physicist called James Joule investigated the heating effects that could be produced by several kinds of energy.

In one experiment, Joule raised the temperature of some water by stirring it with paddle wheels driven by falling masses, and in another experiment, he heated water electrically. From the results of these and many other experiments, he was able to show that equal amounts of mechanical energy and electrical energy produce the same temperature rise (the same heating effect) in a fixed mass of water. So heat, like mechanical energy and electrical energy, must be a kind of energy.

The Principle of Conservation of Energy

Think of the use of an electric motor. Electrical energy is converted into kinetic energy in the motor, but heat energy is also produced by electricity passing through the wires and by friction in the bearings of the motor, and there is also some noise. You may also know that some electromagnetic radiation is sometimes produced. So electrical energy is converted into kinetic energy, heat energy and sound energy, and some energy is also radiated.

The **Principle of Conservation of Energy** summarizes what has been found to apply in all such processes. One kind of energy may be converted into another kind or several other kinds, but the total amount of energy stays the same.

Energy cannot be created or destroyed.

The **Law of Conservation of Mass** (page 19) states that matter cannot be created or destroyed. But in nuclear reactions (page 158) mass is lost while energy is released. The amount of energy produced is proportional to the loss in mass so that the two principles (conservation of energy and conservation of mass) should be combined: *during any process, mass and energy are conserved.*

The loss of a small amount of mass results in the release of a very large amount of energy. During a chemical reaction in which energy is released, any loss of mass is so small that it is undetectable even on the best chemical balances. So for the vast majority of processes, the two conservation principles may be used separately.

Chemical reactions and energy

You know that when a reaction occurs, the temperature of the reaction mixture usually changes. An **exothermic** reaction is one that produces energy: the temperature of the reaction mixture increases. An **endothermic** reaction uses energy: the temperature of the reaction mixture decreases.

Experiment 45.1 Looking at some exothermic and endothermic processes

1. Find the temperature of some water in a boiling tube. Add a spatula measure of ammonium chloride, stir the mixture to dissolve the solid and find the new temperature. Repeat this experiment using potassium nitrate rather than ammonium chloride.

2. Find the temperature of about $25\,cm^3$ of bench dilute (2 M) hydrochloric acid in a small beaker. Add to this about four spatula measures of sodium hydrogencarbonate. Note the maximum or minimum temperature reached.

3. Repeat part 1 using four spatula measures of anhydrous sodium carbonate instead of sodium hydrogencarbonate.

4. (*a*) Your teacher will provide you with solutions of calcium chloride and potassium carbonate. Record the temperature of each solution before the experiment. Mix equal volumes of these solutions in a boiling tube and note the maximum or minimum temperature reached. Repeat the experiment (including finding the temperatures of the two solutions before mixing) using a more accurate thermometer with 0.1 °C divisions.

(*b*) Your teacher will mix equal volumes of sodium chloride and silver nitrate solutions in a boiling tube. Record the temperature of each solution before the experiment. Note the maximum or minimum temperature reached. (There is no need to use a more accurate thermometer here.)

5. Your teacher will provide you with a small volume of ethanol. Note the temperature of this liquid and of a few cm^3 of water. Mix about equal volumes of ethanol and water in a boiling tube and note the maximum or minimum temperature reached.

To work out the temperature changes in parts 4 and 5, you need first to find the average of the temperatures for the two solutions or liquids before they are mixed.

▶ Use your results to make a list of exothermic processes and a list of endothermic ones.

Some reactions involve energy in forms other than heat. Photosynthesis (page 111) involves the absorption of light energy. Also, light energy is evolved by reactions taking place inside a fire-fly and in the tail of a glow-worm. And many strongly exothermic reactions give out part of their energy as light. Electrolytes may be decomposed by using electrical energy, and electricity can be produced by the chemical reactions occurring in car batteries or dry batteries.

The amount of energy required for a reaction to occur is the same however it is carried out. So it takes the same amount of electrical energy as it does heat to decompose 1 mole of H_2O.

What is chemical energy?

There are forces of attraction between the particles in a solid and between the particles in a liquid. Just as work has to be done when a bottle is lifted against gravity onto a shelf, so work has to be done when the particles of a substance are separated from one another against the forces of attraction that they have for one another. A bottle has more (potential) energy when it is on a shelf than when it is on the floor. In the same way, a substance in the liquid state has more (potential) energy than the same amount of the solid substance at the same temperature.

The lifting of a bottle onto a shelf from the floor, the melting of a solid and the boiling of a liquid are all processes in which energy is absorbed. The return of the bottle to the floor from the shelf, the freezing of a liquid and the condensing of a gas are all processes in which energy is evolved.

You should now see that melting a solid and boiling a liquid increase the energy of the substance because both processes involve moving the particles further apart against the forces of attraction between them. The energy changes per *gram* of substance at the melting point and the boiling point are sometimes called the specific **latent heat of fusion** and the specific **latent heat of vaporization**. In chemistry, these changes are usually given per *mole* of substance.

The molar energy change (heat) of fusion, ΔH_f, is the amount of energy required to change 1 mole of solid to liquid at the melting point.

The molar energy change (heat) of vaporization, ΔH_v, is the amount of energy required to change 1 mole of liquid to gas at the boiling point.

The two energy changes can be shown in diagrams (Fig. 45.3). Imagine that the thick lines on which the beakers are standing are like shelves of various heights. To 'move' the particles of the substance to a higher 'shelf' requires energy to be supplied from the surroundings. This is like lifting a bottle from a low shelf to a higher one, though in this case the energy supplied is not heat energy but your own ('human') energy. When the particles (or the bottle) have reached the higher 'shelf', their energy is greater than it was on the low 'shelf'. When the particles of the substance are 'moved' back to the low 'shelf', energy is given out.

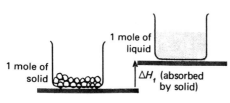

Fig. 45.3   AT THE MELTING POINT

Fig. 45.3 shows a smaller difference in the 'shelf' heights for melting than for boiling. This is because ΔH_f for a substance is usually much smaller than ΔH_v.

Endothermic processes are often recognized by a drop in temperature. When a very volatile liquid, such as ether, quickly evaporates from a watch-glass in the palm of your hand, the watch-glass gets much colder. (CARE: this experiment must only be attempted in a well-ventilated laboratory, and no bunsen burners should be alight.) There is also a drop in temperature for the endothermic reactions in Experiment 45.1. Why is it then that boiling, which is another endothermic process, occurs at a constant temperature (the boiling point of the liquid)?

The heat energy absorbed in evaporating a liquid, or in a reaction, is first obtained from the liquid or the reactants so that they become colder. But the heat energy absorbed during boiling comes from a burning fuel and this is supplied all the time to increase the energy of the substance.

As well as the forces of attraction between the particles (molecules or ions), there are forces of attraction between atoms *within* molecules. These forces (covalent bonds) are often very strong (page 169). To separate the atoms and to decompose the molecules, a large amount of energy has to be supplied. So the separated atoms have a higher

energy than the bonded atoms (the molecules). This may be released as heat energy when the atoms re-form the molecules. Because this kind of energy is to do with bonds, it is called **bond energy**.

There are also forces of attraction within the atoms. The positively charged nucleus attracts the electrons which are in the energy levels surrounding the nucleus (page 153). To remove an electron from an atom, energy has to be supplied to overcome the force of attraction between the nucleus and the electrons. Values for this kind of energy can be used to find out about the arrangement of electrons in atoms.

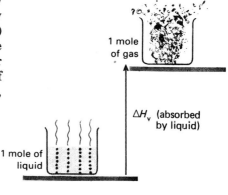

AT THE BOILING POINT

Finally, there are forces of attraction holding the particles of the nucleus together. These forces are so strong that the nucleus always stays unchanged all through any chemical reaction. The process involving changes in the nucleus (nuclear reactions) may occur with the absorption or release of huge amounts of energy, amounts far larger than those for chemical reactions.

Fig. 45.4 gives a summary of the main ideas in this section. The forces of attraction between the different kinds of particles that make up matter provide ways in which energy can be 'stored'.

forces between electrons and nucleus within an atom (concerned with the energy required to remove electrons from an atom)

forces within nucleus (concerned with nuclear energy)

forces between molecules (concerned with ΔH_f and ΔH_v)

forces between the nuclei and the shared electrons (concerned with bond energy)

Fig. 45.4

All these forces can be shown by drawing the molecules as if they were not moving. But any collection of particles has energy because of their motion, and so the kinetic energy of the particles also provides ways in which energy can be stored.

You may now see why heat energy is actually released or absorbed during a chemical reaction. Each substance in a particular state (solid, liquid or gas) has a certain amount of energy bound up in it. If the amount of this stored energy in the products of a reaction is less than that in the reactants, the difference is given out during the reaction and the reaction is exothermic. But if the products of the reaction contain more stored energy, the reaction is endothermic.

Put in another way, the energy change in a chemical reaction depends on which bonds are broken and which new bonds are formed. Energy has to be absorbed to break bonds whereas energy is released when new bonds are formed. The balance between the energy absorbed and the energy released is the energy change for the reaction.

Joules and ΔH

The unit of energy is the joule (J). In chemistry, the kilojoule (kJ) is usually used, and this is equal to 1000 J. There are two important statements about the joule that you need to know.

1 **One joule is the energy transferred when 1 C of electrical charge is passed through a potential difference of 1 V.**

2 **4.18 J of energy raises the temperature of 1 g of water by 1 °C; and 4.18 kJ of energy raises the temperature of 1 kg of water by 1 °C.**

The change in energy for a chemical reaction is written as ΔH.

ΔH is the amount of energy that must be gained from the surroundings or lost to the surroundings so that the products of the reaction are at the same temperature as the reactants.

In an exothermic reaction, such as any combustion process, the system (the reaction mixture) *loses* energy to the surroundings and the ΔH value is *negative*. In an endothermic reaction, the system *gains* energy from the surroundings and the ΔH value is *positive*.

Think about the reaction between hydrogen and oxygen to form water. It is known that 286 kJ of energy is released for every mole of hydrogen molecules burnt. This can be written in the following way.

$$H_2(g) + \tfrac{1}{2}O_2(g) \longrightarrow H_2O(l); \qquad \Delta H = -286 \, kJ \quad (1)$$

If 2 moles of H_2 are burnt, 2×286, or 572 kJ of energy is released. This can be written as

$$2H_2(g) + O_2(g) \longrightarrow 2H_2O(l); \qquad \Delta H = -572 \, kJ \quad (2)$$

These two values for ΔH are both for the combustion of hydrogen. They are different because there are different numbers of moles of reactants and products involved. The ΔH value in equation 1 is for the combustion of 1 mole of H_2 whereas in 2 it is for the reaction of 1 mole of O_2 and 2 moles of H_2. Each ΔH value is linked to a *particular equation*, and this shows that the equation must *always* be given along with the ΔH value.

The ΔH in equation 1 is the **energy change of combustion** of hydrogen. It is usually called the **heat of combustion, ΔH (combustion)**. Heats of combustion are always given per mole of the substance being burnt in the oxygen.

In combustion reactions, the reaction mixture (the system) always loses energy to the surroundings. This means that the store of energy in the system must drop to a lower amount when the reaction occurs. So the products in such a reaction must be on a lower 'energy shelf' than the reactants. An **energy level diagram** may be used to represent reaction 1.

$$\underline{H_2(g) + \tfrac{1}{2}O_2(g)}$$
$$\downarrow \qquad \Delta H \text{ (combustion)} = -286 \, kJ$$
$$\underline{H_2O(l)}$$

To change 1 mole of H_2O back to hydrogen and oxygen, 286 kJ of energy must be supplied. The energy level diagram for this reaction is

$$\underline{H_2(g) + \tfrac{1}{2}O_2(g)}$$
$$\uparrow \qquad \Delta H = +286 \, kJ$$
$$\underline{H_2O(l)}$$

In chemical reactions energy is conserved just as in physical processes: exactly the same amount of energy is required to decompose 1 mole of H_2O as is released when 1 mole of H_2O is formed. For any process that may be reversed,

the energy change in one direction is equal but opposite in sign to that in the other direction.

Fuels and heats of combustion

To find the energy change for the combustion of a fuel, you need to measure the amount of energy passed from the system (the burning fuel) to its surroundings. This can be done by letting the burning fuel heat a known mass of water and then measuring the rise in temperature of the water. If the mass of fuel that is burnt is known, then the energy change per mole of fuel, that is, the heat of combustion of the fuel, can be worked out.

In the next experiment you can find the heat of combustion for a liquid fuel. Alcohols such as methanol and ethanol are chosen for this because they burn quickly but safely in air.

Experiment 45.2 Measuring the heat of combustion of an alcohol

Use the apparatus shown in Fig. 45.5 for this experiment. The aluminium can takes in energy as well as the water. To allow for this, your teacher will tell you the mass of water (x g) that requires the same amount of energy as the can to raise its temperature by 1 °C. You want to heat the equivalent of 1000 g of water, so subtract x g from 1000 g and pour this mass of water into the can. (1 g of water has a volume of 1 cm^3.) Note the temperature of the water.

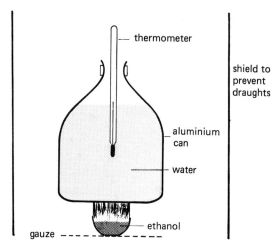

Fig. 45.5

Find the mass of a small clean crucible and then find its mass again when it contains between 2 and 3 g of alcohol. The mass of the alcohol needs to be known accurately. When you have set up the apparatus, use a burning splint to start the liquid burning.

▶ What is the purpose of the draught shield?
▶ Can you explain why the aluminium can has a wide base?

Stir the water gently with the thermometer. When the alcohol has all been burnt, note the temperature of the water. Work out the rise in temperature of the water produced by the complete combustion of the known mass of alcohol.

▶ What major source of error in this experiment is likely to give too low a value for the heat of combustion?

Working out ΔH (combustion)

Suppose that the burning of 2.00 g of propan-1-ol (relative molecular mass = 60) raises the temperature of 1.00 g of water by 12.0 °C.

1.00 kg of water is heated through 1 °C by 4.18 kJ (page 000), so 1.00 kg of water is heated through 12.0 °C by 4.18 × 12.0/1 = 50.2 kJ. 2.00 g or 2.00/60 mole of propan-1-ol burns to release 50.2 kJ of energy, so 1 mole of propan-1-ol burns to release 50.2 × 60/2.00 kJ of energy.

The heat of combustion of propan-1-ol is *1.51 × 10^3 kJ mol^{-3} (evolved)*. This result can be given as an equation and an energy level diagram.

$$CH_3CH_2CH_2OH(l) + 4\tfrac{1}{2}O_2(g)$$
$$\longrightarrow 3CO_2(g) + 4H_2O(l)$$
$$\Delta H \text{ (combustion)} = -1510 \text{ kJ}$$

$$CH_3CH_2CH_2OH(l) + 4\tfrac{1}{2}O_2(g)$$

ΔH (combustion) = −1510 kJ

$$3CO_2(g) + 4H_2O(l)$$

Here are the accurate heats of combustion for four alcohols (Table 45.1).

Table 45.1

Alcohol	$-\Delta H$ (combustion) in kJ mol^{-1}
Methanol	715.0
Ethanol	1371
Propan-1-ol	2010
Butan-1-ol	2673

What makes a good fuel?

Suppose that you were asked to choose a fuel to propel a space rocket at 40 000 km h^{-1} (25 000 miles per hour) away from the earth's surface. Many fuels are available and it is important to know which ones are best for this particular job. A lot of heat energy must be released in a very short time: the evolved gases will then expand rapidly and move very quickly away from the rocket. So you would want a fuel with a very high heat of combustion and which also burns very rapidly.

You might also think about the volume that the required amount of fuel could be made to occupy in the rocket where as much space as possible needs to be saved. In contrast, the volume of the gases produced by the burning should be as high as possible to produce a large thrust.

There must also be a source of oxygen in which the fuel can burn: it is possible to use liquid oxygen or an oxidizing agent that readily releases oxygen.

Fuels which have been used in space rockets include liquid hydrogen, kerosine and hydrazine (N_2H_4). The lunar model of the Apollo II project, which landed the first man on the Moon in July 1969, used methylhydrazine (CH_3NHNH_2) as its fuel. The oxidizing agent was dinitrogen tetroxide. These two substances start to burn as soon as they are mixed together. The equation for the reaction is

$$4CH_3NHNH_2(l) + 5N_2O_4(g)$$
$$\longrightarrow 4CO_2(g) + 9N_2(g) + 12H_2O(g)$$
$$\Delta H = -4740\,kJ$$

Notice that all the products of combustion are gases.

Now think about a more down-to-earth use of fuels – for cooking and for keeping us warm. Quick burning is not so important here as in space rockets. But is is very important for the fuel to have a high **heating value** ('calorific value'). This is the heat energy released per unit mass, or sometimes per unit volume if the fuel is a gas. The heating values for some fuels are given in Table 45.2.

Table 45.2

Fuel	Heating value in kJg^{-1}
SOLIDS	
Charcoal	33
Coal	25–33
Wood	17
LIQUIDS	
Ethanol	30
Fuel oil	45
Kerosine	48
GASES	
Methane (natural gas)	55
Propane (bottled gas)	50
Butane (bottled gas)	50

Besides having a high heating value, a fuel used in the home, the laboratory and industry should be as cheap as possible. What you need to know is how much it costs for each fuel to release the same amount of energy. This can be worked out using the steps given in Question 1 on page 209.

Energy changes and neutralization reactions

In any neutralization reaction between an acid and an alkali there is a rise in temperature because the reaction is exothermic.

Does the temperature rise depend on the amounts of acid and alkali mixed together? The observed rise in temperature depends on how much water is present in the mixture. A lot of water requires more heat to raise its temperature by 1 °C than a small amount of water does. For this reason, the total volume of water in the reaction mixture must be kept constant during the following investigation. Fig. 45.6 shows the apparatus that can be used.

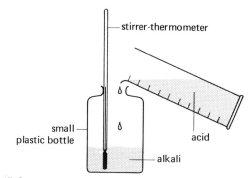

Fig. 45.6

Plastic containers are suitable. Not only do they absorb very little energy when their temperature is raised, but they are also poor conductors of heat.

Various volumes of the acid and alkali are mixed but the total volume of liquid is kept constant. After the mixture has been stirred, the maximum rise in temperature is recorded.

A typical set of results for this experiment is given in Table 45.3, and a graph can be drawn of the rise in

Table 45.3

Volume of 2 M sodium hydroxide in cm^3	Volume of 2 M hydrochloric acid in cm^3	Initial temperature in °C	Final temperature in °C	Rise in temperature in °C
5	35	15.0	18.0	3.0
10	30	15.0	21.4	6.4
15	25	15.0	24.8	9.8
20	20	15.0	26.6	11.6
25	15	15.0	23.8	8.8
30	10	15.0	21.0	6.0
35	5	15.0	18.6	3.6

temperature against the volumes of each reactant (Fig. 45.7).

The maximum rise in temperature is shown by the peak of the graph which is at about 11.6 °C. This is the rise produced by equal volumes of acid and alkali. Because the reactants are of equal concentration, this maximum rise corresponds to a molar ratio of 1 : 1 for the acid and alkali. This ratio is, of course, the one given by the equation for the neutralization reaction (page 74).

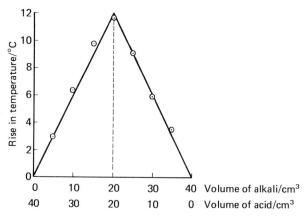

Fig. 45.7

When other volumes of the reactants are used, either some acid or some alkali remains unreacted and a smaller temperature rise is observed. For example, when 15 cm³ of acid and 25 cm³ of alkali are used, the 15 cm³ of acid is neutralized by 15 cm³ of alkali, leaving 10 cm³ of unreacted alkali.

In the next experiment, you can investigate some of the reasons why the temperature rise may vary when solutions of sodium hydroxide and hydrochloric acid are mixed in the molar ratio of 1 : 1.

Experiment 45.3 What affects the temperature rise when alkali and acid of the same concentration are mixed in equal volumes?

1. Mixing 25 cm³ volumes of 2 M acid and alkali.

Use a 25 cm³ measuring cylinder to measure 25 cm³ of bench dilute (2 M) sodium hydroxide solution into a plastic cup. Find its temperature with a thermometer. Thoroughly wash the measuring cylinder and measure 25 cm³ of bench dilute (2 M) hydrochloric acid. Note the temperature of this solution. (The average of the two temperatures is the temperature of the mixture before reaction.) Quickly pour the acid into the alkali and stir the mixture gently with the thermometer. Note the highest temperature reached, and work out the temperature rise.

2. Varying the total volume of the reaction mixture.

Repeat part 1 but use 50 cm³ volumes of each solution measured in a 50 cm³ measuring cylinder.

▶ Is the temperature rise the same or different from that obtained in part 1?
▶ Can you explain this answer?

The result of this experiment is an important one and it is used in working out energy changes in later experiments.

3. Varying the concentrations of the reactants.

Dilute 25 cm³ of the alkali with an equal volume of distilled water in a 50 cm³ measuring cylinder. Pour the diluted solution into a plastic cup. Thoroughly wash the measuring cylinder and then use it to dilute 25 cm³ of the acid with an equal volume of distilled water. Find the temperature of each solution. Now carry on as in part 1 and find the highest temperature reached by the mixture.

▶ Compare the temperature rise with that obtained in part 2.
▶ Do you think that varying the concentrations of the reactants but keeping the total volume of the mixture constant has any effect on the temperature rise?
▶ Is this the answer you expected? Make sure that you can explain the result.

When you are trying to find the energy change for a reaction in solution, you should:

1. use fairly small volumes of solutions (for convenience and cheapness);
2. know accurately the concentrations of the solutions;
3. mix the reactants in the molar ratio given by the equation for the reaction.

In addition, you should assume that 4.2 kJ of energy raises the temperature of 1 kg of most aqueous solutions by 1 °C.

Experiment 45.4 Finding the energy changes for two neutralization reactions

Your teacher will provide you with 1.0 M solutions of sodium hydroxide, potassium hydroxide, hydrochloric acid and nitric acid.

1. The reaction between sodium hydroxide solution and dilute hydrochloric acid.

Follow the procedure given in Experiment 45.3 using 25 cm³ volumes of the acid and the alkali measured as accurately as possible in 25 cm³ measuring cylinders. Do not stir the mixture vigorously because this can cause a temperature rise. Also, do not hold the cup in your hands. Find the maximum temperature rise of the mixture.

2. The reaction between potassium hydroxide solution and dilute nitric acid.

Repeat part 1 using potassium hydroxide solution and dilute nitric acid, and find the maximum temperature rise.

▶ What do you notice about the results of the two experiments?

Calculation of the energy change

You need to work out the amount of energy evolved when 1 mole of alkali reacts with 1 mole of acid. Two ways of doing this are given below. Suppose that in part 1 of the experiment you get a temperature rise of 6.5 °C.

1. Assume that the density of the final solution is $1.0\,g\,cm^{-3}$ and that it takes the same amount of energy to raise the temperature of a given mass of the solution by 1 °C as it takes to raise the temperature of the same mass of water by 1 °C.

A temperature rise of 1 °C is produced in 1000 g of water by 4.2 kJ. So a temperature rise of 6.5 °C is produced in 50 g of solution by $4.2 \times 6.5 \times 50/1000$ kJ.

This amount of energy is released when $25\,cm^3$ of 1.0 M sodium hydroxide solution reacts with $25\,cm^3$ of 1.0 M hydrochloric acid. Each of these solutions contains $1 \times 25/1000$ mole of solute. So 25/1000 mole of NaOH plus 25/1000 mole of HCl release $4.2 \times 6.5 \times 50/1000$ kJ. And 1 mole of NaOH plus 1 mole of HCl would release $4.2 \times 6.5 \times (50/1000) \times (1000/25)$ kJ, or 55 kJ.

The energy change in this reaction is *55 kJ (mol NaOH)$^{-1}$* (evolved).

2. You know from Experiment 45.3 that the temperature rise produced in this reaction does not depend on the volumes of acid and alkali used (so long as they are equal, and so long as solutions of the same concentration are used all through).

So if a temperature rise of 6.5 °C is produced by mixing $25\,cm^3$ of 1.0 M NaOH and $25\,cm^3$ of 1.0 M HCl, then the same temperature rise is produced by mixing 1 litre of 1.0 M NaOH and 1 litre of 1.0 M HCl.

But the temperature rise of 1 °C is produced in 1000 g of water by 4.2 kJ. So a temperature rise of 6.5 °C is produced in 2000 g of water by $4.2 \times 6.5 \times 2000/1000$ kJ or 55 kJ.

The energy change in this reaction is *55 kJ (mol NaOH)$^{-1}$* (evolved).

The equation for any neutralization reaction between a strong alkali and a strong acid (page 75) can be written as

$$OH^-(aq) + H^+(aq) \longrightarrow H_2O(l)$$

Using the energy change for the reaction between sodium hydroxide solution and dilute hydrochloric acid worked out above, the energy level diagram is

$$\underline{OH^-(aq) + H^+(aq)}$$
$$\Delta H = -55\,kJ$$
$$\downarrow H_2O(l)$$

Accurate experiments show that the energy change *per mole of water formed* is nearly constant (at about 57 kJ (evolved)) for any strong alkali reacting with any strong acid. This is because the reaction is the same in each case. This energy change is called the **heat of neutralization**.

QUESTIONS

1 Choose two common fuels used in your own area.

(a) Find the cost of the fuel per kilogram. (Even bottled gas is sold by mass rather than volume because it is always under pressure in its container.)

(b) Use Table 45.2 to obtain the heating value of the fuel in $kJ\,g^{-1}$. Change this to a value in $kJ\,kg^{-1}$.

(c) Divide your answer in step (a) by your answer in step (b) to work out the cost per kilojoule of energy released.
  (i) Which is the cheaper fuel?
 (ii) Is this fuel more or less widely used than the more costly one?
(iii) If it is *less* widely used, try to find reasons why this is so.

2 Work out the energy change (ΔH) in each of the following examples and draw energy level diagrams for the changes. Assume that 4.2 kJ of energy is required to heat 1000 g of a solution through 1 °C and that the density of each solution is $1\,g\,cm^{-3}$.

(a) When $100\,cm^3$ of 2.0 M potassium hydroxide solution is mixed with $100\,cm^3$ of 2.0 M nitric acid, there is a temperature rise of 13.5 °C.

$$KOH(aq) + HNO_3(aq) \longrightarrow KNO_3(aq) + H_2O(l)$$

(b) The complete combustion of 3.0 g of pure carbon raises the temperature of 1 litre of water from 20 °C to 43 °C.

$$C(graphite) + O_2(g) \longrightarrow CO_2(g)$$

When 40 g of ammonium nitrate (relative molecular mass = 80) is dissolved in 1 litre of water, there is a temperature drop of 2.5 °C.

$$NH_4NO_3(s) + aq \longrightarrow NH_4NO_3(aq)\,[0.5\,M]$$

3 When equal volumes of 0.40 M solutions of sodium chloride and silver nitrate are mixed, there is a temperature rise of 3.0 °C. When a 0.50 M solution of calcium chloride is mixed with an equal volume of a 1.0 M solution of silver nitrate, the temperature rise is 7.5 °C. The equations for these two reactions may be written as:

$$NaCl(aq) + AgNO_3(aq) \longrightarrow AgCl(s) + NaNO_3(aq) \quad (1)$$

$$CaCl_2 + 2AgNO_3(aq) \longrightarrow 2AgCl(s) + Ca(NO_3)_2(aq) \quad (2)$$

Assume that a temperature rise of 1 °C is produced in 1 litre of the reaction mixtures by 4.2 kJ of energy.

(*a*) Work out ΔH for the reaction shown by equation (1) and for the reaction shown by equation (2).

(*b*) What is the energy change in each of the reactions in kJ *per mole of AgCl(s)* produced?

(*c*) Can you explain why the two answers to part (*a*) are different but why there is only one answer to part (*b*)?

(*d*) Draw *one* energy level diagram that shows the energy change for the formation of 1 mole of AgCl for *both* reactions.

4 The equation for the reaction of calcium with chlorine is:

$$Ca(s) + Cl_2(g) \longrightarrow CaCl_2(s); \quad \Delta H = -795 \text{ kJ}$$

The energy evolved when 1 mole of $SrCl_2(s)$ is formed from strontium and chlorine is 828 kJ; and the energy evolved during the formation of 1 mole of $BaCl_2(s)$ is 860 kJ.

(*a*) Describe with the help of a diagram how you would carry out the reaction between calcium and chlorine in the laboratory. (Details about how to find the temperature change, and so ΔH, are not required.)

(*b*) Draw an energy level diagram for the formation of 1 mole of $CaCl_2$.

(*c*) Use the above data to say which one of the three chlorides you would expect to be most difficult to decompose by heat. Explain your answer carefully.

(*d*) Predict a possible value for the energy change that occurs when 1 mole of $RaCl_2$ is formed from radium and chlorine. Explain carefully how you work out your answer. (Remember to give the sign for ΔH.)

5 (*a*) Why is the heat of neutralization for any *strong* acid and *strong* alkali constant?

(*b*) Why would you expect the heat of neutralization for a *weak* alkali and a *weak* acid to be less than 57 kJ? (Remember that energy needs to be absorbed for bonds to be broken, and that weak alkalis and acids are not made entirely from ions in solution (page 82).)

6 'Fuels such as oil, natural gas and our food have stored-up energy from the sun which is released when we burn the fuels in air or oxidize the food in our bodies.'

Write a short essay explaining this statement.

Key words

exothermic reaction	bond energy	energy level diagram	heat of neutralization
endothermic reaction	joule	heat of combustion	
latent heats (of fusion and vaporization)	ΔH	heating value (of a fuel)	

Basic facts

- Energy is the capacity for doing work.

- Exothermic reactions are ones in which energy is evolved as the reaction occurs, and endothermic reactions are ones in which energy is absorbed as the reaction occurs.

- There are forces of attraction between molecules and between ions, as well as forces of attraction between atoms within molecules. When a reaction occurs, these forces are changed. It is the change in the overall balance of these forces that determines whether a reaction is exothermic or endothermic.

- An energy level diagram can be used to summarize the energy change (ΔH) that takes place during any particular reaction.

- The heat of combustion of a fuel is the energy change per mole of fuel burnt. It is one factor that determines the usefulness of a fuel, though the heat produced per unit mass (the heating value) is rather more important.

- The heat of neutralization is the energy change for the reaction between an acid and an alkali per mole of water formed.

Chemicals from nature II

46 The analysis of carbon compounds

Detecting the elements present in carbon compounds

A lot of the compounds that are present in living things have been found to be compounds of carbon. Many everyday substances, such as sugar, flour, bread, wood, paper, kerosine and methylated spirit, have been formed from living things. These compounds are often called **organic** compounds, while compounds obtained from rocks are called **inorganic** compounds. How can these organic substances be shown to be compounds of carbon? Many of them burn when they are heated in the air and the carbon they contain is oxidized to carbon dioxide.

But it is not very easy to collect carbon dioxide from a substance that is burning strongly in air, so a reaction using copper(II) oxide is usually used.

Experiment 46.1 How do carbon compounds react with air and with copper(II) oxide?

1. Solids to use: sugar, starch, sodium ethanoate (sodium acetate), polythene and gelatin.

Place a small amount of the solid about the size of two rice grains on a crucible lid. Direct a bunsen flame onto the solid.

▶ Does the solid burn?
▶ If the solid burns, is a residue left or does the solid burn to leave no residue?

When you have done the experiment using these solids, repeat it using two drops of ethanol (methylated spirit) and then two drops of kerosine. (CARE: whether stoppered or unstoppered, do not leave bottles of these very flammable liquids near to a bunsen flame.)

▶· Do these liquids leave any residue when they burn?

2. Use the apparatus shown in Fig. 46.1 and one of the solids from part 1. Mix about half a spatula measure of the compound with about three times its volume of *dry* copper(II) oxide and put this mixture in the bottom of a *dry* test-tube. Cover the mixture with a layer of dry copper(II) oxide. Heat the contents of the tube, starting at the top; when the copper(II) oxide is hot, the whole of the mixture can be heated.

▶ Is any carbon dioxide formed?
▶ Can you see and test for another product?

3. Repeat 2, using either ethanol or kerosine. Add two drops of the liquid to the copper(II) oxide at the bottom of the test-tube, and cover this with another layer of copper(II) oxide. Again, heat the copper(II) oxide from the top downwards.

▶ What products can you find?
▶ Which *two* elements must be present in the carbon compounds used in 1, 2 and 3?
▶ What does the copper(II) oxide do to these substances?
▶ What happens to the copper(II) oxide in these experiments? (Look at the contents of the tube after the experiment is finished to make sure that your answer is right.)

Many compounds which are formed from plants and animals burn and leave no ash. These compounds must contain only non-metallic elements.

When some of the compounds burn, an ash is left and this means that the compound contains a metal. The metal can be identified by dissolving the ash in a dilute acid and looking at the reactions of the metal ions in solution.

When substances such as skin, nail parings, hair, meat and cheese are heated with an alkali such as soda-lime, ammonia is given off. This result shows that these substances have some nitrogen-containing compounds in them.

Many carbon compounds contain only carbon and hydrogen, or carbon, hydrogen and oxygen. Other elements such as nitrogen, sulphur, the halogens and metals are also present in some of the carbon

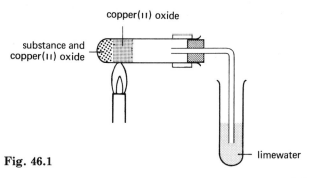

Fig. 46.1

compounds. Tests have been developed which identify these elements. Finding out which elements are present in a compound is called **qualitative analysis**. In **quantitative analysis** the proportions of the elements in a compound are found.

It is surprising that the very large number of compounds which can be formed from animal and plant material are made up of only a few elements.

Finding the formulas of carbon compounds

When the elements present in a compound have been identified by qualitative analysis, it is possible to find by quantitative analysis the proportions by mass of each element. From these data the empirical (simplest) formula can be found. The molecular formula may then be found if the relative molecular mass of the compound is known.

The following example shows the steps in the working out of the molecular formula of a certain organic liquid.

Example *A liquid contains 38.7% of carbon (relative atomic mass = 12), 9.7% of hydrogen (relative atomic mass = 1.0) and 51.6% of oxygen (relative atomic mass = 16). It has a relative molecular mass of about 60.*

	Carbon	Hydrogen	Oxygen
Mass of element in 100 g of compound	38.7 g	9.7 g	51.6 g
Number of moles of atoms of each element	$\frac{38.7}{12}$ = 3.23	$\frac{9.7}{1.0}$ = 9.7	$\frac{51.6}{16}$ = 3.23
Simplest ratio of moles of atoms	1	3	1

The empirical formula of the liquid is CH_3O.

2. If the molecular formula of the liquid were also CH_3O, then the relative molecular mass would be (12 + 3.0 + 16) or 31. The relative molecular mass found by experiment is about twice as large, and so the molecular formula must be $(CH_3O)_2$ or $C_2H_6O_2$.

The next step is to find the way the atoms are joined together in the molecule. This arrangement is called the **structural formula** of the substance. It is the structural formula rather than the molecular formula which is most useful in studying the chemistry of carbon compounds. One method of finding a molecular formula is given on page 91.

Methods of analysing carbon compounds involve the oxidation of the compounds to simpler substances that are easily recognized. For this reason it is difficult to detect the presence of oxygen in an organic compound.

In the example above, qualitative analysis would show the presence of carbon and hydrogen only. Quantitative analysis would show that 38.7% of the compound by mass is carbon while 9.7% is hydrogen. The remaining 51.6% would be assumed to be oxygen because no other elements had been found in the compound.

QUESTIONS

The necessary relative atomic masses will be found in Data Sheet 1 on page 279. The molar gas volume at S.T.P. is $22.4 \, l \, mol^{-1}$.

1 A compound of only carbon and hydrogen contains 82.8% carbon by mass.
(*a*) Calculate its empirical formula.
(*b*) If its relative molecular mass is about 60, calculate its molecular formula.

2 Qualitative analysis of a liquid shows the presence of carbon and hydrogen only. Quantitative analysis shows that the compound contains 37.5% carbon by mass, and 12.5% hydrogen.
(*a*) Explain why these percentages do not add up to 100.
(*b*) Calculate the empirical formula of the compound.
(*c*) If the relative molecular mass of the compound is about 30, calculate its molecular formula.

3 A gaseous compound of carbon and hydrogen contains 85.7% carbon by mass. At S.T.P. its density is $1.25 \, g \, l^{-1}$.
(*a*) Calculate its empirical formula.
(*b*) Calculate its relative molecular mass.
(*c*) What is the molecular formula of the compound?

4 Calculate the molecular formulas of the following compounds.
(*a*) A volatile liquid which contains 23.8% carbon, 5.9% hydrogen and 70.3% chlorine by mass and which has a relative molecular mass of about 50.
(*b*) A white crystalline solid which contains 40.0% carbon, 6.7% hydrogen and 53.3% oxygen by mass and has a relative molecular mass of 180.
(*c*) A gaseous compound of carbon and hydrogen which contains 75% carbon by mass and which has a density of $0.71 \, g \, l^{-1}$ at S.T.P.

5 Qualitative analysis of a liquid showed the presence of carbon and hydrogen only. When 1.00 g of the liquid was completely oxidized, 1.42 g of carbon dioxide and 0.87 g of water were produced.
(*a*) Calculate the mass of carbon in 1.42 g of carbon dioxide.
(*b*) Calculate the percentage of carbon in the compound. (All the carbon in the carbon dioxide came from the compound.)
(*c*) Calculate the mass of hydrogen in 0.87 g of water.
(*d*) Calculate the percentage of hydrogen in the compound.
(*e*) Calculate the percentage of oxygen in the compound.
(*f*) Calculate the empirical formula of the compound.
(*g*) The relative molecular mass of the compound is about 60. Calculate its molecular formula.

Key words

organic compound   qualitative analysis   structural formula

inorganic compound   quantitative analysis

Basic facts

- All organic compounds contain carbon and most contain hydrogen. Many compounds obtained from plants contain carbon, hydrogen and oxygen and many from animals contain nitrogen too.

- Organic compounds can be analysed by oxidizing them and detecting the products of oxidation, such as carbon dioxide and water.

- The molecular formulas of organic compounds can be calculated from the results of quantitative analysis, together with a knowledge of the relative molecular mass of the compound.

47 Investigating petroleum

What is petroleum?

Petroleum, or crude oil, is found in many parts of the world and has been known for hundreds of years. It is only in this century that it has been used to make fuels and as a source of carbon compounds. It is now the most important raw material in the organic chemistry industry.

Experiment 47.1 What happens when petroleum is burnt or heated?

1. Put two drops of petroleum on a crucible lid and try to set them on fire using a bunsen burner.

▶ How easily does petroleum burn?

Repeat the experiment but, before lighting the petroleum, put a wick in it (a suitable wick can be made from a twisted piece of cotton wool).

2. Find out what happens when petroleum is heated and collect any substances given off using the apparatus shown in Fig. 47.1. A few pumice grains or pieces of porous pot help the petroleum to boil smoothly.

At first, heat the petroleum as gently as you can, using a very small moving flame. Make a note of the temperature when liquid first begins to condense in the collecting tube.

▶ What happens to the temperature shown on the thermometer as you continue to heat the petroleum?

Carry on collecting the liquid until the temperature reaches about 90–100 °C and then replace the collecting tube. Repeat this procedure, gradually heating the petroleum more strongly, and collecting in different tubes the liquids given off in the temperature ranges 100–150 °C, 150–200 °C, 200–250 °C and 250–300 °C. Remember that the apparatus is very hot at the end of the experiment, and it should be allowed to cool before you attempt to take it to bits and investigate the residue.

Look at the properties of the liquids formed and make notes of:

(a) appearance and smell,
(b) viscosity (how easily do they flow?),
(c) flammability (put two drops of each of the liquids on a crucible lid and try to set fire to them; if the liquid does not burn, insert a small wick and then try to light it).

▶ Draw a table of results giving your observations for each liquid you collected.

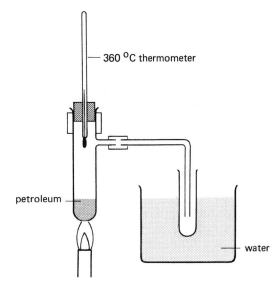

Fig. 47.1

After the residue has cooled to room temperature, look at its properties in the same way. Finally, mix together samples of all the liquids you collected in the experiment, including the residue, and compare the properties of this mixture with the properties of petroleum.

▶ What can now be said about the composition of petroleum?

If a mixture of two liquids with boiling points 50 °C and 200 °C was heated, the first liquid would boil off at about 50 °C. Then the temperature would rise and little, if any, liquid would distill off until the temperature reached about 200 °C. While petroleum is being heated, there are no sudden rises of temperature during which no liquids distill off. Instead, the temperature continues to rise steadily as liquids are distilled off over the whole temperature range. So petroleum must be a mixture of a very large number of liquids, each with its own boiling point.

It should be clear to you that petroleum is not decomposed under the conditions of Experiment 47.1 but is simply separated into several parts by distillation. These parts are usually called **fractions** and the separation into fractions is called either **fractional distillation** or **fractionation**.

Each fraction contains liquids with boiling points in a certain temperature range. If several samples of the same fraction from the experiment are mixed and redistilled, the original fraction can be split up into smaller fractions, each with a smaller boiling point range than the original fraction.

It has been found that the compounds in petroleum are mainly **hydrocarbons**, that is, compounds composed only of the elements carbon and hydrogen.

Processing petroleum in industry

The starting material for the petrochemical industry is petroleum. The first step in the treatment of petroleum is fractional distillation (page 270). But the industrial process is completely different from the experiment you have done because it is run continuously. Experiment 47.1 shows how a 'batch process' works: one batch of petroleum is distilled and the apparatus has to be emptied before another batch is treated. Continuous processes are more efficient than batch processes because no time is wasted in emptying and then refilling the apparatus.

If you refer to page 213, you will see how the fractions you obtained in Experiment 47.1 are similar to the fractions produced industrially: gasoline, kerosine, diesel oil and so on.

Key words

fractions   fractionation   hydrocarbons

Basic facts

- Petroleum is a mixture of a very large number of compounds, most of which are hydrocarbons.

- The fractional distillation of petroleum divides it into fractions.

- As the boiling point of the fractions increases, the flammability decreases, the viscosity increases and the density increases. Their flammability and viscosity control the use of the fractions as fuels, lubricating oils and greases.

48 The alkanes

A family of hydrocarbons

Families of *elements* contain elements whose chemical properties are similar. Chemists have found that it is possible to divide carbon *compounds* into families: the members of each family have very similar chemical properties.

Hydrocarbons can be divided into several families. This section is about one of them, the **alkanes**, which are important because they are the substances in petroleum.

The simplest alkane is methane and its molecular formula is CH_4. Methane does not occur in petroleum because it is too volatile, but it is the main component of natural gas. Other alkanes have molecules which contain more than one carbon atom. The molecules of ethane each contain two atoms of carbon while those of propane contain three atoms of carbon, and so on. The formulas of some of the simple alkanes are given in Table 48.1, along with some of the physical properties of these compounds.

Table 48.1

Name	Molecular formula	Melting point in °C	Boiling point in °C	Density in $g\,cm^{-3}$
Methane	CH_4	− 182	− 162	
Ethane	C_2H_6	− 183	− 88.6	
Propane	C_3H_8	− 188	− 42.2	
Butane	C_4H_{10}	− 138	− 0.5	
Pentane	C_5H_{12}	− 130	36.3	0.626
Hexane	C_6H_{14}	− 95.3	68.7	0.659
Heptane	C_7H_{16}	− 90.6	98.4	0.684
Octane	C_8H_{18}	− 56.8	126	0.703

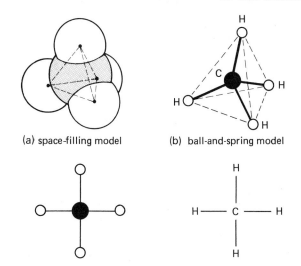

(a) space-filling model   (b) ball-and-spring model

(c) 'flattened' representations

Fig. 48.1

The members of families of carbon compounds have similar chemical properties because the structures of their molecules are similar. In a methane molecule, each of the four hydrogen atoms forms a covalent bond with the carbon atom (pages 168/9).

The four hydrogen atoms are arranged in a special way around the carbon atom. If the molecule is thought to have the shape of a tetrahedron, then the hydrogen atoms are at the corners and the carbon atom is in the middle of the tetrahedron. Your teacher will probably show you a space-filling model of a methane molecule (Fig. 48.1a) and a ball-and-spring model (Fig. 48.1b). Neither of these is easy to draw so the forms shown in Fig. 48.1c are usually used. In order to get these, the ball-and-spring model has to be flattened out. Whenever they are used, you should remember that they are only drawings in two dimensions of molecules that are three-dimensional.

Fig. 48.2 shows some ways in which the molecular structures of three other simple alkanes, ethane, propane and butane, can be drawn.

These diagrams show the **structural formulas** of the alkanes. They are more useful than the molecular formulas because they show the way the atoms are arranged in the molecules.

Not only are the structures of the molecules of these alkanes similar to one another, but also their molecular formulas can be written in a general way. If an alkane molecule contains n carbon atoms, it contains $2n + 2$ hydrogen atoms. So the general formula for all alkanes in C_nH_{2n+2}.

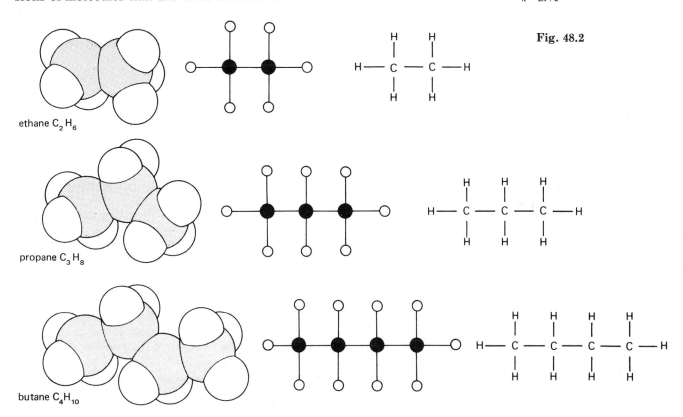

ethane C_2H_6

propane C_3H_8

butane C_4H_{10}

Fig. 48.2

A family of carbon compounds is usually called a **homologous series** of compounds. The members of a homologous series always have a general formula that can be used for all molecular formulas of that series. It is the similarity in their molecular structures that causes their chemical properties to be very similar.

Another observation about a family of carbon compounds is that their physical properties show trends with increasing relative molecular mass. The data in Table 48.1 show the trends in melting point, boiling point and density.

For the alkanes, another trend is that the liquids are more viscous as the number of carbon atoms increases. You should now see that each fraction formed in the distillation of petroleum (Experiment 47.1) contains alkanes of higher relative molecular masses than the fraction before it.

Isomerism among the alkanes

Alkanes are known with up to about one hundred carbon atoms in their molecules. You might think this means that there are about one hundred different members of the alkane homologous series. In fact, there are many thousands of different alkanes. This can be explained by looking at the molecular structures of some simple alkanes.

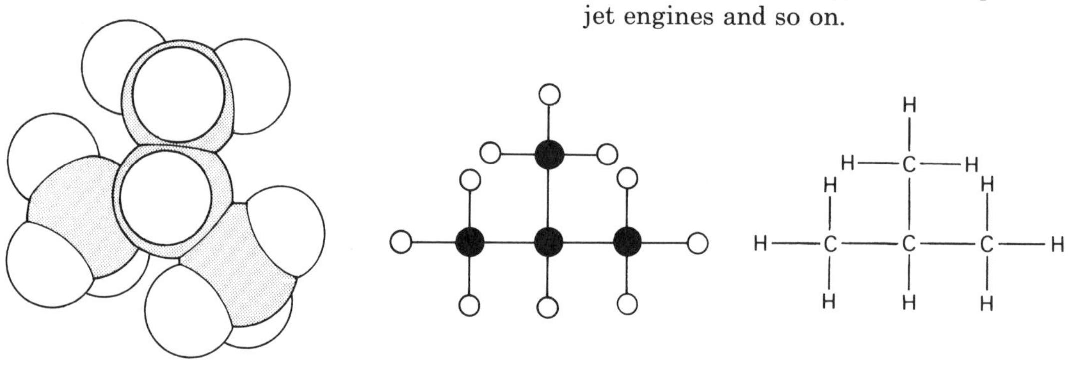

The existence of more than one compound with the same molecular formula is known as **isomerism** and the different substances are termed **isomers**. The substances can be said to be **isomeric** with one another.

By drawing the possible structures for the molecular formula C_5H_{12}, and by making models using five carbon and twelve hydrogen atoms, it is fairly easy to decide that there should be three isomers. But it is rather more difficult to decide that there should be five isomers with the molecular formula C_6H_{14}. As the number of carbon atoms in the molecular formula increases, the number of possible isomers with that formula increases rapidly. The existence of isomers explains why there is such a very large number of different alkanes in petroleum, each with its own particular boiling point.

The chemical properties of the alkanes

Alkanes are not very reactive substances. They show only three important reactions.

1 Combustion

The most noticeable property of the alkanes is that their vapours burn easily in air: in fact, mixtures of air and alkane gases can be dangerously explosive. If controlled, these combustion reactions can be used to provide heat energy, for example in car engines, jet engines and so on.

Fig. 48.3

Study the diagrams of models of ethane, propane and butane (Fig. 48.2) and try to decide if any other arrangements of atoms are possible. One other arrangement for the four carbon atoms and the ten hydrogen atoms in butane is shown in Fig. 48.3. So there are two compounds with the formula C_4H_{10}. The melting points and boiling points of these two compounds are given in Table 48.2.

The structure in which the carbon atoms are arranged in one 'line' is called an **unbranched chain** of carbon atoms. The other structure has three carbon atoms in a 'line' and one that branches off this 'line': such a structure is called a **branched chain** of carbon atoms.

Table 48.2

Structure	m.p., in °C	b.p., in °C
H H H H | | | | H—C—C—C—C—H | | | | H H H H	− 138	− 0.5
H | H—C—H H | H | | | H—C——C——C—H | | | H H H	− 160	− 11.7

When hydrocarbon fuels are burnt in an excess of air or oxygen, the products of combustion are carbon dioxide and water. But if there is not enough oxygen for complete combustion, carbon monoxide is formed (page 112).

air, compounds with large complicated molecules are broken down in a decomposition reaction into compounds with simpler molecules (page 10). Can the large alkane molecules be broken down in a similar way?

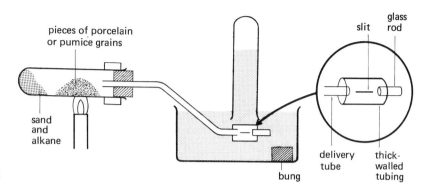

Fig. 48.4

2 Reaction with bromine

Your teacher may show you the reaction between bromine and a liquid alkane. A few drops of bromine are added to a liquid alkane, such as hexane, and the mixture is poured into two test-tubes which are then closed with bungs. One test-tube is put in a dark cupboard while the other one is left in bright sunlight. After a few minutes the mixture in sunlight will become colourless. But the colour of the mixture left in the dark will not have changed. When the bung is taken out of the tube which has been in the sunlight, an acidic gas which fumes in moist air can be detected. This gas is hydrogen bromide.

The equation for the reaction is

$$C_6H_{14}(l) + Br_2(l) \longrightarrow C_6H_{13}Br(l) + HBr(g)$$
$$\text{bromohexane}$$

This sort of reaction happens with all alkanes, and it is possible for more than one hydrogen atom in the alkane molecule to be replaced by a bromine atom. Alkanes do not react in this way with bromine in dilute aqueous solution.

Reactions in which one atom (or group of atoms) is replaced by another atom (or group of atoms) are called **substitution reactions**. These substitution reactions are generally shown by **saturated compounds**, that is, compounds which contain only single covalent bonds in their molecules.

3 The action of heat on alkanes

Petroleum contains a lot of alkanes with high boiling points, that is, alkanes made of large molecules. But many of the most useful alkanes in everyday life, such as those in gasoline, have low boiling points and are made of small molecules. So it is important to find a way of breaking down the large molecules into smaller ones.

When wood is heated strongly in the absence of

Your teacher may show you the experiment illustrated in Fig. 48.4. The sand contains a liquid alkane such as decane, or a mixture of solid alkanes such as candle wax. The pumice is heated strongly but occasionally the sand is also heated in order to vaporize some of the alkanes. The bunsen valve allows gas to pass out of the apparatus but helps to prevent the water in the trough being 'sucked back'.

At least three tubes of gas should be collected so that the following tests can be tried.

▶ Does the gas burn? If it does, what kind of flame is produced?
▶ Does the gas react when it is shaken with dilute aqueous bromine solution?
▶ Does the gas react when it is shaken with an acidified solution of potassium manganate(VII)?
▶ Does the original alkane react with either aqueous bromine solution or acidified potassium manganate(VII) solution?

It is clear that a reaction occurs in this experiment because the product is a gas and has different properties from those of the original substance. Also, the formation of a gas (boiling point below room temperature) from a liquid or a solid (boiling point above room temperature) means that small molecules are produced from larger ones.

When the gases formed by this decomposition reaction are analysed, they are found to be mainly a mixture of hydrocarbons. Some of these hydrocarbons are alkanes with molecules smaller than those of the original alkane, but some are hydrocarbons that react quickly with dilute bromine solution and acidified potassium manganate(VII) solution and cannot be alkanes.

Suppose that the breakdown of decane ($C_{10}H_{22}$) produces another alkane, hexane (C_6H_{14}). If there is only *one* other product, it must have the formula C_4H_8. This hydrocarbon cannot be an alkane because its formula does not agree with the general formula for the alkanes. It is a member of the homologous series of hydrocarbons called the **alkenes**, whose members have the general formula C_nH_{2n}, where n can have values of 2, 3, 4 and so on.

The simplest alkene ($n = 2$) is ethene (ethylene), C_2H_4. The alkenes are discussed in the next chapter.

The breaking down of large alkane molecules into smaller alkane and alkene molecules is called **cracking**. It is a kind of thermal decomposition and is given this special name because of its great importance in the petroleum industry.

The industrial importance of cracking

The fractional distillation of petroleum divides it into fractions. The fractions that are most useful are the low boiling point fractions. Cracking provides a method of breaking down alkanes with large molecules (which are not very useful) into alkanes and alkenes with small molecules (which are far more useful).

Alkanes are not very reactive and are therefore not very useful as starting materials for the production of other organic compounds. But alkenes are very reactive and are the starting materials for the production of many other compounds (page 271).

The manufacture of hydrogen

Large amounts of hydrogen are needed for the manufacture of ammonia by the Haber process (page 133). The hydrogen is usually made either from natural gas or from **naphtha**, one of the fractions produced in the distillation of petroleum (pages 270/1).

Naphtha is a mixture of hydrocarbons such as C_6H_{14} and C_7H_{16}. It is reacted with steam at about 900 °C to form a mixture of hydrogen and carbon monoxide. This process is called **steam-reforming**.

$$C_6H_{14}(g) + 6H_2O(g) \longrightarrow 6CO(g) + 13H_2(g)$$

More steam is added to this mixture which is then passed over a hot iron catalyst. The carbon monoxide reacts with the steam to produce carbon dioxide and more hydrogen.

$$CO(g) + H_2O(g) \longrightarrow CO_2(g) + H_2(g)$$

This reaction is called the **shift reaction**. Carbon dioxide can be removed from this mixture by dissolving it in water under pressure, leaving hydrogen.

Natural gas is mainly methane, CH_4. Its reaction with steam is similar to the reaction of naphtha with steam.

$$CH_4(g) + H_2O(s) \longrightarrow CO(g) + 3H_2(g)$$

The rest of the process for the production of hydrogen is carried out as described above.

The method chosen for the production of hydrogen in a particular country depends on whether naphtha or natural gas is more readily available.

Before the petrochemical industries were established, hydrogen was made by passing steam over coke at about 1000 °C.

$$H_2O(g) + C(s) \longrightarrow H_2(g) + CO(g)$$

The mixture of hydrogen and carbon monoxide produced by this process is called **water gas**. The shift reaction was then used as above.

World reserves of coal are very much greater than those of oil and gas. So it is possible that, as supplies of oil and natural gas are used up, hydrogen will again be produced from water gas.

QUESTIONS

1 Explain the terms:
(a) homologous series,
(b) isomerism (give an example),
(c) substitution reaction (give an example).

2 The fractional distillation of petroleum divides up the petroleum into fractions which have certain boiling point ranges. Explain why this is a useful way of dividing up petroleum. (Remember that the main uses of the fractions are for fuels, which rely on flammability, and for lubricants, which rely on viscosity.)

3 Petroleum is a free-flowing liquid. Explain why the 'petroleum' in the Trinidad pitch lake, Fig. 29.6 (which is formed by petroleum finding its way to the surface), is a very viscous liquid.

4 Two alkanes have the same relative molecular mass of 58.
(a) Write the molecular formula of the alkanes with relative molecular mass 58.
(b) Draw the two structural formulas that are possible for this molecular formula.
(c) What is the name used to describe two different substances having the same molecular formula?

5 A hydrocarbon contains 80% carbon by mass and has a relative molecular mass of about 30. Calculate its empirical formula, its molecular formula and draw its structural formula.

Key words

alkanes	**unbranched chain**	**isomers**	**saturated compounds**
structural formula	**branched chain**	**isomeric**	**cracking**
homologous series	**isomerism**	**substitution reactions**	

Basic facts

- A homologous series is a family of organic compounds. Their formulas can all be represented by one general formula. The physical properties of the members of a homologous series show trends. The chemical properties of the members of a homologous series are similar.

- The structural formula of a compound shows how the atoms are arranged in its molecules.

- The alkanes make up a homologous series of hydrocarbons with the general formula C_nH_{2n+2}. As n increases, their boiling points increase (fairly regularly), their melting points increase (rather irregularly), their viscosities increase and their flammabilities decrease. The variation of flammability and viscosity explains the uses of the various fractions obtained from crude oil as fuels and lubricants. The chemical properties of all the alkanes are similar: combustion, reaction with bromine and cracking.

- The process of cracking is very important in the petrochemical industry. It produces useful compounds from high boiling point alkane fractions.

- Alkanes are saturated compounds (their molecules contain single covalent bonds) and so they react with bromine by a substitution reaction.

- Isomerism is the existence of more than one compound with the same molecular formula.

49 The alkenes

The structures of alkene molecules

The homologous series of alkenes has the general formula C_nH_{2n}, where n can have the values 2, 3, 4 and so on. The simplest alkene is ethene, C_2H_4. It is called *eth*ene because its molecules contain *two* carbon atoms, like ethane molecules. But to show that it is an alkene, the 'a' in the 'ane' part of the alkane name is replaced by an 'e'.

covalent bonds. The double covalent bond can be drawn in several ways, three of which are shown. Using this structure it is possible to explain the reactions of ethene.

All alkenes have molecules that contain a carbon–carbon double bond. This explains why there is no alkene with only one carbon atom in its molecules.

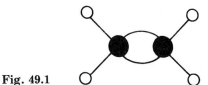

Fig. 49.1

The arrangement of the atoms in a molecule of ethene is shown in Fig. 49.1. All the atoms are in one plane and each carbon atom is joined to two hydrogen atoms by covalent bonds. The bonding between the carbon atoms uses the other two unpaired electrons of each carbon atom and consists of two covalent bonds. In this way, all four outer electrons on each carbon atom become paired in

The preparation of alkenes

Alkanes occur in petroleum but alkenes are too reactive to be found widely in nature. In the petrochemical industry they are produced by the cracking of alkanes which have high relative molecular masses (page 218).

Suppose molecules of the alkane decane $C_{10}H_{22}$ are

broken down by cracking. Two of the many ways in which this can happen are shown in Fig. 49.2. The

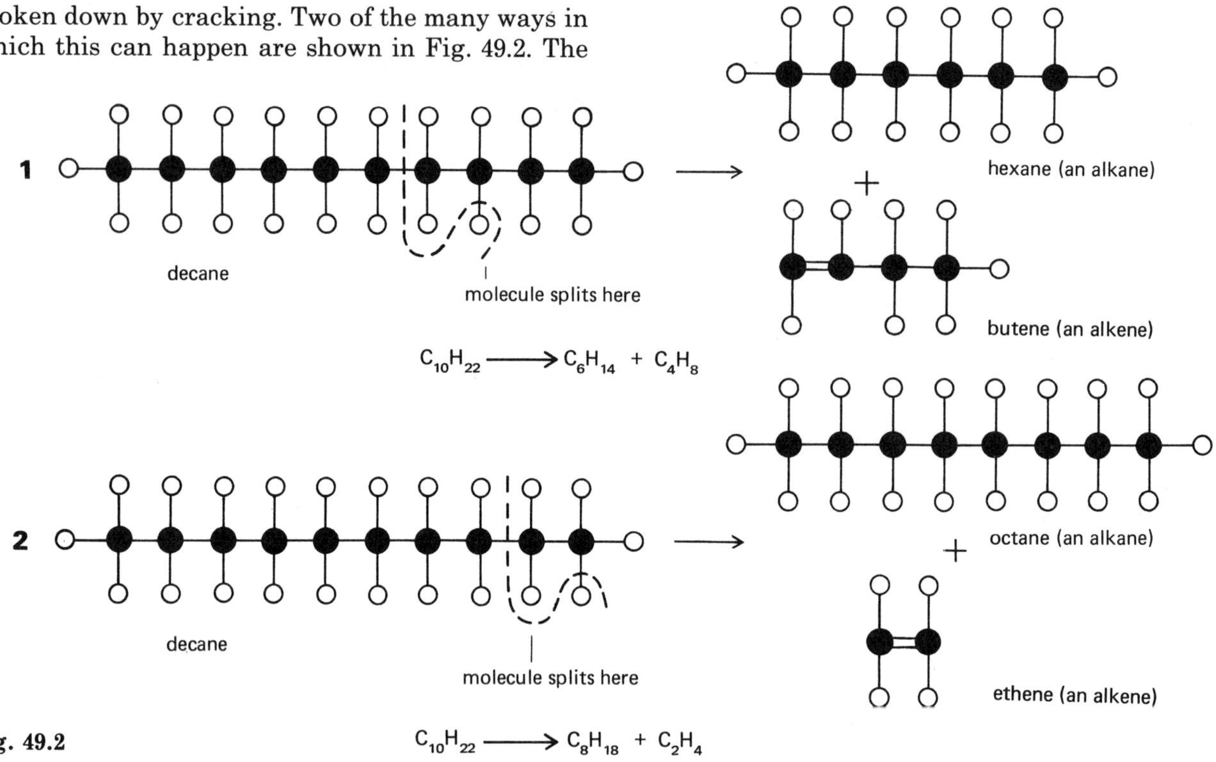

1 decane

molecule splits here

$$C_{10}H_{22} \longrightarrow C_6H_{14} + C_4H_8$$

hexane (an alkane)

+

butene (an alkene)

2 decane

molecule splits here

octane (an alkane)

+

ethene (an alkene)

Fig. 49.2

$$C_{10}H_{22} \longrightarrow C_8H_{18} + C_2H_4$$

two alkane molecules shown (hexane and octane) would probably undergo further cracking so that the final mixture contains mainly alkenes with low relative molecular masses.

The chemical properties of the alkenes

Alkenes are far more reactive than alkanes. Some of their more important reactions are described here.

1 Combustion

Alkenes, like alkanes, are flammable and form explosive mixtures with air. But they are more dangerously explosive than alkanes and are not used as fuels. Instead, they are highly valuable as starting materials for producing other substances. The equation for the combustion of ethene is

$$C_2H_4(g) + 3O_2(g) \longrightarrow 2CO_2(g) + 2H_2O(g)$$

Alkenes burn with rather sooty flames. (They contain a higher proportion of carbon than alkanes.)

2 Reaction with bromine

Alkenes rapidly decolorize an aqueous solution of bromine. It has been found that 1 mole of an alkene combines with 1 mole of Br_2 to form one product. A picture of this reaction for ethene is given in Fig. 49.3. The reaction mixture becomes colourless as the reaction happens because the bromine is used

up and the product is colourless. Notice that the double bond between the carbon atoms is changed to a single bond. Substances whose molecules contain only single bonds are said to be saturated while substances like ethene, whose molecules contain one or more double bonds, are **unsaturated**.

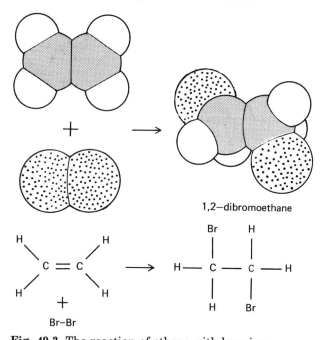

1,2–dibromoethane

Fig. 49.3 The reaction of ethene with bromine.
● Why do you think it is necessary to include two numbers in the name of the product of this reaction?

Reactions in which two molecules react to give a single product are called **addition reactions**. Bromine can add to ethene only because each ethene molecule contains a double bond. So unsaturated compounds show addition reactions but saturated compounds do not.

All alkenes react with bromine in the same sort of way, in what are called **bromination** reactions (and similar reactions occur with chlorine). The reactions are quite fast and are addition reactions in each case. The reaction with bromine can be used as a test for unsaturated compounds. It is also used in industry in the manufacture of plastics.

3 Reaction with hydrogen

Alkenes will react with hydrogen, but only under rather special conditions in the presence of a catalyst. The reactions occur readily at about 200 °C in the presence of finely divided nickel, and at a lower temperature if platinum or palladium is used because they are better catalysts than nickel (but also much more expensive).

The reaction is called **hydrogenation** and is an important example of an addition reaction. The equation for the hydrogenation of ethene is

$$C_2H_4(g) + H_2(g) \longrightarrow C_2H_6(g)$$

This sort of hydrogenation is important in the large-scale production of margarine from vegetable oils. The molecules of these oils contain one or more $>C=C<$ groups of atoms: when these are converted by hydrogenation to $-\overset{\displaystyle H}{\underset{\displaystyle |}{C}}-\overset{\displaystyle H}{\underset{\displaystyle |}{C}}-$ groups, the oil becomes 'hardened', that is, it becomes a solid. In the following equation, the parts of the molecules which do not react are shown as rectangles.

liquid alkene

→

solid alkane

4 Reaction with acidified potassium manganate(VII)

The reaction of acidified potassium manganate(VII) solution with ethene produces a compound called ethane-1,2-diol (or ethylene glycol, Fig. 49.4). This liquid is used in anti-freeze solutions: for example it is put in the water used to cool car engines in cold climates. Its large-scale production, however, does not use potassium manganate(VII). The equation for its formation can be written

$$CH_2{=}CH_2(g) + H_2O(l) + O \text{ (from } KMnO_4)$$
$$\longrightarrow CH_2OHCH_2OH(aq)$$

The decolorization of acidified potassium manganate(VII) solution when it is shaken with alkenes is another test for unsaturated compounds.

5 The hydration of ethene

The equation for this reaction is

or $\quad CH_2{=}CH_2 + H_2O \longrightarrow CH_3CH_2OH$

This addition reaction of ethene is very important in industry because the product, ethanol, has many uses. There are two ways in which this hydration is carried out (there is no reaction when ethene is shaken with water).

(a) The ethene is dissolved in concentrated sulphuric acid. The solution is then diluted and distilled and ethanol is given off. The remaining concentrated sulphuric acid can then be used again.

(b) The more modern method consists of passing a mixture of ethene and steam over a suitable catalyst (phosphoric acid absorbed in sand) at 300 °C.

6 The polymerization of ethene

When ethene is mixed with a trace of oxygen and then compressed to very high pressures (above 1000 atmospheres) at about 200 °C, many ethene molecules join together to form fewer but much larger molecules.

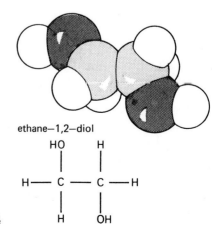

ethane—1,2–diol

Fig. 49.4

49 The alkenes

The joining together of two ethene molecules is shown in Fig. 49.5. After this reaction, the end carbon atoms each have one unpaired electron (because they have formed only three covalent bonds). Further reaction with more ethene molecules can occur at each end, and so on.

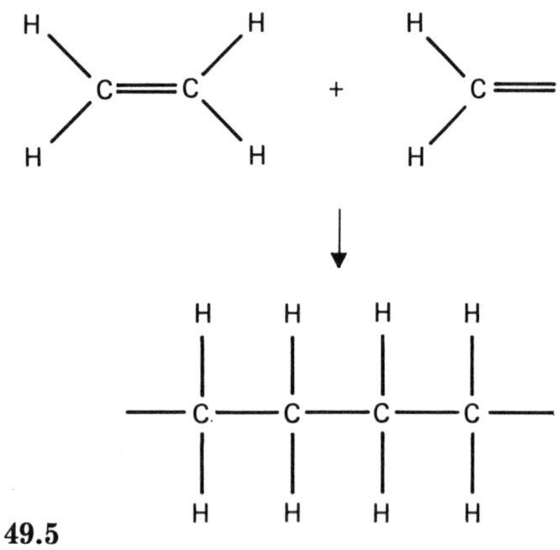

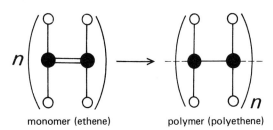

Fig. 49.5

The linking together of many small molecules to form large molecules ('macromolecules') is called **polymerization**. A way of representing the polymerization of ethene is shown in Fig. 49.6.

monomer (ethene)   polymer (polyethene)

(*n* may be several thousand)

Fig. 49.6

The products of polymerization reactions are called **polymers** (many parts). The compounds whose molecules can be linked together to form polymers are called **monomers** (one part).

You should see that the starting material, ethene, is unsaturated but that the product, polyethene, contains no carbon–carbon double bonds and is saturated. So polymerization is a kind of addition reaction in which molecules of the alkene add on to each other. For this reason, the process is often called **addition polymerization**. In theory, the reaction can carry on for ever, forming longer and longer molecules, but this chain-building stops when all the monomer has been used up.

Many compounds containing the $>C=C<$ group in their molecules have been used as monomers and with them, many different polymers have been made by addition polymerization reactions. Some of these polymers are described in Chapter 55.

Testing for unsaturated compounds

Alkanes react with bromine only in bright light. Even then the reactions are slow. But alkenes decolorize dilute aqueous bromine solution fairly quickly. This difference in reactivity towards bromine provides a useful way of distinguishing between saturated compounds and unsaturated compounds which contain carbon–carbon double bonds.

Experiment 49.1 Testing for unsaturated compounds

Your teacher will provide you with dilute aqueous bromine solution and some organic liquids whose molecules contain chains of carbon atoms. To a few drops of each liquid in separate test-tubes, add a few cm^3 of bromine solution. Cork the tube and shake it vigorously. If you do not see a colour change in the two layers straight away, carry on shaking the tube for about a minute.

▶ Decide which liquids are (or contain) unsaturated compounds.

QUESTIONS

1 Compare the reactions of ethane and ethene with bromine. In your answer you should use the terms saturated, unsaturated, addition and substitution, as well as giving the different conditions and equations for the two reactions.

2 Explain why all alkenes have the same empirical formula.

3 (a) Draw a structural formula of propene.
(b) Write the equation for the reaction of propene with bromine and draw the structure of the product.
(c) Use this reaction to help you to explain the terms saturated, unsaturated and addition reaction.

4 (a) Draw the structural formulas of pentane and one of the pentenes.
(b) How is it possible to convert pentene into pentane?
(c) What is the name given to this sort of reaction? Explain why it is important in industry.

5 'Bottled gas' (such as Shellane) is said to contain mainly propane and butane. How would you test it to find out if it contains any unsaturated hydrocarbons?

6 An outline of one way of preparing polyvinyl chloride (PVC) is as follows:

$$CH_2{=}CH_2 \xrightarrow{\text{I}} CH_2ClCH_2Cl$$
ethene   dichloroethane

$$\downarrow \text{II}$$

$$CH_2{=}CHCl \xrightarrow{\text{III}} PVC$$
chloroethene   polychloroethene
(vinyl chloride)

(a) How would you carry out stage I?
(b) What is the name given to stage III?

222

(c) Draw the molecular structure of PVC. (It may help you to draw several molecules of chloroethene to start with.)

(d) Use some of the substances involved to explain the meaning of the terms monomer and polymer.

7 Draw the structural formula of polypropene.

8 A hydrocarbon contains 85.7% carbon by mass and the density of its vapour is $1.83\,\mathrm{g\,l^{-1}}$ at 100° C and 1 atmosphere pressure. (The molar gas volume under these conditions is $30.6\,\mathrm{l\,mol^{-1}}$.)

(a) Calculate its empirical formula.

(b) Calculate its relative molecular mass.

(c) What is its molecular formula?

(d) Draw the structural formulas of two substances which have this molecular formula.

(e) Define the term isomerism. Use your answers to parts (c) and (d) as an example.

Key words

alkene	bromination	polymerization	addition polymerization
unsaturated compounds	hydrogenation	monomer	
addition reactions	hydration	polymer	

Basic facts

- The homologous series of alkenes has the general formula C_nH_{2n} where n can have values 2, 3, 4 and so on.

- The presence of a carbon–carbon double bond in each alkene molecule means that alkenes are unsaturated hydrocarbons.

- Unsaturated hydrocarbons undergo addition reactions.

- The main chemical reactions of the alkenes are bromination, hydrogenation, hydration and polymerization. All these reactions have important industrial applications: hydrogenation in the manufacture of margarine, hydration in the manufacture of ethanol, and polymerization in the manufacture of polymers.

- Unsaturated compounds can be detected by their rapid decolorization of bromine (and acidified potassium manganate(VII)) solution.

50 The naming of carbon compounds

The naming of alkanes

The names of the alkanes are particularly important because the names of a lot of other carbon compounds are derived from them.

You need to know the names and formulas of the first four members of the alkane homologous series: methane CH_4, ethane C_2H_6, propane C_3H_8 and butane C_4H_{10}. A useful way of writing the formula of butane is $CH_3—CH_2—CH_2—CH_3$, since it shows which atoms are connected to each carbon atom. (This is important for many compounds.) The line represents the covalent bond between carbon atoms.

The names of the alkanes with five to ten carbon atoms in their molecules are pentane C_5H_{12}, hexane C_6H_{14}, heptane C_7H_{16}, octane C_8H_{18}, nonane C_9H_{20}, and decane $C_{10}H_{22}$. You do not need to memorize these names. The above names apply only to unbranched chain compounds.

The substance with structural formula

$$CH_3—CH_2—\overset{\overset{\displaystyle H}{|}}{\underset{\underset{\displaystyle CH_3}{|}}{C}}—CH_2—CH_3$$

or $\quad CH_3—CH_2—CH(CH_3)—CH_2—CH_3$

is not called hexane even though there are six carbon atoms in its molecules. It is named from pentane because the longest unbranched chain of carbon atoms in its molecule contains five carbon atoms. The CH_3 group is called methyl (from CH_4, methane). So the name of the compound is 3-methylpentane. The figure '3' shows that the methyl group is attached to the third carbon atom along the C_5 chain.

Q 1 Write the structural formula of 2-methylpentane.
Q 2 Write the structural formula of 4-ethylhexane.

(The answers to the questions are given on page 226.)
The compound with the formula $CH_3—CHCl—CH_3$ is called 2-chloropropane.

Q 3 Draw the structure of 1-chloropropane.
Q 4 What is the name of $CH_3—CHCl—CH_2—CH_3$?

The compound with the formula $CH_3—CCl_2—CH_3$ is called 2,2-dichloropropane while $CH_2Cl—CH_2—CH_2Cl$ is called 1,3-dichloropropane. (Note the comma beween numbers and the hyphen between numbers and letters.)

Q 5 Draw the structure of 1,2-dibromopropane.
Q 6 What is the name of the compound with the formula $CH_2Br—CH_2—CH_2—CH_2Br$?

The naming of alkenes

To name an alkene, think of the alkane which contains the same number of carbon atoms and replace the 'a' in the alkane name with an 'e'.

C_2H_4 is ethene (from C_2H_6, ethane)
C_3H_6 is propene (from C_3H_8, propane)
C_4H_8 is butene (from C_4H_{10}, butane)

Q 7 What is the name of the alkene with formula C_6H_{12}?
Q 8 Write the molecular formula for butene.

There are two isomers of butene, depending on the position of the double bond:

$$\overset{1}{CH_2}{=}\overset{2}{CH}—\overset{3}{CH_2}—\overset{4}{CH_3}$$
$$\text{but-1-ene}$$

$$\overset{1}{CH_3}—\overset{2}{CH}{=}\overset{3}{CH}—\overset{4}{CH_3}$$
$$\text{but-2-ene}$$

To name these isomers, the carbon atoms are numbered and the number in the name refers to the carbon atom preceding the double bond. Note that the name but-3-ene (which is another name for but-1-ene) is not used because the numbers are kept as small as possible and the carbon atoms can be numbered starting from the other end of the carbon chain.

Q 9 What are the names of the following?
  (a) $CH_3—CH_2—CH_2—CH{=}CH_2$
  (b) $CH_3—CH_2—CH{=}CH—CH_3$
  (c) $CH_3—CH{=}CH—CH_2—CH_3$
  (d) $CH_2{=}CH—CH_2—CH_2—CH_3$

Q 10 Draw the structure of 1-bromo-2-chlorobut-2-ene. (Think through the sequence butane, butene, but-2-ene and then put in the halogen atoms.)

The naming of other hydrocarbons

Alkynes

Some compounds contain carbon–carbon triple bonds. The simplest one has the formula $CH{\equiv}CH$ and its name is ethyne. (It used to be called acetylene.) It is the simplest member of the homologous series called the alkynes.

Q 11 What is the general formula of the alkynes?

Cyclic alkanes

There is a compound which has the molecular formula C_6H_{12} and which would appear from its formula to be an alkene. But it shows none of the reactions of the alkenes and behaves like an alkane. Its molecules have a ring structure:

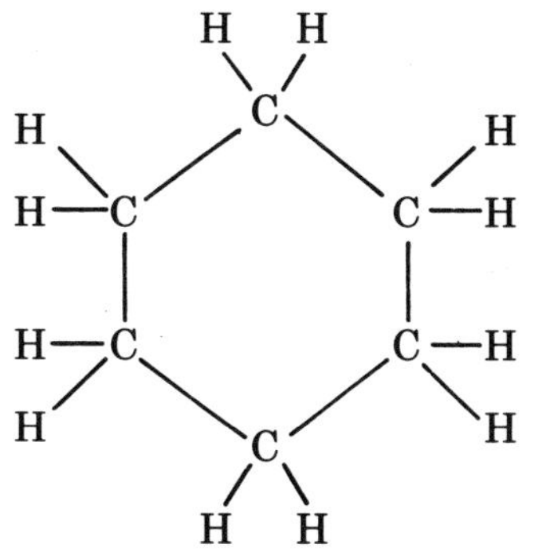

It is called cyclohexane.

Q 12 What is the formula of cyclopentane? Draw its structure.

Q 13 What is the formula of cyclohexene? Draw its structure.

Benzene

Benzene has the molecular formula C_6H_6 and would appear from its formula to be very unsaturated. Although it does show some addition reactions, it most easily undergoes substitution reactions. The atoms in the molecules are arranged in a ring and the molecule can be drawn as:

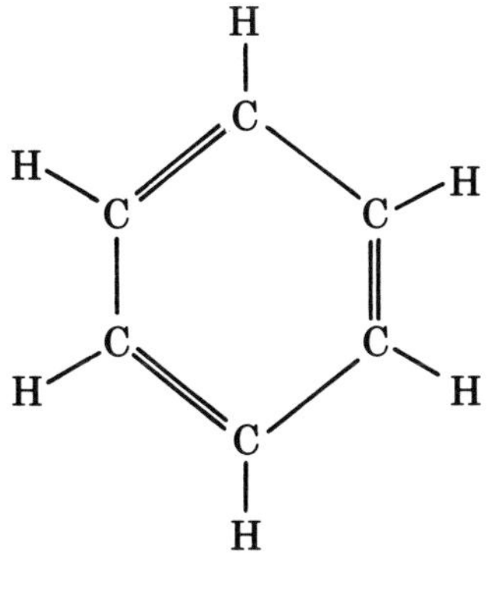

Alternate double and single bonds are necessary for each carbon atom to form four covalent bonds. But this structure is not satisfactory because it suggests that benzene should behave like an alkene. The problem of the structure of benzene troubled chemists for many years. If you carry on to study more advanced chemistry you will learn how the problem has been solved.

The naming of alcohols

This section can be left until you are studying the alcohols (Chapter 52).

The compound CH_3CH_2OH is not called hydroxyethane because the alcohols are sufficiently important to be given special names. The compound with formula CH_3CH_2OH is called ethanol (cross the 'e' off ethane and add 'ol'). It is the second member of the homologous series of alkanols, or alcohols. The ending 'ol' means that an OH group is present in the molecule.

Q 14 Write the name and formula of the first member of the alkanol series.

There are two propanols:
CH_3—CH_2—CH_2OH is called propan-1-ol, and
CH_3—$CHOH$—CH_3 is called propan-2-ol.

Q 15 Draw the structures of:

(a) butan-1-ol and

(b) butan-2-ol.

Q 16 Name the substances with the formulas:

(a) CH_3—CH_2—CH_2—CH_2—CH_2OH

(b) CH_3—CH_2—CH_2—$CHOH$—CH_3

(c) CH_3—CH_2—$CHOH$—CH_2—CH_3

(d) CH_3—$CHOH$—CH_2—CH_2—CH_3

(e) CH_2OH—CH_2—CH_2—CH_2—CH_3

The naming of acids

This section could be left until you are studying the acids (Chapter 53).

The acidic substance in vinegar is usually called acetic acid but its modern name is ethanoic acid. Its formula is CH_3CO_2H. It is called ethanoic acid because its molecules each contain two carbon atoms. The end of the name is obtained by replacing the 'e' of ethane with 'oic'.

Ethanoic acid is the second member of the homologous series of acids:

Q 17 What is the name and formula of the simplest member of the series?

Q 18 What is the name of the compound with the formula CH_3—CH_2—CH_2CO_2H?

Answers to questions

1 $CH_3—CH(CH_3)—CH_2—CH_2—CH_3$

2 $CH_3—CH_2—CH_2—CH(C_2H_5)—CH_2—CH_3$

3 $CH_2Cl—CH_2—CH_3$

4 2-chlorobutane

5 $CH_2Br—CHBr—CH_3$

6 1,4-dibromobutane

7 hexene

8 C_8H_{16}

9 (a) pent-1-ene   (b) pent-2-ene   (c) pent-2-ene
(d) pent-1-ene

10 $CH_2Br—CCl{=}CH—CH_3$

11 C_nH_{2n-2}

12 C_5H_{10}:

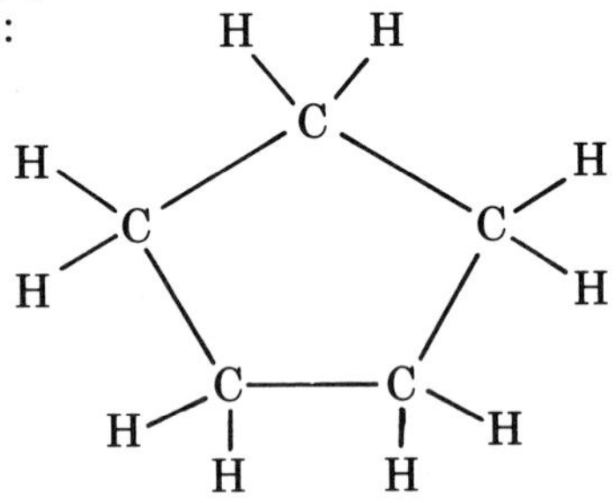

13 C_6H_{10}:

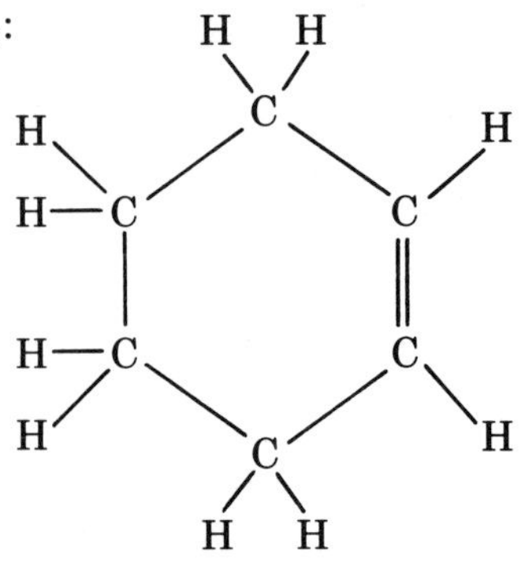

14 methanol, CH_3OH

15 (a) $CH_2OH—CH_2—CH_2—CH_3$
(b) $CH_3—CHOH—CH_2—CH_3$

16 (a) pentan-1-ol
(b) pentan-2-ol
(c) pentan-3-ol
(d) pentan-2-ol
(e) pentan-1-ol

17 methanoic acid, HCO_2H

18 butanoic acid

51 Breaking down carbohydrates

Carbohydrates: some naturally occurring macromolecules

Many compounds which are obtained from plants contain the elements carbon, hydrogen and oxygen, with the hydrogen and oxygen present in the same molar ratio as they are in water. The formulas of these compounds can be written in a general way as $C_x(H_2O)_y$ and they are called **carbohydrates**.

Some examples of these compounds are sugars, such as glucose $C_6H_{12}O_6$ and sucrose $C_{12}H_{22}O_{11}$, starch contained in flour, and cellulose contained in wood, and cotton wool. Starch is composed of some of the largest molecules known: it has a relative molecular mass of about 1×10^6 and its formula can be written as $(C_6H_{10}O_5)_n$ where n can be as large as 6×10^3 (Fig. 51.1). The molecules of cellulose are also very large. Molecules which are very large are frequently called **macromolecules**.

All carbohydrates can be burnt and these reactions are exothermic. Most living things obtain energy from the oxidation of carbohydrates. Athletes sometimes suck glucose tablets before competing, to make sure they have an adequate energy supply.

The complete combustion of carbohydrates breaks them down into carbon dioxide and water. Is it possible to break down carbohydrates in any other way?

Remembering that alkanes can be decomposed by a cracking process, you might suggest that carbohydrates can be broken down by the action of heat in the absence of oxygen.

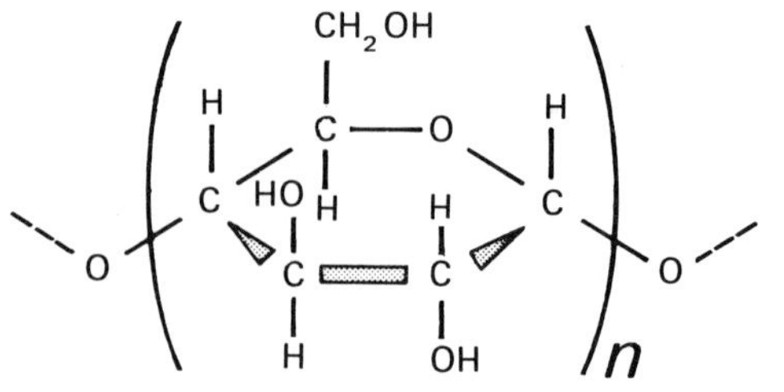

Fig. 51.1 One unit of a starch molecule. Note that each unit consists of a six-membered ring with five carbon atoms and one oxygen atom

Experiment 51.1 What are the products of the thermal decomposition of carbohydrates?

Heat small amounts of the following substances separately in small test-tubes (ignition tubes). Try to identify any gases given off and look at the residue after decomposition is complete.

Substances to use: sucrose (table sugar), glucose, starch, flour, cotton wool.

For carbohydrates there is no process similar to the cracking of the alkanes: instead of the large molecules being broken down into smaller carbohydrate molecules, decomposition goes much further.

The decomposition of organic compounds to leave a residue of carbon is known as **charring**. You may have seen the charring effect of concentrated sulphuric acid on sugar (page 142).

Is it possible to break down the large starch molecules into much smaller molecules of carbohydrates? A clue to the answer to this question is given by digestion in human beings. It is known that during this process starch is converted into sugars, and that the presence of saliva in the mouth is necessary. But before you attempt the breakdown of starch, you should do Experiment 51.2a so that you know how to tell between starch and the so-called reducing sugars, such as glucose and fructose. You should recognize one of the reactions as a test for iodine in aqueous solution.

Experiment 51.2a Testing for starch and sugars

Dissolve a spatula measure of glucose in about 10 cm³ of water and divide the solution into two parts. To one part add a few drops of dilute iodine solution and note the colour. To the other part add a mixture of Fehlings solutions and boil the mixture until a colour change occurs. (To get the correct Fehlings solution mixture, add Fehlings solution B (the colourless one) to Fehlings solution A (the blue one) until the precipitate that forms at first just redissolves.)

Find out whether or not starch solution behaves in the same way as glucose.

Sugars such as glucose and fructose can reduce hot Fehlings solutions to a red precipitate of copper(I) oxide. Starch and non-reducing sugars, such as sucrose, do not react with hot Fehlings solutions. These tests using Fehlings solution and iodine solution are useful ways of recognizing reducing sugars and starch.

Experiment 51.2b Breaking down starch into sugars

1 Using saliva

Half fill a boiling tube with freshly prepared starch solution and put the tube in a beaker of water kept at about 40 °C. Rinse out your mouth with a few cm³ of warm water so as to get a diluted solution of saliva and add the solution to the boiling tube. Stir the solution in the tube with a glass rod to mix the starch with the saliva.

Take out a small sample of the mixture straight away using a dropper, and add two or three drops of it to a tube containing about 1 cm³ of dilute iodine solution. Repeat this every quarter-minute or so and add the drops of the mixture to fresh 1 cm³ samples of iodine solution. Carry on repeating this experiment until no further change occurs in the result of the test. Compare the colours produced at each stage of the reaction. Finally boil some of the final mixture with a mixture of Fehlings solutions.

▶ Decide whether the starch has been broken down into a reducing sugar or a non-reducing sugar.

2 Using acid

Repeat part 1 but raise the temperature of the water-bath to 70 °C and carefully add 5 cm³ of concentrated hydrochloric acid to the starch solution instead of the saliva. Take samples of the mixture at about one-minute intervals and test them as in 1 until no further change happens. Neutralize the final mixture with bench dilute (2 M) sodium hydroxide solution (use litmus paper as an indicator for the neutralization). Then boil this neutralized solution with a mixture of Fehlings solutions.

▶ Decide whether the starch has been broken down into a reducing sugar or a non-reducing sugar.

The breakdown of starch in aqueous solution is called **hydrolysis** (hydro : water; lysis : breakage) because it is being broken down by a reaction with water. But unless there is a catalyst the breakdown occurs at an extremely low rate.

The catalyst in the saliva is an **enzyme** called α-amylase: enzymes are extremely efficient catalysts and their presence in plants and animals is essential if the many natural processes are to take place at the right rate. The catalyst in the second hydrolysis of starch is an acid, that is, H⁺(aq) ions: it is not such an efficient catalyst as α-amylase and a much higher concentration of it is required to give a high rate of hydrolysis. The two kinds of reaction are often called **enzyme-catalysed** hydrolysis and **acid-catalysed** hydrolysis.

Breaking down carbohydrates by fermentation

Can starch be broken down further than to a sugar? It has been known for many centuries that substances containing starch are not just useful as suppliers of carbohydrate, and hence sugars, for the human body. With the help of yeast, they can be changed into alcoholic drinks.

Yeast is a kind of mould that grows naturally on the surface of some fruits, especially grapes. It contains enzymes which can break down sugars. In the absence of oxygen, ethanol is produced and this process is called **fermentation**.

51 Breaking down carbohydrates

Experiment 51.3 Fermenting glucose

Make up a solution of about 5 g of glucose in 50 cm³ of water in a conical flask and add to this a spatula measure of dried yeast. Set up the apparatus shown in Fig. 51.2 and leave it for several days. From time to time, look at the mixture and the limewater.

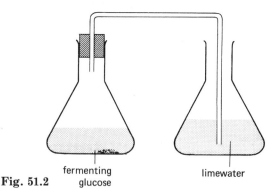

Fig. 51.2   fermenting glucose   limewater

▶ How can you tell that a reaction is taking place?
▶ What is the gas that is given off?
▶ How do you know when the fermentation has stopped?

At the end of the reaction, smell the contents of the flask.

The final mixture contains some ethanol (sometimes known as ethyl alcohol or simply as alcohol). But fermentation forms only dilute solutions of ethanol, with a maximum possible concentration of about 15% by volume.

Your teacher may show you the fractional distillation of the dilute ethanol solution but this experiment also produces a mixture of alcohol and water. The maximum concentration of ethanol you can get in this way is about 95% by volume. If dry ethanol (absolute alcohol) is required, the rest of the water can be removed by using a drying agent such as quicklime.

The molecular formula of ethanol has been found to be C_2H_6O and the equation for the change from glucose to ethanol is

$$C_6H_{12}O_6(aq) \longrightarrow 2C_2H_6O(aq) + 2CO_2(g)$$

Fermentation in action

There are two main steps in the breakdown of the very large starch molecules to ethanol:

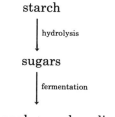

starch

↓ hydrolysis

sugars

↓ fermentation

ethanol + carbon dioxide

The starch is obtained from grain crops such as barley and rice or from root crops such as potatoes. Sugar is used only in tropical countries where sugar cane grows well and sugar is quite cheap (Chapter 60).

Yeasts cannot ferment starch because they do not contain the enzyme that breaks down starch to sugars. So the grain is usually allowed to germinate (sprout). When this happens, enzymes in the seeds catalyse the hydrolysis of the starch to sugars. These sugars would have been used by the growing plant as a supply of energy until it had grown leaves and could carry out photosynthesis for itself. Yeast is added to the germinated grain and this provides the enzymes which catalyse the fermentation of sugars to ethanol.

When sugar is used as the starting material, the yeast is added to a solution of the sugar. Fermentation produces only a low concentration of alcohol (Fig. 51.3) so that the mixture formed can be used

Fig. 51.3 Inside a brewery. The fermentation produces carbon dioxide which makes the liquid froth. The vats are made of stainless steel and have to be kept very clean

only as a beer or wine. For a spirit such as rum, whisky or saki, the dilute solution has to be distilled. The production of rum is discussed on pages 226/7.

When dead animal or vegetable matter decays (rots) in the absence of air, large molecules of carbohydrates are broken down to much smaller molecules by bacteria which provide the necessary enzymes. If the material is kept reasonably warm (at about 30 °C), a lot of methane and carbon dioxide is formed. Fig. 51.4 shows vegetation being loaded into a tank where this sort of decay will occur. The methane can be used as a fuel. Fig. 51.5 shows a tank for storing the gases produced by the decay of vegetable material. This breakdown involves a fermentation step and it has much in common with the breakdown of starch to ethanol.

The several ways in which carbohydrates can be broken down are summarized in Fig. 51.6.

Fig. 51.4

Fig. 51.5

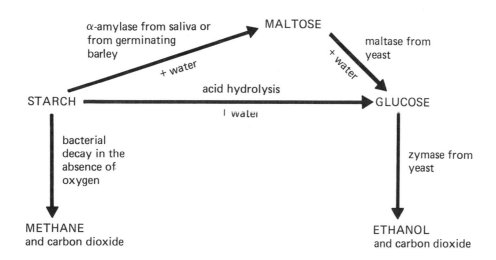

Fig. 51.6

229

QUESTIONS

1 Explain what is meant by the terms (a) carbohydrate, (b) reducing sugar.

How would you distinguish between starch and a reducing sugar (two tests are required)?

2 How would you show that:
(a) maize contains starch but does not contain a reducing sugar;
(b) during germination, the starch in maize is converted into reducing sugars?

Describe how you would produce an alcoholic drink (about the same strength as a beer) starting from maize.

3 Explain what is meant by the terms the acid-catalysed hydrolysis of starch and the enzyme-catalysed hydrolysis of starch. How do the products of these two reactions differ?

4 A solution containing 9.0 g of glucose is fermented. Calculate the maximum mass of ethanol and the maximum volume of carbon dioxide (measured at standard temperature and pressure) that would be formed, assuming that all the glucose reacts.

Key words

carbohydrates   charring   hydrolysis   enzyme-catalysed hydrolysis   fermentation

macromolecules   reducing sugars   enzyme   acid-catalysed hydrolysis

Basic facts

- Carbohydrates (so called because their formulas can be written $C_x(H_2O)_y$) are very important in living things as a source of energy. They burn in air but are charred by heating in the absence of air.

- Hydrolysis is the breakdown of large molecules to small ones by reaction with water.

- Carbohydrates can be hydrolysed to sugars either with α-amylase (which is present in saliva and germinating seeds) or by warming with moderately concentrated acid. The α-amylase hydrolysis produces maltose (a reducing sugar) while the acid hydrolysis produces glucose.

- Starch can be detected by the intense purple (nearly black) colour it produces with iodine.

- Reducing sugars can be detected by boiling them with mixed Fehlings solutions. A red precipitate of copper(I) oxide is formed by this reaction if a reducing sugar is used.

- Fermentation of sugars in the absence of oxygen produces ethanol. The reactions are catalysed by the enzymes produced by yeasts.

- Fermentation produces only a low concentration of ethanol (suitable for wines and beers). Spirits are produced by distillation of the fermented mixture, which increases the alcohol concentration. Pure ethanol can be produced by fractional distillation, which produces about 95% alcohol, followed by drying with calcium oxide.

- Fermentation of vegetable material by bacteria produces methane which can be used as a fuel.

52 Ethanol and the alcohols

The structure of ethanol molecules

Qualitative analysis shows the presence of only carbon and hydrogen in ethanol. Quantitative analysis shows that ethanol contains 52.2% of carbon by mass and 13.0% of hydrogen. The remaining 34.8% must be oxygen (page 212). These results lead to the empirical formula C_2H_6O for ethanol. Since the relative molecular mass of ethanol is 46,

the molecular formula of ethanol is C_2H_6O. (You should work through this calculation for yourself. If you are unsure of any of the steps, refer back to page 212).

How are the carbon, hydrogen and oxygen atoms joined together in ethanol molecules? In other words, what is the structural formula of ethanol molecules? If you try to make a model of a molecule of ethanol using two carbon atoms, six hydrogen atoms, and one oxygen atom, you should find that there are two ways in which these atoms can be arranged. Which one is present in ethanol molecules? Your teacher may show you some of the reactions of ethanol that help to answer this question.

Dry ethanol reacts with sodium giving off hydrogen. A white solid is left that has the formula C_2H_5ONa and is called sodium ethoxide. The equation for the reaction is

$$2C_2H_6O(l) + 2Na(s) \longrightarrow 2C_2H_5ONa(s) + H_2(g)$$

Dry ethanol also reacts with phosphorus pentachloride giving off a mixture of hydrogen chloride and a gas called chloroethane, C_2H_5Cl.

In the reaction of ethanol with sodium, only one of the six hydrogen atoms in the molecule is replaced, while in the reaction with phosphorus pentachloride, the oxygen atom and one hydrogen atom are both replaced at the same time by a chlorine atom. These results can be explained if one of the six hydrogen atoms in an ethanol molecule is bonded differently from the other five. The reaction with phosphorus pentachloride suggests that one of the hydrogen atoms may be bonded to the oxygen atom.

From the results of the above and other experiments, chemists believe that ethanol molecules have the structure shown in Fig. 52.1. The other arrangement of two carbon atoms, six hydrogen atoms and one oxygen atom is present in the molecules of a substance which is isomeric with ethanol.

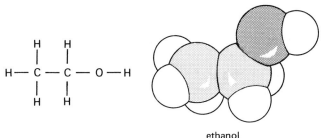

Fig. 52.1

ethanol

Water has some reactions similar to those of ethanol. When water is added a drop at a time to sodium, there is vigorous reaction to form hydrogen and a white solid residue (sodium hydroxide). Water also forms hydrogen chloride when it reacts with phosphorus pentachloride. (This is why the ethanol used in the above experiments has to be dry if the results are to mean anything.) The formulas for water and ethanol can be written as H—OH and C_2H_5—OH and the presence of —OH in each molecule can be used to explain why the reactions of these two liquids with sodium and phosphorus pentachloride are similar.

Ethanol is a member of a homologous series known as the alcohols (sometimes called alkanols). Two other members of this series are methanol (CH_3OH) and propanol (C_3H_7OH). The molecules of all the alcohols contain a carbon chain with an —OH attached: so their formulas may be written as ☐—OH, where ☐ represents the carbon chain. The —OH may be attached at the end of the carbon chain or it may be attached somewhere in the middle. So there are two isomeric alcohols with the formula C_3H_7OH. They are called propan-1-ol and propan-2-ol (page 225).

It has been found that all the alcohols react with sodium and with phosphorus pentachloride in a similar way to ethanol. These reactions can be used as tests for compounds whose molecules contain an —OH group.

The properties of the alcohols are due mainly to the presence of the —OH group in the molecule. The —OH group is called the **functional group** of the alcohols. The functional group of the alkenes is the carbon–carbon double bond.

The reactions of ethanol

1 Oxidation of ethanol

Ethanol burns readily in air and is sometimes used as a fuel. The equation for the complete combustion of ethanol is

$$C_2H_5OH(l) + 3O_2(g) \longrightarrow 2CO_2(g) + 3H_2O(g)$$

Is it possible to oxidize ethanol without breaking down its molecules completely to form carbon dioxide and water?

Experiment 52.1 What is the action of acidified potassium dichromate(VI) solution on ethanol?

Your teacher will provide you with two solutions containing potassium dichromate(VI) and sulphuric acid. The dilute solution contains 25 g $K_2Cr_2O_7$ dissolved in 100 cm³ of 1 M sulphuric acid. The more concentrated solution contains 40 g $K_2Cr_2O_7$ dissolved in 90 cm³ of 1 M sulphuric acid, to which is then added, slowly and carefully, 10 cm³ of concentrated sulphuric acid. This solution must be allowed to cool before it is used.

1. Add 2 cm³ of ethanol a few drops at a time to about 10 cm³ of the more dilute solution containing potassium dichromate(VI) and sulphuric acid in a boiling tube. Warm the tube gently over a low bunsen flame. (CARE: ethanol is a flammable liquid.) Watch for a colour change in the solution, and compare its smell with that of the original ethanol.

2. Add about 2 cm³ of ethanol, a few drops at a time, to about 10 cm³ of the more concentrated solution containing potassium dichromate(VI) and sulphuric

acid in a boiling tube. Add a few pumice grains or a chip of porcelain to this mixture. Assemble one of the pieces of apparatus shown in Fig. 52.2 and gently boil the mixture for about 10 minutes.

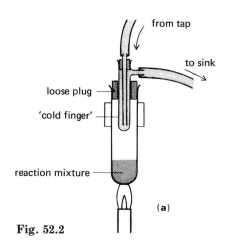
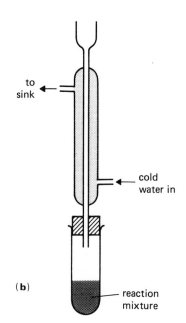

Fig. 52.2

▶ What is the purpose of the 'cold finger' or the condenser?

After the reaction is finished, let the mixture cool and then smell it (do not take a deep breath of it).

The oxidation under the mild conditions of part 1 of this experiment produces a substance called ethanal (acetaldehyde) which has the formula CH_3CHO. This is an oxidation reaction because it involves the loss of two hydrogen atoms from the ethanol molecules.

Under the less mild conditions in part 2 of the experiment, ethanol is oxidized further to form ethanoic acid (acetic acid), which has the formula CH_3CO_2H. Ethanal can also be oxidized to form ethanoic acid. This reaction involves the addition of an atom of oxygen to the ethanal molecule. These reactions are summarized in Fig. 52.3 using diagrams of molecular models.

Many reactions involving organic compounds are slow. One way to speed up these reactions is to heat the reaction mixtures. But if a mixture of ethanol (boiling point 78°C) and oxidizing agent is heated, ethanal (boiling point 21°C) would evaporate before it can be oxidized to ethanoic acid (boiling point 118°C). The apparatus shown in Fig. 52.2 is used to reduce the loss of ethanol and ethanal to the atmosphere. This procedure is called **refluxing**.

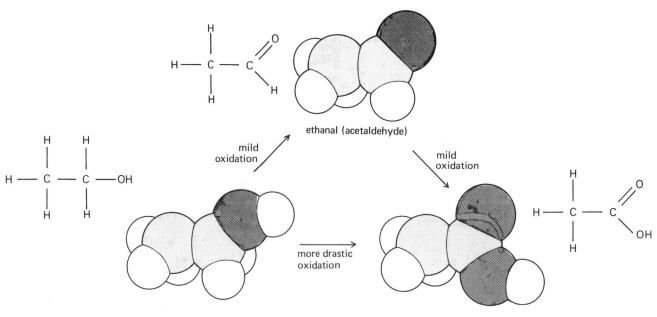

Fig. 52.3   ethanol   ethanoic acid (acetic acid)

Some car owners are foolish enough to drink alcoholic drinks and then drive. Several methods have been invented to find out if drivers have been drinking. One of the first instruments used was the 'Breathalyser'. The driver has to inflate a plastic bag by blowing through a transparent tube which contains potassium dichromate(VI) moistened with sulphuric acid.

If the driver's breath contains ethanol vapour, the orange crystals turn green. The distance that the green colour spreads along the tube measures the concentration of ethanol in the driver's breath and hence in his blood.

In the traditional method of manufacturing vinegar (a very dilute aqueous solution of ethanoic acid), ethanol is oxidized by atmospheric oxygen. Certain bacteria are used to produce an enzyme that catalyses the process: the same reaction occurs when wines go sour.

2 Reacting ethanol with sodium

The apparatus shown in Fig. 52.4 can be used to show that hydrogen is produced when ethanol is added to sodium. The solution left in the tube at the end of the reaction can be evaporated to leave solid sodium ethoxide. The equation for this reaction has already been given (page 231).

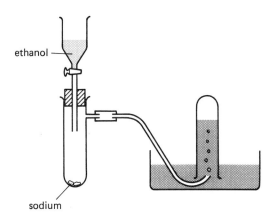

ethanol

sodium

Fig. 52.4

3 The dehydration of ethanol

Experiment 52.2 What happens when ethanol is strongly heated?

The apparatus is the same as that shown in Fig. 48.4. Soak the sand at the bottom of the hard-glass boiling tube with about 2 cm³ of ethanol. Heat the pumice grains or pieces of porcelain, not the sand, very strongly. After the air has been expelled from the apparatus, collect three test-tubes full of the gaseous product and test it as follows.

1. Try to burn the gas.
2. Add about 1 cm³ of dilute bromine solution to a test-tube of the gas, cork the tube and shake it thoroughly. Then open the tube with its mouth under water.
3. Repeat 2 using about 1 cm³ of dilute acidified potassium manganate(VII) solution.

▶ To which homologous series does the product belong?
▶ Remembering that this product is formed by the decomposition of a compound whose molecules contain two carbon atoms, try to decide the formula of the product.

4 The reaction of ethanol with acids to form esters

This type of reaction is described on page 237.

The production and uses of ethanol

There are two important methods for producing ethanol: one is by the fermentation of sugars while the other is the hydration of ethene (page 221).

In many countries, the fermentation method is used only for producing alcoholic drinks. The ethanol that is needed for industrial uses is made from ethene because, at present, ethene is readily available from the petrochemical industry (from the cracking of alkanes).

But as supplies of petroleum become exhausted it is possible that the chemical industry will obtain more of its starting materials from plants. If this happens, ethene could then be prepared by the dehydration of ethanol (that has been produced by fermentation). The reaction would be the reverse of the hydration of ethene and similar to that in Experiment 52.2.

$$CH_3CH_2OH(g) \longrightarrow CH_2{=}CH_2(g) + H_2O(g)$$

Already some countries are producing ethanol by the fermentation of cane sugar for use as a fuel in cars (page 266).

Methylated spirit is ethanol that has been made unfit for drinking by adding methanol (which is very poisonous) and other substances to give it a colour and an unpleasant taste. In this form ethanol is sold without the heavy tax that is applied to alcoholic drinks. It is used widely as a solvent and as a fuel for 'spirit burners'.

Other alcohols

Ethanol is the second member of the homologous series of alcohols (or alkanols). The general formula for the alcohols is $C_nH_{2n+1}OH$.

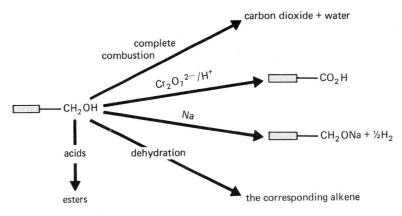

Fig. 52.5

The chemical properties of the alcohols are generally similar to those of ethanol and are summarized in Fig. 52.5. Note that for the reaction with sodium, the functional group is the —OH group. But for the oxidation with potassium dichromate(VI), the functional group is —CH$_2$OH.

QUESTIONS

1 When wood is heated in the absence of air, one of the substances produced is a colourless liquid which contains 37.5% carbon, 12.5% hydrogen and 50.0% oxygen by mass. Its relative molecular mass is between 30 and 35. Its old-fashioned name is 'wood spirit'.

Calculate its empirical formula and its molecular formula. Suggest a structural formula for the compound.

What experiments would you do (and what results would you expect) to confirm your suggested structure?

2 A colourless liquid contains 60.0% carbon, 13.3% hydrogen and 26.7% oxygen by mass. Its relative molecular mass is 60.

(a) Calculate its empirical formula and its molecular formula.

(b) The liquid reacts with sodium to form a white crystalline solid and a flammable gas. Suggest two structural formulas that the compound could have. What are the names of these two compounds?

3 How would you distinguish between water and ethanol using chemical reactions only? Suggest two reactions that could be used.

4 Outline how you could prepare some ethene starting from sugar cane.

5 Explain how a breathalyser works.

6 How does propan-1-ol react :

(a) with sodium;

(b) when boiled with an excess of acidified potassium dichromate(VI) solution in a flask fitted with a 'cold finger' (Fig. 52.2a);

(c) when passed over strongly heated pumice?

For each reaction draw the structural formula of the organic product, and for parts (a) and (c) write balanced equations.

Key words

functional group   refluxing

Basic facts

● **There are two isomers with the molecular formula C$_2$H$_6$O. The structural formula of ethanol is decided by examining its reaction.**

● **The main chemical reactions of the alcohols are combustion, oxidation to acids, reaction with sodium, dehydration and ester formation.**

● **Alcohols can be prepared by the hydration of alkenes.**

● **The main everyday uses of ethanol are as a solvent, as a fuel and in alcoholic drinks.**

53 Ethanoic acid

The alkanoic acids

The functional group of the **alkanoic acids** is the **carboxyl group**:

$$-C\!\!\diagup\!\!\!\!\!\!\!\diagdown\!\!\begin{array}{c}O\\O\!-\!H\end{array} \quad \text{or} \quad -CO_2H$$

Older names for the alkanoic acids are the *fatty acids* (because some of them can be obtained from fats) or the carboxylic acids.

The acids are named from the *total* number of carbon atoms that their molecules contain, so that $C_2H_5CO_2H$ is called propanoic acid (page 225).

Methanoic acid, HCO_2H, occurs in certain stinging plants such as nettles and also in ants. It was first obtained by distilling ground-up ants and its old name, formic acid, is derived from the Latin for ant. Vinegar is a dilute solution of ethanoic acid (acetic acid). Pure ethanoic acid is often called 'glacial acetic acid' because it readily solidifies in cold climates (melting point 17 °C). Butanoic acid, $C_3H_7CO_2H$ is formed when butter goes rancid and is responsible for the smell of rancid butter.

The acidic properties of ethanoic acid

The reactions of acids are discussed in Chapters 23 and 24. Is ethanoic acid a typical acid? In some of the following reactions, ethanoic acid is compared with hydrochloric acid. To make the comparison, the two acids should have the same concentration in $mol\,l^{-1}$.

Experiment 53.1

1 Taste

The sharp taste of vinegar is due to the ethanoic acid it contains. (On no account should you taste hydrochloric acid.)

2 pH value

Use a universal indicator paper to get a rough idea of the pH value of 2 M ethanoic acid solution. Then use the appropriate narrow-range indicator paper to measure the pH value more accurately. Repeat the experiment using 2 M hydrochloric acid.

3 Reaction with magnesium

Put equal volumes of hydrochloric acid and ethanoic acids into separate test-tubes (a 2 to 3 cm depth is sufficient). Then add similarly sized strips of magnesium ribbon to each.

▸ Test any gases given off.
▸ Which reaction is faster?
▸ Are the two reactions equally exothermic? (Judge this by feeling the two test-tubes during the reactions.)

4 Neutralization with sodium hydroxide solution

Using a 25 cm³ measuring cylinder, measure 20 cm³ of 2 M ethanoic acid into a beaker and add a few drops of universal indicator solution. Rinse the measuring cylinder and pour into it 25 cm³ of 2 M sodium hydroxide solution. Add the alkali to the acid and estimate the volume needed to produce a neutral solution. Repeat the experiment using 2 M hydrochloric acid instead of the ethanoic acid.

▸ Compare the volumes of alkali required to neutralize the same amounts of the two acids. Try to explain your results.

5 Reaction with copper(II) oxide

Pour about 25 cm³ of 2 M ethanoic acid into a 100 cm³ beaker and add a small amount of copper(II) oxide. If no reaction occurs, warm the mixture.

▸ What are the two observations which mean that a reaction is happening?

Repeat the experiment using 2 M hydrochloric acid.

6 Reaction with sodium carbonate

The procedure is the same as for part 5, but sodium carbonate is used instead of copper(II) oxide. Test any gas given off.

7 Assemble the circuit shown in Fig. 8.2 on page 25

Immerse the electrodes in 2 M hydrochloric acid, rinse them and then immerse them to the same depth in 2 M ethanoic acid.

▸ Which acid is the better conductor? Try to explain this result.
▸ Why should the electrodes be immersed to the same depth in both solutions?

Enter your results into a table so that it is easy to compare the reactions of the two acids. Try to explain the similarities between the two acids and also try to explain the differences. Write equations for the reactions that have occurred. You may need to refer to Chapter 24 to explain some of the results.

Other reactions of ethanoic acid

1 Oxidation

Ethanoic acid is prepared by refluxing ethanol with an excess of a powerful oxidizing agent (Experiment 52.1). So it is not easy to oxidize ethanoic acid. But your teacher may show you that pure ethanoic acid (glacial acetic acid) will burn. The equation for its complete combustion is

$$CH_3CO_2H(l) + 2O_2(g) \longrightarrow 2CO_2(g) + 2H_2O(g)$$

2 Reaction with ethanol

Experiment 53.2

Mix about $2\,cm^3$ of ethanol with about $3\,cm^3$ of pure ethanoic acid in a boiling tube. Then add five drops of concentrated sulphuric acid, one drop at a time, shaking the mixture between each addition.
CARE: the reaction of concentrated sulphuric acid and ethanol is very exothermic.
  Gently warm the mixture but do not boil it.
CARE: ethanol is very flammable. Let the mixture cool and then slowly pour it into about $50\,cm^3$ of water in a small beaker. Stir the mixture and then smell the product just enough for you to recognize it. You should not breathe in the gas deeply because it is addictive. The product is ethyl ethanoate, $CH_3CO_2C_2H_5$. It is an example of an **ester** (page 237).

3 Reaction with ammonia

When ethanoic acid reacts with either aqueous or gaseous ammonia, the salt ammonium ethanoate is produced.

$$NH_3(aq) + CH_3CO_2H(l) \longrightarrow CH_3CO_2NH_4(s)$$

If ammonium ethanoate is heated, there are two possible reactions that can occur.

$CH_3CO_2NH_4(s) \longrightarrow$
either $\longrightarrow CH_3CO_2H(l) + NH_3(g)$
or $\longrightarrow CH_3CONH_2(s) + H_2O(g)$
ethanamide

To produce ethanamide from ammonium ethanoate it is necessary to prevent the decomposition to ammonia and ethanoic acid. This can be done by heating ammonium ethanoate with pure ethanoic acid.

The structure of ethanamide is

$$CH_3-C\diagup^{\displaystyle O}_{\diagdown NH_2}$$

It is an example of the compounds known as **acid amides**.

QUESTIONS

1 (a) Name the acid that has the formula $C_4H_9CO_2H$.
  Write the formulas of the following compounds: (b) methanoic acid, (c) butanoic acid, (d) sodium propanoate, (e) copper ethanoate, (f) magnesium ethanoate.

2 Why is it safe to use vinegar on food while it would be dangerous to use very dilute hydrochloric acid for the same purpose?

3 Explain the meaning of the terms strong acid and weak acid. In your answer, refer to the following properties of ethanoic acid and hydrochloric acid: pH value, reaction with magnesium, and ability to conduct electricity.

4 Explain how you could prepare some propanoic acid from propan-1-ol. Draw the structural formulas of the organic compounds.

5 How would you prepare a small amount of ethyl propanoate? Draw the structural formulas of the organic compounds and write an equation for the reaction.

6 An organic acid has the composition 2.2% hydrogen, 26.7% carbon and 71.1% oxygen by mass. Its relative molecular mass is 90.
(a) Calculate its empirical formula.
(b) What is its molecular formula?
  A solution of the acid contains $9.0\,g\,l^{-1}$. $10\,cm^3$ of this solution required $20\,cm^3$ of $0.10\,M$ sodium hydroxide solution for neutralization using phenolphthalein as indicator.
(c) How many moles of the acid were used in the titration?
(d) How many moles of NaOH were required for neutralization?
(e) Write the equation for the neutralization reaction.
(f) What is the basicity of the acid? Draw its structural formula.

Key words

alkanoic acids   carboxyl group   weak acid   strong acid   ester   acid amide

Basic facts

- The alkanoic acids contain the functional group $-CO_2H$.

- Ethanoic acid shows all the reactions of a typical acid but it is a weak acid.

- Ethanoic acid is flammable, it reacts with ethanol to form an ester and with ammonia to form ethanamide.

54 Esters

Ethyl ethanoate

A small amount of ethyl ethanoate is prepared in Experiment 53.2. Ethyl ethanoate is a member of the homologous series of **esters**. The reaction of an acid with an alcohol (alkanol) to form an ester is called **esterification**.

Ethyl ethanoate is a very good solvent and it is used in industry for this purpose and also in glues and varnishes. (Nail varnish and nail varnish remover normally contain ethyl ethanoate.) Unfortunately it is addictive and wherever possible it is being replaced by other non-addictive solvents.

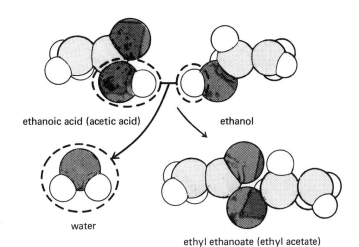

Fig. 54.1

The equation for the reaction of ethanol and ethanoic acid is shown in Fig. 54.1. This reaction is very slow and is also reversible. It can be speeded up by adding an acid because esterification reactions are catalysed by acids. To get a good yield of ethyl ethanoate, it is necessary to prevent the water from reacting with the ester.

In Experiment 53.2, the concentrated sulphuric acid has two effects:

1. It catalyses the reaction and so makes it go faster.
2. It reacts with the water formed and so favours the reaction to the right.

Even then the reaction cannot be described as fast. The reaction mixture would have to be refluxed for half an hour or so to get a reasonable yield of ester.

At the end of Experiment 53.2 the reaction mixture is added to water. Everything in the reaction mixture except the ethyl ethanoate is soluble in water. Since the ester is less dense than water, it floats and its smell can be detected easily.

Esters

Any alkanoic acid will react with any alcohol (alkanol) to form an ester. The general equation for these esterification reactions can be written

Because this reaction is reversible, esters can be hydrolysed (page 227). But aqueous hydrolysis (boiling them with water) is a very slow process. The **hydrolysis of an ester** is catalysed by acids, but the most effective way to hydrolyse an ester is to boil it

237

with a strong alkali. The equation for the reaction of ethyl ethanoate with sodium hydroxide is

$$CH_3CO_2C_2H_5(l) + OH^-(aq)$$
$$\longrightarrow CH_3CO_2^-(aq) + C_2H_5OH(aq)$$

The general equation for the hydrolysis of an ester can be represented

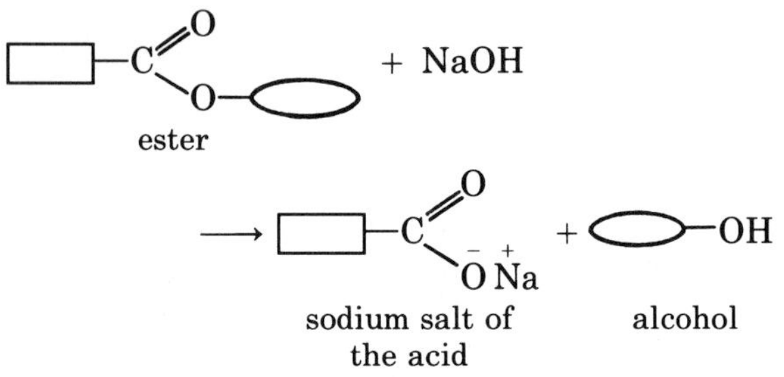

ester

sodium salt of   alcohol
the acid

Naturally occurring esters

Many esters occur naturally in plants and are partly responsible for the smells of flowers and fruits. Ethyl methanoate can be used as an artificial rum flavouring and ethyl butanoate is used in pineapple essence.

Commercially, the most important naturally occurring esters are vegetable **oils** and animal **fats**. These are esters of the alcohol propane-1,2,3-triol (glycerol or glycerine) which has the structural formula shown here:

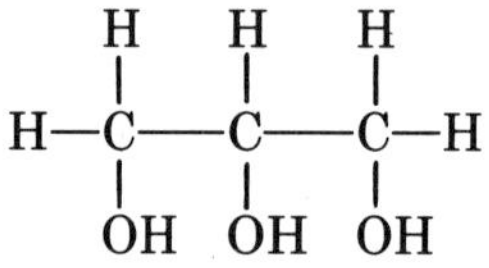

Three of the many acids which occur in these esters are:

octadecanoic acid (stearic acid) $C_{17}H_{35}CO_2H$
hexadecanoic acid (palmitic acid) $C_{15}H_{31}CO_2H$,
octadecenoic acid (oleic acid) $C_{17}H_{33}CO_2H$.

Palmitic acid can be obtained from the esters present in palm oil and oleic acid from the esters in olive oil. Note that while the first two acids are saturated, the third one is unsaturated.

The esters obtained from fats and oils consist of propane-1,2,3-triol (glycerol) molecules which have formed ester linkages with three acid molecules. Their structures are represented in Fig. 54.2.

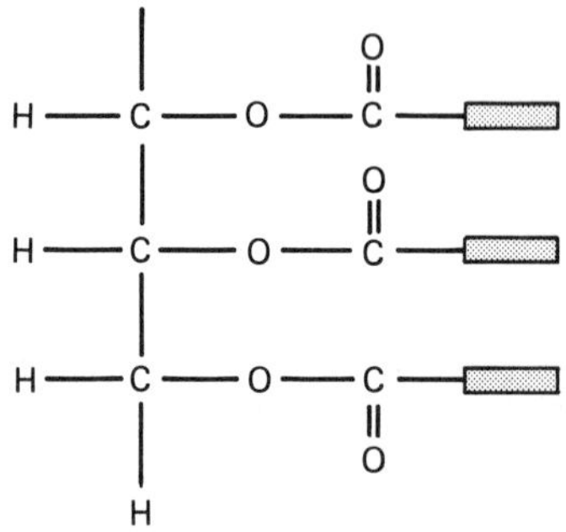

Fig. 54.2

The melting points of oils are lower than those of fats. Fats are solid at room temperature but liquid at body temperature, while oils are liquid at room temperature. It is found that the acids that are present in the esters in *fats* are mainly *saturated*. But the acids that are present in the esters in *oils* are mainly *unsaturated*. So the melting points of these esters depend on whether the acid parts of the esters are saturated or unsaturated.

The manufacture of margarine

Butter is made from the fat in milk. Foods produced from animals are more expensive than equivalent foods from plants. So it would be cheaper to use vegetable oils instead of butter. And unsaturated vegetable oils are generally thought to be less harmful to our health than saturated animal fats.

Margarine is made by hydrogenating (page 221) unsaturated vegetable oils. As the unsaturated oil becomes saturated, its melting point rises. This process, which is called the hardening of oils, can be summarized

Vegetable oil which is liquid at room temperature because it is unsaturated	$\xrightarrow[\text{nickel at about 150 °C}]{\text{Hydrogen}\atop\text{in the presence of}}$	Hydrogenated oil which is solid at room temperature because it is partly saturated

The hydrogenation is continued until the product has the required melting point. It is then coloured and flavoured, and other additives such as vitamins are put in to produce margarine.

The manufacture of soap

The hydrolysis of fats and oils with sodium hydroxide is important because it produces **soap**. If the fat or oil contains the ester of glycerol (propane-1,2,3-triol) and stearic acid (octadecanoic acid), the reaction can be represented as follows.

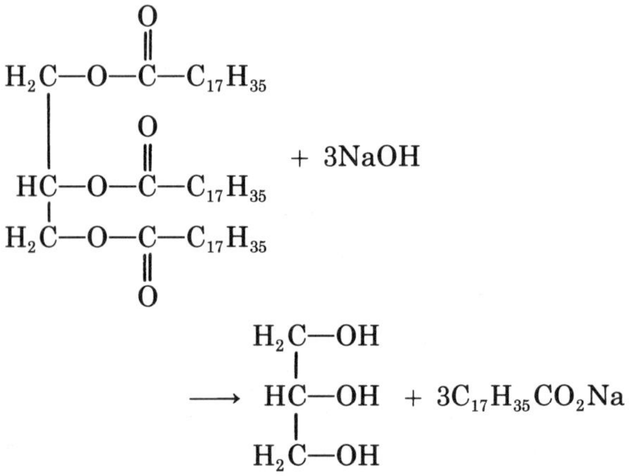

The sodium salt of stearic acid (sodium stearate or sodium octadecanoate) is the soap. Reactions like this which produce soap are called **saponification** reactions.

Experiment 54.1. The saponification of a vegetable oil

Into a 100 cm³ beaker pour about 25 cm³ of 2 M sodium hydroxide solution and about 2 cm³ of a vegetable oil. Add a piece of broken porcelain (to help the mixture boil smoothly) and gently boil the mixture until all the oily layer has disappeared. (All the oil has then been hydrolysed.)

Then add about two or three spatula measures of sodium chloride, stir the mixture to dissolve the salt and allow it to cool. The solid that separates is soap. (Soap is moderately soluble in water but is less soluble in salt solution.)

Filter the mixture using vacuum filtration and wash the soap on the filter paper with about 10 cm³ of salt solution.

The soap will probably be very alkaline because it still contains sodium hydroxide. If you want to wash your hands with it, you must first purify it.

Scrape the solid into a 100 cm³ beaker, add about 50 cm³ of water and boil the mixture to dissolve the soap. Then add salt and cool and filter as before to obtain the purified soap.

Soaps and synthetic detergents

The cleansing action of soap is due to the nature of its molecules. They can be described as a fairly long carbon chain with an ionic end, e.g.

$$CH_3(CH_2)_{16}CO_2^-Na^+$$

Other molecules with this sort of composition will also have cleansing or **detergent** properties.

Both animal fats and vegetable oils are important as foods, so other sources of cleansing agents have been found.

Many soapless detergents are now produced from some of the products of the petrochemical industry. A very common soapless detergent has the structure

$$CH_3(CH_2)_{11}\!-\!\!\left\langle\!\!\bigcirc\!\!\right\rangle\!\!-\!SO_3^-Na^+$$

(The hexagon with a circle represents a benzene ring.) This detergent is made by reacting together dodecene ($C_{12}H_{24}$) and benzene and then reacting the product with concentrated sulphuric acid. Neutralization of this product with sodium hydroxide produces the soapless detergent.

Soapy detergents have some disadvantages: they are expensive, in hard water they do not lather well and they form a scum. Soapless detergents have none of these disadvantages. The first soapless detergents to be produced were made from alkenes whose molecules contain side-chains. The resultant detergents could not be broken down by bacteria and so they polluted rivers and caused foaming (Fig. 54.3).

Fig. 54.3

More recent detergents are made from alkenes whose molecules have unbranched chains. These can be broken down by bacteria and so do not cause pollution.

Many detergents contain phosphates which help the detergent to work effectively. The presence of phosphates can cause pollution in rivers and lakes (page 134).

QUESTIONS

1 Write the equation for the formation of the following esters, using structural formulas:
(a) ethyl propanoate   (b) propyl ethanoate
(c) methyl ethanoate   (d) ethyl methanoate

2 The reaction between an acid and an alcohol to form an ester is slow and reversible.

(*a*) What is meant by the term reversible? Why is this reaction slow?

(*b*) Explain why concentrated sulphuric acid is frequently used in the laboratory preparation of esters.

(*c*) Esterification is sometimes carried out by passing gaseous hydrogen chloride into a refluxing mixture of the acid and alcohol. Explain the action of the hydrogen chloride.

3 (*a*) Explain what is meant by the saponification of ethyl ethanoate with sodium hydroxide. Write the equation for the reaction using structural formulas.

(*b*) Explain how you would separate samples of ethanol and sodium ethanoate from the final reaction mixture.

4 Collect a wide variety of margarine packets and cooking oil bottles. Make a list of the ingredients of these two foodstuffs.

(*a*) Try to find out what the ingredients are made from.

(*b*) Are they made from plants or animals? How does this affect their price?

(*c*) How could the use of margarine and cooking oil rather than butter and the traditional cooking fat affect our health?

5 How is margarine manufactured? Explain the chemistry of this process.

6 Explain the production of soap from glyceryl tristearate (propane-1,2,3-trioctadecanoate), including the separation and purification of the soap.

Key words

esters	hydrolysis of esters	fats and oils	detergents
esterification	saponification	soap	soapless detergents

Basic facts

- There is a homologous series of esters. Their general formula can be represented as RCO_2R', where R and R′ are alkyl groups such as CH_3, C_2H_5, etc.

- The esterification reaction between an acid and an alcohol is slow and reversible. The addition of concentrated sulphuric acid to the reaction mixture speeds up the reaction and also tends to make it irreversible.

- Ethyl ethanoate is a very useful solvent but is addictive.

- Esters can be hydrolysed to form acids and alcohols. Aqueous hydrolysis is very slow but alkaline hydrolysis, saponification, is much faster and also irreversible.

- Esters occur widely in nature. The most important ones (for an industrial chemist) are the fats and oils which are esters of propane-1,2,3-triol and various acids.

- The acid parts of the esters in fats are mainly saturated, while in oils they are mainly unsaturated.

- Margarine is made by the hydrogenation of unsaturated oils.

- Soapy detergents are made by the alkaline hydrolysis (saponification) of fats and oils.

- Soapless detergents are made from products of the petrochemical industry. The use of soapless detergents poses some pollution problems, not all of which have been solved.

55 Some natural and synthetic polymers

Polymers

Polymers are formed by the **polymerization** of **monomers**. One example is the formation of poly-ethene (polythene) from ethene (page 222).

Some naturally occurring polymers are very important in living processes. Starch, cellulose and proteins are all polymers. Synthetic polymers are becoming more and more important in everyday life.

Polysaccharides

Glucose is a **monosaccharide** because it cannot be broken down into simpler sugars. Its molecular formula is $C_6H_{12}O_6$ and its structural formula is given in Fig. 55.1. Fructose has the same molecular formula as glucose but a different structural formula and so is isomeric with it.

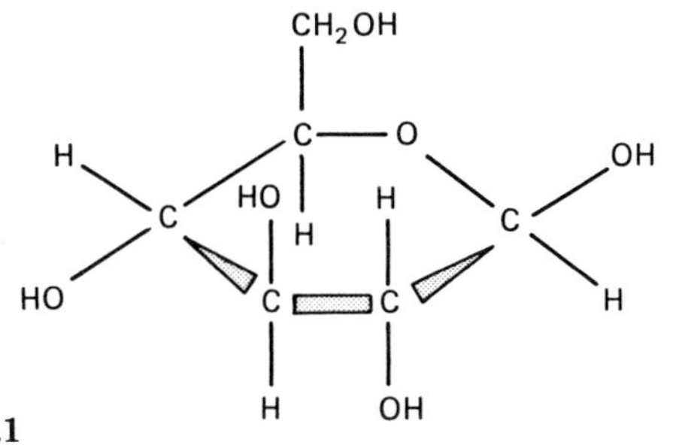

Fig. 55.1

The sugar that is obtained from sugar cane and sugar beet is called sucrose. Its molecular formula is $C_{12}H_{22}O_{11}$. When it is warmed with an acid or treated with yeast, the sucrose molecules are broken down.

$$C_{12}H_{22}O_{11}(aq) + H_2O(l) \xrightarrow[\substack{\text{or} \\ \text{add yeast which} \\ \text{provides the} \\ \text{enzyme sucrase}}]{\substack{\text{either} \\ \text{warm with acid}}} \begin{array}{c} C_6H_{12}O_6(aq) \\ \text{glucose} \\ + \\ C_6H_{12}O_6(aq) \\ \text{fructose} \end{array}$$

Because sucrose molecules can be broken down to give two simpler sugar molecules, sucrose is called a **disaccharide**. The hydrolysis of sucrose produces a mixture of the two isomeric sugars, glucose and fructose.

Starch (page 226) and cellulose are both poly-saccharides. When they are hydrolysed only one monosaccharide, glucose, is produced. Glucose is the monomer of both of these polymers. The way in which glucose molecules are joined together in starch molecules is shown in Fig. 51.1 on page 226.

Plants produce simple sugars such as glucose by photosynthesis (page 111). The simple sugars are then polymerized to produce polysaccharides. To produce a polymer such as starch (page 226), many glucose molecules are joined together. This joining involves two of the —OH groups in each glucose molecule, while the rest of each glucose molecule remains unchanged. If a glucose molecule is represented as HO—X—OH, the formation of starch can be shown in the following way.

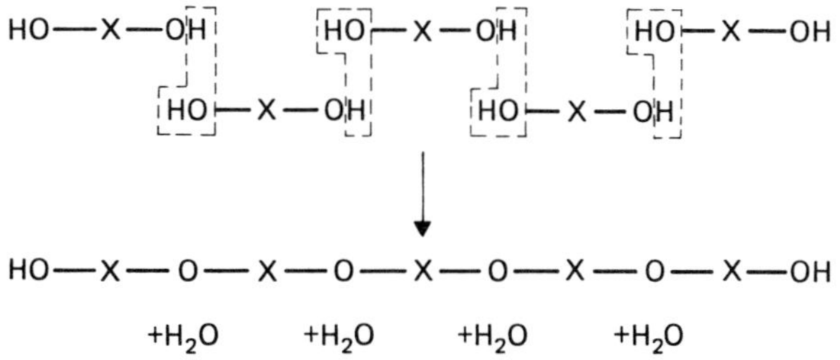

Further reaction can take place at each end of the molecule produced.

The reaction that occurs in this polymerization is a **condensation** reaction: the joining together of two molecules with the elimination of a small molecule, such as a water molecule. So this is an example of condensation polymerization.

In most plants, the simple sugars produced by photosynthesis are used in one of three main ways.

1. As a source of energy for the plant.
2. As a food store (starch) for the following year's seeds.
3. To produce cellulose which provides the mechanical strength of the plant.

Sugar cane and sugar beet are unusual in that they contain high proportions of the disaccharide sucrose.

Proteins

Proteins are substances required for the building up and repair of all plant and animal tissue. They contain the elements carbon, hydrogen, oxygen, nitrogen and occasionally sulphur. The nitrogen cycle (page 134) shows how nitrogen is exchanged between the atmosphere, the soil, plants and animals.

All proteins consist of macromolecules and include the most complex substances known. One of the simplest proteins is insulin, which has a relative molecular mass of about 6000, while some of the more complex proteins have relative molecular masses of several millions. Enzymes, the biological catalysts, are very complex proteins.

Proteins can be broken down either by hydrolysis with an acid or by treating them with suitable enzymes. (Some detergents contain enzymes which break down proteins and can therefore remove marks due to protein, such as blood stains.)

The end-products of this protein breakdown are **amino acids**. These are compounds whose molecules contain $-NH_2$ (amino) groups as well as $-CO_2H$ groups. An amino acid molecule can be represented as in Fig. 55.2. Amino acids are the monomers from which proteins are made.

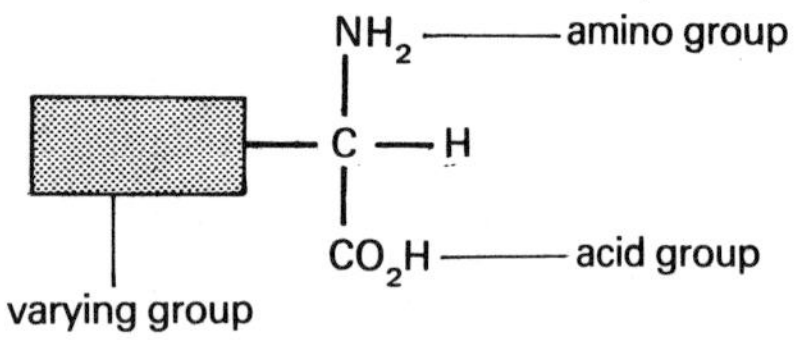

Fig. 55.2

The simplest amino acid is glycine or amino-ethanoic acid, $H_2N-CH_2-CO_2H$. Over twenty different amino acids have been obtained from proteins and, usually, in any one protein molecule there are several hundreds of amino acid units. Thus the number of different protein molecules is very large indeed. The breakdown of proteins to form amino acids can be represented as shown in Fig. 55.3.

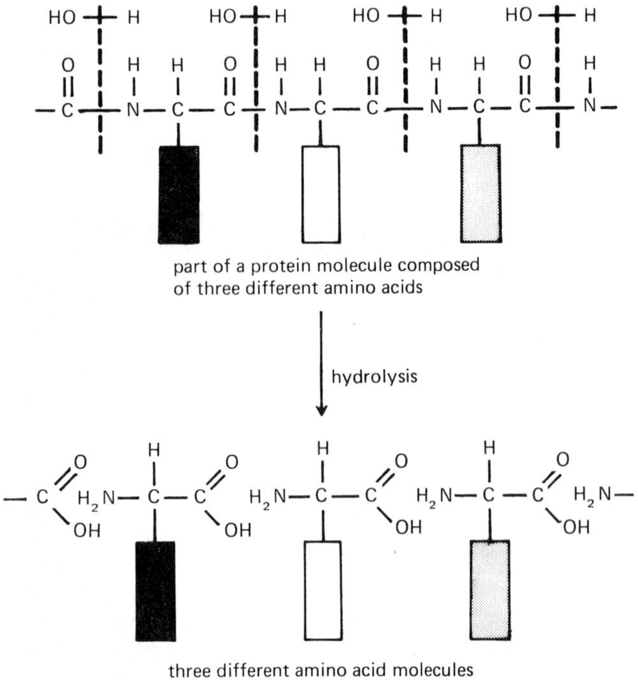

part of a protein molecule composed of three different amino acids

↓ hydrolysis

three different amino acid molecules

Fig. 55.3

When animals eat a food containing protein, digestion breaks down the protein into amino acids using enzymes in the digestive juices. The amino acids are

then reassembled in the correct order to produce the protein that the animal requires. The build-up of proteins from amino acids is another example of condensation polymerization.

The first step in working out the structure of a protein is to identify the amino acids present in the protein. After the protein has been hydrolysed, the best way to separate and identify the amino acids is by chromatography. A piece of filter paper is spotted with the mixture of amino acids and a suitable solvent is then allowed to soak through the paper and to carry the mixture across the paper. The amino acids are separated because each one sticks to the paper to a different extent and also has a different solubility in the solvent. Thus an amino acid that is very soluble in the solvent and 'sticks' to the paper very weakly moves a long way across the paper. But an amino acid that is not very soluble in the solvent and 'sticks' well to the paper moves only a short way.

A result of this sort of analysis of the amino acids from casein (the protein of milk) is shown in Fig. 55.4. This shows that the amino acids lysine, leucine and valine are present in the hydrolysed casein mixture, but other amino acids are also present which have not been identified. In fact casein is composed of seventeen different amino acids.

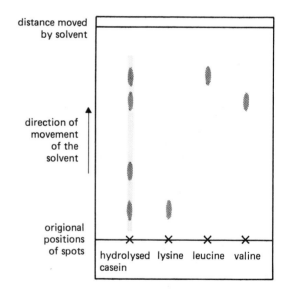

Fig. 55.4

The $-C\overset{O}{\underset{N-}{\diagdown}}$ group linking amino acids in protein macromolecules is called the **amide group** (page 236), so that proteins can be referred to as **polyamides**. The traditional name for this group is the peptide group so proteins are frequently called **polypeptides**.

Polyalkenes

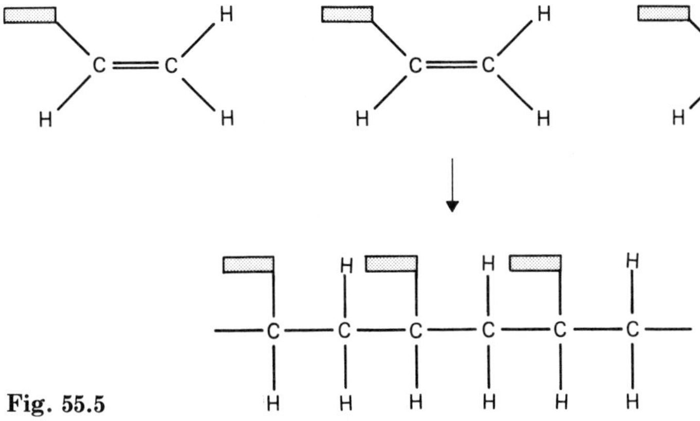

Fig. 55.5

The polymerization of ethene produces polyethene (polyethene) (page 222). Other alkenes can also be polymerized.

The polymerization of the alkene is shown diagrammatically in Fig. 55.5. Further reaction can occur at both ends of the chain.

Polythene (polyethene) was first manufactured in 1939 and is nowadays the most common synthetic polymer. It is easily coloured and can be rolled into thin sheets which are used for wrapping and for making 'plastic bags'. It can also be moulded and blown easily and is used for making washing-up bowls and squeezy bottles. It is strong enough to be used for crates for beer bottles.

The objects shown in Fig. 55.6 are all made from polythene. Different materials were used to make these objects before polythene was invented. Polythene has several advantages over these older materials: it is relatively cheap to produce, but the lower cost of using polythene is only one advantage and you should be able to think of others.

Propene can be polymerized to form polypropene (polypropylene). Its properties are similar to those of polythene, but it is less dense, stronger and softens at a higher temperature than polythene. The polymerization of propene is represented by replacing the rectangles in Fig. 55.5 with methyl groups, CH_3-.

Phenylethene has the formula

and its common name is styrene. When polymerized, it produces polystyrene. The main uses of expanded polystyrene are as a heat insulator and as a packaging material (Fig. 55.7). You should try to decide what special properties of expanded polystyrene make it suitable for these uses.

Fig. 55.6

Fig. 55.7

The common name for chloroethene, $CH_2{=}CHCl$, is vinylchloride. When polymerized, it produces polychloroethene, or polyvinylchloride, P.V.C. The properties of this very useful polymer can be varied by including a variety of additives. It is stronger than polythene, is a very good electrical insulator, is resistant to fire and chemical attack and can be easily coloured. It is used for coating material to make it weatherproof, for covering wires and cables and for making music records. It can be made to look and feel like leather and is used for artificial leather in upholstery and clothes. It is also used to make floor coverings, curtains and table cloths, because it can be wiped clean easily.

Tetrafluoroethene, $CF_2{=}CF_2$ can be polymerized to produce polytetrafluoroethene, P.T.F.E. or Teflon. This polymer has a remarkable set of properties: it is very resistant to chemical attack and is stable up to temperatures over 300 °C (most other polyalkenes melt at temperatures well below this), it is an extremely good electrical insulator; its surface has a very low coefficient of friction which means that other substances tend not to stick to it. The one disadvantage of this polymer is that it is expensive. Its best-known everyday use, for coating cooking pans, makes use of its non-stick property and stability to heat.

All these polyalkenes become soft when they are warmed because the long-chain molecules are not strongly fixed to each other. They harden again on cooling. This change is reversible and these polymers are said to be **thermoplastic**.

There are other polymers which set solid when they are heated and the change is irreversible. These are called **thermosetting** polymers. Two examples are Bakelite and Formica. On heating, the long-chain molecules react together and links are formed between the molecules which stop the molecules moving past one another (Fig. 55.8).

Rubber is a naturally occurring polymer which is made using the latex from rubber trees (Fig. 55.9). The long-chain molecules of rubber contain double bonds. When rubber is heated with sulphur, the sulphur atoms can react with the $>C{=}C<$ groups in adjacent chains to form links between the chains. When this is done, the molecules can no longer slide past one another easily and the rubber becomes harder. This process is called **vulcanization**.

Oxidation by oxygen in the air can cause rubber to become hard and brittle so that it easily cracks. Nowadays, P.V.C. is often used to insulate cables because it does not harden and then crack in air.

Some synthetic rubbers have been made which are more useful than natural rubber. Neoprene rubber is less flammable, more heat resistant and less affected by oils and greases than natural rubbers.

Natural fibres

Wool and silk, which are derived from animals, are both proteins. Cotton and hemp, which are derived from plants, are both polysaccharides and are made of cellulose.

In the manufacture of paper, wood is broken down to free the individual fibres of cellulose, which are then compacted together in a layer to form paper.

The first artificial fibre was made by dissolving cellulose in a solvent and then squirting the solution through fine jets into a liquid which precipitates the cellulose. The resultant fibre is known as rayon.

The synthetic fibres (see the next two sections) are often cheaper to produce than natural fibres and have better washing and wearing properties. But the aim of the producers is to make fibres that resemble the natural fibres (wool, silk and cotton) as closely as possible both in appearance and how they feel when worn. (Many artificial fibres do not absorb moisture, so that clothes made of them easily feel sweaty.)

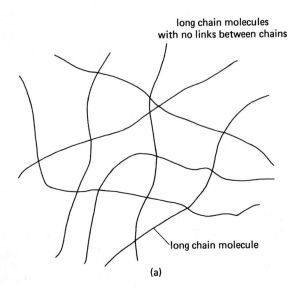

long chain molecules with no links between chains

long chain molecule

(a)

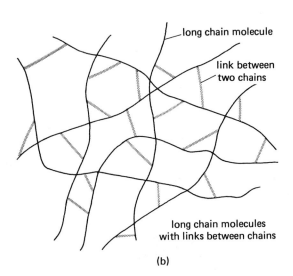

long chain molecule

link between two chains

long chain molecules with links between chains

(b)

Fig. 55.8 **(a)** The structure of a thermoplastic polymer. **(b)** The structure of a thermosetting polymer

Fig. 55.9 *above* Malay women extracting latex from a rubber plantation. *below* A tapper struggles with her morning collection of latex. *right* Latex being sieved

Polyester fibres

You may need to revise the esterification reactions of acids and alcohols (page 237) before you read this section.

Consider the reaction of an acid whose molecules contain two $-CO_2H$ groups with an alcohol whose molecules contain two $-OH$ groups. The formation of an ester link is shown in Fig. 55.10. But further

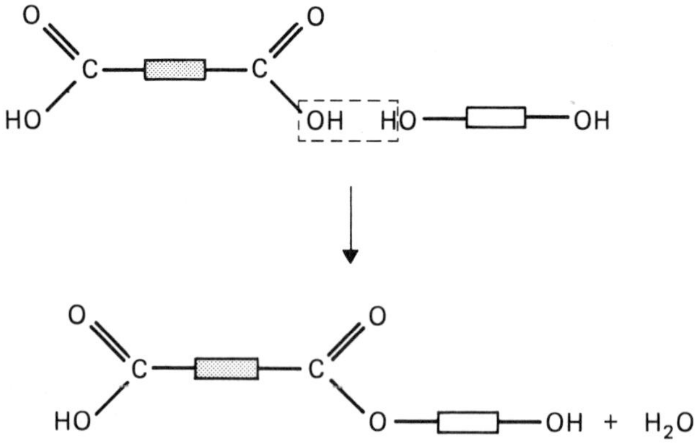

Fig. 55.10

reaction can occur at each end of the molecule. And, no matter how many times reaction occurs, further reaction is always possible. There is always either a $-CO_2H$ group (which can react with the alcohol) or an $-OH$ group (which can react with the acid) at the ends of the molecule. So it is possible to produce macromolecules called **polyesters** and the product is a polymer. Because the esterification reaction is a condensation reaction, this sort of polymerization is called condensation polymerization.

Terylene, or Dacron, is a polyester. It is made from a derivative of benzene-1,4-dicarboxylic acid

$$HO_2C-C_6H_4-CO_2H$$

and ethane-1,2-diol

$$HO-CH_2-CH_2-OH$$

After the polymer has been formed, it is melted and extruded to form fibres (forced through fine holes, rather like water through a shower head).

Terylene fibres are strong and do not rot and so Terylene is used for making cloth for sails. It is frequently mixed with wool or cotton to produce materials which can be permanently creased (for trousers, skirts, blouses and shirts), but which are then resistant to other creases. Because Terylene fibres are strong, these materials last longer than materials made entirely of wool or cotton.

Terylene can also be produced as a film and, because it has a high melting point, it is used to make food roasting bags.

Polyamide fibres

The amide group is

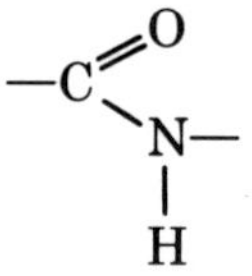

(page 236) and the linkages between amino acid units in proteins are amide linkages (page 242). The synthesis of polyamides relies on the reaction of an $-NH_2$ group with an acid group (or a group that behaves like a $-CO_2H$ group). Because acids do not react readily with amino compounds, acid chlorides, which contain the group

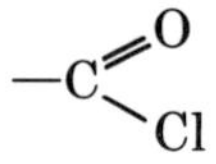

are usually used.

The reaction of a substance whose molecules contain two $-NH_2$ groups with one whose molecules contain two $-C\begin{smallmatrix}O\\Cl\end{smallmatrix}$ groups is shown in Fig. 55.11.

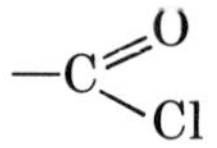

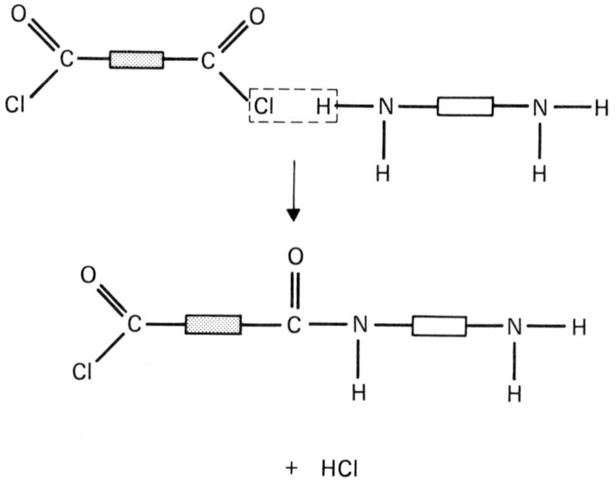

$$+ \quad HCl$$

Fig. 55.11

Further reaction can occur at each end of the molecule and can continue indefinitely. So a polyamide polymer can be produced and the reaction is another example of condensation polymerization. Nylon is this sort of polymer.

Like Terylene it can be melted and extruded to form fibres. Fine fibres can be woven to produce cloth, while thicker fibres can be used as bristles for brushes. It is similar to wool, but lacks the softness of wool and also it does not absorb moisture. It is stronger than wool and so wears well and it can be washed very easily.

Its first major use was in the replacement of silk to make stockings, but it now has a wide variety of uses: carpets, light machine gears and bearings, and climbing ropes.

Both proteins and nylon contain amide groups, so they can both be referred to as polyamides. But the sequence of $>$CO and $>$NH groups is different in the two polymers and only proteins can be referred to as polypeptides.

Your teacher may show you a reaction that produces nylon. One reactant, sebacoyl chloride, whose molecules contain two $-C\overset{O}{\underset{Cl}{<}}$ groups, is dissolved in tetrachloromethane (about $3\,cm^3$ in $100\,cm^3$). The other reactant, 1,6-diaminohexane, whose molecules contain two $-NH_2$ groups is dissolved in water (about $4\,g$ of the amine and $8\,g$ of anhydrous sodium carbonate in $100\,cm^3$ of water). The two solvents are not miscible and the aqueous solution can be poured on to the top of the tetrachloromethane solution. Reaction occurs where the two solutions meet and the thin layer of nylon formed can be drawn out of the solution using tweezers. The equation for part of this reaction is shown in Fig. 55.11.

Synthetic and natural polymers

If you have compared the properties of synthetic polymers with those of the materials they are replacing, you will probably have concluded that synthetic materials are usually more suitable for the jobs they do. In many cases, the synthetic material is cheaper than the one it has replaced.

Paper bags easily tear and their strength decreases when they are wet or greasy. Polythene bags are cheaper to produce, are unaffected by moisture and grease and they are transparent so that it is not necessary to open them to find out what they contain.

Washing up bowls used to be made of enamelled iron, which chipped very easily so that the iron would rust.

Weatherproof clothing used to be difficult to produce and so was very expensive.

There is now a very wide range of synthetic polymers, each with its own set of properties. And it is usually possible to choose a synthetic polymer so that its properties are suitable for a particular use.

There are, however, drawbacks in the use of synthetic polymers. The supply of petroleum is limited and at the present rate of use supplies are expected to run out early in the next century. Perhaps people will then look back to this period and express surprise that so much of this valuable resource was apparently wasted in the manufacture of unnecessary goods, over-elaborate packaging and just burnt as a fuel.

One major problem is that it is not economic to recycle synthetic polymers. (Metals and paper can be recycled.) So they are used once and then thrown away. Because their structures are different from those of naturally occurring substances, bacteria cannot break down most synthetic polymers. This property is very useful while the polymer is being used, but becomes a nuisance when it has been thrown away.

It is interesting to speculate about the materials that will be used in the not too distant future as supplies of petroleum are depleted and the cost of these synthetic polymers rises.

QUESTIONS

1 Use the polymerization of ethene to explain the meaning of the terms monomer, polymer, addition polymerization.

2 (a) Explain what is meant by the term esterification, using the reaction between ethanol and ethanoic acid as an example. Draw structural formulas for the compounds.
(b) Starting with the acid with molecular formula $HO_2C-X-CO_2H$ and the alcohol with the formula $HO-Y-OH$, show how a polyester can be formed.
(c) What sort of polymerization is this?
(d) Name a polyester which is used widely and give two examples of its uses.

3 (a) Show how a polyamide can be formed from the substances $H_2N-X-NH_2$ and $ClOC-Y-COCl$.
(b) What sort of polymerization is this?
(c) Name a polyamide in common use and give two examples of its uses.

4 Show diagramatically how a polymer can be formed by the polymerization of propene. Use structural formulas. Give two examples of the uses of polypropene.

5 A manufacturer requires bottles to hold concentrated hydrochloric acid. He thinks that glass can be replaced by a synthetic polymer.

Write a short account of the properties required for the container. Try to decide what sort of polymer (polyalkene, polyester, polysaccharide, polyamide) the manufacturer should use.

6 Choose an everyday article that is made from a synthetic polymer. Find out which material was used for this article before synthetic polymers were available. Compare the two materials and decide what advantages and disadvantages have resulted from the replacement of the traditional material by the synthetic polymer.

7 Describe tests you could use to detect the presence of (a) starch, (b) a reducing sugar such as glucose.

What experiments would you do to show that starch breaks down to form a reducing sugar when it is hydrolysed?

Describe two methods of hydrolysing starch. Which method is more efficient?

8 Here is a list of formulas for some carbon compounds. The rectangles represent carbon chains (which are not necessarily the same in the different compounds).

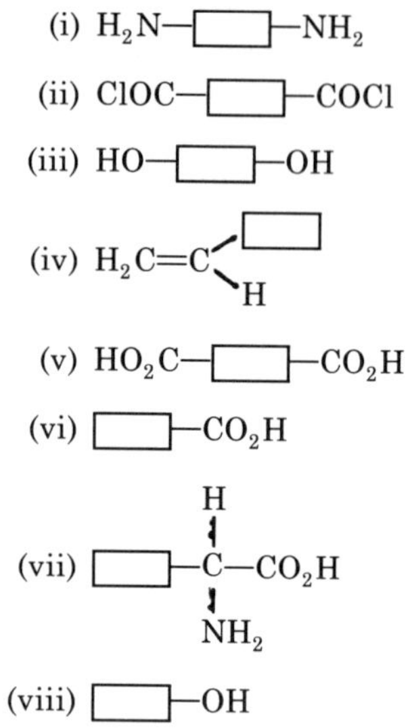

(i) H$_2$N—▭—NH$_2$

(ii) ClOC—▭—COCl

(iii) HO—▭—OH

(iv) H$_2$C=C⟨▭ / H

(v) HO$_2$C—▭—CO$_2$H

(vi) ▭—CO$_2$H

(vii) ▭—C(—CO$_2$H)(H)(NH$_2$)

(viii) ▭—OH

(*a*) Which would react together under suitable conditions to give a simple ester? Give the formula of the ester produced and suggest a suitable catalyst.

(*b*) Which compound is likely to undergo addition polymerization to form a plastic? Draw a section of the polymer chain.

(*c*) Which two compounds would react together to form a polyamide? Draw a diagram to show the structure of this polyamide. How could a fibre be produced from this polyamide?

(*d*) Which two substances could be reacted together to form a polyester? Draw a diagram to show the structure of this polyester. If you were given a sample of it, describe how you would try to break it down to its component compounds.

(*e*) Which of the substances can be obtained by the hydrolysis of proteins? How could this substance be recognized even when it is in a mixture with other similar compounds?

(*f*) Which of the substances could be a monosaccharide produced by the hydrolysis of a polysaccharide? Draw the structure of the polysaccharide.

Key words

monomer	thermoplastic	polyamide
polymer	thermosetting	peptide link
polymerization	vulcanization	polypeptide
monosaccharide	protein	polyester
disaccharide	amino acid	
polysaccharide	amide group	

Basic facts

- Polymerization is the production of a compound (the polymer) with very large molecules from a compound (or two compounds) with small molecules (the monomer).

- Addition polymerization can occur with monomers that contain the >C=C< group.

- Condensation polymerization occurs between two substances whose molecules contain (at least) two functional groups which react together with the elimination of a small molecule such as water or hydrogen chloride.

- Polysaccharides are substances (such as starch and cellulose) which can be broken down to simple sugars (monosaccharides) either by enzyme-catalysed hydrolysis or acid hydrolysis. Polysaccharides are formed in living organisms by a process of condensation polymerization.

- Proteins are condensation polymers of amino acids.

- The amino acids present in a protein can be identified by paper chromatography after the hydrolysis of the protein.

- Polyesters are obtained by the polymerization of acids whose molecules contain two carboxyl groups with alcohols whose molecules contain two hydroxyl groups. They are condensation polymers.

- Polyamides are formed by the polymerization of acids whose molecules contain two carboxyl groups (or similar compounds) with compounds whose molecules contain two NH$_2$ groups. They are condensation polymers.

- Some synthetic polymers can be extruded to form fibres. Terylene is a polyester while nylon is a polyamide. These fibres have partially replaced wool, silk and cotton.

- There is a very wide variety of synthetic polymers all with their own particular properties. These properties can sometimes be modified by mixing the polymers with other substances. In the use of polymers, an attempt is made to match the uses to the properties of particular polymers.

- The widespread use of synthetic polymers produces a pollution problem, since many of these polymers are not broken down by bacteria.

Chemical analysis

56 Qualitative analysis

Tests for some common gases

Gas	General properties	Special tests
Steam	Colourless, odourless and neutral; 'steamy' appearance	Easily condensed on a cool surface; turns anhydrous copper(II) sulphate blue
Oxygen	Colourless, odourless and neutral	Relights a glowing splint
Hydrogen	Colourless, odourless and neutral	Burns with a blue flame; explodes if mixed with air and ignited
Carbon dioxide	Colourless and odourless; slightly acidic and turns moist blue litmus red	Turns limewater cloudy
Hydrogen chloride	Sharp acid smell; turns moist blue litmus red; slightly 'steamy' appearance	Gives white fumes with ammonia and a white precipitate with $AgNO_3/HNO_3$ solution
Chlorine	Yellow-green gas with a choking smell; bleaches moist litmus	Gives white fumes with ammonia and a white precipitate with $AgNO_3/HNO_3$ solution
Bromine	Red-brown gas with a pungent smell; bleaches moist litmus	Gives white fumes with ammonia and a very pale yellow precipitate with $AgNO_3/HNO_3$ solution (cf. nitrogen dioxide)
Ammonia	Colourless gas with a pungent smell; the only common alkaline gas	Gives white fumes with acidic gases
Nitrogen dioxide	Red-brown acidic gas with a pungent smell	Sometimes confused with bromine, but gives no precipitate with $AgNO_3/HNO_3$ solution
Sulphur dioxide	Colourless, acidic gas with a cough-inducing smell	Turns acidified potassium dichromate(VI) solution green and acidified potassium manganate(VII) solution colourless
Hydrogen sulphide	Colourless, slightly acidic gas with a bad eggs smell	Like sulphur dioxide, reacts with potassium dichromate(VI) and potassium manganate(VII) solutions, but also gives a black precipitate with lead ethanoate (lead acetate) or lead nitrate solution
Nitrogen	Colourless, odourless and neutral	No simple tests

Tests for some ions

This section tells you how to identify some of the ions that could be present in a solid or a solution. Rather than testing for each ion in turn, you could do the tests in the order given here. The ions included in this scheme are:

Anions: chloride, bromide, iodide, sulphate, sulphite, sulphide, carbonate, hydrogencarbonate and nitrate.

Cations: lithium, sodium, potassium, magnesium, calcium, aluminium, iron(II), iron(III), copper(II), zinc, lead(II) and ammonium.

You can also use this section to look up the test for a particular ion.

Tests for anions (and the ammonium cation)

1(a) Heat a small amount of the solid in a small, dry test-tube. Test any gases evolved (see page 250).

Gas evolved	Conclusion
Steam	Water of crystallization or a hydrogencarbonate (test for carbon dioxide)
Carbon dioxide	Carbonate or hydrogencarbonate (the carbonates of the group I metals are not decomposed by heat under laboratory conditions)
Oxygen	Group I metal nitrate or an unstable oxide
Nitrogen dioxide and oxygen	Nitrates of metals other than the alkali metals
Sulphur dioxide	Sulphate or sulphite
Ammonia	Ammonium salt (some ammonium salts do not give off ammonia when heated)

(b) Heat a small amount of the solid with powdered calcium hydroxide in a test-tube. If a positive test for ammonia gas is obtained (see above), then the solid contains the ammonium cation.

2. To a small amount of the solid add a few cm^3 of either bench dilute (1 M) sulphuric acid or bench dilute (2 M) hydrochloric acid. If no gas is evolved, warm the mixture. Test any gas evolved.

Gas evolved	Conclusion
Carbon dioxide	Carbonate or hydrogen-carbonate
Sulphur dioxide	Sulphite
Hydrogen sulphide	Sulphide

A smell of vinegar indicates that ethanoic (acetic) acid has been produced and that the solid is an ethanoate (acetate).

3. Test for sulphate ions To a solution of the solid in bench dilute (2 M) hydrochloric acid, add barium chloride solution. A white precipitate shows that sulphate ions are present.

Note. Sulphite and carbonate ions also give a white precipitate with barium ions but these precipitates (unlike that of barium sulphate) are soluble in dilute acids. This is why you have to add dilute hydrochloric acid as well as barium chloride solution.

4. Test for halide ions To a solution of the solid in bench dilute (2 M) nitric acid add silver nitrate solution. Test how soluble any precipitate is in bench dilute (2 M) ammonia solution and then in concentrated ammonia solution.

Observation	Ion
White precipitate soluble in dilute ammonia solution	Chloride
Pale yellow precipitate just soluble in concentrated ammonia solution	Bromide
Yellow precipitate 'insoluble' in concentrated ammonia solution	Iodide

Note. Certain other ions, such as carbonate ions, give a precipitate with silver ions but these precipitates (unlike those of the silver halides) are soluble in dilute nitric acid. This is why you have to add dilute nitric acid as well as silver nitrate solution.

5. Test for nitrate ions Do not do this test if the solid reacts with dilute acid (test 2) or contains halide ions (test 4).

Warm the solid gently with some copper turnings and a few drops of concentrated sulphuric acid.

(GREAT CARE REQUIRED: PERFORM IN A FUME CUPBOARD.)

The evolution of brown fumes of nitrogen dioxide indicates the presence of nitrate ions in the solid. The concentrated sulphuric acid produces concentrated nitric acid with the nitrate, and the nitric acid reacts with the copper turnings to form nitrogen dioxide.

When you have finished the test, allow the mixture to cool before you pour it, drop by drop, into plenty of water.

6. Distinguishing between carbonates and hydrogencarbonates

(*a*) Heat an aqueous solution of the solid. Hydrogencarbonates decompose and evolve carbon dioxide but carbonates are not affected.

(*b*) To an aqueous solution of the solid add a 0.5 M solution of magnesium sulphate. A white precipitate shows the presence of carbonate ions. If no precipitate is formed, boil the solution and look for carbon dioxide being evolved and for a white precipitate: these show the presence of hydrogencarbonate ions.

Tests for cations

1. Appearance Most of the salts of the group I and group II metals are white (colourless in solution). Salts of heavy metals are often coloured.

Colour	Ion
Blue	Cu^{2+}
Green	Fe^{2+}
Yellow-brown	Fe^{3+}

2. Flame test Clean a nichrome (or platinum) wire by dipping it into concentrated hydrochloric acid and then heating it strongly in a non-luminous bunsen flame until it no longer gives a colour to the flame. Moisten the wire with concentrated hydrochloric acid, dip it into the solid and then heat it strongly.

Flame coloration	Ion
Very intense red	Li^+
Persistent intense yellow	Na^+
Lilac (easily masked by Na^+ impurities), crimson through blue glass	K^+
Brick red	Ca^{2+}
Green	Cu^{2+}

(Ba^{2+} ions give a yellowish-green flame colour.)

3. Tests for cations in solution Prepare a solution of the solid in either water or a dilute acid (about 0.1 g in 5 cm^3) and divide it into two parts for use in (a) and (b).

(a) Add bench dilute (2 M) sodium hydroxide solution, *a drop at a time* to the solution of the salt. Look for a precipitate and test how soluble any precipitate is in an excess of sodium hydroxide solution. Warm the mixture and find out if ammonia is evolved (see first table, next column).

Observation	Ions that may be present
Ammonia evolved	NH_4^+
White precipitate, insoluble in an excess of sodium hydroxide solution	Mg^{2+} Ca^{2+}
White precipitate, soluble in an excess of sodium hydroxide solution	Al^{3+} Pb^{2+} Zn^{2+}
Coloured precipitate, insoluble in an excess of sodium hydroxide solution	Fe^{2+} (dirty green) Fe^{3+} (red-brown) Cu^{2+} (pale blue)

(b) Repeat (a), but use bench dilute (2 M) ammonia solution instead of sodium hydroxide solution.

Observation	Ions that may be present
White precipitate insoluble in an excess of aqueous ammonia	Mg^{2+} Ca^{2+} Al^{3+} Pb^{2+}
White precipitate soluble in an excess of aqueous ammonia	Zn^{2+}
Coloured precipitate insoluble in an excess of aqueous ammonia	Fe^{2+} (dirty green) Fe^{3+} (red-brown)
Coloured precipitate soluble in an excess of aqueous ammonia	Cu^{2+} (pale blue precipitate giving a royal blue solution)

(c) The only cations that cannot be distinguished in tests 2, 3(a), and 3(b) are Pb^{2+} and Al^{3+}. But while the chloride, iodide, sulphate and sulphide of Pb^{2+} are insoluble in water, the same salts of Al^{3+} are soluble.

4. Other tests for iron(II) and iron(III) ions Iron(II) compounds often contain some iron(III) ions because of oxidation by the air. The following tests are very sensitive and so they are likely to detect small amounts of iron(III) ions in an iron(II) compound.

To separate volumes of a solution of the solid in water, bench dilute (2 M) hydrochloric acid or bench dilute (1 M) sulphuric acid, add a few drops of solutions of (a) potassium or ammonium thiocyanate, (b) potassium hexacyanoferrate(II), (c) potassium hexacyanoferrate(III). See table below.

	Thiocyanate ions	Hexacyanoferrate(II) ions	Hexacyanoferrate(III) ions
Iron(II) ions	No colour change occurs	Only slow formation of pale blue colour	*Immediate dark* blue colour or precipitate
Iron(III) ions	Intense red colour	*Immediate dark* blue colour or precipitate	Brown or green coloration

Tests for oxidizing the reducing agents

Oxidizing agents give one or both of these tests.

1. Add dilute sulphuric acid to a dilute solution of potassium iodide. Add a small amount of the oxidizing agent (as a solid or a solution). A brown precipitate of iodine is formed. Add starch solution. A deep blue colour shows iodine is present. Iodide ions have been oxidized to iodine.

2. Add an aqueous solution of hydrogen sulphide to a warmed solution of the oxidizing agent. A yellow precipitate of sulphur is formed. Hydrogen sulphide has been oxidized to sulphur.

Reducing agents give one or both of these tests.

1. Add dilute sulphuric acid to potassium manganate(VII) solution. Then add a few drops of this mixture to a solution of the reducing agent. The purple solution goes colourless. Manganate(VII) ions have been reduced to manganese(II) ions.

2. Add dilute sulphuric acid to potassium dichromate(VI) solution. Then add a few drops of this mixture to a solution of the reducing agent. The orange solution goes green. Dichromate(VI) ions have been reduced to chromium(III) ions.

Some practical exercises in the identification of single substances

1. Carry out the following experiments on the substances X and Y. Describe carefully what you observe, and identify any gases evolved.
(a) Heat a small amount of X in a hard-glass testtube.
(b) Add dilute hydrochloric acid to the *cold* residue left after heating X.
(c) Add dilute hydrochloric acid to a solution of X, and warm.
(d) Repeat (a), (b) and (c), by using Y instead of X. (There is no need to warm in test (c) when using Y.)

2. Carry out the following experiments on substance P which is a salt. Make all the observations you can and decide which ions are present in the salt.
(a) Add a few drops of dilute sodium hydroxide to a solution of P. Warm the mixture and identify any gases evolved.
(b) Acidify a solution of P with dilute hydrochloric acid, then add a few drops of barium chloride solution.

What kind of salt does P seem to be?

3. M is a metal oxide. Carry out the following experiments on substance M and decide on the identity of the metal.
(a) Boil a small amount of M with a few cm^3 of dilute sulphuric acid. Cool and filter the mixture.

(b) Put the *solid residue* into a crucible in a fume cupboard and add a few drops of moderately concentrated nitric acid (CARE).
(c) To the *filtrate*, add aqueous ammonia until in excess.

4. You are provided with three white solids, A, B and C. One is hydrated sodium carbonate, one is anhydrous sodium carbonate and the third is sodium hydrogencarbonate. Devise and carry out some simple tests to identify which is which.

5. Carry out the following experiments on the substance S. Describe what you observe, identify any gases evolved and suggest what S might be.
(a) Heat a small amount of S in a hard-glass testtube. (Do not point the tube at anyone while it is being heated.)
(b) Make a solution of S in water and divide the solution into three portions.
 (i) To portion 1 add a little dilute sulphuric acid.
 (ii) To portion 2 add dilute sodium hydroxide solution until the alkali is in excess.
 (iii) To portion 3 add a few drops of sodium chloride solution, heat to boiling and then cool.

6. Carry out the following experiments on the substance G. Describe what you observe, identify any gases evolved and suggest that G is likely to be.
(a) Heat a small amount of G in a hard-glass testtube.
(b) Add a few drops of potassium thiocyanate solution to a solution of G in water.
(c) Add a few drops of potassium iodide solution acidified with dilute sulphuric acid to a solution of G in water. Pour a small amount of the resulting mixture into another test-tube, dilute it with water and add to it 1 or 2 drops of starch solution.

7. E and F are two colourless liquids. One of them is pure water, the other is not. Carry out the following experiments on both E and F. Describe what you observe, identify any gases evolved and suggest what the other liquid might be.
(a) Add a few drops of each liquid to a small amount of anhydrous copper(II) sulphate.
(b) Add a very small amount of manganese(IV) oxide to each liquid.
(c) Add a small volume of each liquid to a roughly equal volume of potassium manganate(VII) solution acidified with dilute sulphuric acid.

8. U, V and W are all colourless solutions of salts. One is a chloride, one is a bromide and one is an iodide. You are also provided with dilute nitric acid, silver nitrate solution, dilute ammonia solution and chlorine solution. Devise and carry out some experiments using all these chemicals in order to determine the identity of each of the colourless solutions.

57 Volumetric analysis

Introduction

A **standard solution** is one whose concentration is known. The concentration of a solution is usually expressed in $g\,l^{-1}$ or $mol\,l^{-1}$.

If a solution is known to contain 10.0 g of solute in 1000 cm³ of solution, each cm³ of solution contains $10/1000 = 0.010$ g of solute. The mass of solute in x cm³ is $0.010\,x$ g. Similarly, a solution that contains 0.15 mol of solute in 1000 cm³ of solution (i.e. it is 0.15 M) contains 1.5×10^{-4} mol of solute in each cm³, and in x cm³ of solution there is $1.5 \times 10^{-4}\,x$ mol.

These calculations assume that the solute is evenly spread throughout the solution, in other words that the solution is homogeneous.

In volumetric analysis, the volumes of solutions that just react together are easily measured. A pipette is used to measure out a known volume of one solution and a burette measures volumes of the other solution. Provided the concentrations of these solutions are known, the masses or numbers of moles of the solutes that react together can be calculated from these volumes.

Making standard solutions

Standard solutions are made by dissolving a known mass of solute in water and diluting the solution to a known volume. But standard solutions of sodium hydroxide and hydrochloric acid cannot be made in this way. Solid sodium hydroxide rapidly reacts with water and carbon dioxide in the atmosphere and would no longer be pure by the time its mass has been found. Pure hydrogen chloride is a gas at room temperature which reacts rapidly with water vapour. Substances that are stable in the atmosphere and can be used to make standard solutions include sodium carbonate and ethanedioic acid.

(a) Preparation of a 0.10 M sodium carbonate solution.

What mass of sodium carbonate is needed to prepare 250 cm³ of a 0.10 M solution? Since 1000 cm³ of a 1.0 M solution contains 1.0 mol of solute, 250 cm³ of a 0.10 M solution contains

$$\frac{250}{1000} \times 0.10 = 2.5 \times 10^{-2}\,mol.$$

The mass of 1 mol of Na_2CO_3 is 106 g so that 2.5×10^{-2} mol has the mass $2.5 \times 10^{-2} \times 106$ or 2.65 g.

So to prepare 250 cm³ of a 0.10 M solution of sodium carbonate, it is necessary to measure out on a balance 2.65 g of anhydrous sodium carbonate. But if you use crystalline sodium carbonate it is necessary to take account of the water of crystallization in the crystals. The formula of the crystals is $Na_2CO_3 \cdot 10H_2O$, its molar mass is 286 g, so it is necessary to measure out $286 \times 2.5 \times 10^{-2}$ or 7.15 g.

This solid is dissolved in about 100 cm³ of pure water and the solution is then transferred to a standard (graduated) 250 cm³ flask. The beaker must be rinsed several times in the flask to make sure that all the sodium carbonate is in the flask. Water is added until the volume of the solution is 250 cm³. Pure water must be used because carbonate ions react with calcium and magnesium ions that are frequently present in tap water. The solution should be shaken thoroughly to make sure that it is homogeneous.

(b) Preparation of a 0.10 M solution of ethanedioic acid.
CARE: ethanedioic acid is very poisonous. Wash your hands thoroughly when you have finished any experiments involving this substance.

Crystalline ethanedioic acid has the formula $H_2C_2O_4 \cdot 2H_2O$. You should be able to work out that 3.15 g of this solid are required for the preparation of 250 cm³ of a 0.10 M solution. The procedure is similar to that described for sodium carbonate.

(c) The preparation of standard solutions of other acids and alkalis.

Standard solutions of many acids and alkalis cannot be prepared directly as in (a) and (b). But solutions of these substances can be standardized by titrating them with either the standard sodium carbonate or the standard ethanedioic acid solutions.

The standardization of hydrochloric and sulphuric acids

Bench dilute hydrochloric acid is usually about 2 M. This is far too concentrated to titrate directly with the 0.10 M sodium carbonate and so it has to be diluted. If 50 cm³ of the bench dilute hydrochloric acid is diluted to 1000 cm³, its concentration should be about 0.1 M, and this solution can be titrated with the sodium carbonate solution so that its concentration can be determined accurately.

Rinse a 10 cm³ pipette with water and then with sodium carbonate solution. Measure out 10 cm³ of the sodium carbonate solution into a conical flask.

Rinse the burette with water and then with the hydrochloric acid and fill it with the acid, making sure that the tap of the burette is also filled with the solution.

Add two or three drops of methyl orange indicator solution to the sodium carbonate solution and run in the acid until the first permanent red tinge is seen. Record the volume of acid used and repeat the titration until consistent results are obtained.

Suppose that $24.0\,cm^3$ of the acid is needed to neutralize the sodium carbonate. What is the concentration of the acid?

The equation for the reaction is

$$Na_2CO_3(aq) + 2HCl(aq)$$
$$\longrightarrow 2NaCl(aq) + CO_2(g) + H_2O(l)$$

or $CO_3^{2-}(aq) + 2H^+(aq) \longrightarrow CO_2(g) + H_2O(l)$

So 1 mol of Na_2CO_3 reacts with 2 mol of HCl. In $10.0\,cm^3$ of 0.10 M sodium carbonate solution there is

$$\frac{10.0}{1000} \times 0.10$$

$$= 0.0010\,mol\ Na_2CO_3.$$

Since 1 mol of Na_2CO_3 reacts with 2 mol of HCl, the 0.0010 mol of Na_2CO_3 reacts with 0.0020 mol of HCl. And this amount of hydrogen chloride must be present in $24.0\,cm^3$ of solution. So $1000\,cm^3$ of the acid must contain $0.0020 \times 1000/24$ or 0.083 mol of HCl. The concentration of the acid is 0.083 M.

A similar procedure can be used to prepare a standard solution of sulphuric acid. Bench dilute sulphuric acid is about 1 M, so $100\,cm^3$ of it should be diluted to $1000\,cm^3$ to provide an approximately 0.1 M solution.

But in the calculation, it is important to remember that 1 mol of Na_2CO_3 reacts with 1 mol of H_2SO_4:

$$Na_2CO_3(aq) + H_2SO_4(aq)$$
$$\longrightarrow Na_2SO_4(aq) + CO_2(g) + H_2O(l)$$

The size of the pipette can be increased to $25\,cm^3$ for this standardization.

The standardization of sodium hydroxide solution

Bench dilute sodium hydroxide solution is approximately 2 M. When $50\,cm^3$ of this solution is diluted to $1000\,cm^3$, the concentration of the final solution should be about 0.1 M and this is suitable for titration with the 0.10 M ethanedioic acid solution.

The procedure is similar to that described for the standardization of hydrochloric acid. A $25\,cm^3$ pipette should be used to measure out the sodium hydroxide solution and the indicator should be phenolphthalein.

Suppose that $13.0\,cm^3$ of the standard 0.10 M ethanedioic acid solution is needed to neutralize $25.0\,cm^3$ of the sodium hydroxide solution. What is the concentration of the alkali?

The equation for the reaction is

$$H_2C_2O_4(aq) + 2NaOH(aq)$$
$$\longrightarrow Na_2C_2O_4(aq) + 2H_2O(l)$$

So 2 mol of NaOH reacts with 1 mol of $H_2C_2O_4$. In $13.0\,cm^3$ of 0.10 M ethanedioic acid solution there is $\frac{13.0}{1000} \times 0.10$ or 0.0013 mol of $H_2C_2O_4$.

Since 2 mol of NaOH reacts with 1 mol of $H_2C_2O_4$, in $25.0\,cm^3$ of the alkali, there must be 0.0026 mol of NaOH. In $1000\,cm^3$ of the alkali there are $0.0026 \times 1000/25$ or 0.104 mol of NaOH. So the sodium hydroxide solution has the concentration 0.104 M.

Key words

volumetric analysis   **standard solution**   **titration**   **standardization**

Basic facts

- **A standard solution is one whose concentration (in $g\,l^{-1}$ or $mol\,l^{-1}$) is known.**

- **The volumes of given solutions of an acid and an alkali required for neutralization can be found using a titration.**

- **If a standard solution is used as one of the reactants in an acid–alkali titration, the concentration of the other reactant can be calculated from the results.**

Chemistry in society

58 Metals and ores — some economic and social issues

General economic considerations

Many countries have large reserves of ores (page 98). But this does not always mean that they will be able to get rich either by exporting the ores or by extracting the metals and then exporting these. This chapter deals with some of the problems.

The price that can be obtained for the metal on the world market is obviously very important and can vary a lot even over a short period of a year or two. The economy of a major ore-producing country can be seriously affected by sharp falls in the world price of the ore.

Three important factors that govern the price of a metal are:

its physical and chemical properties (these determine its range of uses),
the world demand for the metal, and
the world supply of the metal.

The introduction of new materials, for example new alloys or new plastics, can sometimes reduce the range of uses of particular metals, and therefore their value falls. On the other hand, if the demand for a metal is high and the supply cannot keep pace with it, then the price of the metal will rise. But if an increased demand leads to more of the metal being produced, its price may fall again.

These factors must be set against the cost of producing the metal which, in turn, depends on the availability of ores suitable for the extraction process and the costs of the various stages of the process. Fig. 27.2 (page 98) shows the relative abundance of some metals. In itself, this does not indicate how available each metal is because that depends on how easy or hard it is to extract from its commonly occurring ores. For example, aluminium occurs widely in rocks in the form of alumino-silicate compounds, but at the moment it is extracted only from bauxite (page 101), an aluminium ore that is not nearly as widespread in rocks as the alumino-silicates. (Some current research work may lead to the commercial extraction of aluminium from alumino-silicates in the future.)

Sometimes the balance of these factors will mean that mining and processing of an ore is worthwhile, and sometimes the balance will mean that an existing mining operation has to be closed down, or a decision made not to begin a new operation.

Suppose a country has quite a lot of iron ore but the ore deposits are situated hundreds of kilometres from the nearest port. Transport costs would obviously be high. The decision on whether or not to mine the ore would depend partly on how these transport costs compare with the export price obtained. Because iron is a common metal, its world price is low. This means that the transport costs would approach the export price obtained, and it would then not be economical to mine and transport the ore.

The decision might also depend on the **grade** of the ore. Low-grade ores have a small percentage of available metal whereas high-grade ores have a large percentage. It is clearly more economic to transport the high-grade ores which fetch a higher price per tonne.

However the decision might not be the same if the ore contains gold. Even though there may only be a very small amount of gold ore in an area, it might still be worth mining. This is because the costs of separating the gold from its ore and transporting it to the nearest port for export are only a small fraction of the price of gold on the world market. If really large reserves of gold ore are found in a country, there is no problem at all in deciding to build new railways, roads and docks to deal with the new trade.

A final point is that digging out ores and exporting them makes very much less money than refining and forming the metal into useful objects.

An imaginary case study

An imaginary problem is shown in Fig. 58.1. Country X has large reserves of an ore in a remote desert area close to the border with country Y. The capital city, Umbali, has a very good deep-water harbour but its docks are not well developed. The nearest place on the coast to the reserves is Tolo, which has a good natural harbour but is only a fishing village built on a swamp. What do you have to think about before deciding what to do with the reserves? Remember that setting up any new mining and extraction operation requires a lot of money.

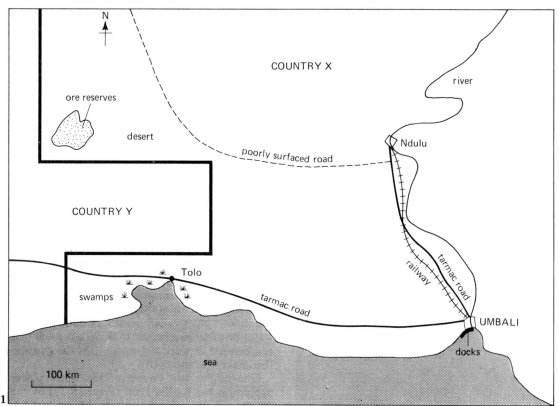

Fig. 58.1

First of all, the ore would have to be mined. Then it would have to be **concentrated** so that some of the impurities are removed and the ore becomes richer in the metal.

Should the ore be transported to the coast or should it be concentrated first?

The mining and the concentration of ores usually need a large labour force and a supply of energy.

Where would the labour force live?
Should a new town be built near the mine?
Is the area suitable for a town?
What are the large-scale sources of energy that are usually used and are any of these available?

Suppose that a decision is made to export the concentrated ore. Table 58.1 shows some of the possible solutions to the problem along with their advantages and disadvantages. The first two require a new

Table 58.1

Possible solutions	Advantages	Disadvantages
1. Transport unprocessed ore via Ndulu to Umbali, where it is concentrated and exported	Ore is concentrated at place where energy supplies and labour force already available Docks and some facilities already exist in Umbali	High transport costs per tonne of metal because ore is not concentrated at mine
2. Concentrate ore at mine, then transport it via Ndulu to Umbali, where it is exported	Lower transport costs per tonne of metal than for 1 Docks and some facilities already exist in Umbali	High costs of making energy supplies available at mine High costs of establishing new town for labour force at mine Difficulties in getting people to live in a remote desert area
3. Concentrate ore at mine, then transport it via new road or railway directly to Tolo, where it is exported	Shorter distance to Tolo than to Umbali, therefore lower transport costs (but road or railway might have to be built entirely within country X and this would increase the distance)	High costs of establishing port facilities at Tolo Possible difficulties in building and running a road or railway through country Y

road or railway to be built between the ore reserves and Ndulu so that the metal in the ore would have to fetch a reasonably good price on the world market. The third solution would require a new road or railway to be built between the ore reserves and Tolo. The docks at Ndulu would need some improvements but entirely new port facilities would be required at Tolo.

Another possible solution to the imaginary problem in Fig. 58.1 is to extract the metal from the ore in country X rather than to export the concentrated ore. This decision might be taken if there is a good local market for the metal and the goods made from it. Methods of extracting metals from ores include:

the reduction of oxides with carbon (coke),
electrolysis,
the reduction using a more reactive metal such as magnesium or aluminium.

Coke is available cheaply only if a country has large and accessible reserves of coal. (Coke is made by heating coal in the absence of air.) Electrolysis requires plentiful supplies of cheap electricity (see below). Reactive metals are very expensive and can be used for metal extractions on a fairly small scale only. These facts suggest that many countries do not really have the necessary resources to extract a metal from its ore.

All metal extractions use a lot of energy in the form of heat or electricity, or both. The large-scale sources of energy are fossil fuels (coal, oil and natural gas), hydroelectric power and nuclear power. If a country has to rely on importing fossil fuels, then the cost of the energy it produces is very heavily dependent on world prices and this can often result in serious economic problems. For some countries, the solution is to develop hydroelectric power. However, it is still the case that a lot of countries with large ore deposits choose to export either the impure ore or the concentrated ore because it is not economic for them to extract the metal and export this.

The location of a metal processing industry

As with any chemical industry, the location of a metal processing plant depends on a balance between economic factors and environmental and social factors.

The imaginary problem in the previous section shows that such a location close to the ore reserves reduces transport costs. But if the area is remote, the cost of building the plant and maintaining and running it are likely to be high. So it may be better to locate the plant in a more accessible place. If large supplies of energy are required (and this is usually the case for chemical industries), then it might be best to build the plant near a cheap energy source such as a hydroelectric power scheme.

One important environmental problem associated with a metal processing industry is the effect on the landscape of the mining operation. Some mines are located underground (Fig. 58.2) but many are open-cast mines which are located at the surface

Fig. 58.2

Fig. 58.3

(Fig. 58.3). At worst, these operations leave very ugly scars on the land. At best, it is sometimes possible to return the land to its former use by careful landscaping.

Another main environmental problem in a chemical industry is the disposal of any waste products. In metal processing industries, the major waste products are the unwanted parts of the ore and the unwanted by-products of the concentration and extraction processes. Gaseous by-products, such as sulphur dioxide from the roasting of sulphide ores, could pollute the atmosphere. Soluble products and liquids might have to be discharged into the waterways where, again, they could create a pollution problem. And where the unwanted products are solid, they may have to be dumped in unsightly waste tips.

Ore reserves and conservation

All mineral resources are finite, that is, they are limited in quantity. Also, world demand for many metals is rising very steeply. Some scientists believe that we could run out of certain metals by the turn of the century and we would then have to find alternative materials to replace them.

There are various ways in which we might extend the 'life' of these metals:

prospecting for and developing new ore reserves (especially in the more remote parts of the world);

processing lower-grade ores;

developing new extraction processes that can be used with ores which were previously thought to be unusable;

recycling of used metals;

replacing rare metals in certain uses by more abundant metals and their alloys.

The careful use of metals and the conservation of ore reserves are matters of great concern, and much effort will have to be devoted to them in the future.

QUESTIONS

1 For each of examples (a) to (c) describe the difficulties which inhibit the mining and processing of the ores.

(a) A country has reserves of iron ore but they are in an area 500 kilometres from the nearest port. There are no coal deposits in this country.

(b) A country has reserves of both coal and iron ore in the same area, but it is a remote region with poor communications.

(c) A country has very large reserves of bauxite but only a small amount of aluminium is extracted there (most of the bauxite is exported).

2 Sketch the map in Fig. 58.1 in your notebook and then draw in some possible solutions to the problem. Write down some of the arguments for and against each solution.

Key words

ore reserves (deposits)   concentration of ore   open-cast mining   waste disposal

grade of ore   extraction of metal   waste tips

Basic facts

- The main economic factors in a metal processing industry are:
  - the accessibility and grade of the ore
  - the transport costs
  - the cost of building the plant
  - the cost of labour for running and maintaining the plant
  - the cost of the reducing agent (and any other raw materials)
  - the energy costs
  - the selling price of the product (which could be the unprocessed ore, the concentrated ore or the extracted metal)

- The location of a metal processing industry must take account of the above economic factors as well as environmental factors such as waste disposal.

- The conservation of the world's scarce metal resources is becoming an increasingly important issue.

59 The aluminium industry

The mining and purification of bauxite

Aluminium occurs widely in rocks (Fig. 27.2, page 98), but it is extracted from only one particular mineral called bauxite, which is a hydrated oxide with the approximate formula $Al_2O_3 \cdot 2H_2O$. Deposits of bauxite are formed by the chemical alteration of aluminium-bearing rocks under tropical conditions.

There are large reserves of bauxite in Australia, USA, USSR, and in Jamaica and Guyana. The ore in Guyana has one of the highest grades of all bauxite deposits.

In both Jamaica and Guyana the ore is found under a layer of soil called **overburden**. The ore is mined by open-cast methods, that is, by removing the overburden and digging the ore out using machinery located on the surface. In Jamaica, the overburden is fairly thin and easy to remove (Fig. 59.1), whereas in

Fig. 59.1

Guyana a much larger amount of overburden has to be skimmed off before the bauxite can be mined (Fig. 59.2). The ore is then transported to a processing plant (Fig. 59.3).

Fig. 59.2

Fig. 59.3

If the layer of overburden is thin, the soil can be returned to the area once all the bauxite has been dug out. This is clearly a major advantage, especially if the land is suitable for farming. In Jamaica, for example, the soil is intensively cultivated with citrus groves and as grasslands for cattle pasture. If land reclamation is not carried out, then unsightly holes are left and the land cannot be put to good use after mining is finished.

The ore can be transported quite easily by water, for example along the Demerara River (from Linden in Guyana) or from Ocho Rios or Port Kaiser (Jamaica). It takes up to 5 tonnes of bauxite to produce just 1 tonne of aluminium and so low transport costs for the ore are important.

The first stage in the processing of the ore is to concentrate it by removing some of the impurities. This is done by grinding the ore into small grains and then separating the bauxite from the impurities using the difference in density between them.

Most purified bauxite is used in aluminium extraction (see below) but some is used in the extraction of iron in the blast furnace. For this second purpose, the purified ore has to be heated very strongly to form small brittle pieces of bauxite. This **calcined** bauxite is added to the blast furnace and acts in a similar way to that described for calcium oxide on page 101. So the aluminium oxide (in combined form) appears in the slag at the bottom of the furnace.

Calcined bauxite has been particularly important for Guyana.

From bauxite to alumina

The concentration process is not the end of the purification of bauxite. The concentrated ore still contains some compounds of iron, silicon and titanium, and these are removed by treatment with concentrated sodium hydroxide solution (page 101). Pure alumina (Al_2O_3) is the product.

This purification creates two problems of waste disposal from an alumina plant. Alumina dust is discharged into the atmosphere and a by-product called 'red mud' has to be stored in nearby man-made 'lakes'.

Table 59.1 Approximate analysis of dry red mud

Aluminium oxide, Al_2O_3	15% (this cannot be removed during purification process)
Silicon(IV) oxide, SiO_2	40%
Iron oxides (e.g. Fe_2O_3)	21% (these give the mud its red colour)
Titanium(IV) oxide, TiO_2	18%
Calcium oxide, CaO	6%

Red mud is composed of soil residues, mainly the oxides of metals along with some other metal compounds. Table 59.1 shows the results of an analysis of red mud with respect to the oxides.

After the last stage of the purification process, the red mud is pumped to the large storage 'lakes' as a slurry in very dilute sodium hydroxide solution. Since no use has yet been found for the red mud, these 'lakes' grow larger and more numerous as time goes on. They are obviously an eyesore and the high pH value of the mud causes the vegetation surrounding the 'lakes' to die. Also, unless great care is taken, it is possible for the alkaline solution to seep into the water sources with potentially disastrous consequences. Finally, if the edges of the lakes are not kept wet, the mud can form a dry dust which gets blown into the air by the wind.

The location of an alumina plant must take account of the need to dispose of the red mud. It should always be possible to convert natural land formations into 'lakes' without having to build expensive dams and without using up valuable farmland.

The most important constituent in red mud is the 18 per cent of titanium(IV) oxide. This oxide is widely used in the manufacture of white paint. However, it has not yet proved economic either to transport the mud to potential users of titanium or to attract the titanium users to the red mud sites themselves.

The main problem for the latter development is that other raw materials would also be required if a titanium-based industry were to be established. In any case, extracting titanium oxide from red mud would not solve the disposal problem since a substantial amount of waste (Table 59.1) would still be left.

There are, as yet, no really satisfactory solutions to the problem of red mud.

The extraction of aluminium from alumina

The electrolytic reduction of aluminium oxide dissolved in cryolite to aluminium is described on page 101. The aluminium oxide needs to be free of other metal oxides (the ones in the red mud) because these might be more easily electrolysed and so be deposited on the cathode. This would make the aluminium metal impure.

The current required for the cell may be about 30 000 A, with a potential difference of about 5 V. This is a major energy demand. Put another way, for every tonne of aluminium produced, about 15 000 kWh of electricity is used. This fact has usually led to the siting of an aluminium smelter close to a source of hydroelectric power, for example in Norway and Canada. It is also worth noting that both these countries have excellent deep-water harbours, and extraction plants can be built close to the sea, so minimizing the costs of land transport.

The provision of cheap electricity was behind the idea of the Upper Mazaruni Development in Guyana. Unfortunately, the world recession of the early 1980s meant that the market for aluminium declined considerably, while there was already much excess capacity elsewhere in the world. The Upper Mazaruni project had to be abandoned, as did a project for an aluminium smelter in Trinidad based upon the availability of large supplies of oil and natural gas which could be used to produce the required electrical energy.

The current trend towards recycling aluminium in the form of aluminium cans may also affect any possible future developments in aluminium smelting.

QUESTIONS

1 What would be problems associated with the location of an alumina plant close to a town?

2 (a) Make a list of the factors which decide whether or not a country with large reserves of bauxite would also build an aluminium smelter.
(b) Would the smelter have to be built next to the alumina plant, or could there be good reasons for siting it elsewhere?

3 Write an account of the chemical processes involved in the extraction of aluminium from bauxite. Give equations where possible for the chemical reactions.

4 What are the main uses of (a) bauxite and (b) aluminium metal?

Key words

bauxite   overburden   alumina   red mud   electrolytic reduction

Basic facts

- Countries with large reserves of bauxite are not necessarily aluminium-producers.

- There are four possible developments of the aluminium industry:
  - countries with bauxite reserves may concentrate the ore and then export it (e.g. Guyana);
  - countries with no bauxite reserves at all but with relatively cheap sources of electricity may import the concentrated ore or the alumina, and then extract the aluminium (e.g. Norway, Canada);
  - countries with bauxite reserves may concentrate the ore and then convert at least some of it to alumina before exporting it (e.g. Jamaica);
  - countries with bauxite reserves may carry out all the processes which are needed to extract aluminium (e.g. Australia, USA, USSR).

- The main pollution problem in the aluminium industry is the red mud which has no use and is stored in large man-made 'lakes'.

60 Sugar and ethanol

Sugar cane and jaggery

Sugar cane is widely grown in tropical countries such as those in the Caribbean where the soil is warm and fertile and where there is a plentiful supply of rainwater.

The sugar plant is a type of 'giant' grass which grows to a height of 3 or 4 metres. Sugar (sucrose, page 226) is produced in its stalk. After about a year, the cane is cut by machine (Fig. 60.1) and transported to the sugar factory. The roots of the plant stay in the ground and soon grow new stalks. Unlike many local crops, sugar cane is always grown on a very large scale.

When sugar cane was first used many hundreds of years ago, Man probably just chewed the raw cane because of its pleasant taste. But some people must have put it through a simple process to make an impure brown sugar called **sukari guru** or **jaggery**.

Experiment 60.1 Making your own sugar

Crush a small amount of sugar cane using a pestle and mortar or a simple mincing machine and collect the juice in a beaker. Add a small amount of slaked lime (powdered calcium hydroxide) and stir the mixture. Use a glass rod to spot the liquid onto a piece of red litmus paper. Repeat this process until the litmus paper just turns blue.

Boil the alkaline juice and then filter it using a suction pump if necessary. Then boil the filtered juice with decolorizing charcoal to remove the impurities.

Finally filter again to remove the charcoal and heat the juice in an evaporating basin on a steam bath until a very thick syrup is produced. Allow this syrup to cool and to form crystals. (It may help to speed up the crystallization if you add some sugar crystals to the syrup.)

Fig. 60.1

Some of this was then fermented to make beer. However, in a modern sugar factory the process is much more complicated and there are several important products.

Jaggery is made on a large scale by a process that is quite similar to the one described in Experiment 60.1, except that the brown impurities are not removed.

The sugar factory

After the leaves have been removed from the cut cane, the stalks are cut into much smaller pieces by a machine and then passed through heavy metal rollers which squeeze out the juice (Fig. 60.2). This process is repeated and water is also added to ensure that all the juice has been removed. The dry wood that remains is called **bagasse** (Fig. 60.3).

Many sugar factories use this as the fuel for producing the steam necessary for the later evaporation process as well as the steam that drives the crushing and rolling machines. The use of its own fuel makes sugar production a very economical process. Bagasse fibres, held together by a synthetic resin, can also be used to make fibreboard (hardboard).

Fig. 60.2

Fig. 60.3

After the juice has been extracted, it is filtered through mechanical screens. It is then heated by steam and some slaked lime is added. The heated juice is then allowed to settle in tanks called **clarifiers**. The slaked lime helps to precipitate the muddy impurities which fall to the bottom of the clarifiers. After washing, the mud is returned to the cane fields as a fertilizer.

Slaked lime is also added for another reason. Sucrose can be hydrolysed (page 227) to form two other sugars called glucose and fructose, both of which have the molecular formula $C_6H_{12}O_6$.

$$C_{12}H_{22}O_{11}(aq) + H_2O(l) \rightleftharpoons C_6H_{12}O_6(aq)$$
glucose

$+$

$$C_6H_{12}O_6(aq)$$
fructose

(Glucose and fructose have the same molecular formula but different structural formulas.)

If such a mixture is formed, no crystallization will occur. Just the right amount of slaked lime in the juice prevents this hydrolysis from occurring.

The pure clear juice cannot be heated above about 200 °C because the sugar would 'burn' and go brown. To avoid this problem the juice is evaporated in

265

Fig. 60.4

Fig. 60.5

closed containers under reduced pressure using steam as the source of heat (Fig. 60.4). The reduced pressure lowers the boiling point of the juice. As the juice passes from one **evaporator** to another, it loses water and becomes progressively more syrupy. Finally, the syrup is again evaporated at very low pressure in a **vacuum pan** until the sugar crystallizes.

Large centrifuges (Fig. 60.5) are used to separate the solid sugar from the very thick syrup (**molasses**). After washing with water and then drying, the sugar is bagged for sale or transported in bulk for export (Fig. 60.6).

Sugar has a lot of uses in the home as well as in the production of soft drinks, sweets, biscuits, cakes, jams and so on. However, a diet containing a lot of sweet things can significantly increase tooth decay.

Ethanol from sugar

The process of fermentation can be used to make ethanol (alcohol) from sugar (page 227). One of the modern uses of ethanol is as an alternative fuel to petrol, and some sugar-producing countries like Brazil are developing the production of ethanol as part of their sugar industry. Already Brazil fuels about 20 per cent of its cars using **gasohol**, a mixture of ethanol and petrol, rather than just petrol.

However, a more familiar use of sugar is in the fermentation of molasses to make the famous Caribbean spirit called **rum**. Despite the extraction processes described above, molasses still contains about 60 per cent of dissolved sugar.

The manufacture of rum begins by adding water to the molasses and then pasteurizing (partially

Fig. 60.6 Transporting bulk sugar by lorry and barge to ship

collected in three separate containers. One container collects the rum while the others collect lower concentrations of alcohol which have to be returned to the still for further distillation in the next cycle. The modern method operates a continuous process rather than a batch process and uses **column stills** (Fig. 60.9) which have much in common with the distillation columns in an oil refinery (page 270). The first column is used to remove the dilute solution of alcohol from the fermented mixture and the other two are used to purify and concentrate the alcoholic vapours. Each column consists of perforated trays and downpipes that allow the liquid to flow from one tray to the next one down the column. As in the

Fig. 60.7

sterilizing) the solution so formed. Yeast is used to ferment the sugar in fermenting tanks (Fig. 60.7). When the sugar has all been converted to alcohol and carbon dioxide, the yeast dies from lack of nutrient and the mixture is now ready for distillation.

The old method of distilling uses the **pot still** (Fig. 60.8). This is basically a kettle which is heated by steam, and the vapour given off is condensed and

Fig. 60.9

fractional distillation of crude oil, the continuous process results in condensates being drawn off at various points up the column. So a mild rum product as well as alcohol can be made.

Newly distilled rum is not yet ready for drinking. It has to be aged (matured) in large oak casks for many years, and then finally blended to give the familiar products such as 'Appleton', 'Mount Gay' and 'Old Oak'. The pure alcohol from the column stills is used in the manufacture of gin, vodka and liqueurs.

Fig. 60.8

The economics of the sugar industry

The tropical countries produce their sugar from sugar cane. But one of the most important changes in the sugar industry this century has been the gradual switch from sugar cane to sugar beet. Beet contains the same proportion of sucrose as sugar cane but it has the advantage that it can be farmed in much more temperate climates where sugar cane cannot be grown.

The price of sugar has fluctuated widely in recent years from a high in the mid-1970s of about $1500 a tonne to a low of about $150 a tonne in the late 1970s. Where sugar production was relatively inefficient, the low world price often resulted in sugar being produced at a loss. Because of considerable competition from beet-producing countries, the cane-producing countries have suffered from a declining output. For example, Jamaica's output of sugar was 500 000 tonnes in 1970 but only 200 000 tonnes in 1980.

It is quite possible that there will be a shift in emphasis away from the use of sugar as a food to its use in producing a variety of useful chemicals. In particular, as the world's reserves of crude oil dwindle and prices of oil-based chemicals rise, the use of sugar to make gasohol may become more widespread. Also, molasses can be fermented to citric acid, propanone (acetone) and butanol using certain moulds and bacteria. Again, sucrose can be reacted with the acids obtained from coconut oil to produce detergents, and it can be polymerized with other chemicals to make plastics and resins. Such developments could inject new life into the sugar industry.

QUESTIONS

1 In some African countries a 'local gin' is made from impure sugar (jaggery). Explain how you think that:
(*a*) jaggery is made from sugar cane,
(*b*) 'local gin' is made from jaggery.

2 Explain why bagasse is such an important by-product of the sugar industry.

3 (*a*) What are the main differences between making gin in a pot still and making it in column stills?
(*b*) Why do you think that only a small percentage of rum is now made in pot stills?
(*c*) Column stills in a gin distillery have a similar design to fractional distillation columns in an oil refinery. Read Chapter 61 and then write down the differences between the two distillation processes.

Key words

sucrose (sugar)   bagasse   molasses   fermentation   distillation   pot stills   column stills

Basic facts

- Sugar (sucrose) can be extracted from sugar cane, which is grown in tropical climates, and from sugar beet, which is grown in temperate climates.

- The main stages in the production of sugar from sugar cane are: crushing the cane and washing out the sugar with water; adding slaked lime to the heated juice to precipitate impurities; evaporating the purified juice under pressure, crystallizing the sugar; and centrifuging to separate the sugar from the molasses.

- The main by-products of the sugar industry are bagasse and molasses. Bagasse is used as a fuel for the boilers in the sugar factory and also to make fibreboard. Molasses is used to make rum and it is also one of the constituents in cattle feed.

- The main stages in the production of rum from molasses are fermentation using yeast, distillation (either in pot stills or column stills), maturation, and blending.

- It is possible that a sugar-based chemical industry will develop as oil-based chemicals become more costly.

61 The petroleum industry

Exploration and development

Exploration for crude oil and natural gas is being carried out in several areas of the Caribbean, but by far the most important known reserves belong to Trinidad and Tobago. The first well drilled for oil in Trinidad was in 1857, close to the famous pitch lake. Commercial oil production in Trinidad began in 1908 and for nearly 50 years was based entirely on wells drilled on land. But since the late 1960s there have been several succcessful developments of offshore oilfields, especially off the south-east and south-west coasts of Trinidad (Fig. 61.1). Natural gas production has been largely associated with the oilfields and up till recently had little commercial value: some was used by the oil companies as a fuel in their refineries and quite a lot was vented or flared off.

However, world energy problems have caused a reassessment of the worth of the natural gas associated with oilfields. The demand for natural gas has risen considerably and it is now used in large quantities as a fuel in industry and as a starting point for the manufacture of certain chemicals such as hydrogen (page 218) and ammonia. Some exploration effort is now aimed at finding natural gas deposits separate from the oilfields, and gasfields have already been located off the north and east coasts of Trinidad.

Fig. 61.1

There are two oil refineries in Trinidad (Fig. 61.2) which produce the usual range of hydrocarbon fuels and lubricants but only a very limited number of **petrochemicals** (chemicals made from crude oil).

Fig. 61.2

New energy-based industries are also being developed at the Point Lisas industrial estate on the west coast of Central Trinidad where there is an excellent deep-water harbour. Natural gas (mainly methane) is the most important raw material (feedstock). It is used along with steam to make synthesis gas, a mixture of hydrogen and carbon oxides (page 218). Once the oxides of carbon have been removed, the gas mixture is a source of hydrogen for the Haber process (page 133). Liquid anhydrous ammonia made at Point Lisas is exported to Europe, the USA and South America. Some of the ammonia is reacted with carbon dioxide to make urea, which is a solid fertilizer with a high percentage of nitrogen. Some natural gas at Point Lisas is converted to methanol and some is also used in the extraction of iron from iron ore.

The refining of crude oil

Crude oil is a complex mixture of many hydrocarbons. The separation into simpler mixtures is achieved using the process of **fractional distillation** (fractionation) in an industrial fractionating column (Fig. 61.3).

Fig. 61.3

The crude oil enters the column at a temperature about 400 °C but the temperature at the top of the column is only about 30 °C. The part of the petroleum that is still liquid when it enters the column (boiling point above 400 °C) falls to the bottom, while the part that is a gas at 400 °C rises up the column and is steadily cooled as it rises (Fig. 61.4a).

Think about what happens to a hydrocarbon with a boiling point of 200 °C. It is a gas when it enters the column and it passes upwards through the bubble caps (Figs. 61.4b and 61.6) in the first three trays. But before it reaches the top tray, the temperature falls below its boiling point so that it condenses and falls back to the next lower tray. It is tapped off as part of the kerosine fraction.

Similarly, a hydrocarbon with a boiling point of 300 °C is a gas on entry and passes upwards. But this time it becomes a liquid before it reaches the second tray from the top. It is tapped off as part of the diesel oil fraction.

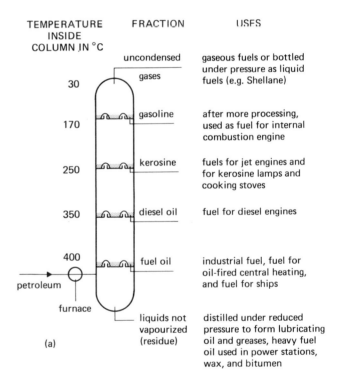

TEMPERATURE INSIDE COLUMN IN °C	FRACTION	USES
30	uncondensed gases	gaseous fuels or bottled under pressure as liquid fuels (e.g. Shellane)
170	gasoline	after more processing, used as fuel for internal combustion engine
250	kerosine	fuels for jet engines and for kerosine lamps and cooking stoves
350	diesel oil	fuel for diesel engines
400	fuel oil	industrial fuel, fuel for oil-fired central heating, and fuel for ships
	liquids not vapourized (residue)	distilled under reduced pressure to form lubricating oil and greases, heavy fuel oil used in power stations, wax, and bitumen

petroleum →
furnace

(a)

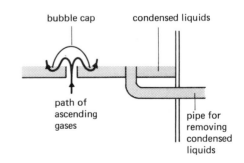

bubble cap   condensed liquids

path of ascending gases

pipe for removing condensed liquids

Fig. 61.4   (b)   TRAY AND BUBBLE CAP

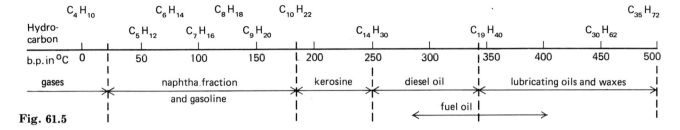

Fig. 61.5

Another way of looking at how the petroleum is split up by fractional distillation is shown in Fig. 61.5. This also gives an idea of the formulas of the alkanes in the different fractions.

Fig. 61.6 Dismantled bubble caps

The petrochemical industry

Some oil refineries also have a petrochemicals complex in which a wide variety of useful chemicals is made from some of the fractions from the fractionating columns. After several distillations, the fractions with higher boiling points are usually **cracked** so that the larger, less useful molecules are broken down into the smaller, more useful ones (page 218). The other main conversion process is **reforming** in which the molecules stay the same size but their shapes are altered: this is important, for example, in producing gasoline with a high octane rating.

The most important products in the petrochemical industry are the alkenes that are formed by the cracking processes. These are produced, along with the alkanes made of smaller molecules, when the vaporized fractions, together with some steam, are passed at a moderate temperature through a fluidized bed, of alumina (Al_2O_3) and silica (SiO_2), which acts as a catalyst. The products of this cracking process are passed on to a fractionating column where they are then separated into several fractions.

Alkenes such as ethene (ethylene) and propene (propylene) are the usual starting points for making organic chemicals. Some of the products made from ethene are given in Fig. 61.7: the range of products made from propene is even wider than this. Most of the reactions shown in Fig. 61.7 are addition or polymerization reactions (pages 221 and 222).

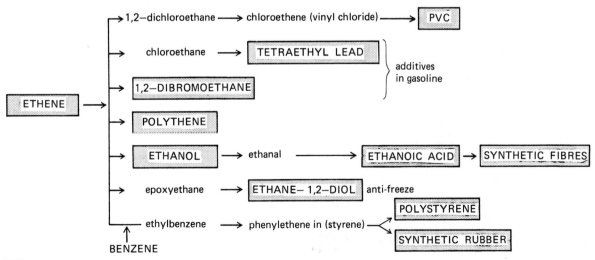

Fig. 61.7

QUESTIONS

1 (*a*) Explain, with equations, how methane (the main constituent of natural gas) can be used in the manufacture of ammonia on a large scale. Mention what other raw materials are required besides natural gas.
(*b*) What is the main use of ammonia?

2 List some reasons why:
(*a*) much of the natural gas found in association with crude oil used to be vented or flared off rather than piped ashore;
(*b*) as much of this natural gas as possible is now put to good use.

3 Use the diagram of a fractionating column (Fig. 61.4*a*) to explain what happens to (*a*) a hydrocarbon with a boiling point of 60 °C and (*b*) a hydrocarbon with a boiling point of 375° C.

Key words

petrochemicals	fractionating columns	tray and bubble cap	reforming
fractional distillation (fractionation)	fractions	cracking	

Basic facts

- The most important reserves of crude oil and natural gas in the Caribbean belong to Trinidad and Tobago.

- Crude oil is separated into various fractions with different boiling point ranges by the process of fractional distillation in a fractionating column.

- Some of these fractions are used in the petrochemical industry to make a wide variety of chemicals. The main chemical reactions involved are the cracking of alkane molecules into smaller alkene molecules, and the addition (or addition polymerization) reactions of the alkenes.

- Natural gas is now widely used as a fuel and as a feedstock in the chemical industry.

62 Alternative energy supplies

What is alternative energy?

Much of the world's energy comes from the fossil fuels – coal, oil and natural gas. Reserves of oil and gas in the Caribbean area may last into the twenty-first century, especially if exploration results in new discoveries. However, increasing attention will need to be given to alternative energy sources, that is, sources that do not involve fossil fuels.

Fig. 62.1 shows many of these alternative sources. Some like nuclear energy and hydroelectric power

(HEP) are already quite widely used in various parts of the world while others, like solar power, geothermal energy (heat energy from 'hot' rocks under the earth's surface) and the energy derived from the wind, waves and tides, are being experimented with on a small scale but do not provide more than a tiny fraction of any nation's energy.

The energy produced in the various ways shown in Fig. 60.1 is either used directly as heat or is converted into electricity in a power station. For

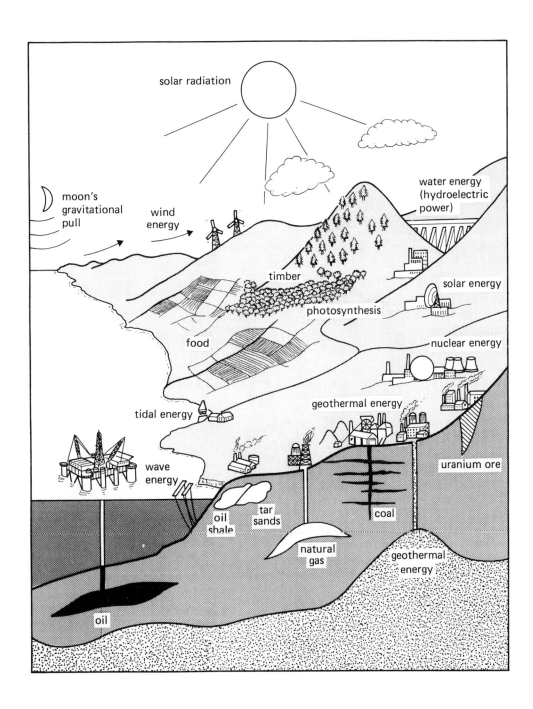

Fig. 62.1

Fig. 62.2

Fig. 62.4

example, solar energy can be used directly to heat water in homes (Fig. 62.2), to dry crops (Fig. 62.3) and to distil water (Fig. 62.4), or it can be used to produce electricity by the direct conversion of solar energy to electrical energy in a solar cell (Fig. 62.5).

Fig. 62.3

Most of these alternative sources of energy are **renewable**. However much we make use of solar energy or the energy from the wind, waves and tides or hydroelectric power, more of the same will always be available. Even geothermal energy is like this, although there are obviously limits on how long a particular borehole in 'hot' rocks will continue to supply hot water. In contrast, fossil fuels represent **non-renewable** sources of energy because their supplies are finite and will eventually run out. Nuclear power from fission (see below) is also non-renewable because it is dependent on supplies of uranium ore.

Energy obtained from recently-living materials is more difficult to classify in this way. This includes the burning of wood or charcoal as a fuel, the burning of bagasse in a sugar factory (page 265), the use

of methane produced by the decay of vegetable material (page 229) and the use of ethanol derived from sugar as a fuel for the internal combustion engine (page 266). Given good management, the resources that are used are clearly renewable though the total mass of all living things in a given area (the **biomass**) varies a lot depending on factors

Fig. 62.5

such as climate, soil type and the rate of use by Man. In extreme cases, the biomass can be severely depleted by over-exploitation, for example, by the wholesale destruction of forests and the serious soil erosion that sometimes follows. The resources then become non-renewable in those areas. There are huge areas of forest in the Amazon Basin of South America, but there is much worldwide concern about the rapid rate at which the trees are being felled and the land cleared for agricultural purposes.

The following is a list of just some of the alternative energy projects that have been undertaken recently in the Caribbean countries. Some of these may be developed on a large scale sometime in the future.

1. A biogas (methane from vegetable material) project in Jamaica.
2. A project in Montserrat to develop more efficient techniques for the production of fuelwood and charcoal, and the development and testing of more efficient charcoal-burning stoves (Fig. 62.6).
3. A solar-powered pumping system for farm irrigation in Antigua.
4. An assessment of wind and solar energy resources in Antigua, Barbados, Barbuda, Montserrat, Nevis, St. Kitts, and St. Lucia (Fig. 62.7).
5. A solar-powered electricity station for a rural health station in Guyana.
6. A biomass resource analysis and assessment for the Windward and Leeward Islands and Barbados.

Fig. 62.7 Wind turbine used to generate electricity in Antigua

Fig. 62.6

Nuclear energy

As yet, very little attention has been given in Caribbean countries to the use of nuclear energy for electricity production. But in some parts of the world it is the most important form of alternative energy.

Radioactive elements change into other elements as they emit radiation (page 158). In 1919, Rutherford succeeded in artificially changing one element to another. He did this by directing α-particles at nitrogen atoms. Some of the α-particles hit the nitrogen nuclei so hard that oxygen nuclei were produced along with some protons. Each time one of these changes takes place, energy is released because of the destruction of some mass (page 203).

The best 'missiles' for making artificial nuclear reactions are fast-moving neutrons. These have no charge and so are not repelled by the nuclei which they are about to hit.

The energy released by the change of a single nucleus to a different nucleus is very small indeed. But if a lot of nuclei are affected, then the energy released can be very large indeed. There are two kinds of nuclear reaction – the splitting of the nuclei of heavy atoms to form lighter atoms (**fission**), and the combining of the nuclei of light atoms to form heavier atoms (**fusion**).

Electricity from nuclear fission

The world's first nuclear power station making electricity from nuclear fission was opened at Calder Hall in Britain in 1965 (Fig. 62.8). The fission reaction releases heat energy which is used to produce steam at a high pressure. The steam drives turbines which make the electricity.

The fuel for the process is natural uranium (Fig. 62.9). When a neutron hits an atom of uranium-235, the atom splits into two nearly equal bits

Fig. 62.8

Fig. 62.9

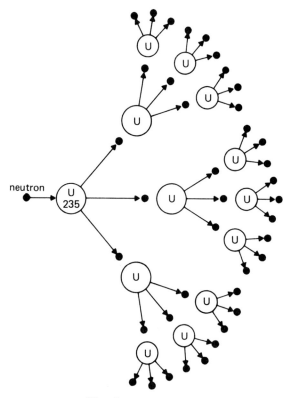

Fig. 62.10

(The diagram does not show the other fission products—the atoms of barium and krypton.)

provided some electricity for the national supply since 1975. Fast breeder reactors can produce nuclear energy at the same time as 'breeding' their own fissile fuel (plutonium-239) from uranium-238. The plutonium can be separated from the mixture of elements in the reactor and then put back as the fuel. Unlike uranium, it is a man-made element and is not found in nature.

There are some problems associated with this form of energy, especially over getting rid of the highly radioactive waste which all nuclear power stations produce. This waste cannot be destroyed, and it has to be left in a safe place until it is no longer radio-active. Since this may take thousands of years, it is vital that we do not endanger the lives of generations to come by storing it in the wrong way.

A recent idea is to mix the waste with silicon dioxide (sand) to convert it into a stable glass which can then be encased in stainless steel canisters. These could be buried in holes drilled deep into the rocks or left to lie on the sea floor. But arguments are still going on about the safety of this method of disposing of radioactive waste, and also about other hazards of producing energy using fission reactions.

Nuclear fusion

Fusion is the process that can create the frightening amount of energy of the kind released by the hydrogen bomb. It is also the source of the very high temperatures in the sun and other stars. In the sun, it is thought that hydrogen nuclei fuse together to form helium nuclei, and attempts have been made in the laboratory to do the same kind of thing on a much smaller and controlled scale.

There are many difficulties to overcome if man-made nuclear fusion is to be a major source of the world's energy. But it is an exciting prospect for two reasons. First, one of the most suitable elements for fusion is deuterium, an isotope of hydrogen. This is present in sea water and so, unlike uranium, it is in plentiful supply. Secondly, the products of fusion reactions are stable elements and not highly radio-active ones: there will be no problems in getting rid of this kind of nuclear waste.

(these could be, for example, atoms of barium and krypton) and also releases three more neutrons. These neutrons can then go on to hit other uranium-235 atoms and so more splitting occurs in a **chain reaction** (Fig. 62.10). If this reaction is allowed to carry on unchecked, the rate gets higher and higher and a huge amount of energy is produced in a very short time. Under certain conditions, an unchecked fission reaction can cause an atomic explosion.

But for making electricity, the fission reaction must be controlled in the **reactor** so that the heat energy is released at a steady rate. Rods of boron steel have to be used to absorb some of the neutrons whenever the reaction begins to accelerate too much.

Most nuclear power stations use 'natural' uranium which has been extracted from the ore pitchblende. This contains only 0.7% of uranium-235: the rest is uranium-238 which is not **fissile** (that is, its atoms cannot be split in a nuclear reaction with a neutron). Some of the more recent nuclear power stations use a fuel that has been enriched in uranium-235 so that it lasts longer before it has to be renewed.

Efforts have also been made to find ways of converting uranium-238 into fissile fuel. These have resulted in a new and, so far, experimental **fast breeder reactor**. One of these has been built at Dounreay on the north coast of Britain and has

QUESTIONS

1 List all the sources of electricity that are used in your country. Find out the percentage contribution each makes to the total supply.

2 (a) List all the renewable sources of energy that you can think of.
(b) Write a short essay in which you predict which of these sources are most likely to be important in the Caribbean countries in the twenty-first century.

3 What are the prospects of nuclear energy ever being developed as a major source of electricity in the Caribbean countries?

Key words

alternative energy	biomass	fusion
renewable resources	nuclear power	chain reaction
non-renewable resources	fission	fast breeder reactor

Basic facts

- Alternative energy sources are those sources that are alternative to the fossil fuels.

- Unlike fossil fuels, alternative energy sources are largely renewable.

- As yet, the only alternative energy sources used on a large scale are nuclear energy and hydro-electric power. However, many smaller scale projects are underway for all the sources featured in Fig. 62.1.

- In nuclear fission a chain reaction occurs in which neutrons cause the 'splitting' of U-235 atoms. This reaction generates heat energy which is used in a nuclear power station to produce high-pressure steam.

- Nuclear fusion offers the best very long-term source of the world's energy.

Data sheet 1 The symbols and relative atomic masses of some elements

Element	Symbol	Relative atomic mass
Aluminium	Al	27.0
Argon	Ar	39.9
Barium	Ba	137
Beryllium	Be	9.01
Boron	B	10.8
Bromine	Br	79.9
Cadmium	Cd	112
Caesium	Cs	133
Calcium	Ca	40.1
Carbon	C	12.0
Chlorine	Cl	35.5
Chromium	Cr	52.0
Cobalt	Co	58.9
Copper	Cu	63.5
Fluorine	F	19.0
Germanium	Ge	72.6
Gold	Au	197
Helium	He	4.00
Hydrogen	H	1.01
Iodine	I	127
Iron	Fe	55.8
Krypton	Kr	83.8
Lead	Pb	207

Element	Symbol	Relative atomic mass
Lithium	Li	6.94
Magnesium	Mg	24.3
Manganese	Mn	54.9
Mercury	Hg	201
Neon	Ne	20.2
Nickel	Ni	58.7
Nitrogen	N	14.0
Oxygen	O	16.0
Phosphorus	P	31.0
Platinum	Pt	195
Potassium	K	39.1
Rubidium	Rb	85.5
Silicon	Si	28.1
Silver	Ag	108
Sodium	Na	23.0
Strontium	Sr	87.6
Sulphur	S	32.1
Tin	Sn	119
Titanium	Ti	47.9
Uranium	U	238
Vanadium	V	50.9
Xenon	Xe	131
Zinc	Zn	65.4

Data sheet 2 The boiling points, melting points, and densities of some elements in their groups

Group	Element	m.p. in °C	b.p. in °C	Density* in $g\,cm^{-3}$
I	Lithium Sodium Potassium Rubidium Caesium	180 97.8 63.7 38.9 28.7	1330 890 774 688 690	0.53 0.97 0.86 1.53 1.90
II	Beryllium Magnesium Calcium Strontium Barium	1280 650 850 768 714	2477 1110 1487 1380 1640	1.85 1.74 1.54 2.62 3.51
III	Boron Aluminium	2300 660	3930 2470	2.34 2.70
IV	Carbon Silicon Germanium Tin (white) Lead	sublimes at 3730 °C 1410 937 232 327	(see left) 2360 2830 2270 1744	{ graphite 2.25 { diamond 3.51 2.33 5.35 { white 7.28 { grey 5.75 11.3
IV	Nitrogen Phosphorus (white) Arsenic Antimony Bismuth	− 210 44.2 sublimes at 613 °C 630 271	− 196 280 (see left) 1380 1560	0.808 (77 K) { white 1.82 { red 2.34 5.72 6.62 9.80
VI	Oxygen Sulphur (rhombic)	− 218 113	− 183 445	1.15 (90 K) { rhombic 2.07 { monoclinic 1.96
VII	Fluorine Chlorine Bromine Iodine	− 220 − 101 − 7.2 114	− 188 − 34.7 58.8 184	1.11 (85 K) 1.56 (238 K) 3.12 4.93
Noble gases	Helium Neon Argon Krypton Xenon	− 270 − 249 − 189 − 157 − 112	− 269 − 246 − 186 − 152 − 108	0.147 (4 K) 1.20 (27 K) 1.40 (87 K) 2.16 (121 K) 3.52 (165 K)

*The densities of the gaseous elements are at their respective boiling points which are given in kelvin after each density. All other densities are at 293 K (20 °C).

Data sheet 2 (continued)

Group	Element	m.p. in °C	b.p. in °C	Density* in $g\,cm^{-3}$
Heavy (transition) metals	Scandium	1540	2730	2.99
	Titanium	1675	3260	4.54
	Vanadium	1900	3000	5.96
	Chromium	1890	2482	7.19
	Manganese	1240	2100	7.20
	Iron	1535	3000	7.86
	Cobalt	1492	2900	8.90
	Nickel	1453	2730	8.90
	Copper	1083	2595	8.92
	Zinc	420	907	7.14
	Silver	961	2210	10.5
	Cadmium	321	765	8.64
	Platinum	1769	4530	21.4
	Gold	1063	2970	19.3
	Mercury	− 38.9	357	13.6

Data sheet 3 The reactivity series for metals

| | REACTIONS OF ELEMENTS | | | | REACTIONS OF COMPOUNDS* | | | | |
| | | | | | Reduction of oxide by | | Action of heat on | | |
Metal	Air or oxygen	Water or steam	Dilute HCl or H_2SO_4	Displacement reactions	Carbon	Hydrogen	Oxide	Carbonate	Nitrate
K		React with cold water to form alkaline solutions						Do not decompose on heating	Decompose to nitrite and oxygen
Na			React to form salts, giving off hydrogen		Not reduced				
Ca									
Mg	Burn readily to form oxides	React with steam to form oxides		Metal displaces a less reactive metal from an oxide or a salt		Not reduced		Decompose to oxide and carbon dioxide	Decompose to oxide, oxygen, and nitrogen dioxide
Al							Do not decompose on heating		
Zn					Only reduced industrially				
Fe						Readily reduced			
Pb	Slow oxidation	No reaction	No reaction		Readily reduced				
Cu									
Hg							Oxides decompose on heating	Decompose to metal, oxygen, and carbon dioxide	Decompose to metal, oxygen, and nitrogen dioxide
Ag	No reaction								

* *Note.* Where heating is involved, it has been assumed that the maximum temperature obtainable in the laboratory is about 800 °C. Many reactions which do not occur at this temperature may well occur at higher temperatures.

The periodic table

periods	groups																	
	I	II											III	IV	V	VI	VII	VIII
1	1 H																	2 He
2	3 Li	4 Be											5 B	6 C	7 N	8 O	9 F	10 Ne
3	11 Na	12 Mg						heavy (transition) metals					13 Al	14 Si	15 P	16 S	17 Cl	18 Ar
4	19 K	20 Ca	21 Sc	22 Ti	23 V	24 Cr	25 Mn	26 Fe	27 Co	28 Ni	29 Cu	30 Zn	31 Ga	32 Ge	33 As	34 Se	35 Br	36 Kr
5	37 Rb	38 Sr	39 Y	40 Zr	41 Nb	42 Mo	43 Tc	44 Ru	45 Rh	46 Pd	47 Ag	48 Cd	49 In	50 Sn	51 Sb	52 Te	53 I	54 Xe
6	55 Cs	56 Ba	57 La *	72 Hf	73 Ta	74 W	75 Re	76 Os	77 Ir	78 Pt	79 Au	80 Hg	81 Tl	82 Pb	83 Bi	84 Po	85 At	86 Rn
7	87 Fr	88 Ra	89 Ac †															

* lanthanides

58 Ce	59 Pr	60 Nd	61 Pm	62 Sm	63 Eu	64 Gd	65 Tb	66 Dy	67 Ho	68 Er	69 Tm	70 Yb	71 Lu

† actinides

90 Th	91 Pa	92 U	93 Np	94 Pu	95 Am	96 Cm	97 Bk	98 Cf	99 Es	100 Fm	101 Md	102 No	103 Lr

alkali metals

alkaline earth metals

halogens

noble gases

Each element in the periodic table is given a number that shows its position. This number (here above symbol) is called the **atomic number** and is not the same as the relative atomic mass of the element.

Identity of single substances used in practical exercises (Chapter 56)

1 X Na_2SO_3
  Y $NaHCO_3$
2 P iron(II) ammonium sulphate
3 M Cu_2O
5 S $Pb(NO_3)_2$
6 G $Fe(NO_3)_3$
7 E H_2O
  F H_2O_2

Answers to numerical questions

20 Atoms and formulas
1 (a) 27 (b) 9 (c) 8 (d) 40 (e) 20
2 NaCl
3 $MgCl_2$

21 The chemical mole and writing equations
1 (a) 32.1 g (b) 7.1 g (c) 1.4 g (d) 138 g (e) 15.5 g
  (f) 3.0 g (g) 14.58 g (h) 47.6 g (i) 274.7 g (j) 0.558 g
2 (a) 0.33 (b) 0.50 (c) 0.165 (d) 3.0 (e) 2.0
  (f) 2.0 (g) 3.0 (h) 0.50 (i) 0.010 (j) 3.0
3 (a) 46.0 (b) 102.0 (c) 148.3 (d) 18.0 (e) 159.6
5 (a) 0.67 g (b) 1.89×10^{-2} mol Cl
  (c) 1.89×10^{-2} mol Hg (d) HgCl (e) $HgCl_2$
6 (c) 0.067 g of hydrogen, 0.533 g of oxygen
  (d) 0.067 mol H, 0.033 mol O
  (e) H_2O
7 (a) NaCl (b) CO_2 (c) PbO (d) Fe_2O_3 (e) $PbCO_3$
  (f) Na_2CO_3 (g) NaOH (h) HNO_3
8 (b) Fe_2O_3
9 (a) $AlCl_3$
10 (a) 2 mol Na, 2 mol S, 3 mol O
  (b) 158.2 (c) 5 mol H_2O (d) 90.0 g (e) 248.2
11 (d) 0.0301 mol $CuSO_4$, 0.15 mol H_2O
  (e) 5.0 (f) $CuSO_4 \cdot 5H_2O$
12 $Na_2CO_3 \cdot H_2O$, $Na_2CO_3 \cdot 10H_2O$

22 The idea of ions
4 (a) 510 C (b) 284 580 C (c) Fe^{3+}
5 (b) 8.33×10^{-3} g (c) 810 C (d) 97 200 C (e) H^-

23 Ions and the reactions of acids, bases and salts
1 (a) 0.50 M (b) 0.50 M (c) 0.050 M
2 (a) 101 g (b) 35.5 g (c) 50.4 g
5 (a) 0.10 mol $CaCO_3$ (b) 0.20 mol HCl (c) 0.10 mol CO_2
10 (a) 5.5 g (b) 50 cm³ of 0.5 M KI solution,
  25 cm³ of 0.5 M $Hg(NO_3)_2$ solution
  (d) 1.25×10^{-4} mol $Hg(NO_3)_2$, 2.5×10^{-4} mol KI

24 Some more ideas about acids and alkalis
6 (a) 0.10 M (b) 2.5×10^{-3} mol $H_4C_2O_2$
  (c) 2.5×10^{-3} mol OH^-
  (d) 1 mol OH^- reacts with 1 mol $H_4C_2O_2$ (e) 1

25 Reactions of gases
2 (a) 0.050 mol Cl_2 (b) 2.7×10^{21}
  (c) 2.24 l (d) 2.4 l (e) 0.25 mol CO_2
3 a d b e c
4 (a) 3 (c) AsH_3
5 (b) 4 molecules of NO (c) 2 molecules of N_2
6 (a) N_2F_2 (c) (iii)
7 (a) 2 (c) 43.9 (d) N_2O
9 (a) C_2H_4 (b) CH_2

26 Chemical calculations
1 296 kg
2 1980 kg
3 (a) 560 kg (b) 2.4×10^5 l
4 (a) 27.5 kg (b) 14.4 l
5 2.22 g of calcium hydroxide, 3.00 g of calcium carbonate
6 500 cm³ of oxygen, 300 cm³ of carbon dioxide
7 (a) 80 cm³ (b) 10 cm³ (c) 20 cm³ (d) no (e) 10 cm³
8 700 l
9 (b) 8 cm³
10 (a) 0.001 (b) 2.5 cm³
11 (a) 100 cm³ (b) 100 cm³
13 (b) 0.10 mol Na_2SO_4, 0.15 mol $BaCl_2$
  (d) 23.3 g
14 (a) 1.5×10^{21} (b) 3.0×10^{23} (c) 2.4×10^{22}
  (d) 3.0×10^{23}
15 0.127 g of copper, 0.142 g of chlorine
16 (a) 1.5×10^{22} (b) 1.2×10^{22} (c) 1.5×10^{23}
17 (a) 5.79×10^4 C (b) 2.41×10^3 C

31 Chemicals from limestone
3 (b) (i) 4.8 l (ii) 2.4 l
  (c) 40.1%, 21.8%

Answers to numerical questions

33 Chemicals from air
4 (a) $0.48\,g$ (b) $0.48\,g$ (c) $0.06\,g$ (d) $0.06\,mol\;H$
(e) $0.28\,g$ (f) $0.02\,mol\;N$ (h) 3
5 21.2, 35.0, 17.1, 46.7, 82.4

37 Isotopes
3 (a) 18, 20 (b) 755,245 (c) 35.5
4 (a) 72 days (b) $0.5\,g$
(c) mass number $= 234$, atomic number $= 91$

45 Energy in chemistry
2 (a) $-56.7\,kJ$ (b) $-386.4\,kJ$ (c) $+21.0\,kJ$
3 (a) $-63\,kJ$, $-126\,kJ$
(b) $-63\,kJ$

46 The analysis of carbon compounds
1 (a) C_2H_5 (b) C_4H_{10}
2 (b) CH_4O (c) CH_4O
3 (a) CH_2 (b) 28 (c) C_2H_4
4 (a) CH_3Cl (b) $C_6H_{12}O_6$ (c) CH_4
5 (a) $0.387\,g$ (b) 38.7% (c) 0.097 (d) 9.7% (e) 51.6%
(f) CH_3O (g) $C_2H_6O_2$

48 The alkanes
5 CH_3, C_2H_6

49 The alkenes
8 (a) CH_2 (b) 56 (c) C_4H_8

51 Breaking down carbohydrates
4 $4.6\,g$, $2.24\,l$

52 Ethanol and the alcohols
1 CH_4O, CH_4O
2 (a) C_3H_8O

53 Ethanoic acid
6 (a) HCO_2 (b) $H_2C_2O_4$ (c) $1 \times 10^{-3}\,mol$
(d) $2 \times 10^{-3}\,mol$
(e) $H_2C_2O_4(aq) + 2NaOH(aq) \rightarrow$
$Na_2C_2O_4(aq) + 2H_2O(l)$
(f) 2

Index

Index

of molecular compounds 161
charcoal ('coal') 10, 107–8
charring 227
chemical change (reaction) 10, 15
chlorine
  manufacture of 122–3
  preparation of 125
  properties of 125–6, 179
  uses of 126
chromatography 6, 242
coagulation of a colloid 2
coal, *see* charcoal
colloidal solution 2
combustion reactions 18
  and mass changes 18
  of hydrocarbons 216–7
  products of 19
competition for oxygen 34–5
compounds 13, 14, 15
concentrated solution 5
concentration 5
  units of 73
condensation polymerization 241,
  242
condenser 5
conductors 25
Conservation of Energy, Principle
  of 202–3
Conservation of Mass, Law of 19,
  203
Constant Composition, Law of 15
contact process 142, 200
copper
  extraction of 99–100
  reaction with air or oxygen 17
  reaction with nitric acid 135–6
copper carbonate
  action of heat on 10, 11
  formula of 60
copper (II) ions
  finding the charge on 66–8
  tests for 252
copper (I) oxide, formula of 56
copper (II) oxide
  formula of 56, 59
  reaction with ammonia 132
copper (II) sulphate
  electrolysis of 63
  reactions with metals 35–6
  thermal dissociation of 196
corrosion of metals 19, 105–6, 145
covalent bonds
  in giant structures 170
  in molecules 168–70, 215
cracking 218, 220, 271
crude oil 108
  composition of 213, 270
  distillation of 213, 270–1
  search for 109–10
crystallization 4
crystals, growth of 50

Dacron 246
Davy, Humphry 72
decomposition 10, 11
delocalized electrons 170
densities, values for elements
  280–1

desalination 4
detergents 239
diamond 164
diatomic molecules 89
dibasic acids 83, 117
diffusion
  of gases 51–2
  of liquids 52
dilute solutions 5
displacement reactions
  and energy changes 33
  of halogens 181
  of metals 35–6
dissolving 1
  and particles 53
distillation 4
  fractional 5, 128, 214, 270–1
division of matter 50

Electrochemical series 38
electrodes 25
electrolysis 25, 63–70
  explanation of 69
  of acids and alkalis 72
  of copper (II) sulphate solution
    63
  of hydrochloric acid 63
  of molten salts 25
  of salts in solution 25–6, 69
  role of water in 25, 69
  uses of 26, 70, 100, 101, 122–3
electrolytes 25
  formulas of 69
electrolytic conduction 25–6,
  63–70
electron transfer 173
electrons 65
  arrangement in atoms 152–4
  delocalized 170
  mass and charge of 150–1
  outer (valence) 153
electroplating 26, 70, 105
electrorefining 99
elements
  and redox reactions 183–4
  classification of 28–9, 147–9
  definition of 13
  symbols for 16, 283
empirical formula 90–1, 212
emulsions 2
endothermic reactions 12, 203
end-point 42
energy
  bond 204
  chemical 203–5
  definition of 202
  forms of 202
  nuclear 204, 275–7
  units of 205
  world's supplies of 273–7
energy changes (molar) of
    displacement reactions 33
energy level diagram 205
energy levels in atoms 153
enzymes 227, 228, 229, 242
equations
  calculations based on 59, 93–6

from gas volumes 89–90, 91
  using atomic symbols 59–61
  using ions 75
  using words 9
equilibrium
  dynamic nature of 198–9
  factors affecting 200–1
  in the chemical industry 200
esterification 237
esters 236, 237–9
ethanal 232
ethanamide 236
ethane, formula of 215
ethanoic acid 232, 235
  properties of 235–6
ethanol
  from fermentation 228
  manufacture of 221
  reactions of 231–3
  structure of 230–1
ethene 219
  from ethanol 233
ethyl acetate, *see* ethyl ethanoate
ethyl alcohol, *see* ethanol
ethyl ethanoate 236
ethylene, *see* ethene
exothermic reactions 12, 33, 203

Faraday constant 67
  and calculations 96
fast breeder reactor 277
Fehlings solutions 227
fermentation 5, 227–9
fertilizers 134
fibres 244–7
filtration 1
fission, nuclear 275–7
flame test 252
fluorescein 50
formula mass, *see* relative
    molecular mass
formulas 16
  determination of 55–6, 59–61,
    212
  empirical 56, 91, 212
  molecular 91, 212
  of electrolytes 69
  of hydrated salts 60
  structural 212, 215
fossil fuels 108
fractional distillation 5, 128, 214,
  270–1
fractions 5, 214, 270–1
fuels 107–113
  energy change during
    combustion of 205–7
  heating values of 207
functional group 231
fusion, nuclear 277

Galvanizing 105
gamma radiation 158
gas volumes
  and equations 89–90, 91, 94–5
  effects of temperature and
    pressure 87
  in reactions 88
gasohol 266